PRAISE FOR

Warrior Pose

"Brad Willis' life is the background for this extraordinary tale that provides compelling and essential lessons for anyone wanting a more fulfilled life. *Warrior Pose* is more than just one man's journey of healing and transformation. This book is a bright beacon of practical wisdom and guidance, inspiring us to reach for greatness and reminding us that we each possess an amazing capacity to achieve a more healthy and joyful life as well as our most heartfelt dreams. Read it and you too will be emboldened to soar."

—Rod Stryker, Para Yoga

"Brad Willis leads us on an amazing life journey of courage, passion, hope, despair, and never-die spirit. His war stories, tender moments with his son, and transformative lifestyle are beacons of light for everyone seeking to find their path of well-being."

—Dr. Suhas G. Kshirsagar BAMS, MD (Ayurveda, India), Director, Ayurvedic Healing, California Integrative Medicine

"Remarkable recoveries and miraculous healings of incurable cancers and other terminal disease have been the topic of many recent books. Bhava, born Brad Willis, has written the most exciting, original, and vividly relevant book yet on this topic. Its concise, hard-hitting prose makes a page turner about the shockingly grim world behind the nightly news as revealed to a top television reporter. Ram ignores his progressive physical collapse, stuffing his feelings and internal life to focus entirely on his macho career. Using his fierce will to survive and strong intellect to question medical authority, Bhava, draws inspiration from the miracle of his son Morgan, halts

his self-sabotaging habits, chooses 'right living,' and heals himself via a selfless emotional life dedicated to teaching and healing others."
—Candace Pert, PhD, Chief Scientific Officer, RAPID Laboratories, Inc.; author, *Everything You Need to Know to Feel Go(o)d* and *Molecules of Emotion: The Scientific Basis Behind Mind-Body Medicine*

"This amazing book is a must read for all seekers. Brad Willis has lived the very deepest principles of Yoga and Ayurveda, healed against all odds, and become an inspiration to people worldwide. *Warrior Pose* not only takes us through an amazing journey through war zones and global crises, it leads us on an inner journey of profound self-healing and personal transformation that reminds us all of our own potential to access our inner power and live our truth."
—Felicia Tomasko, Editor-in-Chief, *LA Yoga Magazine*

"*Warrior Pose* is another important and insightful book by Bhava Ram. He has made many profound and original contributions to the field of Yoga, and we look forward to many more!"
—Dr. David Frawley (Pandit Vamadeva Shastri)

WARRIOR POSE

How Yoga (Literally) Saved My Life

BRAD WILLIS

AKA BHAVA RAM

BENBELLA BOOKS, INC.

DALLAS, TEXAS

Copyright © 2013 by Bhava Ram

BenBella Books, Inc.
10300 N. Central Expressway, Suite 530
Dallas, TX 75231
www.benbellabooks.com
Send feedback to feedback@benbellabooks.com

Printed in the United States of America
10 9 8 7 6 5 4 3 2 1
Library of Congress Cataloging-in-Publication Data is available for this title.
978-1-9378-566-94

Editing by Debbie Harmsen
Copy Editing by Eric Wechter
Proofreading by Rachelle Sparks and Cape Cod Compositors, Inc.
Composition by Integra Software Services Pvt. Ltd
Printed by Bang Printing
Photo on page 118 courtesy of Tara Eby, In-Sight Photography, www.tfortara.com

Distributed by Perseus Distribution
To place orders through Perseus Distribution:
Tel: (800) 343-4499
Fax: (800) 351-5073
E-mail: orderentry@perseusbooks.com
www.perseusdistribution.com

Significant discounts for bulk sales are available. Please contact Glenn Yeffeth at glenn@benbellabooks.com or (214) 750-3628.

To my son, Morgan,
who inspired me to find my way from
the darkness back into the light

Contents

SECTION TWO: THE ABYSS

SECTION THREE: YOGA

Lead Me from the Unreal to the Real
From the Darkness into Light
From Death to Eternity

BRHADARANYAKA UPANISHAD: I.III.28

Foreword

As a young man, I was drawn to mathematics, science, and medicine. The exactness of a complex calculation, the explicit conclusion of a well-constructed lab experiment, the predicted impact of a pharmaceutical medication, the precise slice of my surgeon's scalpel as I moved toward an infected organ—these things resonated with me. A led to B. One plus one equaled two. Facts were facts, outcomes could be predicted, and ultimately, logic prevailed.

As my practice as a physician progressed, however, I witnessed how some patients healed and thrived as a result of specific treatments while others worsened and succumbed even though their conditions and therapies were identical—A did not always lead to B. One plus one did not always add up to two. I came to see that the patient could not be approached as merely a body composed of interchangeable parts, as in the Cartesian model so prevalently taught in our schools of Western medicine. There was a far greater complexity to the human organism, and all its aspects needed to be addressed for true and lasting healing to occur.

A major key to healing, I soon realized, was the mind. Our thoughts not only determine our actions but they also play a major role in the neurochemicals we create in our bodies as well. These chemicals, in turn, impact the integrity of all our systems, from organs, bones, and blood to our immunological, cardiovascular, and even emotional health. Beyond this is also a deeper realm: that of the Soul. The more connected a patient is with his or her inner truth and authentic self, the greater his or her capacity to face the most formidable of life's challenges.

As a result of these realizations, I put my scalpel down in the early 1970s and was fortunate to become one of the pioneers of the science and art of mind-body medicine. I devoted my professional life to exploring the profound human capacity to heal through mastery of our minds. As I verbally guided patients into deep states of physical and emotional relaxation and then provided them with positive imagery and affirmations, I began to see them effect profound change in their lives. It's a process I came to call Deep Healing.

As the years passed, I continued to see scores of people achieve remarkable results, even when faced with life-threatening conditions. I have witnessed people overcome emotional and psychological challenges as well, achieving optimal performance in their lives through positive thought. In the early years, mind-body medicine was met with great skepticism by most mainstream scientists and medical practitioners. Today it's an accepted and proven fact. Once you take charge of your thoughts, your inner chemistry is altered. You are empowered to take positive action, to find the light at the end of the tunnel. Your capacity to heal, and ultimately to thrive, is greatly enhanced.

Those of us in the healing profession don't always get to see the positive fruits of our work, but when we do, it is very pleasurable and, on rare occasion, truly remarkable. When Bhava Ram, at the time known as Brad Willis, came to my workshop at Esalen Institute in 2004, he told me he had come to pay homage, for it was upon hearing the voice and the words on one of my guided imagery tapes that he found himself awakening mentally and emotionally to a deep truth and inner power. It was at that moment that he began to realize he could take charge of his life, remake his inner landscape, and heal the surgically irreparable broken spine that had led to his total disability, as well as overcome his stage IV throat cancer.

Willis's journey led him into the greatest depths of the ancient and profound healing sciences of Yoga and Ayurveda, which arose thousands of years ago and comprise the foundations of mind-body medicine along with the essence of self-healing and self-realization.

But it was his remarkable life and near demise that set the stage for such an inspiring transformation. Like the Buddha, Willis was a seeker, a man driven by some deeper force to repeatedly put his life on the line to honestly express his inner truth, someone whose heart seemed to know the world had something to teach him, and whose mind was determined to learn. The impulse struck him early in his life. In the midst of the Civil Rights Movement and Vietnam War, the world around him seemed to offer only conflict and hypocrisy, but his heart pushed him to look deeper for meaning, authenticity, and purpose. As a result, he found himself hurtling through some of life's most challenging experiences.

Most of us know, at least at the intellectual level, that when we run into adversity it compels us to experience ourselves at a deeper level, and that which does not kill us makes us stronger. If only we could recall this when the next tragedy is upon us and have faith in ourselves and in the world we live in! How courageous we would all be, and how honest we would be with ourselves, and with what integrity we would live our lives every day! Each of us comes to the world with our own *dharma*, the path we are meant to walk in life. But far too few of us ever discover what that path is, how to be faithful to this deeper purpose, or even that such a thing might be. This is always to our tragic detriment. However, each of us also has the capacity to be who we truly are, who we came here to be, just like the hero of the enlightening story that you will soon be enjoying.

As I read *Warrior Pose*, I discovered myself thrilling to the adventures of a journalistic Indiana Jones, a young man following his heart and living a soldier-of-fortune lifestyle that every kid imagines for himself from time to time. It reminded me of the kind of life I would have wanted, or gone after, had I possessed the courage. By taking himself to some of the most dangerous and hotly contested areas of the world, Brad Willis exposed himself to humanity in a uniquely stark and unflinching way. Again and again he was able to see beyond the curtain, reveal the grisly political machine that has been controlling the destiny of our world, and bring focus to the underlying humanity within us all.

Some might read this account and think they are just reading a fascinating memoir. They will miss an important truth: *Warrior Pose* is about your life, my life, all our lives, and even the history of our world—a history we often fail to learn from and that therefore seems to repeat itself. You and I may never have been to all his extremes, but the author's story is our story. The unpredictability of life, the betrayal of our political system, the inhumanity of our social interactions, and the importance of love to our healing and wholeness, these are the same for all of us. Willis's journey is your journey, and my journey—writ large. It's the story of someone who was powerfully guided, even driven, one might say, to receive the deepest of teachings. To read this book properly, you must be open to receive this teaching as well. Don't read with just your head—allow your heart to participate in the journey.

Come to the battlefields with the author; peer into the smoking tanks and see the horrors of war up close. Breathe in the depleted uranium from the U.S. artillery shells that will cause stage IV throat cancer. Helicopter into the jungles of Bolivia as cocaine drug labs are uncovered and set ablaze. And be there as Willis travels undercover with freedom fighters into Soviet-occupied Afghanistan to document the atrocities of war visited upon the most innocent of victims.

Let yourself feel how depressed he became after seemingly losing it all and ending up in a body brace with a prognosis of paralysis and death. Then, as his marriage was crumbling and all seemed lost, listen and hear the fervent words of his young son that echoed continuously in Willis's head, touched the chords of love in his heart, and awakened his inner power to push on to heal and transform. Allow yourself to be touched. Be fully present as you read, and with a little luck, as you experience his turnaround you will learn something of great importance to your personal journey.

As a scientist and a doctor, I can share with you that this book also lays out beautifully the essential philosophy that leads to the deepest healing. You will learn the power of profound relaxation, how to use guided imagery to impact your body and future, mantra to keep you present, and inspiration to keep you focused on your true goals. You will be inspired to reclaim a power that has been within you all along. A power that not only can transform your life but can help transform the world, because as Mahatma Gandhi said: "You must be the change you wish to see in the world."

Perhaps Willis's recount of his dark night of the Soul can help you quiet the distractions in your mind so you can remember this always, so that you can look honestly at your life and your world, and know your own truth. Perhaps, as you accompany him through his harrowing adventures, you will see a light that can bring extraordinary and unexpected richness, and a complete transformation of one's life. If you can see it, you are most fortunate. You have arrived. Stay focused on it, follow it, and I am certain you will be richly rewarded.

—Dr. Emmett Miller
Self-Help for Mind, Body, Emotions and Spirit

Dr. Emmett Miller is best known for his revolutionary work in creating the holistic approach to healing and the field of mind-body medicine and integrative (holistic) medicine. Dr. Miller has received special acclaim for his development of the field of guided imagery, a revolutionary tool for empowering people to use the power of their minds for self-healing and optimal performance. He is the author of numerous books on holistic and mind-body medicine and co-creator of DrMiller.com.

Introduction

Life's greatest lessons usually sneak up on us when we least expect them. Some hit like hurricanes, turning our worlds upside down and wreaking havoc. It's always confusing, chaotic, and challenging to understand why we've been chosen for such a fate, and in the midst of the maelstrom, it's impossible to view our suffering as a blessing. But it almost always is.

This is my personal story. But it's about you, too. It's about all of us. I say this because I've come to learn that there's a power deep within every human being that can help us overcome great obstacles, deal with crisis and calamity, and turn our suffering into a catalyst for positive change and personal transformation. I know this is true because I am alive today even though all the experts said I should have passed away long ago.

I was in the prime of my life, traveling the world as a foreign correspondent for NBC News, when my storm hit and everything came crashing down around me. In what seemed like an instant, I was declared permanently disabled with a broken back. Then came a diagnosis of terminal cancer, with only two years to live. I was once capable of covering wars, crossing deserts, climbing mountains, and slipping in and out of battle zones with ease. Now I couldn't sit up to eat a meal, walk without a cane, or speak without a voice box strapped around my neck. The career that had been my greatest joy and defined my life for more than two decades was gone forever. My identity was shattered. I no longer knew who I was or why I was alive.

I became completely dependent on a medical system that didn't help me heal. Chronic pain and heavy medications warped my mind and stole my Soul. I was angry, confused, frightened, and deeply depressed. As I approached death's door, addicted to painkillers and alcohol, I fell into an abyss. Not a person on Earth could have told me that somewhere in this darkness was a glimmer of light.

It was an overwhelming love for my two-year-old son that finally motivated me to transform my life. This realization was triggered one morning when he tearfully implored me to "Get up, Daddy." *Getting up* required recreating myself in body, mind, and Soul. I had to move past my rational mind and journalistic cynicism, and find the courage to venture into a realm of self-healing and inner awareness I once dismissed as absurd. There, in the deepest reaches of my being, I discovered my own battlefield, with wounds to treat, conflicts to resolve, and peace to be made.

It was the greatest challenge I have ever faced, but ultimately I overcame cancer and a broken back, forged a new life, and was able to be the father my son deserved. My healing journey taught me that there is an inherent power and natural intelligence within all of us. By tapping into these forces, we can move far beyond our perceived limitations and often achieve miraculous results. We see this in the mother who performs an astonishing feat of strength to protect her child, in the passerby who rushes into a natural disaster to save a life, and in the small children who flee war-torn villages and somehow manage to survive against staggering odds.

These might seem like isolated incidents that have little to do with us, but they illustrate a great truth: *The capacity to rise up and overcome great obstacles is our birthright as members of humankind.* The more fully we reclaim this right from a system that has all too often disempowered and disenfranchised us, the more we are able to experience profound healing, liberate ourselves, and chart new courses in our lives.

Although years of physical pain and emotional anguish were nothing I ever would have wished for, I now realize that a broken back, failed surgery, cancer, and a lost career were my greatest teachers and biggest blessings. They taught me more about the world than all my previous travels and experiences combined, compelled me to face myself, and made me a better human being.

This book details my personal journey from a career as a war correspondent to life as a permanently disabled person with terminal cancer. It shares my descent into years of darkness; the battle against depression, painkillers, and alcohol; and the story of how I ultimately clawed my way back into the world. My intention is that *Warrior Pose* will inspire all who face physical and emotional crises to dig down deep, connect with their power, and unfold their fullest potential.

Bhava Ram
(Brad Willis)

AUTHOR'S NOTE: Some names in this book have been changed for reasons of confidentiality. My healing program as outlined in this book is not a formula for anyone other than myself. The practices I undertook should never be done by persons with certain health disorders, and an experienced doctor, teacher, or healing practitioner should always be consulted by those facing serious medical challenges.

DISPATCHES

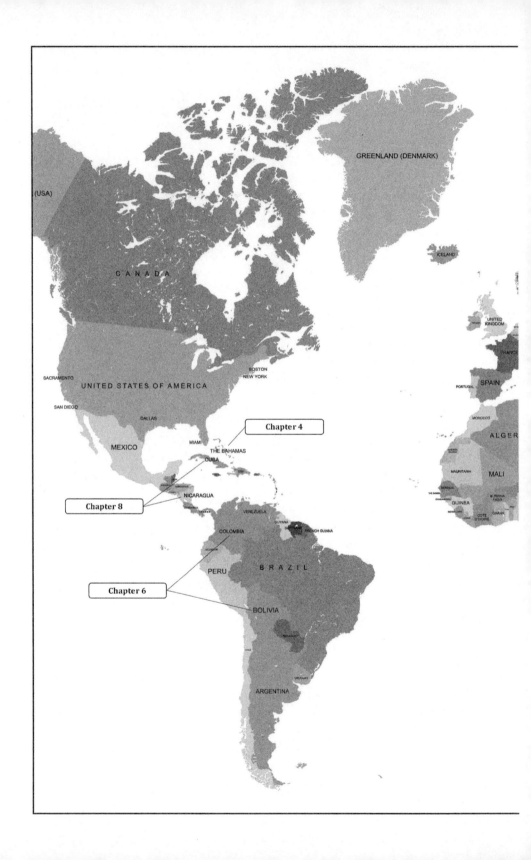

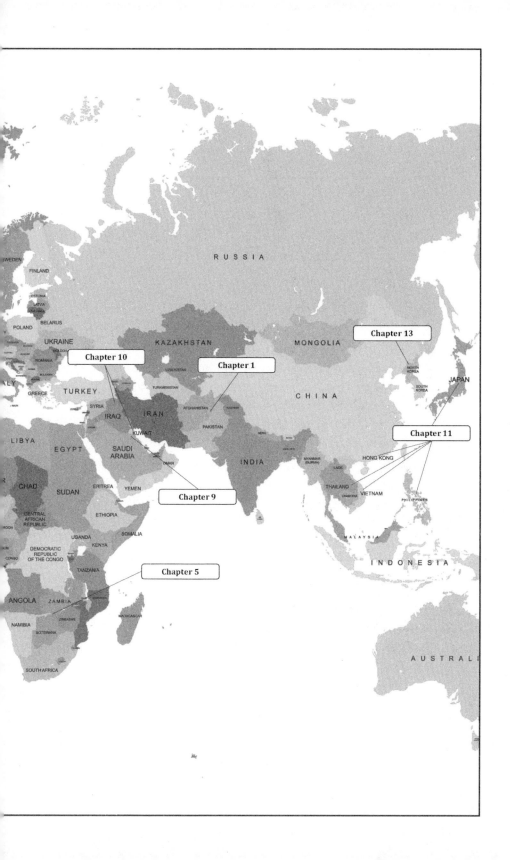

CHAPTER 1

Afghanistan

MAHMOUD'S EYES mesmerize me. They are deep ebony. Plump as a newborn fawn's. He holds my gaze with such blazing clarity that I feel frozen in time. He's a small, slender boy. Ten, maybe eleven years old. His thick, black hair is beginning to show again on his shaved head. His perfect white teeth glisten as he softly smiles.

His quivering body is bright red, covered with third-degree burns. Large patches of skin have peeled away from his torso, which is now covered with open sores. He is lying on his side in partial fetal position on top of a thin mattress on a rusty metal bed. Bloodstained gauze is wrapped around his ribs, both arms, and his left thigh. It hurts just to look at him, and I can't begin to imagine his pain.

The rest of Mahmoud's burned body, too tender and wounded to touch, is exposed to the dank air of the refugee hospital. It's close to 100 degrees outside, as the midday sun bakes the arid ground on the desolate border of Pakistan and Afghanistan. The hospital has no ventilation or cooling system, so the heat is stifling, the air almost too thick to breathe, and it smells like a butcher shop filled with spoiling meat.

"How did this happen to you?" I ask Mahmoud through my interpreter. He can barely whisper his response, and his body seems to quiver even more as he recalls what happened.

"I was just playing outdoors, all by myself," he says as his eyes close tightly, fighting back tears. "Then the jets came and everything exploded, and I was on fire."

As I stare into Mahmoud's gentle face, I can hear my deep breath and feel the pounding of my heart. Every cell in my body is trembling with compassion, disbelief, and a sense of outrage that such a thing could happen. What I feel is not a new emotion, but a reignited one. A righteous anger at the injustices in the world has smoldered within me since I was a child, like Mahmoud. It began as I became aware of the violence and discrimination in my own country during the Civil Rights Movement. Then, as I became a teenager, the Vietnam War turned me into an advocate for peace and justice. This indignation continued with me into adulthood, motivating me. This is why I'm a journalist. Making the public aware of suffering and inequity in the world is my passion. It defines what I do, and who I am.

Mahmoud was simply being a little boy, playing in his remote village high in the mountains of Afghanistan, when Soviet MiGs suddenly roared overhead and began dropping bombs. His horrific wounds are from napalm, a jellied gasoline designed to stick to its victims and burn them to death. As he was running down the rocky clay street trying to escape the attack, the gooey fire stuck to his body and consumed him. Dozens of people in his village were killed, including Mahmoud's parents. Despite his scorched flesh and terrible pain, he managed to walk through the mountain wilderness for three weeks, cross the border into neighboring Pakistan, and find this refugee hospital just in time, before his wounds became so infected that any chance of survival would have been lost.

On a bed next to Mahmoud is a boy of similar age from a different village. His right leg has been blown off by a land mine. In the far corner, behind a cloth curtain for privacy, is a teenage girl from a region farther north. Her swollen, lacerated face is peppered with tiny, razor-sharp pieces of metal from the shrapnel bomb that killed most of her family. She's been blinded in one eye. She stares at the floor with the good eye, an empty gaze of hopelessness.

This is happening throughout Afghanistan as the Soviets attack villages and drive the people out so that the local freedom fighters have no basis of support. Every bed in the refugee hospital is filled with victims of all ages. Some are infants. Others are more than eighty years old. All have ghastly wounds. Many barely cling to life. The medical staff is in a perpetual state of overwhelm, and more victims are carried in every day.

I know we have done things like this to one another throughout all time. Knowing it is one thing. Witnessing it is something else. It touches you in places you never knew existed. Gazing at Mahmoud, I can't help but believe that if I devote my life to telling the world about such atrocities we might wake up one day and stop the killing. I realize this is utterly naïve, but Mahmoud's eyes argue otherwise. "You must tell the world," he seems to be saying with his gaze. "You must."

"Yes, I'll do it," I say aloud as my cameraman finishes filming. It's impossible for me to consider otherwise. I feel this at the very core of who I am. And even though Mahmoud speaks no English, his soft smile tells me he understands that I've heard his message.

One Month Earlier

WBZ-TV is the NBC affiliate in Boston. I'm the new reporter here, hired just two months ago and bent on making my mark. This morning, as I sit at my desk in the newsroom leafing through *The Boston Globe*, a photo jumps out at me. It shows a young girl with a white cloth wrapped over her thick black hair. Her dark, haunting eyes are staring straight into my Soul. There is no story, just a caption below the picture saying, "Free Afghanistan Alliance." That's it. No details, no phone number, no way to contact the organization.

It's 1986, and the war in Afghanistan has been major news ever since the Soviets invaded seven years earlier, and I think this might be a "local hook," a Boston connection to an international event.

Nobody in the newsroom has ever heard of the Free Afghanistan Alliance. The phone company doesn't have a listing. It makes me all the more determined to contact them. I finally get hold of someone in *The Globe* advertising department and I beg, cajole, and schmooze them for all I'm worth. It works. They break the rules and give me the name of the person who bought the ad. His name is Charles Brockunier. He owns a Persian rug store just across the Charles River in Cambridge. I ring him immediately, telling him I'm a reporter and that his ad caught my eye. He gives me an overview of his mission to help the Afghan people by smuggling badly needed medical supplies into the country. As we speak, it's clear that he's brilliant but also eccentric, totally locked into his mission. I'm completely intrigued now and know I must meet him. I get his address, jump up, and tell the assignment editor I'm off to investigate a lead on a possible story.

Brockunier's shop is hard to find, tucked away on a side street near Harvard Square. The air inside smells ancient, and with so many dusty, antique carpets piled everywhere there's barely room to pass through. The place is empty, and I have to call out several times before Brockunier appears from behind a stack of rugs. The founder of the Free Afghanistan Alliance is tall and lanky, clad in worn, wrinkled khaki trousers, a drab, collarless Nehru shirt, and a rugged vest that looks and smells like it was made from the wool of a wild goat. He is sporting a matching brimless, woolen hat like the ones I've seen Afghan freedom fighters wearing in network news reports. He has a heavy, poorly trimmed reddish beard, ruddy complexion, and glasses so thick his eyes look like they might jump out of their sockets.

Brockunier insists that we sit down, cross-legged, on a stack of elaborately patterned burgundy, gold, and earthy brown Persian rugs to sip Afghan tea. I've always been stiff. Sitting like this is a pain. It makes me impatient. It's not even that cold outside, so I don't feel like drinking hot tea. I just want to pepper Brockunier with questions and get a full understanding of what he's up to. But this is his world and he's clearly not going to be rushed.

As he settles in with his tea, Brockunier tells me he is a native of Cambridge, went to Harvard but never finished a degree, and has spent years traveling to Afghanistan to buy rugs for his shop. He's in love with the Afghan people, a self-taught expert on their culture and history, and fluent in their languages of Pashto and Dari, along with being conversant in several other languages of the region. When I ask for an example of a few dialects, he rattles off sentences with ease. I can't understand a word, but I can tell he isn't faking it.

"I had to flee Kabul in 1979 when the Soviet tanks rolled in," he explains in a deep, scratchy voice. "Otherwise, I'm sure they would have arrested me, tortured me, accused me of being a spy, and locked me away in prison." Back home in Cambridge, Brockunier founded the Free Afghanistan Alliance and dedicated himself to raising money to support the Afghan freedom fighters, called mujahideen. These are the men, and often boys, who are fighting the Soviet occupation of their country. Most are rugged, rural villagers—farmers and tradesmen—who stage daring attacks on Soviet positions, then slip back into hidden camps in the mountains. They are outnumbered and vastly outgunned but are holding their own against all odds.

"I smuggle the medical supplies across the border of Pakistan and into mujahideen camps," he tells me, his voice monotone. Matter of fact. "I have to go through the tribal territories. It's lawless. Everyone is armed. You have to be careful."

I always try to follow my instincts, and they tell me that I can trust this man. He's experienced, compassionate, and dedicated to his cause. And I really want this story. When he tells me he's about to leave on another trip to a mujahideen hideaway in the Afghan mountains, I know that somehow, some way, I'm going with him.

"Can you get me and my cameraman in with you?" I ask him point blank. "We can tell your story. More people will know about your work. You'll probably get more donations." Brockunier's bulging eyes get even wider and, for the first time since I arrived, I see the hint of a smile on his face.

"Yes, I can do that," he answers without hesitation. I get as many details from him as I can persuade him to share without compromising his need for secrecy and protection of his contacts, then head back to the station for online research on the war through our station's new computer system, one of the first in the country.

I check in with my favorite cameraman, Dennis, to see if he's willing to risk the trip. He's beyond willing; he's ecstatic about the idea.

Within a few hours, I've drafted a detailed proposal and mounted it in a glossy report folder. Navigating the expansive and ever hectic newsroom, I reach the office of our news director, Stan Hopkins.

"Stan," I say, as I poke my head inside his door, "can I have a few minutes?"

"Sure, come on in and have a seat." Stan is one of the best news directors in the country. He hired me to stir things up and I've done some of that already with a few investigative reports, including exposing corrupt cops who shook down nightclub owners in downtown Boston for thousands of dollars in bribes. I'm still the new kid, but I've earned Stan's trust and support. Now I'm about to stretch him to the limit.

"Take a look at this," I say as I hand him the proposal. The station has never sent a reporter to cover a foreign war, so I've included story summaries, itineraries, budget breakdowns, and backup plans. Most importantly, I've made a detailed argument on the relevance of the story for our audience. The Free Afghanistan Alliance is right next to Harvard and receives donations from throughout New England. The war between Russia and Afghanistan is front page news almost every day. This international coverage will set us apart from the other news stations, with whom, of course, we're always in competition. Stan takes his time and pores through every detail. I can practically hear his mind spinning, weighing the risk against the payoff. After several minutes, I can see he's hooked.

"How do you know this guy is for real and can get you inside Afghanistan?" Stan asks, still looking at the proposal.

"He's been doing it for six years, at least two times a year," I answer. "But there are no guarantees. We'll be taking a gamble."

"Do you realize how dangerous this is?" Stan is looking me straight in the eye this time.

"Yes," I say, knowing this would come up. "There are no Western journalists inside Afghanistan that we know of, and the Soviets say they'll execute any they capture."

"And you and Dennis are willing to take that chance?" Stan knows the answer.

"Yes, we are."

This is what journalists do. Take chances. Go places only soldiers would go. Even risk their lives to report the news. Especially idealistic journalists with a burning desire to be wherever the action is, to expose injustice and the causes of human suffering.

"Give me a few minutes," Stan says. As I return to my desk, I see him heading upstairs toward the general manager's office. *He's going to take a huge chance and pitch the story*, I say excitedly to myself. I can't think of much else the rest of the day and am relieved when the assignment desk doesn't need me for any breaking news. Just as I'm getting ready to go home for the night, Stan calls me back into his office and stares straight into my eyes for a minute before saying a word.

"It's a go," he finally says with a firm smile. "I know you'll do it right. If you don't, we'll both be looking for work somewhere else."

"I won't let you down," I say, amazed at his courage, and touched by his confidence in me.

A few weeks later, Dennis and I land in Peshawar, Pakistan, an ancient city near the Khyber Pass, close to the southern border of Afghanistan. We'd be lost without Brockunier at our side. The narrow, jumbled streets are thronged with mule carts weaving their way through lines of huge trucks covered with colorful paintings, wood carvings, calligraphy, and mirrors. Small, open-sided mini-taxis with high-pitched engines scurry between the trucks and carts belching black smoke into the air. Men with thick, long beards and piercing gazes are gathered at every corner, thronging the walkways, and huddled in dark shops sipping chai tea while gravely discussing the war next door. Most wear loose, pajama-style outfits called *shalwar kamiz*, with tan vests and cloth turbans or woolen hats called *pakols*. Large ceremonial knives, curved like crescents, dangle from their waists. The sharp steel blades could slice off the head of a goat with ease. The women of Peshawar are almost invisible in the background, covered from head to toe in heavy cloth gowns called burkas. It's like wearing a prison cell, with only a small slit at the eye level so they can navigate the outdoor markets.

Tall, conical minarets with onion domes tower over the city; from these, the faithful are called to prayer at the mosques five times a day. Traditionally, a devotee called a *muzim* climbed the winding staircase to a narrow ledge atop the minaret to call to the village at the top of his lungs. No one would hear him today. So great bullhorns have been attached to the minarets, wired to tape players down in the mosques. It's a sign of progress, Pakistan style.

Brockunier has somehow managed to get us into Mahabat Khan, Peshawar's largest mosque, to film the prayers. He blends in easily, wearing his own travel-worn *shalwar kamiz* and *pakol* while speaking the local dialect with fluency. Dennis and I stick out like sore thumbs, standing behind our TV camera and tripod in our blue jeans and khaki shirts. We look like aliens, or at least two futuristic men who hijacked a time machine and landed in a past century.

The mosque dates back to the 1600s and is stunning with its high, arched gateways, richly carved parapets, and fluted domes crowning a massive prayer hall. There must be more than a thousand people here. Rows of men with heavy beards sit on their heels chanting prayers in Pashto as they reach their arms to the sky in unison and then bow forward, touching their foreheads to their prayer rugs. More than a few of them gaze up at us as they lift their heads, their thick eyebrows knitted in frowns of disapproval. Even though America is an ally of Pakistan, and the country is happy to take billions of dollars in U.S. foreign aid, nobody said they have to like us. And most don't. They don't like our politics, our lifestyles, our culture, or the power we wield in the world. The only thing worse than an American right now is a Russian. It's an open secret that the CIA is funneling aid to the Afghans to fight the Russians, so we are tolerated. As the old saying here goes, *the enemy of my enemy is my friend.*

Brockunier is good at getting us around the streets of Peshawar, moving by foot from mosques to marketplaces so we can shoot the necessary background color for our reports. But we have to be careful. Everywhere we go someone becomes resentful of our presence, raising his voice at us. A crowd gathers. Tempers start to flare. We quickly commandeer some mini-taxis and get the hell out of there before the crowds become anti-American mobs.

At almost every location we film, Brockunier stops to buy Afghan rugs from street vendors. I can't understand it. He has thousands of rugs back in his shop that will take him years to sell. He's even begun pressing me for funds to buy more. Worse, he's having trouble making contact with the Afghan mujahideen, which is, of course, the reason why we're here. It's been five days now and I'm starting to wonder if my judgment was flawed and all I've done is sponsor a maniacal rug-buying spree for a complete crackpot. I have a sickening vision of walking back into the WBZ newsroom, tail between my legs, everyone staring at the failure I have proven myself to be as I break the news to Stan, and then start looking for another job.

Every night, Dennis and I sit in one of the two decrepit and mostly empty "foreigners' hotels" as Brockunier disappears into the dark streets to seek out his Afghan contacts. These are the people he has worked with for years, he tells me, and the only ones who can get us into Afghanistan. They always have to stay in hiding, and the dangers of meeting with us get greater every day. The longer we're here, the more people are aware of us, the more visible we become.

Peshawar is filled with intrigue. Soviet agents, secret police, spies, and snitches. Everyone on the lookout for an enemy or a chance to sell some information. A Soviet spy would kill an Afghan freedom fighter in a heartbeat, and vice versa. A bomb went off two nights ago at the other foreigners' hotel, destroying several rooms and injuring some European businessmen. Yesterday, there was an explosion at the Afghan restaurant we've eaten at every day.

Tonight, after a sixth day of waiting for contact with the mujahideen, I can't sleep. I'm furious with myself for trusting Brockunier and am contemplating storming into his room, confronting him, and tossing all his lousy rugs into the street while I'm at it. It's almost dawn when I doze off. Then I'm startled awake by a soft but firm knock at the door. I crack it open to see Brockunier standing there with two rugged men in Afghan dress. One is brandishing a Soviet AK-47 automatic rifle. The other looks like he could kill someone with his bare hands. It's the most comforting sight I've seen since we landed in this country and I feel embarrassed for losing faith in my friend who buys all those fabulous carpets.

"They have to blindfold us," Brockunier says as I rouse Dennis from his bed. "They don't want us to know where the safe houses are in case we're captured and interrogated."

One of the mujahideen pulls strips of dirty cloth from his baggy pajama pants pockets and wraps them around our heads to cover our eyes. Then we're stuffed into the back of a Jeep and driven to a safe house somewhere in the maze of the oldest sector of the city. When the blindfolds are removed, we're in a dark cement room, surrounded by a half-dozen or so mujahideen sitting cross-legged on an ornate rug. They look tough as grizzly bears but welcome us with warm smiles as they gesture for us to sit and drink chai with them. As I'll soon learn, nothing happens in Pakistan without this ritual of sitting on the floor and sipping tea as we are subtly scrutinized and deemed to be trustworthy…or not.

After several meetings, each time at a different safe house, we finally win their trust. One morning before dawn, the mujahideen arrive at our room again without any notice. They give us a few minutes to

With Charles Brockunier inside Afghanistan in 1986.

gather our gear, then load us into the back of their Jeep, this time for the dangerous journey through the wild, tribal territories along the border and into the snow-covered mountains of Afghanistan. There's no need for blindfolds now, but we need to lay low and do our best to blend in. Along the way, we stop at a tailor's shop and quickly get outfitted with Afghan clothing. All we need now are beards down to our waists and AK-47s slung over our shoulders.

The tribal territories line the amorphous border between Pakistan and Afghanistan. They begin on the sloping plains that skirt the Himalayas and soon rise into jagged mountains. The main crop in this region is poppy flowers, grown to produce opium and heroin. Warlords hold sway here. In the few remote towns we have to sneak through, weapons are openly sold on the streets and frequently fired into the air—sort of a test drive of your AK-47 or Kalashnikov before you take ownership of it. Dennis and I stay curled up in the back of the Jeep on top of our gear. There are informants everywhere, and we would be a prize catch.

"Are you doing okay?" I ask Dennis.

"Fine," he says with an impish smile. Dennis looks like a shorter, tougher version of Brockunier, with his ruddy Irish face, short-cut reddish beard, and broad shoulders. He's strong as an ox, funny and charismatic, and utterly fearless. He's also the best photographer I've ever known. He never misses a shot and always manages to step squarely into the action without ever getting in the way.

"I'm just thinking about the gear," he says. "I hope the solar battery recharging kits work right. I tested them before we left the States, but you never know."

I don't have any doubts. Dennis keeps everything meticulously organized and I've seen him instantly repair his gear in the midst of a big story. He's unstoppable.

Brockunier is seated right in front of us, on the backseat of the Jeep with our guide and interpreter, Rasoul. The mujahideen with the AK-47 rides shotgun while his partner speeds across the rocky dirt roads. Every five minutes we hit a huge bump and our heads slam into the roof. We're choking on dust. It's hot as hell. And I love every second of it.

It's pitch black when we finally get through the territories and into the mountains of Afghanistan. We're driving without headlights, still going so fast that I can't believe the driver can stay on the winding road guided by starlight alone. But at least with the cover of darkness Dennis and I can finally poke our heads up and breathe more deeply, relieved that we've made it without having to get through any checkpoints.

"The border guards come and go," Rasoul says in perfect English as we head higher into the mountains. "None can be trusted. We must still be very careful."

Rasoul, which is surely a pseudonym, has thin, fine features, like a nobleman. In talking with him, I can see he is highly educated and cultured. He is fluent in English, French, German, and Russian in addition to all the major Afghan dialects. He loves conversation, but he is cryptic about his past, except for sharing that he is from Kabul, the capital city of Afghanistan. My guess is that he's a member of the Afghan elite, deeply connected to the government and business community, maybe even a former head of some intelligence operation. I imagine he would have been imprisoned or executed had he not escaped Kabul during the Soviet invasion. Rasoul is vehemently patriotic and devoted to the resistance, moving like a shadow behind the scenes. He has to be the contact Brockunier was waiting for all along. The one person making all of this happen.

It must be close to midnight when I nod off to sleep. Suddenly, our driver slams on the brakes and my forehead smacks into the metal bar framing the backseat. "Get down!" Rasoul hisses with urgency. "Say nothing! No one speak! I'll do the talking. Do not leave the Jeep!" He speaks like a general and we immediately fall in line. Brockunier freezes like a statue. The mujahideen who is riding shotgun grips his automatic weapon and holds it at his chest. Dennis and I curl up again, trying to disappear.

As Rasoul jumps out of the Jeep and slams the door, Brockunier whispers, "We're surrounded by armed men in military uniforms. They're speaking Urdu, so they're Pakistanis. This isn't good."

I can hear Rasoul arguing loudly. I don't understand a word, but it doesn't sound like he's getting anywhere. Suddenly, the Jeep is flooded with flashlights, the doors are thrown open, and we're ordered out. Brockunier seems to pass for one of the mujahideen despite his reddish beard. But Dennis and I, even in our new pajama-like garb, still look very much like foreigners.

Rasoul is ordered back to the Jeep and whispers, "Don't say a word. These are tribal people. They don't speak English, but they know it when they hear it. They hate Americans almost as much as Russians. I've told them you are French doctors, volunteering to treat the wounded. Right now, they are threatening to arrest us all. Whatever you do, do not show your passport."

Three guards walk up and yell at us to get out of the Jeep, then quickly rummage through everything, finding our camera gear beneath the duffel bags filled with Brockunier's medical supplies. This stops the show. The yelling gets louder. Rasoul is incredibly courageous, alternately confronting the armed men with verbal assaults then switching to gentle persuasion. But he's getting nowhere. Finally, he somehow manages to get the guards to wait in a group as he comes back to where I'm standing at the rear of the Jeep.

"This is trouble," he says with a sigh of resignation. "They want to know what doctors are doing with camera equipment. They want documents."

My mind starts racing for some sort of solution. It's too dangerous to change our story and tell them we're journalists. There's no way we can show them our American passports. Then it hits me in a flash. "Tell them I'm getting documents from my bag," I whisper to Rasoul.

He looks shocked and is about to protest when I say, "Don't worry. No passports. Trust me." Rasoul calls out to the leader of the guards and gets his permission as I slowly reach into the Jeep for my shoulder bag and open the zippered pouch I keep my passport in. Right next to it is the equipment manifest we had to obtain from the Pakistan Embassy granting permission to bring our gear into the country. It's covered with official government stamps.

"Tell them this is our permission document from Pakistan customs," I whisper to Rasoul. The first two words beneath the government stamps are Sony Betacam. That's our digital camera. "I'm Dr. Sony," I whisper to Rasoul, pointing at the words. "Dennis is

Dr. Betacam. We're treating wounded fighters and filming it to raise more money back in France for more medical supplies. We're on the side of their Afghan brothers."

Rasoul's eyes widen. "This is good," he says as he takes the paper and walks toward the guards. There are a few tense minutes. The document changes hands several times. Suddenly, everyone is patting Rasoul on the back. Our gear is returned to us and we cram back into the Jeep, start the engine, and roll past the guards, waving and smiling like one big family.

"I have to remember this trick," Rasoul says as he hands the manifest back to me with a huge sigh of relief.

"I thought we were dead," Dennis says. It's the first time I've ever heard him sound frightened.

"Or at least going to jail and having everything confiscated," Brockunier chimes in.

"It's a good sign," Rasoul says, calming everyone down. "We still have a long way to go. Let's get some rest."

I'm exhausted and try to close my eyes and doze off again, but it's impossible to sleep as we wind higher into the mountains and the road becomes narrower and more difficult to navigate, especially with our headlights still off. Finally, we stop in the middle of nowhere. No more road. Nothing but mud and snow.

"We must unload everything here," Rasoul says, still whispering and gesturing for quiet. "No flashlights. No talking."

Once we have our things, our mujahideen driver and guard hug Rasoul, jump back in the Jeep, start the engine, and somehow find a way to turn around and drive off. The woods around us are pitch black. While it was hot in the valleys below, it's freezing cold here. Deep banks of springtime snow are illuminated by the brilliant starlight. We just stand still and shiver, our gear held in our arms, as the drone of the Jeep's engine disappears down the mountainside.

"What the hell is happening?" Dennis whispers to me, risking a rebuke from Rasoul. "We might just freeze to death!"

I look at him and shake my head. Shrug my shoulders. Then I pat the sleeping bag roped onto my backpack and wonder how warm it will keep me in the wet snow. Suddenly I remember we only have one or two days' worth of food with us. As I start to think it might have been better had the tribal Pakistanis arrested us, we hear a faint, sloshing sound at the tree line. Now we can make out the silhouette of two figures under the starlight. A man with a rifle over his shoulder and a mule. They approach silently. He is mujahideen. His first glance is toward Rasoul, who then gestures for us to pile our gear on the mule.

We walk behind the mujahideen, who leads us into the cover of the woods and up the mountainside. It's slow going. Grueling, in fact. The snow is up to our knees and the temperature beyond freezing. We touch one another's backs to keep from getting lost. An hour later, we arrive at a bombed-out farmhouse. More mujahideen appear in the darkness. There are no lights. Not even a candle. Nothing to give the Soviets a chance to discover their position. We stumble into a dark, frigid hallway of the home, finally making it to a room with a wooden floor covered in straw. About to collapse, we unroll our sleeping bags and slip in. Curling up, I roll over and whisper to Dennis, "We made it."

We're beyond exhausted, but we get only two, maybe three, hours of sleep before we are told to roll up our bags and quietly depart before sunrise. There are three mules now, the one with our gear, the other two laden with rounds of ammunition, artillery shells, and grenades. It takes a full day of vertical hiking through heavier snow to find the hidden camp of a group of some two hundred mujahideen. The fighters line up in the glistening snow to meet us, surrounded by towering pines. They shoulder their weapons, from old rifles to AK-47s to rocket launchers, as a show of pride and dedication. Most are rustic farmers from small mountain villages. They range in age from fourteen to eighty-four. Several have lost a leg or an arm to land mines. It hasn't slowed them down a bit. Instead, it has strengthened their resolve. I will soon realize the oldest among them could out-hike me on my best day.

Rasoul introduces us as American journalists who have come to document their struggle. Like the Pakistanis, most Afghans dislike

America but again, the enemy of their enemy is their friend. At least for now. Brockunier delivers his medical supplies to the chief of the fighters and all the men chant "*Allāhu Akbar,*" meaning "God is great." Dennis films them thrusting their weapons into the air, symbolizing that this is a holy war. *When our viewers see this back home they'll be blown away,* I think, as Dennis deftly puts his lens a few inches away from a boy's hand clutching the trigger of his weapon and then pans to his innocent face.

We live with the mujahideen for the next week, sleeping in small huts while burning frozen wood soaked in kerosene to avoid freezing to death. There's only enough food for one meal a day. It's always goat fat boiled into a filmy yellowish grease and served in large, communal bowls, with broken goat bones at the bottom. We sit in circles on the ground and scoop up each bite with a traditional flatbread called naan that the mujahideen bake in makeshift clay ovens. The grease is rancid. The gristle on the bones is black with rot. We're so hungry that it tastes delicious, especially the steaming hot naan.

Dennis and I hold each piece of naan in our fingertips, carefully dipping it into the bowl and slipping it into our mouths. It's challenging to do so without having grease run down our arms. I have to be especially careful since I'm left-handed. The left hand is the one used throughout the region for self-cleaning after defecation. Reaching my left hand into the food bowl would be the ultimate gaffe. For me it's almost impossible to remember. I come close to muffing it every day.

The mujahideen have well-camouflaged anti-aircraft guns posted high above the camp. Just before sunset, they fire at any Soviet MiGs seen flying at altitudes well beyond the range of their artillery. After shooting a few rounds, they circle the guns and chant "*Allāhu Akbar,*" then almost sing, repeatedly, in Pashto, "We vow to purge the satanic invaders from our homeland!"

The real fighting starts long before dawn. The mujahideen slip down dark trails into the valley below to launch guerrilla attacks against Soviet outposts on major roads that connect the few major cities of Afghanistan, all of which are under Soviet control. When helicopter gunships counterattack, they scurry back into the mountains, hiding under huge boulders along the way, carefully moving

With mujahideen inside Afghanistan in 1986.

toward the cover of the thick forest. Back in camp, the fighters treat the wounded with Brockunier's medical supplies. They bury their dead before sundown. We film everything we can. Their war against the mighty Soviet Army is like a small shepherd boy against a towering, battle-trained giant. But these are the toughest people I have ever met and they fight boldly, like David going after Goliath with just a stone and a slingshot.

After leaving the mujahideen and saying good-bye to Rasoul and Brockunier, Dennis and I make our way into the sprawling camps along the Pakistani border. There are 5 million refugees—one-third of the Afghan population—living in horrid conditions, many without so much as a ragged tent over their heads. This is the unseen horror of the Cold War as it's played out around the world. The Soviets invade Afghanistan as a pushback to American influence in Pakistan.

The Americans then push back against communist expansionism. Innocent people get hurt. Lots of them. I am thirty-seven years old and have been in some rough places, but this is human suffering beyond anything I have ever witnessed or even imagined. It sickens me. Angers me. Makes me want to cry. And it strengthens my resolve to tell this story.

We film improvised burial grounds, where bodies are stacked atop one another and covered with dirt and large stones. They surround the edges of the camps like anthills. Those who survive cling to life with incredible determination, refusing to succumb to the diseases that spread like fire. More victims pour into the overwhelmed treatment centers every day. This is where we find Mahmoud and the other wounded Afghan children. We are here for three days, rushing to complete our filming in the camps and main refugee hospital before we fly home. In all, we have been gone less than a month, but it feels like a lifetime.

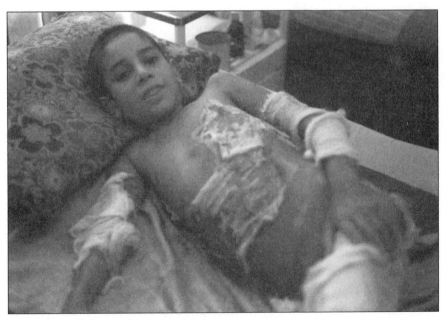

Mahmoud in Refugee Hospital, Pakistan, 1986.

❋

Back in Boston, we air a series of reports entitled "Afghanistan, the Untold Story." I knew this was powerful stuff, but I never dreamed the response would be so overwhelming. Viewers throughout New England rally to the cause. Schoolchildren launch class projects, draw pictures for the children in the camps, and mail them with bags of coins from their piggy banks. Viewers form groups to collect donations of food, clothing, and medical supplies, which Brockunier ships directly to the refugee hospital where we found Mahmoud. New England hospitals offer their facilities, time, and services. Airlines agree to fly in dozens of war-wounded children for world-class medical treatment. Our viewers open their homes to family members accompanying the Afghan children as they arrive in Boston for eye surgery, prosthetic devices, and burn treatments. Mahmoud is on the very first flight and will soon be cared for at the Shriner's Burn Institute. I cover it all, with a new story almost every night. More than ever before, it makes me feel like what I do for a living is making a difference in the world.

Over the next few months, I'm periodically sent on the road to other major stations of Group W, which owns WBZ, and I broadcast the reports from Philadelphia to San Francisco, appearing on talk shows and giving public speeches. One morning, shortly after I return to Boston, Stan calls me into his office to tell me our work has been given a Columbia-DuPont Award. I don't even know what the award is until he explains it's the broadcast equivalent of the Pulitzer Prize.

This is big news for my career. That's not lost on me. But as I say when I accept the award at a ceremony in New York, it's hard to accept such a prestigious honor for documenting such tremendous suffering. As I sit in a suit and tie with Stan and Dennis for a sumptuous awards dinner complete with champagne, I feel humbled as well as a little embarrassed and out of place. I'd rather be back in the field, unwashed, hungry, and exhausted, pushing forward to bring another story of human suffering and injustice into the light of day.

In fact, all I can think about is where to go next.

CHAPTER 2

Beginnings

I WAS BORN IN LOS ANGELES IN 1949. The city was already well on its way to becoming a madhouse. When I turned five, we moved to the nearby countryside. A bucolic place called West Covina. It was paradise: rolling hills, creeks, pastures, farms, orchards, and walnut groves perfect for all-day hide-and-seek and the building of secret forts. But soon the developers arrived, and the landscape was leveled, scraped, and sterilized for suburban housing tracts and strip malls. As I watched all my favorite haunts being destroyed, it felt like they were bulldozing my childhood into oblivion.

Like so many other Americans of their era, my parents and their friends were prejudiced. From my earliest years I heard countless pejorative terms for people who weren't white and conservative. Even as a little boy, something deep inside me recoiled every time they spoke like this. It was incredibly painful and made me feel like I had been born into a family to which I didn't belong. Then came the sixties. The Civil Rights Movement. Vietnam War. The assassinations of John Kennedy, Bobby Kennedy, and Martin Luther King, Jr. It felt like someone had hijacked my country. Like so many others of my generation, I was consumed with youthful outrage. I marched in protests. I got roughed up by the cops at peace rallies. I became completely disillusioned with the idea of ever joining a society that behaved that way.

I can't remember finishing high school in 1967. All I wanted was out. At the first chance, with the ink barely dry on my diploma,

I fled to the woods of Humboldt County in Northern California. It was a place where I could sink my fingers into the fertile soil, plant seeds, tend the earth, and grow my own food. I could spend days on remote, rocky beaches and never see another soul. I could canoe down wild rivers or hike into forests of virgin redwoods and just sit, listening as the quiet whispers of nature enveloped me. Being in this isolated area with nature's beauty was like finding my true home. I was away from the racist remarks, the anger, the frustration of marching and protesting, and a world that seemed upside down and inside out.

I loved the outdoors, working with my hands, and being self-sufficient. I bought an old truck and chainsaw, scavenged dead oak and pine trees from the forest, cut and chopped like a madman, and sold firewood. The smell of the wood splitting open mesmerized me. Oak had a light fragrance of vanilla and cinnamon. The pine resin had a minty aroma that flooded my senses. I also built a business restoring some of the region's cherished Victorian homes, figuring out how to do the needed carpentry and painting as I went. This nourished and sustained me, but when I turned nineteen it felt like it was time to get serious about an education and I enrolled at a small college in the redwoods named Humboldt State University.

I became fixated as I threw myself at my studies even harder than I had chopped firewood. I loved language and literature—from the classics of Shakespeare, Whitman, and Thoreau to the radical poets of the beat generation. I ate it all up like I was starving, finishing a degree in English Literature and earning a high school teaching credential in less than four years. It wasn't from any inherent brilliance, and I had no career ambitions. I don't even know why I got a credential. I never wanted to be a teacher. I just needed to prove something to myself and to the mainstream world I had left behind even though I still wanted nothing to do with society, the system, or the rules. I'd checked out of that scene long ago and, with my degree finished and the small savings left over from my firewood and restoration business, I was ready to head off for the unknown.

I decided to leave my remote cabin on the edge of a village called Freshwater for a few months and see more of the world. I thought about South America, New Zealand, or Africa. Or maybe I'd travel around Europe again on a shoestring budget like my trip there the previous summer. The destination wasn't of utmost importance. Expanding my boundaries was. I longed to feel part of something bigger, explore what was unknown to me, and be a global citizen.

In the end, I chose Canada. I could drive my old van there, explore Vancouver, then head farther north into the Yukon Territory and camp out in the wilderness, avoiding the costs of air travel and lodging. In preparation for my trip, I drove into the nearby town of Eureka to buy some supplies. As I was heading home to pack for my trip, the local television station caught my eye. The large cinderblock building had a neon sign facing the main road that flashed the time and current temperature right beside the station's call letters: KVIQ-TV, Channel 6.

I don't know why I pulled into the parking lot and walked inside. I didn't own a TV and didn't care a thing about local news. I was hooked on *The New York Times* and enthralled by the major events shaking the world, always fantasizing I was the one on the scene of a great war or revolution. I never saw myself as a reporter. I just wanted to be a witness to that which was momentous and meaningful. Yet suddenly, there I was, strolling through the lobby of a small-town TV station, when a portly, gregarious man wearing strong cologne and a loud tie walked up and introduced himself.

"Hi, I'm Alan Jones, the general manager. You must be the one looking for a job." Jones reached out with his meaty fingers and shook my hand with surprising strength.

"Yes, sir," I answered impulsively, trying to match his grip while wondering what I was getting myself into. I'd never taken a course in journalism and had no idea what duties people performed at TV stations.

"Where are you from?" Jones asked with a gentle grin.

"Right here, Freshwater," I answered. "I just graduated from Humboldt State."

"Oh, I thought you were from out of town!" he said with a laugh.

Jones must have been confusing me with someone who really did have a job interview and was somehow blind to my outfit of work boots, blue jeans, and a flannel shirt. I glanced at the station entrance expecting to see a well-scrubbed journalism grad in a dark suit and button-down collar come running in for his interview and angrily declare me an impostor.

"Come with me," Jones said. "As I'm sure you know, we just fired a reporter and plenty of people want this job. I'll introduce you to our news director. We'll see how you do."

"Yes, sir!" I said again with a smile, thinking I might as well have a good time while it lasted and I'd still be able to leave for Canada in the morning.

News Director Don Michaels fit the role of a seasoned journalist to a T. He was sitting behind a desk piled with papers in what could only be called organized chaos. He wore thick glasses framing a face pockmarked from childhood acne. His thinning reddish hair was in a comb-over to hide a balding pate. He was coatless, in a wrinkled white dress shirt with the sleeves rolled above his elbows, thick suspenders, and a narrow black tie tossed over one shoulder. Michaels was so absorbed in his work he didn't bother looking up when Jones said, "Here's a local guy who wants a job," and sat me down in a creaky wooden chair facing his desk. "I'm a local guy, too," Jones said as he turned and headed out. "I like local guys."

Two metal boxes, each about four feet high, stood beside Michaels' desk loudly clacking away, spewing rolls of tan, pulpy paper all over the floor. Suddenly, a sharp bell sounded. Michaels leaned over and ripped the paper off one machine. "Another so-called *urgent*," he said disdainfully, giving it a quick glance then crumpling it up and tossing it into the trash. "Worthless, old news; nothing urgent at all."

"What are those?" I asked, risking sounding like a fool.

"News wires. Associated Press and United Press International. Didn't you learn about these in your journalism classes?"

"No," I said as straightforward as possible. "My degree is in English Lit. I've never taken a class in journalism."

"Humph," Michaels grunted. "Go take a look." Michaels used words sparingly, getting right to the point. His brusque expression never changed.

I walked over and watched the automatic printers firing off one story after the next. World news, national news, statewide news, local news: reports literally pouring in from around the globe before anyone ever saw them in a newspaper. As they cascaded onto the floor like a waterfall, it seemed like the whole world was unfolding right there at my feet. It sent chills down my spine.

Michaels ripped three stories off the wire, handed them to me and said in a curt tone, "Write these up. Make them concise and conversational. One page only. Here's some script paper. You can use that empty desk and typewriter over there. You have ten minutes." He looked me in the eye with a fatherly but piercing gaze as I realized he hadn't bothered to even ask me my name.

I had never typed a word in my life. I hand-wrote most of my college papers and had to pay someone to type them when a professor required it. I sat down at the news desk and flashed through the wire reports, then picked up a sheet of the thick script paper with shaky hands. It was really three sheets; white on the top, pink in the middle, and yellow on the bottom, with sheets of carbon paper in between. It was so thick I could barely get it into the typewriter without destroying it, already losing too much of my precious ten minutes. Once I finally got the sheet threaded, I began to hunt and peck with my index fingers, furtively glancing at Michaels in hopes he wasn't watching and relieved to see he was crumpling up more wire copy and tossing it on the floor. Despite my slow fingers, my studies in English Literature paid off. I knew how to write. I finished just in time, making my first deadline.

I handed the stories to Michaels. He gave them a rapid glance, tossed them onto one of the growing piles on his desk, and said in a challenging tone, "Can you shoot and edit film?" I was in luck again. Art was part of my minor studies, and as an elective I had taken a film class working with 16 millimeter film cameras, cutting the film strips and splicing them together with special glue. Michaels took me into the film room and I gave a quiet sigh of relief. It was the same editing equipment I knew so well. I cut and spliced some leftover film strips for him then noticed the cameras on a wall rack. "Those are Bolex and Auricon cameras," I said. "I know how to use them.

The Bolex is for silent footage and the Auricon records sound on the film strip. You always need to white balance and set the f-stop before you shoot. By the way, I also know how to process the film."

"Okay, I'm a homicide detective," Michaels said, seeming unimpressed as he strode back into the newsroom. "You've rushed to the scene of the crime after hearing on the police scanners that a body has been found in the woods." He pointed to a shelf with a few black boxes that had dials and flashing red lights. I could hear the squawking of a police dispatcher and the responses from units in the field. Scanners. This must be how it really happened.

"I'm busy on this case. I only have three minutes to speak with you. Here's a notepad. Go." Michaels was pushing me. Seeing what I was like under pressure.

I decided to be terse, just like him, stick to the basics and ask the obvious.

"Male or female? Age? Name? Cause of death? Where did the victim live? Any suspects?" I took furious notes as he fired off his answers.

"OK, follow me," Michaels said. "Grab the wire stories you wrote from my desk. You're on the air in two minutes."

We walked briskly into the large news studio. There were racks of lights on the ceiling; massive floor cameras on thick, black wheels; and a colorful news set in the middle, painted in hues of blue with *KVIQ Eyewitness News* prominently displayed in the background. There was an adjoining room behind the cameras with a plate-glass window labeled "Control Room," filled with projectors and other large machines that mystified me. Michaels opened the door and found the engineer. "Fire up the cameras and turn on the lights for a screen test."

As the hot lights flooded the studio, he sat me down in the news chair, wrapped a lavalier microphone around my neck, walked over to a floor camera, and pointed at me, then barked, "You're on the air in thirty seconds. Just back from the murder scene. Forget your notes. Ad-lib what you know. Then read the stories you wrote… right into the camera. Make eye contact. Here we go, 3, 2, 1… You're on."

I took a deep breath and, doing my best to remember how network news reporters sounded, began my story. "I'm Brad Willis. Here's the breaking news. I'm just back from a crime scene in the woods north of town. Homicide Detective Don Michaels tells me the body of a young woman, stabbed to death, has been discovered in a shallow grave. College coed Jane Doe, missing for several days, has been identified as the victim. The police say they have no suspects at this time. We'll stay on the story and keep you informed as more information becomes available."

Then I read the stories I had typed up. *Be sure to pause*, I told myself, *relax into it, be confident*. I glanced up at the camera as often as I could, keeping my right index finger on the script line so I could find my place when I glanced back down. The whole thing was still a lark, but I was already on fire. This was a way to make a difference. To be somebody. All my life I thought I never wanted a career. But now this was all I wanted. Every cell of my body was screaming that I had to have this job.

Back in the newsroom, Michaels asked a final question. "I've interviewed ten people for this job. They are all journalism graduates. Some of them even have reporting experience. You don't. Why should I hire you?"

I stared straight into his eyes, hoping to make my gaze as piercing as his. "Because I'm relentless. I'll work harder and longer than anyone you've ever met. I'll make you proud and I'll never let you down." I meant every word of it. I belonged there. I just knew it.

"Thank you very much, young man." Michaels suddenly turned formal and even more distant. "Give me your phone number. I'll be in touch."

And that was it. I drove home to my cabin, wondering if he and the general manager were chuckling at the rube in work boots who typed with two fingers and had no idea what newswires or police scanners were. I doubted I would ever hear from Michaels. I stuffed my travel gear into a backpack and went to bed, prepared to head for Canada first thing in the morning.

I was tired and groggy when the phone rang before sunrise. "Get in here now and grab a camera! There's a guest at a hunting lodge ninety miles north of here who's gone berserk. He's holed up in a room with his rifle and has already shot someone in the parking lot. I'm sending you to the scene." Michaels threw all this at me so fast I barely understood a word. He hung up before I could ask a question.

I pulled on my blue jeans and the only dress shirt I owned, laced up my boots, jumped into my van, and drove faster than lightning into town. Michaels was at the back door of the studio waiting for me with a handful of wire reports, a Bolex camera, extra film, and a notepad with directions scribbled on the first page.

"Thanks for the job," I said as I grabbed all the stuff and threw it on the seat next to me.

"My number is on the pad," he barked, all business. "Find a phone and call me once you're on the scene. And make me proud."

I sped north on Highway 101 as fast as my old van could go, furiously glancing in every mirror for any sign of the highway patrol. When I arrived at the scene, the lodge was surrounded by more than a dozen law enforcement vehicles. There were police officers, sheriff deputies, and highway patrolmen swarming everywhere with walkie-talkies, guns, and rifles. Cops manning a blockade at the lodge entrance ordered me to keep going. It immediately brought up all my memories of being manhandled at protest rallies. But this was different. I was here this time to report the news, not make it. I needed to be bold, show them I had the authority of the news station behind me. I sucked in a deep breath and slammed on my brakes right in front of them, rolled the window down, stuck the camera out, and shouted, "I'm a reporter from KVIQ-TV!"

It was unbelievable. In an instant, I was an accepted part of the scene. I was allowed to park right there and move as close to the lodge as possible, ducking behind police cars and periodically poking my head up to film the action. The County Sheriff agreed to an interview, giving me about the same three minutes Don Michaels allowed me when I played reporter with him. Within a few hours, the sniper surrendered. I was the only TV journalist there, filming as he walked from the hotel into the parking lot, hands held high, and followed orders to lie facedown on the asphalt as officers swarmed in to make the arrest.

I jumped into my van and blasted back down the highway. I rolled into the parking lot with my gas tank on empty, ran into the station, loaded the film in the processor, and grabbed some script paper. I furiously pecked away at my story and then, with Michaels' help, recorded my report on a bulky eight-track cartridge, editing the film to go with my words. I finished less than two minutes before we went on the air and ran everything into the Control Room just in time. It was an initiation by fire, but I made my first real deadline. I was transfixed, and in that moment the news business became my whole life.

I soon turned myself into an investigative reporter, using pictures and words to peel back the veneer of society and expose corrupt business and political practices. I caught drug detectives falsifying evidence, local council members taking bribes, timber companies illegally cutting down virgin timber in Redwood National Park. Covering the news was what I was born to do. I lived it, breathed it, ate it, and made it my way of crusading against the society from which I had felt so alienated in my earlier years. I was relentless, just as I'd promised Don Michaels I would be.

Within two years, Michaels retired and soon I was named news director, running the small news department, filming and reporting stories throughout the day, anchoring the six and eleven o'clock nightly newscasts, and even cleaning up and taking out the trash before the long drive home to my cabin. It was around-the-clock, usually seven days a week. I made a whopping $600 per month. Far less than I took home from a weekend job painting a house, but I wouldn't have traded it for the world.

CHAPTER 3

Moving Up

A T THE END of my third year at KVIQ, I was beginning to understand something about the business of being a broadcast journalist. The market size of a television station was based on its audience size. I was working in one of the smallest markets in the country, something like number 198 out of 206. If I wanted broader horizons, bigger stories, and more opportunities, I'd need to land a job in a bigger city. But I had no idea how to go about it. Then one morning I received a call from a man introducing himself as Pete Langlois, the news director of KCRA-TV in Sacramento, the twenty-first market, and the state capital to boot.

"We want you to fly down and discuss taking a job with us," Langlois said in soft monotone of a voice.

"Sure, yes," I said with surprise. "But how did you hear about me?" I couldn't imagine anyone outside of Humboldt County even knowing about our little news operation.

"Your competitors," Langlois droned. "They want you out."

There was only one other station in town and they had always been number one in the news. My commitment to investigative reporting had helped turn that around, and after I became news director and anchor, we captured the number-one spot in the ratings and kept it. As Langlois would later explain, the general manager of our competitor station knew the owner of KCRA and had asked him for a favor—to get me out of town.

The job that KCRA offered me wasn't what I expected. I'd be in management as the executive producer of the station's prime-time magazine show, *Weeknight*. It was a light, fluffy show that mixed feature stories from the news department with entertainment and show business reports. They wanted me, they said, because the show needed someone who had been a news director to provide more organization, focus, and leadership than the previous producer. But it meant, they added, that I would no longer be a reporter. I told myself I didn't care. It was a huge jump up in market size, incredible pay, and the only offer on the table. What a mistake it turned out to be.

I gave the show everything I had, always trying to minimize the fluff and inject the investigative journalism I loved. But I was trying to turn a lamb into a lion. The longtime cohosts wanted to keep it soft and light. The reporters only wanted to make the hosts happy. For me, it was like overdosing on candy and I could barely bring myself to even watch *Weeknight*. I argued, sweet-talked, and bullied the staff, trying to make the tone more substantial and journalistic. It was all to no avail. After less than a year it was clear to me, and everyone else, that this job was not for me. When Pete Langlois called me into his office one afternoon, I figured I was about to be fired.

"I don't think you belong with *Weeknight*," he said when I'd barely sat down.

"I know I don't," I answered with a huge sigh, feeling equal jolts of abject fear and complete relief. "I'm not happy. The staff isn't happy. This isn't what I was meant to do."

I confessed to Langlois that it was painfully obvious to me that I was wired to do hard-hitting, investigative news reporting. That's what had come so naturally to me in my first TV job. My passion for the news is what had made me so successful in Eureka.

"I agree with you," Langlois said, sounding as detached as ever. *Here it comes*, I thought, *the end of my career*. Instead, he said, "I want you take over our Call Three. Bring your intense focus and energy to that and there will be no stopping you."

I was stunned, elated, and profoundly relieved. Call Three was an institution at KCRA's Eyewitness News, dedicated to seeking justice for consumers who'd been wronged. Staffed by a group of highly skilled community volunteers, it handled thousands of consumer complaints every month that poured in by phone and mail. Call Three would document their cases, determine the validity of their complaints, and then become their advocate with the merchants or businesses in question. KCRA's designated Call Three reporter would then comb through the resolved cases and pick the best success stories to report on twice a week. The reporter who had handled Call Three for several years had just been hired as a news anchor in another city, and now the segment would be mine.

"I'll take it, Pete," I said so loudly I thought the whole newsroom might hear me. The producer under me at *Weeknight* took over my duties as executive producer, and soon I was off and running with my new gig.

Once I became familiar with the Call Three staff and procedures, I immediately conspired to make it something unique and more substantive. Call Three helped consumers with things like getting shoddy repairs fixed or a refund for a faulty product. The reports would focus on how happy the consumers were that Call Three helped them resolve their complaints. I chose to focus instead on exposing the consumer fraud and went after the perpetrators with my cameras. Once I began peeling back the veils, what seemed like small cases at first often became big stories.

One viewer contacted Call Three to complain that he had been denied medical coverage for his one-year-old daughter who was dying of cancer. Digging into it, we uncovered a billion-dollar construction firm falsifying its payroll records on government-funded housing projects across the country, paying the workers less than half of what it billed the Department of Housing and Urban Development for their labor. This way, the corporation, whose president had close ties with the Republican Party, could skim millions of tax dollars.

The worker highlighted in our story was told that his government-backed health insurance was invalid because he failed to report his full income, which, of course, he never received. I discovered hundreds of other workers in the same boat and, as a result of our reports, the government ultimately forced the corporation to fully compensate them. The health coverage for the little girl whose father first contacted Call Three was validated and she received her cancer treatments.

Viewers soon began calling us with tips. Whistle-blowers came forward. We exposed the local Air Force base polluting the groundwater of its surrounding communities with highly toxic solvents, heroin rings with ties to law enforcement, and even the highest ranking Nazi War criminal ever located in the United States—Otto Von Bolschwing. We found him living in a rest home not ten miles from KCRA.

Although I loved my work and went at it with everything I had, every night I was watching Tom Brokaw on the *NBC Nightly News*, dreaming of being one of his reporters in the field. Not a correspondent at the White House or on Capitol Hill, not based at the New York or Los Angeles bureaus, but a foreign correspondent reporting from the front lines anywhere in the world where there was conflict and turmoil. I didn't know how to make it happen, but I thought continually about getting to network news. It was an obsession.

One day, as if on cue, a stranger named Ken Lindner walked into the newsroom. Tall and lean, with an expensive Italian suit, flashy tie, and a paisley silk muffler scarf tossed casually over his shoulders, Lindner caught the attention of everyone in the newsroom as he shook hands with Langlois and ducked into his office for a meeting. When Lindner emerged a half-hour later he headed straight for my desk and, with a million-dollar smile, said, "Hi, I'm with the William Morris Agency and we want to represent you. Can I take you to lunch?" I glanced toward Langlois's office to see him leaning against the doorway with his arms folded, quietly nodding his approval.

"Sure, let's go," I said, having never heard of William Morris Agency and not having a clue what *representing* me meant.

Lindner took me to the most expensive restaurant in Sacramento, where all the lobbyists at the state capital dined, and soon explained how it worked. Top market and network reporters had well-connected agents who negotiated their contracts and supported them throughout their careers—for a percentage of their salaries, of course. Lindner said he had been watching me for more than a year and met with Langlois to seek permission to represent me. "I think I can get you into a top ten market right away," he said with a gleam in his eye.

It felt suspicious to me. He seemed a little too slick, and being an investigative reporter, I was cynical about anyone and everyone's motives, never taking anything at face value. "Give me one day, okay?" I responded.

"Sure," Lindner answered as he handed me his business card with his private number handwritten on the back. "Take all the time you need."

Back in the newsroom I rushed into Langlois's office. He immediately read my mind. "It's the real deal," he said. "William Morris is a major agency and Lindner is a pro. You're in good hands. We'd like to keep you here, but it's easy to see your ambition and I'm not going to hold you down."

"Thanks, Pete," I said, shaking his hand hard then heading back to my desk to call Lindner immediately and say, "When do I sign?"

A few months later, as promised, Lindner negotiated a new job for me in a top ten market, at WFAA-TV in Dallas, an ABC affiliate and one of the most respected news organizations in the country. It had a consumer unit similar to Call Three, but it was flagging. I was the perfect person, Lindner convinced them, to re-energize it. Before I knew it, I was off to Texas.

I quickly turned the consumer unit into an investigative one. We exposed racial discrimination at several of Dallas's posh nightclubs, where the city's rich and famous gathered. The clubs had secret policies of requiring a second photo identification from African Americans, then denying them entrance even if they managed to comply. We used hidden cameras and microphones to expose them turning away a black woman who happened to be a lawyer in the attorney general's office. Subsequent lawsuits shut down several clubs.

Just as it had been in Eureka and Sacramento, corruption and white-collar crime were plentiful, and I was more aggressive than ever. Only in Texas, the conservative establishment pushed back hard. Business and political leaders began complaining to WFAA management, and the station started trying to tone down my work. I pushed back even harder, refusing to dilute a story and standing my ground. Marty Haig, the news director, was a legend and a man of incredible integrity. But he was on the spot and did his best to walk a fine line between management and news.

When I began working on the plight of a Dallas oilman locked away in a Caracas prison after being framed for a major oil scandal involving the Venezuelan government, the station declined my proposal to cover it. Bullheaded as ever, I took two weeks' vacation, hired a freelance cameraman, flew to Caracas, and shot the story anyway. I even managed to smuggle a camera into the prison on visitors' day and recorded a secret interview with the Texas oilman.

Returning to Dallas, I pitched the story to ABC's primetime network news magazine show *20/20*; the show agreed to buy it. When I shared this with Marty Haig, he was upset and quickly decided WFAA wanted the story. He grudgingly agreed to pay me for all my expenses plus a hefty freelance bonus. The reports, which I titled *Petrospies*, created a sensation in Texas, got the attention of diplomats in Washington, D.C., and ultimately the oilman was freed. But my relationship with Marty Haig and WFAA would never be the same. I distrusted and resented them, and vice versa. My next story proved to be my last.

It was 1984 and the Republican National Convention was about to be held in Dallas, where the delegates would nominate President Ronald Reagan to run for a second term. As it turned out, the construction company I had exposed in Sacramento was based in Dallas and played a major role in Republican politics. The federal government was still investigating them, so I updated the story and produced a five-part series. The night before it was scheduled to run, Haig called me into his office to say the station's legal department was killing my stories. "They say the reports don't pass legal review," he said matter of factly. "They're libelous and will get us sued."

Furious, I demanded to meet with the legal department and challenge its position. To his credit, Haig supported me on this.

That afternoon, as I rifled through all my files to defend my work, I discovered something I had never noticed: WFAA's law firm also represented the construction company my reports had exposed! The next morning, I tore into the legal team, defended my work, pointed out its obvious conflict of interest, and promised that if the reports were killed I'd take it to the Dallas newspapers and expose the whole thing. When it was over, Haig said, "We'll air one report tonight, and one only. You'll have to cut the series down to something less than three minutes. That's it."

Haig didn't have to say anything more. I knew this would be my last report for WFAA. I went back to the station and worked right up to the five o'clock evening news deadline, then walked onto the set to give the lead-in live and answer a few softball questions from the anchors when it was over. The next morning when I arrived at the station, Haig called me straight into his office.

"It's time to cut the sheets," he said, looking down at some papers in his hands.

"You mean not working here any longer?" I said, as if clarification was necessary.

"Yes," Haig said, finally glancing up. "We're letting you go."

"No need," I shot back, "I quit."

I stood up and shook his hand, and thanked him for everything. He was a good man in a tough spot. "See you around," I said and walked back to my desk.

In less than a minute, a security guard tapped me on the shoulder and stated with authority, "Please give me your station identity card. WFAA has the legal rights to all of your files. I'm here to escort you to your car. A settlement on your contract will be negotiated with your agent."

I opened my wallet, handed over my identity card, and walked away, saying politely but firmly, "I can show myself out."

❋

It was the first time I'd ever been fired from anything. I had occasionally wondered if something like this might happen one day, and the thought had always made me shudder with fear. Now, I was surprised at how great it felt.

"Don't worry," Lindner comforted me when I called him from my high-rise apartment overlooking the Dallas skyline. "We'll find a better spot for you. Just give me some time."

"Okay," I answered. "I'm going back to California as soon as I can book a flight. I'll be in touch from there."

It took a few days to arrange for the packing and shipping of my things, then I was off to a small island in San Diego Bay called Coronado, where I had relatives. I rented a condo overlooking the bay and began catching up with family and friends. The settlement on my contract paid my salary for another year. Surely, I thought, Lindner would come through in a flash. I could just relax, sun myself at the beach, and have a good time. But before two weeks was up, I was going stir-crazy. I had no idea what to do with myself without reporting. It was like having no identity. No reason for being. I was completely lost.

The weeks turned into one month, then two, then three. After half a year, I thought I might explode. That's when Lindner finally called. WBZ-TV in Boston, an NBC affiliate in an even bigger news market, liked the reel of my reports that William Morris sent them. I soon had a new contract and an even higher salary. I could breathe again; I was back in the game.

I leased a grand old apartment in the historic Back Bay overlooking the Charles River and the verdigris dome of MIT. It was thrilling to be in this sophisticated city with its rich history, but I knew, even at this prestigious station, local news would never be enough. Going to Afghanistan was just a start. I had to pitch more global stories, stretch the limits, make a mark. I was thirty-six years old. By the end of my three-year contract at WBZ, I'd be close to forty. After that, I told myself, I had to be at the network or I'd be past my prime. Ambition was consuming me again.

CHAPTER 4

Tropical Storm

THE OCTOBER SUN BREAKS the morning horizon and bathes us in golden light. It's already freezing in Boston, but it's sublime here in the Bahamas. Warm breezes carry the rich aroma of the salt air across the tiny island. Gentle ocean waves roll in a soft song, lapping onto the white sand. Pelicans, gulls, and kingfishers soar above us, then splash into the ocean for a meal.

It's the end of 1986, and it's my first vacation in years. I've always been so obsessed with my career that I haven't wanted to take a real holiday since the day I began. There was only the break between the Dallas and Boston jobs, and that was all stress. Now, after being on the road airing my reports from Afghanistan at our other stations, followed by weeks of investigative work at WBZ, I need the downtime. And I'm actually interested in really getting to know someone: Mary Beth, the graphic artist at WBZ who I've always found to be a little mysterious and intriguing in her graceful silence. We've dated for a month, and now we're on this adventure together.

Mary Beth and I have been here five days—five restful days on a remote little island in the Bahamas called Elbow Cay, sunning ourselves on isolated beaches ringed by palms, papaya trees, and tropical pines. In the morning, we snorkel with giant manta rays and tropical fish. As evening nears, I drift our tiny motorboat over crystal-blue waters, dive over the side, and swim down to coral reefs in order to grab spiny lobsters for dinner. At the end of the day, we watch the

40

sunset color the horizon through our wine glasses, then gaze into the skies until the first stars appear.

It's amazingly beautiful, and getting to know Mary Beth better is a joy, but I just can't relax. I'm dying to get back in the groove, break another story, or pitch another international trip. When I'm in the field confronting the target of an investigative report, or even on turbulent foreign soil, like I was with the mujahideen in the Afghan war, I feel perfectly calm and stress-free. Here in paradise, I'm stressed out and distracted, consumed with thoughts of getting to network news. It's an obsession that even a romantic vacation can't drive away. I'm Type A, healthy as a horse, and I feel invincible. I'm also dying to know what's going on in the world as we wake on our last full day of vacation. Little do I know that the worst accident of my life is screaming across the ocean and heading straight for me.

Mary Beth and I plan to spend this final day soaking up the sun, eating cold lobster salad, and snorkeling in the shallow inlet of our favorite little beach, where we've never seen another soul. The beach is just a short walk from our vacation rental home, and today's another perfect morning, with calm breezes and tranquil waters. When we arrive, the beach is all ours again, and we spread out our towels on the fine sand, dab on some sunscreen, and agree to take a swim after a little sunbathing. I doze off but soon awaken with a start. A thick black mass of clouds has appeared on the horizon, and the ocean is starting to roil and froth. The wind is kicking up hard, wailing through the island pines, and bending the palm trees sideways.

Not wanting to get soaked, Mary Beth and I jump up from the beach and run back through a small forest to our vacation rental home. It sits alone in a pine forest at the ocean's edge, facing the approaching storm. As we arrive, the entire sky turns black. A torrential rain slams into the house. Its large, plate-glass windows vibrate and hum as the tempest descends on us. The force of the wind is so powerful we wonder if it's a hurricane.

I have just a few minutes to batten down more than a dozen storm shutters before the brunt of the storm hits. I run to each window, yanking hard at the heavy wooden shutters as their rusty hinges resist. I finally close them all, except one. It's stuck. As I struggle with the rusty latch, it punches a hole in my thumb before I finally secure it.

Completely soaked and with blood trickling down my arm, I dash inside and slam the door. The whole house shakes as the storm lashes against it with amazing force. We hear a loud-pitched scream and look up to see a small, open window at the top of the vaulted ceiling in the bedroom where we've taken refuge. It's shaking so hard I think it might burst.

"I've got to close that," I say to Mary Beth.

"Why?" she asks softly.

"I'm not sure," I answer, laughing a little at myself. "It just seems like the right thing to do. Maybe the glass will break and the room will be damaged by the rain. Besides, I can't stand the noise."

I'm six feet tall, but the window is far above my head, so I have to climb onto a dresser and then pull myself up and balance on a narrow ledge as the storm continues to scream like a banshee.

Barely steadying myself, I reach up and grab the window handles as the salty spray of the storm whips at my face. They're badly corroded and I have to force them. As I twist harder, it happens in an instant. Both handles snap off in my hands. I fly off the ledge, falling twelve feet to the hardwood floor and slamming onto my back.

No matter how hard I try, I can't breathe. My heart is pounding like a jackhammer. My ears are screaming. Mary Beth kneels by my side and holds me, pleading with me to take a breath. I gasp and convulse for what seems an eternity. *Please, body, breathe. Just breathe.* I begin fearing I might die from suffocation. Then, it's like a dam bursting open as the first inhale floods in. A wave of relief rolls over me as I drink in the oxygen. Now I try to get up from the floor. I'm stuck. I can't seem to send the right signal to my legs. They won't move at all.

I've been lying here on the floor for ten minutes. I still can't move my legs. I can feel them, but I can't make them do my bidding. No matter how hard I try to will them to, they won't move.

"Just stay down. Give it time. You'll be fine." Mary Beth is comforting me, saying just the right things, but I can hear the fear in her voice.

"I'm okay," I tell her with a grunt, but I have to use my arms to drag myself across the floor, grab the bedpost, and pull myself onto the mattress. I'm exhausted, yet I feel very little pain. I must still be in shock from the fall. *You'll be fine in the morning*, I tell myself with my usual hubris, then collapse into a deep sleep as the storm continues to rage.

At dawn, the sun is pouring through the tiny window with the broken handles as if nothing ever happened. The skies are calm and the tropical storm, having never become a hurricane, has passed. It's time for the long trip back to the States, but as I stand up from the bed my legs are like noodles and I fall down to my knees. My lower back is on fire. It feels like there's an ice pick in my tailbone and someone is twisting it just to torment me. Despite the agony, I have to laugh as I consider the irony: I just tromped through the freezing mountains of Afghanistan during a terrible war without suffering a scratch, but now I'm on a warm beach in paradise so wounded I can barely walk.

I grit my teeth and force myself to stand. The pain deepens. *Don't worry. This will soon be over. Tough it out.* I repeat this silently as Mary Beth and I head for the ferry boat. There are no cars on the island. We have to take our little boat and motor to the main harbor, then walk to the ferry landing. I limp the entire way, holding the left side of my lower back with one hand while dragging my suitcase with the other hand. When we board the ferry, I grip a rail and steady myself during the long ride to a larger island, where we finally catch a commuter flight to Florida.

By the time we land in Miami, my whole body is on fire. As I limp toward baggage claim gritting my teeth, a TV at the airport bar catches my eye. It's breaking news. A covert CIA operative, Eugene Hassenfus, has been shot down and captured in Nicaragua. He was airlifting military supplies to right-wing Contras fighting to overthrow the socialist government of President Daniel Ortega. It's long been suspected that the American government was behind the war, and here's the first tangible evidence. Adrenalin rushes through my veins and I prepare to jump on the story in any way possible, pain be damned.

I'm at WBZ the next morning, covering local angles on the story, including street protests, predictable sound bites of outrage from our Massachusetts senators, and obfuscations from White House Press Secretary Larry Speakes. Being fully absorbed in the news is power-ful medicine for me, and it takes my mind off the pain. Anyway, I'll be better in no time. It was only a little fall from a ledge. Nothing to worry about.

The back pain subsides after a few nights of rest, allowing me to function closer to my normal level. But at least one morning each week I wake up with a tender back and shaky legs. It inevitably gets worse throughout the day. When this happens, sitting to write a news script or edit videotape agitates the problem and sets my back on fire. An airplane or helicopter flight to cover a story is scorching. On top of it all, every few weeks the invisible tormenter with the ice pick sneaks up behind me and stabs me in the tailbone again.

Some days it hurts so badly I want to scream out loud, but I stuff it. I'm convinced that I'll be better soon. Meanwhile, I feel like I can't let anyone know I'm injured. I have to push forward. In this busi-ness, the weak fall behind and most of them never catch up again. I'll never let that happen to me. *Never.*

Three months have gone by since I crashed onto my back during the storm in the Bahamas. I'm still running at full speed, artfully hiding the problem from my colleagues, each day faking that I'm fine. But the pain is deep. Gnawing. The invisible ice pick torturing me more often. I try everything to make it better: different postures in my chair. A seat cushion. Cold packs. Hot packs. Salt baths at home. Nothing does the trick. Physical therapy and massage at my gym provide temporary relief, but I'm merely treating the symptoms.

My back is not healing. I don't like doctor offices and am only comfortable in hospitals if I'm there as a reporter with a camera crew and an interesting story to cover. But this looks like the only option left. Reluctantly, I finally decide to see an orthopedic specialist.

"You have a hairline fracture in L5, the lowest lumbar vertebra in your spinal column," the doctor says as he holds the X-ray film up to the light.

"You see the pedicles, the two flanges that protrude from the sides of each vertebra?" I have to look closely to see them. They seem like stubby wings sticking out from the sides of each disc.

He points his pen to a thin, blurry line running across a portion of the left pedicle. "This is a hairline fracture. Technically, you have a mildly broken back. I can't believe you are still functioning at the level you are."

"No, it's not a broken back, just a little crack," I snap at him with unintended anger. This has been happening more often with me as a result of the nagging pain. I hear myself getting short with people, sounding aggravated when I don't intend to. "So what can we do?" All I want is a quick solution.

"We might be able to control the pain with medications and a brace," he continues, "but you need to have surgery if you want to fix this. I'd like you to see a colleague of mine, a surgeon who specializes in these procedures."

This is out of the question. Surgery would take way too much time. Get in the way of my career. I obstinately refuse to even consider it. I rationalize it in an instant, recalling having a broken arm and leg as a child and how each injury healed in due time without surgery. My back tightens as my resolve intensifies. *I can still meet deadlines*, I think to myself. *Travel anywhere. Rough it whenever necessary. I am not spineless. I am not crippled. I am not stopping now.*

I grit my teeth and say to the doctor, "I'll take the brace and the pain medications."

The doctor's reaction makes it clear he doesn't agree with my choice, but he complies and fits me with an elastic back brace that straps around my waist. It has two thin metal bands that curve into the arch of my lower back to support the main muscles flanking my lumbar vertebrae. He also prescribes medication: a high-strength dosage of the anti-inflammatory drug Motrin, along with Valium to relax the muscles that often flare up from my buttocks to my shoulder blades.

"You shouldn't drink alcohol with the medications," the doctor warns, "and let me know if the Motrin bothers your stomach."

I'm barely listening, still numb from the thought of having a broken back. I can hardly bring myself to say thank you. I fill the prescriptions at the pharmacy below his office and stop at a water fountain to swallow a dose of each, having no idea that I'm taking my first step into what will become a pharmaceutical-induced nightmare.

Mary Beth and I are still seeing one another, but I'm not a very good partner. Back pain makes me irritable and impatient, and I'm only interested in pushing my career forward. Everything else is on hold. I can't work out at the gym any longer, I've stopped going out on the town, and I'm no longer taking long walks along the Charles River after work. At the TV station I've found a vacant room upstairs and sneak into it whenever possible to lie down on the floor and rest. Three times a day I gobble Motrin and each night down a Valium with a glass of wine, ignoring my doctor's warning about mixing alcohol with drugs.

I'm able to cover the local news in Boston, pursuing the investigative reporting I love, but I have to back off the computer several times a day, stand up, and press my palms into my tender lower back while pushing my hips forward. It's become a newsroom joke as my fellow reporters jump up from their chairs now and then, playfully mocking my stance. They still have no idea how bad it is. My back brace is invisible beneath my trousers and sport coat, and I tell no one about it for fear the station will stop sending me on more rigorous assignments.

My career is all that matters. I have to move forward. Afghanistan was just a few months ago, but it seems like years. I have to find the next opportunity to pitch an international story. I feel like I've almost made it to the top of the mountain and my body is trying to drag me back down. *No way. I'm not giving in. I'll never stop.*

CHAPTER 5

Apartheid

I T'S 1987 AND THE STRUGGLE AGAINST APARTHEID, South
Africa's white supremacy system, is boiling over. There are riots
and violent clashes throughout the country. Nelson Mandela, the
charismatic founder of the African National Congress (ANC), has
been imprisoned by the South African government for years and is
now a living martyr. Massachusetts Senator Ted Kennedy is pushing
for strict economic sanctions against South Africa in hopes of freeing
Mandela and forcing an end to government-sanctioned racism. The
Reagan Administration calls Mandela's ANC a terrorist organization
and is adamantly opposed to sanctions. Instead, Reagan promotes
"Constructive Engagement," a euphemism for preserving the status
quo. It's a classic struggle between liberals and conservatives.

With antiapartheid protests in New England, there's great local interest in the international story. The networks have bureaus in South
Africa with correspondents filing reports almost nightly, so if I want
to cover it myself, I have to come up with a unique angle. I decide to
focus on Zambia, where the ANC is now headquartered and run by
Nelson Mandela's law partner, Oliver Tambo.

Tambo is in exile and a prime target for the South African government. It takes weeks for me to make contact, even with the help of
Senator Kennedy's staff. When I finally do get his top aide on the
phone, he confirms that Tambo has agreed to an on-camera interview with us. This positions me to tell the story from the perspective

of what are called the Frontline Nations of Zambia, Zimbabwe, Botswana, and Mozambique, where black Africans have their independence and are putting up a united front against apartheid. When WBZ approves the proposal, it's like a miraculous medicine for my back. I can barely feel the pain as Dennis and I board a flight to Africa. Even so, I take an extra dose of Valium and Motrin as we land in Zambia more than fifteen hours later, just to be sure.

Zambia is landlocked, sitting atop the lower third of the continent like a gateway to its southern regions. The capital city of Lusaka, built on a plateau, is subtropical and steamy. Humidity hangs heavy in the air as we bounce into the city in a taxi that feels like it lost its shock absorbers years ago. A million poverty-stricken people live here, virtually on top of one another. The streets are organized chaos. Makeshift markets selling paltry goods. Children play on street corners as raw sewage flows by. Starving dogs fight over bits of food hidden in the piles of trash. The stench is overwhelming, but the thrill of being on a major story makes it almost smell sweet.

Surprisingly, there is little sense of desperation amid all this filth and chaos. The Zambian people hold themselves with dignity. It's been two decades since they ended a century of white domination and exploitation, mostly at the hands of the British. Every time we jump out of our taxi to film, young people immediately surround us to express the pride they feel as members of an independent nation.

In South Africa, it was the white Afrikaners who fought with the British for primacy and ultimately took power. The Afrikaners are a deeply conservative German, Dutch, and French ethnic group called Boers who migrated to South Africa in the 1600s. They formed a political minority National Party that managed to take power in 1948 and quickly enacted harsh segregationist laws that became known as apartheid, which means "apartness." The policy created a system of complete social and economic discrimination against black South Africans, who were forced into ghettos called townships and denied all rights.

To fight back against the ANC and Frontline Nations, Special Forces of the South African government regularly launch military strikes into Zambia. They have secret police throughout Lusaka. Assassinations of ANC leaders are all too common. Oliver Tambo has various safe houses hidden within the heart of the city. It takes a day to arrange a secret meeting with Isaac, the ANC operative who will guide us to the right location. We meet at a side street several blocks from our hotel.

"Welcome," Isaac says with polite formality and a firm handshake. "We must move quickly. I will speak to your driver. Please get back in your car." Isaac whispers something to our driver, Jonas, and walks off in his well-tailored suit like a businessman headed for an urgent meeting. His commitment to the struggle is palpable. It's clear he's prepared to die for his beliefs, and equally clear he intends not to.

Jonas starts the car quickly and turns into the first alley, entering a maze: Narrow lanes. No street signs. Thicker crowds. Within five minutes I'm completely lost and know I would never find my way out of here without a guide. We begin doubling back, circling, losing anyone who might be following. A sudden stop. We're in front of a fifteen-foot, rusted steel wall with a small doorway cut into its center. Suddenly, Isaac appears from nowhere, now clad in a faded T-shirt and jeans, blending perfectly into the neighborhood.

"Grab your gear and follow me," Isaac says with firm calmness. "In here. Quickly." He knocks a code on the steel wall with his knuckles as we get out of the car. Thick steel bolts are unlocked from the interior and the door swings open with a screech. We slip inside the compound with Isaac, and behind us the door is immediately slammed shut and bolted by a tall, muscular young man with a pistol tucked into his waistband. We are standing in a dirt courtyard ten yards from a single-story structure that looks like a cross between a workshop and a residence.

Two more men, also with firearms, approach us with the same formal politeness of Isaac and softly say, "We must check you for weapons." One man frisks Dennis and me with seasoned proficiency. The other deftly goes through all of our bags. "Thank you," they both say after concluding we're unarmed.

"Through here." Isaac takes charge again and leads us into the main door. We go down a corridor with aging hardwood floors and yellowish stucco walls, past a small room filled with filing cabinets, and then a larger room with desks and a few men studiously doing their work. No one glances up, but everyone is aware of our presence.

Now we're turning left down another corridor. Isaac unlocks a door and we enter a comfortable living room with couches and chairs. There's a wide bay window looking out onto a small court-yard with deep green shrubbery and a few trees soaking in glancing rays of warm sunlight. "Please set up your camera," Isaac instructs. "Mr. Tambo will be with you shortly."

After fifteen minutes, Oliver Tambo steps softly through a side door wearing a traditional wax-dyed shirt, called a batik, of bright yellow, red, and green patterns. He is almost seventy years old. He has salt-and-pepper hair, a light beard, and thick, black-rimmed glasses. He welcomes us with a soft smile as Dennis clips a micro-phone on his shirt.

Before I ask a question, he says, "We have struggled against oppression for generations. It is now time for our liberation."

"Critics say your movement embraces terrorism and has many communist members," I reply in a respectful tone. "What is your answer to this?"

"We are puppets to no one," Tambo says with authority and convic-tion. "We want a democratic, nonracial South Africa where all politi-cal parties can participate. We have taken aid from socialist countries because no Western democracies will help us, despite their public statements about seeking equality and justice throughout the world. We have also received support from Scandinavia, which is hardly a radical nation. And no one who assists us tells us what to do."

It's the Cold War again, a story that's played out too many times in too many places around the world. America and the Soviet Union fight each other this way, using smaller, less developed countries as proxies. Its victims always seem to be those facing poverty and strug-gling for freedom. Mr. Tambo is eloquent in articulating his case, and the interview ends far too quickly for me. After ten minutes of conver-sation, his aide says he must go. We have all the material we need, but I could talk to this wise and elegant man into the middle of the night.

Isaac guides us back to the compound entryway. Incredible luck. Chris Hani has just arrived under heavy guard for a meeting with Tambo. Hani is one of the most controversial, elusive, and wanted figures in the movement. I remember seeing his photo during my research and I was struck by the power he exuded. Hani leads the armed wing of the ANC. It's called *Umkhonto we Sizwe*, which means Spear of the Nation. Unlike the Gandhi-inspired nonviolence embraced by Mandela and Tambo, members of *Umkhonto we Sizwe* are convinced that the brutality and injustice of apartheid can only be overcome through armed struggle. South Africa's Secret Police hunt these guerilla fighters relentlessly and kill them when they can. This is probably why we went through so much secrecy and backtracking to get here this morning.

"Mr. Hani." I stop him as he is about to enter the residence. "We've just completed interviewing Mr. Tambo. May we have a word with you?" His guards stiffen and are about to brush us aside when Hani stops them and answers, "Of course. I can give you a minute."

Dennis swings his camera onto his shoulder and slips a microphone into my hand with amazing speed. "Why violence?" I ask. "Why not follow Mandela and Tambo? Peaceful resistance. Civil disobedience?"

"I am a communist and a patriot," Hani says gently. His boyish face and wide smile make it hard to believe he embraces armed struggle until he says, "I make no apologies. The South African government has brutalized, tortured, and killed too many of our people. They make false promises, break agreements, treat us like children. The only thing they will ever understand is violence. We must let them taste the suffering they have given us, make them insecure in their homes and on the streets." Hani is charismatic and articulate. He is the second most popular figure in the resistance movement after Nelson Mandela. Six years after we air our interview with him he will be assassinated.

Departing Lusaka, we move deep into the countryside, passing through small villages and remote areas where armed gangs with murky allegiances often ambush travelers. Zambia had previously been the British Colony of North Rhodesia until it declared independence in 1964. Billy Nkunika, a cross between an intellectual and a street-savvy survivor, was a leader of the resistance against the British and is now an advisor to the ANC. We're lucky to have him with us as both guide and protector.

It's our second day of moving south from Lusaka toward the borders of Zimbabwe and Botswana. Just before nightfall, we round a sweeping corner through the jungle and find the road blocked by two battered pickup trucks. As Jonas slams on the brakes, we're quickly surrounded by a dozen armed men. Two of them have rifles pointed directly at us. The rest brandish large machetes as they order us to get out of our car. It's little matter that Dennis and I are not South African; the fact that we're white and carrying expensive camera gear is enough to place us in grave danger.

Nkunika orders Jonas to leave the engine running as he jumps out fearlessly, barking at the men with great authority. A few of the younger members of the gang, who look to be in their early teens, start tapping their machetes on the hood of our car while pressing their faces against the window, staring hard at us. I think about the five thousand dollars I have in my satchel for travel needs and emergencies. Our camera gear is worth a small fortune.

Dennis whispers, "This is trouble." I'm about to agree when Nkunika bursts back into the car, shoving the young men aside, slams the door and rolls down his window still yelling that he fought against racism before they were born. One of the battered trucks is pushed back and we roar through the roadblock. Dennis and I look at one another and sigh in unison. Without Nkunika, who knows what would have happened.

"These young men are crazy," Nkunika says at a jungle hut where we are spending the night. "They don't know anything about this struggle. They are filled with rage. All they want to do is rob people."

We are having a simple dinner of *nshima*, a bland, pasty dish made from maize. It's also called mealie-meal. It's almost impossible to swallow. Then it sticks to your ribs.

"It's hard to blame them," I say. "They've been terribly oppressed. There are no jobs, no future. I understand why they would want to rob us. What did you say that saved us?"

Nkunika smiles. "I lied to them," he answers. "I told them we had three more trucks behind us in an armed convoy and they would all be killed on the spot if they didn't let us go and scram before our soldiers arrive."

The following morning, deep in the arid bush, we film lines of women standing for hours in the brutal sun with their children to get a few cups of grain from humanitarian organizations. Relief workers weigh their infants and provide powders for malnutrition, diarrhea, and dehydration. Despite the obvious poverty, many of the children seem happy and are glad to see us there. Others stand with blank gazes, flies covering their faces, lips bleeding from the scorching heat, bellies swollen like ripe watermelons from the ravages of dysentery.

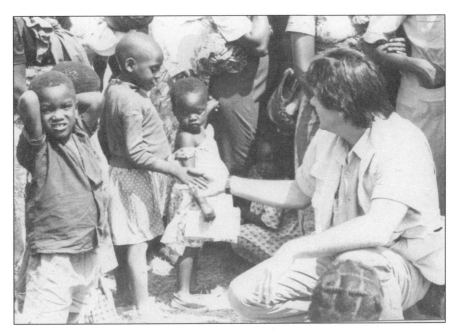

Zambian countryside, 1986.

In preparing for this trip, I came across facts that floored me: Half the people in the world live on less than two dollars a day. More than thirty thousand die daily from starvation; of these, fifteen thousand are children. We came to do a story on apartheid in South Africa and Nelson's movement, but we've also captured scene after scene of the poverty that rules these African nations, and I will weave it into the narratives at every opportunity.

Thinking about this on the flight back to Boston, I realize I take so many simple luxuries for granted: A beautiful home. A refrigerator filled with so much food there's always some that's going bad. A bathroom with running water. More widgets and gadgets than anyone needs. It's embarrassing. What are any of my problems compared to those who are forced to struggle every day just to survive? Who am I to ever complain about a sore back, even if it's on fire right now as I sit in first class having a filet mignon and my second glass of cabernet?

CHAPTER 6

Drug Wars

THE YEAR 1989 is coming to a close, and crack cocaine is exploding on the scene. Crack is a highly addictive form of the drug that is smoked for an instant high. Its name comes from the crackling sound it makes when it's lit. It's cheap and readily available on street corners, and many inner-city Boston neighborhoods are ruled by gangs, guns, and drugs. It's a powerful story, and it's complicated. Gangbangers are building empires, and there are shootouts in the darkest hours of night. Innocent victims get wounded and sometimes killed. Courageous cops risk their lives. Corrupt cops are on the take. Weapons flood the streets. This is much more than a local story. It's a national epidemic. An estimated 2 million Americans use cocaine. More than a quarter of a million are already hooked on crack.

Hoping to turn off the tap at the source, President George H. Bush is holding a drug summit in Cartagena, Colombia, with the leaders of Colombia, Bolivia, and Peru, where most of the world's cocaine is produced. Cartagena is a magnificent, centuries-old city sitting on the confluence of the Magdalena River and Caribbean Sea. I took working vacations there a few times before moving to Boston, helping produce an International Music Festival for Colombian TV with Camillo Pombo, the nephew of Colombian president Cesar Gaviria. It's a natural. I've got a strong local angle on a national and international story, and I have good connections and know my way around where the summit is being held.

When I pitch the story, news director Stan Hopkins supports me again, and I'm soon in Cartagena with Dennis, broadcasting live reports from a temporary headquarters set up by NBC's Miami Bureau. The summit is big news around the globe and all the networks are here, along with Latin, European, and Asian correspondents. But it's more political theater than substance. The United States blames the source countries and wants the coca crops destroyed. Colombia, Bolivia, and Peru resent being blamed. Still, they need trade and assistance from America and are always happy to take the millions of dollars America offers for eradication programs. Some of it might even go toward eradicating coca crops. Most of it will wind up in the pockets of the politicians and business elite.

As far as the people here are concerned, the cocaine epidemic is America's problem. Our national addiction has created the industry and funded brutal drug cartels that often have more power than the governments down here. In Colombia, for example, politicians and judges who don't acquiesce to the drug lords are periodically kidnapped or assassinated. As Camillo likes to say to me, "Why don't you tell the Americans to wipe their noses and stop sniffing cocaine? Then we will have nothing to sell to you. End of problem. Don't come running down here blaming us and telling us what to do."

Each day of the summit I go live from the NBC headquarters, reporting for our evening news on WBZ. I feel closer to the possibility of a network job when I meet the networks' Miami bureau chief, Don Browne, here to run NBC's coverage. He's dynamic, in charge, constantly projecting a sense of contained authority. As we talk, it's like the job is sitting there in front of me on his desk and I can almost reach out and grab hold of it.

At night, I head into the elegant old city to eat at Paco's, owned by Camillo's close friend Paco De Onis. His world-class restaurant is a two-story villa of white plaster, stone floors, and broad wood-beam ceilings. Camillo, here from Bogota to report for his national radio show, always joins me for dinner.

Tonight the restaurant is cordoned off by heavily armed Colombian military police. Immediately curious, Dennis and I push up to the cordons. A guard with an automatic rifle gestures for us to leave.

I flash the badge I have for the summit. It's meaningless, but it looks official. Before he can even look at it, Dennis and I slip past him, ignoring his shouts for us to stop. It's a simple ploy. Stop and he might arrest us, or keep going and he'll think we must be authorized to be there. It usually works like a charm, and this time is no exception.

At first, we can't figure out what's happening. Finally, we get to Paco's and see it's surrounded by more guards. Because we made it through the outer cordon, they readily grant us access. Once inside, Camillo is shocked to see us. "How did you get in?" he asks with wide eyes. "The presidents and their men are here. I had trouble getting in myself." He means the presidents of Bolivia and Peru here for the summit, not George Bush. This is a Latin meeting. Off the record. Behind the scenes.

"We bluffed our way in," I laugh as we greet one another with our usual hug. "Where are they?"

"They are upstairs," Camillo says, referring to the presidents. He glances at Dennis's shoulder bag. "If you have a camera, do not take it out. Whatever you do, do not go upstairs." I've never seen Camillo so intense.

I'm dying to shoot footage of this, but taking the camera out would be crazy. It would quickly be confiscated and we might be taken somewhere for a good beating. But I can't resist going upstairs. Shortly after our dinner arrives, I excuse myself to the bathroom. Then I slip up the curved stone stairwell. It's a lavish party. The room upstairs is filled with men I take for presidential aides and security agents. There are also several incredibly beautiful women, surely hired for the occasion. I glance around quickly, getting the best look I can before I'm noticed. I can't see any of the presidents. There's no way to ensure they're here except for the overwhelming anecdotal evidence. Why else would armed guards cordon off the street? And then there are Camillo's warnings. He always knows what's going on and who the players are. Still, I can't confirm anything and I've already pushed it too far.

On a coffee table I see a large, oval tray made of crystal. There's a huge mound of sparkling white powder in the middle, like a pyramid. Cocaine. Pure cocaine. I see a razor blade and a few thin lines, three or four inches long, waiting to be snorted. Now I realize how dangerous it was to come up here. What a summit. Promises of cooperation during the day. Something else at night. If only I could turn on a camera. Film anyone involved with the drug summit. Get video of the coke. The world-class escorts. It would be a monster story. Everything would stop in its tracks. The summit would crash. An international incident. Oh God, would I love to bag this one.

A muscular looking man in an expensive black suit steps over to the tray, leans over, and snorts up a line of cocaine. He straightens back up and glances at me as he sniffs his nose. Then he does a double take. He's alarmed. I act casual but get downstairs as fast as I can, blending in with the crowd.

Sitting for dinner with Camillo and Paco, I don't speak a word about what's upstairs, but I can't stop thinking about the camera on the floor by Dennis's feet. I'll risk almost anything for a big story. But this wouldn't be a risk. It would be insanity. I can hardly imagine our fate if we tried to pull this off and got caught.

Refining cocaine is a hideous process. It begins in rustic laboratories called *pozos*, typically hidden in the tropical mountain forests. *Pozos* look like anything but labs. They're created by digging large pits in the earth under the cover of the jungle canopy. Tons of coca leaves from farms blanketing the hillsides below are transported in on the backs of mules. Hundreds of gallons of kerosene are poured into the pits, and local children are recruited, often by force, to stand in the sludge for up to twelve hours a day, stomping it with their bare feet. This leeches the cocaine alkaloid from the coca leaves. The soupy mixture is shoveled into large sieves strung between tree branches. The kerosene trickles out through the sieve, leaving behind a thick yellowish paste called *basuco*, which is then loaded into burlap sacks for transport to much more sophisticated city labs.

After the summit, Dennis and I set out to produce a series of in-depth reports on the origins of cocaine. We fly to Bolivia and then helicopter into the mountains above the city of Cochabamba with a heavily armed Bolivian military strike force, funded by the United States as a result of the drug summit, seeking to destroy as many *pozos* as it can discover. Smoke plumes from fires built to keep the workers dry and to cook their food are always the tip-off. As soon as he spots one, our pilot manages to land in impossible places. As he's touching down, we jump out with the troops as they invade the lab. The noise of the chopper tips off the refiners and they flee before we arrive. It doesn't matter. The labs are the real target. The strike force burns down every one it finds simply by sloshing the *pozo* kerosene over everything and tossing in a match. This

Coca Drug Lab, Bolivia, 1989.

hardly puts a dent in the trade, but it shows that Bolivia is doing something with the millions of dollars of American aid it's receiving.

The paste from the jungle labs is smuggled down the mountain into cities such as Cochabamba. Here, it's refined into pure cocaine and eventually smuggled worldwide. Like most drug-refining cities, Cochabamba is host to powerful cartels who bribe and intimidate local officials. Finding a lab here would be next to impossible, even for the strike force. We part company with the soldiers and decide to illustrate what *basuco* is doing to the local culture in Cochabamba, which is also a haven for low-level drug dealers. They hook young street orphans on smoking *basuco*, use them to deliver drugs, and force them into prostitution. Some of the children are barely five years old.

We find these children early one morning in a dry riverbed that threads through the city. They're living in holes they've dug in the clay with their hands. They work in the city from shortly after sunrise to sunset for the dealers, then crawl into their holes at night to smoke *basuco*, the only pay they receive. Within a few years, the toxic paste destroys their nervous systems. Most of them never make it to their teens.

We film an interview with a boy named Alejandro, clearly the dean of the riverbed. He is twelve years old, but he's so small and thin that he barely looks eight. The dark circles around his eyes are haunting. And the *basuco* has given him a form of palsy. It's painful to watch him struggle to coordinate his spasmodic arms and head as he fills his pipe, fights to get the stem between his lips, lights it, and sucks in a long hit.

"My parents threw me on the streets when I was five. I was the youngest of many brothers and sisters. They could not afford to feed me," says Alejandro as he exhales a plume of deadly smoke that eerily wisps around his face.

His words are garbled and hard for our interpreter to understand, but a deep intelligence still manages to come through. "This is my home. I have lived here seven years. Longer than anyone else. I know I'm dying now. I don't care. All I want is my *basuco*. They can push the clay over me when I'm dead." With his head shaking,

With Alejandro in Cochabamba, Bolivia, 1990.

hands quivering, and eyes spasming, Alejandro takes another hit and drifts off into a world of his own. As we say good-bye, I wish I could lift this boy out of his hole in the riverbed, carry him in my arms to an airplane, whisk him home, help him recover, and give him a new life.

My final day in South America, still in Cochabamba, Bolivia, I feel my back catching on fire again. I still have some Motrin, but I'm out of Valium. I'm on a major story far from home, and so the prospect of a serious flare-up scares me to death. I find a drugstore that looks more like a corner newsstand, with a half-dozen sheets of Valium pills sitting on an outdoor table by the entryway, each encapsulated in a little plastic bubble. The sheets hold two dozen pills apiece and cost next to nothing, and I don't need a prescription here. I buy them all and quickly punch three or four from one sheet and dissolve them under my tongue, anxious to get the muscle-relaxing drug into my bloodstream as quickly as possible.

Within fifteen minutes, my body begins to feel like jelly. I'm a little woozy as Dennis and I sit down to dinner. After a few glasses of wine, the pain is only a memory. This is such a logical and necessary course of action that if you told me it looked like Alejandro and I had something in common, I'd think you were out of your mind.

CHAPTER 7

30 Rock

SPRING OF 1990 BRINGS another bitter Boston winter to an end. Thousands of cherry trees blossom throughout the city in brilliant hues of pink. I'm at my desk, leaning as far back as possible in my chair without falling over. This takes the pressure off my back as I gaze out the window at my favorite cherry tree glistening in the midday sunlight. A hummingbird hovers at one blossom, drinks nectar, then zips away in a flash.

"Willis, come to my office!" Stan Hopkins firmly calls out from across the newsroom, breaking my reverie. It's a tone I've never heard from him.

"Sure, I'll be right there," I respond, getting up from my desk and taking my usual pause: pressing my palms into my lower back, rolling my shoulders a few times, checking in on the pain, and reassuring myself I'm ready for any new assignment Stan might want to discuss. But his tone was strange, and I wonder if something is wrong.

Stan pauses deliberately as we sit down in his office. My mind races through the possibilities. The news budget is being slashed. He's been fired. Or...they've found out about my back problem and I'm being benched. I can't take it anymore and ask, "Is everything all right?"

He regards me with a sober face. "I've got a problem with you," he says. This puts me over the edge. *It's my back. Somehow the news got out.* I stare at my feet, about to admit the whole thing before he says another word. Then Stan smiles. He says, "Don Browne just called. He's now the executive news director of NBC News. He wants my permission to offer you a job."

NBC News. A rush of joy explodes throughout my entire body. *This is it. I've finally made it.*

Then I remember the network always seeks to cultivate good relations with its local affiliates, especially a powerhouse like WBZ-TV. If Stan tells Don Browne he'd rather keep me in Boston, there won't be any job offer.

"You're a top reporter," Stan says. "You have a great career here. I'd like you to stay around."

My heart starts to sink, but then he smiles again.

"But I'm not going to hold you back. Do you need time to think about this?"

About as long as it takes to exhale. "Stan, you're the best news director I've ever worked for, and a great friend. You've supported me in every way, even put your career on the line for me. I'll never forget it, but this is the only thing I've wanted since I first set foot in a newsroom."

"I thought so," he replies. "I already told Don it's okay to move forward. Here's his number. Go give him a call." I wisely repress the urge to jump up screaming with delight and run back to my desk, bad back and all.

It takes a month before Don Browne can see me at NBC headquarters at 30 Rockefeller Center in Manhattan. It's the longest month of my life and I get antsier by the minute until the day finally comes. The shuttle flight from Boston to New York is always a quick trip, but I want to ask the pilot to step on it. As the New York skyline comes into view from my window, it feels like the plane will never land. I anxiously deplane at La Guardia airport, rush down the endless corridors, and see a chauffeur holding a little white sign with my name neatly printed on it as if I'm someone important. It's almost impossible for me to believe what's happening.

The driver is clad in a black suit with a white shirt and black tie. He takes my luggage and politely guides me to his sleek, black limo sedan, opens the back door for me so I can slide onto the plush seat as he places my bag in the trunk. We listen to classical music as he cruises toward Manhattan. As we cross the Triborough Bridge, I feel a rush. I'm so close to fulfilling my dream I can taste it. As we pull up to the Omni Berkshire Palace Hotel on West 52nd in Midtown, just a few blocks from NBC, I almost float out of the limo.

The Omni is a hotel of understated elegance, dignity, and decor. The impeccable concierge lets me know that the room, meals, and incidentals are covered by NBC and to call him if I need anything. He tells me to enjoy the stay, and I almost blurt out "No problem," then remember how dignified this place is and politely thank him. A bell captain promptly guides me to a luxurious suite. I'd love to go out on the town, but I order room service instead to save my back for the big meeting in the morning. Then I click on the TV just as *NBC Nightly News* begins.

"Good evening. I'm Tom Brokaw. Topping the news tonight…"

I can hardly believe this is really happening. I'm a kid from a middle-class family who fled the suburbs, tried to drop out of the whole world, went to an obscure state college, and one day drove into the parking lot of a small-market TV station on a whim. I'm now in a swanky hotel in the Big Apple, awaiting filet mignon with gorgonzola sauce, julienned carrots with green beans, and a pricey bottle of vintage cabernet, on the cusp of a dream-come-true.

It's a beautiful, crisp East Coast morning as I walk the few blocks from the Omni to NBC News. Down West 52nd Street. Right on Avenue of the Americas. The city is bustling. Traffic is bumper-to-bumper. Endless honking. Crosswalks are thronged. Magnificent skyscrapers tower over it all like massive redwood trees of stone and steel. I can feel the energy of the city in every cell of my body as my heart pulses to its staccato rhythm. Left now on 49th. There it is—30 Rock. A seventy-story Art Deco masterpiece. It's the centerpiece of Rockefeller Plaza, and one of the tallest buildings in Manhattan.

I see the renowned outdoor Rockefeller Center Ice Skating Rink. Lording over it is a gilded statue of Prometheus, the Titan in Greek mythology who defied the will of Zeus and brought fire to Earth, becoming the champion of humankind. He holds the fire in his right hand as he soars across the sky. A golden circle around him contains the signs of the zodiac and symbolizes the heavens. The golden mountain beneath him represents the Earth.

To me, Prometheus is holding the light of wisdom, bringing the power of knowledge to our world. He is the archetype of a network news foreign correspondent, the ambassador of NBC News beckoning me to enter. Me, the overly ambitious kid, now almost forty years old, who still types with two fingers. As I stare at the statue, I feel dumbstruck, then remember not to be late and hurry to the entrance.

The 30 Rock security center looks like a bigger version of the reception desk at my hotel. A tall gentleman in black coat and tie with perfect posture gives me a formal glance. "How may I help you this morning?"

"Brad Willis. I'm here for a meeting with Don Browne of NBC News."

"One moment, please." He scans his computer, hits a keystroke, walks over to a nearby printer, folds something together in a small plastic case, and brings it back to me.

"This is your identity badge. Please wear it at all times. The elevators are around that corner to your right. You'll find Mr. Browne on the third floor."

When I realize I'm fifteen minutes early, I start to wander through this extraordinary building. There's a breathtaking mural wrapping around the west wall of the Grand Lobby. It's entitled *American Progress,* by Spanish artist Josep Maria Sert. It depicts an elaborate scene of workers constructing modern America and contains the figures of Mahatma Gandhi, Ralph Waldo Emerson, and Abraham Lincoln, all childhood heroes of mine. I almost feel like they know I'm here as I glance at them and whisper, "I made it!"

The elevator banks are works of art, with shiny bronze frames and panels of polished mahogany. Hundreds of people line up here every afternoon, hoping to get a seat at the taping of *Saturday Night Live*. The red-velvet theater ropes hanging from stanchions are already being set up to contain the crowds. Another security guard checks my badge and I'm allowed to step toward an elevator just as it opens. I slip in and punch the button for the third floor. I decide to hold my breath the whole way just for fun. When the elevator stops on the second floor and someone else gets in, I almost turn blue, but keep holding my breath anyway.

The NBC newsroom is expansive, with long rows of desks forming open corridors that serve as pathways for producers and editors rushing back and forth. There are windowed offices on either side of the room for the executives of the various news shows. The set for *Nightly News*, which Tom Brokaw has anchored for eight years, is in the middle, surrounded by floor cameras. I see Brokaw's chair sitting there like a throne. The seat of a living legend. Chills run up my spine.

A woman in a perfect business suit walks up. "You are here for the appointment with Mr. Browne?" The security desk must have called ahead.

"Yes, thank you." I'm still gazing around in awe and I wonder if my jaw is dropping toward my chin. I straighten into my very best posture. At least I'm wearing a conservative suit and tie instead of boots and jeans like my first TV job interview.

"This way, please."

As we walk down a long hall to another wing of the building, I fumble with my back brace to ensure nothing is showing. We pass Don Browne's office, then Brokaw's, then a large suite for the president of network news, Michael Gartner. *This must be the power corridor.* I smile, wondering if I should pause and genuflect at each door. We stop at a reception desk, where I check in with a secretary and have a seat. Less than a minute later, the secretary stands up and says abruptly, "Come with me. The morning editorial meeting is underway and Mr. Browne wants you to sit in. Please be quiet when we go inside."

As I enter the conference room, there's a group of men and women gathered around a large oval table. Coffee cups are clinking, some are having doughnuts, others are sharing pithy jokes and loud guffaws. It's anything but quiet, but I do my best to be a wallflower and observe the ritual. Don Browne stands up at one end of the table to welcome me and makes brief introductions: the heads of the foreign and domestic desks, the *Nightly News* producer, the New York Bureau Chief, show producers, script editors, and assistants. I walk around the table slowly and firmly shake hands, my heart pounding so loudly I think everyone might be able to hear it.

As I take a seat in a lone chair against one wall, large black conference boxes on the table start barking. "Hong Kong Bureau here with you. London here, too. Miami is on. Atlanta. Los Angeles…"

"Okay," Browne takes charge. "What have you got?"

Each bureau pitches its stories, everyone jockeying for a slot on *Nightly News.*

"Hold that one for the weekend," a producer says, rejecting the first pitch.

"Not enough for *Nightly*, pitch that to the *Today Show*," another producer redirects the second offering.

"Yes, we want that spot tonight. Make it a minute-fifteen." Someone else likes what London has.

"We need some more on that one before we consider it." This story is completely shot down, and I can almost feel the pain of the person pitching it from halfway around the world.

The entire meeting is an elaborate dance. They are all brilliant. Confident. To the point. The foreign desk spars with the national desk for primacy. National spars back. They know the drill by heart. Everyone making their case. Promoting, analyzing, probing, playing devil's advocate.

Suddenly, toward the end, Tom Brokaw walks into the room and sits down. Everyone becomes silent.

"Here's what we have, Tom." Don Browne gives him the rundown.

Brokaw ponders, then softly adds or subtracts this or that in his deep, melodious voice. It's over. The story lineup is settled. Prometheus has spoken.

❋

"Do you prefer covering domestic or foreign news?" Browne asks as we settle into his office after the editorial meeting.

"Foreign news."

"You know, even though we're a global news organization, domestic news usually takes priority. Foreign correspondents have a harder time getting on the air unless they have a major story."

This fact was clear in the morning round table. The foreign offerings lacking an urgent punch were pushed to other shows or shelved. The domestic news prevailed, even stories with no urgency at all. Getting on the air is the name of the game. The more name recognition a correspondent has, the more airtime he or she gets. More airtime translates into job security and a better salary down the road.

"Either one is great for me," I respond. "But if you offered me the choice, I'd go overseas."

"I thought so," Browne replies with a wry smile. "I've been watching your work for a while, especially from the drug summit. You hustle. Work hard. I like that."

He explains how different the network is from local news, reminding me I won't get the three to four minutes for my reports that I've become accustomed to. A minute-fifteen is tops. "And you're talking to several million people, a national audience. You need to synthesize, focus, write so someone living anywhere in the country understands and relates to what you're saying."

After an hour, Browne tells me he has other meetings. "We'll have lunch at noon. Go wander around and get familiar with the place. Introduce yourself to people. Ask questions."

It's my nature to be gregarious, but I'm in awe being here, so I choose to sit in the newsroom and observe. A few famous faces wander in. Science Correspondent Robert Bazell. Andrea Mitchell, one of the greatest political reporters alive. Garrick Utley, anchor of the *Sunday Nightly News*. Maria Shriver from *Dateline*. They are sophisticated, graduates of top universities, global citizens, reminders that I come from a little college in the Redwoods and will need to work harder than ever to keep pace with this crowd.

At noon, Browne takes me to lunch at the famous Rainbow Room restaurant on the 65th floor of 30 Rock. The Art Deco dining room is ornate, formal, and dazzling with its panoramic views of Manhattan. I feel like I'm on top of the world as we're joined by the senior producers for domestic and foreign news I met at the morning meeting. As we dine on a sumptuous lunch, it's all light talk. I'm being looked over. Felt out. I have no doubt that the powerful majesty of this news organization is silently posing the question, "Do you belong here?" I'm surprised at how relaxed and at home I feel, but I'm still careful not to spill soup on my gold-and-black striped tie.

After lunch, I meet with selected producers and editors in the newsroom. Each explains how the NBC system works, what they need in a story and want in a correspondent. They're insightful and supportive, but I realize I'm still being measured. In the late afternoon, I have a final moment with Don Browne before heading to the airport for the shuttle back to Boston.

"What do you think about Miami?" That's the bureau Browne used to run and where he made his name. It's a hybrid: a foreign bureau headquartered in the States but covering all of Latin and South America.

"Yes," I say without hesitation.

"Do you speak Spanish?"

"Only well enough to order a meal, be polite at a hotel, tell the taxi to step on it...*Maneje más rápido.*"

"I appreciate your honesty. It's no worry. We have plenty of interpreters. But I'd bone up if I were you."

Browne stands up and shakes my hand, gives me his famous electrifying stare and says, "Have your agent call me tomorrow."

It's unspoken, but I know it's a done deal. My agent helped me get to Dallas and Boston. Now he'll be negotiating the job of my life. It's a good thing, because I'd work for free if they asked me to.

CHAPTER 8

Miami Bureau

B REAKING UP WITH SOMEONE has always been painful for
me, but it seems to be a pattern in my life. Mary Beth and I
have been living together for more than a year. She has generations of family in Boston and wants to stay. There's no doubt that I'm
leaving. We've been growing apart anyway, especially with my career
always coming first, not to mention that I'm testier these days as a
result of the nagging ache in my back. In no time at all we are saying
our final good-byes and I'm gone.

After a few weeks at NBC headquarters at 30 Rock learning the ropes,
I'm off to Florida. It's early 1990, and Miami is a cultural confluence, in
rapid transition from a languid resort town for snowbirds to a bustling
city of international trade and intrigue. There are neighborhoods of
conservative Cubans who escaped the Castro regime. Impoverished
Haitians who fled the tortures of Papa and Baby Doc Duvalier. Business
moguls from Rio, Bogota, Santiago, and Buenos Aires. Hip entrepreneurs opening dazzling clubs in trendy South Beach. Drug lords from
Colombia living incognito in lavish mansions on inland waterways.

With my housing allowance, I can afford to lease a condo on the
top floor of a high-rise with sweeping views of the Miami skyline, the
bridge to Key Biscayne, and the Atlantic Ocean beyond. Brilliant sun-
rises dance across the marble floors and tinge the walls with golden
hues. Sunsets reflect off the downtown skyline and light the horizon
in splashes of pink and red. It's my very own Rainbow Room, a perch

on top of my new world. I'm flushed with excitement... and a little caution. As soon as I can, I find a top-notch massage therapist and arrange for him to come at a moment's notice to work on my back.

NBC's Miami Bureau sits on the outskirts of Miami in a non-descript, two-story, white building with dark, reflective windows to mitigate the scorching Florida heat. The minute I step inside, I feel the legacy of the great correspondents who came before me. The bureau came of age in the 1970s during the revolutions in El Salvador and Nicaragua, and the region remains important to NBC News. There are solid stories for me to cover in Miami, but most of my assignments are where I really want to be—down in Nicaragua, Colombia, Guatemala, and El Salvador.

As I travel Latin America, I finally understand why countries here are called banana republics. In the late 1800s, bananas were unknown in North America. Then an ambitious railroad builder from Brooklyn married the daughter of the president of Costa Rica and launched an empire. As he built new railroads, he planted bananas alongside the tracks. Soon, he established numerous plantations and created what became the largest company in the world at that time: United Fruit, with farms, factories, and plantations throughout Latin America.

United Fruit acted like a colonial overlord—controlling commerce, transportation, communications, and the political processes of countries throughout the region. It bought the unconditional support of right-wing dictators who maintained their power by terrorizing their citizens and arresting those who defied their regimes. Workers in the fields were driven off their family farms, paid survival wages, and exposed to working conditions teeming with toxic chemicals and disease. Attempts to unionize and improve conditions were met with brutal force. Peasant uprisings were viciously suppressed. Thousands were tortured or killed. The U.S. State Department consistently supported United Fruit, and the company enjoyed close ties with the CIA, even working with them to overthrow popular leaders and replace them with easily manipulated puppet regimes. The locals in every country nicknamed United Fruit *El Pulpo*, the octopus.

I discovered the dark side of United Fruit years earlier while I was an investigative reporter at KCRA-TV in Sacramento. I had uncovered a Nazi war criminal living in a retirement home less than ten miles from our TV station. Otto Von Bolschwing was an SS intelligence officer for the masterminds of the Holocaust. After the war, he was given safe haven in the United States, where he worked for the CIA. United Fruit, I ultimately learned, provided his cover job and false identity. As I would discover during my investigations, Von Bolschwing was one of hundreds of Nazi war criminals in the secret program.

The CIA and United Fruit were behind the right-wing military during a bloody, twelve-year civil war in El Salvador that ended in a stalemate, with some negotiated reforms but mostly business as usual. In Nicaragua, however, workers' advocate Daniel Ortega and his Sandinista Liberation Front managed to galvanize the poor people and, in 1979, overthrew longtime dictator Anastasio Somoza. In subsequent elections, Ortega became leader of the country.

Now in 1990, Ortega is facing the first serious challenge to his presidency. He's up for reelection against a former colleague named Violeta Barrios de Chamorro, who is being backed by the United States as well as conservative Nicaraguan and foreign business interests who are hoping to re-establish dominance and recover valuable businesses and estates the Sandinistas seized and turned over to workers after the revolution.

"The United States speaks a great deal about liberty and freedom, but it suppresses poor people around the world so that its corporations can make great profits," Ortega says, making his case to our cameras in the living room at his modest home in Managua, Nicaragua. It's in a quiet neighborhood on the outskirts of the city amid rolling green hills dotted with banana trees. Ortega is sipping a *mojito*, a cocktail that originated in Cuba. Not wanting to be rude to President Ortega, of course, I sip one myself. It's a sweet blend of sugar cane juice, lime, sparkling water, crushed mint, and white rum. It was Ernest Hemingway's favorite drink, and I recall having one too many at his favorite haunt, *La Bodeguita del Medio*, a historic restaurant and bar in Havana, Cuba.

"We have brought justice and dignity to our country," Ortega continues. "Why does your country seek to turn back the clock?"

The Berlin Wall has just fallen, but the Cold War continues. Ortega has close ties with Cuba, embraces socialism, and is vilified by the American government as a threat to the entire region. It's the "domino theory," holding that if one country goes socialist, they all will, posing a dire threat to the United States and democracies throughout the world. The Cold War advocates never mention, however, that the real threat of a workers' revolution is to companies like United Fruit and the billions in profits they make exploiting third-world labor and resources.

"Maybe your movement swung the pendulum too far the other way," I say to Ortega as our cameras roll. "There have been abuses and injustices committed by both sides, no?"

"Yes, and we have reined those in. We have punished the perpetrators. Still, this does not compare to more than a century of violence, exploitation, and suffering that your country has supported."

With Nicaraguan President Daniel Ortega, Managua, 1990.

❋

When I sit down with Violeta Chamorro, she counters Ortega's argument. "The economy is in shambles. The poorly educated workers cannot run the factories and farms they have been given. The original owners do not deserve to lose their holdings. There must be an accommodation."

"Some say you are too beholden to the United States," I respond. "That you will turn your country back into little more than a banana republic."

"This is not true." She is firm. Dignified. "I fought against that, and now I am struggling for a better future for all our people."

I can understand where President Ortega and challenger Chamorro are coming from. Their conflicting views are both valid. In the real world, it's never good guys versus bad guys. It's always shades of gray. Ulterior motives. Power struggles. Best and worst intentions. Often at the very same time.

Some accuse the media of liberal bias, but I hear a full array of viewpoints and perspectives at NBC and from colleagues in the field. Sure, there are raging liberals and ardent conservatives, but most are moderates. I'm not interested in taking sides and have never voted a party line. I've met few politicians I really trust and none whose rhetoric I take at face value. Our job as journalists is to do our best to find the truth and report it, avoiding outside influences and opinions. I don't feel Ortega is more correct than Chamorro, or vice versa. As long as I get on the air with a story, I couldn't care less who wins.

❋

I stay in Nicaragua through the election as Chamorro pulls off an upset victory. There are festivals and protests simultaneously in the streets, live shots to do for *Nightly News*, packaged reports to produce for the *Today Show*. By the end of it, my back is on fire again from all the travel and constant standing. I'm popping meds like they're *chicharrónes*, the deep fried pork rind snacks so popular in

Latin America. My evening glass of wine has become two. Sometimes three. At least I'm in good company. We're all fairly accomplished drinkers, those of us addicted to exotic settings and occasional war zones.

Back at the Miami Bureau, I'm in survival mode again, carefully hiding the truth about my back from everyone. Some social events are obligatory, but after a few minutes of standing and making casual conversation I start to grit my teeth, look for the nearest exit, and seize my first opportunity to slip out unnoticed. Chronic pain makes me this way: on edge, nervous about the next flare-up, worried that at any moment my life will come crashing down all around me. Every time it flares up I feel a mixture of anger and fear coursing through my veins like hot sauce, which only makes me tenser and exacerbates the pain. Sometimes I want to scream. Other times I want to cry. But I stuff it all inside and just keep shoving myself forward, always diving into the next story.

As the spring of 1990 unfolds, money is tight at NBC, and the network's interest in Latin America is waning. There's talk of consolidation and bureau closures. Miami is rumored to be high on the list. My colleagues exchange worried glances, have hushed conversations, and secretly send out resumes. I can't even process the idea that I could be laid off after being here less than a year. I can't imagine any other life. I don't even believe one exists for me.

Then, on August 2, 1990, President Saddam Hussein of Iraq invades Kuwait.

CHAPTER 9

The Persian Gulf War

S ADDAM HUSSEIN has been making threats against Kuwait for months, but his invasion still catches most of the world by surprise. Norman Schwarzkopf, head of the U.S. Central Command, had been predicting a limited attack to seize the rich Kuwaiti oil fields. Instead, within hours, Iraqi forces have taken downtown Kuwait City and are headed south toward Saudi Arabia.

The Pentagon fears that Saddam's forces could roll into Saudi Arabia next, giving Iraq control over much of the world's oil supplies. This triggers the largest buildup of American forces since the Vietnam War. Members of the U.S. Army 82nd Airborne Division, along with 300 combat aircraft, are quickly flown into strategic bases throughout Saudi Arabia.

By the end of September 1990, close to 200,000 American personnel have been deployed to defend the Saudis in Operation Desert Shield, soon to be renamed Operation Desert Storm. Schwarzkopf and other American commanders believe an offensive to liberate Kuwait City remains too risky against the heavily armed, well-entrenched Iraqi forces, so they call for international support and prepare for the largest military offensive in history.

"Are you willing to volunteer to go to the Middle East and cover the war?" Don Browne asks, knowing my answer already. Since our lives will be at risk, network legal policy requires that we volunteer rather than be assigned to the story. That limits legal exposure for the parent company, General Electric, should we be killed in action.

"When do I leave?"

"This weekend. I already have your ticket arranged. We'll take care of your bills while you're gone."

"How long will I be there?" I ask, trying to gauge NBC's commitment to the story given its financial woes.

"As long as it takes," Brown replies. "Three months, six months, a year. Nobody knows. Just get going and keep your head down."

I buy a new pair of boots, have my doctor write six months' worth of prescriptions, pack my bags, empty my refrigerator, and give the bureau details for handling my bills. NBC is already beginning to send its own army into Saudi Arabia, and the coverage will cost a fortune. I'm now convinced the Miami Bureau is going to close, so I say good-bye to my Rainbow Room, knowing I might never see it again.

Dhahran International Hotel in Saudi Arabia sits on the Persian Gulf about 200 miles south of the Kuwait border. It's a perfect headquarters for the international media. The massive lobby is thronged day and night with journalists from around the world. I'm beyond ecstatic as I wade through the crowd, check in at the reception desk, then hunt for our bureau. It's one of scores of news bureaus that have been set up in every available conference room, office, and suite, and it takes a while to find. When I do locate it, I meet a dozen NBC producers, photographers, and editors for the very first time, feeling like I've truly joined the network's global family.

Desert Storm is expanding fast, as two dozen other nations send in troops. They're called Coalition Forces, but it remains largely a U.S. effort. More than 540,000 American troops will pour in, with Britain a distant second, providing only 43,000 soldiers. Because the military can't accommodate hundreds of reporters in the field, the major national broadcast and print media outlets are being assigned limited slots for "pool reporters." These chosen few will be posted with divisions of the Army, Navy, and Marines. Their reports will be pooled, shared with the media back at the hotel for their own broadcast purposes.

We have several correspondents here, all with more tenure than I, but NBC has given me one of its few spots: pool reporter for the Marines. I immediately realize it's more important than ever to conceal how bad my back is. Anyway, I'm ready to do anything and everything asked of me. The betting is that the Army, with its massive numbers, heavy artillery, and tanks, will be the first to surge into Kuwait. That is the prime place to be as a pool reporter. But I'm happy just to be picked, and I prefer the Marines. They're rougher around the edges and quicker on the move.

Then comes the bad news. Before any of us are allowed into the field as pool correspondents, we have to pass a physical. It's not a doctor's office workup with temperature and blood pressure. It's a workout with a minimum of fifty sit-ups, twenty-five push-ups, five pull-ups, and then running a loop behind the hotel that looks to be almost a mile. The push-ups and pull-ups are the easiest for me and I get them out of the way quickly. I have to fake the sit-ups, being constrained by my brace, yet I manage to get through it. But the running?

I was never a runner. I hated it when we had to do the weekly mile around the track in high school. Whenever the coach wasn't looking, I'd dive behind the bleachers, hide until the final lap, then sneak out, and sprint in while trying to conceal the guilty look on my face. And I certainly haven't tried to run since fracturing my spine four years ago. The mere thought of it hurts.

Am I going to fail this test and be sent home or ordered to sit in the hotel bureau and log videotape? *No. I've gotten this far, back pain and all, and nothing is going to knock me out of this game.* I take a few deep breaths at the starting line and decide to go as fast as I can. *Just go, just go, just go,* I scream silently to myself with every breath. After twenty yards, my heart is pounding and my back is throbbing. Down a dead-end street behind the hotel…looping back now through a parking lot…almost last in my group.

Just go, just go, just go. Crossing the finish line, I'm in a daze. I must get to my hotel room. I can't let anyone see me limp. Stopping a bellhop in the lobby while panting like a mad dog, I hand him a wad of Saudi riyals. "Bring enough ice to my room to fill the bathtub please. Right now, please. Right away."

I stagger to the elevator and lie down inside of it when the doors close. I crawl to my room and swallow a load of Motrin and slip a handful of Valium under my tongue. Next, I open a bottle of Chivas Regal and gulp down a shot. Alcohol is illegal here. An American woman I met at the hotel restaurant is a flight attendant for the Saudi Royal Family's private fleet of jets. She smuggled the bottle to me as a gift, along with a tin of expensive Beluga caviar. I smile at the hypocrisy of the royals in this Islamic monarchy, whooping it up on their private jets filled with booze and beautiful women while Saudi citizens caught drinking are punished with public lashings. I swig another shot and feel it burn all the way down to my belly.

The bellhop arrives and pours the ice in the tub. I hide the Chivas behind my back and try not to breathe in his direction. I tear my clothes off the moment he closes the door, struggling with my jeans and boots because of the pain shooting through my back. As I finally pull my socks off, my legs are on fire. My spine feels like it's been hit with a grenade. I spread a bath towel over the freezing bed of ice and lie down in the tub, the bottle of Chivas clutched in my left hand and the tin of caviar on my belly. *Ahhhhh.*

One week later, I'm sitting on a narrow wooden bench in the rear of an open troop truck, bouncing through the desert. It takes all day to reach the Marine encampment. I have to cinch my back brace tight, clench my teeth, grip the railings, and wedge my boots against a heavy wooden ammo box to support myself the whole way. When we finally arrive, I learn we're a hundred miles inland and less than five miles from the Kuwait border and Iraq's army. For now, this is the front line of the ground war.

The desert is flat, barren, and endless, except for a berm, a long mountain of sand that's been bulldozed along the border to slow down Saddam's tanks if they invade Saudi territory. We're on one side of the berm. Iraq's notorious Republican Guard is on the other. Literally dug in. Its artillery is camouflaged, tanks are buried under the sand, and troops are holed up in underground bunkers. The Marines are all business, exercising and holding strategy sessions throughout the day. Their toughness is remarkable and their commitment is unshakeable, but I also sense apprehension and a silent fear. Many of these men have yet to turn twenty, and most have never seen combat.

My cameraman and I have been assigned to one of the many tents in the Marine encampment. It's sweltering during the day, freezing at night. Scores of little rats, the color of desert sand, flit through our tents in the darkness hoping to find an open MRE, meal ready to eat—the standard military ration that sits in your gut like a bomb. Little snakes and large, fat lizards slither in and out looking for mice. We are in the middle of nowhere, knowing at any time all hell could break loose. I love it.

But it's a waiting game. The Coalition Forces are continuing to build and refine their plans to push north into Kuwait while simultaneously staying on high alert for Saddam's forces coming south. A junior officer serving as a press aide, called a flack, is always standing behind me, keeping an eye on my cameraman and listening closely to every word I say. He wants no controversy, insists on overseeing everything we shoot, and aggressively blocks answers to even the most benign questions I ask the Marines. At the same time, he pushes light, superficial stories, like a feature on MOPP suits the troops have been issued.

MOPP stands for Mission Oriented Protective Posture chemical uniforms. It's a heavy rubber body suit with a head cover and gas mask that's bulky and ill fitting. Even though we're all apprehensive about the chemical and biological weapons Saddam is widely rumored to possess, the MOPP suits strike me as ridiculous and I doubt they will protect us. I do imagine, however, that some well-connected defense contractor is making millions selling these getups to the Pentagon. I need to find a real story.

One night after my flack has gone to sleep in his tent, I join a group of Marines in a deep cave they've dug in the moist sand and covered like a bunker, creating an underground clubhouse where they can gather and let off steam. Using a night-vision lens on a small video camera, I begin interviewing them by candlelight. I've gotten to know these men over the past several weeks, and they're finally loosening up around me.

"I admit it, I'm scared," one Marine says bluntly.

"We don't know what's going to happen when we roll over that berm," another says, "but it ain't gonna be pretty."

A third says, "Let's admit it, we're not even sure what the reasons are behind this war."

When I ask what they think the real reason for the war is, everyone gets quiet. "It doesn't matter," one Marine finally says. "We're here to fight and we're ready to go." All the men agree with this. After all, they're Marines. Without the flack listening in, these Marines are speaking their truth, letting us in on their emotions, being real. This is incredibly moving material and there's no way to exaggerate how much I admire these brave warriors. I know the flack would kill this story in an instant, because his job is to show troops who are nothing but gung ho with no reservations about the looming conflict.

To file my reports, I have to write my notes for the pool, which includes all the networks, then write and record separate stories for NBC, and send both with the videotapes via military courier for a long trip back to Dhahran. The flack always reviews the material and wants to edit every script I write, but I keep this one from him, slipping it in with the feature story on the MOPP gear. I know he would go ballistic if he saw this stuff, especially because we shot it without his permission. It always takes a few days for the material to arrive in Dhahran and, being in the desert, I have no idea what happens to the reports. But when this story makes *Nightly News* and the other networks in the pool, the military's public relations machine goes crazy and I hear about it immediately.

My flack, who must have been admonished by his superiors, screams at me and even makes an empty threat of violence. I respond by telling him I'm leaving to cover another Marine unit, having just heard that Marines in Khafji recently came under some artillery fire from the Iraqi Republican Guard. Khafji is a Saudi city sitting on the Persian Gulf just below the border of Kuwait, and this is the first time the Iraqi Republican Guard has launched an attack over the border. I go directly to Command and Control headquarters at our current location and ask to be reassigned. As the pool reporter for the Marines, I argue, it's my duty to get to Khafji immediately because it's where the news is happening and those Marines need their story told. Within a day, my request is approved. My cameraman and I pack up and head out in one of NBC's four-wheel drive Jeeps, both of us glad to be gone after a month of frustration and thankful for the independence we'll now have by being on our own.

We arrive at the new Marine camp at dark and are taken to the tent that houses this unit's division headquarters. General John Admire, who's in charge, is a calm and gentle man. I explain why I left the first unit and make my case for joining his. "We'll cover whatever you have going on with complete objectivity," I tell him straight off, "but we'll always tell the whole story. I don't want a flack on my back all the time trying to manage the news."

"We don't have a flack here," Admire says in a tone that is strong yet soft. "You do your job, we'll do ours, and I'm sure we'll all get along fine."

We're given cots in a small tent near headquarters and manage to make it to dinner before the mess hall closes. General Admire's unit is part of the First Marines. Nicknamed "The Old Breed," it's the oldest and largest active duty division in the United States Marine Corps, with a ground combat force of more than 19,000 men and women. As promised, the general allows me full access, even letting us into the briefing room with a camera as he plans strategy with his men and updates them on the latest intelligence. Admire also agrees to an on-camera interview, discussing the artillery attack, which missed its mark and created no casualties. Then he offers a candid assessment of the coming war. He is insightful and straightforward, telling the world it won't be easy but that it will be done right and the Coalition Forces will prevail. It's the first time a general in the field has gone on-record like this, and it gives me the strongest reports I've filed since going into the field.

The following day, we drive to the port of Khafji to cover a unit of the National Guard providing security for coalition ships in the Gulf.

Most of these men are part-time Guardsmen who got called up for the war. They're not as indoctrinated as the regular troops, and they prove to be completely candid.

"This war has nothing to do with democracy," one Guardsman says bluntly, stunning me with his candor.

"And America couldn't care less about liberating the Kuwaitis," another agrees.

A third says, "We all know it's about oil. Just oil."

A fourth chimes in, "Who wants to die for oil? Not me!" Everyone nods in agreement.

When this story hits the air, it causes a roar far greater than the report from the underground clubhouse. Even though Kuwait is a monarchy with a history of injustice and oppression, the White House and Pentagon have worked hard to cast Desert Storm as a fight for freedom and democracy, not oil. Top brass from the National Guard are flown in to make public statements about the commitment of their troops, the men who spoke their minds are reprimanded, and General Admire tells me he's been pressured to send me packing.

"I told them no," Admire says. "We made an agreement. You tell the truth and we do our jobs. That's how democracies operate, and freedom of speech is one of the key things that sets us apart from dictators like Saddam."

A few nights later, on January 29, 1991, the Iraqi Army invades Khafji, its first and only ground incursion into Saudi Arabia, and the First Marines spring into action. It's the biggest story yet, and we're the only media here.

For reasons of politics and appearances, the First Marines are ordered to hold a position just outside of Khafji while Saudi and Qatari forces take the front lines as Coalition Forces provide air support. On the second night, however, artillery shells begin to burst all around us. Everyone but me drags on the bulky MOPP suits and gas masks as we dive into bunkers. We've been warned repeatedly that Saddam might use chemical and biological weapons, and all of us are terrified by the prospect. But I have no faith in the protective gear and it's a pain to get it on with a bad back. My cameraman understandably chooses to stay in the bunker as I grab his camera, crawl out, and film the greatest fireworks show I've ever seen. It's an instinctual act. I'm not courageous or suffering from illusions of invincibility. I just can't help myself.

The battle to take back Khafji rages for days. We push up to the outskirts with the Marines and film from a distance as the Saudi and Qatari ground forces fight to take back the city. Each night we return to our tent. The next morning we rush back to the front lines. Road-blocks are set up at strategic points to keep Saudis from driving to Khafji. We only get past them because I'm the pool reporter.

One morning at dawn we're stopped at a roadblock by Marines I don't recognize. A British print journalist is there claiming he is the pool reporter. It's not the first time my colleagues or I have departed from the truth to get to the action, but with two of us there, the Marines aren't letting either of us pass.

I pull my colleague aside and say, "Look, I'm the pool reporter. Everyone gets the story once we send it back to Dhahran. You have to take off."

"Piss off," is his answer. He wants the story exclusively for himself, everyone else be damned. If he can't go, he's wants to block access for the pool so that no one will get the news. It's all I can do to not grab him by the collar and force him to leave.

"Time for you both to turn around and depart," a Marine at the barricade says with stern authority.

"Radio General Admire," I ask with urgency. "Ask him who the pool reporter is. This guy is a liar." The Marine pauses, tired of all this. But he finally agrees with my plea. Within minutes he has an answer. The British journalist is sent packing with his tail between his legs. Months later I will learn that he went home and wrote false stories trying to damage my reputation.

After days of conflict, the Iraqis retreat. We enter Khafji with the Marines as they secure the area, which is now a ghost town filled with death. There are bodies of Iraqi soldiers and Saudi civilians littering the streets. Iraqi tanks destroyed by Coalition air strikes sit in the hot sand, their gray metal frames burned black. Scorched soldiers, charred like burned marshmallows, poke out of the tanks with contorted faces and flailing arms, frozen in time as they desperately tried to escape when the rockets hit their tanks. It's so macabre that my emotions go numb as I take close-up still photos.

We file our reports every day until the battle for Khafji is over. To bypass the sluggish military courier system, I drive our Jeep for several hours every night to Dhahran and deliver our tapes, then turn around and speed back, often arriving just before daybreak, collapsing for an hour or two on my cot before heading back into the field. It's exhausting, but the adrenaline rush keeps me going and helps hold my physical pain at bay. When it's finally over, the horror of Khafji remains fresh in my mind, but I feel a tremendous thrill of accomplishment and have an even deeper understanding of how addictive war can be.

With General John Admire, Khafji, Saudi Arabia, February 1991.

❈

A few weeks later, the Coalition ground war is launched and I have more good fortune. It isn't the Army leading the charge toward Kuwait City as everyone expected; it's the First Marines.

As we cross the desert, most of the roads have been blown up or strewn with land mines, and we're forced to move at a snail's pace. The retreating Iraqi forces have set the Kuwaiti oil fields on fire as part of their scorched-earth policy. More than 700 burning wells are spewing so much thick smoke into the atmosphere that the sky is black even at midday. Oil constantly rains down, covering our clothing, saturating our hair, and flooding our eyes, noses, ears, and lungs.

It takes two grueling days to make it less than a hundred miles across the desert. Portions of the highway have been destroyed, forcing us to navigate around these areas by driving through the firm sand, where the Iraqis have managed to set a few landmines. The First Marines are just ahead of us and we follow their tire tracks with precision to avoid setting off an explosion. On the second day, we catch up with the Marines a few miles outside Kuwait City. Columns of escaping Iraqi vehicles have been hit so heavily by Coalition air strikes that the road has been nicknamed the "Highway of Death."

To reach the city, we have to drive through, around, and over heaps of twisted steel. There are bodies littered everywhere. Some are still clinging to life. Others are in pieces and strewn among the wreckage. A few hundred yards from the city, we stop to film. As I walk through the carnage, I have to keep from slipping in pools of blood. When I stop to steady myself, I see a caterpillar on my pant cuff. It's quivering. I lean down, pick it off, and examine it. My breath stops as I realize it's not a caterpillar. It's the upper lip of an Iraqi soldier, covered by a thick mustache. And it's still warm.

More than feeling startled or repulsed, I'm deeply saddened. Throughout the ages we've attacked and destroyed one another in endless unspeakable ways, and as I drop the piece of human flesh, I wonder if we'll ever evolve to a point where we're mature enough to find a better way to resolve our differences. It's a brief reflection, then I hop back into our Jeep and we push on into the city.

A towering five-star hotel sits across from the U.S. Embassy in the heart of downtown Kuwait City. The fleeing Iraqis have sacked every room and it's now deserted. It's the perfect place to set up our broadcast headquarters. I find a suite on the third floor with a wide balcony overlooking the embassy. It's completely trashed, but the view is perfect and we quickly get set up. Soon, Tom Brokaw arrives from Saudi Arabia to anchor the retaking of Kuwait for *Nightly News*, debriefing me live as the Marines rappel from helicopters into the U.S. Embassy compound and raise the American flag.

There are small groups in the streets cheering the Americans as liberators, but most Kuwaitis have fled or remain in hiding. The city has been pillaged, and many have been murdered. After covering the securing of the embassy, I find my way to the main hospital, seeking to interview wounded citizens. Surprisingly, there are only a few Iraqi soldiers in the trauma ward, all with minor wounds. Their

With Tom Brokaw, Kuwait City, Kuwait, 1991.

glances are furtive. I suspect they fled to the hospital rather than get caught in the Coalition air attack.

"Where are your wounded Kuwaitis?" I ask the doctor who has allowed me in.

"There are none," he answers matter-of-factly. "If they are here, they are dead."

"Where?" I say.

"In the basement morgue."

"Please take me there."

"You do not want to see this."

"Yes, we must. Please. Let's go there now, doctor."

The stench in the morgue is tremendous. We have to wear hospital masks over our noses and mouths, and it barely cuts the acrid odor. Bodies are piled everywhere, heaped on top of one another. I see dead men with horrid facial wounds. Tongues cut out. Acid poured over their faces. Eyes gouged out. Some have been castrated. Others have multiple gunshot and stab wounds. The bodies of young girls show signs of violent rape, some with iron construction rods, called rebar, forced into their body cavities. I am overwhelmed with grief. What dark evil dwells within us that could ever prompt such atrocities?

None of the horrors in this morgue can be broadcast, but we film anyway so there is a record of this savagery. It's likely the Iraqi soldiers lying comfortably in their hospital beds three flights above me took part in some of this grotesque torture. I feel a surge of rage. Part of me wants to find a weapon, burst in, and shoot them dead. Then I realize my response would be a mild version of the same madness that drove them to commit such horrible acts of cruelty.

"Doesn't it outrage you, treating those Iraqi soldiers in your trauma ward?" I ask the Kuwaiti doctor as we depart the hellish morgue.

"It is my oath as a physician," he says calmly. "I am here to save lives, whomever they might be."

It's an extraordinary expression of compassion in the face of demonic human behavior. I've met many heroes while covering this war, but this is a man whose courage, integrity, and compassion I will never forget.

CHAPTER 10

The Gulf War Aftermath: Kurdistan

T HE PAIN. It always gets worse when I'm exhausted. Tonight, at the end of another long day, a sharp, electric sensation shoots down the back of my left leg, spiking into my heel bone. This has been happening more frequently lately. It feels like a tripwire from a grenade is lodged in my lower back, ready to explode if I make the wrong move. I take a few extra pain pills and slip into my sleeping bag on the bed of my sacked hotel room across from the American Embassy in Kuwait. As has become my nightly routine, I whisper to myself that the pain will be gone for good in the morning. *It has to go away. It just has to.*

This is my fifth day in Kuwait City. The Iraqi Army has proven to be no match for the Allied Forces led by the Americans, and has fled home in disgrace. Operation Desert Storm is over. Kuwait has been liberated. But there's hardly time to breathe as a new crisis begins to unfold in the northern provinces of Iraq.

The region is known as Kurdistan: a rugged, mountainous territory spanning a wide area where the borders of Iraq, Turkey, Iran, and Syria converge. The Iraqi Kurds, some 4 million strong, have sought independence for more than a century. Their armed fighters are known as *peshmerga*, which literally means "those who face death." And face death they have, suffering massacres and mass casualties at the hands of Iraqi troops every time they have risen up for independence. Now emboldened by Saddam's defeat in Kuwait, a new uprising has begun.

Saddam's troops have swarmed into Kurdistan to crush the revolt, overrunning and pillaging village after village. It was just eight years ago that the Kurds suffered a similar fate when they sided with neighboring Iran during the Iran–Iraq War. Scores of villages were destroyed. Thousands were killed. And at the end of the war, in 1988, Saddam hit the Kurds with chemical weapons in a massacre known as Bloody Friday. It was this attack that convinced America that Saddam would use chemical weapons against U.S. forces in the Gulf War. Now, millions of Kurds are fleeing into the high mountain ranges along the Turkish-Iraqi frontier. Their maxim has long been, "Kurds have no friends but the mountains." It's the only safe haven they have.

I've been posted to a base camp established for the media just across the border in southern Turkey, covering the Kurdish refugee crisis for NBC News. Periodically, U.S. Army helicopters lift us into the mountain refugee camps, banking down steep, sheer cliffs to avoid the possibility of Iraqi artillery fire. It's harsh terrain, far from friendly to the Kurds. Conditions in the camps are beyond dismal. Each family has put up a small tent for shelter. They only have what little food they could bring, mostly grain, and it is running out fast. Winter is yet to come, but the bitter cold is here. Merchants and artisans, farmers and traders, grandmothers and infants huddle together to keep warm, wondering if they'll ever see their villages again. The fear of Saddam and his brutal army is palpable, even visible in their terrified stares.

The camps are just above the timberline. Most of the available wood has been gathered and burned for cooking a traditional gruel, called *sawar*, made with crushed wheat grain. The *sawar* is running out, and the United States has begun airdropping Army rations, the MREs that stuck in my belly while I was a pool reporter with the Marines.

Kurdish Refugee Camp, Northern Iraq, 1991.

These ancient people can't digest this food, and diarrhea abounds. There is no sanitation, and the Kurds often relieve themselves right in front of their tents. As a result, dehydration has begun claiming lives, and there are fears of a cholera outbreak. As so often happens in war, children are the first victims. Already, a few mothers with glazed eyes cling to cold, lifeless babies, refusing to acknowledge they have lost their infants.

A French medic from *Médecins Sans Frontières,* a renowned humanitarian organization that provides medical aid to victims of war, is with one young woman. She's holding her dead child in her arms as she wanders aimlessly through the camp. She appears to have no other family. Our best guess is that her husband was killed by the Iraqis. This fragile young mother, extremely thin from lack of nourishment, can't be more than sixteen years old. Her thick, matted auburn hair hangs down over her face like a mask but can't conceal her intense blue eyes, which are locked in an empty stare. Time feels as frozen as the sharp icicles hanging from tattered refugee tents.

Neither of us speaks her language, so we simply comfort her by wrapping a warm blanket around her shoulders.

We wait by the mother's side, hoping she will come to the realization that it's best to allow a burial. Finally, she begins to sob, almost imperceptibly, and slowly offers the child to the medic without ever making eye contact. He gently receives the bundle and walks softly toward the makeshift burial pit. The young mother stands like a statue, gazing at the ice-cold ground. It's a stark reminder that the pain eating away at my back right now is nothing for me to whine about.

In the valleys below the refugee camps, the same U.S. and British air forces that have been airlifting aid to the refugees have established a no-fly zone, promising to shoot down any Iraqi aircraft that violates this decree. They also have moved ground forces into Kurdistan that are pushing the Iraqi Army out of Kurdish cities and back toward Baghdad. It's delicate. Any direct conflict could trigger another all-out war. The Pentagon calls it Operation Provide Comfort, and while journalists have been allowed to fly on Army helicopters into the mountain refugee camps, we've been denied access to this dangerous ground game.

After covering the refugee crisis, I manage to get ahold of an old camper van with a bed and stove that NBC has rented indefinitely. This becomes my living quarters at the media camp just across the Iraq border in Turkey. I need it. It's getting tougher to wriggle into a sleeping bag with a sore back, and the ground feels like it keeps getting harder. The camper bed, by contrast, feels luxurious. And the vehicle gives me some freedom of movement. We're not allowed to wander from the media camp without military permission, but I can't help myself. I want to cover the war, not just the refugee crisis. So I decide to make an attempt to cross the border secretly into Iraq.

When my Turkish cameraman and I drive the camper up to the Iraqi border checkpoint early the next morning, it's desolate and eerily quiet. Trash is strewn everywhere. There's no one in sight. We slow to a crawl, zigzagging around cement barricades that are posted with Arabic signs warning that the border is closed. We warily move toward a group of inspection buildings that look abandoned. Just as we're about to cross, a lone Iraqi border guard in a tan uniform appears from a small guard stand.

"*Qef!*" He shouts the Arabic word for "stop" with menacing authority. The guard is in his fifties, tall and beefy. With his hair and moustache dyed black, he looks like an impersonator of Saddam Hussein. He is clearly a Sunni Muslim. The Sunnis and Shiites are factions of Islam. Sunnis form the minority in Iraq, but they hold power. This means they typically get the better jobs, run the government, and form the backbone of the military. I was hoping we would find a Kurdish guard, or maybe a Shiite who might be pleased that America just vanquished Saddam in Kuwait. But instead we're in a dicey situation.

Pointing his automatic rifle just above our heads, the guard aggressively waves us to a halt. I can't understand much beyond *qef*, but he's clearly asserting control and demanding to know what we're doing here. I slowly reach into my shirt pocket and carefully hand him a large wad of crumpled Turkish lira, offering a reasonable border crossing fee for these dangerous times, with a friendly smile, of course. He pauses, staring me hard in the eyes as if he'd rather shoot me than return my smile. Then he takes the money and sternly waves us through with his rifle. I punch the gas pedal and drive as fast as the old camper will go, just in case he changes his mind.

We soon arrive in Zakho, a normally bustling trading center that has become a ghost town. Zakho was once home to the ancient Catholic Diocese of Malta. It was also called "The Jerusalem of Kurdistan" before brutal campaigns against the Jewish population sent this small religious minority fleeing to Palestine in 1920. That left Zakho predominantly Kurdish, until now. It appears all 600,000 residents have fled into the mountains. We can't find a single soul as we film looted stores, empty homes, broken windows—the visible evidence of hasty exits and shattered lives.

We return to the border before nightfall, passing the same guard, who apparently lives in a nearby shack and is the only one here. In the media camp, we reveal our crossing point to no one. I only let our producer at our Turkish base camp know that I've discovered a route into Kurdistan and am going back the following morning. I quickly send one of NBC's Kurdish assistants for beer. He has to travel more than a hundred miles north to the Turkish city of Diyarbakir to buy it. When he returns, I take the beer and make a bargain with the American soldiers: beer for MREs. They love this deal and I'm quickly stocked full, ready for my road trip, with more than a few extra beers stashed in the camper for myself.

The next morning at dawn, I give the border guard another crossing fee plus a six-pack of beer, just so we can stay friends. Despite my generosity and thoughtfulness, he still won't return my smile. My cameraman and I pass through Zakho and drive into the expansive valley beyond. Here we film deserted villages, destroyed Iraqi vehicles, huge caches of abandoned artillery shells, wooden crates of ammunition, and empty Iraqi bunkers. I walk gingerly toward each bunker, carefully inspecting the dirt pathways and occasionally spotting a trip wire. These must be connected to small explosive devices, so we get off the trail and approach through the brush to reach the bunkers and film their contents.

I'm on high alert every moment, scanning the horizon and scrutinizing every road. Iraqi troops are still in command of certain areas, and if we're discovered before we can hook up with American or British troops, my best guess is that they will take us prisoner, interrogate and beat us, accuse us of being spies for the CIA, and ship us south to a Baghdad prison or even a public execution. It's hard to describe what a rush it is having this story all to myself, danger all around us, my heart pumping like a piston. I feel like I have to keep proving myself to the network again and again. Stay ahead of the pack. Get the exclusive story. Push forward and then push and push some more, hiding the back pain all the while.

We're gone for days, winding through an ancient and now abandoned land as eerie and silent as Zakho. Signs of war abound, with destroyed trucks and automobiles lying by the roadsides, many flipped onto their sides and riddled with bullets. I have to periodically siphon gas from one of these wrecks to keep the camper going. Whenever we stop to do this, I make a perfect target for a sniper, so I'm on even higher alert, ducking down and concealing myself as best I can.

"Who are you? What are you doing here?" A heavily armed convoy has suddenly appeared from a side road and stops us dead in our tracks. I can't believe I never heard or saw them coming, and I'm profoundly relieved when I spot American soldiers holding M60 machine guns at the ready.

"I'm American, and I have I.D!" I say quickly and loudly as I fumble for the pool reporter badge I still keep in my canvas shoulder bag along with other essentials. "I covered the war. This is my cameraman, and he is Turkish, not Iraqi!"

It takes a few minutes for trust to be established, but soon we shake hands, everyone smiles, and we join the soldiers as they continue to secure the countryside. It's still a powder keg, with occasional tense negotiations and verbal conflicts between the advancing Americans and reluctantly retreating Iraqis. But the Americans clearly have the upper hand. Whenever an Iraqi commander refuses to withdraw his men farther south, an A-10 Warthog fighter jet is radioed in. It screams over our heads at the lowest possible altitude as a reminder of who has supremacy in the region. The aircraft got its name because, like a warthog, it is loud, ugly, and dangerous. The flyovers work every time.

After a few days, we sneak back across the border into the media camp and file our reports. Stocking up on more Army MREs and grabbing more beer for the border guard, we head back into Kurdistan as quickly as we can. Tonight, an ancient village called al-Amadiyah has become our safe haven. It's perched on the flat top of a high, rocky mountain rising majestically from the valley floor. My Turkish cameraman tells me that, with a history dating back more than 5,000 years, al-Amadiyah was once home to the priests of ancient Persia known as the Magi. The most notable Magi were the Three Wise Men who made a pilgrimage to Jerusalem, taking offerings of gold, frankincense, and myrrh to Jesus Christ shortly after his birth.

Given its unique location, al-Amadiyah has long provided great security for its 6,000 residents, but, like everywhere else here, it's been overrun by the Iraqi military. The city is intact, but the stores and homes have been looted and al-Amadiyah is deserted, except for a few free-roaming chickens pecking in dirt yards by dusty clay homes. We've run out of our pasty army rations and can find nothing to eat in the looted stores, so I've been trying to catch a scrawny chicken all morning. I'm dreaming of gutting and plucking it, cooking it on my camper stove, lathering it with a one-ounce bottle of Tabasco that came in an MRE, and devouring the bird like a barbarian.

It's amazing how our perspectives can shift: what becomes important and what lacks significance in circumstances such as these. Three of my most precious possessions are the tiny Tabasco bottle, a roll of thick twine I use to replace my worn-out boot strings, and my Swiss Army Knife. The comforts of home we cling to, the overflow of possessions stored in our cupboards, closets, and garages, are utterly meaningless to me now. My belly is screaming, and all I want is a meal. Despite my desperate efforts, I can't catch the damn chicken, and my back is killing me from the attempt.

"Thok-thok-thok-thok-thok."

I suddenly hear it. The distant sound of a helicopter. Louder now. As I head toward my camper, an American Blackhawk helicopter swoops overhead, creating a huge dust cloud as it lands in a nearby field. I forget all about the chicken and hurry over as General John Shalikashvili steps out of the Blackhawk and walks toward me. With his oversized glasses, short stature, and pepper-gray hair, the general looks more like a fatherly librarian than a commander, but he is a born leader with an amazing life story.

Shalikashvili is the son of a prince from the Republic of Georgia forced into exile when the Russians invaded his homeland. As a child, he lived through the destruction of Warsaw while his father fought against the Third Reich. At age sixteen, hardly speaking a word of English, he emigrated to America and eventually was granted the first official citizenship he ever held in his life. Then he worked his way through college and ultimately earned a master's degree in International Relations before joining the Army. An American success story, he is now commander of Operation Provide Comfort.

"How did you get here?" General Shalikashvili asks in his thick eastern European accent when he sees me. I had interviewed him in the media camp and am thankful he recognizes me.

"Lucky, I guess. Why are you here?"

"Just wanted to see this historic city," the general replies. After looking around with him and getting an on-camera interview, I confess that I'm out of food and low on gas. "How about a ride back to the base camp?" I ask.

"Fine with me," he says. "Hop in."

Good things happen when you least expect them. It's why I like to step outside the boundaries and follow my instincts. The chopper is full, so my cameraman stays behind and waits for my return later that day. The general agrees to have me back in al-Amadiyah before sundown. This trip would have taken days in the camper, but we make it in just over an hour in his sleek and powerful Blackhawk. Along the way, the views of Kurdistan are breathtaking. I poke a camera out the open door and film stunning panoramas that will add great visual texture to my reports.

When we land at the media camp, reporters run through the dust cloud to question the general. There are looks of shock as I jump out first and hurry my videotapes and reports to our editing trailer, trying not to wince from the pain or look like I'm limping. I grab a handful of MREs from the stash my Turkish helper has been acquiring in my absence. There is noticeable anger from the media mob when I reboard the Blackhawk and we lift back into the sky. Every reporter wants equal access to every story. It's part of the natural competition among us, and we can get furious when it looks like someone has elbowed us out of something. I'm no exception to this rule.

The trip to base camp was a breeze, but by the time we land back in al-Amadiyah my spine is on fire again. I have burning sciatica down the backs of both legs, especially the left one. I have to steady myself getting out of the chopper and limp to my cameraman's tent to share dinner. We talk briefly about what tomorrow might bring, deciding to push farther south at the break of dawn. The sun has set quickly and it's a moonless night, but the sky is exploding with stars so bright that it's easy to find my way back to my camper.

The pain is excruciating. I pop a beer and chug it down in one continuous gulp, then roll onto my bed and unzip my shoulder bag. Before I came to the Gulf, a friend who specializes in tropical medicine put together an emergency field kit for me. It has bandages, sutures and salves, antibiotics, and antibacterials. It also contains potent amphetamines in case I'm forced to flee long distances without sleep, Vicodin pills for minor trauma, and injectable morphine for more serious wounds. These are heavy drugs. Far heavier than anything I've been prescribed.

I witnessed what hard drugs could do to people in my teenage years, so I've avoided the medications in the kit. But my prescription bottles of Valium and Motrin are empty. My circumstances pale in comparison to the wounds I've seen, but I need relief. I take the field kit out of my canvas shoulder bag and fold it open. Rolling onto my bed, I begin my own Operation Provide Comfort. Everything starts to feel like slow motion.

> *Staring now at the syringe and bottle of morphine. Feeling wounded…*
>
> *Starting to remove the plastic casing from around the needle. It crinkles in my fingers…*
>
> *Pulling the cap off a sterilized needle and screwing it onto a syringe…*
>
> *Gazing at my right shoulder muscle…*
>
> *Beginning to push the needle through the soft rubber seal of the morphine bottle…*

Don't do it. A voice in the back of my head whispers insistently before I draw the clear, oily fluid into the syringe. *Save this in case you are truly hurt.*

I take a deep breath, cap the needle, and unscrew it from the syringe. Drop the syringe back into the kit with a soft thud. But I do open the Vicodin. It's a powerful narcotic analgesic often used after surgery. I take a double dose and swallow it while chugging down a second beer. Rolling to one side, I peer out the camper window and see the North Star shimmering in the sky. It looks to me like a celestial beacon, and I wonder if there are any Wise Men left on Earth who might guide us out of this madness of war.

Woozy now.
Warm.
Fuzzy.
No pain.
Drifting.
Gone.

Iraqi forces have retreated to Baghdad and Coalition troops are pulling out of northern Iraq. Operation Provide Comfort is declared a success. The media has finally been allowed to cross the border, and they flood in. A United Nations refugee camp, being furiously constructed in a wide swath of open land just outside Zakho, is being established as a temporary stop for the thousands of Kurdish refugees still in the mountains. The Kurds are wary. They fear Saddam has little respect for the U.N. and will return to slaughter them once the troops depart. It takes delicate negotiations to coax them down before winter strikes.

As the Kurds finally flood into the camp, sanitation becomes a crisis. Diarrhea is epidemic and the fields are soon covered with it. A hot sun bakes the earth. Relief trucks roll in and create clouds of dust. An afternoon storm begins to thicken the air. The clouds turn yellow. They hang low and heavy, ominously filled with fecal dust kicked up by the trucks.

"Those clouds are filled with diarrhea and it's going to rain toxic soup," I tell a few colleagues in our new location, which lies at one end of the relief operation. They laugh and dismiss the vulgar thought. But I don't think it's a joke. I duck into my camper and seal all the windows just before it rains. My windshield turns a sickening brown when it finally pours down.

A few days after the storm, there is more sickness in the camps. Diarrhea, infections, gastroenteritis, and even a few cases of spinal meningitis. It hits the refugees like a fire. Soldiers are down as well. A number of reporters are medivacked out. Thanks to the shelter of my camper, I feel healthy and strong—at least for now. I continue pushing forward, looking for the next story…with the help of a Vicodin or two every time my back pain returns.

CHAPTER 11

Asia Stories

IF I WERE YOU, I'd take Hong Kong," the senior producer for *Nightly News* says with conviction as we sit together at his desk in the middle of the network newsroom. "Japan is an economic powerhouse, China is surging, Burma has become Myanmar with a brutal military junta in charge, Cambodia is now Kampuchea and still recovering from the Khmer Rouge bloodbaths, Laos is in chaos, relations with Vietnam need mending. You'll never be at a loss for important stories."

Marc Kusnetz is arguably the most intelligent person at NBC's headquarters at 30 Rock. Remarkably seasoned in domestic and foreign news, he is compact, studious, and handsome, with thick-lensed, John Lennon glasses and a bushy head of salt-and-pepper hair. Whenever I want guidance, I seek out Marc, my news guru.

Covering the Gulf War cost NBC a fortune and the Miami Bureau has been closed, so I'm a homeless foreign correspondent. Other bureaus also have been closed or downsized, with photographers, producers, and correspondents let go. It's been a bloodbath. But because of my work in the Gulf, I've survived, and have been offered three choices for a new posting. Two are for what we call domestic news, at a bureau in either Atlanta or Los Angeles. The third is a foreign news posting, in Hong Kong. NBC covers all of Asia from its Hong Kong bureau, with mini-bureaus in Tokyo, Beijing, and Manila. I've been fascinated with Asia since the Vietnam War protests of my early teens and have always longed to see it. Hong Kong already was my first choice, and Marc's confirmation is all I need to finalize my decision.

※

Hong Kong is like a mini New York on steroids. Carved from China's southern coast, it's enclosed by the Pearl River Delta and South China Sea. Its heart is Hong Kong Island, where the British first established a colonial foothold in China after the Opium Wars in the early 1800s. The island's tallest mountain, Victoria Peak, rises almost 2,000 feet above sea level, offering stunning views of the expansive harbor and burgeoning city below.

In late fall of 1991, I find a beautiful flat on Victoria Peak at the end of a dead-end road in the jungle foliage that rings the mountainside. This is the tropics. Humidity is often above 90 percent, with temperatures topping 100 degrees. The forest is full of cicadas. The drone of their deep mating call constantly fills the air. Dragonflies course the thick breeze like miniature helicopters. Giant, multicolored spiders weave fantastic webs that hang between the branches like canopies. My new home is all windows, with sweeping views of Hong Kong's dazzling skyline and the vastness of China beyond. Looking out from every room, I feel like an eagle perched above its domain, ready for the hunt.

In the early morning, I often walk from my flat to the top of Victoria Peak and circle the top of the island to exercise my back before it's boiling outside. The journey begins with a panorama of the South China Sea with its thick scent of salt air. As I wander down the path, there's a wide natural park on my left, facing the ocean. Wealthy Chinese who live on the Peak gather here at daybreak under the shade of massive, ancient banyan trees, with thick roots hanging down from their branches like vines. The Chinese are doing tai chi, a meditative form of slow-motion movement that dates back to the time of Buddha. Despite the heat and humidity, many of them, men and women alike, wear mink coats as a display of their affluence. Beyond the park, the path becomes remote and heavily wooded, as if far from civilization, and I have it all to myself. Suddenly, halfway around the Peak, the Hong Kong Harbor and skyline come into view again as the din of the city cuts through the silence with a roar. It's a complete knockout, the most dazzling sight I have ever seen.

Hong Kong is still governed by the British, who are on notice from the People's Republic of China that the colony will revert back to Chinese control six years from now, in 1997. Known as the bankers of the world, the British have long made Hong Kong the financial center of Asia. The world's most elite global corporations maintain a high profile here as deals are cut to fund major projects throughout the vast region. It's like an international village, and the NBC Asia Bureau is smack in the middle of it all.

Hong Kong is also known as a gourmet's paradise. After a morning of researching stories, my producer and I usually venture out for a sumptuous meal of Chinese, Japanese, Indian, Filipino, or Thai cuisine. The streets are always thronged, and the traffic is thick. Because the British drive on the left side of the road, I'm disoriented and have to be careful not to step out in front of one of the double-decker transport buses that dart by at full throttle just inches away from the curb. At the end of the day, I drop by the Foreign Correspondents' Club to have a drink with seasoned reporters from around the world and listen as they swap tales of adventure and intrigue.

Before we shoot a story, unless it's breaking news, we have to pitch it on the conference calls with 30 Rock. Either *Nightly News* or the *Today Show* has to want it before we're allocated a budget and authorized to spend funds. Given the size of Asia, it's always an extended road trip for us when we do get approval. Then we're hurriedly packing our gear, dragging a dozen or more heavy metal cases of camera and sound equipment through airports, checking in and out of hotels, loading travel vans, unpacking, then repacking again.

Traveling throughout Asia is fascinating, but the distances between the countries we cover are daunting. Sitting on long flights and working longer hours gnaws at me and fills my body with tension. My lower back is always tender now, and has started to flare up more often. To keep the secret of how much pain I'm in, I've doubled the strength of the Valium to relax my muscles, and increased the dosage of Motrin to lower the inflammation. I also have a refillable prescription for Vicodin, the narcotic medication that helps kill the pain. Since I renew all of them as early as possible to ensure I always have extra meds for an emergency, my travel kit is beginning to look like a mobile pharmacy, or maybe a drug dealer's private stash.

Thai Sex Slaves

Once called the Kingdom of Siam, Thailand enjoys an important strategic location in Southeast Asia and was long a buffer zone between the French and British colonial empires. Bangkok, an exotic and dynamic city of more than 9 million, is a regional force in finance and business. Ancient cultural landmarks stand amid its growing number of skyscrapers. Hundreds of ornate Buddhist temples dot the city, symbols of a deep spiritual heritage. And then there's Bangkok's infamous prostitution industry.

There is a slum in central Bangkok called Klong Toei. It's right next to a pig slaughterhouse, aptly nicknamed Slaughterhouse Slum. Thousands of Bangkok's poorest people live crammed together here in makeshift shacks, sitting in the shadow of one of the most expensive cities in the world. An acrid stench of death permeates the air. Rivulets of pig blood, urine, and feces run through the narrow mud streets. The only hope for the hordes that live here is Father Joe.

"Ho, ho, ho, I'm a renegade and we're taking back what belongs to these poor people!" Father Joe Maier is a pudgy, red-faced Irish-American in his mid-fifties who wiggles his hips when he laughs his trademark "ho, ho, ho," like an elfish Santa Claus without the beard. He lives in the slum, too, alongside those he serves.

"The rich can take care of themselves," he says with a glint in his eye. "It's the poor who need us," Father Joe tells me as we walk carefully along with my camera crew, watching our step to avoid pools of filth. As we turn a corner, he stops abruptly, leans down, and hands a crumpled bill to an emaciated old man sitting in the dirt.

"I don't care if someone is going to spend it for taking drugs, sniffing glue, or drinking booze," Father Joe says with an impish smile. "You have to give every crazy person you see on the streets a few baht [Thai currency]. We take them all in, people with AIDS, child prostitutes, dope addicts. These aren't bad people and we have no right to pass judgment on them. Jesus never judged anyone, He just loved them all."

Father Joe's personality is so authentic and infectious that it's impossible not to love him instantly. He is a down-to-earth, unpretentious, and truly spiritual human being who has devoted his life to the people here, building schools for the slum children, hospices for the AIDS victims, and shelters for young prostitutes. To free the girls from the sex trade, he tells us, he has to buy their freedom from their pimps, and it usually takes a tough attitude, firmly standing his ground, and never giving an inch.

"Some of these girls are as young as ten years old," Father Joe says gravely as we enter a small schoolroom filled with ex-prostitutes. They now have desks, a few books to study from, and the incredible luxury of a teacher. "Poverty forces them into it. Then the gangsters enslave them. And don't forget," he delivers this point with great emphasis, wagging a finger in the air, "it's American, European, and rich Asian men who are responsible for this and they should be made to take the blame. Shame, shame, shame on all of them!"

Father Joe courageously confronts organized street criminals who prey on the poor. He occupies unused portions of government land, erects makeshift shelters overnight, fills them with destitute families, and shames the government into not evicting them. He condemns the Catholic Church in Bangkok as being too interested in serving the privileged and indifferent to those truly in need. He's more than an activist. He's a radical for peace, compassion, and justice.

After filming a story on his work in the slums, Father Joe agrees to collaborate with us on an investigative piece into the sex-slave trade. Given his work in rescuing young prostitutes and dealing with pimps, he'll be an invaluable source on the inner workings of Patpong, the massive red light district that forms the heart of Bangkok's sex trade. Due to its proximity to Saigon, Bangkok was the city of choice for American troops on R&R (rest and relaxation) during the Vietnam War. As a result, prostitution boomed. Thai women are known as among the most beautiful women in the world, and so the clubs have thrived, gaining international popularity. Now they're filled with foreigners from all walks of life, many of whom signed up for "Sex Tours" in their homelands designed to look like business or tourism trips.

Inside Patpong's glitzy bars, outdated disco music blares from cheap speakers as colored lights swirl around the walls and ceiling of the dark, smoky rooms. Young girls, most of whom have been sold to the slave traders by their impoverished families, dance topless on stage, wearing neon colored string bikini bottoms. Numbered cards hang around their necks like they're cattle at a livestock auction. Titillated customers whisper a number to a waiter with the casualness of placing their drink orders, and arrangements are quickly made to slip the girl of their choice into a back room or send her off to the customer's hotel. Thai-Chinese gangs run the show behind the scenes, and they can be brutal with anyone who gets in their way.

"There's AIDS here, so you have to be careful," a businessman from Arizona yells out over the music to Father Joe and me as we stand at the bar of a Patpong club. He proudly lets us know that he's here with several buddies on a "Sex Tour" organized by an American travel agent to look, of course, like a business and tourism junket.

"I've been coming to Patpong for years. My wife thinks these are business trips." He laughs, pleased with himself. "I only choose the youngest girls, you know, twelve, sometimes eleven. Less chance of disease. Stick with me and we'll find you a young one, too, maybe a virgin!"

Even if he watches the news back in the States, it's too dark in here for him to recognize me, and he has no idea that I have a hidden camera in my lapel filming his every word. I wonder what possesses him to do this and how he justifies it to himself in whatever moments of self-reflection he might have. I wonder even more what his wife and kids will think when they see him on the news and discover what he really does on his "business trips." It's impossible for me to have compassion for him, but I feel terrible for his family back home.

After filming in the clubs, we interview Thailand's Minister of Tourism, Mr. Weerasak Kowsurat. He's a tall, handsome man dressed in a perfectly cut dark blue suit with a crisp white dress shirt and burgundy paisley tie. Having earned a law degree at Harvard, he speaks impeccable English, which he demonstrates as he stares straight into our camera and says, "I invite all of you from anywhere in the world to come to our beautiful country. Come enjoy our temples and dance, our cultural heritage and fine cuisine, our beaches, parks, and mountains. Come enjoy Thailand. But leave our women and girls alone. Have some respect and do not exploit our poverty. Please, have the same respect you would expect us to show your wives and daughters."

Asia's sex slaves are usually coerced into opium addiction, making them easier to control and manipulate. Thailand is a major producer of opium. My crew and I cover this next, beginning in Chiang Rai, a village on the northernmost border of Thailand. Nestled in rolling mountains with tropical forests, Chiang Rai is just what Mr. Weerasak Kowsurat is talking about: a mixture of ancient temples, thatched hut villages, rice fields, wilderness parks, tall mountains, and meandering rivers. It's also the gateway to the Golden Triangle with Burma and Laos. The region is home to warlords who oversee the vast, golden poppy fields and the production of heroin derived from the flowers' capsules. Just like cocaine from South America, most of the heroin is smuggled to the warlords' number-one customer: America.

Opium is the sticky, tarlike resin that comes from slicing the bulbous opium poppies. It's expensive when refined into heroin, but in its raw state it's a poor man's high. North of Chiang Rai, in a small village dating back thousands of years, we enter a dark thatched hut with the sweet smell of opium smoke permeating the air. Elderly men and women with sunken eyes and emaciated bodies are lying on bamboo mats in the dim candlelight, utterly stoned. Puffing long, thin bamboo pipes, they still wear the ornate and colorful outfits with patterns woven to articulate their tribal heritage, but the drug has destroyed their culture, ruined their lives, and stolen their Souls, just as it is now doing to thousands of girls in the sex-slave trade.

"What do you do with your life?" I ask a middle-aged man as he lies on his side smoking opium. Deep wrinkles cover his emaciated face like a network of rivers.

"Nothing," he says, his yellowish eyes glazed into a blank stare, plumes of bluish-white smoke swirling around his head. "I just smoke and all my worries go away. There is nothing else to do."

His simple words illustrate how helpless, resigned, and addicted the drug makes its victims, which is exactly what the slave-traders want.

The most beautiful Thai prostitutes are never found on the stages of Patpong. Instead, they're sold by the Thai-Chinese Gangs to the Yakuza, Japan's powerful organized crime syndicate. The Yakuza enslaves them in major cities such as Tokyo, Osaka, and Yokohama, forcing them to work in very private, very exclusive clubs. They are taught Japanese manners and dressed in expensive evening gowns, with their hair and makeup done by professionals. Then they are forced to serve the elite class of politicians and businessmen, who are willing and eager to pay thousands of dollars for an evening of sensual delight.

So our third and final stop in our coverage on sex slaves is Tokyo, where we locate some of the private clubs in the richest districts of the city. Getting inside these clubs would be impossible. They are guarded by heavily armed Yakuza, and our Japanese film crew wisely advises that we not even try. We shoot a few stand-ups outside the buildings for this element of the story, then interview a middle-aged Japanese woman devoted to helping locate and liberate these young women, after agreeing to darken her face and alter her voice during the editing process to conceal her identity.

"Their passports are taken away from them when they arrive," she tells us with a look that blends anger with sadness. "They have no documentation to prove who they are or where they came from, no money, and no freedom. They are kept locked in small apartments all day long, as many girls as they can cram into a single room, and only brought out each evening to work at the clubs. Their only pay is food…and drugs. If they cause trouble, they are beaten. If they get a disease from sex, they are isolated until they die and their bodies are disposed of by the gangs."

Back in the Hong Kong Bureau we produce our reports, focusing on the lucrative conspiracy the sex trade has created between drug lords, gangsters, politicians, the wealthy class, and Western tourists addicted to exploiting young women for their sordid pleasures. As I view our segment on the Golden Triangle, I remember that, like heroin, morphine is also a derivative of opium. Gazing at the videotape of the opium addicts in Chiang Rai, I think about the day in northern Iraq when I almost stuck a needle filled with morphine into my shoulder muscle to alleviate the torment of my back pain.

Vietnam Twenty Years After the War

Quang Ngai Province, rural Vietnam, 1992. The long wooden shelves hold rows of tightly capped five-gallon glass jars filled with formaldehyde. The strong preservative is yellowed with age. It takes a while to realize what's floating in the murk. Then, as we peer closely, it becomes obvious. Each jar holds a deformed human fetus. Large clusters of reddish tumors visible on small, contorted faces. Tiny arms and legs deformed. Little bodies twisted in the agony of death. It's heart-wrenching to look at them. As my cameraman shoots close-ups, we glance at one another, silently acknowledging that this is worse than much of the carnage we have seen on battlefields.

The fetuses were stillborn as a result of prenatal exposure to dioxin, an extremely toxic herbicide banned in much of the world, and a key component of Agent Orange. The United States sprayed 20 million gallons of it on the Vietnamese countryside during the Vietnam War.

"This is what Agent Orange has done to our people and continues to do to them," Dr. Nguyen, whose name rhymes with *Win*, tells us as we walk down an aisle in his laboratory with cameras rolling. As a government scientist for Vietnam, Dr. Nguyen's life is devoted to documenting the ongoing effects of dioxin on the Vietnamese population.

The Pentagon dubbed the program Operation Ranch Hand. It was designed to defoliate rural villages and forests, denying the communist guerillas of North Vietnam food and cover as they surged south. The spraying of Agent Orange also helped create "forced draft urbanization," a tactic the Pentagon deliberately concealed from the media. Destroying the countryside's rice and vegetable crops eliminated the ability of South Vietnamese peasants to support themselves, forcing them to flee to U.S.-dominated cities such as Saigon. Destitute, their only choice was to join the South Vietnamese Army and fight against their own countrymen from the North.

Operation Ranch Hand destroyed 5 million acres of forest and millions of acres of crops, and seriously polluted most of the waterways in the regions where it was sprayed. Widespread famine occurred, leaving hundreds of thousands of people malnourished or starving. According to the Vietnamese Ministry of Foreign Affairs, close to 5 million Vietnamese were exposed to Agent Orange attacks. Almost a half-million were killed or maimed. An even greater number of children were born with birth defects, and they're still counting. American soldiers were also hard-hit by the defoliants. Thousands of veterans reportedly contracted debilitating skin rashes, suffered neurological damage that triggered psychological problems, and developed cancer. Many also had children born with birth defects after the war.

Dr. Nguyen explains it matter-of-factly: "This is the legacy of the American chemical companies and the U.S. military, but they refuse to take responsibility even now. They must be held accountable." Dr. Nguyen wants the military and the corporations to admit their wrongdoing and offer compensation. He is adamant that justice must be done, but any anger he once may have held has vanished with the passage of so much time.

The primary producers of Agent Orange were Monsanto and Dow Chemical. Both continue to deny their chemicals were to blame, but in one of the most heavily sprayed areas in Quang Ngai province, we are shown more of Vietnam's evidence of the devastation wrought by the herbicide. Portions of the tropical forest surrounding Quang Ngai are lush again, framing peaceful vistas over rice fields and waterways. But in the villages, human deformities abound. In small, thatched huts we interview older men and women, sprayed during the war, with huge tumors deforming their faces into hideous masks. We film small children with unusable limbs, giant heads filled with fluid, tumors covering their bodies.

I remember opposing the war in my teens, shocked at the pictures of Agent Orange being sprayed from Army helicopters over villages such as this. I remember being sprayed with mace by the National Guard and smacked on the head with a billy club during protest marches. To me, loving one's country never means turning a blind eye to such horrors. It means seeking the truth and speaking out in the face of obvious injustice. Freedom of speech is one of the most powerful forces in democracy, and it has always been worth risking everything for. As we film these deformed children, I wonder: What were we doing? Where were the moral principles that gave our country its greatness? How could anyone not speak out?

From Quang Ngai we travel north to Hanoi, joining a delegation from the Select POW/MIA Committee, led by Senators John Kerry, Bob Smith, and John McCain, all of whom served in the armed forces during the Vietnam War. The senators are here on a historic mission. It's the first time an American political delegation has been allowed in the capital city, which served as the headquarters of the North Vietnamese Army during the war.

Unlike bustling, modern Saigon in the south, which was renamed Ho Chi Minh City after the war in honor of North Vietnam's greatest hero, Hanoi offers a journey back in time to the era when Vietnam was a French colony. Many of its streets are lined with spacious three-story French colonial homes with finely carved facades, dormers, and side-gabled roofs that once housed the French elite. They're now occupied by government agencies or foreign embassies. Most Vietnamese here live in far humbler quarters and only a fortunate few can afford the luxury of a car. The primary means of transportation is bicycles, which creates a peace and quiet rarely found in a major Asian city.

The centerpiece of downtown Hanoi is Turtle Tower, an ancient, three-story stone temple sitting in Hoan Kiem Lake. The waters around the tower are covered with lily pads that blossom white each spring, sending their fragrance on gentle winds into the city. The Old Quarter, nestled on one edge of the lake, is a dense maze. Shops of furniture makers, silk traders, vegetable markets, artisans, and craftsmen are knitted together along narrow, twisting streets.

The American domino theory proved wrong. Vietnam never became a puppet of China or a rigid communist dictatorship. Instead, it has emerged as a major economic power in Southeast Asia, and American businesses are hungry for the same access their European and Asian competitors enjoy here. First, however, the U.S. delegation must close the book on the controversy over U.S. prisoners of war and those still deemed missing in action. The POW/MIA debate remains an emotional issue in the States and is the major roadblock to normalizing relations.

Following two decades of refusal, the Vietnamese have agreed to open their archives from the war, allowing senate aids and U.S. Army researchers to pore over old files, examine dog tags, helmets, uniforms, and personal effects of Americans who were captured or killed. At the government palace in Hanoi, our cameras are denied access to the actual negotiations, but we're allowed to film ceremonial meetings between the senators and top Vietnamese officials. Many of these officials fought in the war and were vilified in America at the time. Here in Hanoi, they're national heroes.

It's an intricate dance of diplomacy. McCain, Smith, and Kerry must find a way to close the POW/MIA cases without angering opponents back home, signal a formal government apology to Vietnam without it appearing so, and ultimately lay the groundwork for ending a terrible chapter in our history even though gaping emotional wounds remain on all sides. Like the United States, Vietnam recognizes the enormous economic and political advantages involved, and so the two countries finally hammer out an agreement that will have to be ratified back in the States.

After the senators depart Hanoi, my crew and I take a day trip into the nearby countryside to shoot what we call "color" to add texture and context to our reports. The moment we leave the city, we're surrounded by lush rice fields. Small villages, with traditional huts made of grass and bamboo, integrate perfectly into the natural environment as if they grew here of their own accord. Even a bicycle is a luxury in the countryside, and most rural Vietnamese walk to their destinations. They are lean and strong from diets of rice and vegetables, and while their poverty is palpable, they carry themselves with a silent dignity and inner peace. Like their villages, they appear balanced and in harmony with the natural rhythms of life.

The following morning we find our way to Hun Tiep Lake, in a residential district just outside Hanoi proper. Sitting in the middle of the lake's murky water is the wreckage of an American B-52 bomber. Its nose and wings are submerged. A large, twisted piece of the fuselage pokes into the sky with a white Air Force star at its center. Its rusted landing gear sticks out to one side at the waterline. Nicknamed "Rose 1," it was shot down during Christmas air raids on December 19, 1972. It's been two decades since the war ended, but the bomber looks like it just crashed.

During the Christmas raids, President Richard Nixon was negotiating to end the war, trying not to make it look like a complete surrender. Secretary of State Henry Kissinger had just uttered the famous words, "Peace is at hand," during negotiations with the North Vietnamese at a summit in Paris. Then came the surprise American bombing attack that shocked and outraged the world. It was called Operation Linebacker II, a football metaphor for eleven days of relentless aerial bombardment, the heaviest strikes launched by the Air Force since World War II. More than 1,600 civilians were killed in Hanoi and surrounding villages. Tens of thousands were wounded. In America, the pilots who flew the sorties some twenty years ago are still revered as heroes. Here, they're remembered as demons that came in the night and wreaked havoc. For the Vietnamese, this B-52 in Hun Tiep Lake is a monument to victory over a mighty and brutal foe.

My photographer and I are paddling out to the wreckage now in a small rowboat. The silence is only interrupted by the occasional croaking of small frogs sunning themselves on lily pads. An elderly

Hun Tiep Lake, Vietnam, 1992.

Vietnamese woman in a woven straw hat is waist deep in the water, harvesting watercress. Her face is soft and serene despite deep lines of age. She could be anyone's loving grandmother. Her gentle, rhythmic movements send small, circular ripples lapping against the bomber's fuselage and give our boat a gentle rock. She pays us no mind, as if we do not exist. I try to imagine what it was like for her and her family on the nights the B-52s screamed overhead and the bombs rained down, shaking the earth with their thunder.

Each morning at dawn, I walk from my small hotel in the center of Hanoi to visit Hoan Kiem Lake and Turtle Tower, and then I slip into the Old Quarter. This helps work out the kinks in my back and I also get to immerse myself in the local culture. I'm always drawn to the places where the poorer people live. Their lives inevitably tell the story of a nation's past, how its leaders have treated their people, and what the future might hold. Wandering the Old Quarter, I love the aromas of the outdoor markets drifting through the air and the wrinkled, smiling faces with missing teeth that reveal a history of quiet suffering and perseverance.

Even at this early hour, the quarter is bustling, yet it retains a sense of quietude and peace. Residents squat in the streets with rice bowls, silently enjoying breakfast. It's rare for an outsider to be here, especially a tall, white one. Even though I must be a sight, few look up or acknowledge my presence. For three days straight, however, I've made eye contact with a middle-aged man during my morning walks. Like most men here, he's clad in the traditional pajama-style black shirt and trousers. On this morning, he signals me to squat down and join him for a bowl of rice.

Although the United States fears the Soviets are meddling here, most Vietnamese loathe Russians and would never befriend one. They also dislike the U.S. government. But they like Americans. I don't speak any Vietnamese, so the only words I utter are, "*Je suis Américain*," hoping he understands French from the colonial days.

"*Très bien*," he answers with a wide grin.

This almost exhausts my French, so we communicate with open smiles, subtle body language, and simple gestures. As we eat steaming, gooey rice with our fingers, I remember Afghanistan, where the left hand is used after going to the toilet; thinking it might be the same here, I am careful to use my right hand for the rice. I feel privileged to sit in the street and enjoy this simple meal, and although it's only rice, it tastes sumptuous and far superior to the pricey, processed MREs I lived on during the Gulf War. As we finish, my friend floats up to standing with ease. It takes me a while to get up from being cross-legged on the ground for so long, and it's a struggle to do it without groaning.

Once I'm on my feet, he beckons me to follow him. We walk through a narrow, dusty shop filled with old wood and iron parts for repairing the hand-pulled street carts used to transport goods throughout the Old Quarter. A creaky door in the back of the dilapidated building leads to his home. There are at least three generations of his family living in this tiny space, which is partitioned into miniature rooms by gray blankets tacked to the ceiling. His grandchildren, peeking from behind one old blanket, are wide-eyed. There must be at least a half dozen of them. They've never seen such a stranger, let alone one right here in their home.

My new friend guides me to a far corner. We step past his wife as she squats before a tiny hot plate on the floor, cooking more rice while paying us no mind. He pulls back a tapestry on the wall, revealing a door. It opens onto a narrow passageway, barely illuminated by oil lamps. For a moment, I wonder if I'm being set up to be robbed or roughed up, but I feel genuine kinship with this man. I follow him into the catacombs. The still, dank air smells a thousand years old.

We zig and zag as the hallway narrows. My shoulders brush the walls as my friend slides along effortlessly. My boots land with jarring thumps. My friend's footsteps are silent. A few sharp turns now. There are no more lamps. It's pitch black, except for a faint glow at the end of the corridor outlining another door. My friend slowly opens the door and light floods out from a small room brightly lit by hundreds of candles. Stepping inside, I see that the room is filled with beautiful Buddhist statues, artwork, and artifacts. Incense sweetens the air. Wax runs down the candleholders, forming layers of thick puddles on the rough wood floor. It is a humble temple, yet it feels holier than any great cathedral I have ever seen.

The French suppressed Buddhism in Vietnam when they colonized much of Indochina in the mid 1800s. It was further suppressed in the 1950s after Ho Chi Minh and his communist guerillas, known as the Vietminh, established a Democratic Republic of Vietnam in North Vietnam. I sense the candles in this temple have been kept lit throughout the years as a silent protest, secretly paying homage to the flame of an ancient spiritual tradition. My friend gazes into my eyes, brings his palms together at his heart, and gently bows toward me. I'm not sure what this means, but it feels like a great honor and I return the gesture with a soft smile of gratitude for being allowed to enter this sacred space. I'm mystified, however, why he brought me here.

PHOTO COURTESY OF TARA EBY, IN-SIGHT PHOTOGRAPHY

Golden Buddha

A gilded wooden statue of Buddha is the centerpiece of the temple altar. It's about a foot and a half tall. The Buddha is standing atop a beautifully carved lotus. The index finger of his left hand is pointing up, his right index finger is pointing down. I don't know what this gesture symbolizes, but the statue has an aura of wisdom and serenity. My friend steps over and gently lifts the golden Buddha from the altar. I watch spellbound as he wraps it in a beautiful piece of light brown silk cloth, turns toward me with a tender gaze, and offers it to me. I'm stunned. I resist at first, but he softly persists. He gestures to me to conceal it in my shoulder bag. I finally understand—at least I think I do. He wants the statue smuggled to freedom.

I wonder what will happen if it's discovered by the authorities during my departure from Hanoi. Will I create an incident? Be arrested and imprisoned for smuggling a spiritual artifact out of Vietnam at such a delicate time in history? I pull back a corner of the silk to reveal the Buddha's face. I swear he's looking at me as if to say, "Let's go!" I gently cover him up and carefully tuck him away in my bag, offering a gentle bow of my head to my new friend who gave me this precious gift.

Japan's Economic Bubble

Throughout the ages, all great spiritual texts have counseled against greed and self-indulgence. The Bible warns it's easier for a camel to go through the eye of a needle than for a rich man to enter the kingdom of God. The Bhagavad-Gita calls greed, anger, and lust "Doorways to Hell." Buddhism warns that avarice and desire are afflictions that inevitably lead to suffering. Yet we never seem to listen or learn. Great empires perpetually overextend, over-consume, and overindulge—and most eventually come crashing down.

Rising from the ashes of World War II, Japan's so-called economic miracle is the darling of the capitalist world. It's the early 1990s, and the economy is rocketing. Real estate prices have soared to astronomical levels. The Tokyo Stock Exchange is surpassing record levels. Credit is readily available to all, with interest rates at virtually zero. Speculation is rampant and hubris abounds. But now there are subtle signs and undercurrents indicating that the Japanese economy is in a huge bubble that is about to burst, yet everyone here is in denial and none will acknowledge it.

I'm hitting a wall as I try to report this. Government spokespersons, economists, and businessmen hold deep fears about the bubble, but won't go on the record with me. Corporations won't discuss downsizing or layoffs, especially in a nation where jobs are all but guaranteed for life. As a result of being isolated on an island throughout the millennia, Japan is a unique culture in Asia. Foreigners are kept as outsiders, tolerated and treated with respect but rarely trusted or allowed to fully integrate into the culture. Shintoism, the indigenous spiritual tradition here, is designed to sustain a present-day connection to the ancient past. Its rituals are complex, ornate, and arcane. Shinto includes an approach to life called *honne* and *tatemae*. *Honne* is true circumstances. *Tatemae* is the art of hiding the truth when revealing it would be embarrassing.

White-collar workers, called "salarymen," form the new middle class, which traditionally consisted of farmers and shopkeepers. The salarymen endure long commutes and work horrendous hours for Japan's burgeoning corporations. It's a life of maximum stress, and as a result they are notorious for their consumption of saké and beer. It's rare to see them, or any Japanese people, show emotion, because to do so is considered weak and undignified. Talking about one's troubles or being seen as a failure is called "losing face" and is taboo on both the personal and national levels.

The only hard evidence I have for this economic crisis is an interview with an American economic expert in Tokyo documenting increased layoffs, widespread psychological depression, and a growing rate of suicide. I've been pitching the story on the morning conference calls with 30 Rock for days. No takers, everyone wants more texture and some definitive proof, and all I get is *tatemae*. Finally, in a small article buried in a newspaper from Shizuoka Prefecture on the foothills of Mount Fuji, a tragic confirmation: A salaryman who lost his job walked up into the deep snows of the mountain with his wife and two young children. They never returned. They chose death rather than public humiliation and loss of face.

I can almost see them: The salaryman in his conservative black business suit walking silently in front of his wife, their two children obediently following behind. Giant pines tower around them. Snowflakes swirl in the breeze and drift into snow banks. The sun begins to set. Temperatures plummet below freezing. The family huddles together as the darkness descends, awaiting their inevitable fate.

It's a modern-day form of *seppuku*, the ancient ritual of suicide originally reserved for Samurai warriors who had failed a great task and therein lost face. *Seppuku* was an elaborate ritual performed in front of spectators. The Samurai would draw a sharp blade, called a *tantō*, from a finely designed gold sheath, and then plunge it into his abdomen, eviscerating himself. Through the courage of this act, "face" was posthumously regained.

When the news of the death-walk up Mt. Fuji spreads to Tokyo, many Japanese feel the salaryman has shown great courage and earned dignity for himself and his family. The tragedy provides the evidence I need to convince the producers that the story needs to be told. The report on Japan's economic bubble bursting—and the fallout from that—finally makes *Nightly News*.

As the story is picked up by global media, the bubble completely bursts. Throughout the country, suicide rates soar as Japan's economy collapses. Sadly, the ancient texts have been proven right again. Greed has taken a terrible toll. I can't help but think of the time in al-Amadiyah when I realized my small bottle of Tabasco, ball of twine, and pocketknife were all I needed, and catching a scrawny chicken would have made my day.

But I also wonder: Am I practicing my own form of *honne* and *tatemae* as I continue to hide the truth of my pain? The long travel distances while I'm on assignments in Asia have continued to test me and brought deeper pain to my back. Vicodin has lost some of its punch. I've doubled my dosages of Valium. I dissolve the pills under my tongue at various points throughout the day, and often take a few extra to feel relaxed. Still, I'm getting more and more uptight. I snap even more quickly at someone if they disagree with me or get in my way. I'm always embarrassed afterward, but then it happens again. By the end of any given day, all I can think about is a bottle of good wine, a hot bath, and another dose of drugs to help me sleep.

Poverty and Prosperity in the Philippines

Institutionalized crime, corruption, crushing poverty, pollution, and disease. They plague the third world, and the Philippines has them in spades. The capital city of Manila is huge, hectic, and hellish. It's 1992, and more than 11 million people live here, virtually on top of one another. Most of the country's wealth is held in the hands of the privileged few. There is hardly a middle class. Tens of thousands live in complete destitution. Many families are forced to find shelter beneath bridges or in abandoned buildings, or build shacks from whatever discarded materials they can scavenge. Typhoid, malaria, and dengue fever abound.

Smokey Mountain dumpsite is just outside Manila, in the hot and humid rolling hills and steep ravines of what was once tropical forest. The dump is enormous, with more than 2 million tons of waste decomposing at temperatures so high it frequently catches fire. Thick plumes of toxic smoke rise up from the smoldering filth, which is how the dumpsite earned its name. The stench is so heavy it burns my nose and eyes.

Smokey Mountain is home to vultures, wild pigs, dogs, snakes, gigantic rats—and human beings. Scores of squatters live on its edges, surviving on what they can scavenge from the rubbish. They rush in like clockwork every time the gigantic Dumpsters arrive, competing for position as hydraulic motors lift the rusty collection bins into the sky and fetid trash comes raining down. Children clutching tattered plastic bags scurry beneath the legs of the adults and snatch what they can, stuffing it quickly away then dashing off to safety.

"Look, there! Those little kids. Focus on them!" I say to my crew the moment I spot the two smallest children in the dump. We catch them on camera in the middle of the crowd of scavengers as a line of huge trucks rumble in and disgorge their contents. The tiny pair are masters at quickly identifying anything of value, especially food that has yet to fully rot. They dart in, deftly seize a prize before any grown-ups can beat them to the punch, stuff it in their bags, and quickly make a swift and artful getaway.

We hurry after them as they retreat deeper into the dumpsite, clutching their bags of loot. Plumes of rancid smoke from embers of rotting trash rise up around them from beneath the porous surface. Hungry vultures stare from the branches of barren trees, beady eyes protruding from the ruddy skin of their featherless heads. Their sharp hooked white beaks, designed for tearing flesh from the bone, glisten in the hazy sun. A wild pig snorts and roots in the filth, pausing briefly to glance at the children with disdain.

Following these kids through Smokey Mountain is like watching little angels navigate Dante's inferno. Our presence makes them nervous and they speed up. Almost losing us, they dart down a steeper ravine, where the trash is more firmly compacted from aged, thick roots and grass shoots holding it together in steamy layers. Now they disappear into a small, musty cave they've clawed in the rubbish.

Once we catch up, we begin coaxing them out with the help of our interpreter. Eventually they come to the entrance and stare at us with caution. It takes time to gain their trust and learn their names.

Adalin is five years old. Her brother, Junaz, is barely four. Their ragged clothing is as filthy and fetid as everything else in the dump. Yet, despite the coat of oily sludge covering their faces, their gigantic, dark eyes and plump cheeks show through, making their beauty and innocence inescapable.

"Is this your home?" our interpreter asks my question in the native Filipino tongue of Tagalog.

"Yes," Adalin says, quickly shoving something foul and gooey into her mouth. As we reassure them they've done nothing wrong and are not in trouble, they tell us more. We learn their mother died a few months ago, and they never knew a father.

"It's okay," Adalin says defensively. "We are happy here."

It's hard to believe these children have survived this long. I can't imagine them making it through the coming rainy season when the monsoon brings torrential rain and floods the ravines. As I think back on all the childhood comforts I enjoyed, it's nearly impossible to comprehend the tragedy of such destitution and hopelessness, especially when the victims are so young and innocent. Like Alejandro smoking his *basuco* in the dry Bolivian riverbed, I want to hold them in my arms, hug them closely, and take them home with me for a new life. Just as we finish filming, we hear the roar of more trucks arriving at the dump. Adalin and Junaz grab their plastic bags, slip past us, and scurry back into the inferno.

Smokey Mountain is a symbol of the immense poverty and suffering created under the regime of deceased dictator Ferdinand Marcos and is also a continuing source of national shame. When Marcos fled Malacañang Palace in 1986, his wife, Imelda, left behind 15 mink coats, 508 gowns, 1,000 handbags, and 3,000 pairs of shoes. She and her husband were reported to be worth 35 billion dollars, most of it from pocketing international aid. They enjoyed cozy relations with the CIA and American multinational companies that profited greatly from the Philippines' desperate work force and readily exploitable resources. Now, six years after their downfall, Imelda is returning to run for president in what can only be characterized as an incredible act of hubris. I'm here to do background reports and cover her controversial return.

We're lodged in the historic Manila Hotel, a 500-room, five-star palace in the heart of the city. Priceless antiques are elegantly on display in its spacious ballrooms. Ceilings and walls are paneled with polished cherry-brown hardwood. Expansive foyers are lit with finely cut crystal chandeliers. Plush carpets patterned in burgundy and green designs accentuate shiny marble floors. In times past, this magnificent structure housed Ernest Hemingway, James Michener, and John Kennedy. The Imperial Japanese Army occupied it for a time during World War II. General Douglas MacArthur lived here from 1935 to 1941 as he waged his campaign against the Japanese.

To my delight, my suite is the very one MacArthur called home those seven years. Gazing off my wide veranda toward Manila Bay, I'm awestruck at the privilege of being here. Me, sleeping in General MacArthur's room, paid extremely well for work I would still do for free. But thinking back on where I was this morning, I'm reminded that precious few in Manila ever enjoy such luxury. As I use my pocketknife to scrape the filth of Smokey Mountain from the soles of my boots, I think of Adalin and Junaz peering out from their hole in the dump. The stark contrast to the opulence of my surroundings sends a surge of embarrassment through my bones.

NBC News keeps a permanent room here in the Manila Hotel, filled with editing equipment. Walking down the hall to view videotape after a day at the dump, I feel my back burning more intensely than usual. My legs start to feel like noodles again. I'm wobbling so much that I have to keep a hand on the wall to steady myself. It's been seven years of chronic pain. This pain, however, is new. It's not another ice pick attack. No, this time it's more subtle—yet much more overpowering. I can feel my whole body quivering with agony.

I'm sitting with my editor now, looking for scenes to add historical context to the story of Adalin and Junaz. We log video of workers laboring under the sweltering skies at plantations, homeless families living under bridges, children who look like they haven't eaten in weeks. We flash through file video of the downfall of Marcos:

huge crowds protesting at Malacañang. Imelda's high heels lined up beneath the mink coats in her massive closet. Police attacking demonstrators. I hear myself snapping at the editor to speed up, then I snap at him to slow down.

The pain in my body suddenly soars to a deeper level. The back of my neck is on fire. My arms throb and sting. Lightning bolts flash down my legs. The thick muscles along my spinal column spasm and knot. I grit my teeth and squirm on my chair, desperately seeking a comfortable posture. The images on the viewing screen start to blur. Then, as the edges of my peripheral vision turn dark, I feel something pop at the base of my spine. It's so excruciating it knocks me off my chair and onto the floor. I roll over to one side and scream like a wounded soldier. In this moment of agony, I finally realize the inescapable truth: The game is over. I plead to my producer, "Get me a doctor!"

He and the editor struggle to help me back to my room. I have to crawl most of the way down the corridor. I can barely climb onto the bed. I beg someone to bring my travel kit from the bathroom, fumble to open the Vicodin and Valium, pour several pills into my mouth, chew them into a pulp, and gulp them down with a glass of water from the nightstand. Then I curl up in a fetal knot. As I wait for the drugs to kick in, I can't understand it. After all the rigorous challenges in mountains and deserts, war zones, and riots, my back gives out while I'm sitting on a padded chair in a luxury hotel.

I wait for the doctor to come. Ten minutes goes by. Twenty. I keep waiting, moaning out loud while forcing myself not to scream. Thirty. Forty. It's an hour before a local physician arrives and gives me a shot of morphine, choosing the same shoulder I almost chose long ago in al-Amadiyah when I nearly shot myself up. The plan is to stabilize me, get back to Hong Kong, and take it from there. I'm woozy and disoriented as two hotel employees help me out to the front of the hotel and into a waiting limo, laying me across the backseat. The driver speeds to the airport, where a wheelchair is waiting. Thanks to our local "fixers," who are masters at working the system, I'm rolled to the front of the line at customs and an official quickly stamps my passport with barely a glance. Before I know it, I'm lifted onto a commercial jetliner for the long trip back to Hong Kong. A minute later and I would have missed the flight. I can't remember the rest of the trip home.

When I wake up in my bed the following morning, I feel like a tank rolled over me. My head is spinning, and the pain is overwhelming me again. I reach for my pants on the floor, fumble with the pockets, and find the vial of morphine tablets the Manila doctor gave me. I swallow one, then curl up on my side, gazing out my bedroom windows at the Hong Kong skyline as the drug kicks in. I can hear my breath sounding slower and louder than usual as a woozy sensation of pleasure floods my whole body. The city begins to blur, and I slip into a coma-like haze.

CHAPTER 12

Fusion

S AN DIEGO has long been a mecca for sports medicine and
some of the best back surgeons practice there. It's also where
my two sisters and mother live, and they have found a top neu-
rosurgeon and arranged for me to have an emergency evaluation and
immediate surgery. It's going to be a long, tough flight out of Hong
Kong, and the pain is so deep that, even after five days of bed rest,
I don't see how I'm going to make it. I shake the morphine vial.
Plenty of pills. I'll have to medicate myself all the way.

My current girlfriend, an American named Pamela, has been living
with me here in Hong Kong for more than six months. I've been on
the road so much that we've hardly seen one another. I down three
morphine pills as she helps me get ready for the trip. Then I cinch
my elastic brace as tight as I can get it around my lower back and
limp out the front door, with an arm over Pamela's shoulder for support, as our driver pulls up in the bureau's old Mercedes to take me
to Hong Kong International Airport.

Halfway there, I'm so doped up I throw up out the back window
the entire way. I'm still in a stupor as they put me in another wheelchair and push me to the boarding gate, where I say good-bye to
Pamela. A flight attendant helps me into a first-class seat for a sev-
enteen-hour flight to San Diego. Sitting next to me is a glamorous
American fashion model who just finished a photo shoot in Asia. As
we gain altitude, she leans over and says, "Excuse me, I recognize

you from the news. I'm sorry to mention it, but you don't look so well. Are you okay?"

I'd love to be a fascinating flight companion and engage her in spellbinding conversation, but I can't even sit up straight. I begin to slur a polite response, and then suddenly become sick again, all over both of us. Flight attendants rush to the rescue. I lapse into another haze.

✻

An acrid stench, like there's something dead in the room, forces me awake in the early light of dawn. It takes a few minutes to realize it's me, smelling almost as foul as I did after months in the Gulf without a shower or change of clothing. My mouth tastes like Smokey Mountain dump. My temples are pounding, and I feel like my head might explode. *Where am I?*

As I squint at the room and try to focus, it looks like a quaint bed-and-breakfast, with dark oak antique dressers and nightstands, a flowered quilt, fluffy throw pillows, and powder blue walls. Every muscle in my body aches. My lower back is screaming. My left leg alternates between complete numbness and throbbing pain. *Where am I?*

Slowly, it all begins to come back to me: collapsing in Manila; throwing up all over someone during the flight from Hong Kong; my sister Valerie picking me up at the international airport in San Diego. I'm in the guest room of her historic home in Coronado, a small island in San Diego Bay connected to the mainland by a gently curving blue bridge. I have two siblings, Valerie and Pam. Both live here in Coronado. My mother, Doris, is here as well. It has long felt like home base to me even though I only lived here briefly between the jobs in Dallas and Boston.

I can barely get out of bed. Groggy. Dizzy. My back on fire. Nauseated. Everything blurry. Hobbling to the bathroom for a drink of water, I have to steady myself by holding the wall, then the doorframe, now the sink. Dry heaves. My head is pounding. I grab a toothbrush from a porcelain rack on the wall, squish a load of toothpaste into my mouth, and brush like crazy, but I can't get the terrible taste to go away. Then I run a hot bath. My back is so shot it's a struggle to get into the wide tub. Drying off and dressing myself afterward is a Herculean task. If I weren't still so stoned on morphine it would be impossible, but the drug also makes me feel woozy, off-kilter. That reminds me: Take another pill. The nightstand. My wallet. The pill jar. One or two? Two.

We have an appointment to see a surgeon at the Neurosurgical Medical Clinic in San Diego, so after breakfast, which I can barely eat, Valerie helps me into her car. As we cross the Coronado Bridge, a sense of emptiness drags me down, like gravity might pull me right through the floorboard. My thoughts usually spin a mile a minute, but now my mind is an empty void and there's a dull ringing in my ears. I'm trying to be jovial but can't stay with the conversation. I catch myself staring into space like a zombie.

At the doctor's office I can barely pull myself onto the exam table for an X-ray. Afterward, my sister and I wait in a lobby while a technician reads the results. I hurt so much that I have to fold my head down toward my lap and grit my teeth while we wait for the doctor. "You're going to be okay," Valerie says in her usual upbeat and loving way as she reaches for my hand and gives it a gentle squeeze. I just grunt, trying not to be sick again. Finally, after what feels like an eternity, we're ushered into the surgeon's office.

Dr. Sam Assam is silver-haired and dignified, like an actor playing a seasoned physician on one of NBC's prime-time drama series. I hear my words slurring as I slowly tell him the whole story; the slip from the ledge, the years of pain, the medications, the snap in my back as I sat in the Manila Hotel. I spare him details of the scene I caused on the airplane.

"I don't know how you managed it," Dr. Assam says with dispassionate authority while comparing my current X-ray with the original from 1986, which my sister somehow got the doctor's office in Boston to send out on time. "You've spent seven years with a mildly broken back, and now it's a major break."

Like the first doctor those many years ago, he uses a pen as a pointer to trace the dark lines, comparing the X-rays this time, showing me the difference. In the first X-ray, the line is thin and runs part way through the pedicle bone on the left side of my fifth lumbar vertebra, which sits right above my sacrum. In the new X-ray, the line is thicker and runs all the way through the pedicle bone.

"We might think of it like a small crack in a picture frame that suddenly splits across the glass," Dr. Assam continues. "It's very serious. If it opens further and impinges on your spinal cord, you could be paralyzed."

Dr. Assam insists, in his distant and professional demeanor, that surgery is the only option. The procedure is called a "fusion-laminectomy," and it's major surgery. There will be two incisions. The first one will be on my left side, near the iliac crest of my pelvic girdle. The doctor explains that this area of the pelvis holds a large amount of red bone marrow and is ideal for bone graphs. He will slice pieces of bone from the iliac crest, then make a second incision along my lower spine. The broken pedicle will be removed along with the discs between my two lowest lumbar vertebrae, L4 and L5. Next, the sides of these two vertebrae will be scraped down to expose their marrow. The chips of bone sliced from the iliac crest will then be "laminated" against the vertebrae and exposed marrow. Then they stitch me back up.

"In time," Dr. Assam says confidently, "the bone chips and shaved vertebrae will fuse into a bone mass that will stabilize your back."

I can barely follow him, but it sounds more like a construction project than a surgery, like welding iron rods together to bolster the frame of a building. I feel profoundly resistant to anyone cutting into my back, but what choice do I have? Dr. Assam is making it clear there is none. I close my eyes and a collage of images that have become etched in my subconscious float through the darkness.

Kuwaiti torture victims heaped on top of one another in the morgue.
A piece of a dead Iraqi soldier on my pant leg, my boots covered with thick, warm blood.
Afghans missing arms and legs, third-degree burns covering what's left of their bodies.

*Starving African infants with distended bellies and faces covered
  with black flies.*
*Kurdish mothers in refugee camps with glazed eyes clutching dead
  babies in their arms.*
*Palsied Bolivian kids slowly dying as they smoke basuco in holes
  scratched in a dry riverbed.*
*Orphaned Filipino children living in a rancid garbage dump
  alongside snakes, vultures, and wild pigs.*

My chronic pain and this surgery are nothing by comparison. I have always feared missing work more than I ever feared war zones or injuries, but there's really no choice. To pump myself up, I have a little inner conversation: *This is great,* I tell myself, *I only have to miss three or four weeks and it will mean an end to all these years of pain!*

"The surgery takes at least two hours," Dr. Assam says, breaking my little pep talk. "Then there's a recovery process during which you'll be in a large body brace. You'll need to rest and relax, then, eventually, do some physical therapy. Depending on how quickly the fusion takes, you could be back to work in less than six months."

Six months! I can't miss that much work. So I negotiate, pressing for the earliest possible date I can return to the field if everything goes perfectly. I'm still slurring my words and it's hard to stay focused, but I push Dr. Assam hard even though I can tell he's not used to this. When I have him down to a "best of all worlds" scenario of less than two months, I say, "Okay, let's get it over with."

I'm flat on my back, watching Styrofoam ceiling panels whiz by as I'm wheeled down the hospital corridor into surgery on a gurney. The chemical smell in the surgical theater reminds me of the odor people in war zones exude when they're gripped with fear. The atmosphere of the room feels tense. Monitors are buzzing and beeping. Black cords and plastic tubes are strung like tinsel everywhere. Surgical instruments click as attendants position them in perfect alignment on steel trays. Rubber gloves snap; bright lights glare. People in medical gowns with greenish masks and white gauze head-covers roll me onto my side to expose my lower back.

The anesthesiologist slips a needle into a thick vein on the back of my hand and places an oxygen mask over my face. A few deep breaths now. The room sways. Voices dim. I close my eyes and drift off into the mountains of some far-off place where a revolution is underway, getting ready to go live on *NBC Nightly News*.

"I've never seen anything like it," Dr. Assam says, almost breaking character and expressing emotion, after I awaken from the anesthesia. "I thought I would need to cut the broken pedicle out, but it was so loose I lifted it out with a pair of surgical tongs. It was even more dangerous than I thought, being so detached like that."

I have to spend a night in the hospital in case of unexpected bleeding or infection. The next morning, as a nurse's aide pushes me in a wheelchair, my sister and I stop at the lobby pharmacy to pick up more prescription drugs, including another two weeks' worth of morphine. As I lift myself from the wheelchair into my sister's car, all I can think about is getting out of this place and on the road to recovery. But by the time we get to my sister's home, all I can think about is lying in bed and never moving again. I feel like I could sleep forever.

After a few weeks of bed rest, I'm fitted with a massive body brace. It's a large Kevlar contraption called a Clamshell, with two thick, white plastic halves that fold around my torso like a clam, held tight by thick Velcro straps. It's hard as a rock on the exterior with soft foam lining inside. A heavy electrical device called a Stim is buckled around the lower portion of the brace. It ticks like a windup clock, sending an electric current into my spine, which Dr. Assam tells me is designed to promote fusion. I'm weaned off morphine, but stronger doses of Vicodin are added to my regimen of Motrin and Valium.

It's my new form of meeting "deadlines"—popping all these pills at precise times throughout the day.

My girlfriend, Pamela, flies in from Hong Kong and we settle into my sister Valerie's guest room in Coronado. Pamela and I have been seeing one another on and off for more than a decade. Mostly off because of my career priorities and disinterest in committed relationships. She's upbeat, adventurous, vibrant, and willing to put up with me. I now feel dependent on her and it makes me uncomfortable. Am I using her? Being selfish? I'm not sure and, anyway, I can't really face it. The bottom line is that I need her support, physically and emotionally, more than ever.

One month after surgery, with my new body brace strapped on tightly, I obediently follow the doctor's orders and begin taking short walks through the quiet suburban neighborhoods of Coronado to strengthen my back and legs. Pamela steadies me as we go. I wear an oversized T-shirt to cover my Clamshell and Stim. It makes me look like a stiff, top-heavy robot from a B movie. I feel okay during these brief outings, but standing up without moving for more than a minute is excruciating and sitting for prolonged periods is out of the question. I'm forced to spend hours on the bed, my back propped up by fluffy pillows.

Lying in bed, I devour the news voraciously, but every time a foreign correspondent comes on the air, it's too much for me to handle. It should be me out there. Doing the only thing I know how to do. Pushing forward. Getting the story. Watching someone else in the field makes me feel helpless, worthless, and weak. I grab the remote, mute the TV, and default to the zombie stare.

Every day I manage to walk a little farther, but I still feel tender, sore, and unstable in my spine. I expect the pain to be slowly diminishing, but I'm so heavily drugged it's hard to tell if this is happening. Nevertheless, I stay meticulous with the schedule: wearing the Clamshell and Stim all day long, removing the brace at bedtime, recharging the Stim overnight, strapping the brace back on every morning, hooking up the Stim again, taking all the meds religiously, never missing a walk, always pouring a glass of wine before bed. Maybe two glasses now and then. Sometimes three.

Four weeks go by and nothing really changes. Before I know it, six weeks have passed. Still, no change. I'm staying devoted to the routine, praying that it all works. But my back remains terribly sore. Every time the drugs start to wear off and I feel the pain beginning to surge, I grab for the next dose as quickly as I can. It's not the pain itself that troubles me. After so many years, I'm used to hurting all the time. It's something deep down inside me that fears this might not work. There's no way I can face such a possibility, and I have to shut that voice down any way I can. As I swallow the pills I silently say:

It's going to be okay.
I'm going to make it.
My back is going to heal.
I'm going back to work soon.

It's been eight weeks now and still, not much change. My back remains unstable, and I can't imagine walking without the Clamshell strapped on as tightly as possible. An occasional jolt of burning sciatica, which is caused by the compression of a spinal nerve, shoots down the back of my left leg. Eight weeks. This is when I should have been going back to work. *Maybe it's supposed to be this way. My back is healing, but the tenderness and instability will persist a while longer.* When I see Dr. Assam, he confirms this possibility.

"We can't really tell what's happening without a new scan," he says in his usual distant tone.

"Then can I go back to work?" I must sound like a broken record.

"We'll see," he says in the same monotone. "Let's get a new scan and go from there."

I can feel my anger and impatience starting to rise. I'm tired of all this. Could he have botched this operation? I almost confront him, but catch myself, stand up slowly, and trundle out of his office, unable to stop myself from slamming the door behind me as I go.

❊

The machine is a large, cream-colored, space-age device called a bone scanner. It's much more sophisticated than an X-ray, capable of detecting the slightest sign of fusion in my back. I lie on a steel table as a substance called a radioactive tracer is injected into a vein on my forearm. The tracer, which feels like metallic ice water, flows through my bloodstream and eventually finds its way into my bones. The table electronically slides forward until I'm beneath the scanner. A special camera called a gamma detects the tracer, records images, and sends them to a monitor. Areas of rapid or new bone growth will show up as bright, hot spots. Dark or cold spots indicate areas with little or no blood flow. Any cold spots at the base of my spine, therefore, are indications that the fusion isn't taking.

When I meet with Dr. Assam afterward, I can see it on his face before he speaks a word.

"It's going to take more time," he says, always deadpan, "maybe four to six more weeks."

It feels like a punch in the stomach and shakes my confidence. This isn't part of the plan. If I have to wait any longer, I'll explode.

"Then why not go back home?" I can hear myself sounding frustrated and impatient. "I can start by working in the news bureau without any travel. I'll wear the brace. Lean back in my chair or lie on the bureau couch. I'll be careful."

The truth is, I'm furious with the doctor, blaming him for my lack of progress. But I have to be nice. Without his okay, NBC won't approve my return. I persist, as calmly as I can, making my case that, aside from a long flight home to Hong Kong, it doesn't matter where I am while the recovery process continues. "Alright," Dr. Assam finally consents after giving it a great deal of thought. "Keep walking, use the Stim, don't overdo it. Work no more than two or three hours a day at first, and only a few days a week. Get plenty of rest. Report in to me regularly."

I'm so thrilled about going back to Hong Kong that I can feel adrenalin rushing through me, but I've lost confidence in the doctor and have to be careful not to slam the door behind me again when I leave his office. The moment we return to Coronado, I book the next available flight to Hong Kong, and before the week is out, Pamela and I are in the air. I recline my first-class seat back as far as it will go, drink a glass of wine, and then dope myself up, deliberately knocking myself out for hours so I can endure the trip. When I finally come to, I look out the window and see the Hong Kong skyline glowing in the evening sky. I'm home. Nothing else matters. I'm home.

As we drive to the end of Barker Road on Victoria Peak, my flat comes into view, glistening white against the lush, verdant background of the jungle foliage. I smile at the profound pleasure of being back in Asia and am already wondering what's happening in China, Japan, Thailand, Vietnam, and everywhere else in my region. I can't wait to set foot in the bureau again, pitch a story to *Nightly News*, and have lunch at the Foreign Correspondents' Club, where I can catch up with old friends.

Then I feel a small knot in my stomach as a voice flashes in my head:

Can I really do this?
How long will this be my home?
Will I ever be pain free?

I immediately shut the voice down and go into a state of complete denial, telling myself it's impossible that the fusion will fail. *It's absolutely impossible.*

CHAPTER 13

Pyongyang

I LOOKED ODD enough hobbling down the sidewalks of Coronado in my body brace, but in Hong Kong I cause public scenes. I tower over most Asian people, and with my stilted gait I look like a giant robot from another planet. When someone bumps into me on the heavily crowded streets, which happens constantly because I lack the ability to maneuver, they're shocked to hit my hard brace. They cry out with surprise and stare wide-eyed, thinking I might not be human.

It's the fall of 1992 and Bill Clinton has defeated incumbent George H. Bush for president of the United States. Domestic news has the upper hand at NBC and it's all but impossible to sell a foreign story, so I'm off the hook at a perfect time. I spend most of my limited work hours at the bureau leaning back in my chair to keep the pressure off my back. I balance the keyboard on my lap and diligently track all the news in Asia on my computer, staying informed, keeping files on potential stories. Every hour, like clockwork, I lie down on the visitor's couch by the bureau entrance and rest, then take another robot walk and scare the locals again. It's frustrating, like being under the control of some invisible force that doesn't have my best interests in mind.

My growing anger, fear, and anxiety are worse than the physical pain. I hate the body brace, but I'm scared to death to take more than a few steps without it. I want to slam the Stim against a wall, but I keep hoping it's going to work. I'm sick of all the pills, and yet I'm so dependent and frightened of what might happen without them that I never, ever miss a dose. I know I'm drinking too much, but I need it to release the tension. When I lunch at the Foreign Correspondents' Club now, or anywhere else for that matter, I always have a glass of wine, or two. It's a new habit, drinking this early in the day. I'll do anything to numb my body and my mind.

As I struggle to cope, a compelling story begins to unfold in one of the strangest, most forbidding countries in the world: North Korea. Longtime communist dictator Kim Il Sung runs a totalitarian dictatorship and rules his people with a brutal hand. Thought-police are everywhere. Critics of the regime are routinely tortured and killed. The economy is in shambles. People in the countryside are dying of starvation. There are rumors of cannibalism in remote rural villages.

Kim's only allies are Russia and China, and he even keeps them at bay, holding to a policy of *juche*, which is Korean for self-reliance. North Korea is highly militarized and a constant threat to stability in the region. Capitalism is vilified as the world's greatest evil. But *juche* has proven to be a failure, and the regime is so strapped for cash that it has invited a group of high-ranking Japanese entrepreneurs for a historic tour. Kim is promising them workers, factories, and resources for next to nothing, hoping to persuade them to fund major industrial projects and get desperately needed capital in return.

The Japanese have agreed to Kim's offer, mostly because their economy is still on the rocks and an easy profit is appealing. Luckily, the businessmen insist that journalists be allowed to accompany them, which will boost their images back home. The story is a must-cover and, after some pleading and cajoling, I win Dr. Assam's permission to make the trip, something NBC is still requiring. There's one final catch: Journalists are rarely allowed into North Korea, and the Kim regime loathes Americans most of all. To ensure I get in, we submit our travel papers through my office in Tokyo under the names of my Japanese film crew. My name is at the bottom of the list like an afterthought. This simple ruse works, and I'm soon among the first American journalists ever to fly into the capital city of Pyongyang.

I've seen a great deal of misery in the world, but never a place as strange as this. Kim has constructed a massive cult of personality, brainwashing his people into believing that he alone defeated the Allied Forces in World War II, and that he's been worshipped daily throughout the world ever since. Americans and Europeans, Kim teaches his people, are subhuman and demonic. As the economy of North Korea nosedives, Kim funds more towering statues and color-ful murals glorifying himself, while continuing to build his armed forces and periodically threatening to invade South Korea.

Pyongyang is an extremely modern city with wide avenues, imposing monuments, and monolithic buildings. There's a perfect replica of the Arc de Triomphe, intentionally built slightly taller than the original in Paris. The arch was dedicated on Kim's seventieth birthday, with each of its 25,500 blocks of fine white granite repre-senting a day of his life up to that point. It's the epitome of arrogance and ego in the face of the plight of his people.

Unlike the crowded streets typical of almost every other modern city in Asia, in Pyongyang people are nowhere to be seen. Many of the towering high-rises are perfect on the exterior, but unfinished and derelict inside. There are few cars on the roads, except for the occasional spanking new, black Mercedes Benz with govern-ment officials inside, often weaving the wrong way down a wide highway.

I've been in totalitarian countries before, but the paranoia here is unprecedented. The North Koreans want to completely control our agenda. Our hotel room is bugged and we are tailed everywhere. Our filming is heavily restricted. The few people we find on the streets are far too frightened to speak with us. We begin playing games to lose our followers and finally manage to shoot video of the empty buildings and desolate streets, grab a few interviews about the dismal

economy and lack of freedoms on hidden camera, and do our best to
document this strange story.

On the final day, we take a three-hour train ride with the Japanese
entrepreneurs to a port farther north where Kim hopes they will
set up shop. It's a brutal trip for me, sitting on a hard metal seat
while the dilapidated train bumps and sways like a cheap carnival
ride. All we do at the port is watch the North Koreans escort the
Japanese around a few vacant warehouses. We aren't allowed to go
anywhere else, and it's a huge waste of time. When I get back to our
hotel in Pyongyang at midnight, I'm on fire again. The flight back to
Japan is even worse.

In our Tokyo bureau, I grit my teeth through days of writing and editing. I want to lash out at the whole world and almost scream out loud:

I can't make it!
I have to stop!
It's unbearable!

But my fear, my hubris, and a growing inner rage prevent me.
I have to make it, shift my thoughts, tell myself it's okay:

God damn this injury.
I am not losing this battle.
Just get through this until the fusion takes.
The pain will go away and you'll be home free.

Before checking out of my Tokyo hotel, I swallow a handful of medications without counting the pills, then down a few glasses of wine
on the plane back to Hong Kong. I used to keep track of my drinking, but these days I don't care. It would be a great mistake for anyone to suggest this behavior might be self-destructive in the long
run. I'm not open to such advice and would offer very unkind words
in return. It wouldn't be pretty.

After filing my reports from the Hong Kong bureau, it's time to return to San Diego for a final checkup. I still have persistent pain, but the fusion is definitely supposed to have taken place by now. As I land at Lindberg Field, I can feel the little knot of uncertainty in my belly again, but do my best to ignore it and tell myself it's a lie:

I'm just fine.
I'm going to whip this thing.
Great news is right around the corner.

※

The radioactive tracer feels colder and tastes steely this time as it's injected into the same vein in my forearm. The electronic table hums as it slowly slides me beneath the bone scanner. The camera buzzes and clicks, sending new gamma images to the monitor. I close my eyes and visualize pictures filled with glowing hot spots at the base of my spine. A perfect fusion, solid as a rock. But I can see it in Dr. Assam's eyes again when we sit down afterward.

"I don't understand this," he says grimly. "You are a perfect candidate for fusion. You're young, strong, and otherwise healthy. You don't smoke or have any other habits that would inhibit bone growth. You follow the orders, wear the brace, use the Stim. But there's no evidence of fusion. None."

"So how long will it take?" At the conscious level, I refuse to entertain any possibility of failure. At a deeper level, I know I've lost the battle.

"You have another three months at most." Dr. Assam is not very convincing. "After that, it's just not possible."

I have to blame someone, so in my mind I blame the doctor. *He must have botched this. He's ruining my life.* I want to clobber him. Instead, I say good-bye, slamming the door behind me as loudly as possible. As usual, I book the first flight I can find, knowing I'll need to dope myself up again for a return to Hong Kong.

The pool at my apartment building on Victoria Peak sits on the edge of the steep jungle slope. I can lie down on a shallow ledge in the warm water and gaze east over the Hong Kong skyline toward the endless expanse of China. It's a vibrant, exciting world filled with adventure, mystery, and intrigue that I have barely tasted. I feel like a beached whale.

Outwardly, I'm still avoiding the truth, but the knot in my gut has grown to the size of a grapefruit. It's a big, roiling ball of stress eating away at me. I'm too physically and emotionally spent to take "robot walks" any longer. When I get to the bureau on a rare occasion, we talk about all the stories we'll do once I'm better. Everyone knows it's just talk. My producer, the camera people, the editors, all the staff, they know. Out of kindness, no one says a word as they continue to pretend that everything is fine as three months slip by and nothing changes.

It's mid-1993 as I board a plane back to San Diego for a final evaluation. I struggle to get into my seat. I can feel that my back is still broken, and I'm losing all hope. Yet I have no idea that this is my final departure from Hong Kong or that I will never again return to my beautiful home on Victoria Peak.

The results of the new bone scan are the same. When I'm told this, the ball of stress in my gut explodes. It feels like hot acid flooding all the way to the tips of my fingers and toes. I walk out of Dr. Assam's office vowing to never see him again. In an act of final desperation, I make an appointment with Dr. Steve Garfin, chairman of the Department of Orthopedic Surgery at the U.C. San Diego Medical Center. Dr. Garfin is a leading authority on spinal surgeries. I'm hoping he'll find some tiny glimmer of hope to which I can cling, something in the gamma pictures that everyone else missed. After a thorough review, however, Dr. Garfin also confirms that I have a failed fusion.

My only hope, he says, is a second surgery, this time with two alternatives, each far more invasive than the first surgery. In one option, the fusion would be redone with titanium rods screwed into my vertebrae to hold everything in place. In option two, they go in through the front, pulling all my abdominal organs out of the way and, working on the transverse side of the spine, insert cadaver bones between the lowest vertebrae.

Both procedures sound appalling, and the possibilities of complications are far greater than the surgery that has already failed. Still, I want to know the odds and assess my chances. I swallow hard and play reporter with Dr. Garfin. He's candid: The odds are 50-50 for either procedure. As I press for details, the facts drop my jaw. Half the patients who have "successful" fusion operations end up with as much or more pain. Half whose surgeries "fail" experience significant reduction or a complete end to their pain.

To me, it's clearly a roll of the dice. There's no solid proof that any of these procedures work. Some recover and thrive. Others end up worse. Some are paralyzed. A few even die from infections and complications. The kicker is none of these results seem predicated upon whether the operation is technically deemed to be a success. Why didn't Dr. Assam ever tell me this? I'm overwhelmed with rage. There won't be a second surgery. I'm done with it.

I'm required to fly to NBC headquarters in Manhattan. Physicians for our parent company, General Electric, review the X-rays, bone scans, and doctors' notes. GE's doctors reach the same conclusion: failed fusion. They conclude that my condition is so severe that a trip back to the West Coast is dangerous enough. Returning to Hong Kong is out of the question. I start to protest, but the head doctor holds up his hand to silence me. "There's no room for any discussion here. You are not returning to Hong Kong and that is final."

In an act of surprising generosity, NBC agrees to continue my salary for a full year, cover all my living expenses, plus pay for extensive physical therapy. If I recover, they confirm in writing, my job will be waiting for me. I stare at the paper, realizing it's all I have now, a document promising that my former life will await me for up to one year. As I slip it into my briefcase, I can feel a lump in my throat and have to fight back tears.

From the very beginning, when I landed my first reporter's job at a small station in Eureka twenty years ago in 1973, I've been fully convinced that I could face any challenge, overcome any obstacle. My confidence was always solid as a rock. Now, two decades later, it feels like a facade, like one of those monolithic buildings in Pyong-yang, North Korea, with a polished exterior concealing nothing but darkness, desolation, and emptiness within.

CHAPTER 14

Puncture

L E MÉRIDIEN HOTEL spreads out along the bay in Coronado with generous views of the San Diego skyline. It's the sort of luxurious setting people often envision for their dream vacation. The restaurant's French cuisine is superb. A Brazilian jazz band plays during dinner on the outdoor terrace overlooking a wide pool facing the bridge as it spans the bay to San Diego. The spa has Jacuzzis and saunas, massage therapists, and warm lap pools. NBC is being more than generous. I have a villa on the south end of the hotel complex, sitting quietly on a grassy slope, framed by coral trees and palms. I lie on my deck recliner watching the sunset reflect off the glass high-rises of the city. A gentle breeze caresses my face. Sailboats course the calm blue waters of the bay. But this is not a dream vacation and I find no joy in being here.

Pamela remains in Hong Kong, overseeing the process of packing up our belongings and coordinating with the news bureau to put them in storage. I'm on a desperate mission to explore every therapeutic modality available. I have one year to heal my back and reclaim my career, and for the first time in my life, I fear I'm losing control over my destiny. I look at the promise on the contract from NBC almost every day. I constantly give myself the sort of pep talks I've always given others to help them face challenges in their lives.

You must stay focused and manage the pain.
You have to get strong and healthy.
You will get back to work before this year runs out.
You can do this.

❋

A renowned orthopedic surgeon named Dr. Vert Mooney, whose revolutionary therapeutic techniques have earned him national recognition, has designed my first physical rehabilitation program. In his early sixties, Dr. Mooney favors wearing wild, artistic ties with conservative sport coats. His snowy white hair is neatly parted on one side and his huge spectacles make his eyes gleam like an elf. His constant smile is infectious, revealing a gentle and compassionate man whose top priority is to avoid surgery whenever possible. At our very first meeting, Dr. Mooney lets me know he would not have recommended my first operation and he thinks a second surgery would be far too risky. When he shares this, I feel like steam is coming out of my ears and I want to strangle Dr. Assam.

"I doubt you would get any better with more surgery," Mooney says frankly, "and you might end up much worse."

Dr. Mooney believes I might have achieved a tolerable level of stabilization through his program, if only I had found him shortly after the initial accident. He explains that with a failed surgery, it's a much steeper mountain to climb.

"Most people just won't do the work," he says. "They want a quick fix. One in which time and effort isn't required. I don't believe in that any longer. That's why I avoid surgery."

The clinic rehab facility looks like a cross between medical offices and a high-tech athletic training center. After an evaluation, Dr. Mooney escorts me into a large room filled with thickly padded exercise machines fitted with computers to track a patient's range of motion and muscular resistance capacity. He has designed these exercise machines to stabilize the entire spine while seeking to enhance flexion and slowly build muscle strength in precise areas. I have to admit it scares me. I no longer have the discipline I used to take for granted. I don't know if I can climb this mountain.

I'm assigned a personal therapist who completes a detailed evaluation then straps me firmly into several machines, guiding me into performing gentle movements with minimal resistance from the weights of the machines. It's painful and I can barely stay with it. I keep whispering "You can do this" to myself as I strain against the light weights, but I fear I might be fooling myself. My muscles are soft and atrophied from so much time in the body brace. I'm tired and weak.

Still, I go three times a week and give it all the energy I can muster, hoping to be a miracle case of delayed fusion. That patient who astonishes all the experts. Or, I tell myself, I'll get my feet back under me well enough to live with the pain and return to NBC. But after two months there's no progress. Pain continues to grip my lower back and shoot down my left leg. Dr. Mooney lets me know it might be best to try some gentler alternatives, softly suggesting that I can try the program again if I improve. In the meantime, he has a prosthetic specialist modify my brace by adding a metal bar on the left side that juts down my leg to just above the knee, where it straps onto my lower thigh for more support.

Dr. Chen is from Taiwan and comes from a long lineage of renowned masters of Chinese medicine and acupuncture. He has me lying down on a padded table for up to two hours at a time, poking needles in my body from head to toe like I'm a pincushion. After several treatments, he hooks an electrical stimulation device to some of the needles. This sends currents through key energy points, like the Stim device I wear, but with much more power. I can feel pulsations and vibrations in the exact areas where the pain is most intense, and my hopes begin to soar.

Dr. Chen also performs an ancient technique for creating suction and increasing blood flow called "fire cupping." He picks up a cotton ball with long metal tongs, soaks it in rubbing alcohol, and then lights it like a torch. He holds the flaming cotton inside a thick glass cup the size and shape of a tennis ball cut in half. The heated cup is placed on my lower back, just above the left iliac crest of my hips directly between the two scars from my surgery. It's incredibly hot, but Dr. Chen artfully knows how to keep it just below the burning point. The heat creates a suction that draws my skin up into the cup, turning it bright red as blood floods into the area.

After learning about the bone scan procedure, and how "hot spots" indicate blood flow and potential bone fusion, the cupping technique makes sense to me. Make the stagnant blood flow in my sore back. Get energy moving and bring life back to the area. I feel optimistic after each treatment, and my hopes soar even higher. But the minor level of relief always fades away within a few hours, leaving me back where I began. After more than a month of needles and cups, plus a regimen of foul-tasting Chinese herbs, Dr. Chen sits down with me for a talk. His face holds an expression I've seen too many times before. I know this story too well.

"There is nothing more we can do," he says with a sense of professional frustration. "I am afraid acupuncture is not going to heal you."

I should be getting used to news like this, but it's harder to take each time. A wave of emptiness rolls over me. My stomach feels nauseous. My skin tingles with fear. I just can't face it. All I can do is pretend it's not there. I stuff the emptiness so deeply down into my subconscious that nobody could ever find it. Not even me.

Every night in my villa I order fine French food from Le Méridien room service. As I lie down on a lounge chair, my dinner balanced on my lap, I stare out at the brightly lit skyline of San Diego, watching the colors dance across the bay. I eat far more than I need and usually drink almost a full bottle of Burgundy or Bordeaux. Lately, I've had to loosen the Velcro straps on the Clamshell body brace and my pants are getting too tight around the waist. Glancing in the mirror before bed, I realize that, for the first time in my life, I'm getting heavy. In the past, vanity would have prompted me into taking immediate action. Now, I don't care. Fine food and vintage wines are among the few comforts I have left. Honestly, they're more than comforts; they're my escapes.

It's been almost six months. I'm desperate. The only treatments I'm being offered are palliative. Palliation is the process of masking symptoms instead of dealing with underlying causes. In my case, this means finding ways to lessen the pain so I might be able to function a little better. Epidural corticosteroid injections are in this category. My doctors explain to me that a corticosteroid is a substance naturally produced in the adrenal cortex of the human body that reduces both pain and inflammation. For these injections, it's made synthetically. Like the cupping in acupuncture, this procedure also makes sense to me. I recall how the pain went away when I was in a war zone or on a deadline with my adrenals pumping like mad. Maybe a steroidal substance from the adrenal cortex will trigger the same result.

For precision, I'm told, a fluoroscopic X-ray is used to guide a needle into the epidural space of the spine. The dura is the area between the protective covering of the spinal cord and the bony vertebra. It's filled with fat and small blood cells and covers each of the spinal nerves as they leave the spinal canal. The steroid is mixed with an anesthetic numbing agent called lidocaine and injected into this sensitive area in hopes of relieving pressure on any inflamed nerves, like the one that keeps firing sciatica down my left leg.

Driving a car is next to impossible for me, and it's not allowed following an epidural injection. My friend Kenny, who escaped West Covina with me when we were teenagers, has been visiting for the past several days and takes me to the appointment. Sitting in the waiting room, we reminisce about the days when we got lost in the redwood forests together, camped on remote riverbanks, and jumped off towering cliffs into deep pools by river waterfalls. The memories are comforting. I'm more at home with who I used to be. I have no relationship with the person I am now.

After a long wait, I'm finally called in. The pain specialist immediately makes me wary. I can't put my finger on it, but I've always had good instincts. He's in his mid forties and looks more like someone you might find at a disco club than in a medical office. He talks too much about his expertise. Lacks the seasoned humility and compassion of Drs. Mooney or Chen. He also seems rushed and indifferent. Maybe my instincts aren't so good these days. I'll try anything to stop the pain. But the guy is a creep. I have to tell myself, *Just get this over with. What have you got to lose?*

It's two o'clock in the afternoon when I put on a hospital gown and lie on my side on a metal table. My lower back is scrubbed with antiseptic soap and shaved around the area where the needle will be inserted. Pillows are wedged between my knees and under my head, but I can't get comfortable.

"This will take time," the doctor says. "We are going slowly. After it's done you just lie here and rest until someone comes to get you."

Despite this prelude, it still feels like he's distracted and hurried. I almost call it off, but the promise of a month or two of relief is too tempting. I close my eyes and think about a healing waterfall cascading around me. I can feel the needle moving in deeper now, a few stages at a time. It takes fifteen, maybe twenty minutes. The injection is cool and tastes metallic again, like the radioactive tracer used during my bone scans. Time seems to be suspended as I drift off for a few minutes. When I wake up, I realize the doctor has left without saying a word. I'm all alone. There's no one in sight.

As I lie here on the table, I pay close attention to my back, trying to see if I notice any soothing effects from the corticosteroid. Instead, my head starts to pound. It feels like hot ice has been injected into my brain. Both hemispheres are throbbing like crazy. Suddenly, I begin to sweat all over. Now I'm freezing cold. It flashes back and forth, sweating then shivering, my head pounding harder and harder.

I'm trying to stay with it. Relax and let it pass. But it gets worse. Has it been thirty minutes or an hour since the doctor walked out? Why is no one checking on me? I call out for someone. Anyone.

It's painful to make the sound. More throbbing in my brain. I call louder, yelling, "Heyyyyyy," shivering with the chills. It hurts to open my eyes. Pleading for someone even louder now, worrying that I shouldn't sit up yet, and that I might not be able to anyway. Louder. Screaming now. Holding my head between my palms.

"Oh, my God, what is it?" The receptionist rushes in.

"Get the doctor!" I yell at her. "Something's gone wrong!"

"He went home a long time ago," she says. "I'm the only one here. I was supposed to check you out in about five minutes."

I will later learn that I had a "dural puncture." The doctor missed the mark and punctured the membrane covering my spinal cord, resulting in a leakage of my spinal fluid into the epidural space. This causes acute, debilitating headaches that can last several days.

When the receptionist tells me the doctor is gone, I completely lose it and start screaming at the poor woman. Kenny hears my outburst and rushes into the room.

"Are you okay? What's going on?"

"Get me out of here," I say, holding my temples in my hands. "Please take me home."

"Shouldn't we go to the emergency room?"

"No. Please, Kenny. I've had it. Just get me home."

CHAPTER 15

Final Season

CHRONIC PAIN is consuming. It eats away at you day and night. Robs your body of its energy. Twists your emotions into knots. Like being locked in an invisible prison and continuously subjected to torture. Your tolerance level nosedives. The smallest stressful circumstance sets you off and brings out the worst in you. As the months roll by and my back pain continues to gnaw away at me, I see the negative side of things in an instant. I'm rude and pushy without meaning to be and can't seem to control it. I easily take offense at real or perceived slights and am quicker to lash back if I sense an adversary. I don't like myself this way, but I can't figure out how to turn it around.

At the same time, I cling to a thread of hope that I'll eventually escape this nightmare. I have to hold onto something or I might completely break down. I trundle around in my Clamshell brace and keep turning on the Stim, deluding myself that a miracle remains possible. Along with my lower back, my left leg is crippling me. Persistent sciatica shoots down the hamstring at least once a day. I have to use a cane to support myself when I walk, which I do as little as possible because these days I can barely tolerate it. I continue to eat and drink like a foreign correspondent, not even noticing how stoned I am or the weight I'm continuing to put on.

Years ago, I did reports on widespread struggles against addiction, but I'm delusional enough to believe this doesn't apply to me.

After all, the drugs are prescribed by the very best doctors. The wine is elegant and expensive. Anyway, I'm in crisis and have a right to spoil myself a little. It beats self-pity, doesn't it? This is how warped my mind has become as it rationalizes self-destructive behaviors in order to cope.

The only treatments I can find offer little relief. Therapeutic massage. Ultrasound. Hot packs. Cold packs. I'm getting nowhere and need more ways to escape, like becoming hooked on bestsellers. I can read a thick novel in a day or two. The stacks of books on the floor by my bed could fill a bookcase. Volumes by Robert Ludlum, Scott Turow, Tom Clancy, Elmore Leonard, Ken Follett, John Grisham. I won't admit it to myself, but I'm living vicariously. Numbing my mind with drugs, wine, and meaningless fictional intrigue to replace the global life of adventure and accomplishment I once enjoyed.

When I collapse into sleep, I often have a recurring dream. The characters and locales change, but the theme is always the same: I'm in my office in a newsroom. Reporters, producers, directors, and editors are running in every direction. The evening news is about to begin, but I'm just sitting there staring at the computer screen on my desk. I haven't filed a report for months and feel tremendous guilt. No one has noticed yet, but the moment they do it's certain I'll be fired. I want to run to the assignment desk and beg to be sent into the field, but I can't get out of my chair.

In reality, I can't even sit in a chair anymore. It puts too much pressure on my spine. The hotel staff has brought a poolside lounge into the living room of my villa. This is where I take every meal, lying prone with my plate balanced on my growing belly, another novel open by my side so I can read while I eat. Half the time, I spill the plate, knocking the book on the floor and toppling my wine glass. This makes me scream out loud with frustration and rage—and then drink some more.

Pamela is in Hong Kong looking after our life there, and I don't feel much like being social. It's a lonely existence, but I do have a new friend. He's an old duck, with graying feathers around his shimmering teal and green neck that bulge out to one side like it's broken.

He also waddles with a limp and is clearly in pain, making his take-offs and landings very tenuous. I can sympathize.

The old duck arrives every morning as I'm lying on my lounge on the deck. He's always looking for last night's dinner bread, which I feed him with glee. I recognize his quack and sometimes mimic it to invite him in. In no time at all, we establish a bond. There was a TV show my parents watched when I was a child: *I Love Lucy*. An older couple, Fred and Ethel Mertz, were best friends and neighbors of the stars, Ricky and Lucy. The duck reminds me of Fred: a little portly. Slow. Aging. Kind. Easy to be with. When I leave the sliding glass doors to my bedroom open overnight, Fred the Duck waddles in the next morning to find me in the shower. To my surprise and complete delight, he joins me under the spray, wriggling in the water at my feet, nibbling at my legs, prodding me for bread, and quacking like crazy. It makes me laugh with abandon when I realize that Fred has become my best friend.

One day, Fred brings his partner, whom I name Ethel. Ethel is shy, and for three mornings straight she stays in the bushes framing the deck. She finally decides I'm safe and joins Fred, cautiously nibbling bits of bread from my hand. Soon, the three of us become a family. When mating season arrives, the young mallards on the hotel grounds are in a frenzy, cornering and assaulting all the hens. Unable to battle these stronger ducks, Fred brings Ethel to my villa to seek refuge. Sometimes I have to grab my cane and beat back a gang of young hopefuls as Fred and Ethel hurry into the living room and cower behind the couch, quacking up a storm.

Fred looks like he shouldn't even be alive. It's clearly his last season. Without me as his protector, Ethel would surely be taken from him by the younger males. I decide it's his undying love for Ethel, and hers for him, that keeps him going. It reminds me of a lesson I learned long ago in the refugee hospital on the border of Afghanistan and Pakistan where I met the little boy, Mahmoud, with napalm burns covering his body. A lesson about the power of love.

The medical staff was in a state of controlled overwhelm, doing the best they could with limited medical supplies and a stream of serious-ly wounded victims flooding in daily. During an interview, the head of the refugee hospital, Dr. Shahwani, noted how amazed he was that many of the Afghan patients overcame incredible odds and somehow managed to survive, even when it seemed medically impossible. The Pakistani fighters, however, who were mercenaries that joined the battle for money and ideological reasons, didn't fare nearly as well even though their injuries were similar to those of the Afghans.

I remember that there was always a family member at the bedside of every wounded Afghan, but few in the ward where the Pakistani mercenaries were being treated. The people by the wounded Afghans' bedsides were there around the clock, praying and loving them in their own quiet and reserved ways. *That was it. The reason so many seriously wounded Afghans managed to survive against such enormous odds was due to the power of love.* In much the same way, Ethel's love for Fred the Duck is helping him through one last season, and Fred's love is helping me along, even though I might not get another season in my life as a foreign correspondent.

Pamela has returned from Hong Kong and is with me now, as supportive as ever. We go to the pool, sit by the bay, take walks when I feel capable. I tell her about Fred and Ethel, who seem to have disappeared. It's the only big story in my life these days, far from the sort of news I used to report. One morning, as I'm lying on my back on the living room floor, I hear Fred's familiar quack. Then a chorus of tiny quacks. Suddenly, Fred and Ethel proudly enter the room with eight ducklings in tow. I whisper for Pamela to come in from the bedroom and meet the family. We're all introduced, and soon a few of the ducklings hop over my legs and jump onto my belly. Then they waddle off. Fred gives me a glance and cocks his head to signal a final good-bye before winging into the sky. He's in bad shape, but at least he can still fly.

It's been a year now. Countless failed treatments. Thousands of pills. Gallons of wine. Scores of cheap novels. Endless false hopes. I know it in my heart. I have to face the truth. My time is up. I've lost the battle. There will be no return to my career. No more global travel. No more reports on *Nightly News*. No more of the life I loved more than life itself. I feel resentment, anger, fear, and failure.

I take the letter from NBC promising to hold my job, crumple it into a ball and hurl it against the wall. It hits with a crispy thud and falls behind the couch. Then I limp to my lounge, lean over to my computer, and compose a brief good-bye email to my former colleagues at the network before I'm deleted from the system. I make it as upbeat as possible, but I feel like a fraud trying to sound so positive. There's a final visit with Dr. Garfin at UCSD, but it's only a formality. Like a bird that can no longer fly, I'm officially declared:

PERMANENTLY DISABLED.

THE ABYSS

CHAPTER 16

First Prayer

T HIS IS PARADISE. I wish I lived here!"
This is what we hear from most everyone who visits Coronado. It's a stunning place, nestled in San Diego Bay with sunny skies, beautiful beaches, and world-class resorts. Ever since it was founded in 1885, it's been a destination for the rich and famous from around the world. On any given day you can hear a dozen languages during a walk along the beach in front of the historic Hotel del Coronado, sitting like a Victorian jewel facing the Pacific Ocean. *The Wizard of Oz* was written in Coronado. Its author, Frank Baum, used the hotel as inspiration for his Emerald City, and the city's main street for the Yellow Brick Road.

At the same time, Coronado is a quaint village of 30,000 residents that seems like a throwback to the 1950s, with small cafes and shops, quiet streets, and cozy homes. Despite the ridiculous cost of real estate, families often go to great lengths to move here just so their children can attend the excellent public and private schools. It's also a military town. On the north end of Coronado there's a Naval air base and on the south end, a Special Warfare Command, where the legendary Navy SEALs are trained. Retired admirals live on the village's best streets in luxurious homes made affordable by their generous pensions.

Now that I'm classified as "permanently disabled," staying in Coronado is the logical choice, especially with my family here. But despite its charm and quality of life, I can't get used to it. Without my career, I don't know who I am anymore and I'm no longer comfortable in my own skin. My body brace feels like a prison cell, especially with the thick metal shaft on the left side that runs down my sciatic leg and straps onto my thigh just above my knee. Even with this addition, I have to use my cane to further stabilize myself on my increasingly rare walks. I'm not sure which hurts more, my back or my heart. I just want to click my heels together like Dorothy did in the *Wizard of Oz*, whisper "There's no place like home" three times, and miraculously be transported back to my home in Hong Kong, covering Asia for *The Nightly News*.

NBC was generous in providing a year with all expenses paid while I tried to heal and it continues to cover my health care. The network also compensated me well while I was a correspondent, covering all my expenses due to the requirements of living abroad and facing extensive travel. This allowed me to put almost every paycheck into a savings account, which was bolstered with stock from the parent company, General Electric. The savings are a godsend now, and the only sense of security I have. Almost every day, though, I wonder what will happen if and when the money runs out. It feels emasculating, like I can't take care of myself or fight back against whatever my fate might be.

Despite everything, Pamela and I share an abiding love for one another. We've decided to get married and are trying to establish a new life. I'm not sure I'm worthy of this any longer, but she's caring and compassionate and I need her more than ever, especially since my self-esteem plummeted after being declared permanently disabled. I often wonder if she feels love for the vibrant man I used to be and now holds more of a sense of obligation to the damaged and dependent man I've become. Given my lack of mobility, constant pain, and emotional fluctuations, I question my ability to be a good husband and meet her needs. Most of the time, I'm faking it—pretending to be happy and whole. This makes me feel guilty, weak, and inadequate.

I measure each day in handfuls of painkillers and antidepressants. With every dose, I get further away from any sense of who I am, and barely notice as time trudges by. It's all blurry. Slow motion. Months soon become a year, and then two years. The changes in my body and mind are so gradual I don't really notice my continued weight gain, increased weakness, and personality problems. As a journalist I was paid to be cynical, wary, contentious, and probing. Targets of my investigative stories were adversaries, usually trying to conceal their corruption and misdeeds. Now, almost anyone can become an adversary at a moment's notice. I'm always looking for faults in others, finding hypocrisy that isn't there, criticizing and blaming. If I witnessed someone else doing this, I'd dismiss him or her as obnoxious and insecure, but I give myself permission. *After all*, I think, *I'm wounded. Life has been unfair. I have a right to be this way.*

With my arsenal of medications, there are times I feel stable enough to attend social events and even take a rare vacation with Pamela, but there's always a price to pay. Just as I begin to feel I might be making a slight degree of progress in my ability to cope with this life, a wrong move triggers a sharp thrust of pain in my tailbone, then radiates up my back into my shoulder blades and shoots down my legs to my heels. Every time this happens I'm bedridden for days. It's so debilitating that I have to use a bedpan to relieve myself, which is profoundly humiliating and leaves me feeling even more frustrated and hopeless.

Even on good days, I can't sit or stand for even a short time without the tip of the ice pick stabbing me again and scaring me to death. I have to lie down for almost everything. We've bought a folding lounge chair on wheels to take to parties, dinners, the local movie theater, and Coronado's outdoor Sunday concerts at the park half a block from our home. Pamela packs the bulky lounge into the car, then has to drag it out, roll it to wherever we're going, and set it up for me. As a result, most people treat me differently, usually with a sense of care and compassion. I'm starting to realize what it's like to be the recipient of this. I'm touched to my core by the inherent goodness in so many people, yet I also feel embarrassed, and I instinctively recoil at being an object of pity.

Pamela also hosts dinner parties and does her best to keep me surrounded by people so that I feel engaged in the world. Yet even after two years, I have trouble relating to a suburban lifestyle. It's like I've moved to a country where I barely speak the language. As a news correspondent, I lived in such a different world that it's more than not speaking the language. I often feel like an alien from another planet. I'm used to glib journalists, cynical expatriates, and wry world travelers who talk endlessly about foreign policy, global intrigues, and which area of the world is likely to be the next powder keg. The conversations in this new world are more domestic in nature, filled with nuances and references I don't understand. No matter how hard I try to fit in, something deep inside of me says *you don't belong*, and every time I hear this inner voice I simply shut down.

So I stay on the edges, keeping it light and happy, making small talk when I can, telling war stories only when invited. When I do share some of my past, I feel like a has-been, someone who used to be somebody, and now is a pathetic nobody. But the experiences from my journalistic past stay with me. I can't forget the men, women, and children I've seen tormented, crippled, and maimed from the ravages of poverty and cruelty of war. When people complain about traffic, a rude waiter, a foggy day, or their favorite team being beaten in this or that game, I think about how they don't seem to appreciate the comforts and conveniences—the good life—we have in America, especially here in Coronado. How ironic. *I've been dealt a bad hand, so I can complain,* I reason, *but everyone else had better not.*

In hopes of fitting in better, I've started watching more TV. I feel like I have to learn which sport season it is and who to root for in the big game. You know, the one that comes up almost every weekend and has everyone talking and planning a barbecue. I also need to get reacquainted with the primetime dramas so I can comprehend the endless social references to characters, plot lines, and scenes that permeate all the small talk. I find it superficial and boring, but I do it anyway because I worry about coming off as some sort of elitist snob. The truth is that I don't feel better than these people in any way. I just feel broken, lost, and completely out of place.

I'm struck by how much of American culture is formed by television shows and their relentless streams of commercials. It reminds me of a night long ago, during my first news job in Eureka, when our television station, KVIQ, got knocked off the air during primetime.

The phone banks lit up immediately. I was the only one there, preparing the 11 P.M. newscast. Out of curiosity, I began to randomly answer some of the calls. People were angry, shocked, even frightened, demanding the problem be fixed immediately or their favorite programs scheduled for rerun.

"I've been waiting all week for this show," one caller almost screamed. "How can you do this to me?"

I did my best to explain how the programming was fed in from a cable by the parent company of our station in San Francisco. It had malfunctioned. There was no way to know when it would come back online and there would be no rerun. Many callers went ballistic, like addicts in withdrawal. Even though at the time I was making my living by being on TV, I never related to those shows very much and wondered why we allowed ourselves to become so manipulated and dependent on our TV sets, living vicariously and separated from reality. It was all I could do to keep from suggesting that the agitated callers relax and read a book or maybe talk to their kids.

"Why don't you join Rotary?" Marshall is a new friend who does village banking in the third world. "We meet every Wednesday for lunch at the Hotel Del. You can launch a service project, get involved."

His offer is intriguing. There are more than 250 members in Coronado Rotary: bankers, lawyers, accountants, money managers, retired admirals, city council members, and the mayor. The club is well-heeled and funds projects around the world, including clean-water systems in Africa, facial surgery for deformed children in Mexico, and camps for disabled kids at a facility just south of town. It's an opportunity to be involved. Do something meaningful again. Widen my shrunken world. I'm eager to join, but have to confess that I can't sit for the meetings. Marshall calls the next day to say that the hotel staff came to the rescue, agreeing to bring a poolside lounge into the ornate conference room where the club meets weekly for lunch.

By the time I've attended my third meeting, I have an idea for a new Rotary project that I could spearhead. When I think of humanitarianism, the first person who comes to mind is Father Joe from the Klong Toei slum in Bangkok. I call him in Thailand and ask what we could do to help in his efforts to combat the sex-slave industry. "Village banking," Joe says immediately. "We need to give these women a way to start small, home-based businesses and become self-reliant."

Inspired by these words, I launch a Rotary project to bring village banking to the poor women of Thailand and fly Father Joe to Coronado to speak to our club. Within a few months, and a ton of help from my fellow Rotarians, we're able to raise enough money to establish the first Grameen Village Bank in Thailand. Grameen is a revolutionary system of compassionate banking spreading throughout the third world that provides small, low-interest loans to people with no assets. For as little as twenty dollars, an impoverished Thai woman can establish a home-based business, often something as simple as growing vegetables for market or weaving baskets. This allows her to generate survival income and helps her keep her daughters out of the hands of the sex-slave gangs. It also keeps me connected to my past life and gives me a sense that I'm still an active citizen of the world, contributing something to humanity, doing something with my life.

I've always had compassion for those who suffer. Every time I was in a war zone or place of crisis, I was always deeply touched by those hit hardest, especially the children. I did everything in my power to show the world what was happening and tried to help in any way I could. This project in Thailand reminds me of that part of myself— the person once filled with care and concern. But I can't shake a growing sense of malaise and ennui, especially lying down in the back of the room at Rotary on my lounge chair. I'm fat and getting fatter. In a body brace. My cane leaning against the armrest. My meal precariously balanced on my belly. There are food stains on my shirt and a mess on the floor beneath me.

The sense of being weak, tired, unworthy, and insignificant is like a tsunami always washing over me. There's no way I can ever travel to Thailand to see what we have created, and I'm not sure I even have the energy to keep pushing the project and raising more funds. Worse, at every Rotary lunch I'm always being treated like the walking wounded, and I cringe every time someone offers to bring me a dessert or help me stand up. I know they mean well, but it always makes me feel eviscerated and impotent.

Bottom line: Instead of being a prominent foreign correspondent dashing off to a new adventure, covering an important story that helps chronicle the history of the world, I am now the fat crippled man lying on the lounge in the back of the room dribbling his food all over himself. My identity is so shattered that I can't even begin to face it, much less piece any of it back together, and while I don't like it when others show me pity, I'm dripping with self-pity. It's like I'm falling into a bottomless abyss.

To deal with this emotional turmoil, Prozac has been added to my regimen of prescription medications. It's an antidepressant that numbs my mind, helping me forget about what my life has become. It also makes me feel like I'm pulling a thick wool mask over my head to hide from the world. Like running away without going anywhere. When it works, I'm almost happy and Pamela and I still manage to share moments of laughter, romance, and intimacy. Then periods of darkness hit like sudden storms. I lash out again, start new arguments, brood and withdraw even further. As a result, we spend more time in different rooms. It must be difficult for her, wondering what she has gotten into and where it's all going.

"You have great compassion for others," Father Joe says after I confide some of this to him on one of his return visits to Coronado Rotary. "But I see your inner turmoil as well." He is the only one I've told about the heartache and the darkness. As he continues to counsel me, he pulls his chair close to my recliner and speaks with a mixture of tenderness and strength. "You need some compassion for yourself. You have to accept what your life has become. And you need to find your Soul."

My heart is heavy as an anvil, and I'm aching inside for something to grasp onto, but I'm uneasy about where Father Joe is heading. I'm all too familiar with the violence that has been committed throughout the ages in the name of someone's God. I've witnessed firsthand the role religious intolerance can play in war. I've reported on the scandals, hypocrisy, and self-righteousness of various creeds and cults. I don't think I can handle being preached to, I'm not sure that I can ever accept what's happened to me, and I can't imagine joining a church.

Father Joe surprises me. "I don't care if it's Christ or Krishna, Buddha or Mohammad," he says. "It's not about religion, it's about Spirit. Anybody who tells you their way is the only way, even if it's a jolly old Catholic priest like me, is a deluded fool." Father Joe's credo of activism and engaged spirituality has always touched me at the deepest level. Jesus said we should serve the poor, turn the other cheek, and love our neighbors, and that's what this wonderful man does. He has his priorities straight and practices what he preaches. "You see," Father Joe continues, "no matter how big our field of vision might be, there's always a bigger picture. Find the true voice of your Soul and listen to it as carefully as you can. Then do your best to follow the advice you receive."

With this, he reaches out and takes my hand into his as a rare flood of tears begin streaming down my face. I don't quite know what to do with Father Joe's advice, but this remarkable man has become one of the few people in the world I completely trust, and I'm desperate to find some meaning in the void my life has become.

Our Coronado friends have long invited us to join their community church. Inspired by Father Joe, I put my resistance aside and make this my first tenuous step. Raised by secular parents, I have rarely attended a church service and never could relate. Fortunately, the community church is light, more of a social event than a service. The pastor is affable, nondogmatic, and humorous. I listen, analyze, and try to accept it all—but I am doubtful, cynical, suspicious. Still a journalist at heart.

Yet even though I'm so wary, I keep returning to the Sunday services. There's something stirring inside of me, a nascent spiritual sense I've never known. Tonight, just before falling asleep, I said my very first prayer:

*Whoever you are, help me out of this pain. I don't think I can take
    it much longer.*
Tell me what to do.
Give me a sign.
Please.

The next day, Wednesday, March 13, 1996, we learn that Pamela
is pregnant.

CHAPTER 17

Shining Light by the Sea

I 'D LIKE TO THINK the pregnancy is a divinely orchestrated moment, an answer to my first prayer, but my rational mind dismisses this idea as patently absurd. We've wanted to have a child for more than a year and have been seeing a fertility specialist for months. The treatments finally worked. It would be foolish to think otherwise.

Still, it's given me a sense of purpose far beyond anything else in my life and helps me find something within myself I thought was gone forever: hope. Who cares that at forty-eight years old I will be a "dino-daddy" when the child is born? Who cares that I'm disabled and severely limited in what I can do? Why worry that there will be no running on the beach, chasing a ball, camping, hiking, or coaching at his soccer games? People with serious disabilities have proven to be wonderful parents, I tell myself, as I jump into the preparation process with the fervor of old.

Six months into the pregnancy, we learn that our child will be a boy, and we begin turning an upstairs bedroom into a nursery. The centerpiece is a large, white crib with musical mobiles dangling overhead. I even manage to mount a safety gate at the top of the stairs. This accomplishment makes me feel satisfied, like I'm still worthwhile despite my crippled body. Downstairs, we design a playroom with built-in cabinets and a Murphy bed for the eventual playdates and sleepovers with little friends. This is work I used to be able to do. Now it's far beyond me and I have to hire someone to install everything.

Before we know it, Pamela is in labor and we are in the hospital delivery room. On December 13, 1997, Morgan Bradford Willis arrives in the world. *Morgan*, a name of Welsh and Old English origin, means "great shining light by the sea." Like most Americans, Pamela and I share European ancestry, and the image of living by the sea and bringing a shining light into our lives feels perfect. I watch Morgan as he makes his debut in the world, and I cut the umbilical cord myself, listening to his first cry. When the doctor places him in my arms, I stare at his tiny face and a new kind of love floods my heart. It's an emotional experience beyond anything I have ever known.

Home from the hospital, we establish a new routine with feeding schedules, burping, nap times, diaper changes, bathing, and powdering. Pamela and I grow closer together as I immerse myself in it, but I also have limitations. Pain episodes strike. There are days when I'm down and can't contribute much. Little fears about not being able to be a successful father bubble up regularly, but I tuck them away in the growing file down in my subconscious where I cram all the stuff I lack the courage to face. I weigh close to 215 pounds now, thirty-five more than in my prime when I was a correspondent. Things no longer function well in my body. It's more than physical disability and weight gain. My inner rhythms are out of sync, like I'm a song so out of tune that it hurts your ears.

Fortunately, Morgan is an easy baby. He's always calm, never gets colic, rarely cries, and smiles endlessly. With his flaxen hair, cherubic cheeks, and milky skin, it's as if an angel has descended into my arms. When I'm able, I love to feed him, change his diapers, wash his tiny body, dry him off, dust him with baby powder, and get him dressed. I hold him every chance I get, coo at him, make silly faces, gaze endlessly at his tiny fingers and toes.

I run warm baths almost every evening, slip in, then lift Morgan onto my belly and dip his toes in and out of the water. I bob him up and down, going deeper and deeper, up to his ankles, then his knees, now his hips—always making sure we stay within his comfort zone. Soon, I have him in up to his shoulders, with water splashing everywhere as he gurgles and coos. Then I suddenly lift him high over my head and dip him down in again, making a big whooshing sound, *wwwwhhhoooooaaaaaa!!!!*

After his bath I wrap him in a warm blanket and bring out his baby rattles and stuffed animals for a little play. He gazes with glee as I shake the rattles. When I rub the soft, furry face of his teddy bear onto his cheeks, he swoons with joy. My son really is a shining light, and I have found a new identity: I'm a father. The broken back, the failed surgery, the lost career, the constant pain, and the emotional turmoil don't matter quite so much anymore. This radiant light of new life has opened the seas of my heart, giving me a reason to live.

It's early 1998. Morgan is only three months old. I woke up this morning feeling incredibly sick. It's like a heavy cold, only without a sore throat, runny nose, or headache. I'm feverish, achy all over, exhausted, spent. I fall back to sleep hard.

Day Two of the illness. The symptoms seem to be changing. I get steamy hot and then suddenly feel freezing. My head is pounding. More sleep. I can hardly move.

Day Three. The worst head cold in my life. I can't breathe through my nose. My lungs are filled with goop.

Day Four. I can't stop coughing. The fits are so bad I sometimes think I'll never be able to inhale.

Day Five. The malaise subsides and I start to feel better.

A week later, it hits me again. This time it's more like a classic head and chest cold. Three days later, I'm recovering again, wondering what the hell just happened.

Then I get walloped and begin to fear that something insidious is inside of me. This time, the sickness lingers with persistence, still taking on different personalities. My sinuses throb. Then it's in my lungs. Now my temples are on fire. One afternoon I have full-body aches. The next night I struggle with more sweats and chills. My doctor is baffled. Maybe it's mononucleosis, or a rare infection. Blood tests are inconclusive and antibiotics have no effect.

Over the next few months, the mysterious illness keeps coming in waves, hitting harder and lasting longer each time it strikes. One morning, I reach to rub a sore spot on the left side of my neck and discover a lump about the size of an almond. Within days, the lump grows to the size of a walnut and continues to get larger and more painful.

"It's probably just an infection in the lymph node," Dr. Schafer says. He's an ENT—an ear, nose, and throat specialist—that I've been referred to by the medical group that contracts with my insurance company. "We need to biopsy it, just to be safe. Then discuss your options."

As always, I want details.

"A biopsy is a fairly simple procedure," Dr. Schafer explains. "A specialized needle is inserted into the lump, it's aspirated— meaning cells are sucked into the needle—and then the cells are analyzed under a microscope. You'll be under anesthesia, so it's painless."

The next morning, September 11, 1998, I'm on a gurney being wheeled down a hospital corridor at Sharp Chula Vista Medical Center, just south of San Diego. In the operating room, it's the back surgery scenario all over again. Bright lights, plastic tubes, computer monitors, and clinking steel instruments. The anesthesia needle slips into my vein and the mask slides over my face. In less than a minute, the thick, wet sound of my breath is all I can hear.

I'm dying!

I'm unconscious, but I can hear myself whispering this into a black void.

I'm dying!

I can feel my life leaving my body.

A female voice comes from somewhere beyond the void as I try to hold on: "Wake up! Come back! You're not dying!" She sounds insistent, but far away, like I'm at the bottom of a deep well. I feel myself slipping further away, but the woman's voice gets stronger, demanding that I come back to life.

"Right now. Come back here! It's your sister, Valerie!"

Finally, I slip out of the void. I feel life slowly returning to my body and start to find my way back into the world. But I have no idea where I am and begin thrashing and trying to get up. Two big men begin restraining me like I'm a prisoner caught during an escape.

"Get off me! Let me go! Dammit, let me go!" I hear myself trying to scream, but my voice won't come out.

"You are in the hospital recovery room," a nurse says with authority as the two strong orderlies continue to hold me down. "Snap out of it!"

I struggle and fight some more as the room finally comes into view. My sister Valerie is right next to me. It was her voice beckoning me back from the beyond. As she holds my hand and comforts me, I'm convinced that without her I would have permanently slipped away.

"You had major surgery," Valerie tells me. "You've been out for hours."

"What do you mean, major surgery?" I'm barely able to rasp this out, and it hurts my throat like crazy.

"Let's wait and talk to the doctor," a nurse says firmly while guiding me into lying back down. "You still need more rest."

It's one of those unspoken things. Everyone knows something is terribly wrong, but it's not time to discuss it. There is some complication. Maybe a mistake during the surgery. Too much anesthesia. Possibly something worse. I try to swallow again, but there's tremendous pain in my throat and my neck is throbbing as fast as a jackhammer. I reach for my neck. The entire left side is heavily bandaged. *This was more than a simple biopsy.*

"There's good news and bad news." The surgeon, Dr. Low, is offering me a classic cliché. It's mostly bad news, so the approach is to look on the bright side first, then deliver the hard facts as softly as possible.

"The lump wasn't the source of the problem," he continues. "We found the source and took care of it."

"So what was the source? What's the problem?" I'm still barely able to speak but am back to playing journalist and want to get straight to it.

"It was in your tonsils," Dr. Low says. "We were able to cut it all out and remove your tonsils along with some of the areas around them."

"Cut what out?" I sound like a hissing snake.

"Squamous cells," he says.

"What are squamous cells? What do I have? Just come to the point." Now it feels like my throat might explode.

"You have oropharyngeal carcinoma," Dr. Low says, as if it's a confession. "When we biopsied the tumor we found the squamous cells. We had to sedate you further and perform emergency surgery. After we removed the lymph gland from your neck we found that the squamous cells weren't just in the lump. We had to follow it, go into your throat. We found the source there, in your tonsils. We cut out as much as we could find."

"Carcinoma," I croak the word out slowly. "That's cancer."

No one ever wants to say the word. *Cancer*. That frightening disease that always happens to someone else. *Cancer*. One of the leading causes of death in America. *Cancer*. Fifteen hundred people a day, more than half a million annually. *Cancer*.

"You are going to need some treatments," Dr. Low says. "Radiation is a necessity. We need to try to kill any squamous cells that may have been missed in the surgery, get everything we can. You'll begin radiation treatments once the incision on your neck heals a bit."

"So what are the odds of beating this?" I ask the question Dr. Low has probably heard a million times, my voice almost inaudible.

"We don't know," Dr. Low says calmly, "and I don't think it's ever helpful to speculate and talk about percentages. Each case is different. We just have to do our best and be positive. For now, try not to talk much and just go home and rest."

Go home and rest. *But will I survive? Will I die? If so, how long do I have?* These questions drive me crazy on the drive home. Even though I'm still stoned from whatever they gave me during the surgery, and now have a new bottle of heavy painkillers, I feel half crazy and completely hyped up. All night it pounds in my head: *Cancer*. It's hard as hell to swallow anything with my throat sliced open, but I manage to down a few extra Valium, after crushing them up and mixing them with water. Still, I can't doze off.

It's late now. Well past midnight. I still can't sleep. *Cancer*. I can't get the word out of my head. I get up as quietly as possible and tiptoe into Morgan's room to watch him sleeping in his crib. I listen to the gentle rise and fall of his breath, feeling connected to the very core of his being. Tears run down my cheeks like wild rivers. It's a terrible thought that I'll be leaving Pamela without a husband, although I've often felt she might be better off without having to care for me or face my constant emotional flare-ups. But the prospect of leaving my son without a father rips me apart inside.

"I'm sorry," I whisper softly, the rasp so bad now it's barely audible, careful not to awaken him. This little shining light by the sea has just flooded my life with meaning and joy. And now this disease wants to steal the life out of my body. "I'm so sorry."

CHAPTER 18

Radiation

S HE CAN'T BE more than five years old, playing quietly with her doll on the floor of the waiting room in the hospital's radiation oncology wing. Her red woolen hat matches her winter coat, hiding the baldness that has resulted from her chemotherapy treatments. Her huge green eyes are missing their luster. Her little cheeks are ashen. Her forehead is etched with a frown. She is deeply absorbed in comforting her doll, whispering that everything will be okay. Her parents sit close by watching her, unable to conceal their anguish and pain.

As a journalist, I would instinctively focus on this child as a poignant way to illustrate the heartbreak and tragic randomness of a killer disease. But I'm no longer behind the camera lens documenting the suffering of others. I'm on the other side now, trying to survive. We're all trying to survive: children, teens, middle-aged adults, a few senior citizens, sitting here together in silence. Waiting in the waiting room. Almost stuck in time. We share a common bond, but there's little eye contact and no conversation. Despite the floral carpet and nature scenes framed on the walls, it's somber. Sterile. I can almost taste the quiet desperation in the room.

The little girl hugs her doll and gives it a kiss on the cheek. I can't take my eyes off her as I wonder if she will survive or if cancer will soon claim her precious little life. I wonder about all of us. No doubt everyone here holds similar thoughts. It's a huge elephant in the room, and it feels like an eternity before I'm called in to see the radiation oncology specialist, Dr. Chasan.

"It's been three weeks since your surgery, and your scar seems to be healing well," Dr. Chasan says as she holds my head gently with her hands, slowly turning it side to side to inspect my neck. "We have you scheduled for fifteen treatments over the next seven weeks. You'll finish up just before Christmas day."

Like Dr. Low, Dr. Chasan won't tell me about my odds for survival. But I do get a new fact from her: The cancer is stage IV. "What does that mean?" I ask quickly when she mentions it. It seems to catch her by surprise. "Oh, I thought you had been told," she says, sounding a little hesitant. "It can be pretty tough, but we have a good treatment program for you."

I press for more information, but she artfully dodges. She is very professional, and I begin to realize it's probably an important protocol not to discuss specifics too much with patients, especially if the news is likely to depress them.

"The radiation procedure is painless, you won't feel a thing," Dr. Chasan gets me back on track as she reaches for a thin, black rubber hose connected to a metal box sitting on the counter. I can see that the hose has an oval-shaped glass tip on the end. "But first, I need to look at your throat and take a few images. Unfortunately, this procedure can be a little uncomfortable."

I can't imagine any greater discomfort than what I've been living with the past several years, until Dr. Chasan holds the glass tip of the hose closer to my face and says, "This is a tiny camera. I have to insert this tube down one of your nostrils to see what's going on. We need to go in this way to get a full view of the upper throat."

I take a deep breath through my nose, visualize the process, then swallow hard. "Okay," I say, "let's do it."

She sprays a numbing agent into my left nostril and has me breathe deeply through my nose, holding the right nostril shut so the spray penetrates deeply up the left sinus. Sixty seconds later she begins to insert the tube-cam into my left nostril and down the sinus passageway into my throat. Even with the numbing spray, it's worse than I feared. The pain is excruciating as she slowly forces the tube farther.

My right nostril bubbles and foams with mucus. My eyes flood with hot tears. I want to bite onto Dr. Chasan's wrist and chew her hand off to make her stop. I gag and convulse with dry heaves when the camera enters my still-tender throat. It's a complete violation and I can't wait for it to end.

As soon as I settle down after the tube-cam and can breathe normally, I'm guided into radiation. The treatment room is long and wide, with gray metal cabinets and laminated shelving on the walls. Radiation masks are lined up on the higher shelves like rows of skulls. I was fitted for mine three days ago. To construct it, gauze soaked in warm plaster was layered over my face to create a mold. Once dry, the mold was removed and plastic webbing heated inside of it to form the mask. Designed to block the radiation from damaging areas of my face outside the target area where my tonsils once were, it covers my face like I'm the diabolical killer in a cheap horror movie.

The radiation technician, Greg, comes in now and starts to get me prepped. He is chatty and smart. When I ask how radiotherapy works, he gives me an amazingly detailed answer. "It's designed to damage the DNA of cancerous cells with photons, a basic unit of electromagnetic radiation. Cancer cells usually reproduce much faster and in far greater numbers than normal cells, but they have a diminished capacity to repair themselves. So the idea is that the 'bad cells' will die while the 'good cells' will have a chance to regenerate." I know how critical this is. The oncology partner of the doctor who performed my neck surgery told me during a consultation last week that even if the radiation succeeds, there's no way to know if it's one hundred percent, and if the cancer cells begin growing again I have no chance of survival. Zero.

The radiation therapy machine looks similar to the bone scan device, only bigger and more high-tech, built with shiny white, black, and silver metal casings. I'm laid out on yet another long, cold table, this time with my shirt off so the black, pinpoint tattoos on my chest are in plain sight. These were done when I was fitted for my mask, along with two tiny tattoos on my neck. These markers help guide the radiation beams away from sensitive areas. Greg places the horror mask over my face, then sticks a white, wooden dowel into my mouth.

"You have to gently bite on the dowel the entire time to keep your jaw slightly open so radiation doesn't pass through your jawbone," Greg explains as two more assistants get me perfectly positioned. "That could cause unwanted damage."

As I hold the dowel in my teeth, the electric table slides me beneath a wide, L-shaped arm that supports the large, round radiation device. It looks like the tip of a giant microscope hovering above me. As I stare at it, I flash back to dissecting insects in high school biology lab and feel like I'm one of the sacrificial bugs we used to squish between glass plates to view through our scopes.

After the clinicians leave the room to protect themselves, the device aims radiation beams from several angles of exposure to intersect at the area where my tonsils used to be. As Dr. Chasan promised, it's painless. I can't feel the beams of radiation at all.

Lying under this machine, it's impossible not to contemplate what my life has become. I keep drifting back into the past, reliving the life I once led. I was fully alive then. My body healthy and strong.

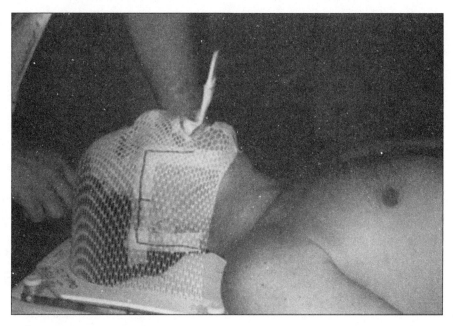

Radiation Treatment, October 1998.

Important things to do. Deadlines to meet. Historic stories to tell. Every day an amazing adventure. Now I'm lying here with a skull mask over my face, biting a wooden stick, and being radiated. I'm so cold, puffy, and pasty white, I feel more like a corpse on an autopsy table than a living human being. "I love you, Morgan," I hear myself whisper-hissing around the wooden dowel between my teeth. "I love you."

※

I'm placed under the giant microscope twice a week. The radiation treatments remain painless, but the side effects are miserable. They give me profound fatigue. My lips are swollen, dried, and cracked, like parched mud. My thyroid gland has been destroyed, which means I have another pharmaceutical medication to take so my body maintains its normal flow of hormones that the thyroid regulates.

My throat feels like burnt toast. Bleeding sores fill my mouth and most of my salivary function has been permanently damaged by the photons. My taste buds have met a similar fate, and my throat is so swollen and inflamed I can't eat regular food and have to drink nourishment through a straw. Dr. Chasan has recommended Slim-Fast smoothies that are used to provide essential nutrients during weight loss programs. They taste terrible to me. If only there were a blended steak and potatoes drink on the market, maybe with a hint of red wine.

Far worse than the Slim-Fast smoothies are the appointments with Dr. Chasan, who continues to periodically force the tube-cam up my nostril and down into my throat, looking for suspect cells, which would appear as black splotches on the bright red lining of my larynx. This procedure remains an inconceivable violation and I loathe entering her office.

※

Two months later, just before Christmas of 1998, the radiation treatments—and the invasive tube-cam sessions—end. My voice has gotten much worse than it was right after the surgery. Now I can barely speak in a scratchy whisper that sounds like fingernails on a blackboard. Sometimes my voice disappears completely. I only have two ways to deal with this. When I'm mute, I type on my computer screen in a huge font, then wave my arms and bring Pamela's attention to my message. When I have a semblance of voice, I put on a gadget called a "Chattervox." It's a plastic, hospital-green amplifier that straps around my waist where the Stim used to go when there was hope of promoting a successful bone fusion in my back. A wire runs from the amplifier to a headset with a microphone. I hiss into the microphone in deep, raw tones and my voice is amplified from the speaker at my belly. It sounds like I've swallowed Darth Vader.

I now understand the word *invalid* in a new way. The noun means someone disabled by illness and injury, but the adjective also comes to mind. I'm not valid. My life lacks validity: a broken back, cancer, no career; incapable of raising my son; helpless, hopeless. I can't imagine how difficult all this is for Pamela. She remains upbeat on the exterior, loving and helping me in every way, sacrificing what little time she has when not taking care of Morgan. But I sense she also has a growing concern for her own future. I don't blame her. Anyone would be frightened, uncertain, and self-protective in a situation such as this. Our relationship has become like a formal dance. We go through all the moves with great politeness and formality, plaster smiles on our faces, have superficial conversations, and barely touch the cancer issue.

My only comfort and sense of worth is when I'm with Morgan. He has no idea that I'm sick as he crawls into my lap on the recliner and we leaf through his little picture books. When I have a voice, I tell him how much I love him through the Chattervox. When I'm mute, I make silly faces and play with him by turning my hand into a crawly thing or giving him gentle tickles. I wish I could sing the lullabies I used to as he drifts off to sleep in my arms. Every time we're together, it's impossible not to be flooded with thoughts of leaving him fatherless. They spin through my head like a tornado and always leave me drowning in grief.

With Morgan, Winter 1998.

Despite the radiation treatments, my prognosis is poor. Although I can't nail them down on this, as best as I can tell from pressing my doctors is that I'll be fortunate to live for two years. I can't help but wonder sometimes if it's worth it. If it weren't for this wonderful child, I think I would choose to call it all off and find a way to quickly slip into the darkness forever.

CHAPTER 19

The Journal

S TILL A JOURNALIST AT HEART, I have to know all the facts.
With my life in the balance, I need them more than ever. I've
bought a hospital "overbed table" from a medical supply store
to use for setting up my computer. It has a strong frame with a serving tray secured to its legs by a single metal shaft on one side. This
way, I can lean back on my recliner to ease the tension on my back,
then roll the table toward my lap and swivel the tray until my computer is facing me.

The Internet is just beginning to burgeon, and there's a new service
called Google that just came out last year. It's a search engine that
helps me find online articles and information. I pore through everything I can find on throat cancer and soon begin to learn how much
I didn't know. Squamous cell carcinoma comes in various types, from
easily treatable skin cancer to aggressive carcinomas that invade various organs. It can show up in the neck, the lungs, the prostate, the
bladder. It's either *in situ*, confined to the site of origin, or *invasive*,
spreading to other organs. The spreading is called *metastasis*, and
this is bad news. My cancer originated in my tonsils and spread into
my lymphatic system, creating the tumor in the lymph gland on my
neck. It's considered invasive. It's spreading. Metastasizing.

This is what Dr. Chasan meant when she said it was stage IV.
In another article, I learn there are four stages of cancer, based on
various factors, including tumor size, the depth of its penetration

181

in the body, whether or not it has spread to other organs, and if it has invaded lymph nodes. Stage I is localized and the easiest to deal with. Stage IV is the worst and indicates the patient has the least chance of survival. It's bad news.

As I read more about radiation, several articles indicate that head and neck cancers such as mine, when metastasized, are very aggressive and generally incurable with radiotherapy since the whole body would need to be treated. The amount of radiation required for this would prove fatal. I can only conclude that my treatments, therefore, were at best just a way to slow things down. But I still can't find specifics about survival rates for stage IV oropharyngeal carcinoma. Many articles contradict one another. There's nothing definitive. No matter how much I search, I can't nail it down with any certainty. I want to discover some new finding that gives me hope or just finally confirms that two years is correct. It's frustrating, and it remains the big unanswered question: *What are my chances of survival?*

THURSDAY, APRIL 1, 1999

It's a blustery morning with huge clouds, high winds, and occasional light rain showers. I've bundled you up, Morgan, tucked you into your stroller and wrapped you in a cozy blanket. We cruise around the block looking at all the flowers, smelling the lilacs and gardenias in the humid air, listening to the birds. You love the outdoors, especially when it rains. We have a perfect time together. I hope we can make this a regular routine.

Despite the fact that the scar has finally healed, my neck is becoming tender again. There are new sore spots and, rubbing them all the time, I think I feel little lumps. All my doctors have acknowledged is that if the cancer returns, my death is certain. But they never seem alarmed during monthly checkups, so maybe it's just fear. I can't be sure, so I'm trying to keep a journal for Morgan to read when I'm gone, hoping he'll have some memory of his father.

———————

WEDNESDAY, APRIL 7, 1999

Dear Morgan. You'll be two years old in seven months. I'm planning to set up a film camera on a tripod and tell you the story of my life. I want you to see the places I traveled to and the news reports I did. I hope you'll view it after I am gone. I can't get to it quite yet. My back feels like it's broken all over again right now. But look for it, okay?

———————

Ever since the surgery and radiation, I've been even more sedentary, but I'm eating as much as or more than ever. I don't need so much food. It's just for comfort. Another way of escaping myself. As a result, I now weigh more than 220 pounds. Morphine has been prescribed on a permanent basis to help with my growing back pain and the residual discomfort from the radiation treatments. It comes in slow-release patches that I stick on my chest and also in stronger pill form for pain emergencies. I still take Vicodin, Valium, Motrin, and Prozac, even though they're hard to swallow down my swollen throat, and have been prescribed Ritalin and Dexedrine to stimulate me since I'm always so lethargic.

I cling to my drugs out of fear and never miss a dose, and although they help manage physical and emotional pain, they've completely masked my Soul. I'm constantly stoned—jacked up on stimulants, numbed by narcotics, dazed by antidepressants, and pickled on alcohol. It's become a weird sort of reality for me, and I'm slowly turning into a person I don't recognize.

WEDNESDAY, APRIL 14, 1999

You saw a wagon on the neighbor's porch this
morning, Morgan, and it transfixed you. You are
only sixteen months old and just beginning to
speak, but you pointed and said, "waaauuun!"
It's the first time I've ever seen you really
want something. During your nap I snuck out to
the local hardware store and bought you a red
wagon. I remember my first wagon and my father
pulling me around in it. This is like passing
the torch. You should have seen your face when I
surprised you with it!

My time with Morgan is now spent in gentle play. I have to hand
him off to Pamela for most of his meals, naps, and diaper changes.
Despite how difficult I can be, she continues to be loving, supportive, and giving. She recently bought a cookbook for cancer patients
and has me choose recipes for her to prepare. She also helps me
in a million other little ways, especially when I'm immobilized by
pain episodes. I feel like a huge burden. It depresses me even more.
I know it's immature. Another form of self-pity. I try to snap out of it,
but I can't seem to do it.

SATURDAY, MAY 1, 1999

Nature, Morgan, is a miracle. I gaze at the
morning sun from my recliner here by my computer, listen to the birds sing, and watch the
flowers bloom. Then I turn on the monitor that
lets me listen to you in your bedroom and I can
hear you breathe while you are still asleep. It
sounds like the song of all life.

I'm still obsessed with finding out what my chances of survival are, and I'm getting fixated on whether or not I had the right treatment. Shortly after the surgery on my neck, the first oncologist I saw, Dr. Saleh, wanted me to have chemotherapy as well as radiation. Dr. Low, who performed the tumor surgery, was against chemo. Because he was my surgeon, I chose to take Dr. Low's advice, but after all the Internet research and conflicting data, I want a new opinion, even though I'm already seeing so many doctors I'm completely confused.

My health insurance company approves this request and I'm sent to see another ear, nose, and throat specialist named Dr. Jimenez. I hate having to find a way to lie down in the reception area so my back doesn't flare up. I also hate that the doctor is running an hour behind. When I'm finally called into his office, he seems hurried and distracted to me, and it makes me grit my teeth. But I also realize that the drugs make me tense, irritable, and impatient. I'm always annoyed with people, especially most of my doctors. I want everyone to be prompt. Give me clear and concise answers. Tell me what I'm hoping to hear. I'm still trying to play investigative reporter, looking for contradictions, mistrusting everyone, always finding faults.

After a few minutes of reading through my file, Dr. Jimenez glances up and says, "Your case is highly unusual, and very rare, especially for a nonsmoker. I think you should have had much more aggressive treatment, including chemotherapy." The doctor expresses frustration with the HMO system and the medical group I belong to, even though he's a member of it. He wants me to see a chemotherapy expert outside the group named Dr. Kourany. "He will tell you if you should have chemo, and he will be straightforward about your chances for surviving."

I'm losing track of all the doctors I've been seeing. The incessant notes I take at every appointment are stuffed in files and folders without the organizational skills I once had as a journalist. It's incredibly frustrating, and the idea that Dr. Low's advice might have been wrong infuriates me. I hate the idea of seeing another specialist, but I need to know: *Did I get the best treatment? Am I going to die? If so, how long do I have?*

FRIDAY, MAY 7, 1999
(A NOTE TO MYSELF)

I carried Morgan out to the yard this morning. He is so small and light, yet it killed my
back. Soon, I'm not going to be able to carry
him upstairs to bed anymore, and he loves this
so much. I don't want to increase the pain meds,
but I need to ask the doctor about it today.
There's no other way.

Despite everything, we still manage to have some good family times, with limited outings and social occasions, but my moments of clarity and freedom from discomfort are far too few. My voice comes and goes. My back comes and goes. Most of my time is spent in bed or on the recliner. When I do have energy, I devote it to Morgan. Spells of darkness, anger, and delusion erupt more frequently these days. My son never sees these, but his mother does. It's like I'm simultaneously shivering with fear and boiling with anger whenever we're together. I know I'm not showing up for her. Instead, I'm taking it out on her. There are those special people who face great life-threatening challenges with amazing dignity, strength, and courage. They are inspirations and role models for us all. I wish I could say I'm one of them, but I'm not even close.

TUESDAY, MAY 11, 1999

A recent bone scan shows deterioration in the
disc between my third and fourth lumbar vertebrae, the level just above the failed surgery.
I took you to the park this morning, Morgan, but
as I sat on the grass with you in my lap, the

disc lightly herniated. I was frozen in pain and
could barely push your stroller the half block
to home. I'm now on ice and another heavy dose
of drugs. My whole body is gripped with tension and fear. I'm so sorry. All I want is to be
healthy and whole for you.

I've finally gotten an appointment with Dr. Kourany for the second opinion on my treatments and prognosis. The reception area is
tiny and the doctor is late, so his secretary takes me into the doctor's
office so I can lie down on a couch. It's an expansive room, with rows
of bookshelves lining the walls, filled with medical texts.

After a half-hour on the overstuffed leather couch that faces the
doctor's massive desk, I feel impatient. I get up and hobble over to
his library, looking for anything that might give me statistics about
throat cancer mortality rates. There's nothing. Moving back toward
the couch I notice the corner of a book concealed beneath a stack
of files and papers on his desk. It seems like a book patients are not
supposed to see, but I slip it out anyway. The title says something
about cancer findings. I take the book and lie back down, thumbing
through it as quickly as I can, feeling like I'll be scolded if the doctor
walks in and catches me.

In the table of contents, there's a chapter on head and neck tumors.
I go to it immediately, still wary of the doctor's arrival. Most of the
language and data is far beyond my comprehension, but things start
jumping out as I rush through the chapter. *Head and neck cancers are
aggressive tumors.* He must have looked through this in preparation
for my appointment. *Involvement of even a single lymph node is associated with a marked decline in survival.* I had a major tumor in one
lymph node and several other nearby nodes removed as well. *Chemotherapy does not confer an additional survival benefit.* So Dr. Low was
right. *There is significant risk of second primary tumors developing. The
prognosis for patients is poor.*

Suddenly, the door opens and I quickly slide the book under
the couch. Dr. Kourany is an imposing presence, tall and broad

shouldered, with thick black hair and a moustache. His name is Middle Eastern, and he looks just like the stern border guard I had to bribe when I crossed from Turkey into Northern Iraq while covering the Kurdish refuge crisis after the Gulf War. "What can I do for you?" he asks in a deep, commanding voice, not even acknowledging being an hour late.

As I explain my story, he thumbs through my file, never once looking up. When I mention I was in the Gulf War and wonder if exposure to something there might have caused this, he finally looks up, stares me straight in the eyes, and says forcefully, "It wasn't a war. It was a massacre!" He's literally shaking with anger and I finally get it. He must be from Iraq. Many innocent people were killed during the bombing of Baghdad. Perhaps some were his family or friends.

"You're from Baghdad?" I venture. "Yes," he says gruffly. I've touched a nerve. "I'm sorry about the war," I respond and try to get back on topic, but he quickly interrupts, "You should not have had surgery or radiation. You should have had chemotherapy. It's too late for that now. But it's no matter. Chemotherapy doesn't save the life, it only slows things down."

He seems to be contradicting his own book, but I'm afraid to confront him with this or let him know I took it from his desk. "So what are my odds of survival?" I ask. "Two years," Dr. Kourany says abruptly as he stands up, signaling it's time for me to leave. "Two years from when the diagnosis was made. There's nothing I can do for you." With that, he turns and walks out through his private entrance door before I can say, "I thought so."

THURSDAY, JUNE 17, 1999

Morgan, you took my hand this morning, as you so often do, pulled me off the recliner, and "run-walked" me to the front closet, pointed to your box of bubble makers and dragged me out front to blow bubbles in the morning air. Then you did a

"Daddy attack," having me lie on the grass as
you climbed onto my belly and we rubbed noses
and laughed. You really are a "shining light by
the sea," and I think you are trying to heal
me in your own little way. I love you so much
for it.

———————————

I've joined a new church just two blocks away, only because it's closer and easier to get to. The pastor, Father David, is in his early forties, lean and wiry, with short, wispy brown hair and a glimmer in his eyes. He is as Irish as Father Joe, and as charismatic—always smiling and filled with energy. He comes to visit me at home once a week and prays for a healing. In the quiet moments I have to myself, I find I'm opening more to inner awareness, but not as a religion. To me, it's a spiritual awareness, a search for deeper meaning in my life, a way to try to cope with my dark emotions and accept that I probably have just a short time left on this Earth. But it's in its infancy, like a tiny seed sprouting beneath the soil trying to push through the crust of the hard earth and not making much progress.

The cycles of back pain and sickness are tormenting. The ice pick episodes strike periodically despite all the drugs, and the malaise I felt when I was diagnosed with cancer keeps returning, like a dark, malevolent presence invading my body again. It's not as intense as before, but it keeps hanging around and it scares me out of my wits. It's often hard to swallow and my throat sometimes bleeds. I can't keep my fingers off the tender nodes on my neck and am always pressing them, wondering if cancer is spreading through my body.

And I'm totally confused. Was there a screwup? Should I have had chemo? Two doctors say yes, but the book on Dr. Kourany's desk says it doesn't confer any survival benefits. I guess that means, like he said, it just slows things down. One thing seems certain: I don't have much time. *Two years.* I can't forget those words. I was diagnosed in September of last year. That leaves me less than a year and a half to go.

Yesterday was Father's Day. You gave me a card that you drew. My throat was bleeding and I had to say thank you through the Chattervox. It was a moment filled with joy, yet I felt a deep depression that I couldn't shake off. As I write this, hot tears are streaming down my face. I wonder if this is my final Father's Day with you. I can't stop worrying about not being here with you and for you.

"Pentagon Denies Claims of Gulf War Illness." The story is buried in the back pages of *The New York Times* today. The article doesn't surprise me. I've long had a hunch that it might have been something I was exposed to in the Gulf that caused my cancer. Maybe some chemical weapon used by Saddam that no one ever discovered. As I dig into the article, I find out it wasn't Iraq that used these types of weapons; it was America.

More than a hundred thousand Gulf veterans are sick and almost ten thousand have died since the war, but it's being hushed up. After years of denial, the Department of Defense is finally admitting that U.S. air campaigns deliberately blew up large caches of weapons in Iraq, sending clouds of toxic debris toward its own ground troops. As I suspected, the article indicates that the MOPP gear, the masks, and the chemical uniforms that soldiers and war correspondents were issued were of poor quality and little use.

It gets worse. There was an invisible enemy on the battlefield: armor-piercing shells made with depleted uranium used in American tank, anti-aircraft, and antipersonnel artillery. Depleted uranium ordnance is denser than lead, pierces better, fragments more easily, and also bursts into flames. It was cheap for the Defense Department to obtain because it's a waste product of the nuclear-bomb program. It was highly effective, but it also filled the battlefields with toxic radiation that is carcinogenic. I remember peering into Iraqi tanks that were freshly punched full of holes from these shells. This must be what I breathed into my throat. Was it our own bomb attacks that made me, and thousands of soldiers, terminally ill? The thought enrages me.

SATURDAY, JULY 17, 1999

Morgan, you and I have entered a joyous new
world of play. I make up silly Daddy games, pretending my hand is a tickle monster. You catch
on immediately and create your own tickle monster to get me back. Then I become all your
stuffed animals at breakfast, each encouraging
you to drink your milk. In the middle of the fun
this morning, I lost my voice again. I see how
it disappoints you, and it crushes me.

I'm continuing to investigate the Gulf War Syndrome. I know it will not do anything to cure me, but I need to know the facts. After endless unanswered phone calls to numerous old sources, I finally reach a Marine general I became friends with during the war.

"I can't say anything on the record," he tells me. "You can never use my name. I would have to deny we ever spoke." He must protect his career. When I agree to these terms, he confirms my findings. Many of his soldiers became sick after the war. Several died.

He believes the depleted uranium played a major role. It's a moral dilemma for him and I can feel his distress.

"I wish I could bring back my men," he says with remorse, "but I can't. That's all I can say. Good luck."

TUESDAY, JULY 20, 1999

There is a painful lump in my throat. I had to return to the throat specialist yesterday for another assault down my sinuses. I am tired of being poked, prodded, and examined. The new oncologist who oversees my case now, Dr. Redfern, says the lump is just swelling and there's no sign of a new tumor. But he confirmed this morning that I'll be extremely fortunate now to live more than a year. I had to really press him to get this out of him. I told him I have a solid pact with you, Morgan, to confound all the experts and live for years. I wish I believed it was possible, but I honestly don't feel I'm going to last much longer. I took you to the pool at the spa afterwards. Having the support of the water is the only way I can still hold you and toss you in the air. My God, I love you beyond belief and want to be your daddy for years and years to come.

I now have two recurring dreams that torment me. Their symbolism is obvious. The first is still the one where I am in a bustling newsroom, sitting at my desk and making no contribution, feeling guilty, and certain I'll be discovered any moment and fired immediately. The second is more frightening. I'm standing at the edge of a cliff, looking down into a dark abyss. Suddenly, the ground gives way beneath my feet and I slip over the edge. As I fall, I reach out and grab a twisted tree root protruding from the sheer face of the precipice. I lack the strength to pull myself back up and can barely hold on. I feel the abyss pulling me down while I struggle to climb out. Finally, I lose my grip and plummet into the darkness, awakening with a muffled scream just as I'm about to hit bottom.

MONDAY, JULY 26, 1999

```
Morgan, you wanted to go outside and blow bub-
bles on the lawn this morning. For the first
time in months, I couldn't do it. My throat was
bleeding and my spine was on fire. So I drew a
little flower with my finger on the back of one of
your hands and a happy face on the other. You
hugged and kissed me, and softly said my favor-
ite word, "Da-eee." I can sense you know what
is happening in some innocent, intuitive way,
and the ache in my heart eclipses the pain in my
back.
```

I've always had a need to feel like I'm in control. I think most people feel this way, especially men. We like to be in charge. Push forward. Win victories. Prove our strength. Save the day. I felt worthwhile, in charge of my life, and victorious as a journalist. Now I feel powerless. Totally helpless. The feeling gets stronger every day.

There's no doubt why I drink so much and am so dependent on the drugs. I'm scared to death. And I know the reason I can't face myself: I would abhor what I see. Sometimes friends come by and I watch myself start arguments with them. I want to stop myself in the middle of it, but I can't because my emotions are so out of control. How did I become so pathetic? So angry? Such a coward? Always the victim? Where did this person come from? Where is the man I used to be? If my son were mature enough to see who I am, would he be proud or ashamed? The answer is so obvious to me that it makes me want to crawl into a dark hole and never come out again.

SUNDAY, OCTOBER 3, 1999

Your second birthday is two months away, but Morgan you are already getting so talkative and understanding so much. Your favorite word is "Da-eee," and you are crawling all over me every chance you get. I'm amazed at how fast you are growing and even now realize a parent's biggest challenge is just trying to keep up. I hope I can keep up with you forever.

This is my last entry in the journal. I never pulled it together to make a video. I no longer have the physical or emotional strength to continue. It's a muddle anyway, with notes to Morgan and ramblings to myself. Still, I print everything on parchment paper, design a cover, and make a little book for him. I tiptoe into his room during his nap and place it on a high shelf in his closet.

Walking to his little bed, built to look like a convertible roadster, I gaze at him as long as I can before standing becomes too painful. Then I struggle to kneel down and manage to kiss his forehead. Morgan's eyes softly open, so I hug him and remind him of our covenant, that I won't let cancer take me from him. I mean it from the bottom of my heart, but I have no idea how to make it happen, and I really don't believe it's possible.

CHAPTER 20

Get Up, Daddy

I T IS AUGUST 27, 1999. Just less than one year ago, I was diagnosed with cancer. Today is my fiftieth birthday. People from
near and far have arrived at our home in Coronado to celebrate.
There are former colleagues from the news business, relatives, and
both recent and longtime friends. I've been in another mute period
with a bleeding throat and can barely talk. What little voice I have is,
of course, raspy and harsh. I have to make do. I'm too embarrassed
to wear the Chattervox and let anyone hear the Darth Vader croak.

The party begins at one o'clock in the afternoon. By two o'clock,
I'm lying on my portable lounge chair in the backyard, drinking a
creamy stout beer. Wine burns my tender throat these days, stout
beer soothes it. It's my latest medicine, so I can rationalize drinking
it whenever I want. I greet everyone as I sip away, acting like my life
is fantastic.

"You should try Yoga," a distant cousin of Pamela's kneels down
and tells me as I have another taste of stout. It's the first time
we've met. He can't be much more than twenty years old. Says
he's a Yoga teacher. Unlike me, he looks fit and strong, lean and
supple.

"Oh, sure," I rasp with a little laugh, like fingernails on the blackboard again. "I can barely walk and I've always been the stiffest person in the world. Plus, I weigh a ton. Then there's this broken back
of mine. No chance, but thanks."

"Okay, maybe someday, when it's right for you." He doesn't push it and simply offers a gentle smile. There's something different about him. I feel drawn to his presence. He's calmer, more centered, and more serene than most people, especially for his young age. Still, the idea of Yoga seems as absurd as deciding it's time to take singing lessons or run a marathon. I excuse myself, roll off my lounge with a great effort, push myself up with my cane, head for the kitchen, and pop open another bottle of stout.

Dinner is served outdoors on tables we've borrowed for the party. After we eat, it's time for me to thank everyone and endure a friendly birthday roast before the sun goes down. We move my lounge to the front porch, where we've set up a microphone stand. When everyone's gathered, I stand up to thank them.

"Thaann...Kuh...You...All for Be...Being...Ahum...here."

My voice is gone. I try to swallow the blood that's trickling into my mouth, but my throat is so swollen it's almost impossible. I can't get any more words out. I'm unsteady, leaning hard on my cane. Adrian, an African-American cameraman I worked with for years, jumps up and takes the mike.

"Don't you love it? He can't talk! I've waited all my life for this!" Everyone roars with delight.

I haven't seen Adrian in years. He's charismatic, witty, and irreverent. We were best friends when we worked together in Sacramento more than twenty years ago.

"I could never get a word in edgewise with him! Always talking, saying Adrian shoot this, don't miss that. How about this angle? You in focus?"

Everyone is continuing to have a good laugh as Adrian glares at me and says with his famous attitude, "Now, brother, you just lie down and listen for once in your life."

There are roasts and toasts, laughter and love. Adrian then closes on a personal note.

"I've always fought prejudice and had trouble trusting white people." He glances at me with a smile, "But you did something that blew my mind and taught me a lesson I'll never forget." This is too kind. I know where he's going and think I might cry at any moment.

"We were working together in Jamaica," Adrian turns toward the crowd, "and we had a driver named Vernal who was so black he looked blue, made me look almost white." Everyone laughs again.

"On our first day, we stopped at a fancy restaurant in the countryside outside of Kingston. The owners were also black, but much lighter in color. They told Vernal he couldn't eat with us. He was too dark. We had a Jamaican government official with us who was also a *brother* and he informed us this was the custom in his country. The super-black folk were lower class and not allowed to mix. I was hungry and said fine, asked Vernal to go wait in the car, and told him we would bring him something when we were finished." Adrian glances back at me now.

"You said no. You gave everyone hell, shamed them into seeing their prejudice. You went out to the car and brought Vernal back inside for lunch, set him down at the head of the table, and told him to order the most expensive meal on the menu."

This was more than twenty years ago, and Vernal still writes me once a year to say thank you for the only steak dinner he has ever had.

"I realized then that my people can be prejudiced, too, and that I was blind to it. So thank you, my brother, thank you." Adrian and I are both crying now as he leans down for a hug. I'm incredibly touched by the story of Vernal, but it also reminds me that I was once a far better person than I am now. That I once had a life I will never recapture.

It's an honor to see so many friends here. I want to walk around and thank every one of them, but when I try to stand up, I realize I'm stoned to the gills. I've had medications in my system for so many years that I wake up high. As I take my usual doses every few hours, I get higher throughout the day. With three or four stout beers during the party, I'm totally gone. In another universe.

The morphine has the strongest effect, especially with the alcohol. I still feel the pain in my back and throat, but there's a sense of physical pleasure in all the places where I'm not hurting. It makes me understand how the villagers we filmed smoking opium in northern Thailand must have felt, and why they laid around all day with glazed eyes, doing nothing with their lives and having no concern for what the future might hold.

The party has ended and I'm in bed. Alone. Pamela often sleeps in her office guest bed these days, wisely avoiding me when I'm too stoned. Reviewing the party in my mind, I have more visions of the vibrant man I once was juxtaposed with the pitiful person I've become. They never seem to stop. I'm obese, bloated, swollen all over, and ghostly white with dark black circles under my eyes. I can't sit up for a meal or walk without a cane. I have stage IV cancer. My throat is bleeding and I can barely speak. The obvious suddenly dawns on me. My friends came to celebrate my fiftieth birthday, but it wasn't the main reason they were here. They were here to say good-bye.

It's Friday evening, December 4, and only three short blocks to our favorite spot to watch Coronado's annual Christmas Parade. This time it's even more special because it's the final parade of the twentieth century. Even though it's a short distance, getting to our favorite spot takes almost everything I have. The last four months since my birthday have been a deeper descent into darkness and pain. My medications have deranged my mind. Add the endless stout beers and I'm fuzzy all the time. Sometimes I wake up and see seven or eight bottles in my bedside trash can. I swear I only remember drinking two or three. The only clarity I have is when I'm with Morgan. He remains the one thing in my life that makes it worth living.

Thousands of people are lining our main street for this kickoff to the holidays. Despite how early it is, I pop the cap off a bottle of stout to celebrate with them. Not because I want the alcohol, of course. It's just to soothe my throat. The High School marching band is playing Christmas tunes. Colorful homemade floats roll by.

Kids in karate uniforms kick at the sky. Cheerleaders shake their pom-poms. The Pop Warner baseball team struts along with bats on their shoulders. Little ones dressed like elves and angels wander back and forth as their parents guide them in the proper direction. Even our city garbage trucks are in the act, rolling down the parade route, their huge Dumpsters strewn with colored lights.

Morgan has climbed out of his stroller and is curled up on my lap. He'll be two years old in a few days and is talking up a storm, giving me the full narrative on all the action. He goes crazy at the end of the parade when our city's largest fire truck rolls past with sirens wailing and Santa Claus on the top chanting "Ho, Ho, Ho!" He wraps his arms around my neck, hugs me closely, and says, "Next year, Da-eee, let's march in the parade together. Okay?"

I might as well promise to hike a mountain, but I hug him back and whisper, "Okay, sweetheart, we'll do it."

I read him the story of Pinocchio just this morning and now, as I make this promise, it feels like my nose is growing. It's more than the discomfort of telling a white lie to a small child. I feel like I'm betraying him.

Morgan's second birthday is on December 13. We throw him a party with all his little friends. Soon thereafter, we celebrate the first Christmas he's been old enough to understand what's going on. The living room is filled with gifts and, like all children, it makes him ecstatic. As I watch him tear open his presents with glee, tossing the ribbons and wrapping into the air with complete abandon, I'm filled with joy and grief. The sense that I'm slipping away from him is more palpable every day as I realize I have no control over my destiny.

With the new year coming soon, and with it, the dawning of 2000, my resolution is to spend what little energy I have each day with Morgan, but as we've grown ever closer, I've become more distant from the rest of the world. I can feel myself worsening daily. I'm always in pain, deeply depressed, combative and unkind to everyone but my boy. I'm tired of being the miserable, drugged, and often drunken person I've become and don't think I can take a slow death with Morgan watching me waste away. So I've begun having serious thoughts of how to end it all.

I've stashed a large box of my heaviest drugs in the closet, thinking that when the time arrives I can make my exit on my own terms. It's a dark vision, and a coward's exit. I imagine leaving a letter for Pamela and flying off to some lavish hotel suite in San Francisco or Las Vegas, even if I need to be pushed everywhere in a wheelchair. I'll check in, order the finest meal on the menu, request a bottle or two of the most expensive wines from their cellar, no matter how much the acidic taste burns my throat. I'll have my "last supper" and then slip into a hot Jacuzzi bath, drink down all the medications I can, and drift off to sleep forever.

Suddenly, Morgan can say *daddy* instead of *da-eee*, and he's growing more aware that his daddy is different. Always on the couch, the recliner, the portable lounge chair. Other daddies don't need canes, body braces, or voice boxes. They can always talk. Sing little lullabies. Get on the swings at the park. Carry their children on their shoulders. Toss them in the air. Kick a soccer ball back and forth. Take walks on the beach.

The doorbell rings. A playmate is here with his father for a day in the park. Morgan scurries to answer the door, then scrambles back down the hallway to find me flat on my back on the couch. He desperately wants me to come with him, to be fully involved. I'm in such bad shape that I can't even get up and walk him to the door.

"Daddy!" His voice is trembling, he's wiggling all over, on the verge of tears. "Get up, Daddy!"

His three little words hit me in the center of my chest like a bomb. I wish so badly that I could get up, but it's another ice pick episode and I'm stuck on the couch.

"You go have a good time, sweetheart," I say, pulling him in for a kiss. "Daddy can't get up right now."

Morgan stands still for a moment and gazes at me, trying to process his emotions. He's feeling something deeper than I think he's ever felt before.

"Please, get up, Daddy!" He pleads again as he reaches out and tugs at my hand.

"I'm sorry, honey," I whisper as my chest throbs. "Daddy just can't get up right now, his back hurts too much."

He starts to plead again but suddenly stops and stares at me. In this moment, he has come to a realization. Somewhere deep inside, he knows I'm breaking the covenant we made during the Christmas parade, that I'm not long for this world. Watching him disappear down the hall for his playdate, I free-fall into despair.

Get up, Daddy.
All night it plays in my head like a loop. *Get up, Daddy.*

But how? How can I get up from this nightmare? I have no idea. *Get up, Daddy.*

The next day, Morgan's little voice continues to loop in my mind and pound in my heart. It's still there the next day, and then the next, like an endless mantra. *Get up, Daddy.*

This morning I wonder why Morgan hasn't come in to crawl on my lap in bed. When I finally get up, I check his room. It's empty. Pamela's office is also empty. I limp downstairs. There's a note on the kitchen table. Pamela and Morgan have gone to spend the night at her mother's home in San Diego. Pamela and I have been more estranged these days, and she's received the brunt of my late-night tirades one too many times. I can understand how much she needs a break. We can talk about it tomorrow. But she and Morgan don't come home. I only get the message machine at her mother's home and can't find out where my family is. Another day goes by. Then, in the late evening, Pamela finally calls.

"I just can't come home right now," she says in a trembling voice.

"Okay, I understand," I answer, "just bring Morgan here, please."

"I can't do that, either," she says, firmer now. "He is going to stay with me."

I start to negotiate, bargain, bully, and rage, doing all the things that drove her away, but she is unyielding and I finally realize I'm powerless to impose my will on her. Morgan has been my lifeline, the limb I've been trying to cling to on the cliff above the abyss in my recurring dream. Now he's gone. I'll do anything to get him back, wage any battle, fight any foe. At least that's what my ego says, but it's empty hubris from a thoroughly broken man.

As I lie in bed, loaded with enough medications to knock out an elephant, I can't sleep. My heart is pounding. My body is aching. My stomach is roiling. My mind is screaming:

Get up, Daddy.

CHAPTER 21

Intervention

I T'S QUIETER THAN USUAL THIS MORNING. I think it was
New Year's Eve last night. Or was it two nights ago? A week? I've
finally started to come alive after another late night of terrible
mental torment. Pamela's leaving with Morgan has forced me to start
facing myself a little. I've been doped up, drunk, angry, rude, and out
of control for how long? Months? A year? Longer? Not only have I
been this way with Pamela, I've done it to my family and even with
the few remaining friends who have dared to stop by lately. I've felt
like such a victim and been so absorbed in self-pity that I never saw
it in its fullness. Until now. There it is. Clear as day. I'm a total mess.
I would have left someone like me ages ago, no matter how sick and
broken they were.

Even though I'm groggy and have the covers wrapped over my
head, I can sense something in the air. It's the feeling I used to get in
a war zone when there was a moment of silence before an attack. As
my head starts to clear, I hear soft murmurs downstairs in the family
room. It must be Pamela and Morgan. I haven't seen them or been
able to make any contact for at least five days. It's been driving me
insane.

I roll out of bed and strap on the lighter, elastic back brace I use
around the house. Slowly I head downstairs. Holding tightly to the
staircase railing to steady myself. Trying to get my blurry eyes in focus. Being careful not to stumble and fall. The murmurs have hushed.

They hear me coming. There's no cry of "Daddy" from Morgan, no "We're home" from his mother. It's eerie. My skin begins to tingle with apprehension.

Halfway down the stairs, still decorated with holiday wreaths, bows, and tinsel, I glance at our Christmas tree in the living room. It's brown. Shedding needles. Dead. *Like me*, I think as I make it to the last step.

I turn into the hallway and enter the family room. I see several people sitting there: Pamela. My two sisters. My mother. One of my nieces. A brother-in-law. Father David. A best friend of mine, who is also Morgan's godfather. And a tall, gangly stranger in a coat and tie, looking confident and in charge of whatever is happening here. Morgan is nowhere to be seen. I'm sensing my son is deliberately being kept from me as a means of getting my attention. No one says a word as I lower myself into my reclining chair, lean back, and survey the room. The atmosphere is serious, solemn, like a funeral, with the taste of fear permeating the air.

"My name is Dale," the stranger says as he stands up and takes the center of the room like a military commander. "I want you to know your family is here to support you."

Dale speaks in well-rehearsed tones but sounds stiff and mechanical. "I lead interventions," he continues. "Your family loves you, but they believe your life is out of control. You are taking too many medications and drinking too much alcohol. Everyone in this room is frightened for your future."

I look around at the somber faces. I can feel their love and compassion, but I also sense their apprehension: They're hoping I won't blow up and throw them all out. Dale now yields the floor to each family member, who, with great courage, takes their turn, nervously telling me how much I've changed. Everyone has written their words out on a form that Dale provided them. *The planning must have been in the works for the past several days.* Each speaker shares with me many hurtful things I've said. Ugly things I've done. Unacceptable behaviors that have worsened with time. My sisters and mother point out that they are always fearful that I might explode over something trivial. My brother-in-law says he believes my mixture of drinking and drugs will kill me. Morgan's godfather talks about my incessant anger and rage. Each of them says they can no longer be in my life if I continue like this, and they want me to get help now. Today. It's tough love. A forced reckoning. Incredibly painful to hear.

Father David has never seen this side of me and chooses not to speak. It's as if he knows I might need a source of spiritual strength during this. Then, Pamela takes her turn. Her hands are shaking as she holds her sheet of paper. Tears fall from her eyes. Her voice cracks as she says, "I love you and I miss you. I have lost my husband and my son's father. I have lost the man I married. I don't know who you will be on any given day. I'm afraid for you, and I'm afraid of you."

I'm in shock when she ends. Multiple voices in my head compete for attention. My ego rages, yelling at me to throw everyone out the door. Another inner voice demands that I defend myself. Remind them of my broken back and terminal cancer. Seek pity. Blame it on the drugs. Guilt-trip them for doing this to me. Then there's a deeper voice, the one Father Joe from Thailand urged me to listen to and the voice Father David represents as he sits facing me in silence. It's a voice we all have but so often refuse to acknowledge or heed. It always knows right from wrong, even when we're in a fit of rage or a drunken stupor. This voice says: *Your family and friends are right. No matter how painful it is to accept, they are one hundred percent right.*

I can see my reflection on the dark screen of the computer monitor that faces my recliner. Black circles under my eyes, greasy hair sticking out in all directions, a twisted scowl on my face. I look like a madman, and I realize I no longer know who this person is. As the voices in my head continue to compete for primacy, the *Get up, Daddy* mantra starts looping through my mind. There's incredible tension in the room as everyone waits for me to say something. Finally, as if I'm outside of my body watching all this unfold, I hear myself say, "It's about time."

A collective sigh of relief permeates the room as Dale seizes the moment. "Good. We realize that you are in pain and have a serious disease, but we want you to check into a Betty Ford Clinic in Palms Springs. Quit the drinking and get off as many of the drugs as possible. No matter how long you have to live, things can't go on like this any longer."

"What about Morgan?" I ask, needing to see him, wanting to tell him I love him before being locked away in rehab.

"Not yet." Dale is firm, speaking from a script that's part of the intervention process. They don't want me to change my mind, and Morgan is clearly the leverage. "You have to go right now, not later today, not tomorrow, but now. Everything is arranged. We have a car out front. Just get a few things together. Your sisters will help you pack. We'll discuss a visit with Morgan somewhere down the road."

My ego starts to seethe again. No one has the right to keep my son from me, especially this stranger in my home. Resentment boils over inside of me. I stare hard at Dale, wishing I had the strength to jump up and strangle him.

"I'll make the drive with you," Father David offers quickly, sensing my mood.

I glance at my reflection in the computer monitor again. I look deranged. Someone I would avoid at all costs. A vision of Morgan appears on the screen, like he's in my lap. I can hear his voice again. *Get up, Daddy*.

All the other voices in my head subside as a sense of surrender envelops me. If nothing else, I tell myself, I can get off these drugs. I can find some level of clarity. Be present for Morgan. Try to honor my covenant with him. Get up, in whatever way possible, before I die. I take a huge inhalation and let it go like a floodtide. It must be the first time I've fully exhaled in these thirteen years of pain and it feels like a river flowing through me, washing away years of fear, anger, and grief. I breathe in deeply again and sigh out loud, "Okay. Thank you, everyone, for doing this. I'm so sorry. Let me get a few things together. I'm so, so sorry."

Dale's car is a small compact. It can barely fit four adults. His messy trunk is too full to handle my small suitcase. Anyway, it would be impossible for me to sit up for a three-hour trip to Palm Springs, much less squeeze myself into this car wearing my back brace. Pretending not to be flummoxed, Dale jumps into action and vows to return in thirty minutes with a van. Without saying a word, Pamela drives off with him. Father David stays with me, like a spiritual sentry. He comforts me. Says a few prayers. Tells me it will be okay. But I'm already starting to get steamed, because it's a much longer wait than Dale promised. He and Pamela are not back until late afternoon.

The drive over the mountains from San Diego to Palm Springs is surreal. Dale and Pamela are up front talking logistics in hushed tones. I'm lying down on a thick pad in the back of the van with Father David sitting cross-legged and hunched over by my side. He whispers more prayers. Smiles. Affirms me the entire way. My mind is still fighting it, like a confused argument with a dozen different people screaming at the same time. My whole body aches from the bumpy ride and the emotional intensity of the intervention. When David isn't looking, I unscrew the cap of the tiny silver vial that dangles from a chain around my neck. This is where I keep my morphine tablets. I shake one out and slip it under my tongue.

The van is slow and struggles over the mountains. The trip takes much longer than expected. It's after 9 P.M. when we finally arrive at the clinic in Palm Springs. The lobby is empty. *Dale said everything was arranged*, I think to myself, noting that there's not a staff person in sight. I lie down on the reception couch, dazed, and completely exhausted. As I wait and wait, anger surges through me as I realize this plan was not so well crafted after all. It's at least another twenty minutes before a nurse appears.

As I continue to wait impatiently on the couch, longing for a stout beer, Dale and Pamela are down the hallway, in hushed conversation with the nurse. I can't hear them, but I can see them. Their body language makes it clear. Something is wrong. They engage in a tense back-and-forth for at least ten minutes. Now the nurse breaks away and comes toward me with authority.

"I'm sorry. This clinic is for alcoholics, not for cancer or pain patients. We are not equipped to admit someone like you, and no one told us you were coming."

The nurse is firm as a rock. Dale won't make eye contact. Pamela is in silent desperation as we pile back into the van and leave Palm Springs for a long, miserable trip back to Coronado.

"We'll find another place," Dale says as he drops me at our house in the predawn darkness and Father David begins to help me inside. "Pamela will call you."

I ignore this and turn to Pamela. "I'm still willing to do this," I say. "I know I have to." I gesture toward Dale, "But this guy has no idea what he's doing. I never want to see him again. Ever."

It's far past midnight when I struggle up the stairs, pull off the body brace, and melt onto my bed. Even though it's been one of the most grueling days of my life, I can't sleep. I pop a stout and chug it as I click on the TV, which only blares at me with mindless nonsense. I click it off and stare into the darkness. I can hear large waves breaking a few blocks away at the beach, the heaviness of my breath, the pounding of my heart.

I close my eyes and see Morgan. He is standing in front of me, tears in his eyes, begging me to get off the couch. I can hear his little voice, pleading:

Get up, Daddy.

CHAPTER 22

Sailboats and Treasure

You have to demand to see Morgan before you check into any
  facility.
Don't make any waves.
You have to do this thing.
There's no way you can stop taking drugs, you're in terrible pain.
What right did they have to do that intervention?
You have to stop the booze and drugs.
He's my son, no one can take him from me.
Don't make any waves.
You have to do this thing.

M Y MIND IS STILL RACING with so many competing voices I can't make sense of anything. It's been three days alone
in the house. Mostly lying in bed, foraging in the refrigerator, watching the television. I haven't heard from Pamela. Even
though I continue to drink and hit the medications heavily, I still
can't sleep at night. The trash can next to my bed is overflowing with
empty bottles of stout. What little self-esteem I might have had is
long gone. I think about my "last supper" plan. Stare at the box of
meds in my closet. Then the *Get up, Daddy* mantra comes back to
me and I see Morgan in my mind's eye. *You can't do this to your son. If
nothing else, get off of everything and die like a man. Give him a chance
to remember someone he can be a little bit proud of.*

I feel the pain of Morgan's absence most in the morning. He had been punctual and devoted, always running into the bedroom and crawling onto me when he woke up. Each time I would slowly lift my knees and he would straddle them, his back facing me as he whispered, "Please draw on my back, Daddy."

I have a nail file we call the "magic drawing stick" on my nightstand just for this special moment. "What would you like?" I would always ask, knowing the answer.

"A sailboat, Daddy."

"This is the mast," I'd say each time, drawing a gentle line down his spine. "Here is the right sail. Here is the left sail. Here's the body of the boat. The ocean is down here. What are these?" I'd ask as I drew squiggles in the ocean of his lower back. He'd giggle and answer, "Fishies, Daddy."

"Here's Morgan, the captain at the wheel. Daddy is on board, and our cat Max is right next to us."

I'd draw little v's in the sky above the sailboat and make bird whistles. Before I could ask he would say, "Those are the seagulls flying in the sky!"

Finally, I would draw a circle high on his right shoulder and stream an array of lines down his back. He'd beat me to the punch again. "That's the sun, shining down on us!"

Then we'd take our boat on an adventure with the magic drawing stick, coursing over the high seas of his smooth little back. We would fire our cannons at pirates and make a daring escape. Then we would land on a remote island, hike across the beach, and slip into the tropical forest. We'd peek and poke in all the darkest places, avoiding tigers and snakes of course, and then, behind a thundering waterfall, we'd discover a huge treasure chest filled with gold doubloons.

Sometimes Morgan would ask for rocket ships after the sailboats and we'd blast through space, conquering the dark force. Other times our fire engine would rush to the scene and extinguish the blaze, rescuing all the children. But the sailboat was always his favorite. Before he was taken from me, I had been drawing one on his back every morning for almost a year.

Daydreaming, I can feel Morgan on my knees. I can smell his golden hair, see the soft skin of his gently sloping shoulders, hear his sweet requests for another adventure on the landscape of his back.

I also hear him whispering, *Get up, Daddy*.

Pamela is all business when she finally calls to say she's found a place that will accept a patient with cancer and chronic pain. It's called the McDonald Center, at Scripps Hospital in nearby La Jolla. She'll be here in one hour to drive me to the facility. There will still be no visit with Morgan before I go. He remains the leverage to ensure I keep my promise. It's almost impossible to swallow this, and I have no idea what the clinic offers. But I gather my things, limp into the closet, and begin to get dressed.

You should see the stash of medications I've been keeping on a shelf in here. It's a plastic storage container filled with at least two dozen bottles. There are unopened bottles of Vicodin and Motrin, as large as the bottles on a pharmacist's back shelf, each holding several hundred doses. I have bottles filled with Valium, morphine, and Prozac that are only slightly smaller. This is because my medical insurance contracts with a national prescription company that ships patients three to six months' worth of medications at a time. Even though I've overmedicated myself for years, I still haven't come close to taking the amount of drugs I've been prescribed. As I lift the heavy box down from the shelf, I realize someone could make a fortune selling all these pills on the street. My plan is to take the stash to Scripps, surrender it when I check in, be rid of it for good.

The doorbell rings. Pamela is here. Before I answer, there's one final thing I have to do. Once I'm downstairs, I call out that I need a few more minutes. I slip into Morgan's playroom, find his crayons, and a large sheet of paper. I draw a sailboat. He and I are on deck with Max the cat. Seagulls soar in the sky and fish jump over the waves. The sun is shining down on us. There is a small island in the distance, sure to have treasure hidden behind a waterfall, and the wind is in our sails.

I write on the bottom of the page, *Daddy loves you Morgan, we'll sail again soon*, then pin it to his playroom wall. I take a few more minutes and glance at his toys, a teddy bear sitting on the window seat, one of his favorite blankets lying on the floor. "I love you, Morgan," I call out softly as if he were here in the playroom with me. Then I trundle toward the front door.

CHAPTER 23

Dark Night of the Soul

I T'S A SILENT DRIVE to La Jolla. The type of silence so thick you
can hardly breathe. There's nothing for Pamela or me to say. No
plans to make. No strategies to discuss. We sit about a foot apart
in her car, but there might as well be a thousand miles between us.
The noise of the highway is deafening. The sound of Pamela tapping
her fingernails on the steering wheel is even louder. I'm numb by the
time we arrive.

Scripps Hospital is a massive facility. It takes time to find the right
entrance. The McDonald Center parking lot is packed. We drive in
circles before finding a place to park. Pamela gets my suitcase from
the backseat and drags the portable lounge out of the trunk. I have my
cane in one hand and I tenuously carry the huge box of medications
in the other. When we walk into the reception room of the McDonald
Center to register, the staff members freeze and stare at me, wide-eyed.

"What are you doing? You can't bring those in here!" A male staffer exclaims as he runs up and grabs the box out of my hands like it's
a drug bust.

"There are patients in recovery here!" He barks, "These need to be
locked up immediately!"

Normally I would defend myself. Tell him to back off. Chill out.
But I'm in surrender mode. I don't say a word. All the other nurses
freeze and watch the scene. I've just arrived and already feel foolish.
Less than welcome. After the drama ends, we're allowed to approach

the reception counter. We complete the registration procedure Pamela initiated over the phone. Then she leaves as quickly as possible without seeming rude.

I'm directed to a chair next to the registration desk. I sit down and stare at my feet. My vitals are taken: blood pressure and temperature. Then the nurse has me step on a scale. 225 pounds. Good God, I'm huge. I feel so humiliated I can't make eye contact and I answer simple questions with grunts. Finally, I'm escorted down the hall. A professional-looking strip with my name on it has already been put on the door of my room, like I'm an executive rather than a basket case.

The room is antiseptic. Spartan. Efficient. It has cream-colored cinderblock walls, nondescript linoleum floors, and two gray metal hospital beds covered with tan blankets sitting on either side of a narrow window. There's a ceiling-to-floor closet and dresser combo made of dark brown fiberboard by the entry door. It faces a small sink next to a narrow bathroom, with a toilet and open shower so close together I could almost sit down and run water over my head.

As I arrange my things in the closet, I'm in denial about where I am. A drug and alcohol detox center. A place for people whose lives have fallen apart. Tossing some socks in a drawer, I glance up to see a small piece of paper posted neatly on the wall by my bed.

SERENITY PRAYER

God, grant me the serenity
To accept the things I cannot change;
Courage to change the things I can;
And wisdom to know the difference.

I wonder how many other lost souls have been in this room and read these words? How many made it back to health and reclaimed some semblance of a life? What were they recovering from? What was their fate? What is mine? A shudder of fear and insecurity ripples through my body.

I lie on my bed and stare at the ceiling tiles, trying to get comfortable. After an hour or so, someone from the kitchen staff brings in a hospital lunch on a lap tray. It reminds me of airplane food. But I'm famished and devour every bite, wishing I had a stout beer to wash it down. Just as I finish, another nurse arrives. I'm so withdrawn I don't even listen to her introduce herself or catch her name. Like the staffer who confiscated my drugs, she's all business.

"Take these," she says, handing me some pills in a tiny paper cup and thrusting a glass of water at me.

They look just like my pills. "What are these?" I ask with surprise, especially after the scene with the box of medications when I arrived.

"They're your prescriptions," she answers as if I must be brain-dead.

"But, I…"

She quickly cuts me off. "The doctor will be here in the morning to evaluate you. You have to take your medications now. We cannot take you off them without the doctor's permission. You can ask him any questions you have when he sees you." Here I am finally ready to face this addiction and I'm ordered to take more drugs. I feel empty and powerless as I reach for the paper cup and toss the pills into my mouth.

"There is no wandering in the hallway at night," she says firmly, arms folded across her chest. "You are required to stay in your room. Good night."

She reminds me of sadistic Nurse Ratched, who, in the Academy Award–winning movie *One Flew Over the Cuckoo's Nest*, eventually forces Jack Nicholson to have a lobotomy for making trouble in her psych ward. I almost say, "Good night, Nurse Ratched," but think better of it as she waits impatiently to ensure I've swallowed all the pills. Then she departs with efficiency, clicking off the overhead fluorescent lights and closing the door with exaggerated authority. I'm left in the dark, alone. Ratched has nothing to worry about. I have no thoughts of escaping my room, especially not into the hallway. I don't want to be seen here, nor do I want to mix with the others in recovery. I just want to crawl in a hole and hide from the whole world.

I fumble through the dark, click on my bedside lamp, and try to read a new book by Scott Turow that's topping the bestseller list. A legal thriller about the shady spaces between ethics and the law. It's a diversion I would usually enjoy, but I can't stay with it.

The vicarious adventure no longer provides the escape I need. I slam the book shut, drop it on the floor, and close my eyes.

I was thirty-six years old—just entering the prime of my life—when I fell from a ledge in the Bahamas during a tropical storm. Now I'm fifty and feel like I'm eighty. I've gone from the life of my dreams, living freely and traveling the world, to the life of a drug junkie in a detox ward, imprisoned by choice within these four cinderblock walls. I've missed what should have been my best years and I'm ashamed to be alive. As I glance over to the wall and reread the "Serenity Prayer," I can't imagine accepting the things I can't change, much less finding serenity. All my strength and courage have drained away over the years. Whatever insight or wisdom I once might have possessed vanished long ago.

It's pitch black in my room once I turn off the reading lamp. As I stare toward the ceiling, little patterns of electric light dance in the darkness. I can hear my labored breath and feel the tightness in my throat. My heart continues to pound hard. My whole body aches. I'm not sure I can do this. I'm not sure at all.

"Time to get up!" The harsh overhead lights go on and the glare blinds me. I can't remember where I am.

"Please come into the hallway right now!"

Suddenly I remember, and it makes me shudder. The McDonald Center. Scripps Hospital. Cinderblock room. Detox.

What time is it? Who's dragging me out of bed? I don't know who's rushing me into the hall, or why. I'm less than half awake and barely manage to grab my cane.

Onto a chair now, almost falling as I plop down. Someone barking orders at me. I gaze bleary-eyed at the floor. I see the feet of other people in the hallway. I can feel their stares, but I'm ashamed to be here and don't look up. Something wrapped around my arm. Pumping. Something else stuck into my mouth. I'm ordered to say *Ahhh*. The lights, the prodding, the crisp commands all assaulting my senses. I'm finally coming to. It's very early in the morning and

I'm being integrated into the routine. Vital signs taken. Another cup of pills thrust into my face. Then suddenly being dismissed to make space for the next patient.

I limp back into my room like a sullen ogre, making eye contact with no one, still pretending not to be here. I turn on the shower. Get the water almost scalding. Curl up on the shower floor in a very stiff and partial fetal position, my feet pressed against the base of the toilet as the steamy water runs all over me. I can hear myself moaning out loud like a crazed beast.

Breakfast arrives shortly after I crawl back onto my bed. Just as I finish the last bite, there's a gentle knock on the door and my rehab doctor slips in to introduce himself. He looks like a young Sigmund Freud, with jet-black hair, a neatly trimmed goatee, and dark-rimmed glasses.

"Good morning, I'm Doctor Gasparo. Are you doing all right?" I'm surprised he isn't wearing the typical white scrubs with a stethoscope around his neck. Instead, he has on neatly pressed black slacks and a well-starched white dress shirt with no tie. He's the first person whose presence has made me feel comfortable since I checked in, and something about his manner makes me like him immediately.

"I'm doing as well as I can," I answer with a heavy sigh.

We go through my whole story, which I've condensed and explained so many times to countless medical specialists that it could be a sixty-second report on *NBC Nightly News*. Dr. Gasparo tells me he's the head psychiatrist for the detox ward and explains that every patient here is struggling with addiction. Most are alcoholics. Some are addicted to street drugs or pharmaceutical medications. Many are struggling with all three. My case is highly unusual, Dr. Gasparo says, given the complexities of cancer and a broken back.

"You've been on heavy medications for almost fourteen years," he says. "Getting off them won't be easy and, given your condition, you have a right to keep taking them and we can taper you off slowly over several months. This is a decision you need to make for yourself."

"I want off them now. They've deranged my mind and stolen my Soul. I don't care what happens. I'm done." I say this with conviction. Ask for his support.

"Are you sure you don't want to go slowly," he says, "reduce the dosages gradually, at least over a few weeks' time?"

"I want to stop now," I answer firmly.

"It's going to be tough," he gently replies. "Cold-turkey withdrawal is a nightmare and it can be dangerous. Are you sure you want to go this way?"

"I'm sure."

Dr. Gasparo agrees to support my decision, but warns that I'll be monitored closely, and if I have serious reactions I'll have to switch to tapering off. Then he writes a note in my file to have the medications stopped immediately. I expected to be scared to death to give up my pills, but it comes as a huge relief. "I'll be checking in on you every day I possibly can," he says, wrapping up our first meeting. "Otherwise, please let the nurses know if you have any problems."

He has a good bedside manner, but as he walks away, I hope it's something more than that. I feel like I might have an ally. That the doctor might really understand me. Be a source of support. I need it.

❁

Detox—Day One: Groggy. Weak. Fingers trembling. More unsteady on my feet than usual. The ward routine takes over. Early morning vitals (I continue to stare at the floor). Meals into the room like clockwork. Dr. Gasparo checks in. Lights out. For the first time since I can remember, heavy sleep.

Detox—Day Two: Morning vitals. Back to bed. Sleep until lunch arrives. Cafeteria staffer takes my untouched breakfast tray. Comes and leaves without saying a word. I fidget. Reorganize the closet. Try to shave. Too much trouble. Can't read. Feel hollow inside. Shaky. Asleep long before dinner.

Detox—Day Three: I feel like I have the flu. Nauseous. Feverish. Aching all over. All lights are piercing and painful. It sounds like the nurses outside my door are yelling. It kills my ears. I refuse to go out for vital signs. Lie in bed with a pillow over my head. Nurse Ratched comes in. Takes my temperature and checks my blood pressure. Lets me know what an inconvenience I am. I reciprocate, and then some. Meals arrive, their smells nauseating me. I leave them untouched.

Detox—Day Four: My mind and body feel disconnected. The back pain is scorching. My throat is on fire. Everything is hazy. I think Doctor Gasparo has been in the room. Can't be sure. Something about cold turkey and seven days. A warning that withdrawal might be tough. Sweating profusely. Too dizzy to walk. I tear off my pajamas. Crawl into the bathroom. Vomit uncontrollably for an eternity. Turn on a cold shower and curl up on the tile floor again. Like I'm a homeless drunk lying in the gutter of an empty street during a rainstorm.

Detox—Day Five: Stomach cramps. Diarrhea. Vomiting. Hot flashes. Cold flashes. My head is throbbing. Every noise in the hall sounds like a bomb exploding. I hate it when Ratched comes in to take my vitals. Stop bringing these foul-smelling meals. Turn out the damn lights. Go away. Let me sleep. God, grant me serenity. Some courage. The pain is completely consuming. Get out of my room!

Detox—Day Six: Deeper nausea. Cramps. Sweats. Chills. Anger. Fear. Delusion. I've lost all sense of time. And I've lost hope. I crawl on the floor in the darkness. Need to get to the bathroom to be sick again. I can't take this anymore. I bump up against my suitcase. Then I remember. I turn the suitcase on its side. Unzip it. Fumbling in the dark now for the full bottle of morphine pills I stashed in a side pocket. My backup plan.

To hell with this detox.
To hell with this whole place.
To hell with my life.

I stagger to the sink. Click on the nightlight. It sears into my eyes. I fill a glass of water. Pour the entire jar into my palm. Fifty tiny morphine pills. Enough to kill a horse. I glance at the mirror. There's the madman staring back at me again. *To hell with my life.* I lift my hand to stuff the pills into my mouth. Then stop as I hear a different voice in my head: *Get up, Daddy.*

I can't get up. *To hell with my life…What about Morgan?…Get up, Daddy.*

My hand shakes uncontrollably as I clutch the pills. The debate rages in my head. I stare at the monster in the mirror again. Suddenly my deepest inner voice stops me in my tracks: *What will life be like for Morgan, knowing his father was so weak and pathetic that he committed suicide?*

Staggering to the toilet now. Tossing all the pills in and flushing them down. Throwing up again. Turning on the shower. Curling up on the bathroom floor in convulsions.

Detox—Day Seven: No food for days. More diarrhea and dry heaves. Flashes of pain everywhere. My skin, my organs, my bones ache like hell. I'm sweating buckets. Cramps. More dry heaves. Uncontrollable. I start to crawl to the bathroom but collapse naked on the floor at the foot of my bed.

It's pitch black. Something moves in the corner of the ceiling. A swirl of electric energy. More swirls in the other ceiling corners. One morphs into a demon. Like a gargoyle. It flies at me. Claws at my throat. Other demons surge in from nowhere and join the attack. Screeching. Eyes blazing red. Teeth bared. Ripping at my flesh. Like Dante's *Inferno.*

My chest is pounding. A heart attack? Hot and cold flashes together again. Intense muscles spasms. Arms and legs writhing. I try to fight back. I want to scream for help but can't find my voice. I get sick. Vomit and diarrhea all over myself. The demons pierce my flesh. Rip at my organs. I try to fight back. Fend them off. It lasts for hours. I'm either dying or going completely mad.

Suddenly, just when I can't take it any longer, the demons dissolve. Everything goes black. I collapse into a coma-sleep on the cold linoleum floor in the middle of my cinderblock room.

CHAPTER 24

Lifeline

WARM COVERS. Soft sheets. A pillow under my head. It feels luxurious. I can see the morning light behind the lids of my closed eyes. I can hear someone breathing next to my bed. There's a hand gently touching mine. "Hello," I say to whoever is by my side.

"Hello, my friend." I recognize Father David's voice in an instant. "They tell me you've been sleeping for almost two days. I'm sure it was a rough time."

"You wouldn't believe it," I whisper as I crack my eyes open. "Demons tearing at my flesh."

"Well, you got through it," he says with a glowing smile. "I'm proud of you."

I can barely move. It takes all my energy to sit up in bed. Father David lets me know I'm going to be okay. I recount as much of the detox experience as I can recall. Even the moment I wanted to swallow the morphine stash and end it all.

"You had a dark night of the Soul," Father David observes.

"I think it was six or seven dark nights," I say with a heavy sigh.

During a pause in our conversation, Father David glances at the prayer taped on the wall and says, "That's beautiful, the 'Serenity Prayer.' "

"What's its origin?" I ask.

"It's the main prayer for members of Alcoholics Anonymous," he replies softly. "But it's for anyone who needs help from God when they're facing great life challenges."

We repeat it out loud a few times. It feels good. But I'm bothered by the AA thing. There's no doubt I drank like a champion over the past two decades, but I've never felt like an alcoholic. After what I've just been through, I have no craving for medications, beer, or wine. I can't imagine falling back into that hell. But the prayer is inspiring and makes even more sense to me than the day I checked in. I have to change what I can in my life. Accept what is beyond my control. Find serenity. Somehow.

My contemplation is broken when a server from the cafeteria knocks on the door and steps in with a lunch tray. "Would you like lunch today?" he asks shyly. I probably threw him out of the room a few times while I was curled up on the floor in convulsions. I can't imagine how I looked…or smelled. This time, I'm famished and the aroma of the food is heavenly. "Yes! Please! I'll take it right here on my lap!" I say all this with the first smile I think I've had for anyone who works here.

Father David watches while I attack the tray like a wild animal. As I swallow the final morsel of potato salad, Nurse Ratched comes in to lay down the law. "You'll have to come out of your room tomorrow morning. We will no longer take your vitals in here. There will be no more meals in bed. You will have to attend all meetings." She says all this without even a glance at Father David, like he doesn't exist.

"What are the meetings?" I ask as kindly as I can.

"They'll explain it all to you," she answers curtly and walks out, clicking the overhead light off out of habit.

She frustrates me. But it's clearly more about me than her. I'm sure everyone who works here has to find a balance between compassion and a firm hand. Nurse Ratched is probably the one who found me after my night with the demons, cleaned me up, and got me into bed. And the truth is, I need someone like her right now. Without her toughness I'd lie in bed for a month. I'm ready to accept a firm hand now, but I'd like it to be my own. Detoxing is only the beginning. I've got to get stabilized. Complete this program, whatever it is. Get back home to Morgan.

After offering me a prayer of his own, Father David says good-bye. I set my watch alarm and lie down to read. I don't even make it through a chapter before I'm sound asleep. I wake up briefly when the last dinner I'll be served in my room arrives. I'm starving again, but I take a pass. I'm too tired to sit up. Too tired to eat. I just want more sleep.

When my watch alarm goes off at 6 A.M. I'm tempted to pull the covers over my head and fight it out with the staff for another day of rest. *Get up, Daddy*. I can hear Morgan's sweet voice in my head. I miss him beyond belief. *Yes, time to start getting up*. I crawl out of bed, take a hot shower, and put on a clean pair of sweatpants and a T-shirt. As I finish dressing, I feel a small jolt of pain in my back. I remember I need my back brace. I pull the smaller elastic one from a drawer and strap it on tightly, grab my cane for support, open the door, and step out of my room.

I feel like I've been hibernating in a cave. It's a whole new world in the hallway. Nurses are scurrying about. People are lined up for vitals. The lights are scorching bright. Maybe half a dozen patients. This time I look at everyone and smile. It's the first time I've seen their faces. One or two return my smile. The others stare at the floor like I used to. I take my place in line. They're efficient here. I'm soon on the chair with a blood pressure monitor wrapped around my arm.

When the nurse finishes with me, she directs me down the hall to the cafeteria. As I amble toward breakfast, I pass five other rooms like mine, each with a nameplate on the door. Every plate has two names. I'm the only one with a room of my own. What a stroke of luck. At the cafeteria door, another jolt of pain stops me in my tracks. I forgot. I can't sit up to eat. I need my portable lounge.

"Excuse me," I say to a male staffer striding down the hall who looks vaguely familiar, "I have a broken back. I brought a portable lounge chair with me. I need it. I can't sit up to eat."

"I remember," he says. "It was too big and bulky, we had to put it in storage. Sorry." He walks off. Then I realize it. He's the one who confiscated my box of drugs the day I arrived.

I peek into the lunchroom. There are nine or ten patients sitting at tables with their breakfasts. A buffet on the right has an assortment of cereals, fruit, coffee, and juices. I glance to my left. A big, red couch. A godsend. I step over and roll myself onto it, still trying to figure out how I'm going to manage this.

"You look like you're in pain," says a young woman in pink flannel pajamas with thick, short cut blond hair and a perky smile. She gets up from her chair and kneels down by me. "Hi, my name is Sherry. I'm a nurse. Well, I was until I lost my job and ended up here. Anyway, can I bring you something to eat?"

I can't believe my luck. "Thanks, Sherry. My name is Brad. I have a bad back. It would be great if you brought me something. Anything. Just a lot of it, please. I haven't eaten much lately."

A few others stop by the couch to say hello as they finish their meals. Everyone seems soft. Humble. I feel the same way. We're all in the process of facing ourselves. It's painful, facing ourselves and putting our egos in their place.

"I'll take your tray," Sherry says just as I finish. "I don't mind doing this for you every meal. It makes me feel like I'm still a nurse."

"Thanks, Sherry," I say as I struggle up from the couch. "You're a gem."

Sherry is the only one here bubbling over with hope and enthusiasm. She's pregnant with her first child. Her boyfriend, the father, comes to visit her every day. She was hooked on Vicodin, but now she's over it. "I'm leaving detox in a few days to spend a month in the residential unit," she says with a wide smile. "Then I go back home and have my baby. I can't wait!"

"What residential unit?" I ask.

Sherry explains that we're all required to leave detox when the staff determines we're ready. They move us to a complex in a three-story brick building next door. We'll be assigned rooms that are like small efficiency apartments where we prepare our own meals, do our own laundry, become more self-sufficient. In another wing, there's a full schedule of counseling sessions and classes designed to help us build new lives. We'll be required to attend daily Alcoholics and Narcotics Anonymous meetings in the grand meeting room just across the courtyard from the detox ward. It's a minimum thirty-day stay.

I've been so out of it, I never knew any of this. No one ever explained the program to me. Or if they did, I have no recollection. I assumed I'd go through detox, rest for a few days, attend a few meetings with staff specialists to make sure I'm stabilized, and then head home. I never really thought it through.

"It's time for your first meeting," Sherry says brightly. "Sort of a taste of what's in store once you move to residential. It's right next door. The room has a couch you can lie on. Come on, I'll help you get there."

Sherry takes my free arm and guides me into the meeting room and over to the couch. I flop myself down on the brown cushions and drop my cane on the tan carpet. There are six or seven other patients already in the room as the counselor walks in. He sees me on the couch and says, "You're here for the first time, right?" He strides over, leans down, and shakes my hand. "Welcome. It's good to have you with us." Then he takes his place at the front of the room.

"My name is Don and I'm an alcoholic," he says with authority. "Hi Don," everyone but me chimes in. I'll soon learn this is the formal greeting in AA. "I was a successful businessman," Don continues with a smile, tugging at the lapels of his tan sport coat. "I had a beautiful wife and two great kids. But there was so much stress in my job that I started drinking at noon and didn't stop until I passed out in bed at midnight."

Don's smile disappears as he continues. "My family intervened many times. I'd sober up for a week, then get right back on the booze. Finally, my wife threatened to leave me, so I hid my drinking from everyone. I had bottles stashed everywhere: at work, at home, in the garage, in the trunk of my car. I'd sneak out, knock down a pint of vodka in a few gulps, fill my mouth with breath mints, and keep on going. Finally, I crashed. Literally. I crashed my car in the middle of the day, drunk as a skunk. It was my third DUI, and when I got out of jail my family was gone. The McDonald Center saved my life. It can save yours, too."

On this note, Don asks each of us to share our story. Sherry leans over and whispers to me, "We have to do this every time. It's part of the program."

The first person to speak up says, "Hi, I'm Tony and I'm a drug addict." Tony is a building contractor who started on painkillers after an injury on the job and got hooked. Next, a businessman named Michael tells us he's an alcoholic who needed a quart of scotch every day just to keep going. Steve is a sometime student in his twenties, addicted to cocaine and methamphetamine. He shares details of his suicide attempts. Sherry tells us she's thirty, pregnant, and was hooked on Vicodin. Judith is a forty-something housewife who mixed wine with Valium for too many years.

Each of their stories touches me to the core of my being. I can feel their pain, their anguish, and their fear of returning to addiction and empty lives. As much as I would like to think otherwise, I realize my story is no different from theirs, except for one thing: I don't miss the drugs or feel any compulsions. I'm never going back. When it's my turn to share, I say, "Hi, I'm Brad. I've got a broken back and cancer. I've taken too many medications and drank too much wine and beer. But I don't think I'm an alcoholic or drug addict." I'm met with glances of disbelief and guffaws of dismissal as a wave of embarrassment floods through me. After the meeting, I ask Don for a moment of his time and try to explain myself. He stops me mid-sentence.

"You're an addict, just like everyone else here," he says resolutely. "I've heard what you're saying too many times before from too many different people in denial. They always go out those doors and straight back to booze and drugs. You need to join AA, go to meetings every day for the rest of your life. Get with the program and stay with it, or you'll fall right back on your face." Before I can respond, Don pats me gently on the shoulder and heads down the hall.

There was great kindness in his firmness, but Don's words hit me like a punch in the stomach. Am I an addict for life? Incapable of going forward without daily meetings? Always on the brink of relapse? It's hard for me to believe. My whole body rejects the idea. I'm sure the residential program is wonderful and has a lot to offer, but I know it's not for me. It's more than believing I don't have lingering addictions. It doesn't fit my circumstances. I'm in great pain and barely mobile, can't sit for meetings, do laundry, or cook meals, much less hike up and down the stairs for the rest of the required activities. The problem is, it looks like I don't have any choice, and I know I'm nowhere near ready to try to go home.

"I just spoke with Don," a woman from the front desk walks up as I turn to leave the lounge and head for my room. "He told me how you're feeling. The residential program is a requirement of your stay here. We've been in touch with your wife, and she is adamant that you follow the program."

"Thank you," I answer, feeling powerless and realizing the futility of attempting a discussion. I'm sure they've all heard it innumerable times from too many people like me. I trudge back into my room with pain in my back, legs, and throat as stress grips my body. Lying on my bed, I ask myself if I'm in denial. If I shouldn't just give in and go with the program. I get the same answer. *I know I'm off drugs for good and I'm not addicted to alcohol.* I can't tell you how I know with such certainty, but I do. I also know I'm not going to move into the residential unit. It doesn't fit, and I'm not physically capable of handling the routine. I have no idea what to do next. It feels like I'm free-falling, and it grips me with fear.

When I return to the cafeteria for lunch, Sherry has everything ready on my tray. I can't figure out why she's so upbeat and bubbly. Everyone else here has their tail between their legs, including me. I thank her and lie on the couch again to eat, trying not to spill anything on my only clean T-shirt. I'm still famished, but the food doesn't taste as good and my stomach feels acidic. I know it's because I'm stressing about the residential thing.

Dr. Gasparo is waiting at my door when I head back down the hall. I lie on the bed as he pulls up a chair. Then I give him the whole story. Tell him I can't do the residential thing. Beg for an option.

"I've never had a case like yours," he says when I'm done. "I'm aware of the pressure for you to go into the residential program, but this is the first time I've felt it's not right for someone. Give me a few days and let me see what I can come up with."

"Thanks for listening," I say with a huge sigh of exasperation. When he leaves, I stare at the ceiling, wondering what I've gotten myself into.

It goes on like this for two more days. Vitals, meals, and meetings. Waiting for news from Dr. Gasparo. Wondering where I fit in. If anywhere. I'm obedient and avoid making waves. But it's frustrating. The pain is getting overwhelming without the drugs. And I still feel the residual effects of all that dope. I'm dazed. Blurry. Fuzzy. Like I'm wrapped in invisible gauze.

On the third morning, Sherry isn't there with my breakfast tray. I get myself a bowl of cereal. It's not so hard. I can handle this at least once or twice a day. As I'm finishing my meal on the couch, Judith comes over. She's the one with the Valium problem.

"We just heard about Sherry," she says with a teary face. "Her boyfriend was bringing her Vicodin every time he came here. The staff caught him slipping it to her in the parking lot. Sherry got angry and drove off with the guy, shouting that she's never coming back."

Now it makes sense. I remember how Vicodin gave me a false sense of optimism and joy. Sherry's upbeat demeanor was only the drugs talking. It's just like Don predicted. And now it's going to be even harder to argue my case. As I slog back into my room after the morning meeting, I feel like a hostage.

Every day I've been pressured by the staff to prepare for the residential program. Pamela remains adamant about it as well. She insists that a phone call with Morgan still isn't possible. It makes me furious. I'm starting to suspect there's more to all this than I understand, maybe a plan to keep me from returning home. But even though no one but me has legal power over my decisions, I lack the strength to argue and feel helpless. I'm weak. I'm humiliated. I'm stuck.

A knock at the door. Dr. Gasparo steps in and whispers with a grin, "I have good news."

I want to jump up and scream with joy before I even know what it is.

"A few months ago, the hospital opened what it calls the Pain Center across the way, in the McDonald complex, right next to the residential facility. I wanted to be sure they would take you before I mentioned it. It's not related at all to the detox program and it's very experimental. They use a blend of ancient Eastern healing modalities and modern holistic Western medicine to help patients cope with pain without using narcotic painkillers. They can't help you with cancer, but they think you are a perfect candidate for help with back pain, and so do I. Are you interested in trying it?"

I'm not sure I understand a thing he's saying, but I'm in scorching pain and need to do something, anything. "Yes. Immediately. Today. When can I start?"

"Not quite yet," he answers. "It might be a few more days. We still need to work some things out."

Dr. Gasparo explains that when a patient is in recovery, the center always seeks to consult closely with the family in determining any course of action. He'll need to convince the detox staff and work with Pamela, let her know he feels it's in my best interest. I sense it will be a power struggle, but I haven't signed away total control over my destiny, and there's no law to prevent me from doing this. This is a lifeline being handed to me. *I've surrendered enough. It's time to take a stand.*

"I've got to do this," I say to Dr. Gasparo. "I've got to. Get me in that program. Please. It's my only hope."

"I'll do everything I can," he promises as he pats my shoulder. "Everything I can."

I feel like a caged animal. I've packed all my belongings and no longer attend the mandatory meetings. I take my meals from the cafeteria to my room and eat on my bed in silence. I've removed my nameplate from the door and thrown it away. I read my novel and wait, wondering what the Pain Center might be like. Three days go by before I hear from Dr. Gasparo again. I almost bolt up in bed when he comes into my room. He tells me everyone has finally agreed, albeit grudgingly so. I can check into the Pain Center on Monday morning after the coming weekend.

"I can't spend another night here," I tell the doctor with desperation in my voice. "I'll go completely crazy. You'll have to put me in a straightjacket, admit me to a psycho ward, and give me a lobotomy."

He laughs and says, "We don't want that. Just a few more days, okay? We have to make sure the transition is smooth. Don't worry. There's a long waiting list for people to get into detox. They'll be glad to move you along. There's no residential unit for the Pain Center, however, so you're going to need to find a place to stay."

"Thank you for everything, doctor," I say, knowing there are no words for how much gratitude I feel toward this man. "Can you stay with me for a minute longer?"

He agrees. We walk to the front desk and I ask for my box of medications. The same staffer who confiscated the drugs is at the desk. When I ask for the meds I brought in with me, he glances at Dr. Gasparo and gets a nod of permission. Then he walks to the vault and retrieves the box of drugs. Still wary of me. Surveying the hall for danger. Like a horde of crazed patients might launch an attack. As I carry the drugs to my room, he follows me like a security guard even though Dr. Gasparo is by my side. I go into the tiny bathroom, open all the bottles, and dump the pills into the toilet. It takes a dozen flushes before the last handful swirls down the pipe and disappears.

CHAPTER 25

The Pain Center

A S I WALK OUT the entry doors of the detox ward, through the courtyard, and past the residential facility, I still look like a robot, hobbling along in my body brace and gripping my cane for support. Only, my gait is worse than ever. The pain in my back and legs is growing more intense as the residual effects of the drugs continue to wear off. I'm exhausted by the time I limp across the large foyer of the building housing the Pain Center and reach the elevator. My mind is as unsteady as my body. I'm nervous and unsure of myself. There are a few others waiting at the elevator bank. I realize I'm staring at the floor again. Hiding. Wondering if they're thinking *here's another addict who destroyed his life*. The ride to the third floor takes forever.

When I step out of the elevator into the entryway, it feels like a boutique university. The lobby is carpeted green with two long, padded sitting benches, upholstered with burgundy fabric, neatly secured against one wall. There's a wide reception counter with class schedules posted on a large corkboard. I'm filled with hope and scared to death at the same time. I don't know if I have the strength to do this. But I can't fail. I just can't. It's my only shot.

"Please have a seat," the receptionist says politely, standing behind the counter and looking very busy. "Someone will be with you shortly."

I lurch over stiffly and use my cane to support myself as I lie down on the padded bench.

"You cannot lie down in this area," the receptionist says firmly. "Please sit up."

"I'm sorry, I can't," I answer. "I've had a failed back surgery and it hurts too much." I've barely stepped in the door and I'm already breaking the rules. Not fitting in. Like the first day I entered the McDonald Center with my box of drugs.

"You still need to sit up, sir." She's adamant, but there's no way I can do it and get through the day.

"I'm sorry," I say again with a pleading tone this time. "I hurt too much, and if I sit up for a few minutes you might have to carry me out of here on a stretcher." I give her my best smile, but my attempt to be witty and charming falls flat.

"Then you can lie there and fill out these forms," she says with pique as she comes from behind the counter and hands me a clipboard. It's the typical paperwork. Medical history. An explanation of my current pain situation. Financial status. A release of my right to take legal action if I'm injured. There's also a form requiring me to promise not to touch any alcohol or drugs and consent to random blood and urine tests. *If you fail a test*, it warns, *you will be suspended from the program.*

It's not a suspension I'm worried about. I'm physically and emotionally weaker than I've ever been in my life. It's hard to pay attention or be enthusiastic with my nerve endings on fire. A bright light, harsh noise, or stern word continues to make my skin hurt. My emotions remain sensitive and easily wounded. It's still all too easy to get fed up or angry in an instant over trivial things. I have to contain myself or I'll say something sarcastic about the way the clipboard was delivered. I also feel confused and disoriented, which Dr. Gasparo warned me often happens after detox, especially with so many years of heavy medications. Their deranging effects tend to wear off in layers over weeks and months. Sometimes it takes years.

Pamela arrives in the lobby. This was part of the arrangement. She has to sign some of the papers and take care of the payments because I left her my checkbook and credit cards when I checked into detox. I can feel how much she still opposes this course of action, but we don't debate it. Once everything is arranged she wishes me luck and departs. It's like she's a thousand miles away. Who could blame her?

I try to sit up for a while in hopes of making the receptionist happy, but after a few minutes my back flares up and I have to lie down again. I don't remember ever feeling this frail, vulnerable, or frightened in my entire life, not even in a war zone. Closing my eyes now. Trembling all over with this uncertainty and self-doubt. *Get up, Daddy.* My son is all I have. I miss him with every breath I take. *Get up, Daddy.*

"Okay, Morgan," I hear myself saying out loud. I open my eyes to see the receptionist glancing at me as if I might do better in a mental ward. I close my eyes again and wait while my case is being reviewed.

Finally, a staff person arrives to present me with my schedule. It's going to be a big day.

9:00 A.M.	Counseling with Ms. Mason, room 306
10:00 A.M.	Assessment with Dr. Kozin, room 300
11:00 A.M.	Physical therapy, room 301
12:00 P.M.	Lunch break
1:00 P.M.	Biofeedback, room 312
2:00 P.M.	Jin Shin Jyutsu, room 309

9:00 A.M.

Clinic counselor Ms. Mason is short and thin, neatly dressed in a gray woolen business suit and burgundy silk blouse buttoned up to her neck. Her manner is formal. Distant. There's no couch in her office, so I slide into an overstuffed chair and spread my legs out, leaning back as far as I can to take the pressure off my back.

"Sit up, please," is the first thing Ms. Mason says, tapping one of her perfectly polished, black high heels against the leg of her chair. As I start to explain why this is difficult, she cuts me off and lets me know that she's the case manager for each patient. It's her job to make sure everyone knows what is expected of them and that proper procedures are observed. This includes sitting up and paying attention. Ms. Mason personifies "tough love" even more than Nurse Ratched.

"You need to follow the program and do what you are told. Be on time, wait in the patient lounge between your classes, and always be quiet and respectful."

I have never been good with authority figures, even when I was in perfect health. I'm starting to grit my teeth.

"We can test you for drugs and alcohol any time we choose," Ms. Mason reminds me dryly. "If you refuse these tests, you will be dismissed from the program."

Just as she starts to get under my skin, I remember that tough love is good for me right now. I have to find a way to shift my attitude. Not be so sensitive, judgmental, or easily irritated. I smile and nod yes to everything. Pay full attention. Do my best to sit up like a good boy. It's not easy. I'm lucky it's a short session. The second it's over I stumble to the patient lounge, cane in one hand, holding the wall with the other. *There's a couch.* I splay myself out on it, rules be damned.

A few minutes before my next meeting, two more patients come into the lounge. James is in his early twenties. He broke a hip and knee in a bad car accident. I can feel his pain as I watch him try to get comfortable on a metal chair, so I sit up to make room for him on the couch. Maria is middle-aged and has fibromyalgia, a condition associated with stress and anxiety. She suffers constant pain in her muscles and connective tissues. She has trouble holding still and can't bring herself to sit down. Her whole body trembles as she paces back and forth. They both tell me that they began treatments here when the center first opened three months ago.

"There are very few patients in the program," Maria says softly as she finally sits on the chair and nervously shakes one of her knees back and forth. "I don't understand why. It's been very helpful to me. I think maybe it's because the insurance companies don't want to pay for these treatments since this is not considered mainstream medicine."

James quickly agrees, saying his family has been paying his bills for the time he's been here. They've been appealing to his insurance carrier, but the claims have been denied and the family money is running out. Both James and Maria fear they might have to leave the program. It's clearly a lifeline for them, like it is for me. We understand each other without much explanation. Brothers and sisters in the tribe of the wounded.

10:00 A.M.

Dr. Kozin is casually dressed in dark slacks, a powder-blue dress shirt with the sleeves rolled up, and a loose, paisley necktie. He's in his mid sixties, with a full head of soft brown hair and a few too many pounds around the middle, like me. He's reviewing my file when I enter his office, and without glancing up says, "Why don't you lie down on the couch. I imagine sitting up is painful as hell."

What a relief to hear. "You're right, it's painful as hell," I tell him as I melt onto the sofa. "I'm not sure how I'm going to get through this."

"Let's just go slowly. First things first. Given your condition, with a damaged back and coming off narcotic medications, there are some new drugs you need to take. They are called Neurontin and Celebrex." I cringe as he says this. "Don't worry," he continues, "they are nonnarcotic and nonaddictive. They should help ease your pain and inflammation."

Dr. Kozin explains that Neurontin is an epilepsy drug. Celebrex an anti-inflammatory medication developed for arthritis. The combination is being experimented with as a treatment for severe pain and muscle spasms. "I feel like it's a step backwards, but if it helps manage this pain, I'll try it," I say as Dr. Kozin calls a nurse to bring a dosage. I swallow the pills and stuff the prescription in my shirt pocket.

"And one more thing," Dr. Kozin says as he leans toward me with an expression of compassion and kindness. "This is a pain center, and we believe we have a lot to offer in that regard, but we have no expertise in cancer and we don't treat cancer patients. You'll need to stay in touch with your oncologist about that."

"I understand. Thank you, doctor," I say as I reach out and shake his hand. *Cancer.* The odds are overwhelming that it's going to end my life. Maybe it's still in remission for now, after the surgery and radiation. Maybe not. If I develop new tumors or more black spots on my throat, it's game over. I'm not going to keep getting tubes stuck down my nostrils to find out.

Get up, Daddy, I think to myself. *Change those things that are within your power to change. Find some dignity and be an example to Morgan no matter what happens.* I grab my cane and amble back to the patient lounge to collapse onto the couch again.

11:00 A.M.

The Physical Therapy room is the largest facility in the center. There are a few treadmills, stationary bikes, and sets of weights, none of which I can possibly use. I already failed with gentler physical therapy machines long ago. This doesn't look promising. Against one wall is a large wooden frame holding a thick, firm pad. It looks like a giant bed, and as I roll myself onto it, it's the only thing here that doesn't intimidate me.

"Hello, I'm PJ, your physical therapist. You look like we need to start at the very beginning." PJ is in her early thirties, tall, lean, and fit as a professional athlete, with a strong jawbone and thick, shoulder-length blond hair. "Let's check your alignment. But first you need to take off your back brace."

PJ has me get up, remove my brace, and sit on a large, inflated rubber ball, stabilizing myself with my feet splayed wide on the floor. It's almost impossible for me to do this. I shake, flail side to side, and have to grab for the frame of the bed or I'll fall off the ball. When I finally get steady, she holds a plumb line behind my back. It's a small metal weight with a pointed tip that hangs down from a long string, creating a perfect vertical line that reveals how out of alignment my spine is.

"This isn't good," PJ says. "Your mid-spine, the thoracic, is curving far to the right, probably from your efforts to stay off your left leg since it was the left side of your vertebra that was broken."

PJ explains we have to work on my posture, plus strengthen my back, stomach, and leg muscles, all of which are soft as jelly from so many years of inactivity.

"Instead of using this plastic brace, which only makes your muscles atrophy more," she explains, "we want to build a brace of muscles around your lower back."

Sitting on the ball, PJ asks me to lift one foot from the floor, then the other. I can't manage this simple movement even while holding the bed frame, and PJ needs to steady and support me. As I struggle to do something so basic, it hits me again: *I have to take charge of my weak, broken body. Somehow get stronger than the pain. There's no other way I'm going to make it through this program, much less reclaim my life.*

Next, we go for a walk down the hall, leaving my brace and cane behind. I feel like a child surrendering his security blanket when I lean my cane against the wall. It's terrifying. The end of the hall is less than thirty yards away, but it looks like a mile to me. PJ has to assist me. She puts an arm around my waist. I reach around her back and hold her shoulder. I'm still dopey from detox and every step hurts, but I try to envision it as a journey of empowerment. *Get up, Daddy. Take charge of your body. Get up.*

At the halfway point, there's a stairwell on my right leading up to the next floor. It can't be more than a dozen stairs, but it looms like a mountain I'll never climb without my brace and cane. At this point, I'm panting and sweating. I can't make it any farther down the hall. We turn around and slowly head back to the therapy room. I lie down on the big padded bed, and PJ slips an ice pack beneath my sacrum. *In a few days*, I tell myself, *I'll walk past those stairs. Eventually I'll make it to the end of that hall without an assist from PJ. I have to keep going. One step at a time.*

1:00 P.M.
Lacking the energy to make it to the hospital cafeteria for food, I stay lying down in Physical Therapy with the ice pack through the lunch hour. Then it's time for Biofeedback. I have no idea what Biofeedback is, but it sounds scientific and intriguing. I leave the back brace off, per PJ's orders, but grab my cane. There's no way I could navigate without it. Fortunately, the room is right next door. *God, I'm sore.* The treatment room is dark, with just enough light to navigate my way to a large recliner that sits facing two computer screens. There are a few other machines next to the computers, with tubes and wires hanging down, like in the surgical theaters

where I had my spine and neck operations. As I lean back in the recliner to get comfortable, a technician steps in, introducing himself as Arthur.

"These will monitor your brain waves, body temperature, and heart rate," Arthur says as he gently places adhesive electrodes on my head, chest, back, and fingers. "You'll see the results as they happen on the computer screens, just like live television, only not quite as exciting."

Once I'm hooked up, Arthur shows me my baseline. The screens are black, with colored lines coursing across them in real time. A green line pulses up and down with my heartbeat. A blue line tracks my body temperature and flows fairly steadily. A white line on the second screen tracks my brain waves as they spike up and down like a seismograph, illustrating the busy pace of my thoughts.

Arthur places headphones over my ears, then he has me close my eyes and lean back even farther in the recliner as he leaves the room. A tape begins to play with soft music as a deep, pleasing male voice says, *You are relaxing in a plush and comforting elevator, slowly ascending past thick, puffy white clouds. The sky is brilliant blue. It's warm and clear.*

The soothing voice guides me on a journey in my plush elevator, floating above the Earth and into the heavens. I feel resistance at first, but soon notice my body relaxing to a level I've never experienced, not even when I was on drugs. It feels like physical tension is flooding out of me as my emotional anxiety starts melting away. I peek at the computer screens a few times as the instruments feed my responses back to me, illustrating this relaxation. I begin to realize something that never occurred to me before: *It's not just my physical body I have to heal, it's my thoughts and emotions as well.*

The biofeedback journey lasts half an hour, but seems like it's over in a flash as my elevator returns to Earth and Arthur reenters the room to say, "Okay, we're done for now."

"That was amazing," I say softly.

"Your response was amazing," Arthur replies. "Your blood pressure went down, your heart rate lowered, and your mind relaxed. It usually takes longer than this to get such a good response."

Whether he really means it or is just encouraging me, I grab hold of this rare praise. I need affirmation that I can do something right, that I have some power within me that I was unaware of, that I'm slowly heading toward some control over my life.

"Whose voice was that?" I ask Arthur. "It was mesmerizing."

"Dr. Emmett Miller. A founder of mind-body medicine in America," Arthur answers.

"Can you write that down for me?" My mind is as shaky as my body these days. My emotions are shipwrecked, and something was so healing about Dr. Miller's tape that I know I need more. Much more. I fold the slip of paper Arthur gives me and slip it into my pocket. Dr. Emmett Miller. *I have to find out about this man and his work. Explore mind-body medicine. Get fully involved with this process.*

2:00 P.M.
After Biofeedback I go to Jin Shin Jyutsu, which I can't come close to pronouncing. I'm so relaxed after listening to the guided visualization that it feels a little easier to walk, and I notice my breath is deeper and smoother as I enter the treatment room. Dawn is the practitioner. She's centered and serene, peaceful yet powerful, reminding me of the young man I met at my fiftieth birthday party who suggested I try Yoga.

"Jin Shin Jyutsu is an ancient healing science from before the time of Buddha," Dawn says softly. "It all but disappeared long ago, until a man named Master Jiro Murai rediscovered it in the early twentieth century."

Dawn explains that Master Murai healed himself of terminal illness through this science and subsequently became a great healer for others. Jin Shin Jyutsu is something like acupuncture, she continues, but without the needles. In the treatment, Dawn will hold certain points on my body where there are "energy locks" and, through the power of intention, send her own energy through these points. The more I'm able to relax and receive her energy, she adds, the more a natural balance is restored, allowing me to experience physical, mental, and spiritual harmony.

"We are shifting the attitudes that lie beneath your symptoms," Dawn says as she has me lie down on a massage table. "The very heart of this practice involves creating a life of simplicity, calmness, patience, and self-containment, plus connecting with your higher power."

The cynical foreign correspondent I used to be would have scoffed at this, but somehow it strikes a chord deep within me, especially after experiencing Dr. Miller's meditation. After so many years of pain, medications, and imbalance, the concept of seeking inner harmony suddenly seems logical and obvious, like something I should have realized long ago.

As Dawn places her hands on my head now, I feel a surge of energy enter my body. She asks me to breathe deeply and whispers that we will both be silent, no talking. After several minutes, she holds my right foot and gently presses her thumb into the arch. At the same time, she holds my left hand and presses her other thumb into my palm. Energy swirls within me. After twenty minutes she reverses the holds and I feel the energy flow in a new direction as I continue to breathe deeply, inwardly chanting to myself, *Get up, Daddy* the entire time. By the time we finish the session, I feel like I'm floating in an ocean of bliss. It astonishes me. All I've really done today is listen to a guided visualization and have someone lay hands on me to move energy around, and it seems like it's done more for me than fourteen years of Western medicine.

With Jin Shin Jyutsu and Biofeedback, I feel like I'm embarking on an inner journey as vast, mysterious, and exciting as the world I used to cover as a journalist. Maybe somewhere deep inside me there's something waiting to be discovered. I'm not sure what it is, but I sense this might be the most important journey of my life and, even though this is my first day at the Pain Center, I have a surprising degree of faith in this process. Despite the odds, I think, I just might have a chance to beat some of the back pain, find a level of dignity, and reclaim a semblance of my life. The cancer is something else, and I can't even think about it right now. *One thing at a time*, I tell myself, *it doesn't matter how much time you have left. Just let go of all your cynicism and embrace what's happening. Relax, take it slowly, let it all unfold.*

CHAPTER 26

Body, Mind, and Soul

I AM STRONG, *healthy, calm, and relaxed.*

It's mid-February 2000, and I'm living at a Marriott Hotel in La Jolla, less than a mile from the Pain Center. I moved here three weeks ago after checking out of detox and am attending classes at the Pain Center full-time.

I consciously choose to let everything else go at this moment in time, and I give myself permission to relax.

The Marriott is twelve stories tall and, because I'll be here for a prolonged stay, the hotel has given me a discounted rate on a spacious suite on the penultimate floor with panoramic views of La Jolla.

There's no place I have to go right now, nothing I have to do, no problem I have to solve...therefore, this is a safe place and I can relax.

I have a dining room that opens onto a living room, a separate bedroom and bath, plus a small kitchenette and office area. It's an incredible luxury, especially after the tough days in my detox room, and reminds me how fortunate I was during my career with NBC to have most of my expenses covered so I could deposit my paychecks into a savings account.

I am allowing relaxation to heal me at every level.

Shortly after my first Biofeedback session, I asked Sandra, the evening concierge here at the Marriott, to order Dr. Emmett Miller's book *Deep Healing: The Essence of Mind/Body Medicine.* It arrived the next day, and I've already read through it twice. I'm lying on the living room floor right now, my eyes closed, silently repeating affirmations from the book.

As I reawaken, I come back feeling relaxed, refreshed, and alert. My body feels invigorated, my mind is clear, and my emotions are calm.

The introduction to the book tells me that Dr. Miller is an African-American who grew up in Harlem in the 1950s. He dealt with the pain of racism through academic achievement. He became a mathematician, scientist, and, ultimately, a surgeon, graduating from the Albert Einstein College of Medicine. But he soon became disillusioned with Western medicine, feeling it lacked compassion and was too quick to implement invasive procedures, especially surgery. Instead, Dr. Miller began to focus on the power of the mind to facilitate healing. As a result, he put down his scalpel and developed *Deep Healing*, which proved to be a revolutionary, holistic program of mind-body medicine. It's a synthesis of East and West, a journey into self-discovery, and a pathway toward self-healing.

The book explains that Western medicine views the human body as composed of systems and parts, such as our various muscles and organs, the skeletal structure, the cardiovascular, neurological, and endocrine systems. Specialists come to great understandings about these parts and systems, but rarely see them as a whole. Eastern medicine takes an opposite view, focusing on the interrelationship between all aspects of a human being, including the body, mind, and Soul, which is why it's called holistic medicine.

While reading *Deep Healing* I've jotted down pages of notes on affirmations, awakening the inner healer, true relaxation, opening the heart, self-acceptance, and faith. This is a complete shift from who I've been. I never thought mental attitude could impact physical feeling, and probably would have rejected the idea had I not experienced it in Biofeedback. Now I'm starting to understand that my fear, anger, and negative thoughts have been like a poison inside of me, making me worse while also alienating everyone around me. As Dr. Miller explains it, our thoughts create an inner chemistry, and dramatic biochemical changes can be achieved based on the thoughts and images we hold in our minds. In other words, we are creating our own experiences of the world, not just in our heads but in our neurochemistry as well.

Chapter Three of *Deep Healing* hit me right between the eyes. The title is "Taking Responsibility for Your Own Health." It delves into the healing powers of profound relaxation, reducing stress by letting go, getting in touch with the deeper Self, and taking charge of my own healing. In a section subtitled "The Holy State of Victimhood," Dr. Miller explains how easy it is to hide behind being the victim, blame others for our plight, and avoid all responsibility. This describes me perfectly, and I flush with embarrassment every time I read it. This is what I've been doing for years: hiding behind the tragedy of my story, lashing out and blaming others, blaming the world, cursing my fate. Dr. Miller writes, "The victim role is one of the greatest weapons we have against real healing." He's right. It's what Morgan felt without really understanding it. *Get up, Daddy* was a plea for me to take charge of my life.

During the Internet research I did on cancer, I discovered an article that maintains almost everyone has cancer cells inside of them, but most are recognized and dealt with by our immune systems. It's when we're stressed, imbalanced, and making poor lifestyle choices that they have a greater chance of taking hold. It's the same with chronic pain. The more you stress over it, the worse it gets. Again, I can't think of a better example than myself. It's clear that if I'm going to deal with my physical pain, and if I have the slightest chance of beating cancer, I have to radically rearrange my mind. I have to let go of self-centeredness, get past my ego, no longer play the victim. Ever since I lost my career I've been waging an inner war. Now I have to figure out how to wage inner peace.

I've also ordered some of Dr. Miller's audiotapes and take guided journeys into healing as I listen to his intelligent and soothing voice. It's an amazing new world to me. Not the vicarious living of the cheap novels I used to read for escape. I'm now on my own adventure. It's an authentic journey of the body, mind, and Soul—one I'm taking myself. I've never been able to relax and let go like this, and I already feel like I'm starting to live again, or, maybe, beginning to live for the first time on a very new level. *I'm totally committed. I have to give this everything I can muster. This is my only chance to get up and be a worthwhile human being.*

The new drugs from Dr. Kozin help ease my back pain a bit, but they make my eyes blurry. Things go out of focus. Spatial relationships shift, with objects appearing closer than they really are and then suddenly appearing to be farther away. As a result, I feel unsteady and look a little drunk when I walk. Given this reaction, I couldn't drive my car even if I had it here with me, so I've hired a service to shuttle me to and from the Pain Center. The black sedan looks like the one that picked me up at the airport years ago and took me to Manhattan for my interview with NBC. It's another reminder of how far I've fallen.

Snap out of it, I tell myself. *Okay, you've fallen, but you're "getting up" like Morgan begged you to. Cut the self-pity. Don't worry about the past. It's over. Move forward. Be strong. Wage inner peace.* When I give myself pep talks like this I realize that, even though three weeks is a short time, I'm getting somewhere. It's working. I can even feel a different inner chemistry that is soothing, the complete opposite to my usual state of agitation. It's a challenge, but I no longer take my brace or cane to the center. Even with an aching back, I can now walk the full length of the hallway without any assistance from my physical therapist, although I still feel intimidated every time I pass the stairwell and glance at the incline.

PJ has worked me hard in our Physical Therapy sessions, and I've mastered balancing on the ball and can hold alternate arm-leg balances for twenty seconds. This requires being on my hands and knees while maintaining a straight spine, then reaching one arm forward and the opposite leg backward, sort of like a hunting dog pointing at a bird hiding in the brush. It's an extremely challenging balancing posture designed to strengthen the core muscles around my lower back. The first few times I tried it I immediately collapsed. It still takes all the strength I have, and I'm sweating profusely within a few breaths, but I get through it by silently chanting, *I am strong, healthy, calm, and relaxed,* and I feel more empowered every time I hold it a little bit longer. It's a mental game as well as physical, and there's no doubt in my mind that I couldn't do any of this without the body and mind relaxation and centering I'm learning through *Deep Healing*.

This morning at Physical Therapy, as I gaze up while icing my tender back after a rigorous session, I glance at a large poster I've never noticed before on the wall. It's a photo of a lean, strong, and vibrant woman on a jetty of large boulders at the beach. She's on top of the highest rock, balancing on her tailbone with her arms and legs extended into the air, making her body resemble a perfect V. The poster simply says, "YOGA." I'm incredulous. *How can she do that?*

"Is that a cruel joke?" I ask PJ with a friendly grimace. "Something to remind me of my inadequacies?"

"It's to inspire you," she replies with a chuckle.

"It'll never happen!" I laugh aloud.

When our session is over, I look at the Yoga poster again. How could anyone have that much strength and balance? Then I walk over to the window and gaze two floors below me to the courtyard between the Pain Center building and the McDonald detox center. I recognize a few of the people who are waiting for the evening Alcoholics and Narcotics Anonymous meeting. I know these meetings are powerful and have helped many lost souls reclaim their lives. I slipped into one last week while waiting for my driver to arrive and take me back to the hotel. A young man on the podium was sharing his challenges with the audience, exclaiming, "My mind is a dangerous neighborhood none of you ever want to be caught in."

My mind was that way not too long ago, even more like a war zone than a bad neighborhood, and I can feel the anguish in the minds of my friends down in the courtyard as they light cigarettes, sip coffee from Styrofoam cups, and stare at the ground. I lift my gaze up to the majestic maple trees surrounding them. A few thrushes, starlings, and sparrows are dancing through the blue sky. I want to call down to my friends and have them open their eyes and look up to see the beauty of life all around them, but I know we're in different worlds. I take a deep breath and whisper to myself, "I am getting up…I am."

＊

Each evening after dinner in my hotel suite, I practice deep breathing, a few alternate arm-leg balances, then lie on the living room floor, reading *Deep Healing* and listening to Dr. Miller's audiotapes. When I'm completely relaxed, I contemplate my higher power. *Exactly what is it? How do I connect at a deeper level? Harmonize body, mind, and Soul like Dr. Miller advocates and Dawn teaches me in Jin Shin Jyutsu?*

But tonight, after a long day, I feel the full force of back pain re-turning. It's the first time since checking into the detox ward that this prelude to a major episode has gripped me. I know it too well. It begins with the ice pick sensation, like I'm being stabbed in the tailbone. Then a fire rages in my back. My muscles fill with tension and begin to spasm. Sciatica runs down the backs of my arms and legs. These episodes always shut me down for at least two or three days, sometimes a week or more. I'm gripped with fear. *Is all my progress just a farce? Is this going to knock me out of the Pain Center?* I have just crawled out of the abyss, and now I wonder, *Am I going to fall back in?*

Instinct and habit kick in. *I need some pills. Must gobble morphine, Vicodin, and Valium. Oh God, I flushed those!* I remember the Celebrex and Neurontin by my bedside and start to go for them. Then I pause. Deep inside of me I hear Dawn talking about physical, mental, and spiritual harmony. And Dr. Miller's words are bubbling into my mind as well, urging me to be strong, healthy, calm, and relaxed. As I stare at the prescription bottles, contemplating swallowing a double or triple dose, an inner voice says *Don't do it. Take responsibility for your own health. Allow relaxation to heal you at every level.*

The flare-up continues to grip me all over, but I don't resist. "I have you," I tell the pain out loud. "You don't have me." I lie down on the living room floor and try to relax into it. *Oh, Higher Power, Dear God, whoever, whatever you are, guide me through this.* Holding my hands together in a Jin Shin Jyutsu position designed to move energy in the lower back, I breathe as deeply as I can, consciously ac-cepting the torment, surrendering to it, even thanking it for all it has taught me. *I am strong, healthy, calm, and relaxed.* There are moments I want to scream and writhe in pain, but I keep completely still. Breathing, relaxing, accepting, releasing, surrendering. *Wage inner peace. It's now or never, this is the test.*

Thirty minutes later, a slow shift. The sciatica and muscle spasms start to subside. *I have you, you don't have me.* I breathe deeper. Focus more intently. Surrender further. Another thirty minutes. I can feel pain leaving my arms and legs. *Thank you for the lesson, pain.* Thirty more minutes and it leaves my hips. *I'm strong, healthy, calm, and relaxed.* My back is still on fire. I stay with it. *My body, emotions, mind, and Soul are all at peace.* Visualizing the ice pick slowly being removed from my tailbone. And then I picture Morgan. *Get up, Daddy.* Another thirty minutes. *Breathe, accept, release.* Maybe an hour goes by. *Get up, Daddy.* Suddenly, I feel deeply relieved. Light. Airy. Still, it takes a while to realize it: All the pain is gone.

I can hardly believe it. In less than three hours, I've ended a pain episode that in the past would have immobilized me for days. The best news is that I haven't had to rely on any drugs. *Maybe I don't have to look inside of a pill jar any more to find relief. I can look inside myself instead.* I stay on the floor a while longer, just to make sure this is real, then get up carefully, find the Celebrex and Neurontin, and toss them in the trash.

CHAPTER 27

The Visits

"HI MORGAN, it's Daddy."

"Hi, Daddy."

"Daddy loves you, honey."

"I love you, Daddy."

I call Morgan a few times a week to remind him how much I love and miss him. My heart aches like crazy, and hot tears stream down my cheeks every time I hear his precious little voice. He's only two-and-a-half years old, so I'm not sure he understands why I'm not home drawing sailboats on his back, playing little games, and holding him on my lap.

"I miss you. I'll be home as soon as I can. You take care of Mommy, okay?"

"Okay, Daddy."

I'd call every morning and night, but it would probably just confuse him and surely drive his mother crazy.

Each time Morgan hands the phone back to Pamela, I ask for a visit. Just me and Morgan. I need to spend a day with him now and then, get reconnected, and let him know how much his daddy cares about him. Pamela always answers, "Maybe next week. We'll see." I sense that she's retaining control because she still opposes my choice of the Pain Center and wants me in the rehab unit. Part of me wants to lash out at her, recount the demons in the detox ward, the continued episodes of pain, how I've been working so hard to heal myself. I have to remind myself to stay calm and relaxed, to wage inner peace, change the things I can, just accept the rest.

Then it dawns on me one evening after we hang up and my frustration begins to subside: *What about her years of suffering? The thrilling promise of a global life replaced with becoming the caretaker of an invalid? My energy, bravado, and boundless curiosity replaced by darkness, depression, and bitter outbursts?* If I had been in her position, would I have stayed, or would I have cut and run long ago? I'm not sure I want to know the answer.

Finally, after a lot of begging and a little badgering, Pamela agrees to a visit, but it won't be time alone with Morgan. My other family members will be there, too, and it will be only an hour or two. No one will come to my room. Instead, we'll meet down the hall in a reception area. I grit my teeth at all this but quietly acquiesce.

It's wonderful to see my family when they arrive on a Sunday afternoon. I hug my mother and sisters, apologizing again for the hurt I've caused, and softly kiss Pamela on the cheek. She's tense, and I sense that the kiss makes her uncomfortable. Then my whole being comes alive when I turn to Morgan. I lift him up and hug him closely, fighting tears as I whisper, "I love you so much," over and over into his ear. But because I have to give my attention to everyone, Morgan and I just can't connect on the level I need.

The reunion soon starts to feel stiff and formal. I'm embarrassed about having been in detox. Visions of the intervention flash in my mind and I start to feel nervous and unsure of myself. We are all uncertain and nervous, staying on the outer edges and keeping the conversation very light. Worse, it seems like it's over before it's begun. It isn't nearly enough. I need time with my son. Real time. Just the two of us. Bonding. Reconnecting. Affirming the fact that his father is completely devoted to him and always will be.

✽

During my calls home, I continue to negotiate with Pamela for a visit from Morgan that we can have all to ourselves. It feels outrageous that I have to beg to see my child, but I swallow the anger. *Wage inner peace.* I don't want to blow it. Being with him is worth the wound to my pride. Two more weeks go by like this, and it's making me crazy. It's all I can do to stay focused on making progress at the Pain Center. Finally, just when I'm about to crack, a breakthrough: Pamela agrees to bring him to my hotel for a half day this Saturday.

When Saturday finally arrives, I'm up early and doing my new morning routine of deep breathing, relaxation, and visualization that I've designed from practices in the *Deep Healing* book that Dr. Miller calls "Experiential Workouts." This time, instead of *I am strong, healthy, calm, and relaxed*, my chant all through my morning practice is *Morgan, Morgan, Morgan.* I'm waiting at the door when I hear the knock. Pulling the door open, I see a boy who seems even bigger now, standing beside his mother with a huge smile on his face as he clutches a little stuffed animal under one arm. I lift Morgan up and hold him tightly to my heart. He wraps his free arm around my neck and nuzzles his cheek into mine.

"Hello, big boy!"

"Daddy!"

"I love you so much, Morgan!"

"I love you, Daddy!"

Pamela is polite and kind, but a wall is clearly there, and it feels to me like it's getting thicker. She lets me know I have three hours with Morgan and tells me the precise time she'll return to take him home. I'll need to have him ready and waiting in the lobby. These are her conditions, which she made clear when we arranged this, and that is that. I have to suppress the urge to remind her that he's my son, too, as I smile and say, "Sure, of course. Thank you." This is hard work for me, always trying to choose humility and kindness.

It's a relief to close the door. Morgan and I hug some more. Roll around on the floor. Catch up on his life. He gives me the latest news on the status of his favorite toys, including a Thomas the Train engine and the new stuffed bear from his grandma, named Fuzzy, that he's still clutching. Our cat, Max, is doing great, Morgan says, but he meows for me now and then. There was a butterfly in the front yard yesterday. It almost landed on his finger. Now they're friends for life. Whenever we're alone together he opens up like this. I could talk and play with him for days on end.

As he continues sharing, Morgan is staring softly at me, touching my face and hair, getting reacquainted. I find myself doing the same thing to him. We have so much to discuss, but it's in the silent moments between our words that we find the deepest connection. When it's my turn to be the reporter, I take him on a tour of all the nooks and crannies of my suite, show him the view from the balcony, and how I can almost see Coronado in the distance.

"When the sun rises, its golden light streams right through this window," I tell him. "Your name means *great shining light by the sea*, and 'Morgan' also means *morning*. So the sunrise makes me feel like you're shining down on me with lots of love. When you see the sun tomorrow morning, I'll be sending my love to you in that light, too, okay?"

Morgan likes this idea. He smiles, hugs me, and says, "Okay, Daddy, we'll send love through the sun." I'm amazed at how much he's talking and it feels like I've missed ten years of his life.

Then we embark on an adventure throughout the hotel, ending up at the downstairs spa. I put on swim trunks I bought in the hotel gift shop. He wears his little pull-ups. We quickly immerse ourselves into a large Jacuzzi. With the support of the warm water, I can swing him around, ride him on my back like I'm a sea monster, and lift him into the air. It's pure joy. We play until the last minute possible then hurry back upstairs to change and meet Pamela at the appointed time.

"Daddy, will you draw on my back?"

"Of course, sweetheart." I've been dreaming of this moment. I even packed the magic drawing stick when I went to the detox ward and have kept it by my bedside like a talisman. "What should we draw?" I ask, although I know the answer.

"A sailboat, Daddy. Please draw a sailboat."

Tears fill my eyes as we take our adventure on the high seas with our sails full and the sun shining down. The way Morgan hugs my knees, I sense he could stay on my lap forever, but soon the front desk rings to say Pamela is waiting in the lobby. I savor every final moment: Gathering his things. Holding his hand in the elevator. Lifting him into my arms to walk through the lobby.

Morgan seems to make the transition with ease. But for me, saying good-bye is almost impossible. "When can I see him again?" I whisper to Pamela after I set him down. "We'll talk," is all she says in reply. My heart aches as I watch my son exit the hotel with Fuzzy tucked under one of his chubby little arms.

It must be three in the morning when a coughing fit wakes me. The skin has split open in my throat. Blood is trickling into my mouth. I instinctively reach for my neck and feel around for lumps, scared to death I'll find a new one. I'd almost forgotten about the cancer. As I get up and spit the blood into the bathroom sink, a jolt of panic hits me. *How am I going to pull this off? Even if I stabilize my back, am I doomed to succumbing to this disease? Am I still in remission or is it spreading? Will I ever get back home, even for a short time?*

A few deep breaths now. Relaxing. Letting it pass. Okay. This, too, I realize, must be given up to the unknown. It's a conundrum: As I seek to take charge of my life, I have to simultaneously let go of trying to control the outcome. I'll do everything I can to get up, change the things I can, but my fate is in the hands of some higher power. I open my mouth wide and stare into the bathroom mirror. My throat is red, raw, and bloody. *God, grant me serenity.*

Before going back to sleep, I find hotel stationery and write a letter.

Dear Morgan,

If you are reading this, it means I didn't make it. I tried to get up, just like you asked me to. Really, I tried as hard as I could. Sometimes things just don't work out the way we plan.

Please never forget how much I love you. I loved you from the moment you were born and I have loved you every moment since.

Always do your best. Believe in yourself. I know you'll do great things.

One more thing. Every time you see a ray of morning sunshine, remember me, okay?

Love, Daddy

I fold the note into a hotel envelope, label it with Morgan's name, and write on the bottom: *Do not open until Daddy is gone.* I slip it in the side pouch of my suitcase and zip it closed.

YOGA

CHAPTER 28

Stretching the Limits

EACH TREATMENT ROOM at the Pain Center has its own personality. Physical Therapy is high energy, bubbling with friendly talk and pop music playing in the background. Biofeedback is the exact opposite: quiet, clinical, and dignified, like a scientific laboratory of mind-body exploration. Jin Shin Jyutsu reminds me of a meditation room, with peace, stillness, and healing energy permeating the atmosphere. The counselor's office makes me feel the way I felt as a child when I walked past the vice principal's office at school a few minutes late for class, terrified of being caught.

But there's another room, one I haven't even been inside, that intrigues me. It's the Yoga room. Right now, standing outside its closed door, I hear soft, exotic music playing. There's a faint aroma wafting into the hallway that reminds me of scented candles. A female voice is murmuring so softly I can't quite make out what she's saying, but it sounds soothing. In the more than six weeks I've been at the Pain Center, I've only had a few glimpses of the room, whenever the door is ajar during my exercise walks down the hallway. It's mysterious, even a little foreboding. Normally, I'm hard to intrigue. Suspicious. Jaded. Cynical. Yet for some unknown reason, I want to know what goes on in this room, and why I haven't been given the chance to experience it.

Yoga was making a wave through America when I was coming of age in the 1960s. It sounded silly to me and seemed like a waste of time, so I took a pass whenever someone invited me to try it. I wanted to climb mountains and canoe down wild rivers, not sit down and try to hold still or twist myself into a pretzel. But I can't climb mountains or canoe down wild rivers anymore. Yoga might even require too much exertion for me now. After seeing the poster in the Physical Therapy room of the woman doing the impossible V pose on the rocks, I'm not sure I belong in a Yoga room at all. Still, I can't get it out of my mind and want to ask if Yoga can be added to my schedule, just to see what it's all about.

"I see you're curious." Counselor Mason startles me as she walks up behind me in the hallway. "Well, today's your big chance. The staff thinks you're ready for Yoga." I'm beginning to wonder if everyone here can read my mind. "You start this afternoon at three o'clock," she continues dryly, then adds with her usual sarcasm, "but Yoga is not for everyone, and it's certainly not the greatest thing in the whole world, like some people around here think it is."

This isn't the first time Ms. Mason has tried to dampen my enthusiasm. Her negativity must be a burden. I feel sorry for her, but it dawns on me that I just can't be around her any longer. I don't want to absorb her pessimism. Dr. Miller talks about this at length in his book. Negative thoughts lead to negative results; positive thoughts lead to positive results. I excuse myself by telling Ms. Mason I don't need a counseling session this morning and am going to do a few exercises in Physical Therapy. After that, I go through the paces in my other classes, but the afternoon Yoga session is all I can think about. I have a strange sense I'll be entering more uncharted territory where something momentous might unfold. There's no logic or reason for this. It even sounds absurd to me. But there it is.

A few minutes before 3:00, I return to the door of the Yoga room, lean toward it, and listen. It's silent inside. No one answers my timid knock. I softly turn the door handle. It's unlocked. As I open the door, I see a pile of thick, wool blankets on the floor near a low, wooden table with a few candles on it. There is a small stack of light-blue rubber blocks near the wall, and some straps like the ones I've seen in the Physical Therapy room. The harsh fluorescent lights are off and the room is bathed in soft, natural sunlight. The windows are open, and a warm, gentle breeze carrying the scent of spring blossoms is flowing through the air. There's nothing remarkable about it, but the atmosphere of the room envelops me. I feel a palpable sense of healing energy surrounding me. *This is it*, my heart says with conviction. As usual, the rational mind of my inner journalist resists, but my heart calls out again, *This is it!*

The instructor floats in from nowhere and offers me a wide smile. "Welcome to Yoga," she says with a thick eastern European accent. "My name is Savita." Like Dawn in Jin Shin Jyutsu, Savita is earthy, relaxed, centered. I immediately feel a deep sense of trust and kinship, like our distant ancestors were once in the same tribe.

"I've reviewed your chart, and I'm sorry you have had to live with so much pain," Savita says softly, still smiling as she gently lays a few blankets out near a wall. "We will begin very slowly and stick to basics. Have you ever done Yoga before?"

"No, never," I say slowly, feeling calm and grounded in her presence. "But I'll give it my best try."

"Wonderful. But the less you try, the further you'll get," Savita says cryptically.

"That's good to know," I answer. "I've always been stiff, inflexible, and tight. More than ever since I injured my back fourteen years ago. And I'm weak and sore, especially since the drugs are still wearing off."

I feel out of body now, watching myself confess to her: "Savita, I have to tell you that the minute I stepped inside the door something happened to me. I felt like I was right where I am meant to be. I don't know what Yoga involves, Savita, but somehow I believe it's exactly what I need."

"It may well be," Savita says with another smile, as if to confirm I'm not crazy. "We'll start by having you lie down and put your legs up the wall."

The old me would immediately want to know why we are doing this so I could analyze and judge its value. Now, I'm surprised how eager I am to do whatever I'm told without question. As always, it takes me time to get myself onto the floor, and it's a chore to maneuver myself where Savita wants me to be. Once I've accomplished this, she has me sit down with my outstretched legs parallel to the wall and scoot my hips about eight inches away from the baseboard. Demonstrating as she speaks, she asks if I can bend my knees, hold onto them, slowly roll onto my back, pivot my hips around, and swing my legs up against the wall. I give it my best effort, but my stiffness and soreness freeze me in my tracks.

"Impossible," I grunt, looking at her with an apologetic smile. "It's okay," Savita says serenely, the indelible smile still on her face. "Don't worry. I'll help you." She brings her legs down and floats up to standing. Then she gently grasps my ankles, deftly swings me around, and lifts my legs up against the wall. Her gentle authority is impressive and, to my surprise, it's completely painless.

"Relax your arms down by your sides with your palms turned face up," she says as I lie here on my back with my legs up the wall. My hamstrings are so tight my knees stay bent and feel locked up. My body is trembling with nervousness, afraid of triggering pain. "Now your legs, relax them…your belly and chest, relaxed…your back…your neck, your head, relaxed…all the muscles on your face, relaxed." As Savita leads me into relaxing my body, much like a Dr. Miller visualization, I realize I'm tensing everywhere and can't seem to let it go.

"This tension you have is the face of pain," Savita whispers. "Just do your best to release it wherever you find it."

Once I relax as much as I can into the posture, Savita teaches me three-part Yogic breathing. First, she has me place my hands over my abdomen and breathe into my belly, filling it like a balloon. After several rounds of this, she urges me to deepen the practice and inhale into my belly and then into my ribs, feeling my side-body expanding. Finally, she has me do the full technique, lifting the third part of my inhalation up into my chest so I feel my collarbone and shoulders opening.

"This is a very healing breath," Savita says. "It is a form of what is called *Pranayama* in Yoga. This means enhancing and balancing your inner energy, or life force, through certain breathing practices. This three-part breath enhances relaxation, oxygenates your blood, and promotes tissue repair." This is just what I need to hear. It's a science.

Even though I was intrigued about Yoga, my rational mind needs this kind of information.

Still, it's a challenge. My stomach muscles remain weak despite Physical Therapy and it takes a surprising amount of effort and abdominal strength to breathe this way. But as I continue, a feeling of euphoria slowly engulfs me and the deep breathing becomes easier. There's a sense of expansion and spaciousness with every inhalation. Every exhalation is an emotional release, like I'm unlocking a file deep in my subconscious where I've been stuffing all my hurts. Soon, I begin to notice a pleasant tingling throughout my body that I've never experienced, except when I was taking drugs.

"Keep breathing deeply," Savita encourages me. "Always through your nose. Listen to its whisper, be aware of its texture and temperature." Whenever my mind wanders, my breath gets short again. When Savita brings my attention back to my breath, my mind becomes calmer and more focused and my breath expands even deeper.

"Relax your jaw." I had no idea it was clenched until Savita softly touches my jawbone. She guides me through relaxing my entire body again, and I find more tension hiding everywhere. There are muscles in my arms, legs, back, neck, and face that I'm gripping without knowing it. Slowly, a deeper relaxation begins to set in as I let go, and let go, and then let go again. I can feel myself letting go of more emotional stuff as well, especially when I exhale, but my "hurt file" is so huge I think it will take a lifetime to delete it all.

As I continue to lie on my back with my legs up the wall, Savita turns on soft, ethereal music and gently presses my shoulders down with her palms. Within minutes, I melt into a euphoria of deep peace. It's more profound than Biofeedback and Jin Shin Jyutsu combined. For the first time since I left my home two months ago, I know for certain that I'm exactly where I'm supposed to be. My vision that Yoga is the answer has been confirmed.

"Gently roll your head side to side and hug your knees into your chest." Savita is softly bringing me back into the world now. "We have one or two more poses to try before we are finished for the day."

Hugging my stiff knees isn't easy, and I begin to default into tension. Then I remember to breathe deeply and take it slowly. This makes hugging my knees much easier. Finally, I'm able to roll over on my side and press up to a seated position on the floor with my back against the wall for support. I try to cross my legs like Savita, but my knees are up to my armpits and it feels like my groin is about to rip wide open.

"Don't force it," Savita reminds me. "Keep your back against the wall, and place your right hand on your left knee. Now, gently twist to your left." There is a string of subtle, painless little pops in my spine as I do this. I have the same experience when I twist in the opposite direction. It feels like I'm making space between each vertebra and a healing force is rushing into every subtle opening. It consumes my attention and a voice inside my mind says *There's hope for you.*

"Keep breathing deep and full," Savita prompts me again. "You have to stay aware because it's easy to forget and default back to shallow sips of air." She's right. I forget every fifteen or twenty seconds, my breath gets shallow, and my mind starts to race again.

"Straighten both of your legs out in front of you now," Savita demonstrates by uncrossing her legs and sliding them straight out on the floor. This isn't easy, either. My knees stay bent due to my tight hamstrings. My back is rounding forward like a hook. I can't keep my torso anywhere near straight without the wall behind me for support. *Just don't tense up. Stay with it ...Get up, Daddy.*

"Now, reach your arms up high, keep breathing deeply, fold forward, and reach toward your toes. Keep me fully informed. If anything causes you pain, tell me immediately and we will modify the posture."

As she says this, Savita folds all the way forward and effortlessly wraps her palms around the balls of her feet. I can fold only a few inches forward, but the good news is that it doesn't cause a hint of pain. Still, my feet look as far away as China. Savita places a strap around the balls of my feet and gives me each end to hold in my hands. As I pull on the strap and try to strain farther into the pose, Savita softly tells me to ease off. "The straps are just to give you some support and alignment. It's not how far you get right now. Don't pull or strain. Just experience it, even if you only fold a few inches."

She's smiling the entire time she says this, and it feels so nurturing and affirming that I trust her completely.

I hold the position where I am, my fingertips not even reaching my knees, and breathe as deeply as I ever have in my life. Suddenly, on an exhalation, the lower lumbar vertebrae in my back pull apart with a loud, baritone popping sound. But instead of agonizing pain, an energetic sense of relief washes through me, like a dam has broken and years of heaviness and tightness have suddenly been washed away. A huge smile covers my face as my inner voice returns and says with even greater authority, *This is it!*

When the session is over, I feel a lightness and openness beyond description, like I'm stoned on some magic elixir. Just before I leave, I ask Savita what her favorite book on Yoga is and commit the title to memory. The minute I get back to the hotel I rush to find Sandra, the concierge.

"Hi, Sandra. Please find this book for me and have it shipped overnight express. It's urgent. I need it right away. Please!"

CHAPTER 29

Fanatical

I'M LIKE A CHILD on Christmas morning as my driver drops me at the Marriott Hotel after another day at the Pain Center and my second Yoga session with Savita. I slide out of the backseat and do my limited version of a power walk into the hotel, limping as I go. I'm panting by the time I get to the concierge desk.

"Is there a package for me?" I ask Sandra with the greatest urgency and a huge smile.

"Yes, it's right here," she says as she reaches under her desk to retrieve it, noticing I'm much more animated than usual and a little out of breath. "Are you okay?"

"Just exercising a lot today," I say as I take the package. "Thanks, Sandra!"

I would run to the elevator if I could. The moment I reach my room, I sit on the bed and call room service to order my usual gourmet dinner of filet mignon and garlic mashed potatoes, little realizing my understanding of what constitutes a healthy diet will soon be turned upside down, right along with my fairly mainstream view of the meaning of life. Then I roll onto my back, prop a few pillows under my head, and reach for my new book. I'm giddy as I rip open the FedEx package, feeling like I've found the buried treasure Morgan and I always "discover" on our imaginary sailing adventures.

The book is titled *Awakening the Spine* by an Italian Yoga teacher named Vanda Scaravelli. The cover has an illustration of a female figure in an amazing back bend with one leg extended straight into the air. Her alignment is defined with geometric circles and triangles, like a takeoff on Leonardo Da Vinci's famous illustration entitled *Vitruvian Man*. It's mesmerizing. I hold the book in my hands as if it's made of gold, feel its weight, study the front and back covers, thumb the pages, and gaze at the pictures. Although Scaravelli is in her eighties, there are photos of her in breathtaking poses, including one where she's lying on her back with both feet behind her head. Even in these impossible contortions, she looks serene and completely at peace. I'm awestruck.

My limited understanding is that Yoga is all about these poses. I'm surprised when I read the foreword and find it's something much deeper. The focus of the book is the artful design of the human body, honoring the spine and moving it in its natural directions, listening for inner wisdom, and approaching life as a spiritual experience. Scaravelli names her internationally renowned Yoga teachers: Tirumalai Krishnamacharya, T.K.V. Desikachar, and B.K.S. Iyengar. They're names I've never heard before and couldn't begin to pronounce, but I'm intrigued and want to know more about this world and these people who are so accomplished.

The book also has a brief summary of the history of Yoga, how it arose thousands of years ago in India as a complete spiritual science and formula for balanced living. Even though I've only had two sessions with Savita, and they focused on body, breath, and mental relaxation, I'm immediately sold on the idea of a spiritual science. It's the perfect complement to Dr. Miller's insights about harmonizing body, mind, and Soul in his *Deep Healing* book, and it convinces me beyond any doubt that Yoga is the next step of my journey.

It doesn't even bother me that *Awakening the Spine* contains no instructions for Yoga postures as I had hoped and anticipated. I'm so transfixed that I read almost half the book before dinner arrives. Yoga has it all: healing exercise, breath work, meditation, nutrition, philosophy, and spiritual practice. I continue reading as I gobble my steak, underlining important passages and jotting down references to other Yoga books as I go. After dinner, I ring Sandra at the concierge desk. "I need more books sent overnight again, please.

Oh, and is there any way to find a few scented candles, a box of incense, and a CD of some soft Yoga music?"

"I know just what you need," she answers cheerily. "There's a shop near my home that carries those sorts of things. I'll pick them up before I come to work tomorrow and bring you a receipt."

"Thank you so much, Sandra," I say as I feel another spontaneous smile break out on my face. I think I've smiled more in the past two days than I have in a year.

After finishing the Scaravelli book and digesting my dinner, I place a towel down on the carpet in the living room and get into my stilted version of a cross-legged seated posture with the couch supporting my rounded back. I close my eyes and concentrate on my spine, especially the fulcrum point above my sacrum. I begin deep three-part Yogic breathing now, and, like Dr. Miller suggests in his audiotapes, visualize that I'm sending healing light to every vertebra and disc. As I move slowly into the beginning twists Savita taught me, then the forward fold, I pay much more attention to my physical alignment and mental awareness. The deep pop in my spine comes again, softer this time, yet just as soothing and healing.

I don't think I can get my legs up the wall without assistance, so I modify the posture by lying down on the carpet and swinging my legs onto the couch with my knees bent. Breathing deeply now while silently chanting *I am calm, healthy, strong, and relaxed*, I ponder Scaravelli's words about listening to my inner wisdom and approaching life as a spiritual experience. I'm not sure how to go about this, but I'm certain the epiphany I experienced when I first stepped into the Yoga room at the Pain Center was a message from that inner wisdom. As I relax more deeply, my stress melts away. My body feels like warm honey. A palpable sense of peace surrounds me. This is when I slip into a deep sleep.

Southern California's spring is in full blossom. It's been three weeks since my first Yoga class with Savita and I've become a complete fanatic. The coffee table in my hotel suite is now a Yoga altar, with scented candles, incense, and Yoga books surrounding the magic drawing stick like it's a sacred talisman. I've bought my first Yoga mat and given it a permanent place on the floor in front of the altar. I'm up earlier every morning now, making it a point to see the sunrise and send Morgan my love through its golden light. I practice gentle poses, deep breathing, meditation, and relaxation for a full hour, then study my books before having breakfast and going to the Pain Center.

My latest Yoga book has dozens of beginning poses with details on their therapeutic values and specific instructions on proper alignment for each posture. I'm surprised to learn that the poses—called *Asanas* in Sanskrit, the ancient Indian language traditionally used in Yoga—are not exercises. Exercise happens as a result of performing them, but they are more like a natural form of medicine. Some poses stimulate and energize the cardiovascular and neurological systems. Other poses calm them down. Different *Asanas* compress and detoxify the organs, open and align the spine, ignite an inner fire of energy and power, or soothe and heal painful emotions.

I attempt to do every one of the poses in the book, but most remain far beyond my capacity. Still, I continue to feel subtle shifts and openings throughout my body with the poses I am able to get into. I breathe deeply and fully almost every waking moment now, sending healing energy into my spine and lower back muscles. My mantras, *Get up, Daddy* and *I am calm, healthy, strong, and relaxed,* flow on almost every breath cycle, like Yoga poses for my normally agitated mind. This keeps me in the present moment. Really here. Not constantly thinking about the past or the future, my thoughts galloping in all directions like wild horses in a frenzy. *This is it.*

It's only been a month of Yoga, yet as I walk briskly from the parking lot toward the Pain Center on a Monday morning in late March, I feel like I'm becoming a new person. I am smiling. Feeling vibrant and energized. My cane and back brace are long gone, my gait is lighter and more confident, there's color in my face. I'm getting stronger and more mobile, and feeling a sense of hope and optimism for the first time in years. As I pass the detox center, I hear a shout from some of my old colleagues sitting on the courtyard benches waiting for their meetings. "Hey, what happened to you?"

"What do you mean?" I ask, wondering if I've done something wrong.

"You were walking dead a month ago," one of them says with wide-eyed surprise. "But now no body brace, no cane. You really look healthy. What's your secret?"

"Yoga," I answer with a smile. "I'm up in the Pain Center on the third floor over there," I say, pointing to the wing of the building beyond the residential area. "Stay with the residential program, but find a way to get into the center and do Yoga, too. It can change your life. I really mean it. It's not just helping my back, it's helping my mind, and it's connecting me with something deeper inside."

"Yoga!" They say it unison with a few laughs, thinking I must be stoned on morphine again.

"No thanks," one says as he takes a deep drag on his cigarette, "I don't want any part of what's deep inside of me."

"I can barely get out of bed in the morning," another says with a dismissive grunt followed by a gulp of black coffee.

If only I could get through to them, convince them that Yoga could help them achieve greater balance, relieve their mental torment, and find some inner peace. I sense it isn't possible, just as it wasn't for me when I met the young Yoga teacher at my fiftieth birthday party whose wise advice seemed so foreign and irrelevant to my circumstances. Plus, I'm no Yoga expert. I'm as green as they come. Who am I to advise anyone?

"It's good to see you," I say, moving along. "I have to go now. Have a great day."

As I walk across the wide lobby toward the elevators, the inner voice I've been hearing more from lately whispers *Take the stairs.* The Pain Center is two flights up, and I still feel intimidated every time I see the stairwell during my Physical Therapy walks down the hallway. I ignore the voice and head for the elevator, then stop in my tracks and remember: *This is exactly the voice I need to heed.* "Okay, let's do it," I say, talking out loud to myself again as I head toward the stairs. I pause at the bottom and gaze up the stairwell. It looks like a mountain. I take a few deep breaths to release the fear, close my eyes, and visualize myself floating effortlessly up, like I'm ascending into Heaven.

Okay.
Here we go.
Breathing deeply.
Chanting "Get up, Daddy," with each step.
Moving slowly and rhythmically.
Staying focused.
Keeping my spine aligned.
Finding little bits of new muscle in my legs and back.
Being strong, healthy, calm, and relaxed.

I'm hyperventilating by the time I reach the top of the first flight. My heart is pounding, I'm dripping with sweat, and my thighs are on fire. I want to give up and crawl to the elevator. *Wait. Relax. Stay focused.* I pause. Deepen my breath. Release tension wherever I can find it. *Get up, Daddy.* Now, even more slowly and mindfully, I breathe and chant my way up the final flight. As I step into the hallway of the Pain Center, I imagine how exhilarated Sir Edmund Hillary must have been when he climbed Mount Everest. I feel so empowered I want to scream to the whole world, *I am alive!*

"I just walked up the stairs from the ground floor!" I announce to PJ like it's a news bulletin as I turn the corner into Physical Therapy, so proud of myself I'm bursting at the seams.

"That's wonderful!" PJ exclaims with maternal affirmation. "How about lying down for a few minutes with an ice pack before we get started?" She's a saint. It's the greatest suggestion I've ever heard.

※

The medications I took for so many years not only clouded my mind, they slowed and clogged my digestive system. Given all the physical pain, I no longer exercised. Rarely walked. Often, rarely moved. Yet I kept eating and drinking like a foreign correspondent, slowly gaining a ton of weight. Several of the Yoga poses I'm now doing, especially the twists, feel like they are detoxifying, energizing, and toning my organs and digestive system. At the same time, I find I'm satisfied with smaller portions of food. And there are no more nightly glasses of wine or bottles of beer. As a result, even though I'm still far too heavy, the excess weight is now pouring off. I can even see the veins in my puffy arms for the first time in years.

I've been wearing sweatpants and T-shirts ever since I entered detox, and they're getting baggier by the day. Just for fun this morning, I tried on the size forty-two khaki trousers I brought to the hotel with me. They slipped off my hips and fell to my knees. Hurrying down to the spa, I stepped on the scale. I'm down to 205 pounds. Twenty pounds less than the day I checked into the McDonald Center a little more than three months ago. This afternoon, I navigated the walkways behind the hotel and found my way to a fashion mall to buy a new pair of slacks and smaller sweatpants: *waist size thirty-eight!*

Despite my attempts not to think about cancer, there are daily reminders. I barely produce any saliva as a result of the radiation toasting my salivary glands, and my mouth is usually so dry I have to drink water in order to swallow my food. My throat gets sore now and then. Sometimes it bleeds. When these conditions arise, I whisper the Serenity Prayer, asking myself to accept those things I cannot change. Then I do everything possible to block it out before it overwhelms me.

The prayer also asks for the courage to change the things we can. This is where Yoga comes in. Maybe I can't change the outcome of stage IV cancer, but I've already made a major shift in my level of physical pain, and it feels like a new beginning. I keep devouring Yoga books and ordering more. I take notes, earmark pages, highlight passages, try every practice and technique I can handle. I no longer lie on the couch during my breaks at the Pain Center. I get on the floor and do little twists, forward folds, gentle backbends, and lateral extensions. It's a complete obsession.

The twists and forward folds are the ones Savita taught me our first day. For the back bends, I simply hold onto my knees while I'm cross-legged, lift my chest forward and up, and then open my shoulders as I extend my head up and back. The lateral extensions involve placing my right hand on the ground out to my right side, then reaching my left arm overhead and extending it diagonally to the right. This lets me breathe deeply into my left ribs as my spine arcs sideways. Then I repeat the pose on the other side. With these simple postures, I'm moving my spine in all directions. Massaging the discs. Enhancing blood flow. Breathing into the spaces. Releasing years of tightness and tenderness.

It's still painful for me to sit cross-legged without back support, but my knees have come down a little from my armpits. I can swing my legs up the wall now with ease, no longer a bend in my knees from tight hamstrings. I'm able to hold an alternate arm-leg balance for a full minute on each side now without collapsing. In forward folds, my lower back keeps extending slightly farther, creating more spaciousness. In every pose, I can feel energy moving in long-dormant areas, my spine realigning and slowly healing. It's like I finally have a grip on life and am climbing out of the abyss, moving from darkness into the daylight. It feels incredibly empowering, even though I know there's still such a long way to go.

There's a network of beautifully landscaped walkways and bridges behind the Marriott Hotel that wind through several city blocks. I've started exploring them in the mornings and evenings. Watching the trees and shrubbery bud and blossom as spring approaches. Listening to the birds. Pausing to feel the sun on my face and gentle breezes on my cheeks. Nature, I'm reminded by Dr. Miller's teachings, is incredibly healing. I knew this intuitively when I escaped Southern California as a teenager and moved into the woods. Then, caught up in my career, I forgot. Now it's coming back to me more deeply than ever. The more I align myself with nature's rhythms, the better I feel.

After so many years of stagnation, I'm also being called to rhythms of creative expression. During college I lived for a year in a large home with several folk musicians. They would gather in our living room almost every evening, playing guitars and sharing songs. I wanted to play, too, but being left-handed I couldn't use their instruments. Finally, I found an old left-handed guitar, and my friends taught me to strum a few chords so I could play along. I never had a lesson or became very proficient, but it always soothed me. Especially when I played alone late at night in my room. I could feel the vibration of the strings inside my body. See the energy of the sounds dancing through the candlelight. Sense a river of peace flowing through my veins.

Left-handed guitars, which are built upside down and backwards, are hard to find. But Sandra, my intrepid concierge, has come through again and found me a beautiful left-handed acoustic guitar with deep and rich tones. At night, after sunset and my evening Yoga practice, I light a candle in the darkness of my hotel room and gently strum chords and fingerpick simple notes I've learned from listening to my new Yoga CDs. Most of the melodies and progressions are droning and repetitive, creating an ethereal sense of meditation.

It's more than music to me. Each sound is a soothing prayer that harmonizes every cell in my body, especially when I chant "OM" while I strum. My books teach me that om, which is drawn out when chanted and sounds like *aaaa-uuuu-mmmm*, is the primary mantra of Yoga and the eternal sound of the cosmos—some say OM is the sound the universe made when it came into existence. The Bible says, "In the beginning was the word." Yoga says the first word, or sound, was OM. Chanting it creates an inner vibration that connects me with my Soul.

CHAPTER 30

Closure

A HAND REACHES OUT and touches my shoulder as I'm walking through the hospital courtyard one afternoon. "Excuse me, my name is Richard. I think you're the person some friends have told me about who is healing a broken back with Yoga?"

"Yes, that's me," I answer with a smile, feeling a sudden sense of worth, like I have something to offer someone in need. "It's really helping me. You should check it out."

Richard looks like an avant-garde European movie star, with dark eyebrows, piercing green eyes, and a thick shock of blond hair falling across one side of his face. But his lean, athletic body is twisted in pain. He limps on a badly damaged ankle and holds his head tilted unnaturally to one side. Richard shares with me that he was chief executive of a hi-tech company, with a wife, two children, and a beautiful home in one of San Diego's most exclusive neighborhoods. He was also under great stress and dealt with his demons by drinking himself into a stupor every night.

He had endless drunken outbursts in front of his family, and numerous drunk-driving arrests. Then one morning, Richard woke up in a roadside ditch with a broken ankle, fractured shin, and wrenched neck. He had no idea where he was or how long he'd been there. When he finally got to a hospital, where his wounds were treated and he sobered up, Richard discovered his drinking had cost him everything. His beloved Mercedes sports car was in the wrecking yard.

His company's board of directors had fired him. A restraining order forbid him from returning home.

Having had plenty of psychological turmoil myself, I can see that Richard harbors deep insecurities and emotional wounds. It's etched in his face and even more evident when he speaks. His words are fraught with fear and anger. He vacillates between hope and despondency. But his intelligence and charisma manage to shine through his suffering and darkness. Despite his desperation and vulnerability, there's something inside of him that makes me think he has a real chance to pull it together.

"I want to get back to where I was," Richard tells me. "Be with my kids again, fix things up with my wife, get my career back."

Richard is now in the residential program, but he tells me he doesn't like AA. He's heard about the changes I've made, and he wants to do Yoga, too. In fact, it's all he wants to do. I support and encourage him in every way possible, but make it clear to him that I strongly oppose his desire to drop out of the residential program and join the Pain Center full time. Even though he disdains the AA program for reasons I can't understand, he doesn't seem anywhere near ready to walk the path of sobriety on his own. So we make a plan. We'll ask the Pain Center to allow him to take Yoga as long as he promises to be fully committed to the requirements of the residential program.

I meet with Dr. Kozin and give him a strong pitch for Richard. He agrees with the idea and it only takes a few days before Richard learns that he is approved for Yoga, with the caveat that he remains fully committed to the residential program. When he gets the news, he's ecstatic. "I'm going to do Yoga!" Richard gleefully tells me one morning as my driver drops me off at the curb of the McDonald complex. "I've been waiting here to tell you. The Pain Center has agreed to let me enroll in a few Yoga classes. I've been able to sort out a schedule and I start tomorrow!"

"That's great news, Richard!" I say, putting an arm around his shoulder as he limps along beside me. "Go slowly. Don't push it. Breathe deeply all the time. And if you run into Ms. Mason, don't let her get you down."

As we enter the complex, Richard turns left toward his first morning meeting. I turn right toward the stairs to the Pain Center. I've liked this man since the moment we met, and as I watch him limp away I whisper a prayer of hope that he'll find healing and eventually create a new life for himself. *No more stress. No more painkillers. No more booze. A life of health, happiness, and wholeness. May it be so for Richard, and may it be so for me.*

My own fourteen years of alcohol and medications were a terrible tradeoff. In return for reduction of my pain, I surrendered my physical and emotional health. Now, with Yoga, the heavy veils I placed over my Soul are slowly lifting, one by one, revealing something inside me that disappeared long ago. My emotions are shifting from anger and fear to acceptance, confidence, and even a little bit of humility. I'm moving away from being a self-pitying victim and starting to take responsibility for my life. A feeling I had forgotten existed now visits me daily. The word that comes closest to describing it is *hope.*

Every move I make, from climbing the stairs to sitting for dinner, getting in and out of a car, standing before the concierge to order more books, or slipping into a hot bath, is now an act of Yoga. I pay close attention to where my balance is, which parts of my body are twisting, flexing, or engaging, and how good it feels to harmonize the rhythm of my breath with the movement of my body. I'm also taking greater charge of my life. I no longer need Biofeedback. I listen to Dr. Miller's audiotapes in my hotel room almost every night and know visualization works without having electrodes and monitors proving it to me. I've pared down my schedule at the Pain Center to Yoga, Physical Therapy, and an occasional Jin Shin Jyutsu session. I find ways to cancel every meeting with Ms. Mason, and vow I'll only see her if I'm threatened with expulsion. Luckily, it's yet to become an issue.

With a shorter schedule, I can get back to my hotel room earlier to study and practice more of the deeper, mind-body aspects of

Yoga. There's a great complexity to this science, yet also an elegant simplicity—a pureness of logic that resonates with my analytical mind. *Pranayama*, the mastery of our life force, known as *Prana*, is the science of controlled breathing. It purifies, balances, energizes, and oxygenates the body. My books say it also boosts the immune system, enhances circulation of the blood, and massages the heart muscle. Meditation lowers blood pressure, reduces stress, and calms the emotions. I lived most of my life being judgmental and combative. This seemed normal to me and always helped me advance my career. Now I understand how it also stressed me out. Breathing deeply and meditating on calmness and acceptance feels so much better than always being on guard.

I'm also learning that all the *Asanas* (poses) have profound physiological, neurological, and even psychological benefits. Twists promote digestion and elimination, tone the abdominal organs, and quiet the nervous system. Forward bends relieve anxiety, stress, and depression; stimulate the liver and kidneys; and calm the mind. Backbends energize, open the area of the heart center, promote courage, and counter fatigue. The more I study, the more I also realize that this barely touches the surface of what Yoga offers. I see it as the ultimate science of how to be a human being in body, mind, and Soul. It's self-healing at the highest level, powerful medicine with no side effects, a completely natural way to heal and thrive. I'm totally hooked.

My usual bacon and egg breakfasts, meat sandwich lunches, and steak dinners always seemed sumptuous and hearty. The science of Yoga recommends a vegetarian diet. Even though I'm not ready for this, red meat and pork now taste greasy and heavy to me, no longer appetizing. It must be the power of suggestion. Or maybe I only liked these foods because I associated them with the "good life." Either way, red meat and pork are gone. I've substituted granola and fruit for breakfast, salads and soups for lunch, and fish or poultry for dinner. I eat more slowly, chew more thoroughly, and really taste the food. This makes me satisfied with smaller portions at every meal. As a result, the new pants I just bought are already too loose, and my extra-large T-shirts now droop over me like sacks.

Pain episodes still strike when least expected. Sometimes I go into my old mode and start to despair. I want to down some painkillers, curl up into a ball, and scream out loud. Then I catch myself and remember all my new tools. The first step is to stop myself from reacting and getting tense. Instead, I breathe deeply, visualizing the pain as a wave that will come and go. Then I do restorative poses, chant my mantras, and relax myself as much as possible. It's worked every time so far.

With less of the stress that pain creates, my energy is increasing. Every morning I feel a little more vibrant and alive. Where I used to be really shut down and completely opposed to making an effort or trying new things, I now feel adventurous. So I try to take the stairs up to the Pain Center every day and even climb the stairs for a few floors at the hotel every morning and evening before surrendering to the elevator. It would be impossible for me to make all twelve stories, but I've made it from the lobby to the fourth floor. My sights are now on the fifth.

I'm also growing more flexible by the day. A few months ago, I could barely touch my knees while trying to do a seated forward fold. Now I can almost reach my toes. I can sit cross-legged on the floor without back support for a few minutes at a time. My spine is coming into a more natural alignment. I'm exploring basic hip openers, more advanced backbends, deeper twists, and more powerful lateral extensions. This physical progress might not be the ultimate goal of Yoga, but it's profoundly inspiring and empowering. Every time I take a pose the slightest bit farther, the light of hope shines more brightly within me.

While I remain heavily focused on Yoga postures, breath work, and meditation, the core of my being continues to be drawn to the spiritual aspects of this ancient practice. The more I study it, the more I'm convinced that it transcends religion and dogma. Yoga urges us to see the unity in all things rather than focus on our differences. I witnessed as a foreign correspondent that when religious, social, and/or political systems see themselves as the only legitimate way, others can become adversaries and enemies. This has promoted intolerance and fanaticism throughout the ages, leading to misunderstandings, condemnations, conflicts, and wars. Yoga offers something different, and I find myself drawn to it like I've been lost in a desert and suddenly an oasis has come into view.

Yoga also holds that self-indulgence and materialism never bring happiness. The more we look externally for a sense of satisfaction in our lives, the more we are destined to suffer. It reminds me of all the stories I've read about people who attained great wealth or fame in their lives yet were miserable and often killed themselves with drugs and alcohol. I remember, too, how as a journalist I was happiest when I was in a third world country or a war zone, like the time in the mountains of northern Iraq when my little bottle of Tabasco, Swiss Army Knife, and a piece of twine were all I needed.

Yoga also teaches me that there is a Divine Being within each of us, and that merging back with this inner essence is the journey of transformation and spiritual unity. It advises me to be still and quiet, really connect with the present moment, and—perhaps most importantly—release my ego and concentrate on my sense of higher power. It also advises me to continually contemplate who I really am at the deepest level, and to seek to be the very best person that I can be. This means even more humility, more compassion, and more gratitude for what I have in my life rather than worrying about what's lacking.

Stillness and silence used to be disconcerting. Now they're rich and delicious. I no longer turn on the TV and allow myself to be seduced by its nonsensical cacophony. My interest in the bestseller novels I used to crave has been replaced by Yoga studies. Stepping onto my balcony at night and gazing at the vast phantasmagoria of the heavens is bedazzling. All this gives me a sense that I'm being reborn. Brad Willis the global journalist died long ago. Brad Willis the permanently disabled man with a broken back is passing away. I even wonder if one day, just maybe, Brad Willis the cancer victim might be gone as well. The authentic person within me has been suppressed for years. Now that person is coming alive as a fledgling Yogi.

I have no illusions that Yoga will make me a sage of any sort, but the more I tune out the noise around me and listen to the silence within, I'm able to access an inner wisdom I've been unaware of most of my life. I now realize there's a natural and intuitive knowing within me, an inner guidance arising like a whisper from my Soul. I repeatedly commit to listening even more closely to this voice, which always seems to be saying *Take it further, commit ever more deeply, and never look back*. My intellectual mind, of course, offers me a million ways to judge or dismiss all this esoteric spirituality, but I've decided not to listen to that mental voice any longer. This is life or death for me. My only chance. *I'm all in. One hundred percent.*

CHAPTER 31

Homecoming

RICHARD IS WAITING for me in the downstairs lobby as I arrive at the Pain Center this morning. I'm surprised to smell tobacco on his breath. He quit smoking last week when he started Yoga, and has been exuding a real sense of hope lately. Now he's gripped with anguish as he grabs my arm with force and almost yells, "Did you hear the news?"

I wonder if there's been a cataclysmic world event I've missed since I no longer watch TV, or maybe someone we know has had a relapse.

"No, Richard, what is it?" I ask softly, trying to calm him down.

"I just found out that the Pain Center is shutting down!" He exclaims with tears welling up in his eyes as he trembles with anger. "They're out of money. The insurance companies say there's no proof any of this works and it's out of the mainstream, so they won't reimburse the hospital for our treatments. There aren't enough patients who can pay the full price and there aren't sufficient funds to continue."

He says all this so fast I have to ask him to take a few deep breaths and slow it down. "One of the nurses told me in confidence," he says, on the verge of breaking down. "I can't believe it. Why would they enroll me and give me this hope when they knew they were closing?"

I remember my first day at the center when two other patients said their insurance company had rejected all their reimbursement requests. Mine have been rejected as well. It's been a source of frustration for all of us. Although I'm fortunate to have enough saved to afford the program, it's been a major financial burden. I hold Richard in a bear-hug and whisper that it will be all right, everything will work out as it's meant to be. Then I go investigate. PJ is always the one who's most dialed into what's going on, so I hurry up the stairs and find her as she's coming out of a staff meeting with a worried look on her face.

"PJ, is it true, about closing down?" I ask, a little breathless.

"Shhhh," she says secretively. "I was going to tell you this morning. Come into my office and we can talk about it, but you can't tell anyone else right now."

When we sit down, PJ is on the verge of tears. It's the first time I've ever seen her down. "The staff has been in meetings trying to find some way to salvage the program, or at least persuade the hospital to run it at a loss while they attempt to locate funding, but it's not going to happen," she tells me as she wipes a tear away. "They just can't attract enough patients to sustain the center without insurance company reimbursements. The closure date is uncertain, but the end of the Pain Center is inevitable, and it's coming soon."

Like Richard, I feel a sense of betrayal and anger at a system that so often puts profits above patients. Is this a business or a place for healing? And there's this irony: Most of the expensive procedures and medications my insurance has paid for only made me worse. The Pain Center has been an oasis and has the capacity to help people find true healing and wholeness. Now, it's going to close its doors. It feels like the rug is being pulled out from beneath my feet just as I'm finally able to stand firmly on the ground. *It's outrageous. They can't do this to us. I won't stand for it.*

Wait. I stop myself in the middle of this psychological drama I'm creating, take a deep breath, and let it go with a loud "AHHHH." Instead of giving in to anger or reacting with fear, Yoga would advise me to meet this challenge with confidence and faith in myself. I close my eyes and focus on the situation.

Yes, my healing has just begun. I've risen from the bottom of the abyss, but I'm still clawing my way up the side of the cliff and my grip remains tenuous. But I can do this. I have to deepen my resolve if I'm going to pull myself all the way up. I have to reclaim the courage that I lost long ago. I must begin believing in myself again. I can do this.

Just by repeating this to myself, my resolve begins to deepen. *I can do this. Even if I have to do it all on my own, I can do this. Stand in Yoga. Get up, Daddy. Get up and stay up.* Then I give PJ a hug and ask that she give me an extra rigorous session. She smiles and says she's happy to oblige.

✻

This morning toward the end of my practice as I'm doing some more self-reflection, it dawns on me that my first step into Yoga wasn't at the Pain Center. It wasn't the epiphany when I walked into the Yoga room. It wasn't when Savita helped me get my legs up the wall or taught me how to breathe. It was nearly four months earlier, on the morning I discovered my family downstairs and the intervention began. That was when I began to face myself, realized I had lost control of my life, chose to let go of all resistance, heard my inner voice telling me the truth about what I had become, and said, "It's about time." I had no idea this was Yoga. But it was.

Yoga teaches the immutable law of Karma. Karma says we are the architects of our happiness and our misery. We can hope for new outcomes from old behaviors, or realize that only new behaviors will change our circumstances. It's our choice. We can continue to suffer, or we can take responsibility for our lives. We can live in our illusions, feeling frustrated and victimized, or we can surrender our egos and see the bigger picture. This means we learn to listen to our hearts, reclaim our power, step up, and take skillful action.

I surrendered a truckload of ego when I entered detox. It was an experience of humility that wasn't easy for me but ultimately proved invaluable. I began to reclaim some of my power when I listened to my heart and chose the Pain Center over the residential program. Now that the center is closing, Pamela is still insisting that I'm not ready to come home and that the residential program is my only option. I think she's afraid life will quickly go back to what it was.

Who can blame her? I think she also wants her way right now, which I can understand. But I've been away from Morgan far too long and my inner voice has been telling me there may be other agendas in play of which I'm unaware. Every cell in my body is almost screaming: *If you don't go home now, you might lose your son.* As I end my morning practice I commit to following this inner guidance. If I can repair and renew my marriage, I'll do so with humility, energy, and effort. The likelihood of this seems uncertain right now, and I'm unsure how many mountains I can climb at once. Either way, my mind is made up: *I'm going home.*

The final days at the Pain Center are difficult for all of us. Staff members have hushed conversations in the hallways. They're angry, sad, and fearful of the challenge of finding work somewhere else. The small number of patients at the center are in despair. Enrolling in this program was a huge step for them, a final effort that offered a glimmer of hope after years of suffering. When I see them now, their physical and emotional pain is palpable. I'm deeply disappointed as well but do everything in my power to accept it and remind myself that I have to move forward as skillfully and courageously as possible.

"I don't know what to do." Richard is dark and despondent in his rage. "I'm not going to stay in the residential program without the Pain Center."

"Richard," I plead, "don't walk out. You know what will happen. You can make it here. I'll give you some of my Yoga books. You can study. Practice. Believe in yourself. Stay strong. We can talk on the phone. I'll come see you when I can."

"I don't have it in me," he answers sharply. "Everyone has betrayed me. I'm done with it all. I'm out of here."

"Richard," I say again, looking for words to break through his agony and shift him out of his darkness. He puts up a hand with his palm facing me, indicating a wall, letting me know he just can't listen right now. As I watch my friend walk away, limping painfully toward great uncertainty, my heart begins to sink. I know that without my newfound Yoga philosophy I'd probably have the same reaction. I'd get furious and feel like a victim. I'd judge and condemn everyone involved. Then I'd take meds again. Drink beer and wine. Blame the whole world. Fall back into the abyss.

Instead, I go back to the hotel and deepen my commitment to my studies and practices. As my final week at the Pain Center comes to a close, I get up an hour earlier, at four in the morning, and practice poses, controlled breathing, and visualization until sunrise. After breakfast, I take longer walks along the pathways behind the hotel, go to the spa, and soak in the hot pool, then meditate in the steam room before going to the Pain Center, always asking myself, *What is the next step?* The answer is always the same. *Go Home. Be with your boy. Stand in Yoga.*

At the Pain Center, I take as many sessions with Savita as she has available, paying close attention to her every instruction. At night, I practice with even greater commitment. I pore through my books, ponder how to integrate the moral and philosophical principles more into my life, explore new poses and breathing techniques, then do a little meditation. After that, I strum my guitar and chant a few simple mantras, surrendering in every breath to whatever the future might hold. *Take it deeper. Don't stop now. Get up and stay up. One hundred percent in.*

It's a Friday morning in late March 2000, and I'm ready to return home even though Pamela still hasn't agreed and doesn't know I'm coming today. The hotel staff has been like family to me over the past several months. We hug during our good-byes, share some tears, and make promises to be in touch. I tell Sandra that I'm not sure what I would have done without her as I give her a bouquet of flowers from the gift shop. The head bellhop, Rick, has come in on his day off to help me pack and drive me home. He loads my suitcase in his car and we head for Scripps so I can say final good-byes at the hospital.

It's the first time I've set foot in the McDonald Center since the day I checked out of the detox ward. The staff stares with disbelief. No Clamshell brace, no cane, no dark circles under my eyes, and I'm more than twenty-five pounds lighter.

"Whatever you've done, keep doing it," says Don, the counselor who once told me I would fall flat on my face.

"Thanks, Don. I will."

Nurse Ratched smiles and gives me a warm hug. I don't even know her real name and now realize what a wonderful person she was, giving me the firm hand I needed. It was just my ego and resistance to being told what to do that made me so defensive with her. She was never the problem. I was.

"Thank you for everything," I tell her, "especially for putting up with me."

"I've had worse!" she answers with a laugh. "Good luck to you. Stay healthy."

The good-byes are longer at the Pain Center, with a few more hugs and tears. "You are our greatest success story," PJ tells me with a warm smile. "Stay with it."

Beth, in her usual soft, often cryptic and insightful way, says lovingly, "One day you will help others to heal." As so often happens with Beth, her words strike a chord within me, but I can't really imagine such a thing. With so much healing still left to be done on myself, the idea that I will one day help others heal seems like something for another lifetime.

Savita and I share few words, communicating with a smile, a hug, and a glance of mutual knowing.

"I'll never forget my first Yoga teacher," I whisper to her.

"I won't forget you, either," she answers with her palms together in *Anjali Mudra* at her heart center. This gesture, which Savita taught me early on, is also known as *Namaste*, a common Yogic greeting that means "I acknowledge that the light in my heart and the light in your heart are the same." I flash back to almost a decade ago in Hanoi when I was guided to a hidden temple in the old quarter of the city and given the golden Buddha. This is the same gesture used by the Vietnamese man who gave me the gift; only I had no idea at the time what it meant. I bring my palms together at my heart, gently bow toward Savita, and whisper back, "*Namaste.*"

I take my last walk down the two flights of stairs from the Pain Center into the lobby that connects to the residential program. I pause at the bottom, turn around, and jog all the way back up the stairs, then turn around and head back down again as fast as I can. As my feet hit each stair, I sing out at the top of my lungs, "I am alive!"

Once I'm back in the lobby, a friend of Richard's rushes toward me. She looks like she's in shock. "Did you hear about Richard?" she asks with such alarm that my soaring heart immediately sinks.

"He told me he was leaving a few days ago," I say. "That's all I know. Is he all right?" I'm thinking he's had a nervous breakdown and been hospitalized.

"He left the program. Disappeared. They just found him last night. He overdosed on pills and booze. He passed away."

The news stops my breath. I remember the anguish on Richard's face during our final conversation. His wounded walk as he departed. *Dear Richard, why? You could have found a way to stay with it. Lived in residence and studied Yoga on your own. We could have been in touch. Guided one another along the way. Figured it out together. Oh, my brother, I'm so sorry. I'll never forget you.*

I realize, too, that this easily could have been me. There were so many times I just wanted to check out of the world before I found Yoga. *There but for the grace of God go I.*

❅

As Rick the bellhop drives us south from La Jolla, downtown San Diego comes into view. I feel like I'm seeing the city for the first time, with its burgeoning skyline, glistening bay waters, sailboats, yachts, and cruise ships in the harbor. It's been more than seven years since I left Hong Kong and moved to Coronado, but I was so often bedridden, always drugged up, and never really had clarity. I missed it all. Now, everything appears new and filled with possibility and potential. I whisper an old adage that I always liked, but now can actually feel in every cell of my being: "This is the first day of the rest of my life."

"What's that?" Rick says.

"Nothing," I say with a laugh. "Just talking to myself."

The drive over the sloping, blue Coronado Bridge is a thrill. All my senses come alive as we reach the top of its arc. The blue waters of San Diego Bay are sparkling on the east side of the island. The vast Pacific Ocean is glistening on the west. Point Loma peninsula juts into the ocean like a giant finger pointing south toward Mexico. On the horizon are the Islas Coronados, a group of four remote, uninhabited islands that look exotic and alluring, like someplace Morgan and I might take our imaginary sailboat in search of buried treasure as we sit on the "story bench." Then I gaze down toward the village. It holds the greatest treasure on Earth: my little boy, in our home, not even knowing Daddy is about to hold him ever so tightly and never let him go again.

Finally, we're on my street, pulling up to the curb. The moment we park, I thank Rick, quickly slide out of the passenger seat, pull my bags and the bulky portable lounge out of his trunk, and hug him good-bye. Then I stop on the sidewalk and stare at my home. It's two stories tall, with natural redwood shingles that have turned a rich, deep brown with age. The windows and doorway are framed in white wood. I chose it because it felt earthy and inviting, like an old friend. Never so much as it does in this moment. Yet I also feel like a stranger. It's been so long since I was last here. As I find my keys, unlock the front door, and step inside, the home's warmth immediately envelops me.

"Morgan!" I cry out so loud it reaches every corner of the house.

"Daddy!" His tiny voice comes from upstairs, filled with surprise. I hear the precious patter of his little feet as he runs to the stairwell and hurries down to meet me in the living room. We rush into each other's arms and I sweep him up, hold him high above my head, then hug him to my chest. I can hardly believe my little boy is two-and-a-half years old. I never want to miss another moment of his life.

As Morgan nestles his face into my neck, he says over and over again, "Daddy's home, Daddy's home."

"That's right, Morgan. Daddy's home. Daddy's home forever."

Pamela comes down the stairs, polite but distant, and offers a more formal welcome as she conceals the surprise of my return. "Hi," she says with a subdued and guarded tone as I reach out tentatively to hug her. It's a brief embrace and feels stiff. Inauthentic on both our behalves. I would love for her to mention how much weight I've lost, that I look healthier and stronger, but she doesn't. I can understand, especially given that this is an unexpected homecoming. As she pulls back from the hug, I smile and say, "It's so good to be home."

I know there is still love lurking somewhere deep within each of us, but we both feel an unspoken pain, the silent recognition that there is a chasm between us that might be too late to bridge. I know we also feel a commitment and responsibility toward our child. It's far too early to make any decisions. We need to have some deep and honest discussions about healing old wounds and starting anew. But now is not the time.

Morgan quickly brings me back to the present moment by crying out with glee, "Upstairs, upstairs, Daddy." I know what's in store and it's joyous. I'm going to get all the news, see his latest toys, visit his favorite teddy bear, and, of course, be asked to draw on his back. I've slipped the magic drawing stick into my pocket to be ready for this special moment. I scoop him into my arms and carry him all the way upstairs, hugging him to my chest like a papoose. The whole time he continues to snuggle in closer, murmuring, "Daddy's home, Daddy's home."

CHAPTER 32

Himalayan Cave

MORNING COMES SOFTLY. I squint my eyes open and see a vaulted ceiling above me with a wide crossbeam at its apex. A hint of light flows through the white plantation shutters covering the windows. An abstract Matisse print on the wall portrays a blue figure lost in ecstatic dance. I've slept past my normal time and feel completely refreshed, but my mind is a little fuzzy and I'm not sure where I am.

"Daddy!" Morgan whispers as he sneaks into the room. It all comes back in a flash. I'm home in my bed and have just enjoyed the best night of sleep I've had all year. "Daddy, pick me up!"

I lean over, reach out, and lift Morgan into my arms and hold him high over my head.

"What a big boy you've become," I say, wiggling him gently in the air. Even though it's only been a few months, and we had a few visits when I was at the Pain Center, Morgan has entered a new stage, getting bigger by the day and speaking with even greater fluency and ease.

"You stay home, Daddy?" I feel like the euphoric Matisse dancer on the wall when he seeks this reassurance.

I bring him down, hug him closely, and say, "Yes, Morgan. I'm never, ever leaving you again."

Then I roll him over onto my knees and grab the magic drawing stick, which I placed by the bedside last night, right where we always used to keep it. "Did you see the sailboat I drew for you and pinned on your playroom wall?" I whisper. "Yes, Daddy," he coos. "I love it." I draw the sailboat on his back and we launch our adventure on the high seas as the fullness of dawn bathes the room with soft light. When I trace a sun with rays streaming down his back I ask, "Did you think about me when you saw the morning light?" "Yes, Daddy," he says, and it makes me ecstatic. This time we share together is the greatest medicine of all, and I savor every moment.

After half an hour, Pamela enters the room and takes Morgan for a bath. She chose the guest bedroom last night and, given my abrupt return, I imagine this might be her choice for some time to come. *Don't push it. Give her space. Remember what a burden you've been.* As I roll out of bed, I'm reminded that my back is still unstable. I get down on the floor and do a Yoga practice at the foot of the bed. *Must keep at this. Every day. Deeper and deeper. Only just beginning. Give it everything you have.*

When Morgan goes down for a nap, I get on the computer and search for Yoga in Coronado. Nothing. No studios. No teachers. There are a few in San Diego, but I don't feel ready to drive a car yet, and commuting over the bridge is out of the question. Even if I was ready, I'm not strong enough for the energetic styles of Yoga that seem to be the norm from what I can see on the studio websites, which show people doing powerful standing postures, even headstands and handstands. I can't imagine such things. I still need more deep healing, profound relaxation, and rejuvenation. I doubt I'll ever even try a headstand. And a handstand? Forget about it.

Also, the Yoga studios seem to focus solely on *Asanas*, and while these are an essential part of my practice, I'm drawn to transforming my life in body, mind, and Soul. I know this is essential for me. I want to heal my back, but at the same time I need to face my emotional imbalances and continue learning to view the world from a new, richer, and deeper perspective. I already feel this happening in subtle ways. I have no idea who it is that I'm becoming, and I still have so much to face on every level, but the process is well underway and I don't want to lose it. The key is to find a way to be self-reliant, to step up and look at myself squarely in the eyes, to dig down even deeper and summon every ounce of courage, energy, and power within me to chart a course and give it all that I have. Otherwise, I fear I'll be lost. Then, as I close my eyes and contemplate this, the inner voice speaks up again. *Do it yourself for now. Study more. Practice nonstop. Get stronger. Go deeper.*

As I ponder this, a shot of adrenalin rushes through me, as it does every time I remember that my stage IV cancer diagnosis was in mid-1998 and I'm toward the end of the two years my oncologists predicted I had left. I close my eyes once again and repeat the Serenity Prayer to myself: *God, grant me the serenity to accept the things I cannot change, courage to change the things I can, and wisdom to know the difference.* I have to focus on my Yoga practice for now, find a space at home where I have solitude, create a new daily ritual, take it further, and change the things I can. *Remember,* I tell myself, *You're all in, one hundred percent, no matter what. This is your path... Get up, Daddy.*

When I bought our Coronado home in 1994, it was a new, two-story remodel of a much smaller, historic Craftsman house built in the 1920s. In designing the expansion, the contractor kept a portion of the original footprint to satisfy historical requirements and fast-track the building permit process. This created a little leftover space downstairs, a tiny room that was turned into a business office. It's only nine by nine feet, with wall-to-wall built-in desktops and file cabinets, leaving barely enough room in the center for a small swivel chair. There are two narrow, horizontal windows high up one wall, and a large framed bank of harsh fluorescent lights on the ceiling. It always has felt like a stuffy, cramped little cave, and so I've never used it.

This space is right across the hall from Morgan's playroom, and as I pass it this morning, it hits me. This is my "Himalayan cave," like a plush version of the caves my books say ancient Yogis took residence in as they sought enlightenment. This is where my healing journey will continue, my place of solitude, contemplation, and *Sadhana,* the

Yogic ritual of devoted daily practice. I have no desire to renounce the world and am light-years away from enlightenment, but I need a cave, a private space for healing, and this is perfect. It's as if the little room has been waiting ever since I bought my home for just this moment to arrive. I call a friend who does carpentry and beg him to come over immediately. We decide to tear everything out of the office and install ceiling-to-floor mirrors on three of the walls. This will create endless reflections, an infinity effect, that will give the room a sense of spaciousness while also allowing me to view my alignment in various Yoga poses.

When Morgan was born I could barely participate in putting together his nursery. Now I'm able to climb up a ladder to the container box and tack some silk tapestries over the fluorescent light panels. I was given the tapestries when I was in Thailand, and as I drape them so they dip and billow, it creates an exotic, soothing effect, like I'm in a temple. Then I climb down the ladder and roll out my Yoga mat beneath the "temple lights," making sure it's perfectly aligned in the center of the room.

One angled corner of the room, by the entry, has a small diagonal shelf built into the wall. This becomes my new altar. The golden Buddha I brought out of North Vietnam is the centerpiece. A friend from Boston sent me a white silk scarf blessed by the Dalai Lama for my fiftieth birthday. I wrap this around the lotus blossom carved at the base of the Buddha statue. I'm not studying or practicing Buddhism, but to me it symbolizes a spiritual quest and holds personal meaning as well. Finally, I add candles, incense, and a few gemstones I picked up during my travels as a journalist, and my new altar is complete.

My comfy Himalayan cave feels like I'm in an ancient temple and is exactly what I need. I'm up again at four every morning, immersing myself in my practice. I begin by lighting candles and incense at the altar, then whispering a soft prayer for healing. Gazing at the golden Buddha, I touch the silk cloth blessed by the Dalai Lama. For the first few weeks, I ponder the significance of the statue's left index finger pointing upwards and his right pointing down. Then I finally get it. The Buddha is pointing toward Heaven and Earth.

The gesture signifies "as above, so below." It's a concept found in Yoga as well as most religions, a reminder that each of us is connected to all that is.

I'm up at four again, this time without any alarm clock. The sages of Yoga named this pre-dawn time the "Time of the Divine." I can see why. There's something naturally meditative about this dark and silent time before sunrise. The moment I sit on my mat I can feel stillness surround me. I can also sense the world preparing to come alive for a new day. Breathing deeply, I see myself becoming part of this eternal rhythm, which helps to make my practice seem effortless. My body feels fluid. The air tastes like nectar. I am connected and fully alive.

It also feels healing. We live in a stressed-out world and spend most of our days hurried, anxious, agitated, and feeling completely separated from any sense of unity or oneness. Our minds are spinning like crazy with endless streams of disparate and disjointed thoughts. Mass media, TV, and video culture spin us further with an overload of fast-paced images and intense sounds. As a result, like Dr. Miller says in his *Deep Healing* book, we're usually in a low level of "fight or flight" response, adrenalin constantly pumping through our veins. I felt this every day as a journalist, especially in war zones and in the pressure to meet deadlines for filing my news reports, but even in less-trying times the stress was omnipresent.

In this "fight or flight" state, Dr. Miller says, our sympathetic nervous system takes precedence in order to meet the perceived emergency we feel we're facing. It's one of the major aspects of our autonomic nervous system, which subconsciously and automatically controls our responses to stimuli, including our heart rate, digestion, breath, salivation, and perspiration. When the sympathetic nervous system is activated, our hearts beat faster and we perspire as energy courses through us to prepare us for an emergency. This shuts down much of our digestive and immune systems so that our energy can be used to fight or take flight. It's a good state to be in when there's a serious threat to our lives or we have important tasks to accomplish, but being in "fight or flight" all the time burns us out and damages our health—*don't I know it!*

Practicing deep relaxation, Dr. Miller notes, allows the parasympathetic nervous system to take over. This is a state of "rest and digest" as opposed to "fight or flight." In this state, adrenalin stops flowing through our veins and our brains produce soothing neuropeptides that promote healing. Our digestive and immune functions are rekindled and our heart rates slow down. Our nerves relax and our organs recalibrate themselves. Body and mind begin to harmonize and heal. This is why animals crawl into caves when they're wounded, instinctually knowing that deep relaxation is essential for their survival.

I experience this state of deep relaxation and inner peace every time I slip into my cave. Sitting cross-legged on my mat, I can feel stress melt away and healing taking place in all aspects of my being, especially when I bring full attention to my breath. Deep breathing continues to help me release old psychological wounds and cleanse my emotions. Focusing on my breath is not only healing, it's a passageway to merging with something mystical and eternal, connecting me to my growing sense of higher power, a silent conversation with the very essence of life.

Chanting *Get up, Daddy* with the flow of my breath, I sequence myself through a series of gentle Yoga postures, slowly and mindfully, harmonizing every movement with sustained deep and rhythmic breaths. Each time I breathe in, I see myself drinking in golden healing light that permeates my entire body while soothing and cleansing my mind. As I exhale deeper into each twist, extension, forward fold, and backbend, I visualize that I'm squeezing out years of pain and toxins. I also try to find something in every pose that's called "the edge." It's the place where I'm moving my body into new territory and going beyond my comfort zone. At the same time, I have to be careful not to go too far and enter the realm of pain or risk an injury. It's a delicate balance, like walking a tightrope.

At the end of my practice, I often place a candle in front of me and sit gazing at the flame. This is a Yoga technique that crystallizes the mind, brings me further into the present moment, and promotes single-pointed concentration. As my mind stills further and becomes more focused, I see deeper into the essence of the flame and the element of fire itself. I notice flames within flames. Colors within colors. The miracle of fire. A tiny piece of our sun. I close my eyes and gaze at the image of the flame as it floats behind my eyelids, changing hue and form. All stress melts away now. My mind is as still and calm as a placid lake. I am fully here in this eternal moment.

Although I've come a long way physically, it's still impossible to sit cross-legged on my mat staring at the candle for more than a few minutes without having spasms in my lower back. Each time this happens, instead of reacting with fear like in the past, I breathe, stretch, and relax myself out of it, then support my back against one of the mirrored walls and continue my meditation on the flame.

By sunrise, I'm in the zone. Totally present, serene yet vitalized, feeling balanced in body, mind, and Soul. I gather my consciousness to my heart center, a space right behind the breastbone next to the organ of the heart. Yoga teaches us this is where the light of the Soul dwells. I listen for the whisper of my inner wisdom, open myself to its guidance, and then, toward the end of my practice, ask this Divine wisdom within me to help me heal. The messages I receive from this ritual are consistent.

> *Practice every day.*
> *Breathe deeply all the time.*
> *Take it further and further.*
> *Purify yourself in body and mind.*
> *Move beyond your perceived limitations.*
> *Release the past.*
> *Open your heart.*
> *Live from your Soul.*

In the "Time of the Divine," I listen. I learn. I deepen my devotion. I feel like I am being slowly transformed.

CHAPTER 33

The Story Bench

I F YOU HAVE A FRAYED ELECTRICAL WIRE, there's no light
when you flick on the switch. Touch the wire and you'll be
shocked. Ignore it and it smolders. It can start a fire. Burn your
house down. This is what's it's often like between Pamela and me.
And we can't seem to find a way to fix it.

We have some really good times together, and they make both
of us hopeful that things are going to work out just fine. When I
find out that the creator of the therapeutic Yoga that Savita taught
me at the Pain Center is leading a weeklong retreat in the mountains of Costa Rica, Pamela agrees to make it a family trip. She and
Morgan join me, relaxing together while I'm in the retreat sessions.
I'm amazed that I can even make this trip without much pain, and
thankful that the Yoga is gentle and therapeutic, which helps me
recover from sitting on the airplane and riding in third world taxis.
Secretly, I'm hoping Pamela will get interested in doing Yoga with me
and attend a session or two, but I soon see that it's not meant to be
and choose not to push it.

After the retreat, we visit some of Costa Rica's remote beaches and
national parks, even taking a small tour boat into jungle swamps
where dozens of small, black monkeys crawl aboard from the man-
grove trees to snatch bananas out of our hands. The tour guide
ensures us the monkeys are harmless, and Morgan is completely en-
raptured when a baby monkey climbs onto his head and chatters like

crazy. Pamela bursts into laughter and snaps a million pictures. The whole experience renews my hope that things might work out for us as a family. *Maybe we really can put the past behind us, forgive and forget, move forward together, and build a new life.*

Once we're home again, however, old wounds arise and we both feel alienated. I know that it was my darkness, depression, and anger that created the distance and distrust for years. I do my best to take full responsibility for this, and each day have a little more clarity into how difficult it must have been for Pamela. But now, even though I'm off medications, have forsaken alcohol, and am devoting myself to a healing practice, it's just not working between us. I think about it in my morning meditations and realize how overwhelming it must be for her to deal with all the rapid, unexpected changes. Pamela fell in love with a journalist who was filled with boundless enthusiasm, married a disabled person who careened into an abyss of darkness, and now she's facing something completely new with a burgeoning Yogi. How does anyone accept or trust that?

It makes me feel empty and lost, especially when we get into the blame game that seems to be such a trap for couples. I get stuck between feeling terrible about who I was during my darkest days and the need to stand my ground as I build a new life. Pamela can't connect with the person I'm becoming, and I can't turn back to the person I was when we first fell in love. We continue to sleep in separate bedrooms off and on. Resigned to being civil. Especially when Morgan is near. It's as if we're already separated but still living in the same home. Tiptoeing around the truth of our circumstance. Denying the pain and hoping for the best.

Pamela's circle of friends solidified in my absence: four or five couples with children Morgan's age, the husbands with successful careers in money management, banking, and real estate, and the wives stay-at-home moms with nannies so they can enjoy luncheons, spa days, and shopping sprees. While I was in detox and at the Pain Center, they became Pamela's primary source of companionship and support. They're intelligent, good-natured, and fun-loving people, and they've been supportive and interested in learning about my healing experiences. Still, I feel like a complete outsider when we're all together. Pamela senses this and it's another source of tension. This is her world now. It's important to her that I fit in. But I don't.

I try attending a few of the weekly parties, always held at the near-by home of the most social couple, but it's painfully clear to everyone that I now live in a very different world. The evenings focus on lavish food and drink. I've become vegetarian and don't drink. The casual banter usually drifts toward television shows or the latest social and fashion trends of which I'm completely unaware. Part of me wants desperately to fit in, so I attempt to contribute something light and funny. My words always feel inauthentic and contrived as they come out of my mouth, and they inevitably land with a thud. Each time this happens, I realize I don't belong to this tribe, and it hurts.

As everyone gets a little tipsy and the laughter gets louder, I can't help but withdraw, and it's painfully obvious to everyone that I'm uncomfortable. This in turn makes them feel like I don't approve. It's not the case, but honestly, if I was drinking and having fun and there was someone like me at the party, I wouldn't want them around either. Eventually, I go silent and slip out to relieve Morgan's baby-sitter, occasionally hearing jokes about Yoga and self-realization on my way out the door. Yoga postures as a form of exercise are fine for Pamela's friends, but my taking on Yoga as a complete lifestyle is just too much. Again, if I were them, I'd feel the same way, and although I know Pamela is happy that I'm no longer drinking or taking meds, this is her tribe. I can feel that she shares their sentiments about who I've become. *Who could blame her?*

After leaving these parties and getting Morgan to bed, I crawl back into my cave to do practice poses and study my texts. It never feels good to slip away like that, so I need the poses and deep breathing all the more. I usually become so absorbed that I never hear Pamela come home.

I finish my *Sadhana* toward midnight, then tiptoe upstairs to catch a few hours of deep sleep. When I wake up the next morning before dawn, I tiptoe back downstairs to the cave again. As the sun rises, despite being focused on my practices, I always sense when Morgan begins to wake up. I hurry upstairs, cuddle him in my arms, then draw on his back. Once we've finished with the magic drawing stick, I get him dressed and make him breakfast. This is when he always does the funniest thing.

His blond hair has dark, golden streaks, matching his golden-brown eyes. He has lost most of his baby fat, but he still has the big, plump cheeks of his infancy. For some mysterious reason, he likes to fill them with as much food as he can before swallowing, looking like a chipmunk about to explode. When I ask him why, he just smiles like a Cheshire cat. I don't want to encourage him, but it's so hilarious I can't restrain my laughter.

Using grown-up logic in an attempt to persuade Morgan to swallow only makes him smile wider and stuff in another bite, so for weeks I play games to cajole him into it—to no avail. Pretending my hand is a talking puppet that begs him to swallow fails to do the trick. Having our cat, Max, sit on my lap and playing feline ventriloquist is also a bust. But finally, I hide a shiny penny in my hand and "discover" it in his ear, telling him he can have the penny when he swallows all his food. Bingo. It works every time.

After breakfast, his meal safely in his belly, Morgan climbs into his three-wheeled stroller and we head for the beach. We make each journey an adventure: stopping to explore flower gardens, staying on the lookout for hummingbirds and butterflies, saying good morning to the sun and inviting it to kiss our faces. Our trip to the ocean is about one mile. It's a glorious meditation, as rich as any experience in my cave. But I doubt I could make it without holding the stroller to support my weak legs.

Our journey always ends at a park bench in a quiet place on the boardwalk overlooking Coronado's wide, sandy beach. We call this the "story bench." The moment I sit down, Morgan crawls onto my lap and I ad-lib a story about some exciting drama at sea in which he is always the hero. This morning we see a small school of silver-gray dolphins coursing south toward Mexico, their fins arching above the shimmering ocean surface then disappearing below. Lines of pelicans, always in perfect formation, glide across the smooth faces of blue waves, swooping just above the dolphins.

"There was a special sea," I begin, hoping the story will come together of its own accord, "where children rode the pelicans through the morning sky, dipping their toes in the warm waves just before those waves curled and crashed." Morgan snuggles in closer, a signal that he's already enthralled with the tale.

"Every now and then, just for fun, a little boy or girl would jump off their pelican right as a dolphin came up to take a breath. They gently landed on the dolphin's back, holding its fin in their hands. The dolphins loved this and took the children on amazing rides, streaming down the faces of great waves, jumping into the air and twisting in the sky, then landing softly back in the water."

"Does anyone ever fall off?" Morgan asks, just to make sure the children are safe.

"Never. The dolphins know just what to do. But one day everything changed."

"What happened, Daddy?" He knows big danger is coming and I can feel his excitement.

"A giant sea monster came sneaking along. He was very unhappy because he thought everyone hated monsters, and watching the children having so much fun hurt his feelings. So when no one was looking, he grabbed a child off a dolphin and took it to his secret cave and kept the child captive."

"Bad monster," Morgan whispers with a blend of compassion and concern.

"Every day the sea monster snuck off with another child, until almost half were missing. The others gathered one evening, crying and wondering what to do. That's when a special little boy showed up in their midst. Do you know what his name was?"

"Morgan!" he exclaims, knowing full well how the story is about to unfold.

"That's right. *Morgan*. He arrived on the biggest dolphin anyone had ever seen and told the children he would help them. The next day, Morgan went and rode a pelican over the waves, all alone. When he glimpsed the sea monster, he jumped into the water and let it capture him. He was that brave!" As I say this, Morgan reaches for my hand and gives it a squeeze of glee.

"When they got to the cave, Morgan said, 'I don't think you're a monster at all. You are just sad that nobody likes you. But I like you. Why not let all these kids go and come play with us? I'm sure they will like you, too. We can ride on your back and swim with the dolphins and laugh all day!'"

"'You'd all really be my friends?' the monster asked. 'Yes, of course,' Morgan answered, patting him gently on his big, horrible wet nose."

"The monster smiled his very first smile, gathered all the captured kids onto his gigantic back, and swam out of the cave. The other children met them and took rides on the monster as well, hugging him and telling him how much they loved him. Everyone was happy from that day forward, and they all said, 'Thank you, Morgan!'"

As his joy with the happy ending sinks in, I ask Morgan to tell me what the story is about. "Love, Daddy. It's always better to love everybody, even if they aren't nice to you. Love always makes everything work out right."

"That's right, sweetheart," I tell him with a big hug, "and I love you more than anything in the world."

I could sit with Morgan on our story bench for hours, thrilled at his enjoyment of my tall tales, but, sadly, I have to tell to him that it's time to go. Morgan will have none of this, nestling further into my lap and pleading, "Tell me another story, Daddy. Please, please, please." I always give in at least once, often twice, taxing my mind for more stories of dangers and rescues on the high seas. As I hold him in my arms and whisper a new story into his ear, I'm touched by what an amazing person he is. He has never had a tantrum or a crying fit. He always seems serene and grounded, perfectly at peace with himself and the world around him, like a little Buddha.

Pamela takes over when we get home, making Morgan lunch and getting him down for his nap. I slip back into my cave to relax after the big adventure, study my texts, and practice more Yoga poses. Pamela and I switch off preparing dinner, which is now one of our few family meals together. After dinner, I read to Morgan, give him a bath, and, of course, we still have the sacred ritual of drawing on his back before bedtime.

After we put Morgan to sleep, I slip back into my cave for several more hours. Toward the end of my practice, I play some soft chords on my guitar, hum, and chant "OM." My throat still bleeds periodically, and I occasionally lose my voice and can't speak very well, much less sing. But when I can chant, it tunes up a body and mind that have been in deep disharmony for years and, in the process, creates a new song of life.

After two months of devotion in my cave, I instinctually awaken even earlier, usually at 3 A.M. Some mornings, however, I want nothing more than to linger under the warm covers. When this happens, *Get up, Daddy* floods into my mind and I drag myself into the shower. This morning my ego is especially resistant. Urging me to jump back into bed and pull the covers over my head. Offering great justifications for doing so. How devoted I've been and how much I deserve the break. So I run the shower on pure cold, just to expand my comfort zone, and teach my ego a lesson. "Ahhhh!" I scream when I step in, jumping up and down under the freezing spray like a wild baboon. It works. Soon enough, I'm downstairs in my cave again, immersed in the "Time of the Divine."

I'm now practicing and studying an average of twelve hours every day. I devour every book I can find and explore various restorative Yoga poses, endlessly sequencing them together in different ways while bringing all my awareness to how they impact my physical body, emotional body, and energy body. I notice where I am weak, imbalanced, or inflexible and seek to stabilize, strengthen, and expand. I also notice where I am emotional or feel energetically knotted up and seek to release past hurts, angers, and fears. When my mind gets agitated, I focus on my breath, beckon myself back to the present moment, and reconnect with my inner Spirit.

Every moment of practice feels rich and nourishing, but the most sublime moments always come during the hours before dawn. I experience the whole world in a state of stillness and silence, yet filled with power and potential. The *Prana* of life seems to dance in the atmosphere, and I can taste it in every cell of my body. Being fully in the present moment gives me a sense of clarity and connection. It reminds me of the times I arose before sunrise in a Saudi desert, the mountains of Bolivia, or in the jungles of Africa. It didn't matter that there was chaos and conflict in the world. Everything seemed perfect, just as it should be. It was a deeply meditative state that, at that time in my life, I sensed but barely understood. Now I understand it in all its richness and fullness.

Outside my cave, my time is devoted to Morgan, except for four to five hours of sleep. With the relaxation and balancing practices of Yoga, this is usually more than enough rest and I feel more energized than ever before in my life. Rather than aging, it's as if I've found the fountain of youth and am growing younger by the day. I continue to get leaner, stronger, and more confident and optimistic about life. I feel completely in charge of my back pain now. It rarely comes up, and I'm able to handle it better every time it does.

But the cancer is something else. Whenever my throat feels sore or my energy plummets, a bolt of fear strikes me. *God grant me serenity. Accept what I cannot change. Change the things I can.* This is all I can do. *Let it go. Accept what happens. Stay with Yoga.* Maybe what some of my books say is true. *Maybe I can whip this, too.* Maybe, just maybe, I can also salvage my marriage. Like cancer, though, the thought of it weighs me down and fills me with fear. I can't figure out how to fix it and it's frustrating. The thought of facing it head-on, maybe separating for a while or ending it altogether, completely overwhelms me. *God grant me serenity.*

On Sunday mornings, I break my routine and walk three blocks down the street to hear Father David's sermons. He continues to inspire me, and my love, gratitude, and respect for him run deep. The teachings of his church are in synch with the spiritual teachings of Yoga, which is devoted to peace, compassion, and unity, but I realize I'll eventually stop attending services. Yoga is my path, my cave is my house of worship, and my *Sadhana* is my silent sermon. It provides me with a tangible experience of being connected to my sense of a higher power. Every movement, every breath, every mantra, and every meditation is ultimately a homage to the Divine. I'm in all the way—body, mind, and Soul.

CHAPTER 34

Bayside Healing

I T NO LONGER HURTS to sit cross-legged on my mat without back support. I can touch my toes in forward folds. Arm-leg balances are a breeze. My range of motion in twists has doubled. The more powerful standing poses in my books are still far beyond my reach, but I feel like I'm always in the "edge" now, stretching my limits and mastering many poses that were once impossible for me to even consider. These include *Bujanghasana*, *Anjaneyasana*, and *Janu Sirsanana*.

These Sanskrit names always challenge me. It's hard to read or remember them, much less say them. But the books have some pronunciation tips, and the more I practice saying these names in Sanskrit, the more I feel connected to this ancient wisdom. When I whisper the name of a pose while deep in my practice, it's like the ancient sages are in the room with me. I think sometimes I can even feel them in my bones.

Bujanghasana (Boo-jan-gah-suh-nuh) translates as Cobra Pose. In this posture, I lie on my stomach with my legs straight out behind me. Then I place my palms firmly by the sides of my chest and lift my head, chest, and shoulders up from my mat for five or six full breaths. This creates a backbend that strengthens the major muscles along my spine and makes me feel radiant and energized. A month ago I couldn't come close to performing this pose. Now it feels natural and nourishing.

Anjaneyasana (Aan-jaahn-eee-ahhh-suh-nuh) is a Low Lunge Pose that demands strength, flexibility, and balance. To do this pose, I step my right foot on the mat between my hands, with my knee deeply bent. The left leg is straight out behind me, with that knee, shin, and foot down on the mat. Then I lift my torso up and raise both arms into the air. Now I am lunging into the ground, opening my hips while rising up through my torso, and expanding my ribs and spine in an arc. As I do this, I visualize that I'm reaching up to embrace the Divine while sinking into Mother Earth as I become that place where Heaven meets Earth. *As above, so below.* This pose is done on both sides, so I switch the positions of my legs after three or four breaths, which is all I have the strength for.

In *Janu Sirsanana* (Jaah-noo-sear-shah-suh-nuh), which simply means Head to Knee Pose, I sit with my right leg straight out in front of me on my mat. I bend my left knee and bring the sole of my left foot to my inner right thigh, pressing my left knee out and down toward the floor. I take a deep inhale and raise my arms high in the air, then exhale and fold forward at my hips, reaching for my right toes. I can't quite get there yet but have become flexible enough to hold my shin close to the ankle. This pose is also done on both sides, and I can hold it for ten breaths. It feels relaxing, nourishing, and comforting, like I'm folding into my heart.

From the Yogic viewpoint, all my *Asanas*, *Pranayama*, and meditation practices have acted synergistically to build something within me called *Agni*. Yoga teaches me that *Agni* is an energetic radiance—an inner fire—that burns away the dross. At its basic level, *Agni* is the digestive and metabolic fire that allows us to absorb nutrients from our food. It is also the inner heat of effort that promotes purification through perspiration, destroying harmful organisms and toxins while repairing and maintaining organs, muscles, bones, and blood. *Agni* is an inner elixir that enhances the immune system and creates resistance to disease. On more subtle levels, *Agni* helps us process, digest, and release mental and emotional imbalances, thus building self-discipline, confidence, and optimism. Ultimately, *Agni* is the radiance and illumination that arises from spiritual practice and helps us sustain and support a journey of self-awareness and personal transformation.

Once again, it's a concept totally outside of Western paradigms, but I like the depth of the science and the way it makes me revamp my view of the world. And because I'm actually experiencing it rather than just reading about it, I know it works, so all my skepticism is gone. The best example is that *Agni* also helps burn away body fat. Stepping on the bathroom scale after my practice this morning, I'm down to 180 pounds. Forty-five pounds lighter than my heaviest weight of 225 and back to where I was during my life as a foreign correspondent. Better yet, I haven't had a back spasm in a month. I don't need any stats or studies. This is all proof to me that Yoga and its fire of *Agni* are for real and it affirms my decision to be all in. One hundred percent. Maybe even one hundred ten percent.

Being adventurous and impulsive, I feel like celebrating my weight loss and a crazy thought arises inside of me about how to do it. I think I now have enough balance, energy, and courage to do something I never dreamed would be possible, especially with a failed back surgery: buy a bicycle! With a bike I can get out of my cave more, pedal around the island, see it for the first time through new eyes. The very idea makes me feel like a child again.

I've picked out a hybrid between a beach cruiser and a racing bike at the local bike shop. It's clearly much more bicycle than I am rider. When I climb on, I'm tenuous and unstable, like when I was four years old and my father removed the training wheels from my first bike. I hold on tightly, place my feet on the pedals, and take off, somehow managing not to fall as I zig and zag like a drunken snake down the street. I have just enough balance to stay up, but I quickly start sweating like I'm in the final stretch of the Tour de France. After rounding our neighborhood block just once, I'm drenched and my thighs are screaming so loudly I have to call it quits.

Soon enough, however, I get the hang of it. Much like my experience when I gain mastery over a challenging Yoga pose, I feel incredibly empowered on my bike. After a few days I can even make it twice around the block without feeling like I'm going to collapse, and it puts much less strain on my back than walking does. Morgan has yet to get on a tricycle, but I envision us riding bikes all over the island one day, making more discoveries of special places to relax, tell stories, and play in the sunshine. I make a mental note of this: *One day we'll ride!*

After a few weeks of daily practice, I can bike all the way to the bayside of the island a mile and a half from home. It's mostly a gentle, flat ride on beautiful residential streets and underneath one end of the Coronado Bridge. This takes me back to the Le Méridien Hotel, where I first lived after leaving Hong Kong in 1993. The hotel has been acquired by the Marriott chain, but the staff still sends me letters to confirm it is honoring the complimentary spa membership I was granted during my long stay here, which seems like a lifetime ago. The spa has a quiet, upscale gym offering generous views of the bay. Although I'm healthier than I've been in years, my muscles have atrophied and I have very low endurance. Yet another crazy idea bubbles up: *It's time to take the game a little further.*

Every morning now, thirty minutes before sunrise, I quietly slip out of my cave, hop on my bike, and head out through the darkness and quietude of Coronado's neighborhoods to the bay. I drink in everything I can see in the predawn light. Certain sights captivate me and become inspirational signposts. As I turn toward the pathway that takes me under the bridge, there's a sleek, towering eucalyptus tree on the edge of the golf course. It reminds me of the essence of *Anjanyasana*, the Yoga pose where I reach up to Heaven while deeply lunging into Mother Earth. A small sandy beach dotted with colorful rowboats reminds me that life still holds mystery, possibility, and adventure. The stately white egrets I see standing in perfect stillness at the water's edge almost every morning are the essence of focus, balance, and stillness.

There's a large cement foundation on a grassy knoll at the Marriott near the villa I once lived in and befriended Fred the duck. The hotel periodically pitches huge tents here for special events, but the space is never used in these early morning hours. I make it my outdoor Yoga studio, rolling my mat out at the edge of the platform to be as near the water as possible. After a few gentle Yoga poses to work out the kinks from the bike ride, I sit in stillness, listening to the lapping of the bay waters, the morning calls of gulls, terns, ducks, egrets, and the occasional cry of an osprey.

The San Diego skyline towers across the bay to the northeast, and I can feel the city slowly coming alive. To the southeast is the Coronado Bridge, with the arch of its sloping blue span perfectly framing a range of mountains on the border with Mexico. This is where the sun rises. As soft, predawn light begins to glow on the mountaintops, I sit in meditation with my eyes fully open, drinking in everything as a new day prepares to dawn.

Mud hens and cormorants float on the surface of the bay then quickly dive under, seeking their morning meals. An occasional seal swims slowly by, wriggling its whiskers like it's smiling at me. A solitary boat floats out from the harbor, its wake leaving a rippling pattern behind it like migrating geese in flight. The ridgeline of the mountains begins to glow in hues of pink and gold as the sky expands. I begin soft chants of "OM," and it sounds like all of nature is humming the mantra with me. I feel my entire being realign with the natural rhythms of Mother Earth and the cosmos.

Finally, the sun bursts forth above the mountains, sending a thick, dazzling beam of golden light dancing across the bay right into my heart center. It's an electrifying, out-of-body sensation, like the first time I stepped into the Yoga room at the Pain Center. As the sun continues to rise, I feel golden light pouring into every cell of my being, cleansing, healing, and energizing me like celestial *Agni*. I can sense Mother Earth spinning through the heavens around this star in a glorious dance, and it's easy to understand why so many ancient cultures worshipped the sun as a deity and the source of all life.

I drink in the deepest breaths possible, thanking my back pain, the broken vertebra, and the failed surgery for all they have taught me. The very first time I tried this practice of gratitude, waves of relief rolled through me, so I've stuck with it. I breathe in light and life and then exhale pain and suffering, accepting all physical challenges and setbacks as blessings and catalysts for positive change.

Concluding my practice as the sun lifts fully into the morning sky, I surrender to whatever the future may hold, then bring my palms together at my heart center in *Anjali Mudra* and bow my head, whispering, "Thank you, sun." I finish with the Sanskrit term Savita taught me at the Pain Center, "*Namaste*," sending a prayer from the light of my heart to the light of the sun. Then I softly roll up my mat, slowly rise to my feet, and walk in a sense of meditation to the Marriott spa.

The spa's quiet, upscale gym offers generous views of the bay, though my focus is on the machines. I spend almost an hour trying every one of them. I have to keep the weights low. Despite how much stronger I've become, every exercise machine confirms I'm still weak and lack stamina. In my prime, I could bench-press 245 pounds for ten repetitions. Now I couldn't lift fifty pounds for five reps if my life depended on it. I go slowly, taking several extra minutes on each machine to improvise supported Yoga poses: twists, extensions, hamstring stretches, and hip-openers. I'm doing a lot more Yoga than lifting, but the combination is furthering my progress, as strange and comical as I must appear to the dedicated morning workout crowd who begin to arrive as I finish up. I always try to make an exit before they pop on the TVs and the Sports Channel begins to blare and break the beauty of the morning.

The bike ride home is a bit of a challenge. Along with a slight incline in this direction, there's a steep hill two-thirds of the way back that still gets the best of me. Although it's only half a block long and no more than a thirty percent incline, it looms like the Himalaya Mountains themselves. I can't get ten feet up the slope without stopping, dismounting, and pushing my bike the rest of the way, huffing and puffing as I go. Little kids heading for school zip right past me, zooming straight up the hill on their tiny bikes. I have to pause and laugh with complete abandon or else I might break into tears.

Pamela and I have rearranged our schedules to accommodate this new phase of my practice. She makes Morgan breakfast in the morning and gets him to preschool. I return from the bay and slip back into my cave until it's time to pick him up at mid-day. I make him lunch, then he and I take off to the beach for story time. Once home, we play until his afternoon nap. I return to my cave, emerging each evening to pedal in the other direction, westward to the beach for sunset. It's another transformative experience for me, meditating on the song of the ocean waves, watching the seagulls gather on the sand to prepare for evening as sailboats return to harbor beneath the golden-pink light. I'm filled with a refreshingly new and deep sense of gratitude as I say, "Goodnight, sun. Thank you, sun. Namaste," again feeling synchronized with the rhythms of nature and truly blessed to be alive.

I'm home in time for dinner and bedtime rituals with Morgan, and then, of course, back in my cave for nighttime practices. This expansion of activities and spiritual connection with nature has deepened my confidence and commitment. I bike to the bay almost every day now, even on mornings when it is cold, cloudy, and foggy, only skipping the ride if there's a rare rain shower. Even then, I drive my car and do my sunrise practice in the spa, listening to the song of the storm as the sky comes alive in hues of silver and gray. I try never to miss the sunset, either, even if it's ducking down behind thick clouds or hidden in a bank of fog. Despite all this, the ego never goes away. It always wants to be in charge and is masterful at conjuring innumerable reasons not to stay faithful to my practice. But I have a deep sense that if I slack off, I'm not going to make it. My back will go bad again. I might even want painkillers. Who knows? The idea of falling back into the abyss is completely unacceptable to me, so I keep finding new ways to put my ego in its place.

Sometimes I walk outside and let the rain pour down all over me, then run inside and take a hot shower to break the chill. Occasionally, on an unusually cold morning, I bundle my sweatshirt and thermal jacket in the basket between the handlebars of my bike and take the morning ride bare-chested. It freezes me to the marrow and it's everything I can do not to scream and wake up all the neighbors along my route to the bay. But I persevere by thinking of how young children can jump into cold oceans and lakes that adults can no longer step a toe in, or play endlessly in the hot sun without the need for air conditioning and shade.

As children, we have an innate capacity to handle a wide range of experiences. We take the hot and cold better than adults. We fall down, skin a knee, let out a roar, then get back up and keep going. But as we age, we become addicted to our creature comforts, we constrict our range, avoiding more and experiencing less. None more so than I during my years of being bedridden and medicated. After such an extended time of feeling nothing but chronic pain and depressed emotions, dancing in the rain and taking crazy, cold bike rides help me reclaim my inner child and expand my range once again. After so many years of running away from the pain inside of my body, I realize I've inhabited it once again. I've developed a new relationship with myself, discovered my inner life force, and opened myself more and more to the possibility of a completely new life.

CHAPTER 35

Going Deeper

A
N OLD INDIAN ADAGE, often attributed to the Buddha, says that when the student is ready, the teacher will appear. One rainy morning, I see on the Marriott spa bulletin board that a Yoga class is scheduled to begin at 6 A.M., in just thirty minutes. I'm there on my mat ten minutes early, laughing at myself for being so excited. I try to close my eyes and meditate on my breath, but all I can think about is what the class will be like, and so I keep popping my eyes open, looking for the teacher. As the time for class approaches, it looks like I might be the only student, but then two or three hotel guests amble in just as the instructor arrives.

"Hello, my name is Rene, and it's good to be here with you," she says with a tone that feels contained and authentic. Then, with a twinkle in her eyes, she adds, "We're here to move our bodies and move our breath, but most importantly, we're going to have a good time doing it."

Like my first teacher at the Pain Center, Savita, Rene is peaceful, grounded, and extremely present. She also sparkles with a childlike joy that's contagious. She looks like a cross between an athlete and an actor who plays Peter Pan in summer theaters, with short-cropped blond hair, wide green eyes, a muscular frame, and ballet-like movements. Her strength and flexibility are remarkable as she demonstrates the poses.

Rene's class is gentle and restorative, yet playful and invigorating. Although I'm familiar with all the poses, she takes me to new levels in each one and it feels effortless. Moreover, I can sense Rene's intelligence and devotion. By the middle of class I'm convinced she has great wisdom and insight into Yoga as a spiritual and transformative practice, not just as an exercise. As the class ends, I know I've found my next teacher. I quietly wait for Rene to end her conversation with the hotel guests then meekly ask for a minute of her time. "I need your help," I say, giving her the shortest version of my story that I can muster.

"I feel I can't take it much further without a teacher like you," I explain to Rene, telling her that I've been creating my practices from reading books and then letting my intuition guide me from there. With a teacher, I hope to get feedback on what I've devised for myself, learn how to do the poses with more specific guidance on my alignment, plus get more help with breath work and meditation. The books have so many practices that I sometimes feel overwhelmed and don't know which are best for me at this stage. I also feel like I've been alone on this journey for too long and need company, especially with someone who will validate rather than ridicule what I'm doing. I don't want any misimpression, so I'm careful to note that I'm married and have a child. There's no other agenda than to practice Yoga with someone who can take me to the next level.

"I think there's a lot we can do," Rene answers in a softly confident tone counterpoised with a radiant smile. "Let's try it and see how it goes."

We agree to practice twice a week on the Marriott boat dock, which juts about thirty yards into the bay near the platform where I sit each morning for my sunrise practices. When we meet the next day, Rene has brought several thick, woolen Yoga blankets for our session. We begin by doing a series of the restorative poses that I'm used to, but with Rene's guidance and gentle, hands-on adjustments, I go deeper into them than ever before. A half-hour later, she uses the blankets to create a comfortable place on the wooden planks of the dock for me to lie down on my back. This is called *Savasana* (Shuh-va-suh-nuh), which is always the final pose in Yoga practice. *Sava* means corpse, and *Asana*, a pose, hence *Savasana* is the Corpse Pose.

In a way, it's like playing dead, lying there like a corpse in stillness and silence, except there's nothing morbid about it. The death is symbolic, signifying the cessation of movement, thought, and ego. It's a deep and profound letting go of the body, mind, and senses while remaining fully aware and present. Before I lie down, Rene takes a long, soft cotton scarf and wraps it several times around my forehead, covering my eyes and ears. "This is a technique of withdrawing the senses," she says. "The more we internalize our awareness, the deeper we are able to go."

With the cloth around my head, I can't see a thing and barely hear the lapping of the bay waters, but Rene's voice comes through perfectly as she guides me into relaxing as she places her palm on my abdomen.

"I can see you already breathe very deeply," she says. "I noticed it in class. This is excellent, but I want you to breathe even deeper now, and breathe much slower. Visualize your breath starting well below my hand, down at the bottom of your pelvic bowl. Now slowly draw it all the way up to the crown of your head."

I find myself wanting to be a perfect student and take the biggest breath of my life.

"That's too fast and too shallow," Rene says with a sense of power and command that impresses me. "Dig down deeper. Start the breath lower. You are still above my hand, about at your navel, and you only took it up to your throat. Start lower and drink it all the way up to the crown of your head."

I focus even more and deepen every inhalation, willing it with all my might to begin in my pelvic bowl and then seeking to pull it to the top of my head. Of course, I'm only filling my lungs with my breath, but the visualization helps me draw my diaphragm down and lengthen my lungs for a much fuller inhale. The effects are profound. After a dozen or so breaths, I feel like I'm floating a few feet above my body.

"You're doing a good job," Rene encourages me, "but don't strain. Keep everything relaxed but your lungs and diaphragm. Deeper now." The Peter Pan playfulness I witnessed in the spa is completely gone. This is all business.

Another dozen breaths and it begins to come naturally. Every cell in my body is lightly buzzing and I feel like I'm floating somewhere above the dock, going higher and higher. Just as I think I might leave my body altogether and soar into the stratosphere, Rene gently brings me down.

"Relax your breath now. No effort. Just let the air breathe you. Listen to it gently rise and fall like a wave. As you do this, gaze into the darkness behind your closed eyes. This is the inner universe. Don't look for anything specific. Just notice."

After a minute or so, an array of incredibly intricate, geometric patterns begin to emerge behind my closed eyes. They are multicolored and bedazzling, occasionally swirling like distant galaxies in endless space. My body relaxes to an even deeper level while I watch the light show. I'm completely mesmerized.

"Let this go now." I can barely hear Rene and I've lost all sense of time and place. "We'll relax your body even more now. Begin by noticing your toes… the soles of your feet… your ankles… your calves… now, your knees…"

She guides my awareness slowly through my body, from the tips of my toes to the crown of my head. It's like the body scans Savita led me through at the Pain Center, only vastly deeper. Although I've never felt so relaxed in my life, I still find tension in certain muscles and joints when Rene brings my attention to these areas. This experience reminds me once again how much stress I hold without even knowing it's there.

"Relax your emotions now," Rene continues. "Let go of all past hurts, all obstacles, all self-doubt, all resentment, anger, and fear. Accept who you are, be at peace with yourself."

Every time I softly exhale, I can feel more of my deep-seated emotional pain melting away. It's as if the gentle waters of the bay are flowing through me and cleansing old wounds. Believe me, I still have a ton of them. I've been denying the innermost layers of my emotional stuff for so many years that this process is going to take a lot more time. Still, I feel a deep level of healing from the hurts I am able to release, and I know I've found just the teacher I need.

As we conclude our session, Rene brings me back into my body and breath. She has me lie on my side, curled up like a fetus for a few minutes, then gently press myself up to seated. Once she unwraps the cloth covering my head, I open my eyes. It's like seeing the world for the very first time. Everything is alive with a visible vibration of energy. I can see it clearly in the palm trees flanking the bay and the lush floral gardens of the hotel, in the large pelican sitting on the railing of the dock a few feet from me, and permeating the clear, blue sky. It's *Prana*, the life force of all things that Yoga speaks of so clearly, including the life force within me. It's been there all along, within me and around me, but I've never been present enough to experience it.

I gaze at Rene and see her radiating with the same energy. There's no need for words. It's a profound, silent understanding. I bring my palms together at my heart and whisper, *Namaste*.

CHAPTER 36

The Studio

M Y GIRLFRIENDS JUST told me the first Yoga studio in town has opened up near the beach!" Pamela shares this with me enthusiastically one June evening, knowing it will be the biggest news I've heard in years. Even though there is distance between us, she still always seeks to be supportive and upbeat. It's always been one the greatest things about her.

"Where? Is there a phone number? Website? Address?" Hurrying over to my computer, I'm filled with questions and want to check it out immediately. I can't find a website or phone listing, but after calling Pamela's friends, I finally get the location. The studio is on the subterranean level of a two-story restaurant and shopping complex near the Hotel Del, just three blocks from our home.

Along with private sessions with Rene, I've attended the Yoga classes at the Marriott spa regularly, but they are very basic and the noise of the televisions and exercise machines in the room next door are disruptive and unsettling. I still don't feel ready to drive over the bridge to San Diego looking for a studio, so this is a godsend.

The following morning, I'm at the new studio a half-hour early for the first Yoga class of the day. No one has arrived yet to open the door and I'm the only person in the underground hallway. It's a long, dark, and drab tunnel, but I feel like a child at Disneyland. Peering through the studio windows, I see a small space, only about five hundred square feet, with glossy wood floors and mirrored walls on two opposing sides. This makes it seem more expansive, like the effect of the mirrors in my Himalayan cave. The far wall of the studio has two narrow windows at the top that allow some sunlight in from the ground level. It's the first Yoga studio I've ever seen and I find it beyond beautiful.

"Good morning. You're here so early!" I hear this welcoming voice from behind me as I continue to survey the studio. "Hi, I'm Linda. My husband, Jean-Pierre, and I are the owners of the studio. I see you have a Yoga mat. There are blankets and straps in a small closet inside if you need them."

Linda is short and fit, with abundant, curly black hair flowing almost to her waist. She radiates health, which doesn't surprise me because every Yoga teacher I've met seems to be this way. Despite her American name, she looks exotic, perhaps Middle Eastern in heritage. Her vibrant smile is welcoming. Her voice is deep and embracing. She unlocks the door and wheels a lectern into the hallway, then has me pay the class fee. A few other students begin to arrive, all women and, like Linda, in much better shape than I. Hoping to hide, I roll my mat out in the back of the room—but with mirrors on the front and back walls, it's impossible to be invisible.

We're seated cross-legged on our mats as class begins. Linda puts on gentle Yoga music and takes her seat facing us. Her strong presence quiets the chatter and brings everyone into stillness and silence. As I close my eyes, it feels like a blanket of peace is descending on the room, just like I experience during sunrise on the bay or when I practice in my cave.

"Good morning. I'm Linda. Thank you for being here. Please take a few deep breaths. Let yourself feel peaceful and grounded, getting ready for our practice this morning." Linda exudes loving kindness yet has amazing command of the room. After a few gentle, seated poses to limber up, she has us stand at the front of our mats and begins taking us through a series of energetic and challenging Yoga poses. All the Yoga poses I've done so far have been restorative. They are performed down on the mat, lying on my stomach or back, or up on my hands and knees. I've seen these standing poses in my books, but feared they were too much for me. I'm about to learn how right I was.

In a pose called Warrior, we stand in a lunge with our front legs bent deeply at the knee and our back legs straight on the mat behind us, lifting our torsos and reaching our arms high into the air. It's much harder than the lunge I've been doing with my back knee down on the mat. Everyone else in the room has a wide stance and deep lunge. My legs are less than three feet apart and my lunge is minimal. By the second breath, the thigh of my front leg is on fire and I'm having trouble keeping my balance. After a few more breaths, I realize I just can't do this and I'm silently begging Linda to let me out of the posture. I barely make it when we switch sides and place the other foot forward.

In the Triangle Pose, we take a wide stance with both legs straight and extended laterally, bringing one arm down toward our forward ankle while extending our other arm up into the air, forming a triangle. I can't reach anywhere near my ankle and have to hold my knee. Both my hamstrings begin to burn like hot lava. I feel awkward and unstable. After three breaths, I lose my balance and fall down. A few students glance at me, but most seem not to notice as they continue to hold their triangle with perfection.

"Just listen to your body, don't push it. Wherever you are in your practice is just where you're meant to be." Everyone else is relaxed and at ease in Triangle Pose. It's clear Linda's words of comfort are for me as she brings a Yoga block and places it on my mat by my front ankle, instructing me to hold it with one hand so I don't fall again. It's the same type of dense, rubbery blue block shaped in a rectangle that Savita used at the Pain Center to help me stabilize my body in certain poses. Here, in front of the other students, it feels like a crutch and a blush of embarrassment floods across my face. Worse, I still can't handle the pose.

All the other standing poses are equally challenging, and it gets even tougher for me when we balance on our right legs, lifting our left knees up toward our chest. I tremble, wobble side to side, and completely lose it. It's even harder to balance on my left leg, which has always been my nemesis because it's the leg that was damaged when I had polio as a three-year-old child, and it was the left pedicle bone of my lumbar vertebra that broke when I fell off the ledge during the storm in the Bahamas in 1986. Of course, everyone else in class is holding this Balance Pose with ease. Because they're all female, it's fabulous medicine for my male ego. I wonder if I'm not in so far over my head that I shouldn't just roll up my mat and sneak out the door. *Get up, Daddy.* I start the mantra and vow to stay with the class no matter what. *I'm in all the way.* Of course, this is when it gets tougher still.

We begin Sun Salutations, which are a series of powerful poses harmonized with the breath and woven together in a flowing sequence. We begin by standing at the front of our mats, inhaling our arms high into the air, then exhaling and folding forward at the hips, reaching down toward our toes. We inhale and step one leg back into an extended lunge, exhale and step the other leg back as well, planting our palms on our mats while lifting our hips high into the air in what is called "Downward Facing Dog." On the inhale, we bring our hips down to the mat, press into our palms and lift our upper torsos, creating a deep backbend called "Upward Facing Dog." On the exhale we push back to Downward Dog again. Then we step one leg forward back into the lunge, followed by bringing the other leg forward into a standing forward fold again. We end by inhaling and lifting our torsos up, reaching for the sky, exhaling, and bringing our palms to our heart centers.

At least that is how it's supposed to go. I'm not anywhere near flexible or strong enough to perform the Sun Salutation sequence properly. Downward Dog is impossible. So is Upward Dog. Halfway through the first round, my arms and legs are like limp noodles, my Yoga mat is an ocean of sweat, and I can't keep pace. By the end of the second round, I give up and lie down on my mat, almost hyperventilating, while the rest of the class completes a third and final round. I stay down while Linda leads the class through a few more standing poses. As she continues to instruct everyone, she somehow finds time to come over and guide me into Child's Pose, seated on my knees with my head bowing toward the floor and my buttocks down toward my heels.

"Don't worry about not being able to do everything," she whispers as she gently presses her palms into my aching lower back muscles.

"You're doing great." Linda compassionately provides the affirmation I need at precisely the right moment. I thought I was progressing so rapidly in my cave, and now I realize how far there is to go. I don't know whether to laugh or to cry, so I just breathe as deeply as I can and remind myself again, *I'm all in.*

The last portion of the class involves restorative poses. I'm back in my comfort zone and begin to feel more confident about being here. Then comes *Savasana.* This time I really do feel like a corpse as I lie on my back and almost melt into oblivion. Before I know it, I'm asleep. A few minutes later, as everyone else comes up to a seated posture for the end of class, the student next to me gives me a nudge and smiles as I groan my way slowly back up. I can't help but wonder if I've been snoring like a drunken sailor.

Despite the challenges of this more rigorous practice, I've added daily classes at the Yoga studio to my *Sadhana.* I attend every class, which is two to three times a day. They are almost always taught by Linda. The only other teacher is her husband, Jean-Pierre. He's on the road most of the time, serving as a personal trainer for a wealthy client who travels worldwide. Short and stocky, with a background in martial arts, psychology, and physical fitness, Jean-Pierre is impish, lovable, and charismatic, his dark-brown eyes always gleaming. When he is in town, Jean-Pierre becomes the star of the show, making special appearances at the studio to lead our practice. Like Linda, he's masterful at commanding class and guides us with great precision through even more challenging poses.

"Pooooiiiiint your toes! You are beeeuuuuutifuuul!" Jean-Pierre is also poetic and theatrical with his thick French accent. He has a knack for making every student feel that they're the most special person in the world while pushing them right up to and then beyond their limits. "Reeeaaacccchhhh to the sky!" he says, almost singing this as he stands behind me with his hands firmly on my upper arms and all but lifts me off the ground. By the time class is over, all I want is a hot bath and a nap.

Even though this is purely physical Yoga, or more correctly, *Asana* practice, Linda and Jean-Pierre are the perfect complement to my work with Rene and my own studies and practices. I never would have attempted such rigorous poses without their guidance and encouragement; as a result, my strength and flexibility soon start soaring. It feels so exhilarating that I beg Pamela to go to class with me, thinking she will have the same experience and get interested in Yoga. It could be a shared interest, something that might help her understand me more and at the same time bring us closer together. When she agrees, I'm beside myself with joy as we find a sitter for Morgan and head to class.

As we practice side by side, I have visions of Pamela coming into my cave and doing Yoga with me in the early morning hours, joining me at the bay for sunrise and walking Morgan in his stroller afterward along the waterfront, and then ending the day doing Yoga with me on the beach at sunset. But it doesn't work out this way. Pamela tries two or three classes on her own while I'm with Morgan and decides it's not for her. I find myself feeling hurt and angry, and then have to catch myself, breathe deeply, and do my best to let it go. *I'm taking charge of my life*, I remind myself, *but I'm not in charge of her life.*

Because I'm at the studio several times every day, I become friends with Linda and Jean-Pierre and eventually share my story with them. They're understanding, supportive, and inspiring, telling me about the many students they've seen make great strides in their lives. I feel some special synchronicity must have brought them into my life right when I needed them, just like Rene and Savita. One morning after class, Linda calls me aside and exclaims, "Over the past two-and-a-half months you haven't missed a day. You've been at almost two hundred classes! I've never seen anything like it in all my years of teaching. I think one day you will be a great Yoga teacher!"

It reminds me of when I left the Pain Center and my Jin Shin Jyutsu teacher, Dawn, said one day I would help others heal. I thought she must be crazy, and now I think Linda must be crazy, too.

✺

Thanks to the psychology of Yoga I've been applying to my life, my emotional state has continued to move from being dominated by depression, self-pity, anger, and resentment to optimism, gratitude, and humility. I have a deeply established faith now in my capacity to take charge of my life and effect true and lasting personal transformation. Yet I'm only halfway up the mountain. I've survived a little bit beyond the two years my cancer doctors predicted, but I still have periodic bleeding in my throat. My neck glands sometimes feel tender and swollen. Occasionally, it feels like the old malaise that signaled the arrival of cancer shortly after Morgan's birth is trying to make a comeback.

I'm gripped by a silent fear every time any of these symptoms arise. It always shakes me to the core and tests my faith. I wonder if I'll be able to continue my healing journey or if I'll succumb to terminal disease. Can Yoga really help me heal from this? This is my contemplation this morning during my practice on the bay as the sun lifts fully into the sky. *What can I do to face this challenge head on?*

I close my eyes and listen for my inner voice, that deeper wisdom that has guided me throughout the year. Nothing. I silently chant "OM" with the rise and fall of my breath, being patient, staying focused, giving it time. Ten minutes becomes twenty, and then thirty. Finally, I begin to get a message.

You've been in avoidance of the cancer rather than acceptance, in fear rather than faith. Healing this must now be your utmost priority. You must embrace and thank the cancer, just as you have your back pain. Take your practice to a deeper level. Purify yourself in every way possible. Take it all the way.

I place my hands together at my heart and bow my head down toward my fingertips, thanking my Soul for providing this guidance.

CHAPTER 37

Organic Chemotherapy

I T'S THE END OF JUNE 2001. I continue to practice every morning in my cave, bike to the bay for sunrise, attend classes at the Yoga studio, and make it to the beach for sunset. My weight is down to 165 pounds, ten pounds lighter than I was as a senior in high school. Downward and Upward Dog, Sun Salutations, and Warrior Poses are now a breeze. So is Triangle Pose, balancing on one leg, and all the other rigorous postures Linda teaches at the studio. I can touch my toes effortlessly in forward folds, do a full backbend, and almost the full splits. I'm even starting to master headstands on my own in my cave.

But I'm a year and a half into my healing journey now, and still feel that I have to purify myself further. This morning, I get on the Google search engine and type in *Yoga* and *purification*. The first hit looks like the perfect answer. It's a retreat at a Yoga center in the mountains outside of Santa Cruz in northern California, and it starts tomorrow. It's being held by the center's spiritual leader, who comes from India and is known as a master of Yoga. He only does this once a year. I call immediately. There's space available. I'm in!

Thanks to Yoga, driving my car is no longer a challenge, but this is an all-day trip and I'm feeling sore when I arrive. After a few standing stretches in the parking lot, the tenderness in my back melts away and I'm flushed with joy. Sitting high on 355 partially wooded acres overlooking Monterey Bay, the retreat center is like

Heaven on Earth. It's a massive complex, with residential units for guests and small, woodsy homes for the community of dozens of live-in students who run the center. As I'm registering and then being shown to my room, I realize once again how vibrant and healthy everyone looks, just like Savita, Rene, and Linda, and all the other devoted Yogis I've met thus far.

Dinner is being served before the evening program that commences the retreat. When I enter the dining hall I'm astounded. There must be at least three hundred people here for this. Maybe more. They're all calm and quiet, yet warm and friendly. I immediately feel at home, like finding a family I never knew I had. The food is vegetarian, of course, but I notice most of the dishes also have signs that say "vegan." I ask the person next to me what that means and they explain that veganism is the purest form of vegetarianism: no dairy, no eggs, no fish, no animal products whatsoever. I decide to experiment and eat only the vegan items. Because I fasted all day before arriving, I heap my plate with a colorful assortment of salad, vegetables, beans, and grains. My meal is beyond delicious.

I read early on in my healing journey that the three greatest killers in the first world—heart disease, cancer, and stroke—are all linked to the Western diet, which is predominantly based on meat and dairy products along with processed and junk foods. Weighing in at a bloated 225 pounds, I was a great example of what the Western diet can do. Although my current vegetarian diet has largely consisted of organic vegetables, fruits, legumes, grains, and nuts, it hasn't been vegan. I've regularly included four foods I still love: wild-caught fish, free-range eggs, organic milk, and cheese. After dinner, one of the retreat assistants tells me new research has shown that the protein in dairy and meat products, including milk, cheese, and fish, tends to nourish cancer tumors, while vegetable protein tends to shrink them. That's all I need to hear. *No more fish or eggs, no more milk or cheese. I'm going vegan from here on out.*

In the days that follow at the retreat, we practice hours of Yoga poses and meditation, but the purifications are what captivate me. These include rigorous breath techniques that are far more advanced than any I've ever done. We also pour medical water through one nostril and out the other to cleanse the sinuses, perform self-induced vomiting to cleanse our digestive tracts, and take medicated enemas to cleanse our intestinal tracts. It's incredibly intense, and I have to overcome tremendous resistance to trying each practice. Of course, the old me would have dismissed all of this as completely absurd. Even now, my ego screams so loudly that I have to repeatedly remind myself: *I'm in all the way.*

The nasal cleansing repulses me at first, and it's tricky to perform. I have to pour water in one nostril and let it flow out the other. The moment I tilt my head and start to pour the water in, my eyes flood with tears. I inadvertently breathe in through my nose instead of my mouth, get water in my windpipe, and choke and cough like crazy. I'm not alone. Most others in the group are also struggling. After a while, though, I get the hang of it, and when it's over I feel renewed and refreshed. It makes me think of the assault Dr. Chasan used to perform with the nose-cam before my radiation sessions to look at my throat, only now it's my choice!

The self-induced vomiting requires drinking several large glasses of warm, salted water, which soon triggers regurgitation. I do this back in my room, of course, not with the group. The idea of throwing up has always given me a sense of fear and revulsion. I have to force myself to gulp down the final glass of water. Then I feel nauseous as bitter acid rises up from my stomach. It tastes horrible, and at first I hate every moment of it, but by the end of the process my entire digestive system is tingling and I feel inner sweetness and space.

The enema is just as daunting. Another extreme violation. But again, once I've completed the process, I feel light and clean.

By the third day of the retreat, I find out that the purifications I've been doing are from a thick and detailed Yoga text called the *Hatha Yoga Pradipika*, written back in the 1400s. I buy a copy at the retreat center bookstore and begin to devour it. *Hatha* refers to the physical aspects of Yoga practice, and *Pradipika* means illumination, like shining light on these ancient teachings. Along with Yoga poses, and the practices I've already done, the book includes numerous scientific techniques designed to detoxify the body at its deepest levels, including prolonged fasting. I read through half of the *Pradipika's* 600 pages before the retreat ends and, even though it's radically beyond anything I've ever considered, I'm convinced that it's just what I need.

Yes, these are far from mainstream aspects of Yoga. They're incredibly extreme. So is cancer. This is my only shot, so I'm going all the way. There's no turning back. No picking and choosing what seems easiest. I'm committed to the whole deal. This is it…Get up, Daddy!

By the time the retreat ends, I have my plan. I'll stay vegan, fast as often as I can, take off at least another twenty pounds, and cleanse myself down to the cellular level, trying all the techniques in the *Pradipika* that I can handle. Then I'll thank the cancer for what it has taught me, embrace it as a catalyst for personal growth and transformation, and ultimately invite it to leave. As I drive down the California coast for home, I decide to call this plan my "organic chemotherapy."

I thought it would be a great struggle, but after a few weeks, veganism isn't as daunting as I feared, especially because I've turned the entire process of creating a meal into a meditative ritual. I thank Mother Nature as I choose each vegetable or piece of fruit at the store. Slicing into a banana or a zucchini is an incredible wonder. I notice the color, the texture, the aroma, the seeds filled with intelligence and potential. Once the meal is ready, I say a silent prayer of gratitude to the earth, water, and sun that have joined forces to produce this miracle of nourishment. I contemplate the fact that this food will soon become me, that we are merging as one. I deliberately take smaller portions, eat more slowly, and savor every bite as delicious, healing medicine, being as fully present to the experience as possible.

I periodically fast for a few days at a time, and always fast one day per week. Before this, the only time I ever went more than a day without food was in the mountains of northern Iraq. It wasn't by choice. I just couldn't catch the chicken. Now, fasting is a central part of my plan. Every Monday morning I have a breakfast of fruit and grain, then make Morgan his favorite organic pancakes with maple syrup. I skip lunch and dinner, drinking only warm water with lemon. The following morning, I have no breakfast, then break my fast at lunch with a light, organic, vegan meal of steamed vegetables, rice, and some salad. This gives me a twenty-four hour period without food but still provides some nourishment each day. The first few times I do this I think I'm going to die of hunger as images of steaks, pork chops, and salmon smothered in raspberry sauce float through my brain, taunting me.

Within a few weeks, however, my weight is plummeting like never before and I feel radiantly healthy. Still, hunger pangs arise almost daily. When I contemplate the hunger, however, I realize it's mostly a result of habit. I'm not really as hungry as I feel. All I need to do is slowly sip herbal tea or lemon water while visualizing that it's providing everything my growling stomach needs. It works most of the time, and soon I'm past the cravings for meat or fish—but I have to admit that instead, I now have periodic visions of heaping portions of brown rice smothered in stir-fried vegetables and a plate piled with fresh, ripe fruit that dance through my mind when I haven't had food for a prolonged period of time.

I rinse my sinuses with the water every morning. Once a week, I shorten my nighttime practice and head upstairs to the bathroom for the more radical procedures of regurgitation and enema. These practices still repulse me and I have to summon all my mantras, remind myself of my commitment, and compel myself to do it. I never get used to it, but I realize how purifying it is, especially on one occasion when I fast for four days and am amazed on the final night when I do an enema and continue to release waste materials even with no food in my stomach.

There's more. A practice I haven't mentioned. The *Pradipika* also maintains that drinking one's own urine can effect great healing. *Oh, ancient sages, how could you do this to me? I've totally bought into this science on every level, and now you want me to do this?* The *Pradipika* says it has profound effects, especially on cancer, but I can't imagine anyone remotely considering such a repugnant idea.

I think about it for weeks on end. *Go for it*, I tell myself every morning. *You must be kidding me*, another inner voice chimes in. *This is as gross as it gets*. Finally, I get the courage. *I'm all in*. I get a glass, go into the bathroom, and fill it half way. I hold it in front of me. I'm totally disgusted. A deep breath now. I begin to bring the glass to my lips. Then I freeze. *There's no way. I'm all in—except for this.* Even a fanatic has his limits. I just found mine.

The *Pradipika* also confirms what all my Yoga texts agree on—purifying the mind is as important as purifying the body. With all the noise of society—busy highways, bustling cities, mass media, and television sets blaring everywhere—our minds can't help but be highly agitated and polluted. I now avoid all this as much as humanly possible, especially the television. Whenever I walk into a room where one is on, it feels abrasive, unnatural, and unhealthy, almost like an assault. It's now hard to believe that I was a reporter on television for more than two decades.

Along with avoiding sensory overload, I speak less and spend more time in silence communing with nature. I choose my words more carefully with Morgan and invite him to explore the silence with me. Tonight, as I'm readying him for bed, he jumps into my arms and says, "Daddy, carry me downstairs. Let's go sit on the front porch and listen to the dark." It inspires me that he would come up with such a beautiful concept. I bundle a blanket around him and we tiptoe down, slip outside, and sit on the front stoop.

Without speaking a word, we cuddle together and "listen to the dark," feeling the gentle breeze on our faces while gazing at a sky splashed with stars. The silence is like a symphony. Our closeness is beyond words. When I sense Morgan is drifting off, I carry him to bed and slip back into my cave. This is when my emotions feel most at ease, my mind stills more quickly than usual, and my evening practice becomes even more sacred.

Avoiding media and overstimulation, eating vegan and organic, fasting, performing daily purifications, and practicing advanced *Pranayama* are cleansing both my body and mind. It's easier now to slip into a state of meditation and be fully in the present moment. I feel a sense of calmness and inner balance that are deeper and richer than anything I've ever experienced. I sense an inner harmony in my organs and tissues—even my bones—that seems to whisper to me that a great healing is taking place. *This is it.*

In the "Himalayan Cave."

CHAPTER 38

Sacred Science

Smell the sea and feel the sky
Let your Soul and Spirit fly...

I WAS MESMERIZED by Van Morrison's song "Into the Mystic" when I first heard it back in the 1970s. Now, all these years later, I feel something deeply mystical during my practice. It's beyond words, inaccessible to the intellect I've always relied upon to define my vision of life, and yet palpable—like something in the atmosphere that can almost be touched yet remains ethereal and elusive. It's the same sense of approaching life as a sacred, metaphysical journey that permeates the ancient texts of Yoga and offers a vision of inner exploration and transformation.

The original manuscripts are called the Vedas, which are estimated to be as much as nine thousand years old. The Sanskrit word *Veda* means knowledge, and it's said the Vedas were divined by sages who spent much of their lives meditating in caves in the Himalayas and ultimately accessed this knowledge deep within themselves. The Vedas speak of the mystical powers of nature, cultivating harmony between the mind and heart, the importance of being simple and humble. The teachings are organic and holistic in that they weave all aspects of a conscious life into a tapestry of balance and harmony. The wisdom is deeply embedded in metaphor, imagery, and symbolism, and it stirs my Soul.

A subsequent great text of Yoga, the Bhagavad-Gita (often shortened to Gita), is much easier for me to grasp than the Vedas. Some two thousand years old, the Gita is one of the most widely read spiritual texts in human history. It's set on the eve of a great battle as the hero, named Arjuna, takes his chariot to the center of the battlefield to view his enemies. Gazing out at the cousins, uncles, friends, and acquaintances in the army he must face in the morning, Arjuna despairs, telling his chariot driver, Krishna, that he cannot slay those he holds so dear. Krishna, who is presented as an avatar of the Divine, admonishes Arjuna, telling him that he must stand in Yoga and be a warrior. This conversation forms the Gita.

Although it's filled with wisdom and speaks deftly on the pitfalls of greed, self-indulgence, anger, fear, attachment, and ego, I'm taken aback by the imagery of the battlefield and human conflict. I thought Yoga was about inner peace, stillness, and silence, not the slinging of arrows and slaying of soldiers! After several readings, however, my understanding deepens. The Gita is an allegory for the ethical and moral struggles of all human life. Each of us is Arjuna, on the battlefield of our own lives, struggling with our inner dilemmas, facing our dark sides, and seeking to be the best person that we can be.

Each of us is also Krishna, who to me represents our higher Self. Therefore, the Bhagavad-Gita is ultimately a story of finding one's own power and living one's truth through the spiritual science of Yoga, which ultimately means unifying ourselves with our higher power. Arjuna's battle is a metaphorical one of transcending the ego, slaying self-centeredness, anger, and greed while learning to live in greater integrity. I know this struggle well, and each morning in my practice I strive to release my baser emotions and come to a place of inner peace and deeper truth. When I think about it, the irony is inescapable: I've gone from being a war correspondent covering external conflicts to standing on the battlefield of my own life. I now have to be a warrior in the quest to reclaim my Soul. This, too, is a central part of my organic chemotherapy: seeking to heal myself on all levels of body, mind, and Soul.

These ancient teachings are a completely new way of viewing life for me, but also connect me to one of my first childhood heroes,

Mahatma Gandhi. Gandhi stood strong in his truth, was completely peaceful in the nonviolent resistance he organized against the British, called *Satyagraha*, which means "Persistent Truth," and ultimately prevailed against seemingly insurmountable odds. In doing so, he not only liberated India from colonialism, he inspired the world. I remember the first book I read about Gandhi when I was in eighth grade. His life impressed me deeply, but what astonished me the most was a photo toward the end of the book that showed Gandhi's possessions at the time of his death. He was the father of modern India, but he owned less than ten things. They included a bowl, his sandals, reading glasses, and a copy of the Bhagavad-Gita.

While the Vedas and the Gita have motivated and inspired me, my favorite text has become the Yoga Sutras. Written more than fifteen hundred years ago, the Sutras take a more scientific approach, codifying Vedic wisdom into 196 terse statements called aphorisms. For me, these teachings articulate the spiritual science of how to be a human being. Although many of the Sutras can be daunting to comprehend, the more I read and reread them, the more their wisdom speaks to me. But vastly more important than reading and understanding the Sutras is doing my best to apply their wisdom directly to my life, again as a central aspect of self-purification and healing.

One Sutra invites me to cultivate positive emotions to replace negative ones, much like Dr. Miller's Deep Healing techniques. I've developed my own way to practice this during my morning Yoga: I visualize that I'm breathing in compassion, gratitude, acceptance, forgiveness, and peace, and then exhaling any negative emotions that might still be lingering in my psyche. When I have a specific emotion arise, such as fear, I visualize that I am drinking in a golden, liquid nectar of courage into my heart center on the inhale, and then allowing that nectar to flood my physical and emotional bodies on the exhale. I can actually feel the shift as I become more confident, empowered, and courageous.

There is also an insightful psychology in the Sutras that explains to me how I create my own emotional suffering by forgetting the oneness of all and becoming absorbed in my ego. Looking back in my life, I see that every time I've been depressed, distraught, angry, frustrated, or fearful, it fits into this concept. I was self-centered, caught up in my ego, clinging to my desires, and worried about things not going my way. Then I reacted, often with exaggerated emotion. I remember how dark I became when a failed back surgery ended the career I loved so much. I was a master of reacting with anger and outrage when I was drinking, drugged, and depressed. I could take umbrage at the slightest comment and go into deep aversion. This never resolved anything; it just caused me to stress out further and usually led to my speaking and acting out in ways that hurt everyone around me.

The Sutras teach me to remember that I am part of something much greater than my individual self. This gives me more humility, compassion, and understanding. It also helps me to remember that I don't control reality, and that when challenges arise I can be calm, accept what is, and then act skillfully rather than reacting. It's a real challenge to turn my thinking around this way, but I see the wisdom in it, and each time I'm able to be calmer and more accepting when someone says or does something that would have set me off before, things really do work out better. I remind myself that it's far easier to see fault in others than in myself, and it's spiritual practice to own up, take responsibility, and look at myself straight in the eyes. As Gandhi said, "Be the change you seek in the world." When I'm able do this, the issue dissolves as time passes, I feel like I've made some progress toward becoming a better human being, and another level of inner healing takes place.

A centerpiece of the Yoga Sutras is called the Eight Limbs. These limbs offer me a formula for how to be a human being that is both scientific and spiritual. The first limb provides guidelines for culti-vating a right relationship with the external world by practicing non-violence, truthfulness, and honesty while avoiding self-indulgence and possessiveness. This is a huge shift for me. In morning medita-tions on these precepts, I recall how many times my words to others have been hurtful, how I haven't always been honest, and how I've often hidden my motives from others. I contemplate how deeply I overindulged myself to mask my physical and emotional pain, and how I always avoided facing who I had become.

The second limb focuses on establishing a right relationship with the internal world—with myself—by seeking physical and emotional purity, contentment, and self-discipline. It also promotes the value of self-inquiry, spiritual studies, and, most importantly, the constant cultivation of an awareness of the Divine within myself, within all living beings, and within all aspects of the world. Again, it's a huge shift, but I already realize that discipline and self-purification have been essential for sustaining my healing journey, and that contemplating my sense of higher power is the essence of spirituality.

Every morning in my cave, I ponder these teachings and set my intention to weave these new principles into my life as best as I am able. I realize that I'm nowhere near perfect. It would take me lifetimes to fully live these moral precepts, but as the Sutras also teach me, I vow to practice with devotion every day while not worrying about the outcome. In effect, just as my Yoga poses are rearranging and healing me physically, applying these precepts from the Sutras is remaking me emotionally and spiritually. And although I understand that variations on many of these precepts can be found in all major religions, this feels like something arising from deep within me rather than something demanded from an external source.

The third limb is *Asana*, the Yoga poses that most Westerners often take to be the whole practice of Yoga. Interestingly, the word *Asana* is only mentioned three times in the Sutras, and in each instance it means sitting in a cross-legged posture for meditation. All the hundreds of other Yoga poses that have developed throughout the ages are really designed to purify, balance, and strengthen us while giving us the flexibility to be able to sit comfortably for prolonged periods of time, still our minds, and go within to make contact with our Souls. I'm a long way from that right now, and I need the poses to keep me on a journey away from pain and back to a place of physical wholeness. Maybe the day will come when I can sit still for hours and feel perfectly at peace. *Maybe.*

The fourth limb is the breath work of *Pranayama*, whose magic I've been experiencing since first being taught to breathe more deeply at the Pain Center. *Pranayama* means much more than deep breathing. It's the practice of expanding my energy—my life force—through deep and controlled breathing. Every breath I take these days feels like a miracle of life and reminds me that I have the capacity to make profound physiologic and emotional changes without having to rely on medications.

The fifth limb, *Pratyahara*, means withdrawing the senses from the cacophony of life and going within, which is what I have instinctively done by spending so much time in my cave. This guides me right into the next limb, *Dharana*, which is the practice of single-pointed concentration, like when I gaze at a candle flame and keep my entire awareness focused there. This leads to the seventh limb, *Dhyana*, or meditation, with which I always end my practice, seeking to concentrate deeply and merge with the focus of my meditation. The eighth and final limb is *Samadhi*, or merging with the Divine. This is not something that can be practiced; it just arises more and more as a result of the overall spiritual practice. It's in *Samadhi* that we realize who we truly are, learn to accept life with equanimity, dwell in the present moment, and live in a state of Yoga.

I often feel what I call a beginner's state of *Samadhi* during my practice. Then it slips away as I get on with my day, which I figure is pretty normal. I'm human and will never be a sage or saint, and as Yoga teaches me, it's all about the journey, not the destination.

Covering conflict, war, and turmoil around the world taught me a great deal about the darker side of humanity. It also taught me something about human potential, although it took me years to realize it. Mahmoud, the Afghan boy who was burned over much of his body by napalm, managed to walk out of the vast Himalayas and make his way to a refugee hospital, surviving against the greatest odds. Little Adelin and Junaz, living in Manila's Smokey Mountain dump, clung to life in the most horrid conditions, surrounded by danger and disease. Even Alejandro, forced into addiction, child slavery, and prostitution in Cochabamba, Bolivia, found the strength to scratch a hole in a dry riverbed and call it home, living longer than ever could be expected.

As a journalist, I witnessed everyday citizens—men and women from all walks of life, all ages, ethnicities, political, and spiritual beliefs—face chaos, pain, suffering, and loss. There were some who rose above the maelstrom and performed heroic feats and others who cringed and fled. Either way, what people believed about themselves and their capacity to face a great crisis was turned upside down. All were compelled to completely rearrange their priorities and view the world through a new lens. What was once paramount suddenly seemed petty. What was taken for granted revealed itself as sacred.

I've learned that humility and softness are far more powerful than the sharp edges of bravado and hubris of my earlier years. That accepting what *is* takes more courage than forcing what I think *should be*. That judgments, opinions, and the need to be right can be great hindrances. That it's always better to give rather than to receive. Affirm rather than criticize. Serve rather than be served. I've also learned to be grateful for the smallest, most ordinary things. The morning light. A sip of water. A breath of fresh air. The privilege of being alive.

Yoga has taught me that a fundamental principle of life is that energy follows intention. When we create a strong intention and really believe in it, the world magically seeks to support us. People who think positively and have faith in something are vastly more likely to manifest it than those who feel doubtful and negative. It still takes great devotion and hard work, but it always starts with the mind. One of the great ancient texts of Yoga puts it well: "Your thoughts determine your actions. Your actions create your habits. Your habits form your character. Your character determines your destiny."

CHAPTER 39

A Demon Departs

O H MY, you look like someone from a concentration camp!"
Pamela's mother, Kathy, means no harm by these words. It's
fall of 2001, five months since I became vegan and started the
radical purifications. My weight is down to 140 pounds. This is twenty-
five pounds lower than when I began my organic chemotherapy, and
eighty-five pounds lower than when I was at my largest while disabled.

"It's okay, Mama Two," I say, using my nickname for my mother-
in-law. "I feel better than I ever have in my life." I give her a hug and
sneak off into my cave to look at myself in the mirror. She's right. I'm
extremely gaunt, my bones are sticking out everywhere, and it looks
like I'm starving myself to death. Mama Two is just the messenger
I need to let me know I've done more than enough fasting. This
phase of organic chemotherapy is over. It's time to rebuild my body.
Eat larger meals, still pure, vegan, and organic. I love it. Gorging
myself on avocados, coconuts, and bananas. Quinoa bowls overflowing with broccoli, squash, carrots, and yams. Desserts of figs, dates,
pears, and pecans!

My bayside healing teacher, Rene, left the country this summer to
sail the Pacific in a small sloop with her husband. For the past few
months, I've been doing a weekly ritual that she inspired on the same

dock in San Diego Bay where we used to meet for our private Yoga sessions. After some gentle postures this morning, I wrap a soft cloth around my eyes and ears and lie down on a few thick Yoga blankets. I take myself into a deep meditative state and begin organic chemotherapy on my emotions. With every inhale I send golden healing light to my emotional body and deepen my sense of empowerment. On every exhale I continue to release remaining old wounds, resentments, angers, and fears. They're generalized feelings at first, but in time they become very specific. Things I was in denial about, or were masked for years by drugs, begin to take form. They well up within me, and then I release them.

I let go of feeling alienated by my parents as a child, the first girl who broke my heart, being fired once by a news director who I felt was more beholden to corporate concerns than investigative journalism. As I continue this practice every day, bigger stuff bubbles up. I let go of resentments I've held from the intervention staged by my family, my years of overreacting and brooding, and finally the agony of hitting the bottom of the abyss during detox. It gets more challenging as I fully face, fully own, and finally release the dark person I was during my years of being crippled, overmedicated, and boozed up. No more justifications, excuses, or avoidance. No more self-pity or rationalization. It's remarkably humbling as I finally face it all.

On Day Four the biggest one comes. I've never fully faced the loss of my career as a global journalist. This is the one I've stuffed the deepest and always pretended wasn't there. Journalism was my truest joy, my full identity, the way I defined and validated myself. It gave me such a sense of worth that when I lost it I could no longer find value in anything, especially myself. As I start to crack the inner blockage on this one, a river of fear floods through me. It takes everything I have to find the courage to look it straight in the eyes. *I loved being that person. I loved that career. It's over now. I will never be that again. It's over and gone.* I begin to sob. And then the dam breaks wide open and my tears begin to flow. I grieve, whimper, wail, and mourn until I'm exhausted. This is when the sun bursts forth from behind the mountains and bathes me in its light. Suddenly it hits me: *I have a new identity. I am someone again. I am fully alive.*

It's Day Five now. I feel like I've actually closed all the deep wounds, faced what I needed to face, owned what I needed to own. As I lie on the dock before sunrise, I begin talking to the cancer, offering it my gratitude for all it has taught me about what's really important in life. I visualize it as a demon that has inhabited me and soon must depart. Again, the jaded journalist I was for decades would laugh at such imagery, likening it to the silly tales I tell Morgan on the story bench where the monster releases the little children after being showered with love. I'm no longer that cynical person, and cancer really does seem like a demon. More importantly, I now realize there's a great deal of power in this sort of personification. It allows me to move beyond the rational mind into a deeper subconscious realm of healing.

Day Eight. I've been practicing releasing cancer every morning on the bay for three days. Today the air is cold and the sky is overcast, streaked with lines of silver and gray. The waters of the bay are smooth as glass, holding the reflection of the San Diego skyline like a painting. I take my Yoga blankets to the Marriott dock and settle in. The stillness is palpable. Even the pelicans and seagulls seem quieter than usual. A lone sailboat softly glides toward the harbor in slow motion. I wrap a cloth around my ears and eyes, lie down on my blankets, and soon go deeper than ever before.

I feel completely in touch with every aspect of my body, mind, and Soul. *You can leave now,* I begin to tell the cancer demon. *It's time for you to go.* Every inhale carries *You can leave,* every exhale *It's time for you to go.* I feel completely present, radiantly healthy, and connected to a vibrant inner power. *You can leave. It's time for you to go.*

After an hour of this mantra, my body begins to ache. Despite the chilly morning air, I start to sweat profusely. I feel tremors in my nerves. My arms and legs start quivering. Another thirty minutes and pain grips my whole body. Now it's concentrating in my chest, shoulders, and throat. I'm losing control of my motor functions. Heavy convulsions now. Memories of the detox ward screaming through my mind. Suddenly, I have a vision of something flying out of my chest at warp speed and disappearing into the universe. In my mind's eye, it flashes for an instant, looking like an opaque, geometric hologram.

The moment it leaves, all the pain and convulsions subside. Curling into a fetal position, I'm in an altered state. A voice deep within me says, *The demon is gone. I'm past the cancer. It's gone.* My rational mind speaks up to remind me that this is utterly absurd. Nothing more than a hallucination. Cancer is a disease, not a demon. It doesn't fly through the sky looking for victims, and it doesn't fly out of someone's body while they're lying on a Yoga mat willing it to do so. Yet the experience is as real and tangible as the demons that tore at my flesh in the detox ward. Illusion or not, I know I'm healed. My organic chemotherapy is complete.

"How can I help you?"

The receptionist at my oncologist's office doesn't recognize me even though I used to have regular appointments and came to know the staff well. I can understand why. It's been more than two years since I've been here and I look nothing like the person I once was.

"I'm Brad Willis, Cindy, here for a checkup with the doctor." I watch with a smile as her eyes widen and her jaw drops.

"I can't believe it's you," she exclaims. "I knew you were coming, of course, but you look so much younger and healthier!" She is kind enough not to mention that I used to look like walking death. Cindy explains how difficult it was to find my file because it was shelved in the "inactive" cabinet. The inference is clear: It was assumed I had passed away.

Dr. Redfern is equally surprised when we sit down in his office. I give him the highlights of my healing journey, even the experience of the cancer demon leaving my body, noting that while it seems absurd to me, it must sound utterly ridiculous to him. After a checkup, he smiles and says, "You are definitely in remission and appear amazingly healthy. I don't know how you pulled it off, but whatever you've been doing, ridiculous or not, it's a miracle."

CHAPTER 40

Warrior Pose

THE RISING SUN BURSTS above the mountain ridge on this mid-November morning in 2001 as I sit facing San Diego Bay. I stand up on my mat, bring my palms to my heart, and whisper "*Namaste*" to the morning light as I begin a series of Sun Salutations, breathing deeply, allowing my breath to move my body, silently chanting an ancient mantra of gratitude to the sun.

Next, I flow into Warrior One. My right foot is forward on my mat, the knee bent into a deep lunge. My left leg is straight out behind me with the sole of my left foot rooted into the mat at a 45-degree angle. My torso is lifted up, and my arms are high in the air, as if I'm reaching to the light and drinking it into my heart. I feel incredibly strong and balanced, serene yet powerful, vibrant and fully alive. Holding the pose, I feel like a warrior for inner peace, a warrior for healing, and a warrior for self-transformation.

After ten deep breaths, I change sides and hold the pose for another ten breaths. Now I transition to Warrior Two, standing in the same powerful lunge, this time with one arm straight forward reaching toward the bay and the other arm out behind me, pointing toward the Pacific Ocean. Taking ten breaths on each side again, I feel expansive, grounded, focused, and whole.

Finally, I enter Warrior Three, a pose I once thought completely impossible. Balancing myself on one leg, I tilt forward at my hips and straighten the other leg out behind me in the air as I reach both arms forward, forming a T with my body. Breathing deeply, I feel as solid as the massive rocks that line the bay and as centered as the snowy white egrets that stand on one leg in the water awaiting their prey. As I change sides in Warrior Three, the sunlight glistens across the smooth surface of San Diego Bay and into my heart center. All my muscles are taut and engaged, working together to sustain my balance and alignment. I feel like I could hold this pose forever and marvel at the fact that it's taken me less than two years to go from the depths of pain, disease, and despair to a level of health and wholeness I've never known. I was supposed to have died by now, but the only thing that passed away was the old me.

After Warrior Three, I squat down on my mat, lift up on the balls of my feet, and brace my knees into the back of my upper arms. Placing my palms firmly on the mat with fingers spread wide, I lean forward and balance on my hands as I lift into Crane Pose. After ten breaths I lean farther forward, place the crown of my head on the mat, and lift my legs straight into a headstand. Then I come slowly down to my knees and bow my forehead to the mat as I sit on my heels in Child's Pose, offering my body and breath as a prayer to Mother Earth.

From Child's Pose, I rise up onto my hands and feet, sweep my right leg forward, and slide into a full split. I melt into the splits for ten breaths then transition to the other side, chanting and breathing as I go. Rising up from the splits, I roll onto my back and wrap one leg behind my head, straightening the other leg out on my mat. Ten more breaths and I change sides.

Next, I hug my knees to my chest as I open myself to gratitude, compassion, forgiveness, loving kindness, and inner peace. Now I bring the soles of my feet down, take my arms behind me, plant my palms on the mat, and lift myself up into a full backbend. I hold it for a full minute, amazed every time I do this pose that a spine with a broken vertebra and failed surgery has this much capacity to heal.

A series of gentle poses follow the backbend as I settle down toward stillness, ultimately entering the Corpse Pose. I lie here for ten minutes, visualizing Mother Earth holding me in the palms of her hands. It feels like the air itself is breathing me, and every effortless inhale is an affirmation of my journey, every exhale is a merging back into the source of all that is. Once I return to a seated posture, I practice *Pranayama*, then sit with my eyes closed and meditate with immense gratitude for the challenges that have taught me to appreciate the miracle of life.

When I've completed my meditation, I gaze out over the bay, contemplating how Yoga has guided me into a personal transformation I never dreamed possible. Although the poses I've done this morning are only a small aspect of Yoga, they do something much greater than build confidence, strength, and flexibility: They reflect life. The more flexible, balanced, and grounded I become on my mat, the more I bring these attributes to life off my mat. If I can move past the resistance I feel in my hamstrings, I have a greater capacity to handle tension in the real world. Staying in poses that test my muscles without backing out helps me stand firm when facing times of challenge. The more present I become in meditation, the more awareness I bring to all aspects of my life.

There is another aspect to the more physically challenging poses that is also transformative. When, after a long period of sustained effort, I finally master something I used to believe was impossible, like getting my legs behind my head or holding a headstand, it empowers me. This faith in my capacity to do something I felt was beyond my reach soon translates into other aspects of my life. It gives me confidence and courage, and helps me turn setbacks and obstacles into opportunities and accomplishments.

At the end of my day, I pedal my bike to the beach to watch the sunset. I breathe in the moist, salty air and watch sandpipers skitter along the ocean's edge. Walking to the water's edge, I let the tide rush up and soak me up to my knees. It's bone-chilling cold and feels exhilarating. I feel a rush of exuberance and begin chanting *I am alive!* I keep it up as I run fifty yards along the shoreline toward a jetty of huge boulders in front of the Hotel del Coronado. It's the first time I've run since the test in Saudi Arabia to be a pool reporter for the Gulf War. *I am alive!* I climb the boulders effortlessly and sit on a wide, flat rock facing southwest toward the Coronado Islands and the coast of Mexico. It's a favorite place of mine that I call Meditation Rock. I watch the sun dance on the ocean's surface as a line of pelicans soars across the face of a rolling wave. In the distance, a regatta of sailboats heads back toward harbor as a majestic cruise ship departs for the tropics. *I am alive!*

It feels like only yesterday that I limped into the Pain Center and was admonished for lying down on the reception couch. I fondly remember the wonderful people who guided me in Biofeedback, Jin Shin Jyutsu, Physical Therapy, and my first Yoga class. Suddenly, a picture drifts into my vision. It's the poster in the Therapy room of the woman doing Boat Pose on a jetty of rocks much like the jetty I'm sitting on right now. Inspired, I climb to the top of the highest rock and playfully go the pose one better, balancing myself on my arms with one leg behind my head, still chanting *I am alive!*

On the jetty at Coronado Beach.

❈

It's early December now. Today is Coronado's annual Christmas Parade. Morgan will soon turn four years old, and something very special is in store. Morgan is still asleep when I tiptoe into his room. Gazing at him softly sleeping, I suddenly remember the good-bye note I tucked away in my suitcase when I feared I might not survive. I wrote it to Morgan when I was at the Marriot Hotel in La Jolla almost two years ago while attending the Pain Center, asking that he never forget me. I step softly back into my bedroom, bring the suitcase down from a high shelf in the closet, and retrieve the note. My eyes flood with tears of joy as I read it one final time, then I rip it up and toss it in the waste bin.

Morgan ambles into my room, sees the tears, and says, "What's wrong, Daddy?"

"Nothing, sweetheart," I answer. "They're tears of joy. I'm so happy to have you, and I can't wait for the parade!"

"Me, too!" Morgan exclaims with glee. "Now, will you draw on my back?"

❈

As happens every year, thousands of visitors have flooded into Coronado for the parade. Two years ago, I was on the curb, watching the parade from my recliner, strapped into my Clamshell brace, drinking a stout beer, pickled on drugs, crippled, and dying. Morgan was snuggled up on my lap, giving me a play-by-play on all the floats and marching bands. I remember as if it were yesterday, how he held me so tightly and pleaded with me to march with him in the next Christmas Parade.

I had been diagnosed with cancer and was certain this would be the last Christmas with my son. It broke my heart when I promised him that we would march together. I felt like a liar, a failure, and a hopeless case. Little did I know that my son would soon make another request of me. It was just a few weeks later that he pleaded *Get up, Daddy!* That was the catalyst for this journey, the one thing that gave me the strength to persevere. Without this bond between father and son, I know deep in my heart that I never would have pulled through.

Last year, I was well enough to watch the parade with Morgan, of course, but not yet strong enough to join in. This year, Morgan has been invited to join a group of his little friends marching in the parade as elves, and I'm all in—one hundred percent. I manage to mock up a fairly silly elf costume for myself and join the other parents who are escorting the kids. When we arrive at the beginning of the parade route, the marching bands, karate club, cheerleaders, sports teams, and even the garbage trucks are all in the queue again, with Santa on the large red fire truck bringing up the rear. I look down the long, wide street and see the throngs of holiday revelers as an instrumental version of "Joy to the World" blares from a nearby loudspeaker. A profound sense of joy washes through me. *I kept my promise to my son. I am alive! Joy to the world!*

The excited voices of the little children in our group sound like angels as we are told that our group is next to march down the parade route. As we begin walking, Morgan reaches for my hand. We skip from one side of the street to the other, just like Santa's elves, waving at the crowd and laughing out loud. After a block or two, I feel a tug at my hand and glance down to see Morgan smiling at me.

"Daddy, can I have a shoulder ride?"

"Sure, sweetheart," I answer with a smile, swinging him up onto my shoulders and dancing with him perched above me all the way through the parade. As I see familiar faces along the way, I realize this parade is very much the same as it has been every year for decades. It's me who is different. Completely different—in body, mind, and Soul. I never dreamed I would fulfill this promise of being in the Christmas parade with my son, much less be able to carry him on my shoulders. I never imagined that such healing was possible. *Joy to the world!*

When we reach the end of the parade route, near the beach and the Hotel Del, I swing Morgan down from my shoulders into my arms, hug him closely, and say, "Guess what? Daddy got up!"

"What does that mean?" he asks, smiling widely as he hugs me back.

I have to laugh out loud and then whisper softly, "One day soon, I'll tell you all about it."

Epilogue

As 2002 unfolds, Pamela and I realize that the chasm between us has become so wide that it might be impossible to bridge. A newsletter from the retreat center where I first learned about deeper purifications and devised my organic chemotherapy regimen is advertising a couples retreat led by a man and woman with international reputations for their work in helping couples reconcile their differences. I beg her to try it with me, and she agrees. Morgan will stay with his grandmother while we're away for four days, which is challenging for both of us.

I'm hoping Pamela might love the place so much that she'll consider moving into residency as a family. We would be in a conscious community, surrounded by nature, and have a chance to make a new start. It even has a school that offers preschool through high school. The day we arrive, I realize it's a fanciful illusion. This is not her world and never will be. We both do our best to come together during the retreat, but it doesn't do the trick. The drive home is painful. Our conversation is inauthentic. Like most men, I want to fix things. Find a logical solution. Put it all back together. But I can't.

A few weeks later I take one last stab at finding a way to create a new life that we both can accept, and Hawaii seems to hold great potential. There's a retreat in Maui with Rod Stryker, one of the few Vedic masters in America. Rod is among the small minority of teachers who focus on what resonates most with me: the deep and ancient teachings of Yoga and how they apply to our lives. He's like a spiritual scientist with a talent for taking arcane and complex theories and synthesizing them into a language that's accessible and easily understandable. His lectures are punctuated with practices that provide a direct experience of the teachings, as opposed to simply offering intellectual insights.

I decide to attend the retreat and also find a home in one of the more rural villages that we could buy, again with the idea of creating a new life. Pamela could enjoy the holiday atmosphere of Hawaii while I continued to study and practice Yoga. There's a private Waldorf school near the place I've chosen. Waldorf schools focus on nurturing each child's creativity, emphasizing music, dance, theater, writing, literature, legends, and myths. Its website says "Waldorf students cultivate a lifelong love of learning as well as the intellectual, emotional, physical, and spiritual capacities to be individuals certain of their paths and to be of service to the world." It would be a perfect place for Morgan to attend.

Pamela flies in with Morgan after the retreat. I've booked us lodging at a quiet, meditative spa on the more uninhabited side of the island. Pamela hates it. She wants to be at a five-star hotel with pools, water slides, and organized tours. She doesn't want to see the homes I've found to look at, and I realize my whole plan is foolish. It's hard for me to face, but I also realize that I keep trying to impose my vision on her. It isn't her vision and it isn't fair. Anyway, Yoga taught me long ago that true change comes from within, not by altering one's external circumstances. *What was I thinking?* I make a switch and we travel to the populated side of the island and check into a resort. She is much happier here, but I can't stand it. It's far too commercial, noisy, and inauthentic. We are worlds apart.

The Royal Way Ranch sits seventy-five miles northeast of Los Angeles in the high Mojave Desert, with the San Bernardino Mountains towering in the background. With its lush gardens and a small stream flowing from a natural spring, it's an oasis in the midst of a bleak moonscape of cracked earth and dry, twisted chaparral. A full moon illuminates the landscape as it sets in the west. Hints of sunrise are stirring in the east. My mat is rolled out on the desert sand as I sit in Lotus Pose, doing my *Sadhana* in the "Time of the Divine," while "listening to the dark," as Morgan once put it so beautifully.

It's late May in 2002, and I'm here for a weeklong Yoga of Fulfillment Retreat with Rod Stryker. During this retreat, Rod has guided us into deep levels of self-reflection. It's now the final day, and I have a vision that I'm standing on the edge of a great abyss, much like the abyss I fell into with a lost career, broken back, and cancer, and that used to haunt me in my nightmares. This time, however, I'm seeking to open my arms as if they were wings, release all fear, and allow myself to fall forward over the precipice. The abyss, this time, symbolizes the unknown. For the past several days, I've felt great resistance to visualizing letting myself fall over the edge. My fear is because I can't control the outcome. It's because I have no guarantee what the result will be. In truth, life is always this way, but most of us still want to think we're in charge of the future, that somehow we can avoid risk, disappointment, and danger.

This morning, I've realized the specific meaning of the abyss. It's my fear of facing something my Soul had known for far too long but my mind has been refusing to face: My marriage is over. I'm reminded of the Serenity Prayer and having the wisdom to know those things I cannot overcome. Although I've been able to effect profound changes in myself through the spiritual science of Yoga, this doesn't mean that I can determine all that happens in my life. I realize, too, that this realization is an essential part of completing my healing, and I know Pamela feels that her healing also requires this difficult step.

My mind blocked it out for so long because I had to heal my back and overcome cancer. And there's more to it. Deeper things. I've been apprehensive about what it might mean for me socially and financially. Most importantly, I've held a deep fear over how it might affect Morgan. But Pamela and I have gone too far in different directions, with too much painful history behind us, to ever reconcile our differences.

Now, it's time. I breathe deeply and finally accept the truth, stare my fear straight in the face, and peer over the edge of the abyss.

I visualize myself opening my arms wide, leaning forward, and finally letting go. I immediately fall into the darkness with terrifying speed. As I expected, the visualization terrifies me. Then I find my wings, make a mighty effort, and eventually soar out of the abyss and into the clear, blue sky.

※

As the summer of 2002 comes to a close, Morgan lives with me half the time. Pamela has moved to another home on the island, and we have ended our marriage. We gave counseling our best try but just couldn't put things back together. It has been traumatic for both of us. We have faced fear, anger, uncertainty, guilt, indecision, and all the other emotions that go with separation. We also have had to face ourselves. Build new lives. Make sure the impact on Morgan is as minimal as possible. Always let him know it's our fault and how deeply he is loved.

I feel a natural sense of sadness and pain the days I'm without my son. To help me cope, and to be with like-minded community, I attend a meditation north of San Diego one night a week. It's held at a large, serene facility where men and women sit on opposite sides of the room, chant Sanskrit mantras, then sit in silent contemplation. Tonight, November 1, 2002, I've brought two Yoga students from the Coronado studio with me for their first visit to the center. After the meditation, they want to go down the corridor to a small cafe that serves light vegetarian meals. I've always preferred to skip this part of the evening and head home for some final practices in my cave before bed. This time, I agree to join them at a table where they've met two people they find intriguing.

One is a man named Eros who engages my friends with captivating tales of his retreats in the tropics, where he swims with wild dolphins. The other is a woman named Laura who, like me, remains quiet and reserved. I've hardly glanced at her to notice how extraordinarily beautiful she is, yet I'm mesmerized by her presence. We barely speak to one another, but deep within, each of us feels a sense of destiny unfolding.

After college, Laura lived in Europe and was general manager of *The Discovery Channel Europe*. Along with running the channel, she produced documentaries on science, culture, and spiritual topics such as vignettes on the Dalai Lama. Like me, Laura endured her own dark night of the Soul and found her way out of her own abyss through turning toward a more spiritual life. But we are both in emotionally tender places. Neither of us is looking for a relationship. Isn't this when it always happens?

January 2004. I've remained in the same home where Morgan was born. Laura and I have married and embraced a life together that is centered on aligning our lives with Vedic wisdom. We've developed a style of daily practice that's based on my experiences and studies in my cave, with spirituality and self-awareness as the foremost principles. I sleep in these days, arising between 4:30 and 5:30 A.M. for my *Sadhana* instead of 3:00 A.M. I rarely attend a class at the Coronado studio, preferring instead to continue developing my own practice.

Laura and I periodically travel to Yoga conferences or attend trainings to study with great teachers. This month, as a pilgrimage, we journey together to Esalen. It's an institute in Big Sur, on the northern coast of California, dedicated to holistic studies and human development. Esalen is a stunning place. Sitting on a steep mountainside surrounded by lush forest, it towers just above the Pacific Ocean and offers staggering views of the rocky cliffs forming the coastline. A fresh canyon stream runs through its spacious gardens and walkways. Its natural mineral baths are nurturing and healing. The pervasive silence is only broken by the song of the mighty waves below.

We've come for a weekend workshop called "Imagery, Deep Relaxation, Movement, and Music," with Dr. Emmett Miller. I've long wanted to meet the man whose voice transfixed me in Biofeedback, and whose work helped transform my life. Although I feel like I already know him from listening to his audiotapes for so many months during my healing journey, I'm taken by his presence. Dr. Miller is well over six feet tall, lean and sinewy, with thick, black hair slightly graying at the temples. A full beard, neatly trimmed, covers his strong jaw. His chocolate-brown eyes are soft and glowing. His voice is even richer and deeper in person, and just hearing him speak feels remarkably healing.

The workshop is like a celebration of mind-body medicine as Dr. Miller guides us into rediscovering peak moments of healing, empowerment, love, and joy. He leads us through techniques of selective awareness, meditation, and guided imagery as we explore the healing force within us. His presence is simultaneously soft and powerful, reminding me of principles in the Yoga Sutras that advocate standing in steadiness and strength while remaining soft, open, and supple.

During the weekend, Laura and I establish a personal relationship with Dr. Miller. "Call me Em," he says gently after I share my story and thank him for the incredible healing I experienced as a result of hearing his words in Biofeedback, reading his book, and exploring his practices while I was at the Pain Center. "Your experience is a profound illustration of the power of mind-body medicine and self-healing," he says, placing a hand on my shoulder and gazing into my eyes. "One day you must share it with the world." I take this as advice from a modern-day sage as I humbly bow my head and answer, "I will. When the time is right, I will."

February 2008. Laura and I have founded Deep Yoga, a Vedic school devoted to teaching the fullness of the ancient wisdom of Yoga. For me, this is an expression of the new person that I have become. When I lost my journalism career, I lost my identity. I found it in Yoga, and now with this new venture, I feel a renewed sense of worth and accomplishment, like I am contributing something to the world.

We call our trainings "Mastery of Life." Our intention is to guide our students into owning the power and living their truth. Through applying the deepest principles of Yoga, we help them develop greater harmony and balance, find their true calling in life, and express themselves to their fullest potential. Through our Mastery Programs, we train Yoga teachers and Vedic healers, offer classes, workshops, and retreats, and continue to see a wide variety of private clients in our practice.

It's a profound privilege to serve those seeking to heal, grow, and transform their lives. Part of our mission is to remind our students that their greatest guide, their true guru, lies within them. That each of them possesses the capacity to recreate themselves and live in greater authenticity, contentment, and self-expression. We've seen so many wonderful people make incredible strides in healing, transforming their lives, and living to their fullest potential, and several of our graduates have gone on to serve others as powerful healing guides.

Morgan joins us periodically as we teach a Yoga class, and occasionally sits in on portions of some of our trainings. He already displays a deep understanding of the primary principles of Ayurveda and has memorized several complex Sanskrit mantras. Yet he is following his own path, becoming a junior black belt in karate, surfing, and designing amazingly elaborate creations with his Lego blocks. We let him know that Yoga is always here for him, but we never require it or even try to nudge him in this direction. He is perfect and whole just as he is, and we are confident he will chose his own path in life with discernment and commitment when the time arrives.

As part of my own journey, which in many ways has been a rebirth from the person I once was, I have taken the spiritual name of Bhava Ram. Such names often embody something that it is important to aspire to. This particular name means several things that I will always seek to embrace. *Bhava* means the essence or experience of an emotion, and *Ram* is the name of the central character in the spiritual epic *The Ramayana,* a man who stayed devoted to Yoga and lived his truth in the face of great odds. *Ram* also signifies the sun, the light of the heart, and the fire of self-discipline. Together, a great Sanskrit scholar has told me, the name can be translated as "Pure State of Being in the Heart."

Traditionally, such names are given by a disciple's guru. Because I have no formal guru and am not seeking such a relationship, Bhava Ram is a name I've chosen as a way of reminding myself that I'm only alive because of devotion to my new path and that I must continue to follow it to the best of my abilities, as imperfect as I might be. After deciding upon this name, my primary teachers agree it's the right choice and give it their blessings.

One of these teachers, Dr. David Frawley, has invited Laura and me to be his guests at a retreat on the Ganges River in the foothills of the Himalayas. Also known as Vamadeva Shastri, Dr. Frawley has written dozens of books on Vedic wisdom and, although American by birth, is viewed in India as a great master of Sanskrit, Yoga, Ayurveda, and the history of ancient India. Laura and I have long wanted to make our first pilgrimage to the country that is the source of the practice that has transformed our lives, and we readily accept this generous offer.

Following a fascinating retreat with Dr. Frawley, Laura and I travel to nearby Rishikesh, known as the home of Yoga, for the International Yoga Festival at an ashram called Parmarth Niketan. Ashrams are centers for live-in spiritual studies, and like many other ashrams in Rishikesh, Parmarth sits on the banks of the Ganges, with sublime views of the river and the mountains rising toward the Himalayas. The ashram's spiritual leader, fondly known as Swamiji, uses funds from the festival to house and educate orphaned children and raise them in the ancient traditions of Yoga.

Each evening, everyone gathers on the banks of the Ganges at sunset, facing a towering marble statue of Shiva, the archetype of transformation, sitting on a platform over the river, for what Swamiji calls "the best happy hour in the world." The orphan boys, clad in saffron robes, surround Swamiji on the wide steps facing the river as he leads us in traditional chants to the Divine. There is a musician playing tablas, which are small Indian drums similar to bongos, only with deeper bass notes that sound ethereal. Another musician plays a harmonium, a small wooden box with piano keys and a bellows pump that sounds like an accordion. Swamiji's voice is angelic as he sings ancient Vedic chants celebrating spirit and divinity.

It sounds like a celestial choir as the orphan children lift their voices with him.

Swamiji, radiant in his orange robes, flowing black hair, and full beard, is internationally known as a servant of peace. He often meets with heads of state around the world while collaborating with other spiritual leaders such as the Dalai Lama. Thousands travel from America, Europe, Australia, and throughout India simply to be near him, to receive what is called *Darshan*—sitting in the presence of a master teacher, a true guru. Swamiji wants no control over anyone's life. He simply offers his heart to all and serves as a living embodiment of the human capacity to be a fully self-realized being.

During the Yoga Festival, Laura and I are given the great honor of being asked to join the Parmarth Niketan teaching staff and return to India each year to share Deep Yoga with students from around the world. Then we're invited to sit in *Darshan* with Swamiji. We're guided to a reception area behind the ashram office that looks like a small, intimate park with a grassy lawn, lush flowers, and bougainvillea flowing over a plaster wall painted deep gold. A roofed bamboo frame covers the reception area, with an altar at one end and Swamiji's cushion in the middle.

A few minutes after Laura and I are seated, Swamiji enters and sits in silence. His presence alone overwhelms us with a pure sense of loving kindness, grace, and the experience of being with a great sage. After a few minutes of meditative silence, Swamiji invites us to open our eyes, places one hand over his heart, embraces us with his peaceful and knowing gaze, then softly whispers, "Welcome home."

Afterword

I faintly recall my wide-eyed daze watching Tom Brokaw query a prominent war correspondent named Brad Willis during the Persian Gulf War. The NBC News reporter flashed across the TV screen with images of an inferno foreign to my unblemished mind. That was in 1990, when Willis was a fiercely impassioned and intrepid reporter crossing enemy lines into a bomb-struck Iraq, navigating through twisted, torqued bodies on a chemical battlefield, and delivering stories no one else was reporting.

As a communication major at UC San Diego, I longed to one day do what Willis exemplified: cover the world's momentous events, peel back layers of illusion to unveil the truth and, finally, deliver the power of knowledge to the masses in prepackaged media nuggets. There was no sign back then that this tough, hard-edged reporter would become my dear teacher and mentor—not in a journalism class or "J-school" as it's often called but in "Y-school," as in Yoga. As in "why" love and inner strength matter more than all the victories of war or worldly riches one could garner.

Fast-forward the tape sixteen years: It was a sunshiny day in 2006 when a man with deep pipes and an uncommon serenity strode into my favorite Yoga studio and began to teach. His was no ordinary Yoga class, where bodies performed athletic postures while eyes wandered the room. His voice commanded pure presence, and as we moved on our mats the clock stopped ticking. In moments, a roomful of strangers breathed as one. The idea that we were exercising melted away as it became a completely sacred experience, a Yoga studio transformed instantly into a temple.

"Reach up to the heavens, drink in light and love, and now bow down to Mother Earth," Bhava Ram invited. "Take healing light into your palms and send it down through the vessel of your Soul. Feel the radiance inside your heart and know you are a Sacred Being," he beckoned us over and over again.

I didn't know what he was doing with this highly unusual, spiritual approach to Yoga, but I was instantly hooked. I was now a television news reporter myself and my brain was busy with the endless news stream, yet every single class from Bhava Ram brought my otherwise stressed and occupied mind into deeper stillness, focus, and harmony.

People of all ages, shapes, and shades quickly filled his classes. Bhava and his wife, Laura Plumb, lovingly cultivated a community of modern-day Yogis through their Deep Yoga teacher training school and inspiring workshops, which soon drew seekers from around the country. There was no bottom to their giving. From an urban oasis near downtown San Diego called Ginseng Yoga Studio, I learned there was nothing newfangled about Bhava at all. He was reviving the ancient spiritual practice of healing and self-realization otherwise being overlooked as mere exercise in an overly stimulated Western world.

And why not? Through his personal catastrophes, Brad Willis had essentially been reborn as Bhava Ram. The foreign correspondent had covered unthinkable atrocities—Kuwaiti torture victims piled into morgues, Kurdish mothers clinging to dead babies in squalid encampments, child prostitutes enslaved in Thailand's red light district—but ultimately, he had to slay more penetrating, private demons than any he covered as a journalist. First, a miserably broken back and doctors diagnosing him as "permanently disabled," and next, late-stage cancer his physicians deemed terminal.

I'd heard that this man, spurred on by indomitable love for his infant son, had recovered—not through conventional cancer treatments, but through Yoga. But, how? Ever the journalist, I was curious about the details.

Even after years of studying with this master, I didn't know how he actually overcame these seemingly insurmountable ailments. This book, at long last, answers that question and tells his extraordinary story with the lucid detail of an esteemed journalist. Whoever you are, whatever your challenges, this text is a treasure that can lead you into a new understanding about your life and how to live it fully.

This is what Bhava has gifted me. As fate would have it, I was an accomplished journalist with PBS in my mid-thirties when I fell ill with a chronic disease that mystified the medical establishment. There was no known cure, doctors said. Debilitating symptoms forced me to quit my career and retreat into a world of stillness. In my darkest, most dreaded moments, Bhava gave me what I had lost entirely: hope, faith, belief in myself, and something beyond the scared little me curled up in bed. I knew if this man could crawl out of the doorway of disability and death, certainly I could heal, too. He taught me tools to resuscitate myself—the same basic protocol that filled his broken, cancer-ridden body with strength and well-being. Through years of diligent practice inspired by Bhava, I feel healthier than I have in a decade and happier than I ever was before the illness.

Something about him inspires one to greatness. Bhava routinely produces miracles in his students. A sixty-year-old woman riddled with cancer tumors went into full remission, another student with fibromyalgia bid farewell to all pain medications and the pain itself, an older man immobilized for decades by depression started doing handstands and climbing mountains.

As a journalist, Brad Willis reported what mattered in the news with courage and devotion. As a teacher, Bhava Ram shares what's truly important in life with even greater devotion and a sense of humility and compassion that is palpable and inspiring. He is living proof of how courage triumphs over all rational prognosis and odds, how deep and abiding love for a child can conquer all, and how we each harbor unseen capacity to heal from whatever wounds life inflicts.

Rebecca Tolin
Journalist/Writer

Acknowledgments

As I imagine all authors experience, once I began ruminating upon whom to thank for making this book possible, a flood of familiar names and faces flowed through my heart. Most notably, of course, is my son, Morgan, who provided the love and inspiration that prompted me to launch my healing journey. Thank you, my son. As the years have passed since that day you pleaded, "Get up, Daddy," you continue to inspire me. It's my greatest blessing in life to watch you grow into manhood as one of the most centered, authentic, kind, and loving people I have ever known.

To Morgan's mother, Pamela, thank you for so many good times and for standing by me during so many of the bad times. You are a wonderful mother and a truly good person.

To my wife, Laura, thank you for being my best friend, my partner in Yoga, my teacher, and my beloved. It was you who provided the ultimate affirmation for the writing of this book, and it was your encouragement along the way that nourished and sustained me.

I thank my sisters, Valerie and Pamela, and my mother, Doris, for embracing me upon my return from Hong Kong as a broken man. You stood beside me even in my darkest days and I love you eternally.

To all of the amazing people at the McDonald Center who helped me through detox, thank you from the bottom of my heart. "Nurse Ratched," whoever you really are, I give you my endless gratitude and will always wonder how you managed to put up with me. To the equally amazing people at the Pain Center, I will never forget you, Savita, Beth, and PJ. Thank you, thank you, thank you.

I am ever grateful to Dr. Emmett Miller, whose wisdom and guidance helped me heal on all levels. I thank Yoga teachers Savita Geuther, Rene Riley, Debbie Adams, Linda and Jean-Pierre Marquez, and Michael Lee for getting me started in my journey into Yoga. I thank Rod Stryker, Dr. David Frawley, and Pujya Swamiji for helping me understand and experience the deepest aspects of Vedic wisdom. A deep and heartfelt *Namaste* to all of you.

Thank you, Denise Baddour, for your boundless enthusiasm and support in bringing this memoir to publication and thank you, David Nelson, for being such a great agent. Others who were instrumental in this process include Arlene Matthews, Rebecca Tolin, and Anne Marie Welsh.

To my editor, Debbie Harmsen, you are amazing. You challenged me, you gave me greater clarity, you made me look deeper into my Soul, and you brought out the best in me. My thanks to all the other wonderful people at BenBella Books, including publisher Glenn Yeffeth, Adrienne Lang, Jennifer Canzoneri, Lindsay Marshall, Monica Lowry, and Leigh Camp. I am honored at the privilege of working with each of you. Special thanks to Paul Henderson of Rise Design Studio for designing a beautiful book cover.

My gratitude goes out to Brad and Cindy Bennett, the owners of Ginseng Yoga Studio in San Diego, who played a central role in the establishment of Deep Yoga and have provided Laura and me with a beautiful studio to call home for our teachings. To all Deep Yoga students, I bow to you. You have given me the privilege of living my *dharma*.

Praise for
TSI: The Influenza Bomb

"I am pleased to endorse *TSI: The Influenza Bomb* just as heartily as I did the first book, *The Gabon Virus*. The characters, the action, the plot twists, the references to some of the most fascinating aspects of our world's history, all ensure that one cannot put this book down after one starts to read it. Furthermore, one emerges from this reading thankful, even with the challenges confronting today's American medical care system, for what we have in this country. As always, the medical details in the novel are accurate and astute."

—Reginald Finger, MD, MPH, researcher, and lecturer

"Terrifically thrilling and excitingly tender, this novel courses through history, medicine, and human drama to unravel the mystery of a deadly influenza pandemic. The authors ingeniously weave an epic that keeps you enthralled to the last page. In the aftermath of the swine flu scourge, this book is a 'Don't miss!'"

—Elaine Eng, MD, clinical assistant professor,
Weill Cornell Medical College

"A brilliant work, full of intrigue. The authors have a keen ability to link multiple themes over different eras and worldwide locations. One's mind is consumed by the real threat of germ warfare and how, in evil hands, unintended consequences of science can destroy."

—Mary Anne Nelson, MD, FAAFP

"Move over Robin Cook and Michael Crichton! Walt Larimore bursts onto the scene with his newest fast-paced medical thriller *TSI: The Influenza Bomb*. Skillfully weaving the flu pandemic of 1918–1919, Nazi germ warfare from World War II, and present-day H1N1 flu hysteria, Larimore creates a novel with unexpected twists and turns that keeps you turning the page from cover to cover! An excellent read with believable and well-researched science. Pick it up today!"

—Byron C. Calhoun, MD, FACOG, FACS, MBA, vice chair,
Department of Obstetrics and Gynecology,
West Virginia University–Charleston

"This is an international thriller with chilling relevance today. The authors have done their homework and written a totally realistic novel that may keep you awake at night! You will never again read about H1N1 outbreaks without wondering about their origins."

—Dorothy Cowling, book reviewer and creator of *The List*

"Watch out for paper cuts reading this gripping page-turner! *The Influenza Bomb* is a medical thriller with more twists, turns, and excitement than an Olympic bobsled run. Jump in and hang on for an adrenaline-charged adventure wrapped in layers of intrigue from start to finish!"

—David Stevens, MD, MA, CEO of Christian Medical &
Dental Associations, and
author of *Jesus, M.D.*

"I very much enjoy a good thriller, and I love a book that gives me new insights—be they historical, medical, or even spiritual. Either is hard to find; both is impossible . . . or it was, until Paul McCusker and Walt Larimore started to write the TSI series. *The Gabon Virus* was great; now they set even higher standards with *The Influenza Bomb*."

—Martin Duerr, pastor and sports columnist

Other Works by Paul McCusker

Time Scene Investigators: The Gabon Virus
   (coauthored with Walt Larimore)
Time Thriller Trilogy
   Ripple Effect
   Out of Time
   Memory's Gate
A Season of Shadows
The Mill House
The Faded Flower
Epiphany

Other Works by Walt Larimore

Time Scene Investigators: The Gabon Virus
   (coauthored with Paul McCusker)
*Bryson City Tales: Stories of a Doctor's First Year of Practice
   in the Smoky Mountains*
Bryson City Seasons: More Tales of a Doctor's Practice in the Smoky Mountains
*Bryson City Secrets: Even More Tales of a Small-Town Doctor
   in the Smoky Mountains*
*His Brain, Her Brain: How Divinely Designed Differences Can Strengthen Your
   Marriage* (coauthored with Barb Larimore)
10 Essentials of Happy, Healthy People: Becoming and Staying Highly Healthy
God's Design for the Highly Healthy Child
God's Design for the Highly Healthy Teen
Alternative Medicine: The Christian Handbook
   (coauthored with Dónal O'Mathúna)
Lintball Leo's Not-So-Stupid Questions About Your Body
SuperSized Kids: How to Rescue Your Child from the Obesity Threat
   (coauthored with Sherri Flynt and Steve Halliday)
The Honeymoon of Your Dreams: How to Plan a Beautiful Life Together
   (coauthored with Susan Crockett)
Why A.D.H.D. Doesn't Mean Disaster
   (coauthored with Dennis Swanberg and Diane Passno)
Christian health blog at www.DrWalt.com/blog
Christian health resources at www.DrWalt.com
Autographed books available at www.DrWalt.com/books

TSI: THE INFLUENZA BOMB

A NOVEL

PAUL McCUSKER & WALT LARIMORE, MD

HOWARD BOOKS
A DIVISION OF SIMON & SCHUSTER, INC.
NEW YORK   NASHVILLE   LONDON   TORONTO   SYDNEY

Published by Howard Books,
a division of Simon & Schuster, Inc.
1230 Avenue of the Americas, New York, NY 10020
www.howardpublishing.com

In association with the literary agency of Alive Communications

Library of Congress Control Number: 2010011271

ISBN 978-1-4165-6975-6
ISBN 978-1-4391-7708-2 (ebook)

10 9 8 7 6 5 4 3 2 1

Manufactured in the United States of America

For information regarding special discounts for bulk purchases, please
contact: Simon & Schuster Special Sales at 1-866-506-1949 or
business@simonandschuster.com.

The Simon & Schuster Speakers Bureau can bring authors
to your live event. For more information or to book an event
contact the Simon & Schuster Speakers Bureau at
1-866-248-3049 or visit our website at www.simonspeakers.com.

Edited by David Lambert
Interior design by Jaime Putorti

*To the dedicated scientists, doctors, and nurses
who fight on the front lines
against the sicknesses that would kill us*

In 1918 an influenza virus emerged.

Before that worldwide pandemic faded away in 1920, it would kill more people than any other outbreak of disease in human history . . .

Epidemiologists today estimate that influenza likely caused at least fifty million deaths worldwide, and possibly as many as one hundred million.

Yet even that number underestimates the horror of the disease, a horror contained in other data. Normally influenza chiefly kills the elderly and infants, but in the 1918 pandemic roughly half those who died were young men and women in the prime of their life, in their twenties and thirties.

One cannot know with certainty, but if the upper estimate of the death toll is true as many as 8 to 10 percent of all young adults then living may have been killed by the virus.

And they died with extraordinary ferocity and speed. Although the influenza pandemic stretched over two years, perhaps two-thirds of the deaths occurred in a period of twenty-four weeks, and more than half of those deaths occurred in even less time, from mid-September to early December 1918.

Influenza killed more people in a year than the Black Death of the Middle Ages killed in a century; it killed more people in twenty-four weeks than AIDS has killed in twenty-four years.

—John M. Barry, *The Great Influenza: The Epic Story of the Deadliest Plague in History*

Maybe what happened in 1918 has today merely the substance of a tenuous memory, but it also marks a lesson that clearly would be dangerous to forget. On the scale of a human life span, pandemic influenza is a rarity, but no one seriously doubts that it will be back.

—Leonard Crane, "The 1918 Spanish Flu Pandemic, and the Emerging Swine Flu Pandemic"

The potential is still there for the catastrophe of 1918 to happen again.

—Dr. Peter Webster, influenza expert, from Peter Radetsky's
The Invisible Invaders

Lora Miller, a 96-year-old Los Angeles resident whose father was killed by the Spanish Flu epidemic said she always knew that a pandemic flu could come back and she dreads to see the effect it would have on society. She believes that people in 1918 could handle a disaster like the Spanish Flu because they saw death far more often; infant mortality was still high and the war had killed and maimed millions in Europe. She is not sure that Americans could handle seeing hundreds of thousands or millions of people dying in just a few months.

"The world doesn't know fear and fright anymore," said Miller. "You won't want to leave your house. I pray every day that it doesn't come back. Every day."

—Robert McDonald, "A Killer Flu Could Come at Any Time: Is the
World Prepared?"

PART ONE

Monday
March 4, 1918

CHAPTER 1

FORT RILEY, KANSAS

MESS SERGEANT ALBERT Gitchell felt awful. He struggled to sit up in his bunk and failed, collapsing back onto his pillow in a feverish haze. His entire body felt heavy, like one of the sacks filled with the potatoes he knew he had to peel in order to feed the ravenous and often ungrateful soldiers at Fort Riley's Camp Funston.

He groaned and cursed both the severity and the inconvenience of his illness or, rather, the timing of it. He had a weekend pass coming and he was *not* giving that up for a cold.

He drew himself into a tight ball and shook from a sudden wave of chills that racked every muscle in his body. He felt as if a truck had hit him. His throat was raw. His eyes burned in their sockets, his head ached as if someone were banging on it with a hammer. Lying in the darkness, he wondered what time it was. Surely not far off his usual waking time of 4:00 a.m.

I'll fight it off. He rolled over, allowing his legs to slip from his bunk. With great effort he sat up. Then, clutching the nightstand for support, he stood. The dark room spun. He labored to pull on his fatigues, then sat again to pull on his boots. His muscles complained with every move. His neck was stiff and his head throbbed. He felt as though he was going to throw up—if he didn't pass out first.

Miserably, he conceded he had to get to the camp infirmary. Surely there'd be a shot or pill he could take for a quick recovery.

Without a shower or shave, he staggered from the barracks.

Gitchell collapsed on the pavement not twenty feet from his

barracks door. He heard the shouts of another soldier, then lost consciousness.

Sergeant Ken Ellis had pulled call duty as the admitting orderly in Hospital Building 91. He hated early-morning duty, especially this winter—the coldest on record east of the Rockies. On top of that, his medical duties had been beyond the pale. Fort Riley was packed, with troop strength of more than fifty-six thousand men. Of course, that meant lots of sick and injured soldiers to be cared for each day.

He entered the aging limestone building just as two sentries carried a soldier in. They dropped him on a gurney and looked at Ellis, wide-eyed and bewildered. They shook their heads and slowly backed away, then turned and hurried from the building.

The soldiers' expressions puzzled Ellis. He stifled a yawn and considered taking off his coat and getting a cup of coffee before throwing himself into the first of many men he'd have to deal with. The hospital had more than one thousand beds. Surely the patients could wait while he got a cup of coffee.

Instead, he looked at the soldier, pulled the chain around his neck, and studied the dog tag. Sergeant Albert Gitchell. He remembered him as the ironfisted chef who ran the mess. Ellis was struck by the delirious soldier's skin color: he was turning blue. Ellis assessed the man's vital signs. Temperature: 103.5; respiratory rate: 32; pulse: 125; blood pressure: 90 over 40.

Abnormal vital signs, but not atypical for the flu. But his color and mental status sure are bizarre. He jotted notes on a chart and, after flagging an orderly, instructed him to give the patient aspirin and start him on oxygen. As Ellis moved toward the break room, he had a quick afterthought and turned back to the orderly. "Put the sergeant in the contagion ward. No sense spreading whatever he has to the other soldiers." *Though, as mess sergeant, Gitchell had probably already done that.* Ellis sighed and headed for the break room.

A commotion down the hall caught his attention. Two soldiers were carrying a third man between them, shouting for a doctor. *I'm never going to get my coffee.* Ellis went to investigate.

Corporal Lee W. Drake, a truck driver assigned to the Headquarters Transportation Detachments First Battalion, was lifted onto another gurney. His skin was the same odd color as Gitchell's and the front of his uniform was covered with blood. A nosebleed, the soldier told Ellis. Otherwise, Ellis confirmed he had the same symptoms as Gitchell. He ordered aspirin and had Drake admitted to the contagion ward.

By the time he'd warmed his hands around a cup of coffee ten minutes later, Ellis was dealing with a third soldier presenting nearly identical vital signs as the other two, except he was lucid and complained that bright light hurt his eyes. His throat and nasal passages were cherry red, and a thick yellow-green mucus lined his nostrils. His cough sounded as if his lungs were tearing apart. Every cough tormented him. Ellis felt the man's chest and could palpate at least one broken rib.

After medicating and admitting the third soldier, Ellis grew more concerned. He had three sick soldiers, all from different units, arriving at the hospital infirmary within minutes of one another. On a military base packed with tens of thousands of men, an outbreak like this could be disastrous—even more so in the middle of a war.

When a fourth patient arrived with the same symptoms, Ellis knew it was time to talk to the chief nurse on duty.

By the time Elizabeth Harding, RN, entered the medical ward and evaluated the sick men, another two soldiers had arrived exhibiting the same symptoms. She took one look at the extremely sick young men and commanded the floor nurse to bring in the on-call *and* backup staff physicians immediately.

Maybe it's just a late-season flu, she hoped. She didn't want to embarrass herself by overreacting. And yet, she'd been trained to consider worst-case scenarios. She walked to the nearest wall phone, picked it up, and dialed.

As the phone rang, she knew *he* wouldn't be happy about

being awakened so early, especially for nonsurgical emergencies. But the situation was serious enough that he would chew her out if she didn't report it to him.

The shrill ring of the phone jolted Dr. Edward Bockner from a deep sleep.

He groaned as he rolled over. The previous evening spent downing martinis at the Officers' Club had left him hungover. The phone rang again and he clawed at the receiver, trying to get a grip on it. "Bockner," he said when he finally got the receiver to his ear and his lips to the mouthpiece atop the candlestick base.

"Dr. Bockner, this is Nurse Harding at the hospital."

The forty-five-year-old camp surgeon sat up and looked at the bedside clock. "It's—oh—five-thirty, Liz."

"Yes, sir, and we're already busy."

"Busy with what?"

He listened as she described the various patients who had come in and her concerns about their illnesses. At first he said nothing. Then, "I'll be right there."

Sitting in the sidecar of his chauffeured motorcycle, Edward Bockner lifted his face to the cool wind. It soothed his hangover. He glanced at his driver, who looked stern-faced beneath the leather cap and goggles. They raced through the sprawling camp, past the wooden barracks and limestone office buildings. Signs of awakening life appeared in the windows and doorways.

Camp Funston, built in 1917, was one of several camps within Fort Riley's two hundred thousand acres, and included twenty-six thousand personnel engaged in teaching and training. The camp's medical facility had eighteen wards for the inpatient care of more than a thousand soldiers.

As the commanding physician and camp surgeon, Bockner understood the havoc a flu epidemic could cause. An outbreak of meningitis would be even worse.

His driver stopped in front of the hospital entrance and Bockner walked quickly through the front door, tossed his coat on a rack in the doctors' lounge, and turned just as Nurse Harding came through the lounge door clutching a clipboard. She handed him a cup of steaming coffee.

Deep lines formed on her forehead and her eyes had the pinched look of stress. "It's bad, Colonel. I've never seen anything like it. Sick soldiers are arriving in unprecedented numbers. The symptoms are violent."

Bockner furrowed his brow. "How so?"

"Most are covered with blood."

"From what?"

"Nosebleeds they can't stop. Some are coughing it up. Others are bleeding from their ears. Still others are vomiting it up."

"Have you checked coagulation studies?"

"We're working on it, sir."

"What else?"

"It's the cough, sir. Some are coughing so hard they've broken ribs. Others are also writhing in agony with delirium. A significant number complain of the worst headaches of their lives. One soldier said it felt as if someone were trying to split his skull with an ice pick. The pain is just behind his eyes. Others say their body aches are so terrible they feel as though their bones are breaking."

"Have lumbar punctures been done?"

"Yes, sir. And the results so far indicate no signs of meningitis—at least from looking at the spinal fluid under the microscope. But the skin changes are the most unusual I've ever seen."

Bockner cocked his head. "Skin changes?"

"The skin of some soldiers is tinged blue, particularly around their lips and on their faces—a blueness that doesn't go away when we give them oxygen. A few have turned so dark that our orderlies cannot tell whether they are Caucasian or Negro. Sir, they're almost black. I've never, ever seen anything like it."

"What in blazes are we dealing with?"

"I have no idea, sir, but whatever it is, we now have more than two dozen seriously ill soldiers, all admitted in just the last hour or so."

She handed him the clipboard. He was surprised by not only the length of the list, but also the extent of the spread. The patients were from divisions and departments all over the camp. "Can you detect a pattern?"

"No, sir. It's certainly being spread by more than physical contact. I wonder if it's airborne."

Bockner imagined the difficulties of a quarantine for a base this size. Then another problem occurred to him. "How many soldiers have shipped out over the past twenty-four hours?"

She took the clipboard back and flipped a few pages. She found a note she'd made earlier. "Over five hundred."

Bockner frowned. There was every possibility some had been infected.

"This could turn into a major epidemic," she said in a half whisper.

"If it isn't already." He took a sip of his coffee as his mind raced through the proper procedure for handling this escalating emergency.

"We're going to need help or this illness could spread to only God knows where."

Bockner nodded. "I'll have to call the War Department."

PART TWO

November 4
Present Day

CHAPTER 2

NOVOSIBIRSK, SIBERIA

VLADISLAV KUNETZKOV DROVE his Toyota into the reserved parking space at the base of his apartment building. He looked up at the tall, nondescript block of cement, just one in the never-ending line of ugly buildings that rose after the devastation of the Second World War.

With a grunt, he pulled his six-foot-four-inch, two-hundred-sixty-pound frame out of the tiny car. Shutting the door, he took a last drag from his cigarette, threw the butt onto the cracked asphalt, and crushed it under his huge boot. He pulled his coat collar tight around his neck, pushed down his fur hat, and shivered. Winter had not yet arrived in Novosibirsk, though autumns on the West Siberian Plain were frigid by most people's standards. He was used to far more severe conditions. So why did he feel so cold now?

He pulled his suitcase from the backseat of the car and walked inside the building. He lumbered down the dark hallway to a sign informing him the elevator wasn't working—again. He swore at the maker of the sign and the landlord who did nothing about the building's condition. Nothing got fixed unless a bribe was involved. He wasn't about to play that game. He'd walk up a long set of stairs.

By the fifth floor, he was struggling. He stopped on a landing, set down the suitcase, and wiped his brow. This was unusual. He worked out every day and had done so for years. He frowned and cursed his body. He had been a world-class shot-putter, twice an Olympian. Why the aching muscles now? Why so tired?

Perhaps it was the past week of personal appearances, the

burden of being a local celebrity. Photo ops and PR at the ribbon cutting for a new state-of-the-art brewery; at the local water-treatment plant to boost confidence in the quality of the drinking water; and at the university at Akademgorodok, where he stood shaking hands and having photos taken with the doctors and scientists who'd come in for a big genetics conference. Imagine that, he thought. A big, brawny former Olympian hanging out with those wispy academics.

Too much sitting. Too much eating and drinking and talking. Not enough exercise. He reprimanded himself. He should have taken advantage of the gym facilities at the university.

He pushed onward and mused that, surely, a week without exercise shouldn't make him feel this weak. The suitcase now felt as if someone had replaced his clothes with anvils.

It took him twice the usual amount of time to get to the top floor. He turned and walked to the door at the end of the hall. It opened to a suite the government had given him for being a Russian Olympian. They described it as spacious, and for most people it probably was. But, for one of his girth, a thousand square feet was hardly roomy.

He had just put his key into the first of three dead bolts when the metal door was suddenly yanked open. Olga stood in front of him, beaming.

"Vladik!" She launched her petite body into his arms.

He barely had time to drop the suitcase and catch his wife. She wrapped her arms and legs around him and kissed him all over his face.

"Olga," he said, chuckling and gasping, as he fumbled to hold on to her while kicking his suitcase from the hall into his apartment.

"Oh, how I missed you!"

"No more than I missed you."

She let go of him and he held on to her as she leaned back to look at him. She frowned. "You look terrible." She felt his forehead. "You are burning up."

She dropped to the floor and, grabbing his hand, led him to the family room.

"Come, darling. Sit down. I'm going to get you some medicine."

The sofa groaned as he fell onto it.

Olga disappeared down the hall, calling over her shoulder: "So, how was it, darling? Terribly tedious?"

"The usual," he said. His voice sounded distant in his own ears.

"I saw a photo of you in the newspaper." She reappeared in the hall. "You were with some professor at that conference. He wore a bow tie."

"Hans Weigel. The geneticist." Something wasn't right. He slurred the word "geneticist."

She returned to the family room and looked at him, puzzled. "Vladik?"

He coughed and black spots pulsed in front of his eyes.

He slumped to one side. From a faraway place he heard Olga cry out. She leaned close, her little hands on his face, saying his name over and over.

After the ambulance pulled up to the entrance of the emergency department, one of the attendants hopped out of the front cab and raced to the back of the vehicle. He opened the rear door. The second man slid out of the back and joined him.

Olga climbed out next, stepping aside to watch as the men, red-faced and puffing, struggled to remove the rolling stretcher carrying her unconscious husband. Getting him down the stairs of the apartment building had required not only the two ambulance attendants, but also two neighbors.

The undercarriage of the stretcher extended and locked into place. The attendants strained to get the stretcher up the ramp toward the automatic doors.

Olga followed them to the entrance through a large group of people gathered in the doorway. The attendants shouted at the crowd and cleared a path, pushing into the open reception area. Olga stayed close behind. The attendants navigated the stretcher through the press of people. Olga looked at the group, wide-eyed. Most were clearly sick—heads down, eyes hollow—many moaning, some softly weeping. They looked just as her husband looked.

The attendants reached another set of doors and pushed the stretcher into the emergency room. What Olga saw shocked her. Doctors and nurses, all wearing face masks, were rushing back and forth in a room overflowing with patients on gurneys and in wheelchairs or hunched on the floor and against the walls.

She grabbed at a nurse rushing past. "What is going on?"

"The Apocalypse," she replied and raced away.

CHAPTER 3

SOMEWHERE OVER RUSSIA

THE AEROFLOT FLIGHT bumped and lurched. Dr. Susan Hutchinson grabbed the armrests and looked out of the small window. Beyond the scarred glass, the wings looked as if they were flapping to keep the aging plane in the air. *I hate this part of traveling*.

She turned to the man in the seat next to her. Anton Pushkin, one of the World Health Organization's Moscow men, looked at her, his eyes alight with amusement and his thin lips pressed together into a smirk. "Good, yes?"

"Good, *nyet*," she said.

The aircraft climbed higher through the clouds into calmer air. Susan forced herself to relax. She had to concentrate. There was a lot to learn from Anton in the four-hour flight between Moscow and Novosibirsk, Siberia. Her greater mandate was to find out all that had been discovered about the influenza outbreak in Novosibirsk quickly and efficiently; determine its virulence and transmissibility; and make an initial recommendation to her superiors at the WHO—all in twentyfour hours or less.

"I would have thought you were used to flying like this." Anton had been assigned as her aide and interpreter for this mission. He had worked in the Russian diplomatic corps before transferring to the Russian Ministry of Health. The WHO nabbed him from there.

"There's no getting used to flying like this."

"Not even in Africa?"

She lifted an eyebrow.

"I read your file. You were a key player in the Ebola outbreak in Gabon. Everyone has talked about your work there. You discovered a sixth species of Ebola."

"I didn't discover it. I got dropped into the middle of it."

"Pretty sweet for a specialist in viral epidemics."

"It didn't seem like it at the time. What else did they put in my file?"

"The usual. MD and Master of Public Health degrees from Duke University. A field investigative epidemiologist. Blah, blah, blah. Still, they should name the Gabon virus after you."

"I'd rather not have a near-world pandemic named after me, thanks." She turned slightly to face him. "Tell me about where we're going."

He tapped a finger against his chin. "Novosibirsk is on the same latitude as Copenhagen, Denmark. The sun will disappear just after five in the afternoon. We may have a temperature high of 2 degrees Fahrenheit tomorrow."

"I'm glad I brought my swimsuit. Tell me about the city."

"Novosibirsk is Siberia's largest city, with more than one and a half million people. The region is the size of Austria and Hungary combined. Though its claim to fame is probably the Akademgorodok."

"What is Akadem . . ." she began to ask, but gave up trying to pronounce the name.

"It means the 'Academy Town.' It is the center for the Siberian branch of the Russian Academy of Medical Sciences. Fourteen research institutions and universities all in one. And it is as high-tech as you can get. In fact, some say it has more IT facilities per square kilometer than any other area in the world, including Silicon Valley and Redmond, Washington. The Novosibirsk region is called the Silicon Taiga."

"Taiga?"

"That describes the physical area. A taiga is an area of coniferous forests, high up, between a tundra and a steppe. Taiga instead of Valley, get it?"

"Got it."

"In fact, some of the IT nerds have renamed the area." He scribbled a word on his pad and showed it to her. "They call it Cyberia."

"Impressive. What kinds of illnesses would be normal in No-vosibirsk at this time of year?"

"Probably the same as anywhere else. Colds, sinus and bronchial infections, stomach bugs, ear infections. Those kinds of things. But it's way too early for the influenza outbreaks we ordinarily see in Siberia—those usually hit in February and March."

"Any clues about the clinical attack and case fatality rates?"

To answer this, he opened a file. "They're both much, much higher than we'd expect from a normal influenza outbreak, even in Siberia."

"How so?"

He shuffled through the papers. "Well, in a normal flu season, the percentage of people at risk for an infection would range from five to fifteen percent. For pandemic flu, clinical attack rates are reported in the range of twenty-five percent. So far, in this outbreak, the clinical attack rates are exceeding fifty percent."

Susan gasped and looked at Anton's paper as if he'd somehow misread it. "Fifty percent?"

"That's right. At the university conference center where this started, there were about five hundred people exposed. As of this morning, over three hundred have been identified as having what health professionals are calling influenza. And the virus seems to have spread to colleagues and family members with great ease—upwards of a thousand cases and counting. However, we can't get any information on the lab tests that have been done. We don't even know for sure it's influenza. Unfortunately, quite a number of people have died."

"How many?"

Anton produced another report and handed it to her. "With a normal influenza season, the case fatality rates would be less than one in a thousand. With a pandemic, you might see one in a hundred. Reports for this outbreak are reporting *one in six*. About fifty-nine deaths so far, to be exact."

Susan shook her head. "Twenty percent! That's astounding." She searched her memory for a time she'd heard of a fatality rate that high. The worst in history had been the so-called Spanish flu of 1918 with a case fatality rate of about 2.5 percent. Estimates have ranged from 20 to 100 million deaths. Surely we're not dealing with a new version of that flu.

Anton continued, "Oddly enough it seems to be killing healthy men and women, young adults. That makes us think it's something new. Certainly something with a pandemic potential."

Susan nodded. A seasonal influenza would normally be most dangerous to the very young, the pregnant, and the elderly. When an influenza virus strikes down healthy young adults, it means it is more likely to be a new mutation. *Just like the Spanish flu was.*

"Around the WHO office in Moscow we have some concern that it may be either a variant of the swine flu, or worse, the avian flu. If the avian flu has finally mutated and is being transferred from person to person, then . . ."

That scenario would truly be a worst-case one. In a handful of cases in China and Southeast Asia the avian flu had transferred from birds to humans. However, there was no indication the flu had evolved into a form that could be transmitted from human to human.

Susan said, "If the authorities discovered it was an avian flu or the swine flu, the WHO would have heard about it by now. The Russian government wouldn't suppress that type of information, right?"

He looked unsure, then shrugged. "Unlikely, but it remains a possibility."

Susan frowned. The ability of the influenza to evolve, to exchange genes with other influenza viruses, to "reassort" genes, meant that another major pandemic not only *could* happen, but also certainly *would* happen. And given that the influenza virus is among the most contagious of all diseases and often spreads before symptoms develop . . . well, the possibility of a public-health disaster was very real.

"Doctor?" Anton was watching her.

Susan glanced at him. "What else do we know?"

"That's as much as I could get." His tone betrayed his frustration.

"That's all? How can that be all? We should be buried in data and reports."

"We're buried, yes. But it's in red tape and bureaucracy. The public-health officials in Siberia are a belligerent and cantankerous group. They will not volunteer anything unless they have to, especially without the proper paperwork."

"But surely a problem like this would push them to action."

"Are you joking? They have yet to admit that there is a problem."

"Our WHO credentials will open some doors."

"Don't count on it. Especially since they view your coming as intrusive—and an insult. Worse, we'll be dealing with Dr. Yuri Cheklovisk." Anton's expression turned dour.

The name meant nothing to her. "Why do you say that?"

"He is a vain man who probably cheated his way through medical school and his postgraduate training to become the chief public-health officer in Akademgorodok. For a man like Yuri, this is a very glamorous position. He gets to serve as personal physician to IT-company presidents, as well as to university presidents and chancellors there. Very prestigious. Lots of hobnobbing with celebrities who come in as guests. But medicine? He knows very little."

Susan groaned. "So you're telling me bluntly that the man in charge of this situation is not equipped to deal with it."

"Exactly."

"Terrific." She closed her eyes and pressed back against the headrest. "This is going to be a real treat."

"It's worse than that," Anton said. "He's my uncle."

It was after 5:00 p.m. when they landed at Novosibirsk Tolmachevo Airport. The sun had just set and the city lights to the east winked at Susan through the thick clouds. She saw strings of headlights on the city roads and wondered whether they were part of rush-hour traffic or something more emergent.

As they descended, she saw the glint of a river and a dark patch of water to the south, which Anton explained was the Ob Sea, or Obskoe.

"It's a man-made reservoir off the Ob River," he explained. "A marvel of Russian engineering. Its hydropower station provides electricity for the region and the water plant provides the drinking water. All for over two million people in the region."

Once they'd disembarked from the plane, Susan felt an inexplicable tension that crackled like electricity through the travelers packed at the various gates and those moving along the passageways. People spoke in shouts and some were in face-to-face arguments. From the corner of her eye, she saw a fistfight break out in a café. She understood the frayed nerves that often accompanied crowded airports, uncomfortable gate seats, and delayed flights. This, however, was a palpable fear.

"Is this normal?" she asked Anton as they walked.

"Not at all." He retrieved his cell phone from his coat pocket. "Let me find out what's going on."

She followed him as he pushed out of the stream of travelers and leaned against the wall. He pressed the phone against one ear, put his finger in the other. Immediately he began shouting at someone in Russian.

"*Nyet!*" he shouted several times, followed by a barrage of words, then silence, then another barrage.

Susan felt a growing sense of alarm. People had tissues and handkerchiefs pressed to their noses. Others walked glassy-eyed, weighted with fatigue. She was aware of every cough. A number of police officers stood with their hands on their weapons and their eyes on the crowds.

Anton groaned loudly and turned to her. "Good news and bad news."

"What's the good news?"

"A car is meeting us."

That was a relief to her. "And the bad news?"

"The city is in something of a panic. Rumors have circulated that this illness *is* the avian flu and that the government is going to quarantine the city, perhaps the entire region."

"What? But we don't know what it is yet."

"That doesn't matter. Something has happened to feed the rumors."

She looked at him, waiting for his explanation.

He caught sight of a large map on a wall nearby. He led her to it and pointed to the symbols for the train stations and tracks. "See? The city is located along both the Trans-Siberian and the Turkestan-Siberia railways. The former connects Moscow with the Pacific coast of Russia; the latter connects Novosibirsk to Central Asia and the Caspian Sea."

Susan's eyes followed the tracks and saw an immediate problem.

Anton continued, "Health officials in Kazakhstan, Mongolia, and China are alarmed. Our home office is saying that, even now, they are threatening to close their borders to Russia. Public-health officials in Japan are discussing whether to allow flights from Siberia to enter Japan's airspace."

Susan lowered her head, appreciating the enormity of the situation, if only from a public information standpoint. "I suggest we get to your uncle right away."

"Ah, well, that's the other bad news."

She lifted an eyebrow. "Oh?"

"He's at the hospital. He's caught the sickness."

CHAPTER 4

AKADEMGORODOK, SIBERIA

THE DRIVE FROM the airport to the Akademgorodok was a white-knuckle experience for Susan. The driver, a silent young man in the government's employ, seemed to have little regard for other cars or traffic lanes. He apparently believed their Volvo, together with the small provincial flag attached to the radio antenna, gave them an invicible right-of-way. Though they were able to skirt the city by taking the highway around to the south, they still encountered lines of stopped cars. The driver remedied this by driving on the shoulder.

This got them as far as a checkpoint, where Anton presented their papers. "It's a classic Russian response to a potential crisis," he said under his breath. "When in doubt, set up a checkpoint."

A sour-faced officer reluctantly waved them on. Within a few miles, they were on an open road. The urban sprawl behind them disappeared. They sped between fields and thick forests that looked impenetrable in the darkness.

After crossing the Ob River, they eventually came into the Akademgorodok. Even without the benefit of daylight, Susan got a sense of its university feel. An abundance of birch and oak trees had already thrown down their green and yellow leaves. Apartment complexes and shops spread out between the large blocks of academic buildings.

With a hard turn, the driver pulled into the driveway of the Central Clinical Hospital. He had to hit the brakes to narrowly avoid colliding with a waiting ambulance. It was one of several lined along the curb, lights on and engines running, waiting to access the emergency entrance.

Anton gave instructions to the driver, who diverted them into a parking lot that led to the main entrance. Cars were parked in every space and double-parked everywhere else.

"We'll get out here," Anton said. "Bring what you need."

She got out and realized that her coat, though it was made of heavy wool, wouldn't be enough for this frigid climate. Almost immediately, her ears went pinprickly and her hands, which were in thin leather gloves, felt as if she had shoved them into a bucket of ice. Her toes tingled through her thin shoes. "Remind me to get a new collection of winter clothes," she said to Anton.

"Give me your sizes and I'll take care of it."

They approached the building, which to Susan looked more like a hotel than a hospital. The double doors opened automatically and a blast of heat hit her in the face.

They stopped just inside the lobby and Anton took off his gloves. "You'll learn," he said. "You freeze outside then step into buildings so blistering hot you wish you'd worn nothing but a T-shirt and Bermuda shorts, then you step outside and freeze again."

Crossing the lobby, Susan was instantly aware of the frightened, tense expressions, the worried pacing, the raw nerves. She didn't need a Russian interpreter to appreciate the undercurrent of panic.

Anton flashed his credentials to a frazzled woman behind the admissions desk. She handed him a pair of plastic bags, then pointed at the elevators, where a crowd had gathered around each set of doors.

"Yuri is in a room on the fourth floor," Anton said. "Shall we take the stairs?"

"Good idea."

On the way up, Anton handed her a surgical face mask. "Just in case."

They put on the masks and came out of the staircase into a pale-green hallway lined with men and women standing around gurneys of the sick.

"Wait a moment," Anton said, and caught a doctor in the doorway of what looked like a break room. The two stepped inside, but Susan could see from Anton's gestures and expressions he was grilling the doctor for information.

Susan stayed outside near the wall, not wanting to draw attention to herself. She listened to the violent, wracking coughs, the moaning, and the cries. One man turned his head and blood exploded from his mouth with projectile force.

Her memory raced back to the black-and-white photos from 1918, of gurneys with sick soldiers struck down with the Spanish flu, all covered with dried, caked blood.

"This way," Anton said, startling her. She followed him down the hall.

In full view, now Susan regretted putting on the surgical mask. Patients assumed she was a local doctor and began to shout at her in Russian. Anton shouted back at them as he reached back to grab her hand, pulling her ahead. Beleaguered doctors and nurses came and went, their eyes revealing fatigue and worry.

She tried to keep her attention forward, but couldn't avert her gaze from the patients who lined the walls. Some cried out and others curled up, writhing. Blood spotted the sheets, the walls, and the floor.

"What did the doctor say?" Susan asked.

Anton shook his head and said from the corner of his mouth, "He's never seen anything like it. It's hitting everyone so fast. Symptoms of pneumonia, discoloration of the face—"

"Discoloration?"

"Brown spots over the cheekbones, even a blue pallor on some. Blood pouring from every orifice. Torture and agony. He said they're calling it *La Grippe*."

Susan stopped, twisting Anton to face her. "La Grippe was the name of the Spanish flu of 1918."

Anton took her arm and pulled her forward to the nurses' station, where he again presented his credentials and demanded to see Yuri's chart. The nurse complied and handed him a file. They walked toward the end of the hallway, where they reached a pair of armed guards. Anton held up his identification and gestured to Susan, explaining who they were. The guards stepped aside.

Yuri Cheklovisk had the room to himself. The room was lit by a single lamp next to his bed and by the monitoring equipment with buttons that flashed like Christmas lights. Yuri lay in a

single bed with IVs hooked to his arms. A nurse in a white uniform stood nearby, her gaze downcast as if she were in prayer.
She didn't look up when Anton cleared his throat.

"Uncle Yuri," Anton said in English.

Yuri slowly opened his eyes. "What? Who is there?"

"It is Anton."

He grunted, then looked at Susan. "And that woman is from
the WHO?"

"Yes, Uncle."

"I'm sorry you're not well, Doctor," Susan said.

They approached the bed. Yuri was a large man with thick
jowls that seemed to turn his eyes to mere slits and pushed his
lips into a permanent pucker. The white sheet draped over him
was not enough to camouflage his massive belly.

"Tell us your condition," Anton said as he looked at the chart.

"It's nothing," Yuri said.

"It's more than nothing." Anton flipped through the pages.

Yuri lifted his head. "I know what you're trying to do. You'll
attempt to use my sickness to take control of my jurisdiction.
You won't!" His voice rose and he continued in Russian. Susan
could guess what he was saying.

"You're such an old fool. This is not about power or control,"
Anton said sharply in English. "We're here to save lives. Now tell
us everything you know so we can get on with it."

Yuri snorted, then put his head back and closed his eyes.

They stood in silence for a moment. Anton fumed. Susan was
incredulous that their ability to do their jobs might be compromised by sheer stubbornness.

"It's likely that he doesn't know anything," Anton said. "I
suggest we find our help elsewhere."

"There is no 'elsewhere,'" Yuri said. He coughed a couple of
times, then burst into a full-blown fit. He stopped and lay still,
moaning, his breathing labored.

Susan grabbed the stethoscope hanging on the headboard
and listened through various areas on his chest. As she moved
from one lobe to another, she heard a cacophony of crackly
sounds that she recognized as rales and rhonchi—what her older
professors had called "the death rattle" of severe pneumonia.

"Uncle Yuri?"

His hard breathing was the only response. The monitors indicated that he was still alive, if unconscious.

Anton turned to the nurse. "Who is his assistant—his second in command?"

The nurse ignored him.

He spoke to her in Russian, his voice low and firm.

She held up her hand, spun on her heel, and walked out of the room. Susan and Anton followed her. Rather than head back to the chaos of the floor, she took a few steps in the other direction. It was a dead end, with a few metal chairs and a small window that overlooked the parking lot. The jam-packed cars puffed white smoke from their exhausts. Horns honked and red brake lights served as rude gestures. The nurse stood with her back to them, her arms folded.

Anton came up behind her. "What are you doing?"

She turned to face them. She had the face of a young woman, but the stout and buxom body of a matron. She looked at Susan. "The obstinacy of men will kill us all," she said in a heavy Russian accent.

Susan looked at her sympathetically. "You are his second in command."

"Unofficially," she said. "Officially his second in command is Grigory Tarasov, but he is a moron who is now hiding in his office hoping this crisis will go away by itself." She held out her hand. "I am Tanya."

Susan took her hand. "I am Dr. Susan Hutchinson."

They shook, then Tanya gave Anton a withering stare. "Did you expect to get his cooperation by calling him an old fool? Is that what they've taught you in Moscow—to disrespect your elders?"

"I think I know my uncle better than—"

"Me?" she challenged him. "I have worked with Dr. Cheklovisk for a very long time."

In an instant, Susan suspected that Tanya did more than work for Yuri. "Can you help us, Tanya? Does Yuri know anything about this sickness?"

"I know what he knows. All the reports and data are in a briefcase in the room."

A crash sounded down the hall. A man in a red cap had angrily upturned a tray and began shouting what sounded like *Vahdah* again and again. A woman wept over a still body. Nurses and uniformed men rushed to the spot.

"Water?" Susan asked.

Anton nodded.

Keeping her eye on the unfolding tumult down the hall, Susan asked Tanya, "So, what are we dealing with?"

"We know what we are *not* dealing with. It isn't an avian or a swine flu. It is influenza Type A, H1N1—completely different from the 2009 H1N1 virus. And we're reasonably certain this was flown in to us."

"What do you mean?" Anton asked, his tone gentler than before.

Her eyes bore into him. "Your uncle may not be a good doctor, but he is a good investigator. He was able to trace the initial cases back to a common denominator: a genetics conference last week. Unfortunately, we did not recognize the threat in time to quarantine those who attended the conference. Some left the country. Many exposed their families and friends."

Susan said, "What was the common denominator?"

"You mean *who*," Tanya said. "A funny-looking man, a bow-tie-wearing geneticist from Berlin who came in for the conference. We now believe he was ill with influenza when he arrived. A simple cold, we thought—fever, aches, runny nose, cough. Dr. Cheklovisk administered an injection of antibiotic and dispensed some ibuprofen and nasal-decongestant spray. He recommended rest, but the professor insisted upon keeping his speaking schedule."

"Which helped to spread the disease," said Anton.

"Within hours to some," she said. "A little longer for others."

"Where is this professor? Do you have him quarantined?" Susan asked.

Tanya shook her head. "*Nyet*. We don't know where he is. But we think he's left the country."

Susan chewed at her lower lip, her mind racing with the implications of this news. Down the hall, a fight broke out between the man who'd been shouting and a uniformed man who attempted to calm him. Punches were thrown. More crashes as a gurney was toppled. Yuri's two guards moved toward the chaos, their hands on their guns.

A loud beeping emerged from Yuri's room. Tanya moved quickly, pushing through the door and straight to Yuri's bed. Susan and Anton raced after her. The heart monitor beeped at them with an increasing urgency, then stopped. Yuri was flatlining.

Tanya shouted something in Russian and Anton rushed out of the room. She threw herself at Yuri, tearing at his hospital gown. She began to apply CPR.

Susan came alongside to assist. But she knew before they started that there was no saving the man.

Susan's fingers hung over the keyboard of her laptop—and paused there. She wondered how to begin the report to her WHO superior. Her gaze wandered around her makeshift office, hastily and reluctantly provided by the Russian health authorities. It had all the appeal of a cement bunker, with rusted filing cabinets, water-stained files, dim lighting, and damp cold.

She looked at the screen and the blinking cursor. *Where do I start?*

She thought of what she'd seen in the Novosibirsk hospital. The words "La Grippe" and "Spanish flu" kept spinning in her head.

She leaned farther over her laptop and began her report.

Less than an hour later, she finished and picked up a mug of tea—now stone cold—and drank from it. She winced, reviewed her words, and settled back in the chair as a feeling of helplessness came over her.

She needed help.

Glancing at a clock hung precariously on the wall, she picked up her phone and dialed the number for the only one she thought could provide it.

CHAPTER 5

THE HAGUE, NETHERLANDS

COLONEL KEVIN MAKLIN sat in his favorite café, wishing it were warm enough to sit outdoors. He considered a patio meal a perk for living in The Hague. Even though the sun was bright, the freezing temperature drove him indoors.

From his seat by the window, he could see the canal—only a stone's throw away. A flock of seagulls winged low over the street.

A waiter in a starched white shirt brought him an espresso. He unfolded the *International Herald Tribune* and sipped his drink. He felt guilty. As executive aide to Brigadier General Sam Mosley, Kevin was normally too busy for these indulgences. Lunch was usually something from the cafeteria, eaten quickly at his desk. But his boss was on a leave of absence following the Ebola crisis in Africa that had killed members of his family. That left Kevin with an unusually reasonable workload, and time to think about *her*.

As he drained the cup of espresso, he drew his cell phone from his pocket. He wanted to call her. There was no reason he couldn't. They were certainly friends. But he was afraid it might be awkward, or he would catch her at a bad time.

He pulled up her number in his contacts list and highlighted it—then hesitated. Should he or shouldn't he? He felt like a schoolboy again. *Do we ever grow up when it comes to this?*

Just as he was about to hit the call button, the phone vibrated in his hand. To his astonishment, the screen announced the very person he'd been thinking about. He pressed the talk button and swallowed back his heart.

"Hello, Dr. Hutchinson. I was just thinking about you."

"Oh . . . hi. Good morning, I mean. Is it morning there? I have no idea what time it is for you."

"It's almost one in the afternoon here."

"Well then, good afternoon, Colonel Maklin."

He knew her voice. Every nuance, in fact. She sounded stressed even while trying to be friendly.

"Is this a bad time?" she asked.

"For you, never. How are things in Siberia?"

"Cold. And we're in the midst of a crisis."

With the word "crisis," he tensed. "What's the problem?" He reached into his inside coat pocket and removed a notepad and pen. "I heard a rumor that you're dealing with H5N1 bird flu."

"That was the initial theory. This is something different. H1N1, far worse than the normal type."

"How so?" He wrote H1N1 on his notepad. "What's so special about it?"

She lowered her voice. "Kevin, I'm concerned we may have a variant descendant of the Spanish flu."

"The *Spanish* flu? In Russia?"

"It's just a name. Do you know what it is?"

"I've read about it. It broke out suddenly and, within two years, millions died. Somewhere I heard that it killed more U.S. soldiers in World War I than were actually killed in combat."

Her voice still lowered, she said, "You realize the impact a new outbreak would have."

"But where did it come from? Why would it show up now?"

"I don't know. I'm trying to confirm my suspicions, but the people are getting crazy here. The public-health official we were supposed to deal with died of it tonight. No one is in charge."

"Except you."

"I have no authority. The Russians are guarded about strangers. I'm afraid of what's going to happen if we don't do something. It's spreading here—and out from here—quickly."

It made him ache to hear the urgency and helplessness in her voice. "What can I do to help? There must be something, even if it's on an informal basis."

The line hissed as she seemed to consider the question. "If

there was some way of working the political channels, to let them know what we may be facing."

"I can do that easily. What else?"

"We think we know who carried the virus into the country, but I'm having a hard time getting officials here to help track him down."

"Give me the details and I'll see what I can do."

"I'll send you a copy of the report I wrote for the WHO. It's for your eyes only, Kevin. Check your e-mail."

"Will do."

"Thanks. It's good to hear your voice."

And then she was gone.

He sat for a minute and stared at the scarred wood tabletop, his heart pounding. Was it because he was afraid she was in danger, or because she was glad to hear his voice?

Grow up, soldier, he berated himself. The waiter arrived with his sandwich, but he waved it away and, after dropping some money onto the table, dashed back to the office.

Kevin didn't bother to hang up his coat, but went straight to his computer. He signed on and scrolled through the list of un-opened e-mails. Hers was the most recent. He clicked on it and looked at the empty message box. She hadn't written a personal note, which disappointed him. But there was an attached docu-ment. After opening it, he leaned forward, chin resting on his left fist, and began to read.

By the time he finished, his heart was pounding again. He stood and paced his office. *This can't be real.*

He turned to the phone on his desk and snatched up the re-ceiver. This was bigger than he'd imagined. And he needed to get help to Susan—*fast.*

CHAPTER 6

LONDON, ENGLAND

COLONEL JAMES MACLAYTON sat at his desk in Chiswick, London, doing the thing he hated most: signing papers. And this morning he faced a mountain of paperwork.

Abby Benson, a short, plump matron, stood over him like a schoolmarm. Her dress looked like worn wallpaper from a 1940s B movie. As he signed each document, she handed him another and pointed to where he should place his signature.

He stopped and looked at her. "Mrs. Benson, I am a senior army scientist. I have served my country with honor for more than twenty-five years. I am personally acquainted with two presidents and more White House and Pentagon officials than you can imagine. Now, don't you think I know how to sign documents without you standing over me?"

She glowered at him. In her posh and precise English accent she said, "No, sir. Without me, these papers would still be sitting where I left them yesterday. And *I* have served *my* country for over thirty years and am personally acquainted with *four* prime ministers and more Whitehall and Downing Street officials than *you* can imagine. Now stop complaining and finish signing these documents so I can get back to work."

He stared at her for a moment, then burst out laughing. "I love the British! And I'm forever grateful to your government for lending you to me."

She looked at him impassively, then pointed to the next page. "*This* form is about—"

Before she could go any further, his phone rang. She deftly

picked it up. "Colonel MacLayton's office." She paused. "Please hold while I see if the colonel is in."

He watched her as she hit the hold button.

"It's a Colonel Maklin from The Hague."

He was surprised. "Is he calling for General Mosley?"

"He didn't say. Would you like me to ask?"

"No, I'll take it." He reached for the phone as she turned and walked from the office. He waited until she had closed the door behind her.

"Kevin?"

"I'm sorry to bother you, Colonel."

"No bother, son. You've just saved me from a large pile of paperwork. Is the general back from leave?"

"No, sir. And I'm taking a liberty here without his approval. This is off-the-record, if that's agreeable."

"All right. What can I do for you?"

"Something has come up. Something that could prove disastrous."

MacLayton hung up the phone and swiveled in the chair to his printers. He picked up the report he'd just printed out, courtesy of Colonel Maklin. He turned back to his desk then jabbed at the button on the intercom.

"Yes, sir?"

"Please get Georgina in here."

"I don't believe she's in yet."

"Then find her!" He leaned back and rubbed his hands over his face and up onto his shoe-brush haircut. The phrase "Spanish flu" tumbled around in his mind. The Spanish flu in Siberia, of all places. He shuddered at the thought of its reappearance.

He remembered his parents discussing the Spanish flu in whispered tones, though they called it La Grippe at the time. The disease had struck down both his grandfathers while they were fighting in World War I. Two maternal aunts had also succumbed. And his mother had suffered from the illness for nearly two weeks before recovering. La Grippe was as much a part of his family's legacy as were the Great Depression and World War II.

He leaned forward and rifled through Dr. Hutchinson's report. It unnerved him. The situation in Siberia could fast become a global problem—which meant it was a potential assignment for his team.

He went to the window and looked at the small residential street below—called Rectory Road presumably because of the old church at the far end of the road. To an outsider, his office was housed in just one of many quaint townhomes and apartments stretching in both directions on both sides of the modest street. It was all very middle-class, part of Chiswick, a suburb of London.

There was no sign on the front door, no declaration this was the English headquarters of the National Institutes of Health's special department of Historical Research and Data Development—a group of brilliant, if eccentric, scientists and doctors whom some considered misfits. They investigated medical forensic cases that others had difficulty solving through the usual course of diagnosis, lab testing, and research. His team was called to solve medical mysteries from the past so as to prevent or treat modern outbreaks. Insiders called them the Time Scene Investigators. It was meant to be a joke, but somehow it had become a genuine designation. Now, no one even knew what HRDD stood for. They were simply called TSI.

The team already had a feather in its cap: they helped identify the Gabon virus, the most recent Ebola outbreak in Gabon, Africa. Without his TSI team, that epidemic would certainly have become a worldwide pandemic. MacLayton was proud of his team. He'd come out of retirement to work with them.

There was a slight knock on the door and Georgina came in. She looked as if she'd just awakened this morning—or hadn't gone to sleep the night before. He never knew which was the case. She was an unusually fresh-faced girl who didn't wear makeup, though he heard rumors she often donned Goth eyeliner for her nights out in Soho's nightclubs. He didn't want to know. It was enough for him to endure her latest hairstyle: blond dreadlocks, with a small clump colored a fluorescent red.

She threw herself into the visitor's chair opposite his desk. She was dressed in a white lab coat; a pair of black leggings jutted out from beneath it like two licorice sticks.

"You wanted to see me, Mac?"

"Yes. I want you to get the team assembled and start pulling out everything we have about the Spanish flu of 1918."

"Okay."

"I want to brief everyone in an hour."

Georgina made a face. "Everyone?"

"Yes, everyone."

"Even Mark and Nora?"

"*Especially* Mark and Nora. Why?"

"You gave Mark some personal time and Nora is lecturing. You gave the okay."

"Did I?" Mac frowned. "So, where are they?"

"In the DC area."

He raised a bushy eyebrow. "Together?"

CHAPTER 7

VIRGINIA

DR. MARK CARLSON could not have planned it better. The morning sun was high and the crisp autumn air was already taking on the warm breath of an Indian-summer day. He shifted the gears of the red Miata and drove faster, zooming down a straight two-lane road that cut through the beautiful Virginia countryside. The Shenandoah Mountains had been on his right for over an hour and the surrounding forests and fields had the enchanted look of a child's fantasy.

"Perfect," said Nora Richards. "I'd forgotten how gorgeous this part of the country is."

He glanced at her in the passenger seat.

She smiled at him. "I'm glad you invited me along."

It was a coincidence, of sorts. Mark had gone to DC to take care of personal business—the drudgery of dealing with a house he never saw and an ex-wife who believed she could treat him as if they were still married. *Badly* married.

Nora Richards, PhD, had been in Baltimore lecturing about medical anthropology, one of her several professional specialties.

Their busy schedules had miraculously aligned and he decided to seize the opportunity.

She looked out at the countryside again. His gaze lingered on her. Grace Kelly, he thought. They should be driving through Monaco with the top down, wind blowing through their hair. If only he were more like Cary Grant.

He remembered the first time he saw her. At a virology conference at Boston University. She was in her postdoctoral training and he was giving the keynote address. She'd made an impression after the speech with the quality of her questions. She was a woman interested in his mind and, had he not been married, well . . .

He forced his eyes back to the road. The affection between them was beyond question but they were mature and professional enough to know they had to be careful. Working relationships that turned romantic often caused problems for everyone. And he was a man with emotional baggage and lots of unfinished business. He was still in a time of healing.

Which was, in part, one of the reasons he'd asked her to join him today.

"It's not much farther," he said, in answer to a question she hadn't asked. "We're almost there."

"I'm in no rush."

That she was willing to make this trip meant a lot to him. The trip brought him one step closer to making peace with the past—to letting go of the events and losses that had scarred him so deeply.

She turned to face him. "All things considered, you seem surprisingly happy."

"I am." He took the liberty of reaching out and taking her hand, but only for a moment. They came to an intersection, forcing him to grab hold of the stick shift again.

A right turn and they headed for the foothills of the southern end of the Shenandoah Mountains. A sign appeared marking the miles to Charlottesville, the town of his birth. They passed another sign for the much smaller town of Ivy, and Mark navigated his way there.

"What's its name?" she asked as they drew near a tiny church.

"St. Paul's Episcopal Church. I was baptized here as an infant." Until this moment, Mark had been able to push aside his anxiety about returning here. Now being there tied his stomach in knots. The feeling grew as they reached the stone building and Gothic bell tower. He pulled into the parking lot and turned off the engine.

"It's a lovely church," she said. He knew she was trying to fill in the silence.

"When I was a kid, I imagined becoming an Episcopal priest and serving in a church just like this." He'd almost fulfilled that dream, until medicine called him in another direction.

"Being a priest would have been a disaster for you." She smiled. "All those poor women parishioners trying to worship while having to gaze at you at the same time. Terrible."

"And I would have been just the kind of guy to exploit that."

"I doubt it. You have too much integrity."

"Integrity, maybe—but it wouldn't have mattered. I never had the faith to be a priest."

She eyed him. "You did. Once. And I think you'll find your faith again." She turned to look up at the church steeple. "Or maybe it will find you."

He shrugged and looked at the church. Whatever faith he once professed had died several years before. And, not for the first time, he had to acknowledge just how much he depended on Nora's faith to shore up his own. Hers was a steady flame to his tiny spark. She seemed to grasp exactly what it was she believed and had integrated it fully into who she was. No separation existed among her spiritual, professional, emotional, or physical lives—they all meshed into a perfect, noncompartmentalized whole.

"Well?" she said.

He took a deep breath, hoping for greater resolve.

"We don't have to go in now."

"It's all right." He opened his door, climbing out of the small roadster, and moved around to the passenger side. He grabbed the handle of her door as she began to open it.

"Allow me."

"Such a gentleman."

He closed the door behind her and they walked across the parking lot. She slipped her hand under and around his elbow.

They rounded a corner and Mark hesitated as the graveyard came into view. The markers and monuments looked like a crowded cityscape, but instead of skyscrapers and high-rises, crosses and angels dominated the view.

He pushed himself onward. "I remember someone saying that the graveyard was established before the church—an overflow from another graveyard near here." He was chattering to hide his anxiety. They stepped through an iron gateway and moved inside the cemetery.

Nora leaned over to read some of the tombstones. "These look like the graves of soldiers."

Mark nodded. "This is the older section. You'll find the graves of some of Ivy's early settlers here. And soldiers who died in the Civil War."

They walked around a cedar tree and suddenly they were there—*her* grave—the final resting spot of Jennifer Carlson.

Mark felt a lurch somewhere in his chest, as if his heart had skipped a beat. "Ah," was all he could say.

Nora squeezed his arm tighter. "God have mercy," she said and performed the sign of the cross.

The tombstone was flat and overseen by a three-foot-tall stone angel. The young angel's small wings were spread out and her long dress seemed to ripple out as if blown by some heavenly wind. Her face was the epitome of pure innocence, flanked by flowing locks of long hair. The eyes were turned downward, as if looking at the child in the grave.

"I should have brought flowers," he said. "Why didn't I bring flowers?"

Nora said, "It's enough that you're here."

"Is it?"

She pointed to the inscription of the birth and death dates. "You didn't tell me that today is the anniversary of her death."

"I thought it would be too depressing. I was afraid you wouldn't come."

She frowned. "You don't know me very well, do you?" She read aloud the main inscription: Jennifer Beth Carlson. With Us Only Five Years. Loved for Eternity.

Mark's eyes misted over. He closed them for a moment and bit his lips to keep them from trembling. When he opened his eyes, he saw Nora dabbing at hers. He pulled her close. "Thank you for coming with me."

She returned his hug. "I wouldn't have missed it for anything."

From the corner of his eye, he noticed a shadow fall across

the grave path. Mark turned as a tall figure, a woman dressed in black, quickly stepped toward them. A black veil covered her face. She carried a bouquet of pink and yellow flowers.

It took him a moment to recognize her. When he did, his jaw dropped.

"Donna," he said to his ex-wife.

"Well . . ." Donna said, pulling up her veil and removing her designer sunglasses. "What a coincidence."

Mark stammered for a moment, then asked, "What are you doing here?"

She pushed a strand of red hair from her face and forced a smile. "The same as you, I would think." She knelt and carefully placed the small bouquet of flowers on the grave. She remained crouched and Mark thought she might be quietly weeping.

The shock of seeing her left him speechless. He looked help-lessly at Nora, who kept her eyes forward.

After a few moments, Donna stood. She was still strikingly beautiful and Mark was touched watching her dab her tears. She turned to face them.

Mark remained frozen. Nora introduced herself and the two women shook hands.

"I'm sorry for your loss," Nora said to Donna.

"Thank you. Whenever I come here, I hope that it won't hurt as badly as the last time. It always does."

"I'm sure the pain never fully goes away."

The three stood silently, uncomfortably looking at one an-other. Mark still couldn't find his voice. Finally, Nora said, "I'll leave you two alone for a few minutes."

Before Mark could speak, Nora turned and walked toward the church.

"That was very kind of her," Donna said.

"She's a kind woman." Mark fought against the bristly edges that began to form around his heart. Instinctively he wanted to protect himself. Since their daughter's death, his relationship with Donna had become poisonous. She blamed him for every-thing that had gone wrong. It was his fault Jenny had died, Donna claimed, because he was away on business when she had grown ill. It was *he* who told her not to take Jenny to the doctor.

No one realized she had been struck with a rapidly spreading bacterial meningitis.

"I'm glad you're here," Donna said with uncharacteristic warmth.

She's going to ask for more money. He had been her personal bank over the past couple of years. She'd repeatedly played the guilt card to get him to fund her many business ventures. They had all ended in failure.

"I know what you're thinking," she said. "But you're wrong."

"Wrong about what?"

"I'm glad you're here because . . ." she let her words drift off as tears again filled her eyes. "It may surprise you to learn that I've been in counseling over the past few weeks."

Mark wasn't surprised. She had been in counseling before—marriage counseling with him, in fact—and had wound up sleeping with their therapist while supposedly working things out with Mark.

"Oh?"

She looked back down at the angelic figurine. "I realize how wrong I've been about you. In my pain, I've lashed out at you, blaming you for something that wasn't your fault."

He took a step back from her as if she'd swung at him. "Are you serious?" *Was she trying to play him?*

"I'm very serious." She faced him. "I haven't been able to stop thinking about it and then to find you here . . . I . . . It seems providential somehow."

"What is?"

"To be able to say what I have to say, Mark." She paused and took a slow, deep breath, as if gathering her strength. "I'm sorry for everything I've done to hurt you. Deeply sorry. Can you . . . will you . . . forgive me?"

Mark tried to blink away the burning in his eyes. He pressed his lips together then relaxed them again. "Donna, I don't know what to say."

She nodded. "It's a lot to ask, I know. You don't have to answer now."

He couldn't have answered, even if he knew how to.

A soft wind rustled through the branches overhead.

"So, was that your girlfriend?"

"A coworker. And a good friend."

"Then I still have a chance," she said with a flicker of a smile. She leaned toward him and kissed him lightly on the cheek, her lips lingering near his ear. "If you find it in your heart to forgive me, then maybe we could go out sometime. On a date, maybe. Just to see if we can salvage what we once had," she whispered.

She took a step away and he gazed into her bright green eyes, trying to understand what was going on behind them.

Is she sincere?

She smiled.

He searched for something to say, found nothing, and was rescued only by Nora's voice.

"Mark!" She walked briskly toward them. "It's the office. We have to go *right away*."

Nora's tone and expression told him that this was not a ruse to rescue him.

"It was good to see you again, Donna," Mark said.

"Call me sometime." Donna slowly turned to face Jenny's grave, her back to him. She lowered her head.

Feeling he had been released from an invisible grip, he strode to Nora. Together they hurried to the car.

PART THREE

Monday
September 30, 1918

CHAPTER 8

BOSTON, MASSACHUSETTS

PHILIP EDWARD KNOX looked at the journalist across the coffee table with cool disdain. As a matter of habit, Knox brushed his waxed handlebar mustache with the side of his forefinger, then rubbed the palms of his hands over his carefully oiled hair. He felt at his neck for his monocle and calmly returned it to his right eye.

"You're either insane or a fool," the journalist said. Anthony Ziegler was slouched in an easy chair, looking baggy-eyed and dressed like a pile of old laundry. Knox wasn't impressed.

"Insane, sir?" Knox snorted. "I thought you were one of those muckrakers. I thought you would be interested in what I have to say." Knox was determined to restrain his fury. "Do you realize the risk I'm taking by meeting with you? To suggest what I'm suggesting is dangerous enough. But to present *evidence*—"

"Yes, all right," Ziegler said, holding up a hand. "I shouldn't react until you have fully stated your case."

Knox stood and moved the few feet from the lounge area of his hotel room to the window. The Boston Common sat sprawling and still green below. The duck pond glistened in the morning sun. "Let's get the facts straight."

"You are Lieutenant Colonel Philip Edward Knox, commander, Health and Sanitation Section of the Emergency Fleet Corporation."

"Well done."

Ziegler's tone was condescending, but Knox had to endure the man if the truth was to get out. Knox looked at the bed and the mass of typed reports, newspaper clippings, telegrams, letters, and dog-eared medical books covering it.

Ziegler patted his pockets and found a pencil and notebook.

"By risk, I assume you're talking about what your superiors in the War Department will do to you if they find out about this."

"Why do you think I'm meeting *here*, of all places?"

Ziegler nodded. "As I said: you're either insane or a fool."

"Repeat those words a third time and I'll throw you out of this room."

Ziegler looked at him as if assessing whether he could make good on the threat and must have decided that he could. "Let's stay calm. Tell me what you have."

Knox handed Ziegler a small stack of documents. "Go with me back to late January of this year, to an area in the center of the country called Haskell County in Kansas. It's an agricultural area, mostly. The Santa Fe Trail cuts right through it, as do train lines from Colorado, Texas, and Oklahoma—all going east to west, north to south, and back again."

Ziegler scratched his chin. "Haskell County."

"The city of Sublette, to be exact. An abandoned freight car was found by a group of boys, including one named Roy Alstine. The boys startled the three men in the car, who immediately ran away. One would reasonably assume the men were hobos, but Roy later told his parents that the men spoke German as they rushed off. The parents dismissed Roy's account, since the boys' imaginations had been inflamed by the war; children were always battling Germans on the playgrounds and in the fields."

Ziegler folded his arms and looked glassy-eyed.

Knox pressed on. "If the German men were a product of Roy's imagination, the freight car was not. The local sheriff investigated. The car was half-full of foodstuffs, mostly tinned or bottled items. No labels or identifying marks appeared on the products or crates, or the freight car itself—nothing to indicate who had made the food or owned the freight. None of the railroad companies seemed to know anything about it; since the car was on a rarely used spur, they didn't care. Not surprisingly, people in the area helped themselves to what was in the car. The sheriff locked the doors and threatened the locals with prosecution for theft. Then, within only a few days of the car's discovery, the people of Haskell County were hit with an epidemic of influenza. People became sick and died at a rapid pace."

"I don't remember anything about an epidemic in Kansas."

"Why would you?" Knox asked, moving back toward Ziegler. "No one reported it. Not even the local newspaper, for fear of hurting morale further in light of the war. But a local physician, Dr. Lawrence Miner, was so alarmed by the suddenness and virulence of the flu that he notified state health officials, even producing a report for the national public-health journal. Then, as quickly as the epidemic began, it suddenly disappeared."

Ziegler shrugged. "People are sick with the flu every spring."

"Not this kind of flu," Knox said. "Oh—and the mysterious freight car also disappeared, along with what was left of its contents. The sheriff, the railway officials . . . none of them have the slightest idea what became of it."

Ziegler gazed at Knox. "Where is this leading?"

"To Camp Funston at Fort Riley, some three hundred miles east of Haskell County. Men in every corner of the camp came down with a potent virus at essentially the same time. The speed of the outbreak was astonishing. The symptoms were the same as those found among the sick in Haskell County."

"The outbreak at Fort Riley is old news," Ziegler said. "Unless you're going to tell me that an abandoned freight car with Germans was found nearby."

Knox smiled. "Two days before the virus appeared in Fort Riley, a shipment of common table mustard was delivered to the camp supply depot. The mustard had not been ordered by the quartermaster or anyone else at the camp. Reliable witnesses say it was delivered by an unidentified truck *after* delivery hours. The crates were mysteriously left at the depot. The supply officers assumed the mustard had been ordered by someone higher up and did not check their requisitions until much later—after they had incorporated it into the soldiers' mess."

"Are you saying the mysterious mustard was connected to the outbreak?"

"Yes. I believe the mustard was the genesis of the infection and, once established, the infection spread like wildfire from soldier to soldier."

"Tainted mustard? Truly?"

"Consider this: the mustard was labeled as being a product of the Berlitz Food Company."

"So?"

"There is no record of such a company. It doesn't exist."

Ziegler's eyebrows lifted. Knox was gratified. But then the reporter shook his head. "It's odd, yes, but I wouldn't say it is proof of anything. Do you have evidence that someone tampered with the mustard?"

"Not yet."

Ziegler looked at him doubtfully.

"Let's move on." Knox presented Ziegler with another stack of documents. "In late April and early May, more than five hundred prisoners at San Quentin in California came down with the Funston virus in less than forty-eight hours."

"A mysterious mustard was delivered to San Quentin?"

"No," Knox said. "In that case, it was a shipment of bacon."

"Bacon!"

"No official at San Quentin had ever ordered it, yet it arrived by an unidentified truck and was happily received and served to the inmates. Within a day, the outbreak began."

"Let me guess: there was no way to track where the bacon came from or who delivered it."

"The truck, authorities later learned, had been stolen from a mill near San Rafael. The bacon was never traced to its source. And it was labeled as coming from the nonexistent Berlitz Food Company. Curious? Suspicious?"

"Curious, yes," Ziegler said. "If it's true."

Knox ignored Ziegler's skepticism and handed over the next series of documents. "Camp Hancock in Georgia, Camp Lewis in Washington, Camp Sherman in Ohio, Camp Fremont in California, and several others: outbreaks, all with a speed that defied the course of a natural infection or a spread from other camp locations. Twenty-four camps had epidemics. And the infection spread from those camps to thirty of the largest cities in the country—most adjacent to the military camps. There is no benign way to explain how the sickness leaped from location to location, or spontaneously appeared."

"Phantom trucks in the night?"

"Not always trucks. Trains, horse-drawn wagons . . . does it matter? Every one of these institutions received an unauthorized shipment of food or liquid—all provided by the ghost Berlitz Food Company."

"Surely someone would have seen the pattern and stopped deliveries."

"I'm the only one who has put the pattern together." Knox held up a bundle of pages. "Here is a report from just a few weeks ago. You may read it for yourself. Boston's very own Chelsea Naval Hospital—quickly overwhelmed by sick sailors. The sailors display a bluish complexion with purple blisters and are leveled by hoarse, hacking breaths which barely supply enough oxygen to keep them alive. Within only two weeks of the virus's first appearance, two thousand officers and men of the First Naval District have contracted this influenza. Over four hundred of them have died."

"I wasn't aware of those numbers."

"Military officials are keeping it top secret."

"Any mysterious shipment to the sailors?"

"Shortly before the outbreak, the sailors were treated to a large social function—a dance—hosted by a local benefactor to raise the morale of the men."

"Don't tell me the men were served bacon and mustard."

"Beer," Knox said sharply.

"Beer."

"Also, Fort Devens. Do you know it?"

"Sure. A new camp, not thirty miles from here."

"The construction crews threw the camp together at lightning speed—over ten buildings a day. Three weeks ago, on September 9, Devens held more than forty-five thousand men, though it was designed to hold a maximum of thirty-six thousand. On September 10, an influenza epidemic began. According to one of the camp doctors, up to one thousand five hundred soldiers a day reported to sick call with influenza. Some ached so badly they screamed when touched. Many quickly became delirious. The doctors say the influenza is ripping through the barracks much like an explosion. Eight days ago, twenty percent of the camp was sick, and almost seventy-five percent of those were hospitalized. Medical personnel are having to work sixteen-hour days to keep up. Four days ago, staff became so overwhelmed, with doctors and nurses now sick and dying, we decided to close the hospital to admissions, no matter how sick the soldier. It's the worst these doctors have ever seen."

Ziegler frowned. "Beer this time?"

"No. Large containers of water for the construction workers and soldiers."

"Who provided the refreshments?"

"The benefactor for both the sailors' dance and the soldiers' water was meant to be anonymous, a wealthy patron. I learned who it was. The company is well-known and the family behind it is wealthy and philanthropic. You won't have the courage to name them."

"Who are they?"

"The Brandts."

Ziegler's mouth fell open.

Knox continued, "I have irrefutable evidence that the Brandts of Boston are members of the same Brandt family that owns a chemical company in Berlin. A chemical company with a secret division that specializes in military provisions. Its name? *Berlitz.*"

Ziegler looked at Knox with incredulity. "You're prepared to publicly accuse William and Kathryn Brandt of infecting American soldiers with a disease?"

"I am."

Ziegler closed his notebook and made as if to stand up. "Thank you, Colonel Knox. I believe we're finished."

"You don't believe me? Then explain to me one final piece of information."

Ziegler looked as if he might refuse the offer, then reluctantly asked, "What?"

"On at least *two* occasions, local military authorities received reports of a German U-boat surfacing off the coast of Massachusetts."

Zeigler looked surprised. "A U-boat off the coast of Massachusetts? Where was it sighted?"

Knox placed a map on the coffee table and placed his finger on a thrust of land north of Boston that stuck out into the Atlantic. "Harriet Point. Do you know the significance of Harriet Point?"

"No."

"The Brandt Company has a factory there."

Ziegler looked as if he might slump back into his chair. "I don't know what to say."

"Of course you're speechless," Knox said. "Not only are the Germans killing us, but also they're killing us at a rate that will only increase exponentially in the coming weeks and months. The virus seems to infect only military personnel now, but the leap to the civilian population is imminent. I predict we will see death on a scale unknown in the history of humankind. What's worse, the government *knows*. In Washington, DC, two German spies, posing as doctors, were caught in a hospital giving influenza germs to sailors. The spies were shot at sunrise. You see? They know what's at stake, they know all about the conspiracy, but they won't warn the public."

Ziegler looked pained. "Surely you're aware of the Sedition Act."

Knox nodded. "A man could spend twenty years in jail if he utters, prints, writes, or publishes any false, scandalous, malicious, or abusive language with the intent to defame the government of the United States."

"Knox, all around this country, reporters are in jail for writing what the Justice Department calls 'pessimistic stories.' How do you think officials will react to this? What do you think they'll do to me for reporting it?"

Knox sniffed disdainfully. "As I surmised, you don't have the courage to deal with it."

"Good luck finding anyone with that kind of courage."

Knox scowled, disgusted that his worst expectations had been realized. "You are no different from my superiors. The Germans are coming by U-boats, trucks, and trains, and no one is doing a thing to stop it. We are sitting ducks to the ultimate effort in germ warfare."

"Even if what you say is true and you can get it to the public, you'll be treated as a laughingstock at best, and as a madman at worst."

"You forgot to mention 'fool.'"

Ziegler fumbled with his coat, as if it had fallen off his shoulders and needed to be put back on. He looked at Knox with an expression of deep sympathy. "For your sake, I'm going to pretend we never had this conversation."

He left.

With a sigh, Knox went to the window and looked down at the street bordering the Common. What was he to do? Ziegler was his last hope. If he wouldn't print the story, who would?

Good luck finding anyone with that kind of courage.

Knox stood there for several minutes as he watched iron gray clouds move in from the harbor. He was out of options.

On the street below, traffic seemed to have come to a halt. Several black cars had invaded the normal flow and had come to a sudden stop in front of the hotel. Men in dark overcoats leaped out and rushed to the entrance.

They're coming for me. He had expected it. He grabbed a suitcase and threw his documents into it. He would escape down the back stairway.

He also placed a prepared letter on the bed: his resignation from the U.S. military. His career was over.

But where could he go? He and his evidence would not be safe anywhere in America.

It's time to leave and fight this battle on another front.

PART FOUR

**November 5
Present Day**

CHAPTER 9

AKADEMGORODOK, SIBERIA

"**THIS IS OUR** man?" Susan asked, as she gazed at the black-and-white newspaper photograph.

The caption identified Dr. Hans Weigel, a short man with hair in an Einstein-wannabe style and thumbs hooked into the waistcoat pockets of his out-of-fashion suit. His bow tie looked like a propeller ready for takeoff.

Standing next to him was Vladislav Kunetzkov, the world-famous Russian Olympian, in a sharp suit. Hanging conspicuously around his neck were his many gold medals earned from two Olympic games and several World Championships. He had his hands on his hips and looked for all the world like a Russian superman ready to fight for truth, justice, and the Russian way.

"He died," Anton said, pointing to Kunetzkov. "It's a huge deal. He is a national hero, but also much loved by the local people here in Siberia. One of their own made good."

"I'm to assume he died because of his contact with Dr. Weigel?"

"That's right. Copies of his charts are in the stack there."

Susan looked at the foot-high pile of files and papers on her desk. "How am I supposed to find anything in this?"

"You aren't," said Anton. "I think that's the idea."

"Give me the latest from the lab."

"They're going over every specimen, every detail," he said. "They know it's a Type A influenza, an H1N1 variant. We don't know if they've done the genetic studies. I know you think it's backward here—"

"Not backward, just uncooperative. If we could send samples to some of our WHO testing labs . . ."

Anton shrugged. "We're a proud people. We don't like outside intervention. Let the doctors here do their best and then we'll see."

"While your proud people die, is that it?"

He shrugged.

"What about Weigel?" she asked. "Do the Germans know where Weigel is? Or are they a proud people too, and not cooperating?"

"They're not cooperating, but it has nothing to do with pride."

"Then what is it?"

"Bureaucracy. I can't seem to get through to the authorities who'll help us. To nab Weigel, we need authorization from German health or intelligence officials. They, in turn, have to go through the proper justice- and penal-system channels and . . ." He sighed. "I'm beginning to think they don't want to find Weigel for us."

"Why not?"

"I haven't figured that out yet."

Susan made as if to tear at her hair. "Doesn't anyone realize how urgent this situation is?"

"I do," a voice said from the doorway.

Susan and Anton spun around to face the door.

A man stood there wearing a dark, rumpled suit. He had a round, friendly face that gave the impression of youth, making his white hair seem incongruous. He wore round wire-framed glasses over sharp, inquisitive eyes.

"Forgive the interruption," he said. Susan detected an accent that might have been Swiss, French, or German.

"Can we help you?" Anton asked.

"Let's hope we can help each other." He approached the desk and held up a leather wallet containing his credentials. Susan's eyes went first to the gold badge with the blue insignia—the sword and globe and the letters OIPC/ICPO, the French and English acronyms for the International Criminal Police Organization, or Interpol. The picture ID of the man showed a younger version with salt-and-pepper hair. The name below identified him as Martin Duerr.

"Interpol?" Susan asked. "Why is Interpol interested in what's happening here?"

Duerr's eyes went to Anton. "Mr. Pushkin, I wonder if I might speak with Dr. Hutchinson alone, please?"

Anton looked to Susan, who nodded at him. "Tea, anyone?"

They both declined and Anton left, closing the door behind him.

"So?" Susan prompted.

"What's happening here may be linked to a case I'm working on."

Susan gestured to one of the metal chairs next to her desk. All were encumbered with at least one box of files. "Sit down, if you can."

"This reminds me of my office." Duerr chuckled as he moved one of the boxes and sat.

"Duerr," she said, the name coming to her. "I remember you from the confidential reports about the Ebola outbreak in Gabon."

He nodded. "I've been tracking an environmental terrorist group called Return to Earth."

Susan remembered the name as well. "They were also mentioned in the Gabon report. There were suspicions the group was involved in what happened there. They were also busy in England trying to disrupt the work of the TSI team."

"Trying to thwart them from finding an antidote to the Gabon virus," he said. "That's Return to Earth's game. They believe that humankind has recklessly forfeited the right to dominance in the world. If, through terrorism, they can eliminate the human race and return the earth to Mother Nature, then all the better. Whether murdering men or women on a small scale, or entire populations on a large scale, it's all the same to them. They are the ultimate suicide bombers."

"You think they're involved here?"

"One of our agents in Munich discovered that a cell there had exported freight to this area."

"What kind of freight?"

"We don't know. We lost track of it before we could find

out," he said. "But then a mysterious and fatal outbreak occurs in the same area and I assume there must be a connection."

"It could be a coincidence."

Duerr's face was calm, but in his eyes was a fierce determination. "I don't believe in coincidences when it comes to Return to Earth. As it is, there is another connection. The man you're looking for."

"Dr. Weigel?"

"Dr. Hans Weigel and Dr. Stefan Maier, founder of Return to Earth, were acquaintances. We know they've had contact in the past year."

A realization came to Susan. "Are you the reason the German authorities haven't cooperated with us?"

"In part, yes. The police in Berlin are watching Weigel's apartment, his office, and every other place he's known to frequent on Interpol's behalf."

Susan felt deflated. "This *is* a mess if Interpol has no idea where he's gone. Can't you monitor his passport activity or whatever it is you do to follow people?"

"Yes. Which is why I'm flying from here to London this afternoon."

"Why London?"

"Weigel flew from Novosibirsk to London. He was scheduled to speak at a conference there. We know he appeared ill on the flight, but not ill enough for the flight attendants to take medical action. We also know that he arrived at Heathrow Airport, but then disappeared. He never arrived at the conference venue."

"You understand that we have to get him into quarantine the instant you find him."

"Of course. You'll have our full cooperation, and we hope to have yours."

"What cooperation do you need from us at the WHO?"

"We need to know what you know. Any clue about this outbreak, any connecting points no matter how odd they may seem—even your most absurd suspicions—you must inform us immediately." He handed her a business card. "Use this number any time, day or night."

She took the card and fingered the embossed lettering. "What kind of clues should we look for?"

"Anything." He stood. "Right now, our attention is on Dr. Weigel. He appears to be the vector, as you say, not only for the sickness, but also for Return to Earth."

"I'll do whatever I can to help," she said, standing. She put her hand out and he shook it gently.

"We'll be in touch," he said and went to the door. As he opened it, he lingered, then turned to her again. "The Spanish flu."

Her heart quickened. "What about it?"

"When it appeared during the First World War, it killed how many people?"

"Up to one hundred million. Or, to put it another way, it made all the Black Plague epidemics look like the common cold."

A crease appeared between Duerr's eyes. "Yes, that would suit Return to Earth perfectly."

Without allowing her a chance to speak, he left.

Susan sat again, her heart still pounding.

Anton returned to the doorway. "Well?"

Without looking up at him, Susan asked, "How does Interpol know that we've been discussing the Spanish flu?"

Anton shrugged, then closed the door. "I have a present for you."

Susan gazed at him suspiciously as he reached behind him, drawing something from under his sports jacket. It was an envelope.

"Maybe this will help." Anton handed her the envelope and she opened it, carefully taking the pages out. It was a copy of the Russian Health Ministry's genetic-lab results.

"Anton, I love you."

He smiled. "How could you resist?"

"Have you looked at it?"

"I've marked and translated the most important sections."

She opened the report and flipped through his notes.

After only a few moments, she closed the report and sighed wearily. "They've definitely identified this outbreak as an H1N1 virus. And they've confirmed that it doesn't match any known avian or swine flu. The initial genetics of the virus appear to be very close to the genetics of the 1918 virus."

Anton stood with his arms folded. "Not close. Identical."

"So our worst fears are confirmed. Some form of the Spanish flu *is* back."

"But how is that possible after almost a hundred years?"

PART FIVE

Monday
January 30, 1933

CHAPTER 10

BERLIN, GERMANY

PHILIP EDWARD KNOX tightened the belt on his trench coat and turned the collar up to cover his neck. It was a biting, cold night, but what could one expect in Berlin this time of year? Knox pushed his hat down, not wanting to lose it in the gusts that whipped trash and debris down the alley.

Somewhere beyond this narrow side street, Knox could hear the shouts of celebration and the crashes of victorious merriment near the Brandenburg Gate. The night was lit by the many torches carried by all the Brownshirts and Berliners who came out to sing praise to the new chancellor of Germany.

A streetlight caught the ragged edges of a poster hanging on a blackened brick wall: a painting of eager faces with the bold words, Hitler—Our Last Hope.

Knox continued to the end of the street and turned left, hoping he was going the right way. These backstreets confused him. Street signs were soot-covered, smudged, or missing completely. He knew only that Brandenburg Gate and Tiergarten were somewhere to the west of him. Or north? He couldn't be sure. All he had was an address and sketchy directions from his contact with British Intelligence.

A crash among some trash cans made him jump and he twisted to face the sound. Two Brownshirts were beating and kicking a man on the ground. One stopped long enough to give Knox a threatening scowl. This was none of Knox's business and he continued walking without looking again. The man on the ground was probably a Jew or a Gypsy. Knox wouldn't want to be either, knowing what Hitler and his regime said they'd do to such groups. Hitler would bring shame to all non-Aryans. Soon. Very soon. And it would be brutal for those who chose to stay.

Knox knew what persecution felt like, having been exiled in shame for daring to speak the truth to his countrymen about La Grippe of 1918. His own parents had rejected him for his embarrassing and outlandish theories.

A wood sign hung from a wall up ahead. He adjusted his gold-rimmed glasses, which had long ago replaced his monocle and looked at the sign. In German, it announced he had arrived at the Strong Worker.

Knox approached the door and thought of the many beer gardens he'd frequented in the years since his exile. *Those were dark days.* Had it not been for the unexpected help of some distant but sympathetic relatives in Winchester, England, he would have died facedown in a gutter somewhere. *Dear Uncle Reginald.*

The door to the Strong Worker's Arms opened and two men stumbled out. The older man, with bushy eyebrows and mustache, had his arm around the shoulders of the younger man who was the clean-shaven image of his elder. *Father and son.* Knox stepped aside to let them pass, thinking of the nights he and Uncle Reginald went to their local pub and spent the night talking about the German conspiracy, speculating about the future, and laughing—like father and son.

Knox caught the large wood door and stepped through the doorway. He removed his hat as he closed the door behind him and undid his coat. The room was surprisingly large, considering how unassuming it looked from the outside. A horseshoe bar dominated the space. Tables surrounded it, like small lifeboats around a battleship. The walls were appointed in scrolled woodwork and gold-framed paintings.

Knox moved to the edge of the bar. A blond *fräulein* with her hair in braids came to take his order. She smiled at him. He asked for a lager and leaned back nonchalantly to survey the room.

His heart jolted.

Through the blue haze of cigarette and pipe smoke, he saw a man sitting in the far corner, alone and hunched over a drink.

The man stared absentmindedly as he flicked the ash from his cigarette. He took a drag, then flicked at it again.

Knox had come to find this man. He was older than he looked in the photo Knox had been carrying since 1926. But it was him. Dr. Werner Schmidt, one of Germany's leading scientists during the Great War and, if Knox's research was correct, one of the brains behind the germ warfare Germany introduced into the United States.

Knox's beer arrived and he paid the barmaid. Taking a drink, he pulled out a handkerchief and dabbed at the foam he knew to be caught at the edges of his mustache. It was grayer now and more modest in size.

Knox glanced at the man again. *Yes, he's the one. Though he looks like an old drunk.*

Picking up his glass of beer, Knox pushed away from the bar and drifted toward Schmidt. He tried to appear as if he were walking aimlessly. It was hard to do. He could hardly contain his excitement. Schmidt's name had emerged again and again in Knox's research. If anyone knew about the germ warfare used by the Germans in the Great War, it would be Schmidt. It was possible he had created La Grippe, and now Knox was going to meet him.

Stepping to the table, Knox said in German, "I'm sorry to bother you, but the seats are all taken. May I share this table with you?"

Schmidt looked at him with half-lidded eyes. In the dim light of the bar, Schmidt's cheekbones seemed more pronounced. He hadn't shaved for a day or two and looked gaunt. He waved a bony hand for Knox to sit. "It'll cost you a drink," he slurred.

"With pleasure." Knox held up a hand to catch the barmaid's attention.

"What is your accent? You are not German," Schmidt said.

"I normally speak English. I live in England."

"Don't tell me you've come here for our big night. Surely the English are not celebrating Herr Hitler."

"I have no interest in politics," Knox said.

"Then why are you here?"

"I am a health and sanitation engineer. I have come to meet with a few of your government officials to, shall we say, compare our efforts."

Schmidt squinted at Knox. "Health and sanitation?" He rode through the phrase on a wave of saliva.

The barmaid came and took Schmidt's drink order.

"What did you say that you do for a living?" Knox asked.

"I *didn't* say. It is too humiliating for me to say."

"Then make up something that isn't humiliating," Knox said with forced joviality.

Schmidt sat up and puffed out his chest with mock pride. "I am an engineer at a major manufacturing firm."

"What kind of manufacturing?"

"I make women's brassieres," he replied and chuckled. "It's far more complicated than most men understand. All those clasps and hooks and . . ." He sighed and took another drink, draining the glass. A sliver of liquid slid down his chin.

"You don't like your job?"

"Would you if you were once considered a great scientist by everyone who knew about such things?"

Knox feigned surprise. "Were you? Honestly?"

"Honestly." Schmidt closed his eyes and rested his chin on his fist. For a moment, Knox feared he would fall asleep.

"Did you have a specialty?" Knox spoke loudly.

"The only specialty any of us had then," he said, his eyes still closed. "Winning the war. And we should have, too. We had everything in place. Success like the first and our enemies would have been on their knees begging to surrender."

"Success like the first? What was your first success?"

Schmidt lifted his head and looked at Knox. "You are inquisitive."

"This is an amazing claim." Knox restrained the wild excitement he was feeling. "I can only suspect that you have had too much to drink and it has turned you into a braggart."

Schmidt attempted to rise. "Braggart! Ha. I have no need to brag. What we accomplished is a matter of *history*. Are you unaware of the flu that seized the world in 1918?"

"I remember it."

"How could you forget?" Schmidt fingered a buttonhole on his coat. "It was the greatest time of my life."

"Most would consider it a terrible time."

"Because they don't know. Had they succeeded as we had, they would have rejoiced."

"Succeeded at what?" Knox was desperate for Schmidt to spell it out.

Schmidt leaned forward and winked at him. "Our time will come again."

"I don't know what you're talking about."

Schmidt reached into his coat and pulled a large yellow envelope from where it had been tucked. He fumbled and nearly dropped it on the table. Knox caught the word *Liebfraumilch* handwritten on the front.

"This is the future," Schmidt said, rubbing his fingers gently over the word. "They want my help. My hours spent in a dump like this are numbered."

"Because of Liebfraumilch? Doesn't that word mean 'milk of our lady'?"

The barmaid arrived with Schmidt's drink and placed it on the table. Knox thanked her.

Schmidt grabbed his glass and downed the contents in one large gulp. Then he pushed the table toward Knox and stood.

"You're leaving?"

Schmidt shoved the envelope back inside his coat. He lifted his hat from a hook on the wall and reached down unsteadily, retrieving a cane that had been leaning against the wall. "Thank you for the drink, sir." He lurched to the door.

Knox watched him go, unsure what to do. Having found Schmidt, he couldn't let him disappear again. Thinking quickly, he spilled beer on his shirt, then frowned and stood as if he'd spilled some on his trousers, too. He used his handkerchief to dab at his shirt, then snorted and gestured to suggest his evening was now ruined. He gathered his things, strode to the door, and went out. A blast of cold air hit him in the face.

The passageway was empty in both directions. He felt sick to think he'd lost Schmidt so quickly.

He followed a sound to his right. Within a few yards, he came upon Schmidt relieving himself against the wall. The old man grunted and groaned, as if the effort were burdensome. Finishing, he sorted himself and staggered back a few steps. He saw Knox and snarled. "Why are you following me?"

Knox thought quickly. "I am unfamiliar with this area and thought I might follow you to a main thoroughfare."

Schmidt frowned and leaned close. "Is that so?"

"It is so." Knox gazed at the emaciated face innocently.

"All right. This way."

Schmidt launched himself forward, leveraging himself with his cane.

The noises of the vast crowd at the Brandenburg Gate sounded like ocean waves bouncing off the walls.

"Why aren't you celebrating?" Knox asked, wanting to make conversation.

"There will be a time to celebrate, but not now."

"When?"

Schmidt rounded a corner, cutting it so close that Knox nearly ran into him. Suddenly Schmidt turned, grabbed Knox's lapel with one hand, and hooked his foot around Knox's ankle, tripping him to the ground. Knox went down hard onto his right side, feeling a flash of pain like fire in his right arm.

Schmidt stood over him, his cane raised high as if to strike. "I want to know who you *really* are."

He's going to thrash me. Knox lifted his arms in defense. "Are you crazy? What is wrong with you?"

"All those questions. Your interest. Who sent you? What do you want?"

"I didn't want anything! I buy you a drink and this is what you do?"

Schmidt swung the cane at Knox, who raised a hand, and the head of the cane, thick and heavy, hit his forearm. Even with his coat on, Knox felt the pain of the hard metal. Schmidt stepped back unsteadily and came forward again, this time hitting Knox on the shoulder, on the arm again, then on his raised hand. There was greater force in the blows than Knox would have thought possible.

Knox kicked at Schmidt, forcing the man back a few steps. He then rolled quickly, trying to get some distance between them. If he didn't get away, Knox knew Schmidt would beat him to death.

Schmidt staggered toward him and Knox rolled in a different direction, this time pushing himself up into a crouching position. A blow from the cane fell onto his back. The pain spread fast. Knox clenched his teeth and, as Schmidt raised the cane again, he used all his strength to throw himself at Schmidt, diving at the man's midsection. Schmidt gasped as Knox drove his head into the man's stomach.

They crashed into a collection of trash cans. Garbage scattered and a cat yowled. Schmidt wheezed as the air was knocked out of him. Knox pulled himself up and grabbed the closest thing he could find—a bottle—and brought it down onto Schmidt's head. The glass shattered and the old man whimpered, blindly clutching at his head. Blood spilled through his fingers.

Aching all over, Knox straightened to his full height. A dim bulb over a black door lit the alley. His fury made everything pulse red before his eyes. The cane had fallen next to Schmidt, who now writhed on the ground. Knox snatched up the stick, the top shaped like an eagle's head.

"This is what you beat me with?" he roared and began to wildly hit Schmidt with the cane. It was as if his years of frustration and humiliation had now exploded in a volcanic rage.

Schmidt was helpless, unable to hold up his arms, rolling over so that the blows would hit his back. He whimpered again.

"I'll give you this much for your success!" Knox shouted as he continued to pound the man. "One hit for every person who died!"

Knox heard the nearby door wrench open. A man dressed in kitchen-worker white shouted at him. Knox stepped back and tried to recover his good sense. Sweat poured from his brow, stinging the scratches on his face. He was breathing heavily, like a wild horse. His rage subsided.

The man in the doorway shook a fist at him. Another worker appeared. Knox knew he had to get away. He stumbled back, glancing down at Schmidt, who lay on the ground perfectly still.

Is he dead?

At Schmidt's feet was the yellow envelope he had pulled out in the bar.

Knox grabbed it, spun on his heels, and stumbled away.

He could hear shouts behind him.

On rubbery legs, he pressed forward. Soon he was in a full run.

Knox felt sure that if he could lose himself in the back alleyways, he could find a place to hide. But within a few turns, he ran directly into a march of Brownshirts and Berliners, all waving torches and shouting. Thinking he had rushed in to join the celebrations, a group pushed him along, pounding him on the back. A woman kissed him. He pushed deeper into the crowd, realizing it was his best refuge. He would march and collect his wits.

He looked back and saw the two men in white breathlessly searching the crowd for him. Lowering his head, he marched on. He was glad, if only for this moment, that Hitler had been made chancellor.

Knox found his way back to the Hotel Adlon. He knew he looked terrible. One of the cuts from Schmidt's cane bled into his hair, and he'd lost his hat to cover it.

He navigated through the spacious lobby. A clerk at the marble-topped reception desk was busy on the phone. Knox avoided the elevators, found a stairwell, and slowly climbed to his floor.

The hall was empty, allowing him to get to his room undetected.

He collapsed onto the bed and closed his eyes. He didn't intend to sleep, only to catch his breath. His body felt as if someone had taken a tire iron to him. His wrist ached. The sound of his breathing roared in his ears.

He held up the yellow envelope and looked at the word "Liebfraumilch." The lettering went fuzzy, doubled up, then disappeared from view.

Daylight streamed through the window as he awoke. He had not moved from where he had fallen onto the bed. Despite protesting muscles, Knox got up and went to the bathroom.

He was shocked by what he saw in the mirror: a man who appeared to have been hit by a train. He turned on the faucets for a bath, then returned to the bedroom as the tub filled. Stripping off his clothes, he noticed blood on his coat sleeves, on his shirt, and on his trousers. Smeared blood also stained his pillowcase. He touched the wound near his ear. It hurt, but had stopped bleeding.

He picked up the yellow envelope and for the first time noticed how thin it was. He'd hoped that it contained a full report of Schmidt's research and activities from 1918—but how could that be? The flap was unsealed.

He thought himself too tired to feel excitement, but his heart thumped with anticipation. Inside was a second envelope with a Deutsches Reich stamp bearing the image of President Hindenburg. Dr. Werner Schmidt's address was typed central to the front. On the back was the black stamp of the Nazi Party: an eagle clutching an encircled swastika. The envelope had been opened cleanly with a sharp letter opener.

Inside, a single sheet of paper bore the Nazi Party insignia at top and, beneath that, the word *staatsgeheimnis*. Top secret. It had the look of a memo, rather than a letter, and was dated January 29. The memo was addressed to the Liebfraumilch Consortium of 1916, with a secondary list of several names, including Schmidt's.

Knox was better at speaking conversational German than he was at reading formal German, but he worked out that this was an invitation to a meeting set three weeks from then at the Hotel Berghaus in Berchtesgaden. The Nazi Party, under the leadership of Adolf Hitler, wanted the doctors and scientists connected to this top-secret project to reconvene and begin further exploration and research.

So that's what they called themselves: the Liebfraumilch Consortium. Now he had a name for it. He imagined them all, hiding in a secret German laboratory somewhere, working away at their destructive project, sweating over the method and the means to unleash their sickness, gloating and laughing as they toiled away under an innocent name like Mother's Milk.

Knox felt a fury burn through his body. He glanced over the

invitation again, then read the last line and felt sick: "For our leader and his idea, we shall fight to the death."

He sat on the edge of the bed. Even before Hitler had become chancellor, he was making moves to put into place his strategies for empowering the country. War seemed inconceivable, considering Germany's economic state, but there was no doubt in Knox's mind that Hitler would begin to re-arm and rebuild his military machine. Obviously, that machine would include germ warfare.

Knox rose and paced. Whatever had been developed in 1916 or 1917 would likely be far more lethal in 1933, and deadlier still in the weeks and months to come. How quickly could they resume their work and improve upon it?

He carefully withdrew the lining from the top of his suitcase and slid the letter inside, closing it up again. The fasteners were invisible to anyone not looking for them. He had to leave Germany as soon as possible. If he'd killed Schmidt—or even if he hadn't—the police would be looking for him.

He bathed quickly, fighting off the desire to soak in the tub for hours. He didn't have hours. Dressing hurriedly, he rang downstairs for a cab. As he waited, he threw the rest of his things into the case. He thought about Schmidt's drunken enthusiasm for the future. Their success. Possibly a greater success than they'd had in the Great War.

For our leader and his idea, we shall fight to the death.

PART SIX

November 6
Present Day

CHAPTER 11

LONDON, ENGLAND

"GOOD MORNING, SERGEANT Johnson," Mark said as he walked down the stairs of TSI headquarters.

Johnson, a stout American soldier in uniform, sat behind a half-walled cubicle at the bottom of the stairs. His hand rested on the gun in his holster as he glanced up from a London newspaper to give a cursory salute. "Good morning, Dr. Carlson. Did you sleep well?"

"As well as anyone can after catching a red-eye from Dulles."

"I hate those flights," Johnson said. "They're no better than a cargo plane." The soldier stood and Mark took note of the series of security monitors tucked under a shelf in the cubicle. They were a marked contrast to the antique desk, Persian rugs, and fine furniture of the entry area.

Johnson waved his hand. "This way, please." He walked down a hallway to a door.

Mark followed, then stopped at the familiar retina scanner mounted in front of the door. As he looked into the box he placed his hands on the finger- and palm-print reader. Meanwhile, puffs of air hit him from all sides, the action of a "sniffer" used to ensure he wasn't hiding explosives on his person. He expected this, but it still startled him. After a few seconds, a light turned green just above him and he stepped back.

"You're clear."

The door jerked open and Georgina Scott greeted him. "Hi, Mark!"

"Hi, Georgina." He smiled and lifted a hand to her bouncing

blond dreadlocks. "These are new. And what's the red streak about?"

"Do you like it?"

"On you, yes. I'd look terrible with dreads."

She shoved her hands into the pockets of her white lab coat. "Did you just arrive?"

"Yes, I feel as though I've got a head full of cotton instead of a brain."

She giggled. "I have some techniques to get rid of jet lag, but you might find them morally questionable. Anyway, I was just coming to fetch you. Mac wants to meet us in the lab conference room to brief us on this new assignment."

"It would have been helpful if he'd explained some of it before yanking us back from the States," Mark said.

Georgina put a finger to her lips. "You'll understand more when you hear what's going on. Nora's already gone in."

She turned and he followed her the few steps down a narrow hall to what appeared to be a wall. But as they approached, Georgina swiped her ID over a scanner and the hidden door slid open. Georgina stood back and allowed Mark to enter first.

Mark stepped into a large lab that extended well beyond the walls of the single town house. The center of the room was filled with equipment desks, each with two or three large flat-screen, translucent monitors. Around one side of the room were a variety of forensic labs, each set behind a large observation glass. Tables inside were covered with state-of-the-art computers, monitors, microscopes, and analyzers. At the far end of the room, on the other side of a large plate-glass window, was a beautiful conference room. No expense had been spared for this effort. It is a magnificent facility, he thought, and he struggled to get used to the idea that he now worked here.

In contrast to the tables of equipment, some of the workspace desks were strewn with journals, papers, coffee cups, and remnants of takeaway Chinese and Indian meals. The worst was the desk of Theodore "Digger" Burns. Digger was the team's resident techno geek and scientist surfer. Although egotistical and socially awkward, Digger was an excellent researcher who loved technical toys and all they could do, which made him invaluable to their work. If there was a system that needed to be hacked, Digger could do it.

Nora's desk sat at the end of the room, the surface contents impeccably arranged and organized. He looked at the empty desk next to hers. That would be mine, he thought, then realized it may have belonged to Henry Colchester, a former member of the team who'd been killed during their last assignment. Few grieved the loss, though, since Henry had betrayed, and nearly killed, Digger and Mark.

Thinking of Henry's death reminded him of the graveyard in Charlottesville, and the encounter with his ex-wife. He thought again of her apology and wondered what to make of it. How far is anyone expected to forgive? Could he forgive Henry Colchester for his betrayal? Could he forgive Donna? He didn't know. It was hard enough forgiving himself, an ongoing task.

"You can have that desk," Georgina said, bringing Mark back to the moment.

"I don't expect to spend much time there. I'm not a desk kinda guy."

"As if any of us are. Come on." Georgina skipped toward the conference room. Mark could see that Digger and Nora were already there studying a map on a large computer screen.

As they entered through the double glass doors, Digger turned. "Good *afternoon*, Mark. Nice of you to join us." He was a six-foot redhead with the body of the Michelin Man under an oversized Hawaiian shirt. He never failed to take facetious stabs at Mark.

Mark nodded. "Always a pleasure, Digger." He turned to Nora, who stood next to Digger in a crisp, white lab coat. "Good morning, Nora."

"Good morning, Mark." She gave him a quick smile, then continued to study the map.

It was discreet, which Mark understood; he also caught the exchange of knowing looks between Digger and Georgina. No doubt they were looking for any clue about his time with Nora in America. He wouldn't yield to their curiosity.

He made his way over to a side table covered with coffee- and teapots, mugs, and appropriate fixings. As he poured the tea into a mug, he kept Nora in the corner of his eye. They had spent quite a bit of time talking on the flight from Virginia. Unfortunately, none of it was about the things he wanted to discuss. He tried to bring up his graveside conversation with Donna, but Nora resisted talking about it. She felt strongly that Mark needed to take Donna's requests for forgiveness seriously, without any input or influence from her. Their mutual agreement to not get further involved, if only for professional reasons, was still in place. He was not surprised to see her greet him in nothing more than a cordial manner.

"What are you looking at?" Mark asked, as he walked around the conference-room table, tea in hand.

"It's a map of Russia." Nora turned to him and suddenly reached up to adjust his shirt collar.

"She never fixes *my* collar," Digger complained.

"Fixing your collar is the least of your problems," Georgina jibed. "And if she started there, where would it ever end?"

"I'd like to find out," Digger said.

Nora crumpled up a piece of paper and threw it at him.

A booming voice sounded from the doorway of the conference room. "Can't you people even pretend you're the professionals to whom I am paying exorbitant salaries?"

The team members looked at one another.

"He can't be talking to us," Digger said. "At least, *I'm* not getting an exorbitant salary. Is anyone else?"

"Yeah, I think the rest of us are," Nora said. "You were singled out not to get one."

"I knew it!" Digger said.

Mac took a deep breath, gestured at the table, and barked, "Have a seat!"

He marched around the conference-room table as the team took their chairs, and approached a bank of panels on the far wall. He retrieved a button-covered glove from a holder, pulled it onto his right hand, and punched the buttons on the wrist. The screens lit up and other maps appeared, along with world clocks and menus.

"At the moment, we're working covertly, to help a good friend."

"I wish you'd told me," Digger said. "I would have worn my Secret Squirrel outfit."

Mac continued. "You should be aware by now of the influenza outbreak in Siberia. Furthermore, this virus has already spread to France, Japan, and Kazakhstan via air travel. France's minister of health has ordered all airlines to cancel flights to and from Russia. We believe that within the hour, the WHO is going to issue a Phase 4 Alert from the United Nations building at a press conference." As he talked, the screen zoomed in to focus on central Russia and northern China.

Mark noted that a city called Novosibirsk was at the center.

Mac said, "But this—Novosibirsk—is our ground zero."

Digger shrugged. "We've been talking about a potential outbreak for a long time. That's why I was digging up bodies of British Tommies from the First World War this past summer."

"Exhuming," Nora interjected.

"Naw. I was digging."

"The cases we *were* investigating in the summer were at the request of our labs in the States and Cambridge," Mac reminded him. "Those were normal and representative."

Mark recalled that Digger had taken part in a preemptive exercise to identify the genetic code of the 1918 virus. The plan was to then move on to possible treatments, or even a vaccine.

Mac went on. "Okay, kids, you could say that we've now gone from a fire drill to the real thing. The flu in Siberia isn't just any flu. Dr. Hutchinson and the WHO have confirmed it's a rerun of the Spanish flu of 1918 but more virulent and not yet fully understood. The symptoms are the same, but the case fatality rates are even worse—above fifty percent."

Mark shook his head. He was no expert on the 1918 flu, but he knew of its global devastation. "Are they sure?"

"Specimens from victims in France and Japan are being processed and we should have that information shortly. Nora already has an idea regarding how to help with further identification of the virus. Nora?"

All eyes turned to Nora. Mark was impressed. How like her to throw herself into the middle of the situation.

"I remembered that our friends at the U.S. Armed Forces Institute of Pathology recovered the frozen corpse of a Native Alaskan woman near Brevig Mission."

"What corpse?" Digger sounded indignant. "Was AFIP digging up bodies without my expertise?"

"Get over it," Mac said.

Nora continued, "She'd been buried for nearly eighty years in the permafrost. Apparently, Brevig lost approximately eighty-five percent of its population to the Spanish flu in November 1918 and she was one of the victims. A sample from the body contained viable genetic material of the 1918 virus. So I've suggested WHO match the samples from the Alaskan woman with samples from the bodies Digger exhumed this past summer. That will allow us to confirm the genetic makeup of the 1918 virus."

"So, if they match, we can see if there's also a match with the virus of the current victims," Georgina said.

"That's right," Nora replied.

"It's good to know that my work wasn't a waste of time," Digger said.

"Meanwhile, what do you want us to do?" Mark asked Mac.

"Our first issue is to make sure we're protected. Tell us what you would recommend to keep us from catching the thing we're trying to fight," Mac said.

Mark tapped his pen against the pad in front of him. "If you haven't had this year's influenza vaccine, get it *today*. We have no way to know if it will work against this virus, but it's better to be safe than sorry. Also, I'd recommend that everyone on the team who has not yet gotten it get the pneumococcal vaccine."

"Why get pneumonia protection?" Digger asked.

"Many of the deaths associated with the flu come from secondary infections that can cause pneumonia. It's extra insurance for us all."

Digger and Mac nodded.

"I'll put a date on the calendar to be sure we check antibody levels on everyone in two weeks," Mark said. "I'd also recommend everyone who travels to do so with personal medical kits that include oral and inhaled anti-influenza medications. Mac, can you arrange that?"

"Got it."

"All that may be useless since we don't know exactly what we're dealing with," Digger said.

"True," Mark said. "Which is why I was on the phone earlier with Dr. Jim Dillard." Mark caught Nora's eye. "See, Nora wasn't the only one working this morning."

Nora nodded in acknowledgment.

"You guys remember Jim. He's with the U.S. Army Medical Research Institute of Infectious Diseases in Fort Detrick, Maryland."

"USAMRIID," Mac interjected, pronouncing it U-S-Am-Rid.

"He gave me an update on the influenza prophylaxes they're recommending for the Siberia team, based on a new flu preventive they've been working on." Mark reached into his pocket and took out a small notepad for reference. "They're proposing a monoclonal antibody for the on-ground WHO team in Siberia."

"Explain that for those of us who aren't medical," Mac said.

"Monoclonal antibodies are specially engineered antibodies that attack a specific protein in the body. USAMRIID, together with researchers at the University of Chicago and at Emory University, used blood samples from the Siberian flu victims to create a special injection they believe will offer additional protection."

"How did they get samples from the Russians?" Georgina asked. "Wasn't Susan having trouble getting even basic information from them?"

Mark nodded. "Apparently one of her team members was able to get a sample. And the Emory team was able to get blood samples from France and Japan."

"Has a treatment like this been tried before?" Nora asked.

Mark flipped a page on his notes. "The Emory team has shown that by using a few tablespoons of blood, they can manufacture influenza antibodies in the lab in a short time. Their hope is that, with enough manufactured, the antibodies will prove useful—at least in helping to protect health-care and public-health workers until a vaccine can be made. Unfortunately, this virus exploded before they could launch any sort of large-scale human testing. But they do have several dozen treatments being shipped to us by military jet."

"I assume this is an injectable?" Digger asked.

"It is," Mark answered, "and they're recommending reinjection every two weeks. Unfortunately, we don't have a lot of it. So let's not fall into a false sense of security. We have to be careful and use all our usual infectious-disease precautions. These antibodies will protect us from exposure to small amounts of the virus, say from coughs or sneezes, but larger exposures—from a needle stick, an infected transfusion, or infected bodily fluids—will render them ineffective."

Mac leaned on the table. "I think that's it. Any questions or concerns?"

Nora shook her head. "I can't believe that we're really dealing with some form of La Grippe after almost a century."

"Does anybody know why it's sprung up now?" Georgina asked.

"And why in Siberia, of all places?" Digger added.

"They may have an answer to the place," said Mac. "Apparently, a geneticist from Berlin was lecturing in Siberia, and it looks as though he brought the virus with him. The people who met with him are now spreading the virus abroad. There's the possibility of additional border shutdowns."

Digger placed his hands behind his neck, leaned back in his chair, and looked at the ceiling. "Leave it to a geneticist to start an epidemic."

"Who was the geneticist?" Nora asked. "We may know him."

"Dr. Hans Weigel," Mac said.

Digger nearly fell backward in his chair. "Hans Weigel!"

"You know him?" Mark asked.

"Anybody who takes conspiracy theories seriously knows Hans Weigel. Weigel believes the Germans developed a way to weaponize influenza, and a method to plant the Spanish flu across the United States in 1918."

"Seriously?" Mark was surprised that anyone took stock in such ideas.

"The theory is that the Germans took respiratory secretions from patients and learned not only how to keep the infection alive, but also how to incorporate it into foods during World War I. And eventually into bombs in World War II. Pretty cool stuff."

"That's absurd," Mark countered. "The Germans died of the flu, too."

Digger smirked. "Their plan backfired, at least in World War I. Our soldiers actually carried it back to them."

Mark rolled his eyes. "Oh, brother."

Nora frowned. "And now Weigel is our vector for this recent outbreak? Isn't that too much of a coincidence?"

Georgina suddenly brightened. "What if Weigel has *become* a human influenza bomb to prove his theory?"

"Have they quarantined Weigel?" Nora asked, trying to get back on topic.

"They don't know where he is," Mac said. "Dr. Hutchinson and Kevin Maklin are working with Interpol to find him."

Mark and Nora exchanged glances. "Interpol?" Nora asked. "Martin Duerr?"

"I don't know who is on the case," said Mac.

"If it's Duerr, then you can be sure Return to Earth is connected somehow," Mark said.

"Oh, great," Digger said. "I still haven't recovered from our last encounter with them."

"Where do we start?" Georgina asked.

Mac turned to Digger. "Since you're our resident expert on Weigel, I want you to figure out where he might be hiding."

"I'll help with that," Georgina said.

"And we'll need a body," Mark said.

"His, or someone else's?" Digger asked.

"What do you mean?" Mac asked Mark.

"If we're going to help Susan, then USAMRIID is going to need more of the 1918 virus. We need to find one or more well-preserved bodies of Spanish flu victims, and get additional viral samples so that our researchers can look for links to this current outbreak."

Georgina raised her hand. "I can look for those—well, at least online. I've just found a database in the British Department of Health that could point us in the right direction."

Mac looked concerned. "How did you find—?"

"Better not to ask," said Digger.

"Mark and I can cover the historical angle," Nora said. "We'll check the medical journals and research to see what comes up."

"Great," Mac said, then clapped his hands and rubbed them together. "We know what we have to do, so let's get on with it."

Just then the speakerphone barked at them and Johnson's calm voice said, "Colonel MacLayton?"

"What is it?"

"Sorry to bother you, sir, but you have a guest at reception."

"I'm not expecting any guest."

"It's Inspector Martin Duerr from Interpol. He says it's urgent."

The appearance of Inspector Martin Duerr at TSI headquarters wasn't a big surprise to Mac. Their work together on the Gabon virus had made Duerr an unofficial member of the team. And Duerr knew he could count on them to help him when needed.

Mac took Duerr to his office to talk. After a few minutes, Mac summoned Mark and Nora.

"A pleasure seeing you again," Duerr said as he shook Mark's hand and nodded to Nora. "Though I wish we didn't always see each other in a crisis."

Mac dispensed with pleasantries and said to Duerr, "I've briefed the team about the situation in Siberia and the search for our vector."

"Good," said Duerr. He gestured to the door. "I'll explain the rest on the way."

"On the way?" Mark asked. "On the way to where?"

"With any luck, we're going to find Dr. Weigel."

CHAPTER 12

HAMPSHIRE, ENGLAND

CORNELIUS KNOX MOPPED his brow as he paced his study. This was not going well, not going well at all. In fact, it was going "pear shaped," as his house servant Sandi would say.

He drifted between his large cherrywood desk and the matching bookcases, his mind spinning. *How did everything get so complicated? The search for the truth wasn't supposed to lead to a tangle of lies.* He hardly knew who or what to believe anymore.

This is what I get for shaking hands with the devil.

A loud clearing of the throat and a voice came from the doorway. "Is there something you want, sir?"

"Tell them to get the plane ready," Knox said to Kenneth, his assistant, then felt as if he should qualify the instruction. "Later, I mean. A night flight. I have to talk to Weigel first. How is he?"

"The same as he's been since he arrived."

"Keep an eye on him," Knox said. "Ring me on my mobile phone if he gets worse. Don't use the landlines. I'm sure MI5 is snooping around here somewhere."

Kenneth nodded and withdrew.

Knox dusted at nothing on his sports jacket, a classic brown tweed with patches on the elbows. He adjusted his collar. He looked the part of the country squire. He only wished his life were so simple.

He paced some more. He was nervous. The call from London was just one more in a series of unsettling events. *Why wouldn't they leave him alone?*

This didn't bode well. He didn't want them to come, didn't want anything to do with them anymore.

Knox went to the French doors leading to the patio. From this vantage point, he could see part of the guesthouse across the sprawling lawn and the grove of trees beyond.

This is Hans's fault. The man should never have come to him, certainly not in his condition. He should have checked into a London hospital. Or stayed at home in Berlin. Why did he come?

He was delusional, that's why. Feverish. Paranoid. Certain that they'd been double-crossed. But how? By whom? Hans wouldn't say, but Knox could guess.

It was bloody annoying not to know what had triggered this whole thing. Some big secret Hans wouldn't reveal.

Well, they both had their secrets, hadn't they? Knox had an entire satchel of them.

The clock on the mantel chimed four.

Time was running out.

CHAPTER 13

HAMPSHIRE, ENGLAND

DUERR STEERED THE Vauxhall Antara from the stop-and-start traffic of London and finally put it through its paces on the M3 heading southwest to Winchester.

"This is a *great* car," Mark said as he rubbed his hands on the dash. "I wish I worked for Interpol so I could drive a car like this."

"You don't think Interpol would let me drive anything like this." Duerr smirked. "I got this from MI5. They have a better expense account than I do."

"Sweet."

"You're such children. This isn't a joyride, you know," Nora chided from the backseat.

"Sure it is," Mark said.

Duerr revved the engine as if in agreement.

"If you can get your mind off your toy for a moment, will you please brief us on what we're doing?"

"I will," Duerr said. "But first I have to explain the Nazi conspiracy."

Mark turned to Duerr. "*Nazi* conspiracy? I heard the outlandish idea about the Germans unleashing La Grippe in World War I, but not about the Nazis."

"Certain conspiracy theorists believe that Hitler had his Nazi doctors and scientists resume work on their germ-warfare program shortly after he took power. That he brought together some of the men who'd worked on La Grippe in 1918. Elaborate theories abound about what happened after that: underground labs and bunkers and secret tests. One theory suggests that the Russians grabbed all the research when they invaded Berlin. Even this morning, the conspiracy bloggers on the web are suggesting that a release of those germs, intentional or accidental, is the cause of the outbreak in Siberia."

"You're kidding," Mark said. "Don't these people have anything better to do with their time?"

"Is there any truth to it?" Nora leaned forward in her seat.

"I have my own theories," Duerr said. "For now, we must keep our focus on Weigel, since he's our best link to the truth."

"But you've lost him," Mark said.

"Temporarily misplaced. Weigel landed at Heathrow three days ago. He was supposed to lecture here in London but abruptly canceled. Everyone's buzzing and blogging about that."

"There are conspiracy theories about the conspiracy theorists?" The idea amused Mark.

"Yes. According to British passport control there's no indication that Weigel has left the United Kingdom."

"Then where is he?" Nora asked.

"We believe he's with Cornelius Knox," Duerr said.

"Cornelius Knox?" Mark glanced at Duerr. "Are we supposed to know him?"

Another slight smile from Duerr. "You would if you were conspiracy theorists. Weigel is a relative newcomer to the world of conspiracies. It's *Cornelius Knox* who has championed the Nazi germ-warfare theory. His family has been talking about it for years. His grandfather Philip started the idea back in 1918 and was drummed out of America for talking about it."

"Drummed out of the country?" Nora asked. "He was forced to leave because of a *theory*?"

"Why not?" Mark said. "War-torn America. Morale. Government control of information. The last thing they'd want is some nutcase stirring things up with ridiculous ideas."

Duerr continued, "Philip Knox wound up in England, where he found more sympathetic listeners. A wealthy uncle named Reginald took him in and gave him the funds and the means to prove his theory. Philip later married Reginald's daughter, Margaret. Under the guise of being a wealthy family man, Philip quietly pursued evidence to prove his conspiracy. He did, that is, until he died mysteriously near the end of World War II. The details are fuzzy and I'm asking my friends in MI5 to fill in the gaps. There are rumors of a female agent who helped Knox—who may still be alive—but agents haven't been forthcoming with information about her."

"Not a big surprise," Mark said.

"In any event, Knox's grandson took up the cause."

"So what's the connection between Weigel and Knox?" Mark asked.

"Cornelius Knox and Weigel met in the '90s. Weigel had his own set of theories about the Germans and their experiments. They swapped ideas and became writing partners. They're supposed to release the definitive book on the subject, with all the proof anyone could want. Now Weigel's the main vector in the Siberian outbreak and I'm not inclined to believe it's a coincidence."

Duerr fell silent and Mark tried to read his expression. "There's something you're not telling us."

"My briefcase," Duerr said to Nora in the back. "Please pull out the folder in the outside pocket."

Mark heard Nora fumble with the briefcase. Then she handed a manila folder up to the front. Mark took it.

"You may both look at it," Duerr said.

Mark opened the folder and angled it so he and Nora could see. Inside was a photograph of three men, posing for the photographer in what looked like a hotel or conference area. Names were typed on labels beneath the photo. Weigel, fifteen years younger, wore a tweed jacket and large bow tie—the classic flamboyant professor type. Next to him was Cornelius Knox, a suave-looking man, tall with strawberry blond hair. The man next to Knox had the look of a sophisticated author: lean face, broad smile, and peppered goatee, with dark, piercing eyes that contrasted with shoulder-length platinum hair. He wore a black suit and black turtleneck. Mark froze as he realized who he was looking at. "Dr. Stefan Maier."

"That's right," Duerr said.

Mark looked at Nora, who was now watching him.

Duerr said, "It's possible that this photo was taken at their first meeting together in 1996, in Paris."

Mark tried to remember the chronology of Maier's activities. It was believed that he'd died in a boating accident on the Rhine a decade ago—a belief proven wrong when Maier showed up alive and well and violently active at the end of last summer. "So clearly this was before Maier faked his death and created Return to Earth, right?"

"We believe Maier began the network for Return to Earth as early as 1992," said Duerr. "They worked covertly for years before becoming publicly known as ecoterrorists."

"What's the connection between these guys?"

Duerr said, "Think about it. Knox and Weigel meet and become partners in a theory that the Germans were developing— or had developed—the kind of germ warfare that unleashed the 1918 Spanish flu. Most people consider it a crackpot theory. But what if Maier believed it? What if there was some sort of bomb that could instantly spread La Grippe? How do you think it would serve Return to Earth's purposes?"

"Perfectly." A chill ran down Mark's spine. "Is that what's going on in Siberia? Maier has set it off somehow?"

"It's too much of a coincidence otherwise," Nora said. "The three have some sort of relationship. Weigel goes to a conference in Novosibirsk and the outbreak follows."

"I have to proceed as if that is the case," Duerr said. "I've never been wrong when it comes to suspecting the worst of Maier and his people. We know that a Return to Earth cell in Munich shipped freight to Novosibirsk before the outbreak."

"What kind of freight?" asked Mark.

"We don't know."

"Presumably, you've spoken to Knox," said Nora.

"That's been tricky. He refuses to speak to the authorities without a court order. MI5 has been watching his place. They suspect someone is there, besides Knox and the servants."

"I assume they have search warrants in this country," Mark said. "Why haven't they gone in?"

"Knox is wealthy. He's a philanthropist and benefactor. He knows powerful people in the press. MI5 doesn't want to cause a stink without some evidence Weigel is there."

"So what's changed?" Mark asked.

"Three hours ago there was a flurry of activity at the house. Our agents think Knox is going to make a move. He's booked to fly out of Heathrow for New York."

"He's leaving?" Mark asked.

"It looks that way."

"Why New York?" wondered Nora.

Duerr shrugged. "Oh—and someone on that estate needs a lot of medication."

"What kind of medication?" Nora asked.

"Over-the-counter stuff from Boots the Chemist in Winchester. One of the agents followed a servant there and watched what he bought—the kind of drugs you'd expect for a flu sufferer. The servant returned to the guesthouse with everything."

"As much as I'm enjoying this drive, I have to ask why you wanted us to come along," Nora said.

"You have the experience to assess Weigel's condition and make a judgment about how to handle him. I don't want anyone else near him."

The sun curved west and long shadows fell on brown fields. As Duerr drove down rivulets of country roads, Mark was struck by how much the Hampshire landscape reminded him of a gently rolling ocean, with waves that seemed to carry the various farmhouses and villages like small boats.

As the Vauxhall Antara neared Winchester, Nora's cell phone chirped, and she retrieved it from her purse. "It's Mac," she said, looking at the screen, then hitting the speaker button. "Hi, Mac. You're on the speakerphone."

"I wanted to update you, just in case you thought your little jaunt to the country was more about pleasure than business."

"Spoilsport," Mark said.

"Digger and Georgina are with me so I can brief all of you at the same time."

"Brief away," Mark said.

"I just got off a conference call with Jim Dillard and Susan Hutchinson."

"How is Susan?" Nora asked.

"Stressed. But she's confirmed that the H1N1 virus in Siberia is genetically identical with the viral specimens we dug up—and a match for the Bervig corpse from Alaska."

"So my work on the Tommies was helpful," Digger said.

"It was. The folks at USAMRIID have now accelerated their flu preventive experiments."

"How?" Nora asked.

"Over the last couple of months, they've infected monkeys with the re-created virus from Alaska. The monkeys exhibited the classic symptoms of the 1918 pandemic and virtually every monkey died."

"So we're now able to confirm what we're dealing with," Mark said.

Mac continued, "But USAMRIID now needs more specimens of the original virus to further their work on monoclonal antibody production. There are simply not enough viral particles in the specimens they have. We need to find more bodies for more viral specimens."

"If you need another specimen, I think I know where we can find one," Georgina said. "I found it on the Internet when I was searching for victims." Mark could hear her clicking on a keyboard. "Apparently a landowner in Nottinghamshire named Sir Josiah Duffield died of the Spanish flu in 1919."

"Why is he perfect?" Nora asked.

"According to this website, he was buried in a *lead* coffin."

There was some jostling and muttering on the speakerphone and Mark imagined the three of them crowding in to look at the screen.

"A lead coffin could have preserved the corpse," Nora said to Mark.

"Maybe."

"This looks like it could be a high-quality sample," Mac said. "Digger, you're off to Nottinghamshire to check out that lead coffin."

"Fun!" Digger exclaimed.

"And what about me?" Georgina whined.

"I want you to begin gathering pathology specimens of Spanish-flu victims from around the world."

"Around the world! It's one thing to break into the British government's database, but everyone else's?"

"She broke into the British government's database?" Duerr asked.

"Better that you don't know," Mark said, then spoke louder for the office to hear. "Don't panic, Georgina. While I was in America, I learned that USAMRIID is compiling a list of medical museums, including AFIP in Washington, DC. Apparently wax-embedded blocks of lung tissue, taken from autopsy specimens of Spanish-flu victims, have been preserved in pathology museums and libraries in a slew of countries. No one has ever gathered them to find preserved Spanish flu. Get in touch with them, find the specimens, and have them shipped to USAMRIID and Cambridge. Got it?"

"If I have to," Georgina said. "Though I'd rather be in Winchester."

"You concentrate on the dead, we'll take care of the living," Mark said.

"Let's hope you have success," said Mac.

"We'll find out shortly," Duerr said. "This is our exit."

With that, he gunned the car onto a ramp off the motorway and toward a roundabout. Mark noted the signs to Kings Worthy and the northern entrances to the city.

Duerr called someone to confirm where he was supposed to go. Within a couple of miles, they reached a sprawling estate to the left, with high brick entrance columns, wrought-iron gates, and a long, narrow drive that cut between a series of meticulously landscaped and groomed hills. Sitting in the midst of the vast acreage of field and forest was a large Tudor-style house, built to look older than it was. Mark suspected it was constructed in the Victorian age when some architects, rebelling against the pointy and boxy styles of the time, chose the look of a bygone era.

"Is this Knox's place?" Mark asked.

Duerr nodded.

"This is impressive," Nora said.

Beyond the house was the Hampshire countryside: rolling, green, and breathtaking.

Duerr swung right onto an unpaved road that led into a small parking lot. Wooden signs gave Mark the impression that the lot bordered a park, or served as a rally point for hikers who wanted to wander the woods and fields.

A tan Land Rover was parked at the far end of the lot, facing the Knox estate. As Duerr came alongside, Mark noticed a clearing in the trees that gave them a direct view of the house. A man stood with binoculars at the front of the SUV, his overcoat flapping like a superhero's cape.

Mark asked, "Who is that?"

The man turned when the three of them climbed from the car and stepped closer. He had sharp eyes, a square jaw, and slick-backed hair. Mark recognized him immediately. "Agent Adam Pennith?"

"Ah, you remember." He shook Mark's hand, then turned to Nora. "Hello, Dr. Richards."

"Hello again," she said.

"Eyam," Mark said, recalling the short time they worked together on his last assignment.

"That bizarre body of the monk, or whatever it was," Pennith said.

"What are you doing here?" Mark asked.

"Trying to keep Duerr out of trouble," he said pleasantly. "My superiors liked my work on the Eyam case, so they've made me a liaison between Interpol and U.S. agencies like yours. Meanwhile, in case this search is fruitful, I've ordered a biosafety team from Cambridge. They are en route via helicopter even now."

Nora looked relieved. "Perfect."

"What's our situation?" Duerr asked, his attention on the Knox estate.

"I have men positioned at strategic points around the grounds."

"Where do you think he's keeping Weigel?" asked Nora.

Pennith handed her the binoculars and pointed to a cottage about fifty yards down a drive from the main house. "Kenneth,

Knox's personal assistant, has been going to and from the guest-house—more than you'd otherwise expect since we have no evidence anyone is in there."

"Except Weigel, who may be too ill to move about," Duerr suggested.

Pennith nodded. "Exactly."

"What about Knox?" asked Mark.

"No sign of him yet." Pennith touched the earpiece in his right ear. "Wait. Kenneth is bringing a car around."

"May I?" Mark asked. Nora handed him the binoculars.

He had a clear view of a white Rolls-Royce Silver Cloud III coming around the oval drive to the front door of the main house.

"Sweet," Mark said. "I love the Silver Cloud."

Nora rolled her eyes.

A medium-sized man with gray hair exited the car and stepped inside the mansion's front door. A moment later, he returned with a large suitcase and placed it in the trunk. After closing the lid, he went back to the door—leaned in for a moment—then came back out and walked toward the guest-house.

"Somebody's leaving," Mark said. A different man, tall with strawberry blond hair and dressed in a black overcoat, came out and stood next to the car. He turned to the guesthouse.

"Is that Knox?" Mark asked, and handed the binoculars to Pennith.

Pennith looked, then said, "It is." He touched his earpiece. "Knox is on the move. B team—up and at 'em. He's yours."

"Aren't you going to grab him?" Nora asked.

"After he's out of sight of his property," Pennith said, still watching through the binoculars. "Then we'll go in with our warrant. I believe we'll have an easier time with the servants than with Knox himself."

Mark squinted to see what he could, but the distance was too great.

Duerr magically produced a smaller pair of binoculars.

Pennith reported, "Knox is getting into the car. He's driving himself."

Mark could make out the movement of the Rolls away from the house and up the drive—a small line of dust rising behind it. The car came to the iron-gated entrance and turned right, away from them.

"Is your team there?" Mark asked.

"Just around the corner. They'll follow him from the next junction. There are no turnoffs before then." Pennith touched his earpiece again. "Are you on it, B team?"

He paused and frowned.

"B team?" he said again.

"Is something wrong?" Duerr asked.

Just then a black SUV roared down the road between them and the estate.

"B team! What are you doing?" Pennith shouted. He spun to Duerr. "This is wrong."

The SUV reached the iron gates and, with squealing tires, turned onto the drive and sped toward the house.

"B team! *Ian! John!* Talk to me!" Pennith tossed his hands up, swore, and dashed for his Land Rover. "Duerr, you're with me! You two follow."

They moved quickly, leaping into the cars. As Pennith skidded out of the lot with Duerr, Mark and Nora leapt into the Antara.

"What's going on?" Nora asked.

"I'm a stranger here myself," Mark said.

The car sprayed gravel as they tore from the lot and followed the Land Rover to the main road, then down to the drive. They sped to the house.

"Where's the SUV?" Nora asked, craning her neck to look.

They were roaring past the main house now. Pennith's Land Rover obscured the view ahead as they continued to the guesthouse.

Nora leaned forward. "The SUV is at the door of the guesthouse, but I don't see anyone."

The guesthouse was a two-story cottage—small compared with the main house but impressively sized by itself. Pennith brought the Land Rover to a stop a dozen yards from the SUV. Mark pulled up on the opposite side, putting the Land Rover between them and the guesthouse, if only to protect Nora in case anything dangerous happened.

Pennith got out of the car, gun in hand, arms outstretched. Duerr exited the passenger side, circled around, and joined Pennith for protection behind the vehicle. He signaled for Mark and Nora to join him there.

They went into a low crouch as they climbed from the Antara and approached Duerr and Pennith.

"Well?" Mark asked.

"Pennith has called for backup," Duerr said.

The SUV was empty, but the engine was still running. Pennith's eyes were locked on the front door of the guesthouse, which stood open. Mark felt the hairs on the back of his neck stand up. A pair of legs extended into view on the floor of the front hall. The sound of breaking glass came from somewhere inside the house.

"What do we do?" asked Nora.

"Stay back," Pennith said.

A figure dressed in a black jumpsuit and ski mask appeared in full view in the doorway, automatic pistol held high. He fired in their direction. The Land Rover rocked from the impact of the bullets. Glass from the windows sprayed over their heads. Pennith and Duerr dropped for cover. Mark grabbed Nora and pulled her down and away back to the side of the Antara. Mark kept a protective arm around her and held her close.

"A bad time to leave the gun in my other suit," he whispered.

"Drop your weapons and put your hands up!" Pennith shouted, sounding as if he doubted they'd do it.

A volley of shots rang out—including a couple from Pennith, Mark assumed. Then Pennith cried out, swearing loudly.

Mark imagined that Pennith had been hit and came away from Nora to move back to the Land Rover, but Duerr called out, "It's not bad—a graze."

More shots were fired while the doors of the SUV slammed shut.

"They've got Weigel!" Duerr exclaimed.

The engine roared and the SUV pulled away with a spray of dust and gravel.

"We can't let them escape," Mark said. On impulse, he opened the driver's door to the Antara.

"No!" Nora shouted.

"Take care of Pennith," he said, and climbed into the car. He started it and stepped on the gas.

Duerr was up, waving at him. "Stop!"

Mark ignored him and peeled out.

CHAPTER 14

HAMPSHIRE, ENGLAND

NORA CAME AROUND to Pennith, who was sitting, leaning against the side of the Land Rover. Duerr was crouching next to him. Pennith pulled at his coat, which had a tear in the right shoulder. His white shirt came into view, marked with a spot of blood.

"Let me look," Nora said, kneeling next to him.

"It's just a nick," he said, handing his gun to Duerr. "Get inside."

Nora looked to Duerr for instruction. He nodded and took the lead as they carefully approached the house. The man on the floor was prone and unconscious.

"That's Kenneth, Knox's aide. See to him." Duerr continued down the hall. "Police!" His voice echoed in emptiness.

She checked Kenneth's vitals. He groaned and Nora helped him to sit up. He put a hand to the back of his head, flinched, then brought it around again to look for blood on his fingers. They were clean. "What did they hit me with, an anvil?"

He tilted his head up to look at her, his eyes unfocused and his skin pale. "Oh, hello."

"I'm Dr. Nora Richards," she said. "We need to get ice on that bump."

"There's a small kitchen beyond the staircase." He moved as if to stand.

"Stay put. I'll get it." She found the kitchen and a freezer, and wrapped ice in a dish towel.

"So ein Mist!" Duerr complained from somewhere.

Nora took the ice back to Kenneth and gently pressed it

against the bump on the back of his head. He winced. "They took him," Kenneth said.

Duerr walked up the hall. "Who took him?"

Kenneth simply gazed back at him, then slowly shook his head. "I don't know."

"Will you be all right for a moment?" Nora asked.

Kenneth nodded.

"I'd like to see Weigel's room," Nora said.

Pennith appeared at the front door, his right arm limp. He looked annoyed. "So what does Mark think he's doing?"

Mark had no idea where he was. He'd been so busy steering and shifting that he didn't have a chance to turn on the GPS. Signs came and went before he could identify them. He thought he saw "Salisbury" with distance in the double digits.

All he could do was watch for the taillights of the SUV that sped ahead of him. They rounded corners often drifting into on-coming lanes at speeds that would have killed them had cars been coming from the opposite direction. He hugged the inside of the curves and grimaced while hedgerows lashed at the passenger side of the car.

He had no idea what he would do if he caught the SUV.

His phone, which he'd left in his trouser pocket, rang—the chime indicating it was Nora. He fumbled with it, hoping not to drop it. He hit the button for the speaker and dropped it into the console. Just then the SUV swerved to the left. He jerked the wheel to follow, sliding to the opposite side of the road, sideswiping a sign. A car came at him, its horn blaring. It dodged to his left and raced past, the driver offering a hand gesture of disapproval.

Mark threw the car into a lower gear and zoomed off to pick up the SUV's trail.

A small voice called to him from somewhere in the car. "Mark?"

He glanced at the console. The phone was gone, having rocketed out when he hit the sign. He called out, "Nora? I'm a little busy right now."

"Where are you? Pennith wants to send backup."

"I have no idea. I thought I saw a sign for Salisbury. Hold on while I try to . . ." He quickly jabbed at the GPS buttons, missed. On the second try he thumbed the power button. "My GPS is turning on now."

"What can I do to help you?"

"Beats me. They're either trying to lose me, or kill me." He shifted again and made a sudden turn to the right.

They hit a stretch of straight road that ascended a hill. Mark saw a tractor hitched to a trailer ahead and knew the SUV was about to get stuck behind it. This might give him a chance to catch up. At the very least, he might get a license-plate number.

The SUV didn't slow but sped toward the back of the trailer and Mark knew the driver would attempt to pass the tractor. "Oh, no."

"What's wrong?" Nora asked.

What Mark could see, but suspected the driver couldn't because of the trailer, was a large truck coming the other way.

"This is going to be bad!"

The SUV suddenly moved to the right to pass the trailer and found itself in the lane of the oncoming truck. Horns sounded. The driver of the SUV hit the brakes, causing the SUV to fishtail, then jerked the vehicle to the left to get back into the correct lane, but the car was out of control. It crashed through a hedgerow and disappeared off the road and out of Mark's view.

Mark kept control of the Antara as he screeched to a halt, reaching the newly formed gap in the hedgerow. He slammed the car into gear and muscled his car through what was left of shrub. He came immediately to a field, sloping downward on uneven ground. He bounced along, hitting the deep ruts created where the SUV had zigzagged on the rich earth ahead of him.

Maybe twenty yards ahead was the edge of a forest and the end of the SUV's trip. It rested after having plunged head-on into a tree. Mark began to slow as the bright red taillights of the SUV flickered, then went dark.

Coming as close as he dared, he turned on his headlights. If they were going to shoot at him, he'd rather find out while he had cover than when he approached on foot. A shadowy figure stood outside trying to help the driver. The figure suddenly turned to Mark—his ski mask now torn and wet on one side. Staggering, the man spun on his heel and limped into the woods.

"Mark!" Nora called out through the speakerphone.

Mark looked down. His phone was on the floor. He'd forgotten Nora was there. "I need an ambulance. The SUV has crashed."

"Where are you?"

Mark looked at the GPS screen. "It looks like something called Heather Lane near a junction with Church Road. The nearest village is called Nether Wallop. We're in a field beyond the hedgerow that lines the road."

"Got it."

He climbed out of the car and stepped lightly onto the grassy cushion, crouching slightly, hoping to keep some semblance of cover in case someone decided to attack. He approached the rear of the SUV, then cautiously moved around to the driver's side.

The front of the vehicle was buckled back like an accordion, the front windshield webbed. The driver was a lost cause—his head and neck twisted into an unnatural position. Resting on the inflated white air bag, his face oozed blood from various wounds, pouring over the bag like red veins. His eyes were open and staring at death.

Mark turned his attention to the backseat, using all his might to yank open the back door. A man was wedged between the rear bench seat and the backs of the front seats, his head balanced on the edge of the seat, directly in front of Mark. The man's head moved slightly and Mark heard a soft groan.

Pressing himself against the back of the driver's seat, Mark squeezed in to assess the man's condition. The passenger groaned again and slowly turned to look up. His eyes were half-closed and his pallor, skeletal. Mark recognized him from the Internet photos.

His instincts as a doctor overcame his instincts to survive.

"Dr. Weigel, can you hear me?" He drew close to the contaminated man and could see the professor had been terribly ill. His face was drawn and his tongue swollen. The man was obviously dehydrated and had been bleeding. Mark could see residue of dried blood around his nostrils and at the corner of his mouth. Weigel was cyanotic and Mark suspected he needed high-dose oxygen, and quickly.

Weigel winced as he released a staccato of deep, wet coughs. Mark could hear what he recognized as a pulmonary death rattle and wondered whether Weigel had broken ribs or torn rib muscles from coughing.

"Dr. Weigel?" He reached down to the man's neck and felt for the carotid artery. Weigel's pulse was weak, almost nonexistent.

Weigel whispered something, his eyes fixed on Mark.

Mark leaned in closer.

"Stop them," Weigel whispered, but now his words became lost in a trickle of blood that spilled from the corner of his mouth. He tried to move, to get closer to Mark, his eyes widening.

"Be still, please," Mark said firmly.

Weigel spoke up, enunciating painfully. Mark heard "Leave for meat."

The man is out of his head. "Don't move. Help is on its way." It was difficult for Mark to gauge Weigel's true condition. He was clearly injured, but where?

Weigel suddenly grabbed his arm and made another attempt. Nothing came but a choking gasp. He then sighed with a bloody gurgle, his eyes slipping upward and freezing on some point over Mark's shoulder. His gaze fixed there, eyes unblinking.

Mark felt for a pulse again, and this time it was gone. He rushed around to the opposite door and reached in, hoping to perform CPR. By the time he positioned himself for the job, he knew there was nothing further he could do. The rib cage itself was fractured in several places, bones dislodged in sagging skin.

Footsteps landed heavily on the padded turf. Mark had completely forgotten about the other man in the ski mask. He spun, bracing himself for an attack.

A man in industrial overalls stood a short distance away.

"You saw it!" he yelled. "They pulled right in front of me."

Must be the truck driver, Mark concluded, relieved.

"I saw. An ambulance is on the way. Will you go back to the road and tell them how to find us?"

"Righto," the man said. He hurried away.

Mark crawled out of the car and slumped onto the grass. He thought he heard a siren in the distance.

Assured that Mark was all right, Nora went to Weigel's room in the guesthouse. She stood in the center and adjusted her latex gloves. The room was quaint and rustic, with wood paneling covering the bottom third of each wall. Paintings filled the rest of the space to the ceiling. The bed, dressers, and end tables were all fashioned from dark wood in a similar scrolled style.

Nora caught sight of a notepad on the table next to the bed and moved to it. The room was growing dark, but light spilling in from an outside patio light provided enough illumination for her to read. She angled her head to look more closely at the pad.

"Are we at risk?" Duerr asked from the doorway.

"Are you up-to-date with your flu shot?"

"Yes," Duerr replied. "My superiors are adamant about such things. They don't like me taking sick days."

"Just be sure you're gloved up." She leaned over the notepad and looked at the scrawl, presumably Weigel's.

"What's that?" Duerr asked, as he moved into the room.

"I think Weigel was doodling." She looked closely at the plain white paper. A word had been written again and again on the pad, sometimes with violent pressure, tearing into the paper. It took her a moment to work it out. Liebfraumilch.

Duerr came alongside her and looked at the pad.

"Liebfraumilch?" she asked.

"It's German for mother's milk," he said.

"Breast milk?"

He lifted the pad in latex-gloved hands, took a small plastic bag from his jacket, opened it, then dropped the pad inside, sealing the top edge.

"Does it mean anything?" she asked.

Duerr shrugged. "If Weigel was in a state of delirium, it could be nothing more than a rant—or it could represent something more important."

"Meanwhile, I have a few questions for Knox. Have they found him?" she asked.

"Pennith's people were ambushed by the attackers. The SUV was theirs. At the moment, we don't know where Knox is," Duerr said.

Nora didn't notice anything else of interest and walked out of the room. Duerr remained behind. She could hear him opening the dresser drawers.

Kenneth was sitting in the front room, holding the ice pack to the back of his head. Two MI5 officers stood next to him. Through the open doorway of the guesthouse, Nora could see Pennith talking on a cell phone.

Beyond Pennith, she saw an ambulance coming down the drive, its lights flashing red and blue.

"Pardon me," she said. "Kenneth, an ambulance is coming. I want them to take a look at you."

"I'm perfectly fine."

"Let's confirm it. I'm going to have you tested to see if you've picked up the virus from Weigel." She stepped closer and leaned over him. "Where is your boss?"

"I'm not certain of his exact location."

She tipped her head toward Pennith. "*They* won't ask you politely."

Kenneth pressed his lips together, took a deep breath. "I know."

Within an hour, Mark was reunited with Nora at Knox's house. Pennith had converted Knox's study into a makeshift command post. A forensics team from Cambridge had been summoned to safely evacuate the bodies from the crash site and to clean the scene of all bodily fluids. Bloodhounds were being used to search for the man in the ski mask who had run into the forest. Mark felt better being at the house than in the forest searching for a gunman.

Nora was seated in a wingback chair. Duerr stood behind the desk and lightly moved papers around.

"Are you all right?" she asked.

Mark nodded. "Where's Knox?"

"Gone," Nora said.

"To where?" Mark asked. "Doesn't his manservant know where he is?"

"He claims that Knox drove to Heathrow to catch a flight to New York."

"But he didn't," Duerr said.

Nora tapped a pen against a notepad in her lap. "We've got to assume that Knox, Kenneth, and the rest of the staff are infected. We're getting the staff tested and have antiviral medication on its way."

"Don't forget everyone else crawling around this place," Mark said. "Including you and Duerr."

Duerr flinched, but nodded his agreement.

"So the trick now is to find Knox."

"He has access to a private jet parked at Southampton Airport," Duerr said. "Pennith is checking there."

"Why would he run away?" Mark asked. "Was he part of the kidnap scheme?"

"Not a very nice way to treat one's friends," Duerr said.

"What if Knox didn't know?" Nora suggested. "What if the kidnappers knew Knox's movements and timed the grab for after he left?"

"We don't know for certain that anyone was trying to kidnap Weigel," Duerr said. "Perhaps Weigel was trying to escape."

"With men in ski masks?" Mark asked.

Duerr shrugged.

"It looked to me as if they knew not only Knox's movements, but also MI5's," Mark said. "They wanted to get Weigel before the government did."

"Perhaps," Duerr said. "At this point, we don't know what Knox or Weigel knew or intended."

Mark grimaced and remembered his encounter with Weigel at the crash. "Do we put much stock in a man's dying words?"

"Why?" Duerr asked.

"He said he wanted to stop them," Mark said.

"Stop who?" Nora asked.

"Return to Earth, I assume."

"If it was Return to Earth," Duerr said. "We don't have confirmation yet."

Mark continued, "The point is, if Weigel was in on it, why would he want them stopped?"

"Did Weigel say anything else?" Duerr asked.

"Gibberish," Mark said. "Something strange."

"Like what?" Nora asked.

"He told me to leave the meat alone, or something like that."

Nora and Duerr exchanged glances.

Duerr tilted his head, then chuckled. "His dying declaration involved staying away from meat? Was he a deathbed convert to vegetarianism?"

Mark wondered at Duerr's sudden sarcasm. "That's not what he said."

"What *exactly* did he say?" Duerr asked.

Mark realized that Duerr was after something specific. "All right, what's going on? What are you after?"

"Just tell us what he said," Nora urged him.

He thought about it. "To my ear it sounded like 'leave for meat.'"

"Leave for meat," Duerr repeated. "Try that with a German accent."

Mark was puzzled. "I wouldn't know how to say 'leave for meat' in German."

"Not a translation," Nora said. "What you heard. Take what you heard and put Weigel's German accent on it."

Mark looked at her, thinking again, hearing it in his memory. "He was coughing up blood at that point. But . . ." He played the words out phonetically in his mind, then shook his head. "It's ridiculous. The only thing I can think of is Liebfraumilch."

Nora smiled. Duerr leaned on the desk.

"Liebfraumilch? Are you serious?" Mark looked from one to the other.

Duerr reached into his pocket and brought out a small plastic bag. He gave it to Mark. "Not only a dying man's last spoken words, but also his last written words, as well."

Mark looked at the multiple scrawls of "Liebfraumilch" on the notepad paper. "Why in the world would Weigel be thinking about that while he was ill—and dying?"

"I'd like to find out," Duerr said.

"We have to find Knox," Nora said. "I'll bet he knows."

Pennith came into the room. His arm was in a sling and he looked pale and tired.

"News?" Duerr asked.

"The team from Cambridge took the bodies from the accident scene," he said.

"What about your men—the B team that got hijacked by our kidnappers?" Mark asked.

"All three are dead," Pennith replied.

"I'm sorry," Duerr said. Mark and Nora joined in with their condolences.

Pennith nodded. "They were hit at close range from behind—pistols with silencers. Our two kidnappers must have crept up on them from the woods. We weren't prepared for Return to Earth."

"Are you sure it's them?" Mark asked.

"We're running fingerprints through the system," he said. "But we believe the dead driver was part of a Southampton cell. He looked familiar to one of our agents who has dealt with them before."

"What about the man who ran away?" Duerr asked.

"Hidden in the Hampshire countryside, we assume," he said. "It's possible he's infected with the virus, so we've asked the health authorities to watch for anyone coming into the hospital with severe flu symptoms. So far the hounds have not picked up a scent."

"Do you have any update on Knox?" asked Nora.

"We can confirm that Knox took off in a private jet from the

Southampton Airport. We're checking with the Civil Aviation Authority to find out if a flight plan was submitted."

"Where's he going?" Mark asked. "*To* Return to Earth—or is he running *from* them?"

Nora said, "I don't care whether Knox is running to or from anyone. My worry is that he may be infected and not know it. There's no knowing who he'll contaminate along the way."

CHAPTER 15

LONDON, ENGLAND

IT WAS PAST midnight by the time Mark and Nora were permitted to drive Duerr's car back to London.

Mark noticed Nora's stillness during the drive. She gazed silently at the dark countryside, distant lights flickering like ships on a forlorn sea. She sighed once or twice and he thought she might speak, but she settled back into a thoughtful silence.

Mark was tired. Once he was removed from the adrenaline-inducing activity of Hampshire, the reality of what happened bore down on him with a fatiguing weight. He was struck by the sudden change their course had taken—from theories bandied about in an office to the death of five men, including their main witness and vector.

"Liebfraumilch," Nora said suddenly. "Is it possible that, after all these years, old Grandpa Knox was right? What if the Germans succeeded in manufacturing this virus, and Return to Earth now has it?"

"Is that a rhetorical question?"

"I don't know how to get my mind around it," she said. Mark could feel her gaze on him. "It's too big trying to imagine what it was like for the world to lose up to one hundred million people in 1918; take a continent's entire population and erase it from existence. How are we supposed to grasp that kind of devastation?"

Mark glanced at her. "I can't grasp it, which is why I want to make sure it doesn't happen again."

She fell silent once more and, after a while, he suspected she'd fallen asleep.

Then she said, "I'm sorry I refused to talk to you about Donna."

"You were right to avoid getting involved."

"It's not that I don't want to be involved. But I doubt my ability to be helpful. Are you all right?"

"Honestly, I feel as if I'm stuck between a rock and a hard place."

"Which is the rock and which is the hard place?"

"The rock is my suspicion that she's playing me again for some reason. The hard place is my confounded conscience that tells me I should forgive her."

Nora didn't respond. They reached the A3 into London. The glow of the city lights replaced the starlit night.

"What do you think?"

"I think," she said gently, "that anything I say may sound trite or preachy or inane."

"You could never be any of those things."

She was looking at him—and smiling.

Nora's cell phone rang. She read the caller ID, then flipped the phone open. "Hello, Georgina. You're up late."

Georgina responded with something that made Nora laugh.

"I'll put you on the speaker." Nora positioned the phone so Mark could also hear.

"Hey, Georgina," Mark said.

"You two are the party animals. I thought you were too old to keep hours like this."

"What club are you at?" Mark asked. "We'll be there within the hour."

"It's my own private club. I call it Hackers," she said. "Digger put me onto it."

"What are you hacking into?" Nora asked.

"The computers for the British Civil Aviation Authority. They have the flight plan for Knox's plane."

Mark looked at Nora, who rolled her eyes. "Why hack?" she asked.

"Mac told me to," she replied. "He's convinced that throwing Interpol, British Intelligence, and TSI into the same mix will result in a lot of territorial posturing, and that we'll be the ones who get squeezed out."

Mark smirked. "He's getting awfully paranoid."

"Yeah, I suppose he's learned a lot over the past few years," she said. "Besides, Duerr asked us to do it."

Mark laughed. "Really?"

"He's afraid that Pennith may be getting the heave-ho from someone high up—someone who doesn't want MI5 leaning on Knox."

"Don't the higher-ups realize what's at stake?" Mark asked.

"Politics will win out over pandemics any day of the week," Georgina said.

Nora leaned toward the phone. "Okay, so what have you got from the Civil Aviation, or whatever they're called."

"Knox left Southampton."

"We know that much," Mark said. "Where did he go?"

"Munich."

Mark groaned. "What's in Munich?"

"That's what Mac wants you to find out. You leave first thing in the morning."

"Terrific," Mark grumbled. "Alone—or do I get company?" He looked at Nora hopefully.

"You're going with Duerr," Georgina said with malicious glee. "Nora and I get to go to Berlin."

Nora slumped back into her seat. "What does Mac expect us to do in Berlin?"

"While Mark chases Knox in Munich we get to find out what we can about the late Dr. Weigel. Mac thinks clues about his illness may be buried in his research."

"Let's hope he's right," Nora said.

PART SEVEN

Early September
1944

CHAPTER 16

LONDON, ENGLAND

LONDON IS CERTAINLY changing, Philip Knox thought as the train drew into London's Waterloo Station. He hadn't been there since the Blitz had attempted to decimate the city over two years ago. Then he'd come in to volunteer his services as a health and sanitation expert, trying to make sense of the massive damage to the city's infrastructure, and establish some semblance of hygiene to the bomb shelters.

He remembered now how he had worried then. The British officials were so shell-shocked from the nightly air raids, so entangled in their mind-numbing bureaucracy, that he wondered how they ever hoped to survive, let alone win, the war.

Now, however, things were rapidly changing. The invasion of Normandy, reports of the Americans pushing eight miles into Germany—all these things created a new sense of hope. The blackouts were now being called dimouts, as people were allowed to leave lights on past dark. Most of the theaters were open again. Public services and transportation were functioning well. Even the unmanned V-1 flying bombs, the Doodlebugs, hadn't caused the panic the Germans must have wished for. They were considered more of a nuisance to the weary populace than a threat on the level of the Battle of Britain.

Everyone seemed to have a new sense of optimism.

And that's what worried Knox. Optimism often bred laziness and a lack of diligence. Take complacency on one side, and the Germans' violent desperation on the other, and you had a recipe for disaster.

The train came to a hard stop and the passengers clambered

to their feet to disembark. Knox took his time. He casually stood and shuffled into his overcoat, tucked his umbrella under his arm, and grabbed his briefcase. He went to the nearest carriage door and stepped through to the long platform. He looked to his right, in the direction of the main terminal, and strolled onward. There was no point in rushing when he wasn't sure what he was rushing to.

He looked at the massive glass roof curved over the trains and terminal. It was a masterwork of Victorian engineering. He had read somewhere that the roof stretched over thirteen acres and contained over half a million feet of glass, now masked and reinforced in case of another attack.

He rounded a sandbagged kiosk, an aid station, now abandoned. People were becoming lax. He knew for certain that the Germans were capable of unleashing a medical apocalypse. But who believed it? Very few, in spite of his work over the past dozen years.

Time and again he'd written articles and pamphlets. Not under his own name, of course. Philip Barrison was the moniker he now used. He'd learned his lesson in America. He had a wife and son to consider and would not subject them to humiliation, especially now that his only child, Nigel, was serving with the British Army in Europe.

But that didn't stop him from fighting the good fight. He offered irrefutable proof that the Germans had inflicted the Spanish flu on the United States in 1918; that the plague meant for America only had inadvertently spread across the entire world. And he now had significant evidence that the Nazis continued their experimentation into this current war.

His latest piece—quoted in the London *Times*—argued that if the Germans had brought their science to a point of further effectiveness, now would be the time for them to use it. They may even be desperate enough to commit national suicide if it meant destroying their enemies in the process. The letters to the editor mocked him.

He didn't care. He would continue the struggle, even to the death. It amused him to think how surprised his friends, neighbors, and Home Guard pals would be to find out that he, a boring and unassuming health and sanitation specialist, was the "wild-eyed and fear-inducing" Philip Barrison, as the *Times* had called him.

He believed that no one outside his family knew the truth—until the day he received a cryptic envelope in the post.

It had been addressed to Philip Knox. He took it into his study and opened it. As he began to read, he felt an instant tightening in his chest. He slowly sank into the chair at his desk as he read and reread the salutation: "Dear Philip Barrison."

"You are on the right track," the letter said. "We should discuss our respective theories." Signed, "X."

Knox followed the strict instructions for his reply, sending a letter to an address in Chiswick, on the outskirts of London. Other letters arrived, each with a different return address. The new addresses were located farther in the city: Oxford Street, Charing Cross Road, then a church in Mayfair, a boardinghouse in Soho, and a hotel in Lambeth.

Knox's wife thought he was being made a fool of. He was willing to take that chance. And, over time, X proved credible with the information he provided. Knox received news about bombings or military action days before such things were reported in the press. He surmised that X was someone inside the British military or intelligence services.

Knox had been working for some time on his theory that the Germans might be dropping test bombs containing the influenza germs to see if illness emerged among the British population. He suspected that the unmanned V-1 flying bombs were being used as carriers. But his research was incomplete. Getting information was clumsy and difficult. Knox couldn't validate his theory or determine any patterns without greater access to public-health records. So he asked X.

X insisted they meet face-to-face.

Knox was surprised and the invitation made him nervous and exhilarated. He was instructed to take the nine o'clock morning train from Winchester to Waterloo Station. "Bring copies of your evidence, since I will be making a presentation to my superiors. I will make contact with you at the station with the word *Regency*."

Knox walked with the crowd to the main concourse of the terminal, London's largest. It had twenty-one platforms serving some twelve hundred trains a day. A crush of people moved in all directions, some people rushing, some strolling. Others stopped and looked with furrowed brows at posted train schedules. He stopped in the center and felt like a rock in a swirling tide pool of humanity.

There were men in suits and many in military uniforms; women in modest fashions and the occasional starched white outfit of a nurse. Handshakes and embraces, kisses and claps on the back. Kiosks were set up around the floor: a WHSmith newsstand with the day's newspapers and the latest magazines and books; a young boy hawked newspapers, shouting something about the recent gas explosion in Chiswick; a Boots the Chemists shop; volunteers from various charitable organizations stood next to small donation boxes. Then a sign for the Regency café caught his eye.

It had to be more than a coincidence. Without a second thought, he moved toward the café. He had taken only a few steps when an attractive blonde with bright blue eyes stepped in front of him. She held up a cigarette.

"Pardon me, sir. May I bother you for a light?"

Knox was taken aback. "Oh," he said, and fished into his coat pocket. He brought out a lighter and flicked it on for her. She put the cigarette in her mouth and leaned forward, the tip of the cigarette turning red from the flame. She puffed and leaned back. "Thank you, Lieutenant Colonel."

"You're welcome," he said, then took another step on his way. He suddenly stopped. Blushing from his stupidity, he spun around to face her.

She hadn't moved, but watched him with a bemused smile.

"Well," he said. "You're a woman."

"How kind of you to notice. Are you going to the Regency?"

"I might, if you would join me," he said, feeling brazen.

"We'll have more privacy at the Rose & Thorn pub."

"The pubs aren't open yet," he said, gesturing to the large clock in the center of the station.

"This one will be," she assured him.

He nodded, then realized he wasn't sure of their protocol. "Are we allowed to walk together?"

"Isn't that what two old friends would do?" she said with great warmth. Her lips parted into a smile and he noticed their red fullness against her white teeth.

He was struck by an unexpected desire to have this pretty stranger fancy him. He was now almost sixty and had never been the object of a flirtation. She put her arm through his and guided him toward the main entrance—a vast arch built to memorialize the many London & South Western Railway Company men killed in the Great War. At the top, Britannia sat, torch in hand, watching over them.

They walked down the steps and worked their way through the congestion of buses and taxis coming in by the Westminster Bridge Road and out to York Road. She directed him away from the river, toward Lambeth. He glanced back at the vast terminal surrounded by the roads and bridges, railway arches and warehouses. A few blocks and several corners later they arrived at the Rose & Thorn pub. A man in a white apron was sweeping the front step. He acknowledged the woman with only the slightest nod, then stepped over and opened one of the double doors to allow them to enter.

The pub was empty and dark, apart from one or two lights illuminating the bar and the bottles on the shelves behind it. The stools and chairs rested upside down on the various tables. Knox followed her to a booth against the far wall. She dropped onto the bench seat. He slid in across from her.

The place smelled of last night's ale and smoke, and the stark emptiness was unsettling. X undid her coat. She wore a white blouse covered by a green jacket. He rested his hat on the table and loosened his overcoat, then placed his hands on the table, interlacing his fingers. His mind filled with a thousand questions, but he found he could only look at her like a shy schoolboy. She had intense eyes that seemed in a constant state of assessment.

"I don't know your name," he said.

"Call me Lillian."

He nodded. "I'm Philip."

"Yes. Philip Edward Knox." She kept her eyes on him. "You've become quite a legend, you know."

"Have I?"

"The people I work with have studied your writings. Even the prime minister is aware of your work."

Knox was surprised. "Does he think I'm a crackpot, or does he take me seriously?"

"Some of us would like for him to take you seriously. That's why I decided it was time for us to meet."

"You speak in the collective. With whom are you working?"

"British Intelligence Services."

"Which department?"

She looked at him as if his question were ridiculous. "Does it matter?"

He considered a comeback, but decided that it wouldn't amount to much. "Why did you choose to meet me now?"

"I need your help."

He laughed abruptly. "*My* help? I'm here because I need *your* help."

"Then let's try to help each other." She reached under the table and brought up a leather satchel, which she placed on the tabletop. After unbuckling it, she produced a piece of paper. He recognized his handwriting. "You wrote to me about a connection between German bombs and the unusual flu outbreaks around England this past autumn."

"Yes." He reached for his briefcase and clicked it open. "I have some sketchy reports about outbreaks following German bombings in Liverpool, Coventry, Brighton, Bristol . . ."

"I'd like to see those reports. How did you compile them?"

He retrieved the copies of his work and handed them over. "It's all anecdotal. I've spent the past couple of years contacting various physicians in the bombed towns and cities. It's been a painstaking and frustrating process. I imagine that you and the government are already ahead of me and might fill in the gaps."

She shook her head. "Sadly, we aren't ahead of you. But that's about to change."

"Why?"

"We recently laid our hands on a German spy who's been operating in the Midlands. He admitted the Nazis tested germ warfare in their bombs during the first wave of attacks in 1941 and

1942. Our spy—let's call him Otis—claimed he was assigned to track the bombs' effectiveness."

"Were they effective?"

"He seemed to think so, but couldn't produce any evidence to substantiate the claim." She gestured to Knox's papers. "You may know more than he was ever able to find out."

"I'm not so certain," he said, dropping a heavy hand onto his work. "As far as I can discern, there were no obvious spikes in sickness. I only noted there *were* illnesses following the bombings. They uniformly started among squad members sent in to defuse unexploded bombs. From these team members the illness quickly spread to family and friends, but the quarantine measures always seemed to stop it."

"Unexploded bombs?" Lillian asked. She seemed surprised.

"Always. Which led me to believe they were designed to contain the germs, then spread them to the defusing agents the Germans knew would come."

She nodded. "Please continue."

"But any qualified doctor or scientist could argue that all sorts of bugs and viruses normally emerge following times of hardship and stress. The only remarkable thing was the outbreaks seemed to produce the same exact symptoms. Unusual considering the wide geographical spread. Surely this admission from Otis got the attention of your superiors."

She frowned. "They thought he was overstating his country's efforts in order to scare us. His claims would have been dismissed if you hadn't sent your last letter—and if we hadn't put your theory together with a new development."

"What new development?"

"New German weaponry. *Rockets*."

"The V-1 flying bombs? Those aren't new."

She glanced at the door. "The V-2 rockets."

Knox flinched. "The V-2?"

"You know about the recent gasworks explosion in Chiswick?"

"Yes. A handful of people were killed by a ruptured main."

"There wasn't a ruptured main. The government merely concocted a story to avoid panic. It was a V-2 rocket. The Nazis launched it from The Hague."

"God in heaven," Knox said. The V-1 bombs had to be fired from the coast of France to reach London. The Hague was over twice that distance away.

"And its speed and trajectory make it impossible for us to use antiaircraft weapons or fighter planes against it. Unlike the Doodlebug, the V-2 doesn't buzz; you don't hear it coming."

"Do you believe the Germans will use these new rockets to launch their germs?"

"If they're persisting in their tests, why wouldn't they?" She flipped through the pages of his report. "Your work will help us make the case to our superiors."

She paused a moment, her gaze drifting back to the door.

"Is there something else?" he asked.

She looked around, then leaned across the table and whispered, "Liebfraumilch."

Knox felt his body stiffen and go cold. He had never written the word in any of his pamphlets. In fact, he had not mentioned it to anyone since that night in Berlin with Dr. Schmidt. It was the one piece of information he'd held back, like detectives often did with murder-case details to establish a suspect's true knowledge. Knox believed that any independent mention of the word would be a verifiable flag of its existence.

"What do you know about Liebfraumilch?" His mouth was dry.

"Otis mentioned it. We assumed it was the name of their germ-warfare effort." She was watching his face. "Is it? Have you ever heard of anything called by that name?"

Knox forced himself to relax. "Did Otis speak of a Dr. Schmidt when he mentioned Liebfraumilch?"

"Schmidt? He may have. He mentioned several doctors and scientists. Why?"

Knox took a deep breath, then told her the story of his Berlin encounter with Dr. Schmidt more than ten years ago.

When he finished, she nodded. "So Hitler initiated work on their germ-warfare efforts even before taking office as chancellor. Which means they've had a decade to perfect their research and experiments."

Knox nodded.

Lillian seemed to be thinking aloud. "Then they're further

along than I feared. Their work could be at an advanced stage."

"Possibly."

She drummed her nails on the tabletop.

"What are you thinking?" he asked.

"Why haven't they used the germ more frequently? The Spanish flu was stunningly destructive. Why not unleash that again? Why not put the germ into every bomb?"

"Because then they couldn't control it. Along with the rest of the world, many Germans lost their lives to that flu. Before they unleash something that devastating, the Nazis would want to be certain their own people won't die along with everyone else."

"I'm not a doctor," she said. "How do you control something like that once it's set free?"

"I don't know that you can," Knox said. "Which is why I believe they haven't yet launched a full-scale attack. I think they are simply testing their influenza bombs. Unless, of course, they have a cure—which I don't believe they do."

"Why not?"

"Authenticating a cure would require something they don't have—the right test subjects."

"Wouldn't they use laboratory animals?"

"Animals are effective only up to a point," he said.

"Then . . . how?"

"You would have to experiment on humans."

"Humans." She said the word softly.

"It may be the thing that has saved us. Who would volunteer for such dangerous tests? And without humans to test both the disease and cure on, they can't use full-scale germ warfare."

Lillian suddenly went pale, her eyes wide. "The enemies of the German state," she gasped. "The concentration camps."

"I've heard a little about them, but understood they're merely work camps . . ."

Lillian shook her head. "We now have it from credible sources that the Nazis have been systematically rounding up criminals, antisocials, the handicapped—physical as well as mental—homosexuals, communists, socialists, Jews and Gypsies—"

"And putting them to work in factories and keeping them in ghettos," Knox interjected. "Hitler promised he'd do that years ago."

"He's done more than that," she said. "We've heard horrible accounts that they've been tortured and experimented upon, in the most cruel and inhumane ways."

Knox stared at her, the ramifications exploding through his mind like shrapnel. *Human subjects*—as many as the Nazis would need. He reeled at the thought of what was being done to those people, and the success the Nazis might have with their manufactured sickness and its cure.

"If they have an endless supply of test subjects and can effect a cure, then there's nothing stopping them from doing whatever they want to the rest of us."

Lillian grabbed the papers and shoved them into the satchel. "I have to get this information to my superiors."

"You'll want all of it," Knox said, and gave her the remaining papers in his briefcase. She nodded her thanks and buckled the satchel closed again. "One day I'll show you what we have, and how it complements your work. I believe we know where Liebfraumilch is being developed."

"Do you? Then bomb it. Bomb it to smithereens."

She grabbed the handle of the satchel and moved across the seat. She stood, then froze, her eyes on the door. "Something's wrong."

The double doors were closed, as they had been since their arrival. He saw nothing amiss. "What do you mean?" Knox asked as he stood.

"My coworker outside was to keep his broom handle leaning against the glass in the door on the left. That was the signal all was well. If the broom handle moved or disappeared from view, then I should assume we've been found out." Lillian grabbed Knox's arm, tugging at his sleeve. "Get your things. If anything happens, meet me at the Terminus Hotel in Lambeth. Trust no one else."

"If anything happens?" Knox grabbed his hat. Suddenly the double doors crashed open. Startled, Knox turned as a tall man in a black mac and matching fedora flew to the ground, both hands on a pistol. He fired, splintering the paneling just behind Knox.

Lillian threw herself at Knox, thrusting her leather satchel into his arms as she knocked him aside. They fell to the ground behind a table. "Run!" she shouted. She knocked the table over so the flat side gave them cover.

Another shot from the man on the floor. This one blasted chips from the side of the table.

Knox was dumbfounded but got to his feet and pushed farther back into the pub. Lillian thrust her hand into her coat pocket and withdrew a small pistol. She got onto her knees and fired back at the man. He rolled behind the edge of the bar.

"*Go*, you idiot!" she hissed at Knox and fired again. "The back door."

The man in the mac fired back, a wild shot that shattered something behind them.

Knox stumbled away, heading still farther into the pub, banging into a table, and sending the upended chairs clattering to the floor. He held the leather satchel to his chest as if it might somehow protect him. Two more shots rang out behind him. He crouched and moved faster until he saw the door at the back. Another shot and a bottle at the end of the bar exploded to his left. He dropped to his knees and crawled onward. Reaching the door, he stretched to push the sliding lock aside and then turned the knob.

He turned to signal for Lillian to come. She made a dash from behind the table. The man in the mac stood and fired. Lillian cried out, and fell to the ground in a lifeless heap.

Knox took a step toward her, but the assailant stepped into view. He was looking directly at Knox, his gun raised.

PART EIGHT

November 7
Present Day

CHAPTER 17

NOVOSIBIRSK, SIBERIA

SUSAN WALKED DOWN four flights of steps at the Hotel Central-naya, one of the most luxurious hotels in town, at least by Siberian standards. It had the added advantage of being near the center of Novosibirsk, a convenient location from which to catch public transportation during the little free time she had available. Of greater importance, she got a room with a private toilet and shower.

She took the stairs because she didn't have the patience to wait for the creaky, unreliable elevator. She was sweating. Hotel management kept the temperature too high for Susan's liking. She carried her thick hat, wool scarf, and fur-lined gloves. Her coat, a stylish parka from a nearby department store, was left open.

As she rounded the final newel into the lobby, she was surprised to see Anton waiting on one of the couches. He was reading the morning paper, smoking a cigarette, and sipping a small cup of coffee.

She turned her nose up at the smell of the cigarette smoke. She hated that about this country; people were still allowed to smoke in public places.

As she walked toward him, he saw her, stubbed out his cigarette, rolled up the newspaper, and stood. "Good morning."

"Good morning, Anton."

He smiled, but she noticed that his eyes worked the room as he glanced behind her. "Have you seen the news reports?" he asked.

"Yes. I was on the Internet early. Not a word about what's happening here."

He leaned toward her and whispered, "Let's walk together."

She whispered back, "Where are we going? And why are we whispering?"

He looked at her and rolled his eyes. She suddenly understood. He drained the last of his coffee, then gestured for them to leave.

As they stepped from the hotel onto Lenina Street, she zipped up her parka and put on her hat, gloves, and scarf to protect against the blistering subzero temperature. They moved down the sidewalk.

Anton gestured to Lenin Square across the street. "Notice anything?"

Susan looked around. The Opera and Ballet Theatre sat silent in all its glory. She also saw the Chapel of St. Nicholas with its gold onion roof. The little white building was long considered to mark the exact geographical center of the former Soviet Union.

"What am I supposed to be looking at?"

"The square is normally packed at this time of the morning."

Susan looked across to the nearly deserted square and nodded.

"There's a café on the next block." He took her arm and nearly pulled her along with him. He lowered his head, leaned in, and whispered quickly, "They've bugged our rooms at the hotel. The office, too."

"Should I be surprised?"

"Keep whispering," he said softly. "They're probably using shotgun microphones, possibly even lip readers."

She turned to him, surprised. "Lip readers? Really?"

"Really."

"But I don't have anything to hide."

"Not now you don't," he said, his head still lowered. "But you will."

He led her into a café and ordered coffees at the counter. They sat down at a small corner table with a view of the empty square through steamed windows.

"What did you think of the lab reports?" he asked.

"I reviewed them and then faxed them to TSI and Interpol via my satellite phone. I was told that's the most secure way to send anything."

He nodded.

"You realize the significance of what we're dealing with," Susan said.

Anton rubbed his chin. "I thought about it last night. One hundred million people died in 1918 from the Spanish flu. What was the world population then? I mean, what kind of numbers are we talking about now?"

Susan did the math and blanched. "I think we had just under two billion people in 1918. That's less than one-third of the population now."

"So, considering modern travel patterns, a new outbreak of the Spanish flu would travel much quicker than it did in 1918. Given that the influenza virus is so easily passed from person to person, it could infect more than six *billion* people."

"But we have some advantages now," she countered. "Antiviral medications, antibiotics, intensive care, and ventilators. And we have the ability to develop vaccines that were unimaginable then."

"But we also have significantly more people with compromised immune systems. More elderly, more victims of chronic disease, more cancer survivors, not to mention the thirty or forty million people living with HIV/AIDS."

Susan nodded. "You're talking about the worst-case scenario, a scenario we're fighting to prevent. So, for now, we need more blood specimens from flu victims for USAMRIID. And we need more information about what's going on here in Novosibirsk. Maybe I should shout at your pals with the bugs. Don't they understand how serious this is?"

He looked at his hands, which were cupped around his coffee. "I told you, we're a prideful people. We'd rather allow scores of people to die than let some American come in and save us. So you can be sure they're frantically considering everything you're considering, following every lead you'd follow, if only to stay ahead of you."

"Men!" she exclaimed, exasperated. "Prideful, testosterone-driven, competitive creatures."

His eyes met hers. "I was describing Russians."

"I don't care what brand they are, you were describing *men*." She took a sip of coffee as she sifted through her thoughts. "It's time to do what Duerr suggested."

"What did he suggest?"

"Look where no one else is looking."

"I may have a place to start."

Susan looked at him and waited.

Anton kept his head down and lips facing away from the window. "I received some information on the sick woman."

She was puzzled. "Which woman? We've got a number of sick women around here."

"The first one," he explained. "The first person admitted to the hospital with the flu. She was also the first victim. Her husband got into that fight in the hall; he was wearing a small red cap. You remember?"

"I remember. So, apart from a violently distraught husband, why are you specifically interested in her?"

"She worked as a water-processing engineer at Akademgorodok, which is why her husband went crazy."

Susan still wasn't following. "I don't get the connection. Were working conditions there bad?"

"Not bad, *suspicious*. I'm told her husband reacted the way he did because no one was listening to him. Something happened at the university's water-treatment plant; his wife's coworkers had been getting sick for a couple of weeks. A number of them died in various clinics around town."

"Clinics? Why not the university hospitals?"

"He claims university officials didn't want any bad press. It's a fairly new facility and they're in the middle of a campaign to raise confidence in the water's safety. So they paid for plant employees to be admitted at private clinics in Novosibirsk—small hospitals with a few beds, usually located at the site of a treating doctor's office. Supposedly the care is a bit better and the doctors make a little more money. But, more important, the sick employees were moved away from Akademgorodok."

Susan tried to assess the seriousness of this information. "The man could be a fruitcake, dreaming up conspiracy theories to find someone to blame for his wife's death."

"Possibly. But it's incriminating that the water-treatment officials went to such great expense to cover up the problem."

"I understand why they would. If they're trying to boost confidence in their water and plant employees get sick for reasons that may have nothing to do with the water, it looks bad to the public. I wouldn't call it a cover-up, though it might have been irresponsible not to report it." Even as she finished her sentence, her mind latched on to another detail, a painfully obvious one. "Wait," she said, as she put down her cup. She reached into her purse and pulled out her iPhone.

"What's wrong?" Anton asked.

She clicked to her calendar and found what she was looking for. "Anton, have you confirmed the timing of this man's claims?"

"The timing?"

"Did you say they've been treating people from the water-treatment plant for the past *two* weeks?" She scrolled through her calendar. "That would mean the illnesses showed up *before* Dr. Weigel arrived in Akademgorodok!"

"But he was sick with it when he came."

"Maybe so," she said. "But if it was already here, then he isn't our only vector."

Anton looked at her. "You mean *wasn't* our only vector."

"*Wasn't*? Has he been found?"

"I thought you knew," Anton said. "A communication was sent about it. Weigel is dead."

"From the flu?"

"I don't have the details," Anton said. "He was involved in some sort of car accident in England. Your friends at TSI know about it."

Susan didn't know whether to be sad that the man had died, or glad that he was no longer spreading the sickness. "Where is his body? Who's in charge of it?"

"A Dr. Vicki Prentice at the Laboratory of Molecular Biology in Cambridge."

"Good."

Anton took a drink of his coffee.

She watched him. "How do you know so much? I feel as if I'm always a step behind you."

"It's what I'm paid to do."

"All right, then let's chase this lead about the water plant. Can you arrange for us to talk to the dead woman's husband?"

"It won't be easy, but I'll try. If I'm a step ahead of you, I'm afraid our watchers are a step ahead of me."

"Then you're going to have to be extra careful and extra sneaky, won't you?"

Anton lifted his cup and gave her an enigmatic smile.

CHAPTER 18

BERLIN, GERMANY

NORA AND GEORGINA caught an early morning flight from Heathrow, arriving at Tegel Airport just under two hours later. Weigel had lived in the Prenzlauer Berg district since it was considered hip and artistic. Even better, it had a large number of nightclubs. Georgina was thrilled.

"Remember, we're here to work," Nora reminded her, feeling puritanical and staid compared to Georgina with her youthful energy.

As they made their way by taxi from the airport, pushing past the mix of post–World War II architectural styles, Nora thought about Weigel and the mystery of his illness. Did he know he was carrying a virus when he left for Siberia? Was he a partner with Return to Earth or another pawn being played by Stefan Maier? What was Return to Earth really up to? Had they mastered some terrible germ warfare that had been developed by the Germans?

They turned onto Greifenhagenerstrasse. The driver announced in broken English that they were passing the famous Gethsemane Church, site of dissident meetings that played a significant role in the downfall of the communist government in the late 1980s. Nora admired the beauty of the brick building and its majestic tower, and tried to imagine the fierce determination that went into those meetings.

The cab turned left onto Stargarder and continued east where, according to the driver, they would eventually reach the world-renowned planetarium. But before Nora could process the information, the taxi pulled to the curb.

"Something is wrong," he said.

Nora peered out the window and saw the flashing lights of the fire trucks and police vehicles blocking the road.

"A house fire," the driver said. "I hope it isn't the house you are visiting."

"I'll find out," Nora said, and climbed out of the back. The sun had disappeared behind a bank of thick clouds and she gathered her coat around her. A gust of wind sent the leaves—recently fallen from the large oaks lining the residential street—skittering down the pavement. The air carried the smell of burning wood. She walked quickly along the wrought-iron fences that separated the sidewalk from the block-long parade of town houses. Most looked stately with pillared adornments and arched windows. Each had a small front garden with a slip of walkway that led to a small porch and front door.

As she followed the ascending house numbers to Weigel's address, passersby and neighbors collected in twos and threes to watch the drama being played out by the firemen and police. With a sinking heart, she saw that the fire was at Weigel's home. She ventured as close as she could before a police officer held up his hand and instructed her in German to go no farther.

Nora surmised that the fire was already contained since the crew was rolling up the hoses. She glanced around and caught sight of a woman with bleach-blond hair wearing an orange overcoat. She was standing next to a uniformed policeman and clutching a handkerchief, which she used to dab her eyes when she wasn't gesturing at the house. The officer was taking notes and nodding sympathetically. When someone shouted, he gave her an apologetic look and walked away. The woman leaned against a police car and wept into her fists. Since Weigel wasn't married, Nora assumed she was his assistant. Nora strained to remember her name from Duerr's file.

"Helene?" Nora called out, hoping she was correct. "Helene Horst?"

The weeping woman looked up and searched for the source of the voice.

Nora waved and dared to move toward her, crossing the police line. The police officer who had warned her away before snapped at her. She lifted her shoulders in a shrug, then pointed to the weeping woman. "I'm with her," she said in English.

The officer frowned, but waved her on.

Helene Horst stood straight, waiting while Nora approached. As Nora drew close, Helene asked something in German.

Nora replied in English, "I'm Nora Richards. I believe Inspector Duerr phoned and said I would be coming."

"Oh, yes," Helene replied, also in English. "I had forgotten because of this. The vandals!" She shook her fist at the house.

What had been a quaint white town house was now a charred facade. Soot painted eyebrows over two second-floor windows. The glass was gone from both. The front door stood open and officers went in and out with great purpose.

"The professor's house?"

"*Ja.*" She began to cry again.

"What happened?"

She sought to control herself. "It was a blatant attack. I had just arrived at eight a.m., as I always do. And while I was putting the key into the lock, a van drove up. Men in black clothes leaped out and threw bombs through the top windows. Right over my head—while I was standing there!"

"Bombs?"

"They were bottles and petrol—what do you call them?—Molotov cocktails."

"Thank God you weren't inside."

"It's true. I would have been by that very window." She pointed to the window on the left. "That is the professor's office. He gave me the desk facing the front, while his desk faced the back garden. He loves his garden."

"So they knew where his office was," Nora observed.

Helene looked at her as if the thought hadn't occurred to her. "That's right. They knew."

"Who do you think is responsible?" Nora had her own suspicions.

"These days, any group of maniacs could have done such a thing. Perhaps they were Jew haters. I don't know. Everyone who knows the professor loves him."

Nora eyed Helene, aware she used the present tense each time she spoke about her boss.

Helene whispered, "There have been people watching the house. They have been parked in cars. I pretended as if I didn't notice them, but I knew they were there. And then last night they went away and they weren't here this morning."

Duerr had said the house was under surveillance. "The police?"

"Why would the police be watching the house? And if it was the police, why did they leave so that this terrible thing could happen?"

Nora glanced down the street to where Georgina now stood next to the taxi. When she looked back at Helene, she was surprised to see the woman eyeing her.

"Why is Interpol interested in Professor Weigel? Why are these strange things happening? And why are you here talking to me instead of talking to him in England?"

Nora felt sick once she realized Helene didn't know Weigel was dead. Her mind raced with the best way to respond. "You've seen the news about the sickness in Siberia?"

"I have. I was worried about the professor."

"Why were you worried?"

"I didn't want him to catch anything. He has a very busy schedule and getting sick would have been very bad."

"He wasn't sick when he left for the Siberian conference?"

"Not that I know of. Though I didn't see him for a few days before that. He had gone to Munich."

"What was in Munich?"

"I believe he was researching his book."

"He didn't tell you?"

"No. He was often secretive about the nature of his research. I got the impression he didn't want me to know. To protect me."

"Protect you from what? Why would his research be a danger?"

"In this country, digging into our Nazi past tends to agitate people. We would rather it be left alone." Helene nodded to the house, as if the attack proved her point.

"I want to be sure of the timing," Nora said. "He went to Munich right before he went to Siberia?"

"*Ja.*" A deep crease appeared between Helene's eyes. Something more had occurred to her.

"What is it?" Nora asked.

"I had to make the arrangements for the trip rather suddenly. I got the impression that something urgent had happened. He seemed rather excited."

"Excited? Did he say why?"

"No." She thought for a moment, then knelt down to a large soft-side briefcase. She reached in and brought out a spiral-bound book. "His diary. I took it home last night to enter his engagements into the computer. He is notorious for writing engagements down and not telling me."

"Would he jot down the reason for a trip—or who he was meeting?"

"Sometimes." She flipped the diary open and found the correct date. "Oh. How odd. He noted only the word *Liebfraumilch.*"

Nora nodded, but didn't say anything.

"I want to ask him what it means," she continued. "He doesn't often drink white wine."

Nora's gaze went back to the house and the exposed second-floor windows. "Did the professor keep all his research in his office?"

Helene didn't reply and Nora looked at her. The woman was crying again.

"I'm sorry to ask so many questions," Nora said.

Helene shook her head. "It isn't that. It's the way you're talking about him."

"How am I talking about him?"

"As if he were dead." In a small voice she asked, "Is he dead?"

Nora was speechless and, in lieu of words, reached out to Helene. "I'm sorry."

The woman reeled and let out a mournful wail.

CHAPTER 19

MUNICH, GERMANY

AS THE PLANE bumped onto the tarmac at Franz Josef Strauss International Airport, Mark remembered the last time he had been in Munich. To attend a virology conference. He and Donna were married then—happily, he thought—and she had come with him. They hoped to make the trip a second honeymoon.

In between obligations at the conference, Mark and Donna had explored the Bavarian capital. They walked along the quaint and welcoming pedestrian precincts of the Kaufingerstrasse and the Neuhauserstrasse. They enjoyed the charming, old-world elegance of the storefronts along the Maximilianstrasse, the art galleries in the Hofgartenstrasse, and the churches and markets of the Altstadt. They held hands and stole soft kisses and, if Mark got the dates right, conceived their daughter on one of several romantic and steamy nights in the city.

It was a new beginning . . . and, Mark now thought, the beginning of the end.

His mind wandered to Knox leaving his estate just before the kidnappers came for Weigel. Had he betrayed a writing partner—maybe a friend? Had he known of the plan and left so it could be executed? Mark thought about Weigel, lying delirious in his bed. Did he think Knox would help him? Did he trust Knox?

Trust. The word bounced around his brain like a plane in turbulent skies. Donna had asked for his forgiveness, but did he really trust her? Could he?

Duerr, who sat next to him on the flight but said nothing the entire way, nudged him. "You may want to check your phone," he said, his own cell phone pressed to his right ear. "Something has happened in Berlin."

Mark took out his phone and turned it on. He connected to his service and the screen lit up with the message notification. He thumbed the buttons and listened to the news from Nora about Weigel's house.

As they deplaned and walked toward ground transportation, Duerr finally closed his cell phone. "Let's compare notes. What do you know?"

"Nora said that Weigel's office was torched this morning."

"My office gave me the same news."

"She suspects Return to Earth was behind it."

Duerr nodded. "My Berlin counterpart said there are surveillance cameras on Weigel's street. The tapes show the van that carried the arsonists, along with a clear view of the license plate. Polish. The van had been stolen from a packing company in Gorzów a few days ago."

"But I thought Weigel's place was being watched by the police."

"It was," Duerr said, and pursed his lips. "As is often the case with these multinational efforts, there was a screwup in orders. I followed the proper channels and worked with the BKA in Wiesbaden . . ."

At "BKA" Mark's expression posed the question.

"Bundeskriminalamt is the German equivalent of your FBI. They coordinated with Berlin. But, when the local police got word Weigel had died and we were now concentrating on Knox, they pulled their men off Weigel's house. I'm *not* happy about that. No doubt Return to Earth watched the men leave and seized the opportunity."

"Are we assuming that Return to Earth torched the office to cover Weigel's tracks?"

"Possibly. Or to keep his research from falling into our hands."

"It looks as if they succeeded," Mark said. "According to Nora, all his books, papers, and research files were destroyed in the blaze. All that's left are the electronic files of his manuscripts kept on his secretary's computer."

"The Berlin police said nothing about that."

"Weigel's secretary gave Nora permission to look at the files. Georgina's already given them a quick once-over, but wants to go through them in greater detail. Oh—and Nora also confirmed that Weigel took a mysterious trip *before* he went to Novosibirsk."

"To where?"

"Here."

Duerr looked at him. "How is it that Nora knows more than the BKA?" Duerr was clearly annoyed.

"She's a resourceful woman," Mark said with a tinge of pride.

"I'm glad she's on our side. So that leaves Knox as our main source of information."

"So where is he?" Mark asked. "I assumed the Munich police would detain him when he landed here last night."

"Apparently not. They were worried about causing an international incident, what with Knox being a British subject—and a wealthy one at that."

Mark was aghast. "Surely they had someone follow him."

"At the very least." Duerr frowned. "They lost him."

"How?"

"Knox had a car pick him up curbside. Only it wasn't Knox in the car—it was the pilot of the plane. Knox must've used him as a decoy while he took off elsewhere. The officer tailing him didn't know Knox well enough to be able to tell the difference."

Mark groaned as he and Duerr walked through the revolving doors to exit the terminal. *No wonder the bad guys are keeping so far ahead of us.*

"We're checking with the various taxi companies and car services to see who got Knox and where he was taken." Duerr ran a hand through his hair as he searched up and down the waiting cars.

"Unless Return to Earth provided him with that service," Mark suggested.

"Perhaps." A sedan pulled out and came toward them. "Knox hasn't used a credit card or anything we can track."

The sedan drew up in front of them and a young man in an ill-fitting suit came around to them. "Inspector Barth sent me," he said. "He's been detained. I'm Jens Dankopf with the BKA." He grabbed their suitcases and threw them into the trunk. Mark climbed into the backseat.

Duerr sat up front and turned to face Mark. "I don't have a local office. We'll have to set up a base of operations through the Munich police."

Dankopf got behind the wheel and Duerr gave him instructions in German. The driver nodded and pulled away from the curb.

Mark's phone rang. He glanced at the screen and punched the talk button. "Hi, Nora."

"Good morning," she answered. "Nice flight?"

He was glad to hear her voice. "It was okay. Thanks for your message. You've filled in a few missing pieces for us."

"Happy to help. I may have a few more for you."

"We could use them."

"Helene, Weigel's secretary, discovered where the professor stayed in Munich."

"Great. Where?"

"The Kempinski Hotel."

Mark leaned forward and said to Duerr, "The Kempinski Hotel."

"He had expensive tastes."

"So does Knox," said Mark.

"That's what I was thinking," Nora added.

"Take us to the Maximilianstrasse," Duerr said to the driver.

The driver eased the car into the outgoing airport traffic.

Nora continued, "We've spoken to Mac. Georgina is going to stay in Berlin to see if she can dig up any helpful information from whatever is left of Weigel's files. She's going to use the computer lab at the U.S. Embassy here."

"How dedicated of her."

"Not really. I think she has a date with the cabdriver who brought us from the airport."

Mark laughed. "What about you?"

"I couldn't get a date with anyone."

"I mean, where does Mac want you to go?"

"Unless you have any objections, I'm coming to Munich."

"You won't get any objections from me," he said, and felt it to his very core.

"I'm catching the next available flight and will call you when I get in."

The Hotel Vier Jahreszeiten Kempinski exuded luxury and elegance—an impression that stayed with Mark past the colonnades at the front entrance to the massive lobby with its dark wood columns; plush chairs of rich burgundy and tan fabrics; and ceiling adorned with a stained-glass design glowing red, orange, and yellow.

The clerk at the front desk was a stately-looking woman, with her hair pulled into a tight bun and an expression of great efficiency.

Duerr introduced himself and laid his identification on the counter for her to peruse.

"Of course, Inspector Duerr," she said as if he'd asked her for a bucket of ice. "Allow me to get the duty manager for you."

She disappeared for a moment and returned with a man conveying an earnest sense of decorum and pleasantness. He shook their hands. "Gentlemen, please come to my office so that we may discuss with more privacy." Werner Hartzig spoke English with a stiff German accent. He guided them to an official-looking door that led to the inner workings of Munich's most prestigious hotel. The office was cozy and reflected the grandeur of the lobby.

In spite of the invitation, Duerr didn't sit. "I appreciate your help with this matter. We're looking for Cornelius Knox, who we believe is a guest here."

"You can appreciate the premium we place on guest privacy," Hartzig said.

"I certainly can. No doubt it is second only to guest safety."

"Safety? Is this man dangerous?"

"That's what we're trying to establish. Is he here?"

Hartzig turned to the computer on his desk and, after a few clicks, shook his head. "I'm sorry. There's no one here by that name."

Mark, who sat in a guest chair, added, "He may have checked in around two or three o'clock this morning. You wouldn't have that many people checking in at that hour, would you?"

"No."

"Will your system tell you the names of those who did?"

Hartzig turned to the computer again. More clicks. "It looks as if seven people checked in around that time." He turned the screen in their direction. "Would any of these names apply to your case?"

Both Mark and Duerr leaned toward the monitor, then pointed to the same name at the same time.

Duerr spoke. "That's him. Philip Cornelius."

"I'll have to speak with the night manager about the desk clerk," Hartzig said with an indignant sniff. "Guests are expected to check in with valid identification."

Mark stood. "Don't be too hard on your clerk. Knox likely has a document with that name on it. He's clever that way."

"As a matter of interest, how did 'Philip Cornelius' pay?" Duerr asked.

Hartzig pulled the screen around again. "Cash. Which is unusual, since he's in one of our executive suites. Those are extremely expensive."

"Is he still here?" Mark asked.

After a few clicks on the keyboard, Hartzig smiled. "He's in his room now."

"How do you know that?" Mark asked.

"Our electronic security system records room entry and exit," Hartzig replied. "It's helpful to our service personnel."

Duerr smiled. "And to us."

After assuring Hartzig they would avoid an "incident" of any sort, Duerr made a call to Jens Dankopf to arrange for backup with the Munich police.

Hartzig offered his own help in the form of a tall, muscular bouncer type with a shaved head and large white mustache. He had an equally large gun. "This is Ernst Gann, head of hotel security."

Mark, Duerr, and Gann took the service elevator to the top floor.

"Shouldn't we wait for backup?" Mark asked. He suddenly had an image of Knox being surrounded by Return to Earth thugs.

"I don't think it's necessary," Duerr said with a sideways glance at Gann.

Gann certainly looked formidable.

"My security team gives me a full report of any unusual activity," Gann said in a low growl. "If your man arrived with an entourage, I'd know it. If a group of men arrived after he checked in, I'd know it."

"What if it's not a group per se?"

Gann smiled. "If it's not a group, then there's nothing to worry about."

They walked down the hallway to a large, ornate door. A brass sign announced the Kaisersuite.

Gann signaled for Duerr and Mark to step out of view of the peephole in the door. He knocked.

After a moment, a man's voice called from the other side. "Yes? What is it?"

"Mr. Cornelius? It is Mr. Gann from hotel security."

"Is something wrong?"

"Not at all, sir. But there is an urgent matter I must discuss with you."

"Of course." Mark heard the lock being unlatched. The door opened. "What urgent matter—"

Mark and Duerr stepped up next to Gann.

Knox, dressed in pajamas and open robe, looked startled and immediately tried to close the door on them. Gann was quick, placing the side of his size-twelve foot at the bottom of the door and his large hand on the door's decorative panel.

"The hotel does not approve of people registering under false names, Mr. Knox," Gann said.

Knox moved back. He held up his hands in resignation. "Well, you'd better come in, then."

CHAPTER 20

NOVOSIBIRSK, SIBERIA

THE PSYCHIATRIC INSTITUTE sat in a compound outside the city. The main building was built sometime before the Russian Revolution, Susan assumed. It had broad steps leading to Romanesque pillars—a perfect setting for a shoot-out between the White and Red armies. There were several less austere buildings behind the first, boring and block-like.

"How depressing," Susan said as Anton turned onto the short driveway to a guard's shack. A guard stepped out. Anton gave him their credentials, which he looked at blankly. He gave the car a cursory examination, then flagged them through to the main parking lot.

They exited the car. The vast compound astonished Susan. "Are all these buildings filled with patients?"

Anton walked to her side. "More than enough. Fortunately, we only have to talk to one."

The low-lying, dark gray clouds made the start to their day seem particularly foreboding and ominous. To her it looked as if the predictions of a heavy snowstorm that afternoon were about to come true early. She pulled her parka around her neck and was thankful for the woolen scarf that helped protect her face. It was a frigid day, nearly ten degrees below zero. The cold of the Siberian wind seemed to pierce through her clothing like a thousand pinpricks.

Once inside the main building, an orderly directed them down a hall of pale green tiles cracked and chipped with age. They went into a visitors' room—in which sat only a worn sofa, a couple of chairs, and a metal table with matching chairs.

Several minutes later, a rather plain and disheveled man, wearing the same red cap he had worn the night Susan first saw him in the hospital, was brought in and sat in a heavy metal chair across from them. The orderly handcuffed the man's wrists to the arms of the chair. He gave Susan and Anton a cautionary look, then left the room, closing the door behind him. They could see he had positioned himself on the other side of the door, the back of his head framed in the small window.

Susan turned her attention to the patient—and had to disguise her shock. According to the file, this man was only forty-seven years old. He looked at least sixty-five, his eyes shadowed and the lines on his face deep.

The man gazed at them.

"Tell him we are deeply sorry about the death of his wife," Susan said to Anton.

As Anton translated, Susan could see the man's eyes tear up.

She continued. "Tell him we're with the WHO and are here to help figure out the cause of her death. We want to prevent others from getting this sickness. And, if possible, we want to investigate his claims and hear what he has to say."

Anton nodded.

Susan quickly added, "Be sure he knows we are *not* representing the Russian government or the universities at Akademgorodok. We only want to help."

As Anton began to translate, the man held up his hand. He looked at Susan. "My name is Dmitry Lebedev," he said in English. "I did my PhD work in engineering at Purdue University."

"That's a welcome surprise."

"I was part of a student-exchange program. West Lafayette, Indiana, is where Irina and I met."

"She was American?" Susan asked.

"Born in America, but a second-generation Russian. Her parents escaped right after Stalin died. When we returned here, she became a Russian citizen again."

"Why did you come back?"

He paused for a moment and swallowed hard. "My wife is— *was*—an expert in water treatment and had been hired by officials at Akademgorodok to improve the quality of their water. She had planned and overseen the installation of a reverse osmosis system that produced the best-tasting water in eastern Russia, maybe in the whole country. She was a remarkable woman."

"I'm sure you were very proud of her," Susan said.

He nodded and she thought she saw his lower lip quiver ever so slightly.

"What do you think happened to her?" She glanced at Anton, who produced a notebook from his pocket and sat with his pen poised.

Dmitry sat up, frowned at Anton, and glared at Susan. "Why do you care? No one else does."

"We want to find out where the epidemic started and believe your information may help us stop it. I'm hoping you can help. If so, perhaps we can help you."

The man eyed her for a moment, as if assessing her. Finally, he took a deep breath and slowly let it out. "Two weeks ago I took Irina to work. I dropped her off in the morning, as usual. Then I drove outside the water-treatment plant and up the road a bit. I noticed an unusual truck parked next to the fence that surrounds the plant. Several men seemed busy at work. This didn't strike me as unusual, since I knew the facility's water intake was there."

"Water intake?" Susan asked. "Where does the water come from?"

"The Novosibirsk reservoir, via an open aqueduct."

Susan nodded.

"I shouldn't have thought anything of it. Routine maintenance, a water check of some sort, it could have been anything. But something about the men struck me as suspicious. They weren't wearing the usual uniforms. And, to be candid, something about their faces wasn't Russian. They looked foreign."

"How so?"

"I wouldn't know how to explain it. For example, no one here would look at your face and believe you're Russian. You don't have the look. We know it when we see it—or when we don't. These men didn't have it."

"So what did you do?"

"I drove on, then pulled off the road into a small parking lot that hikers use for the forest trails. I kept behind the trees so the men couldn't see me. But I could see them."

"What were they doing?"

"It looked as though they were dumping something into the water."

Susan stiffened. "Dumping something? What?"

Anton stopped writing and looked up.

Dmitry shrugged his shoulders. "I have no way of knowing. They removed a barrel from their truck, took off the top, and dumped a liquid into the intake water. Then they did the same with a second barrel."

"What did you do?" Anton asked.

"I ran to my car and drove back to the plant. I told Irina and she notified security. We all returned to the site, but by the time we got there, the men had gone. We could see the tire tracks, but nothing else."

"Did you inform the police?" Anton asked.

Dmitry smiled and shook his head. "No. The security people at the plant said they would handle it."

"How did they handle it?"

"By ignoring it and hoping it would go away. They didn't tell anyone. Now, there's no proof and the officials think I'm insane from grief. I am grieved, but I am not insane. I think they've had me admitted here to keep me from the press."

"Your behavior in the hospital didn't help your case," Susan said.

He smiled sadly. "No, I suppose not. By that time, I was beside myself trying to get help for my wife. She was dying." He paused for a moment again and jerked at the handcuffs to wipe his eyes. "She knew it was because of the water. I knew it, too."

"Why wouldn't the plant's security people back up your story?" Susan asked.

His eyes turned cold as steel as he stared at her. "Because, like my wife, they are dead."

Susan was about to ask another question when the door opened and the orderly returned. He tapped the watch on his wrist and indicated that it was time for them to leave.

Susan and Anton gathered their things. Dmitry watched

them silently, as if they were also packing up and taking what was left of his hope.

As they drove back to town, Susan made notes in her journal. After finishing her entries, she kept the journal open and looked at Anton. "Is there any way to determine how many other cases of the flu can be traced to the water-treatment plant?"

"Seventeen employees," he said matter-of-factly. "Pretty much all the employees who worked at the plant the day Dmitry told us about. Then, within days, their family members and neighbors got ill. Health authorities thought it was an early seasonal flu—until people began dying."

She was impressed. "You are remarkable."

He nodded. "It's about time you noticed."

They drove and Susan tried putting together a time line of who became sick and when. Then another question struck her. "If the water was somehow tainted with this virus, why wasn't all of Akademgorodok affected, not just plant employees and those around the conference center?"

"Because the plant is fairly new. Most of the area's water supply is still connected to the old plant, and apparently the water from there was not affected. The piping to the new plant is being introduced incrementally. The conference center was one of the first areas to switch over. I suppose officials wanted to impress conferees with their great-tasting water."

Susan considered him for a moment. "Anton, how do you know that?"

"I researched it."

"Why?"

"Because you told me to investigate—"

"Yes, yes, I know," Susan said impatiently. "But you're not doing this only for me, or alone."

"What are you suggesting?"

She turned in her seat to face him. "I'm suggesting that we stop playing games."

He lifted an eyebrow and glanced at her.

"I don't mind. As long as I know everything that your boss knows," Susan said.

"My boss?"

"Inspector Duerr. I *know* you're working with Interpol."

He opened his mouth to speak, but his cell phone rang. "I should get this."

"Uh-huh." Susan leaned back, folding her arms.

Anton spoke to someone in Russian, then hung up. "We're wanted at the office."

"Wanted by whom?" Susan asked.

"I don't know." He hit his turn signal and made a death-defying turn to a side street. Horns blared. "I think we're in trouble."

"For what?"

He stepped on the gas. The car lurched forward. "Our watchers were more diligent than I thought."

Susan frowned and felt a stubborn anger well up in her. "What are we expected to do? If your government won't help and—" She didn't finish the sentence, but growled instead, "Anton, I don't care who you work for. All I care about is finding answers. Let them arrest me if they want, but we have to get to that water-treatment plant."

CHAPTER 21

MUNICH, GERMANY

CORNELIUS KNOX RUBBED his arm and shot Mark a suspicious look. "Are you sure this isn't a truth serum?"

"Do we need one?" Mark disposed of the needle and put the syringe back into his carrying case. "As I told you, this monoclonal antibody is to ensure you don't infect anyone with the sickness Weigel had. And you're going on a round of antiviral medications, as well."

"Medications?" Knox asked. "Isn't one enough?"

"Not for this bug. We think it requires a cocktail."

Duerr stood across the large room, the lounge area of Knox's suite, which accommodated a sofa and wingback chair, a large television, wet bar, desk, and executive chair. He watched Knox thoughtfully and tapped his lower lip with a forefinger.

Mark put his case away and leaned against the desk. He noted three doors. Two were closed and one was ajar, offering a view of the luxurious bedroom.

Duerr kept his keen eyes on Knox. "Perhaps it's time you explained yourself. Why did you leave England?"

"I have obligations here."

"Obligations? You fled the scene of a crime," Mark said.

"Crime? What crime?"

Duerr held up a hand. "We'll get to that."

Knox adjusted the arm of his robe and tightened the belt around his waist. "Frankly, I resent this invasive form of questioning. I've done nothing wrong."

"What obligations brought you here?" asked Duerr.

"Research. For my book."

"The one you were writing with Weigel."

"Correct." He paused and looked at Duerr. "What do you mean *were?*"

"Weigel is dead."

Knox's mouth fell open as his eyebrows shot up. He went pale. "How?" he asked in a choked voice.

"Someone attempted to kidnap him from your guesthouse right after you left," said Mark. "While escaping with Weigel, the kidnappers crashed into a tree."

Knox slumped. "Good God."

"You see, Mr. Knox, the stakes are very high," Duerr said. "It's best for you to tell us everything."

"I'm trying," Knox said in a distant voice. He blinked hard, then stared at the floor. The shock of Weigel's death shrouded his face like a veil.

"What's significant about Munich for your research?" asked Mark.

Knox hesitated. Mark could see he was struggling with what to say. "There are many things here."

"Give us an example," Duerr said.

"We believe the Nazis worked on their influenza bomb here. They may have tested the virus on their prisoners at one or more concentration camps."

"Is that why Weigel came here before he went to Siberia?" Mark asked.

Knox's eyes flickered. "I didn't say he came here."

"We have that information from another source," Duerr said. "That's why you're here."

Knox didn't deny it.

Mark added, "He was excited about something he'd found. What was it?"

"I don't know," Knox said. "He was too ill. I couldn't get coherent answers from him."

Duerr looked at Mark with an expression that echoed Mark's feelings: Knox was lying.

"Tell me about your relationship with Stefan Maier," Duerr said.

"Who?"

Duerr tsked. "Now you're being insulting. Stefan Maier. I have evidence of your connections to him. Shall I show you photographs?"

Knox shrugged. "We've met once or twice."

"It's within my authority to have you arrested."

Knox shook his head. "I want to speak with the British Embassy."

"You'll get your phone call after you sweat in jail. And the embassy will want you to go home, where the British police aren't very happy with you. They have a number of questions they want answered."

"You don't have to bully me."

"Yes, I do."

A stare-down ensued between the two. Mark thought it was like a game of chicken to see who would blink first.

Knox did.

"Maier has subsidized some of our research," Knox said.

"Subsidized it? Financially?"

"Why would a man with your wealth and position need outside help?" Mark asked.

"My family inheritance has served me well. But I've never had enough money to fund the considerable research we've done over the years. We needed outside grants and sponsorship."

"He didn't just cover *some* of your research. Maier covered it *all*, didn't he?" Duerr asked.

Knox nodded.

"Do you know why he was so interested in your work?"

"He was a fan of my family's work on the subject. He believed the Germans developed a technique in World War I to spread influenza through food, then furthered their research during World War II using bombs and rockets. He encouraged me to continue the quest. He introduced me to Professor Weigel, who was exploring many of the same theories. Maier thought we would be more effective working together than individually. He was right."

"Then Maier's death must have come as a shock to you," Duerr said.

"His death?"

"A decade ago. The boating accident that took his life."

"Oh, yes. That."

"*That?* Then resurrection must be normal in your line of work. For me, Maier's reappearance was quite a shock."

"Resurrection?"

"You know he's alive."

Knox looked as if he might deny that knowledge, but his eyes narrowed and his lips twisted ever so slightly. Mark thought Knox must be a horrible poker player.

Knox said softly, "Yes."

"Who told you?"

"An assistant at the foundation." Knox was knotting and un-knotting the belt to his robe.

"And?"

"It was no accident, but an attempt to kill Maier to stop his work."

"What work?" Mark asked.

"I don't know. Something controversial. The rumor was he had been experimenting at a secret lab somewhere. After the attempt on his life, he went into hiding and allowed everyone to believe he was dead. Most people still do."

Duerr folded his arms. "But you've met him personally since his 'death.'"

"I haven't." Again, the narrowing of the eyes. "But Weigel has—at least, I'm fairly certain that he has—sometime during the past few weeks."

"Where did they meet?" Duerr asked. "In Novosibirsk?"

"No. I think they met here in Munich."

Duerr tapped his lip again. "Are you here to meet Maier as well?"

"No," Knox said.

"Then what is your plan? You didn't come to hang out in the hotel."

"Weigel and I have a contact in the history department at the Ludwig-Maximilians-Universität München. I was going to contact her, to see if she recently spoke with Weigel. I plan to follow in his footsteps to see where it leads."

Still lying, Mark thought.

"Get dressed," Duerr said. "We'll go talk to her together."

Knox looked worried, then stood and went to the bedroom. Both Mark and Duerr followed.

He turned to them, irritated. "Are you serious? You're going to watch me dress?"

"We don't want to lose you again," Duerr said.

"Suit yourself." Knox went to the closet near the bathroom. He began to dress. "Knox, do you know what Maier's foundation actually is?" Mark asked.

"That's a trick question," he said, shuffling into his trousers. "I assume it dabbles in a variety of things like most foundations."

"How about terrorism?" Duerr asked.

Knox jerked his head from behind the closet door. "Don't be absurd."

Duerr looked at him as if to say that he was never absurd. "Haven't you heard of Return to Earth?"

Knox frowned. "Only in the news. It's green and politically correct. But that isn't the name of his foundation. It's the Maier Foundation." He buttoned his shirt.

"No matter. Return to Earth is funded by him," Duerr said.

"So?"

"They believe humankind has revoked its privilege to own and manage planet Earth. Or, to use Maier's words, 'man is a malignant ecotumor destroying the earth.' They're dedicated to killing off most, if not all, of humankind in order to return the earth to its natural state."

"I wouldn't know anything about that." Knox turned his attention to his socks and shoes.

"You ought to. If some sort of influenza bomb exists and Maier and Return to Earth get their hands on it, they will use it to try to kill all humans."

Knox put a hand against the closet door. His features sagged and he looked old and ashen.

"That's why we need your help," Duerr continued. "You have to tell us exactly what you know—what Maier knows—and what Weigel discovered before leaving for Novosibirsk."

Knox sat down on the bed and stared at his shoelaces, as if he had forgotten how to tie them. He was weighing his options.

"Knox?"

"He thought he found the lab," Knox said softly.

"What lab, exactly?" Duerr asked.

"The lab where the Nazis developed the influenza bomb."

Mark was astonished and looked to Duerr.

"Where is the lab?" Duerr asked.

"I don't know for sure."

"How are you going to find it? Did Weigel tell you where it is? Do you have a map?" asked Duerr.

"Only some cryptic scribbles he'd written in his room."

Mark remembered the word *Liebfraumilch* written over and over on a notepad by Weigel's bed.

"What scribbles?" Duerr asked. "Words?"

"No. Lines and circles." He walked over to a dresser and opened a large leather portfolio. He pulled out a slip of paper and handed it to Duerr. Mark moved next to Duerr and looked at the shaky and ragged lines of ink.

Random circles, squares, and lines. More scrawls from a delirious mind, Mark thought.

"Does this mean anything to you?" Duerr asked Mark.

Knox suddenly stood and began to sway. He put a hand to his forehead. "What did you put in that syringe?"

"The antibody shouldn't have any immediate side effects," Mark said, moving to the man's side.

"I think I'm going to be sick." Knox turned and went into the bathroom, disappearing around the door and kicking it almost shut. The sounds of heaving came back to them through the open door.

"Is this normal?" Duerr asked Mark.

"No. But injections affect people differently. It may be the stress."

The retching stopped. The toilet flushed. The tap water flowed.

Duerr moved to the door. "Are you all right, Knox?"

Silence.

Duerr knocked on the door. "Knox?"

Mark immediately thought of the two closed doors he'd seen in the lounge—and knew instantly that one was a second entrance to and exit from the bathroom. Mark dashed to the living room.

Duerr swore loudly in French—and came through the second bathroom door. The door to the suite clicked as it automatically closed.

Knox was gone.

CHAPTER 22

MUNICH TO FREILASSING, GERMANY

MARK AND DUERR rushed into the hallway. It was empty. Duerr moved to the left and gestured for Mark to go right. "I'll check the elevators, you see what's that way."

Mark dashed down the red-carpeted hallway toward a rear window—a mere adornment at a junction of hallways. Mark stopped, wondering whether to go left or right. He heard a door bang to his right, then noticed the sign for the interior fire escape. Mark groaned and sprinted toward the door.

He reached the end of the hall, pushed through, and stopped, listening for the telltale echo of feet pounding the stairs somewhere below. Mark propelled himself forward, leaping down the steps two and three at a time. *Why didn't I insist on taking the elevators?*

Quick glances downward revealed Knox's hand on the railing, but always a floor or two beneath him. He hoped Knox might make the error of dashing into the lobby and into Duerr's arms. But no such luck. Knox continued downward, past the door for the lobby. *This has to stop somewhere.* Mark's heart pounded.

The fire escape ended at street level. An alarm went off as Knox pushed through the exit. Less than a minute later, Mark followed, and found himself on a busy side street. Knox was rushing up the pavement to the left—away from the hotel's front entrance. Mark sprinted after him. Knox crossed the street at the corner, against the light. Car horns blared. Mark attempted to cut him off by crossing in the middle of the traffic. But the unyielding drivers made it difficult. Knox disappeared around a corner.

He's going to vanish into the city.

Impressed that a man Knox's age could move so quickly, Mark forced himself onward. His mind also raced with what he'd do if he caught up with Knox. He had no authority to stop him—and no time to call Duerr.

A few more blocks, doglegs to the left and to the right, and Mark realized he wasn't gaining on Knox. The pedestrians seemed to have conspired to get in his way and keep them the same distance apart.

Suddenly, Knox's hand went up, and a taxi pulled to the curb. As Knox was maneuvering into the backseat, Mark also flagged a cab, and said the words he longed to say since he was a child: "Follow that cab!"

The driver looked at him in the rearview mirror and laughed. "Which one?"

"That one!" Mark gestured. "That white cab there!"

The driver nodded and jerked the car into the flow of traffic. Now the chase took them into the few open spaces and gaps between cars, with last-minute turns and unheeded stoplights. Mark bounced around in the back, hanging on for dear life.

The driver grabbed a handset and shouted something in German. A moment later the speaker crackled and a response, also in German, came back. The driver laughed again and looked at Mark in the mirror.

"Don't worry," he said in a thick accent. "I know where we're going."

"Where?"

"The main train station."

"How do you know?"

"Because my brother is driving the other cab!" The driver guffawed; a big, hearty sound that evoked crowded beer halls and polka music.

"Did your brother tell his passenger we're following him?"

"Be generous with your tip, and I can make sure he doesn't."

"Count on it," Mark said. "Can your brother delay the man?"

"Now, that wouldn't be fair, would it? What did he do, sleep with your wife?"

Mark shook his head. To tell the truth or imply this was a police affair might have caused the driver to stop, if only to avoid getting involved. "He owes me. A lot." Mark pulled out his phone and checked the call list for Duerr's number. He hit automatic dial and prayed Duerr would pick up.

The phone rang twice and Duerr shouted, "Where are you?"

"I'm in a cab following Knox to the main train station. Can someone intercept him?"

"I'm working on it. Munich police aren't used to responding to Interpol on a moment's notice."

"Well, do something fast. We're here."

The first cab had come alongside the station—large and red walled—and pulled around to the front drop-off. Knox was already out of his taxi and racing up the stairs.

Mark realized he had only British pounds and gave the entire wad to the driver. It was a lot more than the fare. "This will cover the rate of exchange." He dashed from the car and up to the main entrance.

Once inside, he headed for the vast concourse. The place was all steel and glass, packed with kiosks, ticket-vending machines, and passengers looking at train and platform announcements. Further announcements in German came over the loudspeaker.

Mark caught sight of Knox rounding a Häagen-Dazs stand, craning his neck to see if anyone was following. An idea came to Mark and he ducked behind a pillar as if to tie his shoe. If Knox thought he had lost his pursuer, Mark would have a better chance of catching him. Mark leaned to one side and caught a clear view of Knox still at the ice-cream stand, searching the area. Knox turned in a slow circle and stiffened as two uniformed police officers approached. He leaned away until the officers passed without acknowledging him. Mark waited.

After a moment, Knox lowered his head and drifted to a bank of ticket-vending machines. He punched a few buttons, paid, and grabbed the dispensed train ticket. As he scurried to the platforms, another slip of paper printed out and fell to the ground. Mark carefully made his way to the machine and knelt to snatch up the paper. It was a receipt for a first-class ticket to Berchtesgaden.

Berchtesgaden? Mark didn't have time to try to figure it out. Using his credit card, Mark bought a second-class fare. The board indicated that the train was about to depart from Platform 12. He ran for it.

At the head of the platform, Mark found a group of young people all with backpacks and the tanned good looks of hikers. He moved away from the train and to the far side of the group, hoping that Knox couldn't see him from a first-class carriage window.

Mark boarded the coach carriage directly behind first class along with the hikers, who found their seats and unloaded their backpacks. Mark sat in an aisle seat with a clear view of the door leading to first class. He called Duerr.

"Why Berchtesgaden?" Duerr asked after Mark had quietly updated him.

"No idea. Maybe Berchtesgaden is where the lab is."

"That's three hours by train. I can get there faster by car. I'll meet you at the station."

A young man with long, wavy hair and a trimmed beard asked in a clipped accent if he could sit in the window seat. Mark hated the idea of company, but could see that the carriage was full. He made room while the young man abandoned his backpack to an overhead hold, then squeezed in.

"Knox is playing us." Mark lowered his voice to a whisper. "If you meet us, he'll try to run."

"We'll catch him again."

"But we don't know where he's going."

"Let's give him a long leash to see where it leads."

"It's risky."

"Only if you lose him."

"See you in Berchtesgaden." Mark signed off.

The train pulled away from the station, heading southeast on the Munich-Frielassing rail line. Drops of rain hit the window, then smeared across the glass. The city's buildings looked impressionistic.

The young man next to him politely asked in clipped English whether he was going all the way to Berchtesgaden.

Mark was concerned that he'd spoken louder than he realized. "Yes."

"I'm going to that area, too."

"Hiking?"

"No, it's too late in the season to hike there. I'm a student."

"What are you studying?"

"History. But, mostly, I'm interested in the Nazi regime." He pulled out a map from his pocket and unfolded it on the tray table. "Have you ever been there?"

"No, I haven't."

"It is a treasure trove, if you're interested in the Nazis."

"I am. Why is it a treasure trove?"

The young man smoothed the map out and pointed. "Going out from Berchtesgaden, there are many landmarks of interest. Here especially." His finger was on a town in the Alps called Obersalzberg.

"Obersalzberg?"

"It was the location of Adolf Hitler's *Berghof*, his favorite retreat. The Nazis took over the area and set up a complex. They had homes for the top officials, bunkers, and an elaborate network of tunnels."

"No kidding." Mark wondered if those tunnels might contain the germ-weaponry labs. He dug into his coat pocket. He still had the slip of paper with Weigel's scribbles, the one Knox had shown them; he'd shoved it into his pocket when Knox ran off. He opened it and looked from the scribbles to the map and back again.

The young man was watching him, his face a question.

"A friend of mine drew this map," Mark explained, hoping he was on the right track. "I think it's meant to be Berchtesgaden but, as you can see, he's not much of a mapmaker."

"I should say not."

"Does it compare to your map?"

The young man compared the two. He pointed to the lower left-hand corner of the paper, where Weigel had scribbled a circle and a small group of Xs. Then he pointed on the map to the town of Berchtesgaden.

"If that on your friend's map is Berchtesgaden, then it makes sense, in a crude way."

"How so?"

The young man's finger followed along a series of squiggly lines leading away from Weigel's markings of the town, which, on the young man's map, went in the direction of Obersalzberg. "That could be the area I just told you about. You see?" Then he pointed to a circle a few inches away. "This could be Lake Königssee."

Mark looked at the drawing and the map and had to agree. It was possible. Mark pointed out another marking Weigel had drawn with more squiggly lines, something that looked like a bush, and a direct line to another circle with jagged edges. "And this?"

"I suppose that's the *Kehlsteinhaus*, or what some called the Eagle's Nest."

Mark knew it from his history courses. "I've heard of that. A fortress built for Hitler by . . . " He faltered, confusing the names of Hitler's cronies. "Speer, Hess, Goering, or someone."

"Martin Bormann," the young man said. "In its time, it was an amazing feat of construction and engineering. The house was built on the mountain with four miles of access road. A hairpin curve would have thwarted most military vehicles from reaching the top. A tunnel was drilled through the mountain to an elevator. Some four hundred feet to get in, then up four hundred feet to the fortress. Some say a whole network of tunnels in the mountain lead to rooms full of lost treasures: priceless paintings from Paris, gold chalices from ancient churches, bullion, you name it."

"Amazing."

"Bormann did it all, the road and the house, in just over a year," the young man said. "Imagine attempting something like that now. But he was determined to get it finished in time for Hitler's fiftieth birthday."

"That is remarkable."

The young man smiled. "And all the more amusing because Hitler *hated* heights. He went there only a few times to impress dignitaries."

Mark studied the drawing and wondered if Weigel believed that fortress was where the influenza bombs were created. "But was it used by others? Would the Nazis have created laboratories there for research?"

"What kind of research?"

"New weaponry?"

"Not at the Eagle's Nest. That would be too visible and vulnerable to bombers. If they were developing new weaponry, they'd do it where it would be well hidden, or where they'd have easy access." He pointed to an area back near Obersalzberg. "Down here. In what were the military complexes. If they had succeeded in developing such things there, they'd want to use them as a last resort."

"Why only as a last resort?" Mark asked.

"The Nazis weren't idiots. They thought through all the strategic possibilities, including that they might lose the war. This was the Alpine Redoubt, Hitler's last stand. In fact, you Americans were so concerned about it that you left the Russians in Berlin and went there to destroy any remnants. Imagine your surprise when no one was there. Hitler and his new wife were charred remains in a Berlin ditch."

"A grand honeymoon," Mark said. He pondered the idea of germ weaponry being used by the Nazis as a last resort. It made sense. If they had no antidote or cure for the virus they'd created and they knew they'd lost the war, they might unleash it with a reckless disregard for the consequences. It would have been the ultimate suicide pill.

Now Mark understood why Knox was headed for that area.

He thanked the young man for his help and they fell into silence as the ride went on. The train seemed to stop every five or ten minutes at towns with names such as Rosenheim, Übersee, and Traunstein. He caught glimpses through the window of businesses, industrial parks, and houses. The rain stopped. At each new platform, Mark made it a point to watch for Knox among the departing passengers. He wouldn't put it past the man to sneak off early.

A woman came by with a trolley of coffee and sandwiches. Mark ordered one of each.

He took out his cell phone and dialed Nora, but it went immediately to her voice-mail service. He assumed she was on the flight from Berlin. He left a message to say he was on his way to Berchtesgaden and for her to call him when she arrived. No

sooner had he hung up than his phone vibrated in his hand. Assuming it was Nora returning his call, he answered without looking at the screen.

"Hello?"

"Hi, Mark." It was Donna.

"Donna?" He instinctively tensed up.

"Yeah . . . hi . . . is this a bad time?"

"I'm okay for a couple of minutes. What's up?"

"Nothing. I've been thinking about you and just thought I'd
call," she said gently. "Where are you? Somewhere exciting?"

"Outside of Munich."

He heard her release a slow breath. "Munich . . ." she said.
And he knew she remembered. "Has it changed much?"

"I'm here on business. I haven't been able to visit any of the
places we saw."

"Oh." She sighed. "What a great time that was."

"Yes, it was."

"Will you be there long?"

"I don't know yet."

"I was thinking . . ." After an awkward pause, she giggled. He
hadn't heard her do that in a long time. He thought of how endear-
ing, how innocent, he'd always found it. "I'm sorry. I didn't have a
reason to call." She hesitated, sounded as if she might reveal more,
then didn't. "I won't keep you. Call me when you get back to the
States. Maybe we can get together. Tell Munich hello from me."

"I will. Thanks for calling."

"Stay safe, Mark."

"I'll do my best." Mark hung up. He turned the phone over
and over in his hands, just as he turned the decision he had to
make over in his mind. Yet he knew that, no matter how many
different ways he scrutinized it, he'd have to answer her.

An hour and a half after they left Munich, they came to a city
called Freilassing. The young man moved to gather his things. As
he grabbed his backpack, he asked Mark whether he was changing trains there.

"Should I?" Mark asked.

"You must if you are going to Berchtesgaden. The connecting
train leaves in about twenty minutes."

"Thanks." Mark smiled. "I didn't look closely at the schedule."

The train pulled into the station and a crowd of passengers jammed the aisle to get off. Mark said good-bye to the young man and watched the people on the platform through the carriage window as he waited to get off. Knox appeared in view, walking calmly and with the sure confidence he wasn't being followed. For Mark, that was good news. The bad news appeared a moment later. Knox stopped beside a pillar and extended his hand outward. Another man, obscured by the pillar, shook it warmly. The two men walked out of Mark's view into the main terminal.

On the phone, Duerr offered a string of what Mark assumed were German obscenities.

"What should I do?" Mark asked, interrupting. He had followed Knox and the mystery man to the front of the station. Clearly Knox wasn't continuing by train to Berchtesgaden.

"If they get in a car, can you follow them?"

"In a cab? Through the German countryside? They'll know."

Duerr grunted. "You're convinced Knox will go to Berchtesgaden?"

"If I've interpreted Weigel's drawing correctly, yes."

"Then we'll have to take a risk. Try to get any identifiable markings on the car they take. Then continue by train to Berchtesgaden and we'll rethink our strategy there." He hung up.

A black Mercedes-Benz sat curbside. Nothing about the car was worth noting, apart from its pristine beauty and tinted windows. The stranger wore a dark hat and overcoat and kept his face down and obscured. He guided Knox to the passenger door, then quickly circled to the driver's side out of Mark's view. The car drove off.

With only a minute to spare, Mark made it to the train for Berchtesgaden.

CHAPTER 23

FREILASSING TO BERCHTESGADEN, GERMANY

CORNELIUS KNOX LOOKED out the sedan's windows at the traffic of Freilassing. The tint of the windows muted the colors of the buildings, the storefronts, even the pedestrians, giving everything the look of an old film.

Knox was afraid. And he'd found that by concentrating on incidentals—on obscure nothings—he could manage his fear.

He looked at the driver. Stefan Maier navigated the traffic with a cabbie's expertise. He wore sunglasses that seemed to highlight his small ears and the lightly tanned patina of his shaved head. Knox glanced at his profile, hoping to determine where he was from. High forehead, hawklike nose, thin lips, square jaw. Humorless smile.

Maier looked at Knox without speaking, then turned away again, driving on—which unnerved Knox all the more. If what Duerr told him was true, his benefactor was a madman. *It's possible he purposefully set Weigel up to die.*

They cleared the city and followed a B road to an A road to an E road, although Knox couldn't keep them straight. Maier signaled and took a turn south to Salzburg.

Knox couldn't bear the silence anymore. He cleared his throat. "Well."

"You were wise to call me," Maier said.

Knox grunted. "Was I?"

Maier turned his head slightly, but kept his eyes on the road. "Yes. It's going well, I think."

"I don't agree," Knox said. "I'm a fugitive without having done anything wrong. And Weigel is dead."

"That was unfortunate."

"*Unfortunate?* Why on earth did you try to kidnap him?"

"Because the authorities were closing in. In his delirium, he might have told them what he knew."

"What did he know?"

Maier glanced at Knox. "Did he not speak with you?"

"Not in any way that made sense. What did he find?"

"I assumed that's why you came."

Knox realized what Weigel found, and his heart rose into his throat. "Is it . . . " He swallowed hard. "Have you seen it?"

Maier continued his silence.

Knox hit his knee with a fist. "Blast it, man! Do we have proof of what the Nazis were up to or not?"

The sliver of lips curved upward. "I believe your family will finally be vindicated. Fully."

Knox didn't dare believe it.

"Imagine it. All those years of ridicule and mockery will evaporate into nothing but admiration and acclaim once the world learns the truth."

It took a moment for Maier's words to register in Knox's fear-addled brain. When they did, he couldn't help but slump back into the leather seat. His eyes burned. He feared he might cry. "Tell me directly. Is it the lab?"

"You'll see."

"Where is it? Berchtesgaden?"

"Obersalzberg."

Knox took a deep breath. It had to be a lab. Just as they'd always believed. Probably in one of the many bunkers built by the Nazis there. He thought about Weigel's scribbles, pleased his theory was correct. It *was* a map of that area. Knox reached into his pocket, then remembered that the American, Mark Carlson, had taken it right before Knox made his escape. But surely Carlson couldn't figure out Weigel's cryptic notes and symbols.

"Is there something wrong?" Maier asked.

"Not at all." He thought better of mentioning the lost map to Maier. It would only add to Knox's feelings of stupidity and weakness. "What did Weigel say? Did he go inside?"

"He said the lab was boring, an oversized bunker. But it served their purposes, and it will serve ours."

Our purposes. Knox's mind went back to what the inspector had said about Maier and Return to Earth. He still didn't want to believe it. In any event, whatever was in that lab was over a half-century old. It couldn't be of any use now. "Did he find formulas? Chemicals? What?"

"Be patient. You'll see."

Knox thought for a moment. "Why didn't Weigel come straight to me? Why did he go off to Siberia? He could have easily canceled his appearance at that conference."

"I advised him to go."

"Why?"

"So as not to draw unnecessary attention to his activities. If he began canceling this and that, some would have wondered why. Our adversaries would have noticed, and possibly found what he had found."

"What adversaries?"

"Are you so naive?" Maier asked. "Conspiracies operate in two camps. Those who want to prove them and those who want to stop them from being proven."

"I've never experienced a credible threat."

Maier smirked at him condescendingly. "Only because I've protected you. But the stakes are much higher now."

Knox remembered Duerr saying the same thing.

Maier continued with a quick pat on Knox's knee. "I believe you have the wherewithal to keep your head and get through this time. Weigel, sadly, wasn't of the same constitution. He didn't do well under pressure."

Knox considered Maier's words, then cautiously asked, "Did Weigel become sick from what he found?"

"Weigel put himself in harm's way. Think of it as a sacrifice. A sacrifice for *you*."

Knox hadn't thought of it that way. Whatever Weigel had found, whatever he had done, whatever had made him sick: all for their cause. *My family's cause.*

"You owe it to him to keep focused."

"What about that American and the inspector from Interpol? They may figure out where we've gone."

"How could they possibly figure it out?" Maier looked at him.

Knox squirmed without actually moving. He had a feeling

that Maier knew about Weigel's last map. And he probably knew exactly where Carlson and Duerr were at that moment. "They're very clever."

"Yes, they are," Maier said. "Which is why we must stay a step ahead of them."

"How can we do that?"

"By being smarter than they are. When all is said and done, they'll have done just as I've wanted. The more I waste their time, the better it is for us."

"Better *how*? When all *what* is said and done? This endeavor was to prove that the theories are true. What else is there?"

"Don't be so small-minded. There's so much more."

Knox felt as if someone had just stepped on his grave. "Such as?"

Maier shook his head. "As long as you get what you want, what *I* want is of no concern to you."

Is that what it really comes down to? Getting what we want?

"Knox. Are you with me?" Maier's tone was stern and demanding.

"With you? Meaning what?"

"Meaning, can I still count on you?"

Knox paused. He thought of his grandfather and his courage to face the jeers and taunts, to bravely tell the truth to a world that didn't want to know. Would it be his legacy to prove him right, or to have been an unwilling conspirator to something terrible?

His mouth had gone dry. He felt as if his teeth and tongue clicked as he spoke. "The inspector seems to think that you plan to infect the world through whatever was found in that lab. He thinks you've already started, by spreading a virus in Siberia. That's not really your plan, is it?"

Maier laughed. "Do you really want to know, Cornelius? Do you want to involve yourself in my work? Shall I tell you everything?"

Knox knew this was a decisive moment. One on which he'd look back with pride or with regret. Which would it be? The question hung between them like a pall of smoke.

Maier took Knox's silence as an answer. "I'm hungry. Let's

find a restaurant, shall we? Something vegetarian, if you don't mind. I can't stand the smell of cooked meat."

"Shouldn't we get to where we're going?"

"We have time. I want them to get there ahead of us."

"*What?* Why would you want that?"

"So they'll catch you when you arrive."

Knox gasped. "What's the point of my escaping if only to get caught again?"

Maier sounded fatigued, as if he were explaining the obvious to a small child. "I have yet to tell you the next part of the plan."

Knox listened to Maier talk and his feelings of nausea returned.

As they pulled into a restaurant, Knox recalled that Hitler was a vegetarian, too.

CHAPTER 24

NOVOSIBIRSK, SIBERIA

SUSAN WALKED TO her office and was surprised by the armed guard standing at her door. He looked at her indifferently, then nodded for her to enter. Anton took a step to follow, but the guard blocked his way. Anton looked indignant and began arguing with him.

"Dr. Hutchinson," a deep voice growled from inside.

She walked in to see a moonfaced man, with thinning brown hair and the suggestion of a goatee, smiling at her. He wore a black suit and brightly colored tie. He held out his hand. "My name is Dr. Grigory Tarasov. I'm now the health ministry's acting director of this effort."

Susan shook his hand thinking he looked too young to be an acting director of anything, let alone this crisis.

He moved around her and closed the door on the argument outside. Anton looked helplessly at Susan before disappearing from view.

"Dr. Hutchinson," he began, as his voice softened. "I've admired you for many years, especially your groundbreaking work on identifying and stopping the Gabon virus. An Ebola epidemic, yes?"

Susan blushed. "Actually, Dr. Tarasov—"

"Grigory is fine."

"Well, actually, Grigory, lots of great people worked on my team. They are the ones who deserve the credit. Not to mention the incredible lab work done in the United States and England."

He smiled warmly. "I think you're not taking the credit you are due. We followed the Gabon virus investigation very, very carefully."

"Thank you," she said, and wondered where this was leading.

"Nevertheless, I'm a little concerned about your rather un-orthodox activities here in Siberia."

"Unorthodox?"

"Interrogating our citizens without our knowledge or con-sent."

She glared at him and tried to remain calm. "Doctor, the work of an epidemiologist, by definition, requires interviewing victims and their families."

"We *don't* condone the term *victim*," he said, the smile never leaving. "Perhaps *patient* would be more appropriate."

Her face flushed. "Perhaps *corpses* would be better still, Doctor. People are dying and I'm here to find out why. Other-wise, there will be more deaths than you can imagine."

He tipped his head as if considering a specimen in a jar. "I understand. But I must insist that in *our* country, you follow *our* rules. That would be proper WHO protocol, eh?"

She didn't reply. He was right. And that made her angrier. "Rules or not, a local authority has never before attempted to re-strict the potentially lifesaving work I was sent to do. I've han-dled cases in more than two dozen countries—many of them more primitive than yours. Though I'm beginning to wonder."

He frowned. "If you choose not to comply, then it's within my power to deport you and your team. Do I make myself clear?"

She nodded. "Aren't you even the slightest bit interested in what we are investigating—or do you already know?"

"Inform me."

"The virus may be waterborne."

"Waterborne?"

"We've learned that shipments have been made to Akademgoro-dok by a terrorist organization; these shipments may have been used to contaminate the new water-treatment plant there with a virus similar or identical to the 1918 Spanish flu."

"Where did you get this information? What terrorist organi-zation?"

"Interpol—and the terrorists call themselves Return to Earth. I'll gather the details for you. But we believe it's worth investi-gating."

"I know what you're suggesting, but I think it's a waste of time," Grigory said.

"I have to disagree."

Grigory gave her a smug look. "Dr. Hutchinson, we are aware of the many conspiracy theories about the weaponization in World War I of the influenza virus, but I and my researchers have discredited these theories. They are delusions proliferated only by the insane. Believe me, if the 1918 virus could be weaponized, we would know about it. There is simply no way that a terrorist organization has accomplished what you suggest."

"But you are aware that employees at the water-treatment plant fell ill *before* Dr. Weigel arrived?"

"We are convinced those people died from a different virus," Grigory said dismissively.

"A *different* virus?"

"The autopsies and testing are ongoing, but thus far there's no convincing evidence that it's the same virus."

"All the same, I'd like permission to continue our investigation."

"Leave it with us," Grigory said.

"Does that mean you'll investigate it, or push it aside?"

The answer was in his passive expression. "I'm meeting with my team in half an hour. I would like you to be there."

Susan glanced at the clock. "This late?"

"This is an emergency, isn't it?"

She nodded.

"Then I'll see you there."

After Grigory and his bodyguard left, Anton entered the office and closed the door. He looked troubled, but said brightly, "Dr. Grigory Tarasov. What a great choice to head up this work."

He circled his finger in the air. Bugs, he mouthed. He gestured for her to follow him.

They walked into the outer office, now empty, and Anton turned to a door on the right. It was a storage closet, filled with office supplies. Once they had entered, he turned on a single bulb and closed the door.

"Bug free," he said.

"Okay, so tell me about Dr. Tarasov."

"Don't let his schoolboy looks fool you. He's got a heart of iron and a conscience of ice."

"I don't mind that, if he knows what he's doing. What's his background?"

"Until recently, he was a fellow and chief researcher at Jotham."

"Jotham?" She had heard of Jotham, but only through a variety of unofficial reports and industry gossip she had picked up over the years. It was notorious for the development of viral and biological weaponry during the cold war. Until the fall of the Soviet Union, few Russian officials ever admitted its existence. "Tell me about it."

"Big. Top secret. Scary."

"You have to be more specific."

"Jotham is the State Research Center of Virology and Bio-technology that links the Scientific Research Institute of Molecular Biology, and the Design Institute of Biologically Active Substances. In essence, the Jotham campus is the industrial production facility for the region."

"That must be a large lab."

"Not one lab, more than a hundred. They've got everything there including a large, isolated virology-research campus. Dr. Tarasov worked in what is called 'Building Number 6,' one of the largest and best-designed virology labs in the world. State-of-the-art. It makes Biosafety Level-4 labs look like outhouses. The lab has advanced maintenance and biocontainment systems, each designed to exclude any possibility of infectious material invading either the work space or outside environment."

"Great," she said. "So Dr. Tarasov worked with Jotham. How does that tie into our problem here?"

Anton glanced at the door, as if expecting someone to yank it open. "Maybe I should mention the lab's work loading the Marburg virus into special long-range missile warheads. Or the warheads they supposedly created that contained smallpox, bubonic plague, and anthrax. Or that Iran actively courted the lab to enhance its biological capabilities."

"Maybe you should have mentioned that first," she said. "So, whose side is Grigory on?"

"That's the prevailing question."

"Does Duerr know about this?"

Anton shrugged. "How would I know?"

She frowned at him. "Where is the facility?"

"Maybe thirty kilometers from here."

"I want to see it."

"Not a chance."

"Try."

He smiled at her. "You want to get into the water-treatment plant and now Jotham as well. Who do you think I am—Superman?"

"Yes."

He sighed. "Let me go get my cape."

Susan looked at her watch. "Later. Right now we have to go into the lion's den."

CHAPTER 25

BERCHTESGADEN, GERMANY

THE TRAIN TO Berchtesgaden climbed the gentle grade, with an occasional loud whistle as if to alert the fir-covered inclines that humanity was coming yet again to revel in their beauty. Mark sat at the window and lost himself in the green forests and mountains, some thrusting dramatically up from the ground, their naked tops exposing deep cliffs and crags. The higher peaks were covered in snow. The majestic Mount Watzmann, with its horned head, watched over the train's approach to the town center.

Mark fingered an area brochure he'd found stuffed in a seat pocket. For just a few moments, it was easy to forget why he was there. He could be a tourist coming to see the salt mines or the ancient marketplace. Quaint shops, beautiful countryside. Who wanted to think about sickness and death in a place like this?

The train pulled into town. Snuggled into the shoulders of surrounding hillsides, it boasted a collection of Bavarian styles, both traditional and modern, with A-frames and shuttered windows. He thought sections of it looked like something from *Hansel and Gretel*. Mark emerged from the station and spotted Duerr waiting in a navy blue Citroën. As Mark climbed into the vehicle, Duerr nodded and pulled away.

"Is there any chance you grabbed my things from the hotel?" Mark asked.

"Everything's in the back."

"Thanks. I'll be needing my lederhosen for the yodeling concert later."

Duerr smirked. "No time. We have to figure out where Knox has gone, and with whom."

"As a wild guess, I'd say he's with Stefan Maier and they're off to Obersalzberg."

"Why there?"

Mark explained what he'd learned about the area from the young man on the train. He took out Weigel's scribbles and explained his theory about them. "Unless you have a better idea, I think that's where they've gone."

The drive from Berchtesgaden took them up winding roads through forests of beech and maple, leaves long fallen, and lush groves of evergreen trees. The forests moved aside to give them gorgeous views of the rolling hills, houses, and town below. Mark mused about Hitler's attraction to the area. No doubt it deeply inspired him while he planned to kill non-Aryans and rule the world.

"What are we looking for?" Duerr asked. "Can you make out anything else from Weigel's map?"

Mark scoured the drawing again. "If I'm right, then we're looking for something that looks like a bush, or maybe it's a tree, and there's a weeping willow kind of thing or maybe it's a bird—"

"An eagle?"

"Could be." Mark grunted. "Weigel obviously went to an impressionistic school of drawing."

"What else?" Duerr sounded exasperated.

"Some squiggly lines and a boxy-looking thing and—"

"This is of no help whatsoever."

"We need help," Mark said. "Someone with information about this area when it was occupied by Nazis."

"Who, for example?"

Mark took out his phone and hit the speed dial. The phone rang three times and was engaged on the fourth.

"Hello?"

"Hey, Georgina."

"Hi, Mark."

"Where are you?"

"Somewhere in Berlin. The home of Weigel's secretary. I'm going through Weigel's files."

"Anything interesting?"

"Not yet."

"Can you dig up some information for me about Obersalz-berg—Nazi period? I've got what I think is a crudely drawn map, but I don't know enough to make sense of it."

"Send me the map."

"Honestly, it's a mess. Hardly a map at all."

"Send it anyway. I've got a professor buddy who's a remote-sensing and image-processing expert in Colorado."

"A what?"

"His computer can take a hand-drawn map and compare it to satellite reconnaissance imagery. He'll take whatever it is and place it on a grid with a proper map."

"Are you serious?"

"He's found all sorts of stuff—including the possible location in Iran of the remains of Noah's Ark. He is brilliant, but not a lot of fun on a date."

Mark looked at the scribbles in his hand. "How do I get this to you?"

"You could use the camera on your cell phone."

"I'll try."

Mark took a photo of the paper and sent it to Georgina's phone. A moment later she called back. "You weren't kidding. It's a mess."

"Sorry."

"Are you anywhere near a proper scanner or fax?"

Mark remembered from the brochure on the train that the Hotel Big House or something like that was in the area. "I'll find a hotel. What number should I use?"

"My eFax phone number. That way I'll be able to e-mail the electronic file to my friend."

"You'll have it as soon as I can get it to you."

They hung up and Mark turned to Duerr, who preempted him by saying, "There are two hotels in the area of Hitler's hide-away. The InterContinental and the Hotel Berghaus."

"The Berghaus." The brochure information came back to Mark. "It's near Hitler's getaway home. Family-run. Modest. Maybe the staff can tell us about the area."

"It should be around the next bend."

Mark held up the map and pointed to a box. "This?"

Duerr glanced at it. "Possibly."

"Slow down," Mark said. "If Weigel is right, we're coming to the bushy-tree-looking thing with some kind of stem protruding from it."

Duerr frowned as he slowed the car. "We've got to work on our terminology."

They reached signs for the InterContinental Hotel & Resort, a circular complex of low-lying, stone-covered buildings. "I hope this map isn't a diagram of Weigel's last vacation plans," Mark said.

"What's this?" Duerr asked as they came to a sliver of a road that ascended to a forest.

"A drive that leads nowhere?"

"It leads to *something*. Is this where your bushy-tree-looking thing is?"

"Uh-huh."

Duerr sped up past the drive. "Let's get to the Berghaus and sort this thing out."

"Are you sure you don't want to stay at the InterContinental?"

"My expense account allows only low-budget hotels."

They took a turn and passed a small guard station—empty since the war. They drove to the hotel, a two-tone building, the upper story a dark brown wood and the lower story painted white. The windows had rust-colored shutters and pots for flowers already gone to sleep for the coming winter. It looked friendly and cozy and, from the parking lot, offered a view of the entire valley—including, to Mark's amusement, the InterContinental Hotel atop a neighboring hill. They parked in the lot and went through the main entrance to the lobby area.

Mark took in the white walls, curved arches over the doorways, small-bulb chandeliers covered by equally small shades, light from the many windows, and dark carpet. Behind the unassuming counter stood a big-eyed blonde who could have easily worn a bustier and served beer somewhere. Maybe she did.

"May I help you?" she asked in English.

Duerr presented his badge. "Do you have a fax machine?"

Her big eyes grew bigger. "Is there something wrong?"

"Not at all. A fax machine, please. We'll pay, of course."

But the badge alarmed the girl. Muttering an apology, she rushed to a rear office. She returned a moment later trailed by a short woman with reddish-blond hair and abundant laugh lines around her sharp, inquisitive eyes.

"I am the owner, Barbara Peschak," the short woman said in a nicotine-saturated voice. "What is it, please?"

Duerr explained what they needed. She looked relieved and guided them to a small office, crammed with filing cabinets, a forlorn-looking computer that barely peered out over a stack of papers, and a fax machine. Mark sent Weigel's drawing off to Georgina.

Frau Peschak invited them to the bar—a narrow room with a handful of tables and a self-service refrigerator—where they learned all about the hotel and were given the tourists' version of the area's history.

Mark listened politely. When the opportunity finally presented itself, Mark showed her Weigel's drawing.

She laughed. "Did a child draw this?"

Mark pointed to one of the little boxes. "I think this is your hotel."

"I suppose so."

Mark pointed to the bush symbol and the line, which he now assumed was the driveway they'd passed. "And this?"

Frau Peschak snorted. "That was *his* place."

"Whose?" Duerr asked.

"Adolf Hitler's. That driveway led to his Berghof."

"His home away from home," Mark said.

She rolled her eyes. "Unfortunately, yes. It was originally a three-bedroom house that Bormann turned into a thirty-room mansion for his master. They took over this entire area and built houses for themselves. They seized this hotel illegally from its original owner, my grandfather. They sent him off to a concentration camp."

"The house is gone now," Duerr said, trying to move her along. "Destroyed by the Allies?"

"Mostly. But what was left became a shrine for neo-Nazis. So the Bavarian government blew up the ruins." She thought about it a moment, as if remembering something from her childhood, then added, "It was on the thirtieth of April, 1952. The anniversary of Hitler's death. Anyway, all that's left is the driveway, a few sidewalls, and some concrete footings."

"How about this?" Mark pointed to the bush symbol itself.

"What is that supposed to be?" she asked.

"A bush? A tree? Was there a plant at the bottom of the driveway?"

She tapped the paper. "Yes. That might be Martin Bormann's tree."

"He had a tree?" Duerr asked. "What was he, a dog?"

She gave him a sympathetic smile, then explained, "Before the war, when Hitler stayed at his Berghof, he used to stand at the end of his driveway and greet the locals and military units. They paraded past for hours and Hitler complained to Bormann about the lack of shade there. Bormann then transported a mature linden from Munich and planted it on the grass near the driveway."

"A linden tree?" Duerr asked. "Never heard of the species."

"I believe it is called lime or basswood in some countries."

"I didn't notice a tree when we drove past," said Duerr.

"It was cut down sometime in the '60s," she said. "There is a stump there. The last time I looked, it had shoots growing from it."

"I hope that isn't symbolic."

"God forbid," she said.

The big-eyed blonde appeared at the table and spoke in German to Frau Peschak.

"Excuse me," Frau Peschak said to Mark and Duerr. "Business summons."

After she had hustled off, Mark turned his attention back to the map. "Why would Weigel draw that tree?"

"*If* that's what he drew. How can you tell?"

Mark shrugged. It was all guesswork. For all he knew, they were on a fool's errand.

His cell phone rang. "Hi," he said to Nora.

"Hi. I got your message. Where are you?"

"The Hotel Berghaus in Obersalzberg. Where are you?"

"On my way to you, if there's still a reason to come. Are you having any success?"

"I'm learning a lot about the Nazis. Whether that has anything to do with our mission, I don't know."

"Should I come or not?"

Mark asked Duerr, "Are we staying here tonight?"

"I suppose so," Duerr said unhappily.

"Yes," Mark said to Nora. "It should take you only a couple of hours. Let's have dinner."

"Looking forward to it," she said.

So am I. Mark hung up and looked at Duerr. "It's been a long time since I've seen a grown man pout."

"Return to Earth could be killing us all and you're making dinner plans."

"We have to eat."

"I understand, but"—he slapped his hand onto Weigel's drawing—"this could be a huge waste of time. The man was out of his mind, after all."

"It's been proven correct, so far. Even if we don't understand it," Mark said. "But if you have a better idea . . ."

"I don't," Duerr snapped. "That's why I'm pouting."

Mark stood. "Let's take a walk."

"To where?"

"Bormann's tree. Maybe we'll find a clue that'll explain Weigel's fascination with it."

They followed the road back to the site of the Berghof. The driveway asphalt was cracked and broken. On the right side, the hill leading to the main road was overrun with bushes. The stump wasn't far up, with shoots reaching out like skeletal fingers.

"Well?" Duerr asked.

They circled the stump. Grass and dirt. No clues.

Duerr stood with his hands shoved into his pockets. Mark looked around and tried to imagine Hitler standing in this very spot, greeting the locals and his soldiers in the shade of the tree. Why was it important to Weigel?

He had an idea and called Georgina.

"I got your map," she said. "My friend is working on it now. He refused to promise success."

"I understand," Mark said. "It's a long shot, but worth trying. Meanwhile, are you still on Weigel's computer?"

"Helene's, yes. Fortunately, she has a lot of Weigel's research. Notes, correspondence, all kinds of things."

"Can you do a word search through all the documents?"

"Sure. What word?"

"*Tree.*"

Georgina was silent for a moment. "Did you say 'tree'?"

"I did."

She chuckled softly. "If you insist."

Mark could hear the clicks of her fingernails on the keyboard. "Narrow it down to the last couple of weeks."

She hummed to herself while the computer did its business. Then she said, "Here's something."

"Go ahead. But I'll put you on speaker so Duerr can also hear." The men drew close around the phone.

"It's in an e-mail," she said. "To Cornelius Knox."

"From when?"

"Two weeks ago. There are only a few lines. 'I'm being careful in case the *unwanteds* penetrate the system. Will tell you more when I see you in London. The key is at the base of the tree. You'll understand shortly.' That's it."

Mark and Duerr circled the stump again. Mark said, "The key is at the base of the tree. Literally? Or does he mean the base of the tree is the key to something?"

More clicking from Georgina's fingernails. "I'm searching the e-mails written around that same time."

"Dig," Duerr said.

"I'm doing my best," Georgina replied.

"Not you—*us.*" Duerr knelt and began clawing at the dirt.

Mark joined him, placing the phone on the stump and attacking the ground on the side opposite Duerr. The ground was hard and cold.

"There's another e-mail from Weigel to Knox, written a couple of days later. But it's not about a key."

"What does it say?" Mark asked.

" 'Ask F.P. for envelope to Philip Barrison.' I don't see that he actually sent this one." She paused. "Who is Philip Barrison?"

"The name doesn't mean anything to me," Mark said.

"That's it. I can't find anything else," Georgina said thinly.

"Neither can we."

"I hope Weigel is laughing, wherever he is," Duerr said.

"You guys get to have all the fun," Georgina said. "Signing off now. Toodles."

"Bye," Mark called out. His eye went to a root that crooked out from the base of the tree like a small arch and disappeared into the earth. He shoved his fingers under the arch and came upon a hollow space, like a small compartment. He felt something smooth and metal inside. "Here's something."

Duerr came around the stump. "What is it?"

Mark had to squeeze his fingers farther down to get ahold of the small, square item. He carefully pulled out a jewelry box.

"Go on," Duerr ordered, his eyes widening in expectation.

Mark opened the box. Inside was a silver key.

CHAPTER 26

NOVOSIBIRSK, SIBERIA

CONSIDERING THE LATE hour, Susan was surprised to see the conference room packed with men and women—all dressed as if they had followed the same bureaucratic dress code. Dark suits for the men, gray jackets and skirts for the women. Only the men's neckties and the women's scarves differentiated their uniforms.

The conversation around the conference table stopped as she and Anton entered.

Anton took her by the elbow and led her to a long buffet table covered with coffee urns, teapots, and water pitchers, along with a selection of hors d'oeuvres.

"What's all this?" Susan whispered to Anton.

"This is fairly by-the-book protocol for visitors," he said softly. "Take something, even if you don't want it."

She filled a cup with coffee and took a small sandwich. She leaned toward Anton again. "Where is Grigory . . . er, Dr. Tarasov? Is he here?"

"He'll make a dramatic entrance after we're seated. Keeping everyone waiting is his power play."

They found their designated places at the end of the conference table and, as if on cue, Grigory strutted in. He shook a few hands and smiled with a politician's ease.

He gave Susan and Anton a cursory hello, then took his place in a large executive chair at the head. The distance from that end of the table to where they were seated seemed enormous.

Anton folded his arms and looked perturbed.

"What's wrong?" Susan quietly asked.

"This is very unusual," he whispered. "Usually, at these types of briefings, we seat our guests directly across from us on the side of the table, so that we might be closer to them."

"He wants us to know our place."

Grigory cleared his throat and the room fell silent. He made a few statements in Russian—preliminary greetings, Anton explained.

Grigory turned his gaze on Susan and Anton and said in English, "I also want to welcome our distinguished guests from the WHO. On behalf of the Ministry of Health in Moscow and the Russian Academy of Medical Sciences, welcome to Russia." He looked around the table and addressed his colleagues. "You'll find their bios in the handout you've been given." Looking back at Susan, he smiled. "Our warmest welcome."

He paused so that the others could politely applaud.

"For their sakes, I will speak in English—since we are better at Dr. Hutchinson's language than she is at ours."

Susan nodded appreciatively.

Grigory continued, "As we now know, the pathogen for the current epidemic is indeed genetically identical to the pathogen for influenza type A, *H1N1*, the Spanish flu of 1918 and 1919. The vector was a visiting genetics professor from Germany. None of our animal-testing programs have identified this virus as coming from an animal source, at least in Siberia. We believe the professor, who has since died, must have brought it here. All the initial victims were in contact with him at the meetings and lectures, or at the hotel and restaurants he visited. Those victims unknowingly spread the virus to their families, friends, and colleagues. We are now publicly declaring a major epidemic."

Finally, Susan thought. She started to raise her hand to mention the water-treatment plant, but Anton seemed to anticipate that and put his hand on her wrist. She looked at him and he shook his head.

Grigory shuffled a few pages in front of him. Susan got the impression he was stalling. "The Novosibirsk epidemic is far worse than we've been led to believe," he admitted. "The clinical attack rates are approaching one hundred percent of not only those exposed to respiratory secretions of the victims, but also those situated in the same rooms without proper respirator-mask protection. Furthermore, the common surgical face mask appears to give little or no protection from the spread of the virus."

Susan could tell from the faces around the room that this information was a surprise to most of them.

Grigory allowed them to settle down. "The case fatality rates are even more alarming. In a normal influenza season here in Siberia, we might see a case fatality rate of one in a thousand—and those deaths are mostly limited to the elderly, those with chronic diseases, and the very young—infants and toddlers. With the current Novosibirsk epidemic, we are seeing a fatality rate of nearly seventy percent."

This was news to Susan. *"Seventy percent!"*

All eyes turned to her.

Anton put a hand on her arm. "Keep calm."

"Dr. Hutchinson?" Grigory seemed surprised at her outburst.

"I'm sorry. We'd heard twenty to fifty percent," she said.

"A shock, to be sure," he said. "Perhaps it is even unparalleled in history."

"That's nothing to be proud of," she muttered as she sat back in her chair. Her mind raced. Things were far worse than she had imagined.

Grigory slowly stood. "Let me be frank about our realities. We have mobilized all possible resources. A call is going out tomorrow morning for all citizens to be immunized immediately. This year's vaccine has H1N1 antigens and we are hoping the vaccine will offer some protection to those not yet exposed. We're exempting only babies younger than six months. And, for those with egg allergies who cannot take the injection, we are providing a nasal-spray vaccine."

"Is this mandatory or voluntary?" a man asked.

"Mandatory," Grigory replied. "In addition, we are starting high-risk individuals on a cocktail of antiviral medications at the start of their symptoms."

"How are you defining *high-risk*?" a woman asked.

"The standard WHO definition," he replied, with a nod to Susan.

Susan asked whether they'd been using oral oseltamivir phosphate, the usual medication stockpiled by countries around the world in case of pandemic influenza. In the United States, the drug was marketed under the brand name Tamiflu. It came in tablet and liquid form, the latter for young children.

Grigory shook his head. "Unfortunately, this virus is resistant to both oseltamivir and rimantadine—one possible reason why the case fatality rates are so high, apart from the obvious virulence."

Susan was alarmed. "Is the virus sensitive to *any* antiviral medication?"

"Fortunately, at least for now, it's sensitive to an older oral antiflu drug called amantadine, and zanamivir—"

"Relenza," Susan interjected, using the name of the drug as it was known in most countries.

"Unfortunately, our government, like many around the world, only purchased Tamiflu in large quantities and we have plenty of it stockpiled. However, we did not buy *any* zanamivir—Relenza—to stockpile."

"Why not?" she asked.

"Because of the expense, and because it cannot be used in people with respiratory disease. And that's problematic with the high levels of smoking-related asthma, chronic obstructive pulmonary disease, chronic bronchitis, and emphysema in our population. With hindsight, we can see what a mistake that was, although in accordance with worldwide practice."

Susan appreciated his candor.

"What's in your antiviral cocktail?"

"We are using both amantadine and osel . . . er, Tamiflu. Our clinicians are finding the combination more effective than the individual drugs, and we're hoping this will prevent the virus from developing additional resistance."

Susan nodded.

Grigory continued, "In addition, I have ordered, effective today, that all citizens are to wear approved N95 respirator face masks when they are out in public. Surgical face masks are to be worn until more of the respirator masks are available. We hope they will be more effective than no facial coverage at all."

"What measures are you taking for those who fall ill?" Susan asked.

"They will be quarantined in their homes with on-call nurses to assist them. The hospital wards will be reserved for only the dire cases, who will be transferred to the hospital in specially equipped ambulances. And, in the hospital, they will be under the best quarantine protocol we can manage."

Susan shook her head. She knew they didn't have the facilities or personnel to fulfill the promises Grigory was making.

As if sensing her doubt, Grigory said, "To that end, I have been in communication with the office of the president of Russia and with the Russian minister of health about the situation. As of today, they are ordering military resources here to assist us. We will also limit noncritical transportation into or out of quarantine zones. Similar measures are being taken in the other affected cities in our region. It is likely officials will be declaring a public-health emergency for all of Russia. In the meantime, we need your assistance, Dr. Hutchinson."

She leaned forward. "What would you like me to do?"

"We'll need a million doses of Relenza and a half million doses of amantadine as soon as possible. In addition, we need at least half a million N95 respirator face masks."

Susan leaned over to Anton. "Better warn the team at headquarters."

Anton nodded. "I'm doing it now." He gestured to his iPhone and began texting.

Susan said, "We'll notify our headquarters immediately. And, with your permission, we'll activate appropriate warnings, work with your team on both press releases and a press conference, and obtain all critical assistance as soon as possible."

"Thank you, Dr. Hutchinson," Grigory said.

Susan decided to press what little advantage she had. "Of course, I will work under your command, but we must have immediate access to significant office space, unmonitored and untapped communications equipment, and security-screened administrative personnel. Is that doable?"

He stiffened, his eyes locking on hers. Susan knew this was a decisive moment and could well determine who'd be calling the shots. "Of course," he said.

"Thank you."

"Each of you is to meet with your teams, determine your needs, and recommend a course of action. Meet me in the main auditorium with your direct reports at nine tomorrow morning. No one is to talk to the press or file *any* Internet reports—including notices on social-media or video websites. Understood?"

Heads nodded around the room.

"You are dismissed."

"May I have a private moment?" Susan asked Grigory as the room cleared.

"As you wish."

"I noticed you didn't mention anything about the virus being waterborne."

"Your *theory* that it is waterborne." He picked up his papers. "I told you that we'll handle it. I won't have you expending valuable time and resources on a rabbit trail."

"Not to be rude, sir. But it is *my* time."

"Put it out of your mind," he said quickly and left the room.

Susan turned to Anton.

Before she could speak, he said, "I know, I know. We have to get to the water-treatment plant."

CHAPTER 27

BERCHTESGADEN, GERMANY

AFTER SECURING ROOMS for the night at the Berghaus, Mark and Duerr went their separate ways: Mark to his room to get cleaned up, Duerr to Berchtesgaden to consult with his police counterparts and get the key analyzed.

The key was nondescript, Mark thought as he showered. It could go to any kind of door or padlock. No brand name or markings. Just a key. Presumably Weigel planted the key under the stump to control who had access to it. He likely didn't want it in the wrong hands if anything happened to him. *Smart man.*

Still, he'd drawn the map for Knox. He must have anticipated that Knox would be able to follow it to the key and to whatever the key opened.

Mark stood in the center of his room, a comfortable square with the basic amenities. The double bed had squeaky bedsprings. A head- and baseboard sported hand-painted florals, and a small table doubled as a desk. The sofa was mere inches larger than the average chair. A large wardrobe stood next to the red curtain covering the bathroom doorway. Another long red curtain covered the two windows on the far wall. No television or other electronics, apart from an old-fashioned phone on the bedside table, accompanied the room. All part of the charm.

He toweled his hair and dressed, changing into a white shirt and jeans.

The hotel phone rang. He picked it up. "This is Mark."

"I'm here," Nora said. "I've just checked in and changed. Are we still on for dinner?"

"You betcha." He immediately felt the stress of the day peel off like an old bandage. "Shall we try the restaurant here? How bad could it be?"

"This is Bavaria. I'm sure it'll be very . . . well, German."

"See you downstairs in a minute." He threw on a sports jacket, checked himself in the mirror, and walked out.

As he passed the front desk, the big-eyed blonde called out to him. "Dr. Carlson?"

He stopped. "Hi."

She came toward him with an envelope. "This fax came in for you." She handed it to him as if it contained vital safety information. "It's from someone named Georgina."

He took the envelope, thanked her, and placed it in the inside pocket of his coat. Before she turned away, he asked, "Restaurant?"

She pointed to the hall and he followed it to a room styled like a Bavarian hunting lodge. Stuffed owls and hawks watched over his entrance from their perches near the ceilings. Artificial vines stretched out from various corners and tangled around the single chandelier. A massive hutch covering the far wall dominated the room. Several square tables were covered in white tablecloths, each with chairs on opposite sides. There was a separate alcove with similar tables and a rounded wall with picturesque windows.

Nora sat at a table in the middle of the alcove. She stood as Mark entered and smiled. She wore a dark blue sweater, black jeans, and black boots.

He felt as if he'd been transported back to high school as feelings of warm affection and insecurity mixed inside him. He nearly blushed. "Hey."

"Hey," she said and reached up to hug him.

He took her embrace, aware of her slight waist beneath the sweater. He kissed her lightly on each cheek.

"Very European, Dr. Carlson," she observed.

They sat across from each other. A waiter appeared with glasses of water and asked them a question in German.

Mark and Nora both replied, "*Sprechen sie Englisch?*" and laughed.

The waiter smirked and nodded. "Yes. If you insist. I asked if you would like anything from the bar."

They opted for two glasses of house Riesling.

After the waiter left, Nora leaned toward Mark. "I talked to Mac on the way here. He hopes you treat your mother better than you treat him. You haven't written, you haven't called . . ."

"What's the news from Siberia? How is Susan holding up?"

"Nobody knows for sure. She's in and out of contact."

"That's unusual for her," Mark said, concerned. "Is she all right?"

"Mac is checking. Or, I should say that *Kevin* is checking. He's paying close attention to the situation."

"I'm sure he is," Mark said. He knew Kevin Maklin was enthralled with Susan, but he wasn't sure how Susan felt in return.

Nora smiled. "He'd go in with a Special Forces unit to invade the whole region if he thought she was in danger."

The waiter returned with their wine. "Are you ready to order?"

"Not just yet," Mark answered as he studied the menu. When he closed it, they toasted each other and sipped the wine. "This is good."

"Hard to beat the Germans at excellent white wines," Nora added.

"So what is Mac saying?"

"The last I heard, outbreaks had erupted in other regions. Japan is suffering a severe shortage of Relenza. So that's a problem."

"Don't they have a stockpile of Tamiflu?" Mark asked.

"They've found the virus is resistant to Tamiflu. Relenza and a couple of the older antivirals are all we have to fight this monster."

Mark turned the stem of his wineglass between his fingers. This was bad news. They had to come up with a better solution. "How are we doing on other fronts? What happened to Digger and that lead coffin?"

"Mac said the exhumation may have been a waste of time. The lead coffin was cracked, so the extracted tissue samples may or may not be useful to us. We'll see. Meanwhile, he's sent Digger to Cambridge to monitor Weigel's autopsy."

Mark felt melancholy at the thought of Weigel lying on a stainless-steel table.

"What have you found here?" Nora asked.

"It's an interesting place. Throw a stone in any direction and you'll hit something the Nazis built and the Allies blew up."

"That's it?"

He shook his head and explained the latest about Weigel's map and the mysterious key. Then he remembered the fax from Georgina and plucked it from his inside jacket pocket. "This came from Georgina."

"What is it?"

He opened the envelope and took out three sheets of paper. He read the first quickly. "I need to check my e-mail for an attached file, if I can access e-mail here. Just in case I can't, she's faxed part of it."

"Part of what?"

"This," he said, angling the page on the table so they both could see it. "A professor friend of Georgina's took Weigel's map and somehow applied it to a grid of a satellite image of this area."

Nora looked at it, then shook her head. "So Weigel wasn't as delirious as we thought. It actually makes sense."

Mark agreed. All the proper landmarks seemed to be represented. Even the squiggly lines were crudely connected to various roads and trails. His eye went to Hitler's driveway. The professor had correctly placed Weigel's tree drawing where it belonged.

"This is us?" Nora asked, and pointed to a small square.

"Not a very good likeness."

She placed a finger on the square, and on something next to it. "What does this little symbol mean? It looks like a chevron."

Mark looked closer. Earlier, he'd assumed it was a slip of the pen. But he realized he could no longer take any of Weigel's lines for granted. "It could be. But it's sideways. Maybe it's an angular letter C or possibly an L."

"L?"

"For *Lab*?"

"Or *Liebfraumilch*?"

Mark noticed a single computer-generated circle around another small square nearby.

"What does that mean?" asked Nora.

He turned to the third page and saw notes from the professor who'd worked on the map. He had reproduced one of Weigel's small squares, enclosed it in the circle, and written, "We can find no correlation for this symbol on any current or historical maps or satellite photos."

"Apparently Weigel found something that Georgina's professor doesn't know about," Mark said, noticing that the mysterious square was positioned between Hitler's house and the rest of the former SS complex.

The waiter returned. Mark took a chance and asked, "Do you know this area?"

"Like the back of my hand."

"How well do you know the back of your hand?" Nora asked.

He smiled at her and held up the backs of his hands. They were tattooed with colorful flowers and vines. "Well enough."

Mark showed him the map and pointed to the circle. "Do you have any idea what is in this area?"

The waiter squinted at the map, muttering to himself as he identified the hotel, the Berghof site, and the other landmarks close by. Finally he grunted and said, "There is a small cement shed there. The Nazis left sheds all over the area to use for the SS guards or to store short-term supplies. It's well hidden, surrounded by trees, and covered in vines. That's the only thing I've seen that fits your map. Now, are you ready to order?"

"I think we are," Mark answered. Nora asked for the scallop and langoustine carpaccio with citrus marinade and caviar. Mark opted to try the Mediterranean loup de mer baked in dill with the artichoke risotto and champagne sauce.

"You will not be disappointed," the waiter said. "Fresh baked bread and dill butter will be out in a moment."

As they talked, other diners, mostly couples, had come into the room, and they chatted in soft tones. The waiter lit candles on each table and dimmed the lights, giving the alcove a more romantic atmosphere. Their conversation gently moved from the business at hand to the friendly, nothing-in-particular variety. Then, after the waiter had taken their dinner plates away, Mark gazed at Nora for a moment. She smiled shyly at him.

He wanted to take her hand. Instead, he clasped his hands under his chin and said, "Talk to me about forgiveness."

Her eyes were bright and alive in the candlelight. "I don't think we should talk about Donna."

"I'm not talking about Donna," Mark said. "I'm talking about forgiveness. In general. As a philosophical idea."

"In that case, I'm all for it," Nora said. "People ought to forgive."

"Why?"

She thought for a moment. "Well, as Christians, we ought to forgive because God is willing to forgive us."

"God is God. He acts and loves and forgives in ways we can't."

"Can't or won't?"

"You think people should forgive *anything*?"

"Why not? Think about the Lord's Prayer. We ask God to forgive us as we forgive others. And remember that Jesus told a parable in which an unmerciful servant, whose master had forgiven him a huge debt, turned around and beat people who owed him much less."

"But here we are in Hitler Central. You think people should forgive Hitler? The Jews should forgive him?"

"I didn't say forgiving is easy. But I believe that when we *don't* forgive, it hurts us more than it hurts the one we can't or won't forgive."

"Interesting. How so?"

"Refusing to forgive leads to bitterness, resentment, even hatred. Those things eat us up inside. They destroy us." She paused, then added, "You know that better than most."

Mark nodded. After the death of his daughter, he spent the ensuing years blaming himself for what happened. Only recently had he come to believe he could let go of all the self-loathing he'd poured into his heart.

"This is where it gets personal," she said. Her hands, which were resting on the table, moved, her fingers touching the cloth. For a moment, he thought she might reach out to take his hands. She didn't. "You couldn't forgive yourself for the death of your daughter. Remember what that did to you inside. And think now

how much healthier you are because you've accepted God's forgiveness and have begun the process of forgiving yourself."

He let her words settle in his mind and marveled at the simplicity of her faith. It seemed so innocent and childlike. "I think I
can forgive Donna," he admitted. "But, to tell you the truth, I'm
afraid."

"Afraid of what?"

"Afraid that she'll use my forgiveness against me. That she'll
play me as a sucker, the way she has over the past few years."

"Isn't that the risk of forgiveness? Don't we do the same
thing with God? He lavishly offers us grace and forgiveness and
we play it, take it for granted, even use it as an excuse to do what
we know we shouldn't."

"But it's more than that . . ." Mark faltered.

"What?"

"If I forgive her, do I have to get back together with her?"

Nora averted her gaze. "I don't know."

He decided to put his true concern out there, for better or
worse. "If I forgive her, do I lose any chance with you?"

Her eyes came back to his. They flickered between helplessness and determination. "I won't get in the way of your doing the
right thing. I *won't*. That's why I don't think we should talk
about this anymore."

The waiter brought their coffee. An awkward silence came
with it. Mark joked and attempted to talk about other things, but
they were little boats thrown against the rocks by the waves of
emotion he'd created.

They walked up the stairs together and continued down the
long hall side by side. They came to her room first. Mark paused
and struggled with saying good night.

She turned away from him to open her door, and seemed to
be struggling, as well. She faced him again with tears in her eyes.

"Nora," he said softly.

"You don't know what you're doing to me," she said, her lips
trembling.

He took her face in his hands. "I'm sorry. I'm not trying
to . . ." He had no idea what he was saying so he did the only
thing he could think to do. He kissed her.

He thought it would be a quick kiss, was sure she would push him away, but she allowed his lips to stay on hers and, to his surprise, leaned into him. He pulled her closer and thought that of all the kisses he'd ever had, this was the saddest, and most beautiful and intimate.

But her words came back to him. He didn't want to hurt or confuse her. At this moment, in this kiss, he knew he loved her too much for that. He pulled back.

She looked up at him, her eyes still moist. She said nothing, but pushed the door to her room open. Her upturned face, the sweetness of her expression, drew him back again. He was willing to forget her words, to forget everything, for another kiss. He took a step toward her.

A loud thump in the stairwell caught their attention. A man emerged into the hall, tugging a small wheeled suitcase, swearing at it with an English accent. The man stopped and looked at them in astonishment.

Mark's own shock followed. "Hello, Cornelius."

He kept his eyes on them and groaned. "This is absurd."

"An impressive coincidence." Mark readied himself in case Knox bolted again.

"Weigel's map?" Knox asked.

"Yes," Mark said. "You should have taken it back before running away."

Knox sighed. "One can't think of everything."

"I guess not. But I'll say this: You're in good shape for a man of your age."

"Thank you." He nodded to Nora. "Will you introduce us, please?"

"This is my colleague, Dr. Nora Richards."

He bowed slightly.

"I'll put on my running shoes," Nora said. "I think you've worn Mark out."

"I'm not running anywhere now." He spread his hands in submission and appeared contrite. "I surrender."

Mark didn't believe him.

"Anyone for a nightcap?" Knox asked.

PART NINE

Early September
1944

CHAPTER 28

LONDON, ENGLAND

PHILIP EDWARD KNOX stood frozen at the rear doorway of the empty pub, his hand on the doorknob. The clock may have ticked off a mere second, but it felt much longer and was long enough for him to see the face of the man with the gun trained on him. The face was narrow, skeletal. A red scar marked the gunman's right cheek. He fired and the wood on the door frame splintered.

Knox was startled to action. With the leather satchel clutched to his chest, he threw himself out the door, falling and crashing into a collection of rubbish bins. The air was filled with the stench of old food and alcohol. Bottles broke around him. On his knees, he kicked back at the door, slamming it shut.

He clawed his way to his feet and tried to get his bearings. The sunlight, a harsh contrast to the darkness of the pub, blinded him. Guessing that the man would throw open the door, Knox hastily pushed the rubbish bins against it, causing more bottles to smash to the ground.

He was at the dead end of an alley. Knox ran like a madman to a narrow road lined with parked cars. Not a person in sight.

The Terminus in Lambeth. Which way was that?

Behind him, the pub door banged against the rubbish bins. The assailant was pushing his way through. Once outside, he spotted Knox, raised the pistol to fire, and stepped forward.

Knox dashed to the left and heard behind him the sound of breaking glass and shouts of pain. He assumed the man tripped and had fallen on the broken glass.

Good, Knox thought as he ran toward the sounds of traffic.

Knox reached a main road filled with cars, buses, and pedestrians. He was relieved, but had no idea what road he was on; all street signs had been removed earlier in the war to confuse the Germans if they ever invaded. The roof of Waterloo Station loomed over the buildings up ahead, giving him some idea of his whereabouts. He looked back—no sign of his pursuer. Through the scattered pedestrians, he spotted a police constable standing on the corner a block away.

Relief again came over him. He rushed along the curb and reached the constable, breathless and flustered. "A shooting," he gasped.

The constable, a tall, barrel-chested man, eyed him. "What's that?"

"The Rose pub—around the corner."

"Pubs aren't open," he said, as if that alone settled the matter. The constable looked him up and down. "Looks like you've already had a few too many as it is."

"Don't be a fool! I'm telling you—"

The constable leaned close. "Listen to me, *mate*—"

That was all he was able to say before the shot rang out. It could have been the backfire of a car, but Knox knew better. The constable straightened, as if he, too, knew the sound. His eyes widened at something over Knox's shoulder. Knox spun. His pursuer was pushing through the crowd, arm outstretched, gun pointed at them.

The constable stepped forward, his hand held up as if stopping a line of traffic. "All right now—"

Another shot. People shouted and screamed and the constable staggered back, his hands clutching at his chest.

Knox ran.

The Terminus Hotel was a mile from Waterloo Station, down Kennington Road—or so stated an advertisement stuck to the side of a building. Knox weaved and dodged through people, over crosswalks, down side streets, hoping he'd lose the gunman somewhere behind him. A red awning with gold lettering announcing the Terminus Hotel appeared like an old friend just ahead.

Was it possible there were other intelligence agents inside? He leaped over the two steps leading to the glass revolving doors. Pushing his way in, he sailed through the lobby while keeping an eye on the entrance. He glanced around at the spacious reception area—garishly decorated with Grecian-style pillars and replica Louis XVI period chairs—looking for doors or windows as a way of escape. A monstrous reception desk stood at the far end. To the right a large hallway extended to an elevator and, presumably, rooms beyond. A slender staircase sat to the left of the reception desk.

Knox slipped behind one of the pillars, still watching the street. He hoped the man in the mac had been tackled by the crowd near Waterloo Station. That hope disappeared instantly as his pursuer came into view. He was in a fast stride and appeared to be looking ahead for Knox. He stopped suddenly, lingered on the sidewalk for a moment as he craned his neck, then moved on.

Knox closed his eyes and exhaled. *I am in way over my head.* He looked at his hands. They ached from clutching the leather satchel so tightly. He wondered if this was what the man in the mac was after. Did he want the papers, to kill Knox, or both?

He plucked a handkerchief from his coat pocket and wiped his brow. What should he do?

Call the police. For all he knew, Lillian was still alive and in great pain on the floor of that pub.

Gathering his strength, he walked to the reception desk and rang the small silver bell. A man with a pasted comb-over stepped from a back room, wiping a spot of mustard from the corner of his mouth.

"Yes, sir. How may I help you?" Even as he finished the question, his eyes scanned Knox.

Knox looked down and realized how frightful he looked. His clothes were smudged and stained from his fall into the rubbish bins. He was sure he smelled.

"Do you know a Lillian?"

"We're not that kind of hotel," the clerk said with an indignant sniff.

Knox groaned. "I'm not that kind of man."

He placed the satchel on the counter and the act of releasing it from his grasp made him think. He had to assume that, apart from his own papers, it was filled with classified material. He couldn't risk anyone seeing the papers—or the man in the mac getting the satchel if he happened to return.

"May I have a piece of paper and a pen?" Knox asked.

"Of course." The clerk produced a piece of stationery with the hotel's name and address in gold at the top.

Knox scribbled a note and folded it up. "Envelope?"

"Yes, sir." The clerk gave him an envelope, also identifying the hotel.

Knox wrote a name and address on the envelope, then put the note inside. As an afterthought, he reached into his coat pocket and found his personal calling card. He dropped it into the envelope and sealed it.

The normalcy of the effort helped him calm down. He was breathing steadily again.

The clerk watched him with an inquisitive expression.

Knox dug into his trouser pocket and pulled out a money clip. Releasing a wad of pound notes, he put some with the envelope and slid everything across the counter to the clerk.

The clerk arched an eyebrow. "It's too much money to post a letter, sir."

"I don't want you to post it. I want you to hold on to it until I come back. The money is to ensure that you do."

"All that money for a letter?"

"The letter, and this," Knox said, handing him the satchel. "Under no circumstances are you to open this bag. If you do, I'll know. It's to be kept safe until I return. If I don't return in two days, then it should go to the person I've identified on the envelope. Do you understand? This is of the utmost importance and in the interest of national security."

"National security!" The clerk blinked a few times, then stood straight as if he might salute. "Understood, sir. I'll put them both in the safe in the office."

Knox watched anxiously as the clerk disappeared with the satchel and the envelope. He came back a moment later and looked especially satisfied with himself.

"Will there be anything else?"

Knox nodded. "I would like you to ring the police, please."

The man looked alarmed. "The police? What on earth for?"

"A woman has been shot at the Rose & Thorn pub," he said.

"Shot! With a gun?"

Knox gritted his teeth. "Please, I'd rather explain it to the police. You must phone them immediately."

"Yes, sir. Of course, sir." The man moved a few feet away, his back to Knox. He picked up a receiver and spoke to an operator about placing a call to the police.

For reasons he couldn't have explained, Knox suddenly felt uneasy and turned toward the lobby. Just outside the revolving doors stood the man in the mac, squinting in his direction.

Knox felt as if all the air had been sucked from his body.

"Get down!" Knox shouted.

The clerk stood with the phone to his ear, dumbfounded. "Sir?"

The man in the mac stepped forward, pushing on the revolving door.

"That's the man who shot her!" Knox cried, realizing how exposed they were.

The gunman was now just inside the lobby, and his hand moved to his coat pocket. Knox sprang for the hallway, running as fast as he could.

He heard the clerk shout, but the sound was cut off by the blast of gunfire. Knox didn't look back, but heard heavy footsteps thumping behind him.

Knox raced down the burgundy carpet past gold velvet wallpaper, praying the hallway led somewhere helpful. He found a door at the end of the hall and launched through it. A short metal stairwell greeted him. He followed it down to another door.

Crashing through that door, he landed outside again, facing an open court with loading docks. Footsteps pounded down the stairs. Knox raced toward the mouth of the court.

A motor roared as a van pulled away from a loading dock. With no time to think, Knox dashed to the van's rear bumper and, grabbing the door handle, pulled himself up and balanced precariously on the bumper.

He looked back to see the gunman in the doorway lifting the gun to fire at him. The van jerked to the left, taking the corner onto an adjoining road. The gunman disappeared from view.

The van drove the length of the road and stopped at an intersection. Knox leaped off and moved into the crowds on the pavement. He came alongside a waiting taxi and climbed in.

"Waterloo Station, please."

Knox asked to be let off at the entrance to the Northern line of London's underground railway system. If, by some chance, the man in the mac followed him here, Knox was sure he could lose him in the tunnels below.

After purchasing his ticket home, Knox descended the stairs to a junction of tunnels. A sign indicated that one passageway led to Waterloo Station, and another to the Elephant & Castle line. He opted for the latter.

He strode down more tiled tunnels past the advertisements on the walls, to another flight of stairs that descended to a fork of two more tunnels. He went left and found himself moving against the flow of people coming off an incoming train. A few swore at him. He reached an adjoining tunnel and slid in with a small crowd moving toward the platform for northbound trains heading into the city.

This was truly a dead end. If he hadn't lost the assailant, their final encounter would have taken place here.

Knox heard the sound of a train approaching the platform on the other side of the tunnel.

His heart pounded as he waited and watched the passageway. Voices echoed and bounced off the tiled walls. The distant train started again, the noise fading into the inner recesses of the vast railway network.

Knox braced himself as a man entered the platform area, his nose in a book. Then other travelers—some walking together, others on their own—came into view. They spread out along the length of the platform. Two women dressed smartly in office attire chatted amiably as they came near him.

The train was late. More people entered the platform area, filling the empty spaces. Businessmen. A couple of soldiers. Two young men with a giggling young woman. Knox was surrounded now and felt a greater sense of security. The man in the mac was nowhere to be seen.

A thrust of air blew from the tunnel and into the waiting area. The crowd jostled in anticipation of the incoming train. Knox stepped closer to the edge of the platform and peered at the five-foot drop to the tracks. A mouse scurried along the wall and into a hole. Knox glanced around at the press of people, aware of the sweat matting his hair against his forehead and his shirt against his skin. He felt ill. He saw the train's light flickering in the recesses of the tunnel. The propulsion of air intensified. There was a roar in his ears as the train came closer.

His lungs burned from the oppressive air. He imagined himself getting to the next station and emerging into a fresh breeze. He would find the police and tell a detective everything. If necessary, he would return with them to the pub. He hoped that Lillian, whatever her real name might be, would still be alive.

A hand fell on his shoulder as the roar in his ears grew louder. He wasn't startled since in his heart he knew it would happen—the touch was expected. He turned slightly and looked into the pockmarked face of the man in the mac. The red scar was angry, like a river of lava. He had dark eyes, and the slight upturn to his lips could have been a smile or a sneer.

Knox stiffened, expecting the knife blade in his back. Why not? In this tight crowd, only Knox and his assailant would know.

"Dr. Schmidt sends his best regards," the man in the mac whispered in impeccable English. And yet there was something not quite right about it. The "Schmidt" was a little too precise—too German, in fact.

The light of the oncoming train filled the tunnel. Knox considered screaming to draw attention to his plight. But he'd lived among the English for too long. His sense of self-preservation had been muted by a greater fear of embarrassment. Causing a scene simply wasn't done. He also feared the crowd would panic and someone would get seriously hurt. Why should more suffer because of him?

He felt a blunt pressure against his back. But instead of the sharp stab of a knife, it was the palm of the man's large hand. He pushed Knox with remarkable strength and hooked something that felt like the heel of a shoe around the front of his right ankle.

So that's how it would be done.

Knox felt himself fall headlong into the black grave that was the track for the oncoming train. He turned in the air, reaching upward, and thought how absurd a person must look when falling, having nothing to grab on to, arms flailing stupidly. He thought of his wife and her inevitable "I told you so."

He thought of his son, who would be called home from the Front for his funeral. He heard the blast of the train horn—then nothing at all.

Reverend John Gillingham sat in the front room of the vicarage in Notting Hill and stared at the items in front of him on the coffee table.

"John?" his wife called from the doorway.

He looked at her. Her bright eyes were aglow and her cheeks flushed from her efforts in the garden.

"What are you doing?" she asked. She wiped her hands on the long leather apron she wore for such duties.

"Hello, Wendy," he said, and thought his voice sounded strangely distant.

"I didn't know you'd come back. Did you pick up that package from the hotel?"

"It's the strangest thing," he said. He pushed aside the envelope he'd torn open—the one with his name and address written on it—and held up a calling card and a note. "It's from Philip Knox."

She moved into the room, with a furrowed brow. "Philip Knox? Where have I heard that name recently?"

"He's the man who fell in front of the train the other day." Even as he said it, he realized he couldn't believe it.

"Oh, yes. A terrible accident. You knew him from that—oh, what was it?"

"We were on that war committee a couple of years ago, sanitation in the shelters and all that."

"I remember." She looked closer at the card and the note. "How dismal. The package was from him?"

"Yes. This." He pointed to a leather satchel sitting on the table.

"That's an odd package."

"Indeed. The bag has the initials L.H. inscribed on the flap."

"Those aren't his initials," Wendy observed.

"Clearly not."

"So what's in it? Sanitation reports?"

"I haven't the foggiest," John replied. "And, according to the note, I'm not supposed to look."

"Not look? That makes no sense. Why would he arrange for you to retrieve a package from a hotel and not allow you to see what's in it?"

John shrugged. "I don't know. But look at the name of the hotel."

"The Terminus."

"It's near Waterloo Station."

"Is that significant?"

"A clerk was shot dead there in cold blood. In the middle of the day. Not a witness to be found. The hotel manager told me the clerk had only just phoned the police to report a stabbing or a shooting or something of that nature at a nearby pub. A constable had also been shot in the same area, possibly by the same man."

Wendy frowned. "Oh dear, not a modern-day Jack the Ripper?"

"Let's pray not. Though, curiously, Philip Knox died the same day. I may be holding the last thing he ever wrote."

"Good heavens, John! What does it mean?"

"I wish I knew."

"What are you supposed to do with this bag?"

"He didn't give any instructions about it, except to hold on to it until he came for it."

"Obviously he won't be doing that. What did the manager say?"

"The manager knew nothing about it. He found it in the office safe last night and assumed the murdered clerk put it there. He saw my name on the envelope and rang. I suspect he was disappointed I knew nothing about it."

Wendy lightly touched the leather on the satchel, then drew back. "We shouldn't keep it, John. We must turn it over to the police."

He looked at her aghast. "Absolutely not. I don't want to get in the middle of it. You know how the bishop feels about his clerics and controversy."

"Yes. Of course."

"I'll post a letter to the family. They live in Winchester, I believe."

She sighed. "Whatever you think is best, my love."

The flames licked higher and sparks flew as Margaret Knox threw a handful of papers into the rusted barrel. Lance, one of the servants, stood next to her, holding the box of papers, looking disinterested. It was his way. He never betrayed what he was thinking.

"Am I wrong, Lance?" Margaret asked.

"It's not for me to say, ma'am."

"It is if I ask you."

His dull eyes went to her face. "I have no opinion, ma'am."

The French doors from the study opened and a young man stepped onto the patio. He wore a smoking jacket and light-colored trousers. His hair was slicked back from the bath he'd just had and he looked pink-cheeked and fresh—much as his father did forty years ago. He shoved his hands into the jacket pockets. A carefully folded newspaper was tucked under his arm. He came close, eyeing the barrel and flames.

"So you're doing it," he said, coming closer.

"I thought it was best." She lifted her cheek to him and he kissed it.

"This won't make it go away," he said. He opened the newspaper. "An anonymous source has revealed to the press that Father was the writer Philip Barrison."

"Oh, dear." Margaret swayed a little, feeling as if she might faint.

Nigel reached out to steady her. "Sit down," he said, drawing her to one of the patio chairs.

"No," she said, pulling away from him and returning to the barrel. She grabbed another stack of papers and threw it in. "From a tragic death to a laughingstock. All in the space of a fortnight. How like your father."

Nigel crumpled up the newspaper and added it to the fire. "Don't think about it."

"I can only wonder what this will do to your military career."

He shook his head. "I shouldn't have told you."

"We had an understanding," Margaret complained. "No one was to ever know about his foolish preoccupations. I sometimes believed your father suffered from some form of mental illness. It wouldn't surprise me to learn that he *threw* himself in front of that train."

"We'll never know," Nigel said, then pressed his lips together. They had worried the day would come when the truth would be known about him. Now it was here.

Hermione, one of the servants, appeared at the French doors with a silver tray. On it was a small stack of letters. "Today's post."

"Put it on the desk in the study," Nigel instructed her.

She paused, then took a few steps toward him. "One is marked 'urgent.' Perhaps you'd like to see it now?"

Margaret waved her hand at Nigel. "You deal with it. I can't bear any more bad news."

Hermione presented the letter to Nigel.

He looked at the envelope addressed to the family of Philip Knox, with the word *urgent* in the lower left-hand corner. Nigel opened it and read the letter, then grunted and tossed it onto the tray. "Put it with the rest of the condolences in the study."

"Yes, sir." Hermione did a slight curtsy and returned to the house.

"What was it?" Margaret asked.

"Do you know a vicar in Notting Hill named John Gillingham?"

"No. Why?"

"He claims to have a leather satchel that belonged to Father."

Margaret frowned. "Your father didn't own a leather satchel. He had only a briefcase, which we assumed was stolen from the underground railway platform in the confusion following the accident."

"Then the good vicar must be mistaken," Nigel said.

"Shouldn't we ask after it?"

"I'll get to it eventually. We have more pressing matters to deal with." He frowned and asked, "Did Father have any identifying marks on his briefcase?"

"No. He used it to transport his papers about the German conspiracy and didn't want anyone tracing it back to us."

"Excellent," Nigel said. "I wouldn't want that briefcase to show up and embarrass us any further. God only knows what kind of nonsense he kept in there."

Margaret put a hand on her son's arm. "Don't hate your father, Nigel. He was a good man."

"I don't think I could muster enough emotional effort to hate him," Nigel said. "I am indifferent to him. As he was to me."

"That's not true."

Nigel smiled at her and she felt the sadness behind it. "His life was his work and his work was his life. There was little room for a son in that equation."

She gazed at him silently, wanting to reach out to him—wishing she could have given him a better father, someone strong and sensible like her father was.

Nigel looked at his mother and put his hands on her shoulders. His tone turned somber, beseeching a promise. "Let's never speak of this again."

She embraced him. He spun on his heels and stepped back toward the house.

We won't. But she knew others would.

PART TEN

November 8
Present Day

CHAPTER 29

NOVOSIBIRSK, SIBERIA

SUSAN ATTENDED STAFF briefings at the academy all morning and had to deal with a spate of calls between the WHO director-general and her staff in Geneva. The overall news from doctors caring for flu patients was horrifying.

She sat at her newly organized desk and stared, trying to take in what she'd just heard. She felt overwhelmed and helpless, wishing she were anywhere other than in Siberia. The phone rang and Susan was tempted to ignore it. It rang three, then four times. She relented. "Susan Hutchinson here."

"Susan? It's Kevin."

A friendly voice. She breathed a sigh of relief. "It's so good to hear your voice."

"Susan," he said seriously. "Count to twenty, slowly and firmly."

"What?"

"Trust me," he said.

She didn't understand, but complied.

After she got to twenty, Kevin said, "Good. The techies here tell me your line is clear and secure."

"We were promised we'd be bug free, but I'm glad to have confirmation."

"You sound tired."

"I am. Emotionally, not physically."

"Give me some idea how bad this is."

She sighed. "You won't hear any of this on the news from official personnel. This is strictly confidential."

"Understood."

"The virus is here in Siberia, as well as in Japan, China, and France. Our offices are seeing the same things. Almost all patients are experiencing extreme fevers, with temperatures of 104 or 105 degrees. Violent chills. One WHO clinician reported patients shivering so violently their teeth are breaking. Patients describe their excruciating pain as being in every muscle and bone. Some are using the name "breakbone fever," a name synonymous with the most severe forms of dengue fever, marked by severe contortions due to intense joint and muscle pain. It's that bad."

"Unbelievable," he said.

"Sometimes the pain settles in the abdomen," Susan continued, closing her eyes. "The vomiting is relentless. And they're seeing cases of subcutaneous emphysema."

"What is that?"

"Pockets of air trapped below the skin, from the lungs rupturing during severe coughing. The emphysema starts in the neck and spreads across the entire trunk. One nurse told us that it sounds like Bubble Wrap popping when they turn the patients."

"Good God," Kevin said.

She was venting and knew she should stop. "You don't want to hear this."

"I do. I want to know. What else is happening?"

Susan paused for a moment, then glanced at her notes. "For some reason this flu is settling in the middle ears of many patients. The pus builds so rapidly that the eardrums rupture and the pus pours out. More than half the patients develop severe otitis media. Doctors are dealing with ruptured tympanic membranes. They have implemented a new protocol; if a patient develops ear pain, doctors prophylactically lance the eardrums."

"Ouch," Kevin said—she could envision him wincing.

"What's also striking is the severity of the headaches," Susan said. "Patients say it feels as if their heads are going to split open, as though someone is driving a spike through their eyes or an ax through their foreheads. I heard a report that a young man in Tokyo committed suicide because of his head pain. It seems to start behind the eyes, then becomes unbearable. Some patients have ocular-muscle paralysis; some suffer sudden blindness."

"Are these symptoms temporary? Can they be reversed?"

"We don't know. The flu is also resulting in pneumonia, which comes fast and hard. Virtually every lobe of the lung consolidates with infection and most patients develop ARDS—"

"ARDS?"

"Acute respiratory distress syndrome," Susan explained. "And it develops in some patients in mere hours. The doctors hardly know what to do. They put the patients on ventilators and treat them with one hundred percent oxygen, antibiotics, steroids, antivirals . . ."

"Is it helping?"

"No." Susan slumped in her chair, the feeling of helplessness coming like a wave again. She touched a finger to the pad in front of her and traced the words "Black Death."

"Susan?"

"Some patients' lips, ears, noses, cheeks, tongues, fingers, and toes turn a dark blue, almost black color," she said. "And, if those things weren't bad enough, doctors are saying the blood loss is the worst. Everything from bloody noses to bleeding ears. If patients get subconjunctival hemorrhages, their eyes bleed, which turns the whites of their eyes bright red. A nurse reported seeing blood spurt from patients' noses across the length of their beds. Patients fill emesis basins with blood; it's in their vomit and stools. Women frequently hemorrhage as if they're having miscarriages. It's horrible. Just like the Spanish flu, but more intense. A ramped-up version of the original."

"I saw on the news that, in some cases, patients have gone delirious and stark-raving mad," Kevin said.

"Hospitals are running out of sedatives to keep them calm." She clenched her fists. "The only merciful thing—if you can call it merciful—is that death comes quickly for many patients. We're hearing reports of people perfectly well at six in the morning, dead by nine at night."

She was silent for a moment, the tears coming.

"Susan? Are you still there?"

Her voice betrayed her fight to contain her emotions and quivered. "So far, just today, we've lost four doctors and sixteen nurses. All were completely well at the beginning of their shifts last night. Almost in an instant, they were being placed onto gurneys or hospital beds in agony. Some of them are people I've worked with over the years."

"I'm sorry, Susan," he said. "I wish . . . I wish I could be there for you."

"This helps. Talking to a friend."

"Anytime," he said.

"But you didn't call to hear about all this." She sat up in her chair, forcing her body back into a professional position. "What can I do for you?"

"I have some information for you," he said. "I've talked to the Pentagon and to the CIA."

Susan picked up her pen. "Go ahead."

"You know about the Jotham labs near Novosibirsk."

"What about them?"

"We've learned that in the last year, the compound has been upgraded. It's now ringed by three sophisticated security fences, complete with cameras and motion sensors. We've also learned that besides the viral labs, the facility has a large animal farm for breeding and maintaining pure lines of lab animals for their experiments. They also provide animals—mice, guinea pigs, rabbits, goats, sheep, fowl, monkeys, and gorillas—to other labs all over the world."

"Are they afraid of some *one* getting in, or some *thing* getting out?" Susan asked.

"It gets worse. The CIA believes that Jotham may have a significant stockpile of the H1N1 influenza virus that caused the Spanish flu."

"Really? Where in the world did they get it? Who is working on it?"

"We're trying to find out," he said. "But here's the most interesting part: the rumor is that your pals at Return to Earth may have a lab on the premises."

It took a moment for his statement to register. "That doesn't make sense, Kevin. Why would they partner with the world's largest facility for animal experiments?"

"Because it's secure, and it's the last place anyone would expect them to be," Kevin said.

Susan frowned, trying to think it through. "Wouldn't they want to destroy it?"

"I'm sure that's an option for them. And one we have to take seriously. Who knows what diseases would be unleashed if someone blew up Jotham."

"Does Duerr know about this? He believes Return to Earth shipped something to Akademgorodok prior to the outbreak. And we're checking into an incident that may be related." She wanted to tell him about the water-treatment plant, but knew he'd caution her against going there herself.

"I'll track down Duerr to tell him." He paused, then his voice went quiet. "Please take care of yourself."

She smiled. "I will. Thanks for being such a good listener, Kevin." She hung up, a feeling of warm affection coming over her. But it didn't last. The chill of reality set in again. The work of Return to Earth seemed larger than she'd feared.

It would take an army to get into Jotham, but a water sample from the Akademgorodok water-treatment plant had to be doable. If nothing else, it would help confirm her suspicions and persuade Grigory Tarasov to investigate further.

There was a light knock at the door. It opened and Anton peered in. "Well? Are you ready for a road trip?"

"A road trip?"

"Meet me at the front curb in five minutes. And bring whatever you need to test water."

CHAPTER 30

BERCHTESGADEN, GERMANY

MARK WALKED INTO the hotel dining room and scrutinized the breakfast buffet. In the morning light, the room seemed completely different from its dinner look, as if someone had changed it overnight. The wood seemed pale, the decorations and stuffed animals were less dominating, mere affectations.

The large hutch was less formidable and more attractive. He took a closer look at it and noticed a small sign on the wall nearby. In German, Spanish, and English the sign announced that the hutch was the only piece of prewar furniture left from the original hotel: "It has enjoyed its position on this very wall for over one hundred years."

Mark grunted to sound impressed should someone be nearby, then turned to the dining-room tables. Nora was already seated and eating.

"Good morning," he said, enjoying the look of her first thing in the morning.

Nora buttered her toast and smiled. "Good morning."

"Any sign of the boys?"

"The boys?"

"Knox and Duerr."

Nora laughed. "Not yet. Are you sure Duerr didn't throw Knox in jail?"

Mark sat across from her and remembered the look on Duerr's face when he'd walked in last night and saw the three of them in the bar. "He certainly wanted to. He probably handcuffed Knox to the bathtub in his room. Anything to keep him pinned down while we figure things out."

"At the end of the evening," Mark continued, "Duerr allowed Knox to sleep in his own room, but not without a Berchtesgaden police officer guarding the door. And if the window to Knox's room hadn't been directly over a fifty-foot drop to the hillside below, Duerr would have put an officer there, as well."

Nora bit into her toast. "I feel sorry for Knox."

"I don't." Mark poured himself some coffee from a carafe on the table. "Though I was impressed by the way he seemed to answer our questions, without answering them at all."

"I noticed that, too. He knew Weigel, but not well. He saw the map but doesn't know what it means."

"And he still hasn't admitted that Maier met him at the Freilassing train station."

"Right, Professor Josef Strauss. A colleague," Nora said. "A retired academic who has helped him with his research."

"Sure. I believe it."

"I looked Strauss up on the web. He exists. He's retired and living in a village near Freilassing."

"But the police haven't been able to reach him to confirm Knox's story," said Mark. "How convenient."

Nora took a last bite of egg from her plate. "I noticed that you didn't tell Knox about the key you found under the tree."

"I'd rather let him think we don't know anything about it." Mark drank some of the strong coffee. "Showing him the satellite version of Weigel's map was more than I thought wise."

"It's possible that he doesn't know any more than we do."

"It's possible," Mark said. "But what if he met up with Maier, and Maier knows what Weigel was on to?"

Nora was quiet for a moment. "What if there really is a Nazi lab with a formula or virus that Return to Earth can use? What if they *have* used it in Siberia?"

Mark shook his head, not because he doubted it, but because he feared the damage Return to Earth could do with such a weapon.

"Did you look at Georgina's e-mail?" Nora asked.

"Yeah. She attached the computer-drawn map, but with better resolution. I didn't see anything new." Mark bit into an apricot pastry. "With or without Knox, we have to get to that mysterious shed."

Nora gestured to the doorway leading from the lobby. "Here they come."

Mark turned in time to see Duerr shake the hand of the German police officer who'd stood guard over Knox. The guard nodded and went toward the lobby. Duerr strode into the dining room with Knox following close behind.

Knox had the look of a politician who was about to work the room. "The InterContinental would have a better buffet," he announced as he came up to the table.

"And have more ways for you to escape," Duerr said. He still looked and sounded annoyed.

"How is breakfast?" Knox asked.

"Sit down and find out for yourself," Mark said.

"I'm afraid not," Knox replied, nodding to Duerr. "Inspector Duerr is punishing me. He insists that we get on to our business."

"Did you study Weigel's map?" Nora asked Knox.

"Yes. I agree with your conclusions. That shed is the first thing we must explore."

"If you find it, I want you to look the shed over," Duerr said, "but don't go inside without me. It could be booby-trapped."

"Don't worry. I have no interest in catching any viruses wafting around there," Mark said.

"You're not coming with us?" Nora asked Duerr.

"No," he replied. "I have to meet with the Berchtesgaden police. Maier may have stayed at the InterContinental last night under an assumed name. The desk clerk is reasonably certain he saw a man resembling Maier."

Mark looked to Knox. "Well?"

He shrugged. "As I told you last night, I don't know where Maier is. My research colleague brought me here."

Duerr placed a hand on Mark's shoulder. "May I have a brief word?"

"Sure." Mark got up and followed Duerr into the hallway. He noticed that Knox quickly took his seat and reached for the toast.

Duerr handed Mark Weigel's key. "Take this."

Mark put the key into his trouser pocket.

Duerr then reached into his jacket and brought out a small pistol. "Do you know how to use one of these?"

"More or less."

"I'll hope for more." Duerr leveled his gaze at Mark. "Give Knox room. Play along. Give him just enough rope to hang himself. There's a lot he's not telling us."

"Right."

Duerr managed a half smile. "Call me if you find anything." He turned and moved briskly down the hall.

Mark tucked the pistol into the waistband of his jeans and pulled his sweatshirt over it. He went back to the dining room. Nora and Knox were talking about the assortment of German pastries on the buffet.

"They're too much of everything: flour, filling, sugar," Knox was saying. "The Germans do everything with a heavy hand. Their food, their decorations, their music. Just think about their polkas. And their operas last forever!"

"Don't forget their weapons," Mark said. "Very heavy-handed."

"*Especially* their weapons," Knox agreed. He glanced from Mark to Nora and back again. "I know you don't trust me, and I've given you legitimate cause not to. But remember this: my grandfather spent his life trying to expose the truth about the Germans' experiments."

"This isn't just about your family or some historical conspiracy," Mark said sharply. "People may be dying *right now* because of your pal Maier."

"It's easy enough to prove your good intentions," Nora said with reasoned calm. "Simply tell us the truth."

Knox pushed his chair back and stood. "Let's discover it together."

They retrieved their coats from their rooms and walked down the road from the hotel. Dark clouds were moving in. It was going to rain.

Knox began to talk. "Several days before he went to Novosibirsk, Weigel told me he'd found something amazing. He didn't explain how he'd found it, or what it was exactly, but he was genuinely excited about it. He kept using the word *Liebfrau-milch*—which, of course, got my interest since it was the code name for the Nazis' work with germ warfare."

"Why didn't Weigel give you the details of what he found?" Nora asked. Her hands were pushed into her coat pocket, burrowed there to avoid the chill in the air.

"It was the nature of our relationship," he said. "Perhaps we were unduly paranoid. We always shared our most important finds in person rather than on the phone or through e-mails. We intended to meet in London when he came for that conference. But, as you know, everything went pear-shaped."

"So you really don't know what he found," Mark said.

"I have a pretty good idea," Knox replied. "I've put the pieces together as best as I can, though some of Weigel's conclusions—this map—don't line up with my family's research."

"And what about Maier? Does he know what Weigel found?"

"Maier." Knox repeated the name as if it were a bad omen. "Weigel must have told him. Or shown him. Or he's come here to see for himself. I don't know for sure."

"Then why did Maier meet you at the station?" Mark knew it was a gamble.

Knox paused. "He didn't meet me at the station."

"Oh, that's right. I forgot."

"Even if he had, I don't believe he would have told me much. He's the sort of man who absorbs information but rarely gives any. He gives impressions without giving facts. You converse with him, but later, you realize how little he actually told you." His voice sounded distant, as if he were speaking mostly to himself.

"Then the two of you went to the same school," Mark said.

Knox gave him a wan smile. "I believe Maier plays with information out of a sense of power, of control."

"And you?" Nora asked.

"Fear."

They walked up the driveway to the site of Hitler's Berghof. As they passed the stump of Bormann's tree, Knox didn't break stride or look in its direction. Was it possible he didn't know about the stump, or what had been hidden under it?

Mark returned to their conversation. "If you're afraid of Maier, why are you partners with him?"

"It was a financial arrangement, as I told you. His business and causes have nothing to do with me."

"Now they do," Mark said. "At some point you're going to have to figure out which side you're on."

Knox didn't reply.

They were at the edge of the woods that now overran the foundations of Hitler's home.

Knox shivered. "I don't like to be this close to that man."

A small clearing yielded more tree stumps, though these looked freshly cut. Piles of rubble peered at them through patches of grass. The woods thickened and they saw remnants of walls, a floor, even a few stone steps tucked into the ground.

"This is what Maier wants to do to the world," Nora observed as she sidestepped a chunk of concrete. "Destroy it all and let Mother Nature have her way with whatever might be left."

"Some things deserve to be destroyed," Knox said, his tone dark.

"Are we going the right way?" Mark asked, realizing he'd lost his bearings.

"We go up." Knox walked farther into the woods and along the slope of a rising hill.

Mark took Nora's hand to help steady her as they followed. She looked at him with gratitude but said nothing.

They pressed through the forest. Without specific landmarks, it was difficult for Mark to know if they were headed in the right direction for the shed. Every now and then, Knox would stop, consult the map, look back in the hotel's direction, then continue on.

"How does he know where he's going?" Nora whispered to Mark. "Every time he looks at the map, I get the feeling it's a charade."

"Maybe Maier gave him the details."

"What if this is a trap? What if Maier and his thugs are here?"

"To what end?" Mark asked, though he'd wondered the same

thing. "To take us hostage? No—if they've been here, they've already taken anything of value."

They came upon a hiking path, which they followed for a hundred yards or so. Knox suddenly diverted to the right, moving deeper into the woods.

Mark had a deepening suspicion that Knox might be leading them away from where they should be. He was about to say so to Nora when Knox cried out.

"Here! It's here!"

Knox was only a few yards ahead and seemed to be looking at something, but Mark couldn't see it. He and Nora exchanged glances, then moved forward. As they came closer to Knox, they could see a vine-covered concrete building—small and square and windowless, like a utility shed, made almost invisible by the thick overgrowth and trees surrounding it. The building jutted out of the hill, and there was no way to tell how far into the earth it went.

Knox was wide-eyed, his mouth hanging open. "This is it."

CHAPTER 31

AKADEMGORODOK, SIBERIA

"**LEAVE OR I'LL** call the police," the man said in English, after determining Susan was American.

"There's no need for that," Susan said. She was standing in a small managerial office at the new Akademgorodok water-treatment plant. Everything was gray metal: the desk, the files, the man they were stuck talking to—as if his time in that room had made him part of the furniture. His hair was gray, his suit was gray, his pallor was gray. His name was Gradinski.

"Comrade, listen to me," Anton said. "Let us take a few water samples. Or only one. That's all. What's the harm? And if we're right, you could be a big hero."

"And I could be an unemployed laughingstock," the man said. "Now go away."

Anton argued with him in Russian, and Susan hoped the arguing wouldn't lead to an encounter with the plant's security—or the police. Having slipped down side streets and out-of-the-way roads to get here undetected, she didn't want it all undone by an argument.

Anton winked at her and she wanted to believe he knew what he was doing. She drifted over to a large satellite image hanging on the wall. Small arrows and boxes identified areas around the plant and the surrounding town. Anton shouted. The man shouted back.

Susan spun around to Anton. "All right. We've inconvenienced this man long enough. Let's go."

"Go?" Anton gazed at her. "But—"

"No, Comrade Gradinski is right. It's wrong for us to put him at risk."

"You are a sensible woman, for an American," Gradinski said.

Anton opened his mouth to respond, but Susan touched his arm. "We don't want any trouble."

Anton looked at her unhappily, then nodded. They walked out.

Anton fired up their vehicle, backed up quickly, and screeched out of the parking lot. He followed the winding driveway away from the water plant. He passed the white guard's shack and came to the main road. He stopped and looked at Susan.

"Why did you give up so easily?"

"Plan B."

"What Plan B?"

"Turn right."

"We go left to return to the city."

"Just take a right and drive slowly. There should be a service road nearby on the right."

Anton turned right and gunned the engine.

Susan gripped the seat. *He knows only one speed.*

"A service road to where?" Anton asked.

"If the satellite photo in Gradinski's office is correct, there should be a small shed down that road."

She twisted in the seat to make sure they weren't being followed. No cars were coming their way or lingering back. She faced front again, then shouted, "There!"

Anton applied the brakes and drew up to a small road sandwiched between thick bushes. A sign shouted at them in Russian. "It says 'No Trespassing,'" Anton said.

"Maybe it does and maybe it doesn't," Susan said. "I don't read Russian, so how am I supposed to know what it says?"

Anton gave her a wry glance, then pulled down the unpaved road. They followed it for a quarter mile—which felt more like two miles—and arrived at a small metal building with pipes snaking out the side.

"This must be it," Susan said.

They exited the car into the still, frozen air. Susan could hear an industrial hum coming from inside the building.

"A pumping station?" Anton asked.

She smiled, said, "Hope so," and reached back into the car. She took her sample case from the backseat. "Grab the toolbox from the trunk, will you?"

"What if we get caught?" Anton eyed the road.

"Then you better have a good explanation." She put the sample case on the ground, opened it, and retrieved two pairs of latex gloves. She handed one pair to Anton. "Just to keep the fingerprints to a minimum."

After putting on the gloves and opening the toolbox, Anton used a hammer to break open the lock hanging from the door. As he unbolted, then pried open, the door, he said, "I hope they don't have a silent alarm system in this thing."

"Me, too." Susan stuck her head through the door. She reached in, found a light switch, and turned it on. An overhead fluorescent light fired up.

She dragged in both boxes and surveyed the facility. "Good. It's not only a pumping station, but also has pressure valves. This couldn't be better. But, for safety's sake, let's put on face protection."

"Quickly," Anton said.

Susan handed out eye protection and the respirator face masks. Once they were both properly equipped, Anton used a wrench to open one of the valves. As the clear water began to slowly escape, he smiled.

Anton let the water drain freely for a minute, then Susan collected samples in several glass jars. She handed each jar to Anton, who labeled it, then put it into a protective bag. All were carefully stowed in cushioned slots in the sample case.

"That was easy," she said as she closed the lid.

"Let's get out of here." Anton closed the water valve, then the toolbox, and dashed out the door. Susan followed with the sample case. At the door, she turned to make sure everything was as they had found it.

Her eyes were suddenly drawn to a small red light in the far corner of the building, near the ceiling.

Susan's eyes widened. She decided not to tell Anton about the security camera.

CHAPTER 32

BERCHTESGADEN, GERMANY

THE DOOR TO the cement bunker was held fast by a large silver padlock that bore no company name or logo. Mark and Nora looked at each other while Mark's hand went instinctively to the key in his pocket.

Knox grabbed the padlock and tugged. "Blast!" He lifted the bottom of the lock and looked at the keyhole. "Well, now, don't I feel stupid."

"No key?" Mark asked.

Knox scowled. "Weigel sent me an e-mail about a key, but I didn't take the time to establish what he was talking about. I assumed Weigel would explain it when we saw each other in London. Brilliant. Can either of you think of a way to break a solid steel lock?"

Mark wondered how long to wait before offering the key in his pocket.

Nora answered the question for him. "Go ahead, Mark."

Mark reached into his pocket again and pulled out the key. "Maybe this will work."

Knox looked puzzled. "You put this lock on the door?"

"No," Mark explained. "Weigel's map guided us to the key. It was under a stump along the driveway to the Berghof."

Knox appeared to suddenly put the several pieces together. "Right. Let's hope it's the right key for the right lock."

Mark was about to insert the key into the lock when he thought better of it. "Before we open the shed, we should call Duerr."

"Why?"

"A precaution," Mark said. "We don't know where this leads. There could be biohazardous waste in there."

"Nonsense. Weigel went down there and—"

"And got sick," Nora interjected. "I agree with Mark. We should wait until a team gets here to make sure it's safe."

Knox frowned, turned, and paced a few steps away. He ran his hands through his hair. "I haven't endured all these years to wait for your Inspector Duerr or any other gaggle of European inspectors."

"You haven't endured all these years to behave impulsively at the last moment, either," Mark said.

Like a petulant child, Knox kept his back to them and thrust his hands into his coat pockets.

"Go ahead, Nora."

Nora took out her cell phone and flipped it open.

"Stop," Knox said firmly. He was facing them again, this time with a gun in his hand.

"You're kidding me," Mark said, feeling stupid. Not because Knox had pulled the gun, but because the gun Duerr had given him was tucked under three layers of clothing. There was no getting to it now. "You're turning into such a cliché."

Knox smiled and shrugged.

Nora offered a jaded sigh. "You're making it very hard for me to feel any sympathy for you."

"It's not sympathy I want," he said. "Use the key or I'll be forced to use this."

Mark shrugged and lifted the lock, hoping the key wouldn't work, that it belonged to something else. But the key slid in easily, and the lock clicked open.

"I think Nora should stay here," Mark said. "There's no point in exposing all of us to danger."

"Rubbish," Knox said. "I'm going to keep an eye on you both. Now, let's go."

Mark pulled open the door and stepped inside. The concrete building was just what they'd supposed: a shed. There were metal shelves lining the walls and a small desk and chair, along with empty munitions boxes, empty food canisters, and assorted other boxes, all with German writing, some with swastikas. He quickly looked around for a weapon he might use against Knox, but nothing showed itself, unless he wanted to throw empty tins at the man.

Nora came in behind Mark, and Knox followed her.

"How cozy," Nora said.

"It's an awfully small laboratory," Mark said. "I guess the Nazis didn't put much of a budget behind their efforts."

"This can't be all there is," Knox said. He waved the gun to give directions. "Look around."

Mark and Nora moved in different directions and began searching for clues about the shed's purpose. Knox stamped his feet on the floor, trying to find a hatchway underneath the dirt. Mark also looked for a means to restrain Knox. His gaze drifted to the bottom of a metal shelving unit resting on wheels along the back wall. He grabbed the unit and pulled. It slid noisily away from the wall.

"What's that?" Knox asked, coming closer.

Inset into the wall behind the unit was a large metal door.

"It looks like a freight elevator," Nora said.

Mark lifted the locking handle, then pulled. The door moved to one side. "Score one for you," Mark said to Nora. It was a large freight elevator.

"Inside," Knox said.

"And you think it'll be powered by *what*?" Mark asked.

"Let's push a button and find out."

They stepped into the box. Three sides were covered with protective padded tarp. Attached to the tarps were faded signs in bold German lettering, containing enough exclamation points to scare away the fainthearted. In one corner was a long, vertical rod fastened to the tarp with three rings. Cut into one of the tarps was a square, with a panel behind it. The buttons indicated the shed had only two levels.

On one side of the panel was a small light switch. Mark flicked it up. A dim yellow light came on above them.

Knox closed the door, reached past Mark, and pushed the button to take them down. A mechanism groaned and strained. The elevator lurched, then began its descent. It shook and rattled, the strain of years with little use. Mark couldn't help but be impressed that it still worked. The ride took several minutes, indicating they were some distance down.

The elevator jerked to a halt with a thump. Knox opened the door.

The three of them faced a gaping blackness. The dismal light from the elevator bulb illuminated only a few feet out, revealing a scarred cement floor. Knox stepped into the room and reached to his right—a good guess on his part. Mark heard the loud click of a switch being thrown, and light followed. Slowly at first, a dim glow came from multiple bulbs hanging on stiff wires from a ceiling whose height couldn't be seen clearly in the relative darkness.

As he could see clearer, Mark found himself slack-jawed. The room was enormous, a giant square full of large rectangular tables and stools, covered with test tubes, beakers, and electronic equipment. Tall metal cabinets and desks ran along the walls.

They moved farther inside. Mark could hear Knox breathing. "This is it," Knox said, sounding elated.

As the lights seemed to gather strength and brighten, any joy in the discovery transformed into a gloom as real as the darkness in the room's corners. They weren't the first to discover the shed; someone else had visited this place recently. Desk drawers and cabinets were opened, shelves emptied, and papers scattered on the surfaces and floors below.

Knox moved in among the tables, wandering aimlessly. Any evidence that this was once a laboratory for germ warfare seemed to be gone.

"Congratulations," Nora said. "You've found a ransacked laboratory."

"Your friend Weigel wasn't very tidy about it."

"No," Knox protested. "This wasn't Weigel. It had to be . . ." He didn't finish the sentence.

Mark signaled Nora to stay near the elevator and try to use her cell phone to get Duerr.

Knox drifted to the far end of the room and found another switch. He pushed it up and lights came on inside an enclosure made of steel and thick glass, equal in size to the main lab. A single door led to the center of it.

"What's this?" he called out.

Mark moved toward him. "It may be an early prototype of a biosafe room."

"To be used for germ warfare?" Knox asked hopefully.

"Possibly," Mark said. "Likely."

Knox pointed to an etching in the glass next to the door. *Grippe-Bombe.* "Ha! Look!"

Mark approached the glass. Inside the chamber were circular bays, not unlike the bays in a garage, and square black boxes that looked like old safes. On the back wall were sketches, diagrams, and bomb schematics.

Knox looked around in wonder. "There! Do you see those? This must be the lab where they kept the bombs!"

Mark looked at the empty bays and felt a growing sense of alarm. "Knox, were there bombs in that chamber?"

"I don't know." Knox's eyes stayed glued to the chamber. "Oh, I wish I'd brought a camera. Be a good lad and go back for one."

Mark took a step toward Knox. "Listen to me. Did Weigel confirm there were bombs in here?"

Knox looked at Mark vacantly. "Confirm? Isn't this enough confirmation?"

"Maier and his pals at Return to Earth may have taken the bombs out. Do you understand?"

Knox turned away again, and Mark looked back at Nora. She held up her cell phone and shook her head. No signal.

"This isn't enough," Knox said. "I must have more proof. Formulas, research . . . something. If I show photos of this, people will laugh. It could be a lab anywhere, for anything."

Mark watched him carefully. Knox's voice was rising, growing shrill. He was pacing back and forth in front of the chamber. "Weigel didn't leave me anything. Or Maier took it. That's it! Maier. He double-crossed Weigel . . . and now he's double-crossed *me.*"

"Cornelius," Nora called out. "There may be more evidence in here than you realize. But we must let the authorities in, with the proper equipment, to find it. This place might be not only contaminated, but also booby-trapped by Return to Earth."

"She's right," Mark said. "Let's get back to the surface and get help."

Knox shook his head. "No. I'm not leaving this to them. They'll bury the evidence. They always do. 'Too much scandal, don't bring up the past, nobody cares anymore.' No. If there's any evidence here, I have to find it."

Mark considered the odds of successfully jumping Knox now without someone getting shot. They weren't good. He also considered trying to get to the gun Duerr had given him, but the odds of that seemed about the same.

As if reading his mind, Knox lifted the gun. "You go if you want. Call whomever you like. But I'm not coming up until I've searched the place myself."

Mark backed across the lab to Nora. "Don't be an idiot, Knox. Who knows what Maier has done in here?"

"Go!" Knox ordered.

"Please come with us," Nora said.

Knox waved her away.

Mark took Nora's arm and gently pulled her to the elevator. "We'll take care of him when help comes," he said softly.

"Are those safes?" Knox asked no one, his face near one of the glass walls of the chamber. "They must be. The Nazis would keep information in them."

Mark and Nora were in the elevator now, and Mark watched as Knox stepped toward the door of the chamber.

"Don't open it!" Mark shouted.

Knox wasn't listening. He took hold of the handle.

Nora moved as if she might go back into the lab, but all Mark's instincts screamed at him. He pulled Nora back again and grabbed the elevator door handle, pulling the door closed behind them with all his strength.

The last glimpse he had as the door closed was of Knox pulling the chamber door open.

There was a deafening explosion.

CHAPTER 33

AKADEMGORODOK, SIBERIA

AT NOVOSIBIRSK TOLMACHEVO Airport, Anton showed his credentials to the guard at the VIP security gate. The guard inspected and reinspected the paperwork, then signaled for an escort car to lead them in their vehicle across the tarmac to a small commercial jet.

The WHO had chartered the aircraft to transport personnel and supplies for Susan's field office. A truck and van were already parked next to the jet, and WHO employees were carrying boxes to the van.

Susan got out of the car with the sample case and hurried to Polly Toynbee, a short but fierce woman with a shock of red hair. Her birdlike eyes darted quickly, as if she expected to spy a mouse for her next meal.

"Hello, Polly," Susan said.

"Is this it?" Polly asked, taking the case of water samples.

"Yes. Guard it with your life."

"Don't worry."

"I'll stop worrying when you get this out of Russian airspace."

Polly nodded and climbed the stairs into the jet.

Susan glanced nervously around the tarmac. Anton flashed the headlights and Susan went back to the car and climbed into the passenger seat.

"Well?" he asked. "I hope this was worth it."

"Testing the samples is our only way to prove that the water supply to the new water-treatment plant—and to the conference center at Akademgorodok—is contaminated."

They watched the WHO personnel finish loading the last of the supplies.

"Even if only a few viral particles per trillion parts are still in the water, the WHO contractors will be able to detect and identify them. A genetic analysis of the virus will force your comrades to get off their rear ends and do something."

"Don't be so sure," Anton said.

Customs agents gave a thumbs-up, the doors closed, and a few minutes later, the pilot navigated the jet to the runway. Susan watched it take off, and allowed herself the luxury of relief only when its flashing lights vanished from sight into the darkening sky.

The escort car led them back to the security gate. Anton gave an appreciative salute to the driver and drove to the guard shack. He rolled down his window, but the guard waved them through. Susan noticed it wasn't the same guard who'd allowed them in.

They started down the drive toward the main road when a rusted white van, parked off to the side, lurched toward them. Anton hit the brakes and swore loudly. "Crazy driver!"

The van suddenly swung to one side, skidding to a stop in front of them. A sliding door opened and two large men in ski masks jumped out.

"Back up!" Susan shouted. "Hurry!"

Anton reached down to shift gears, but the guard was at the open window and smashed the butt of a rifle into Anton's forehead.

Anton fell back against the seat, dazed, and the car, still in gear, lurched toward the van. Susan screamed and clawed at her door handle. The car bumped into the van, and the two men came around to her side. They wrenched the door open, grabbed her by the arms, and dragged her to the pavement.

She struggled against them and screamed as loudly as she could. A gloved hand, smelling and tasting of old leather, covered her mouth.

They pulled her toward the van, her knees scraping against the rough blacktop.

Suddenly a gunshot rang out, and the man who had hold of her left arm jerked wildly as he fell backward. Something warm and wet sprayed Susan's face.

At the same moment, an engine roared. A black SUV skidded from the main road, and the driver gunned the vehicle straight at them. Her second captor pulled a gun from a holster under his arm and began firing at the vehicle, the bullets striking the front grille with blue sparks. Susan tried to dive away from him, but he held her arm in a viselike grip. With his free hand, he fired again as he pulled her still closer to the van.

A man leaned out the passenger window of the SUV and aimed a pistol directly at them. Susan shrieked and dropped all her weight down. Her captor tugged at her but then drew back and spun to the ground. Another explosive sound followed as he landed on the pavement with a lifeless thud. Blood poured from his neck and began to form a dark pool around him.

Susan, barely upright, held up her hands as if her palms might ward off any remaining bullets. They shook violently from her fear and shock. The guard next to Anton's car began firing at the SUV, but a gunman inside dispatched him with one shot. The driver of the original van leapt out with his hands clasped to his head. He screamed in Russian and fell to his knees in front of the headlights.

Susan now lay prone on the ground. She squinted, aware of heavy boots against the pavement. Men seemed to be coming from all directions. Guns were cocked and deep voices shouted in Russian. They surrounded the bodies and the driver, who sobbed loudly, pleading.

Someone approached Susan and knelt next to her. He had a weathered face and thick gray hair.

"Dr. Hutchinson." The voice seemed muted as her ears rang from the gunfire.

"I am Detective Rozvensky. Come with me," he said, and held out his hand.

She took it and he drew her onto legs that felt as if they couldn't hold her weight.

CHAPTER 34

BERCHTESGADEN, GERMANY

MARK AND NORA were thrown to the back of the elevator by the rocking concussion. Debris banged and dented the elevator door, which buckled slightly. The yellow light above them went out. The small box quickly filled with smoke.

"Are you all right?" Mark asked Nora, reaching for her. An annoying ringing filled his ears.

"I think so." She sounded far away and muted.

Mark took out his cell phone and flipped it open. The glow from the small screen gave them some light. He punched buttons to increase the light to full power. Nora did the same. In shadows, they looked at each other. Nora had dust in her hair and a scratch on her cheek from her fall.

"We have to get back in there," Mark said, also coughing. He tried to pull the handle on the door. "I've got to get to Knox."

Nora put a hand on his arm. "No. We don't know what's in there. The explosion from the chamber could have unleashed any number of unknown contaminants. We're already at risk."

Mark recognized her good sense and nodded. He pushed at the control buttons, just for good measure. They didn't work. He looked around and spied the rod fastened in the corner. He looked up. At the top of the elevator was a hatchway with an indentation. Using all his strength, he unhinged the rod's fasteners, which hadn't been opened in more than fifty years, and grabbed the rod. One end was shaped like the flat end of a screwdriver. He lifted it, fit the end into the indentation, and turned. The hatchway unlocked. He pushed it up and it swung back on its hinges, banging against the roof of the elevator. Cool air drifted in, giving them relief from the smoke and dust.

"Our way out," he said. "I'll hoist you up."

"Maybe you should go first. I'm not very good at climbing."

"You'll be fine." He interlaced his fingers, making a stirrup of his palms.

She placed her foot in his hands and he lifted her to the hatch. Grabbing hold of the edges, she pulled herself through and sat on the roof, her feet dangling.

"See anything?"

"A steel ladder going up to the surface."

"Those Nazis thought of everything," Mark said. "Go up. I'll follow."

"How?"

It was a good question. He couldn't reach the top of the elevator to pull himself up. There was nothing to climb on, and Nora wouldn't have the strength to pull him up.

He shined his cell phone light around the elevator. An idea came to him. He pressed his hands against the tarp on each wall and hit on something bumpy under the one on the back. He pulled at the tarp with both hands, yanking it from the tacks that held it in place. A small ladder leading to the hatch was hooked to the wall.

"I could have saved my fingers," he said.

Nora peered down at him. "What?"

"I'm coming. You go on."

He listened as she began to climb away. Glancing back at the door, he thought of Knox again. It would be idiotic to go back in there without a protective suit. Who knows what biological agents would be wafting in the air after the explosion?

But all his instincts as a doctor came to him, pouring over his reason. *Knox could be dying. I may be his only chance.*

Mark groaned and prayed that the monoclonal-antibody injection would work. He picked up the rod and shoved it into the elevator door.

• • •

Emergency lights on the walls cast a dull red glow over the debris. A thin veil of smoke clouded the air, and glass glittered all around like small gems. Mark could see well enough to make his way to the glass chamber, the soles of his shoes crunching with every step. The chamber was horribly damaged. Its door was gone, blown from its hinges.

Mark turned in a slow circle and called out for Knox. A low moan came from somewhere nearby. Mark gingerly stepped over an upended table and saw the chamber door lying at an angle. Another low moan. Mark found Knox with his lower body covered by the door, the rest of him coated in brown dust. Blood mixed with the dust on his face. His coat and sleeves were shredded. Streaks of blood soaked through the fabric.

Mark was astounded Knox was alive and could only assume that the door shielded him from the worst of the blast. Pushing the heavy door off, Mark said softly, "Knox."

Another moan.

He knelt next to Knox and tried to assess the extent of the injuries.

Knox's arm was bleeding profusely. Mark looked around, searching for something strong to use as a tourniquet. Finding nothing, he took off his coat, then his sweatshirt, and tore at the sleeves. While he busied himself with that work, a large metal cabinet near the remnants of the glass chamber caught his eye. The blast had moved the cabinet to one side by a few feet, exposing the wall behind and a large door.

Duerr, wearing a biosafe suit and mask, emerged from the elevator, having come down the way Nora went up. He ran to Mark and handed him a respirator face mask. "Here, put this on."

As Mark fitted the mask, Duerr explained that Inspector Barth, a detective with the BKA, had arrived with a team of officers from Berchtesgaden and set up a perimeter around the bunker.

"I want anyone who comes in here to wear a suit—and to get a shot and medication," Mark said.

"Like *you* did?" Duerr remarked.

Another man in a protective suit appeared at the door. Duerr said, "He's an engineer. He has to ensure that the structure is sound enough for the paramedics to enter. You see, some people take precautions before rushing into these things."

"I'm nothing if not an example to all who work with me," Mark said.

Knox had slipped into unconsciousness. His pulse and respiration were reasonably stable, and the bleeding had stopped, but Mark was getting impatient with delays. While the engineer worked out how to get the elevator operating again, the paramedics entered and saw to Knox.

They fastened Knox to a stretcher, put a face mask on him, and locked his body into place with constraints.

"There's a clearing not too far from here," Duerr said. "He'll be airlifted to the hospital in Salzburg. Barth will make certain that a couple of officers go with him."

The lights had come on again. Mark went to the large door that had been hidden behind the cabinet. Duerr came along his right side. Mark felt a punch in his left arm, and Nora glared at him through her protective headgear. "That was a stupid, stupid thing to do."

"You're absolutely right."

Duerr reached up to touch the door, but withdrew his hand. "What is this?"

"It was hidden behind that cabinet. The blast knocked the cabinet away."

"Another booby trap?"

"That's for someone else to figure out. I'm not opening it," Mark said.

"Let's get out of here and let the bomb squad deal with it."

"I assume this country has a hazmat team, as well?"

"They're on their way," Duerr said. He led the way out.

An hour and a half passed before a sergeant cleared them to re-enter without bioprotective gear. The hazmat team found no hazardous biologics or toxic chemicals in the lab, and the bomb squad declared it clear of any more explosives.

The engineer had already turned the lights on inside the un-explored room: more naked bulbs hanging from threadlike wires. The narrow room, dominated by a long row of filing cabinets, smelled of damp, old paper, tobacco, and sweat. Mark opened one of the file drawers, as did Nora and Duerr. Each was filled with brown folders containing typed forms and reports; lines and boxes were filled with names and data.

"I think I know what these are." Duerr looked at Mark and Nora grimly. "Medical files. Results of testing performed by Nazi doctors."

"There must be hundreds of them," Nora said. "I'm going to need Georgina's help. These files may contain test results related to the influenza bomb."

"It could take you months to go through all these."

"Then I'd better get started." She walked out of the room and to the elevator.

"We don't have months," Mark said to Duerr. He walked out to the main lab again and pointed to the chamber. "It's likely there were bombs in there, and I'm sure Return to Earth has taken them."

"Must be small bombs," Duerr said. "The elevator's the only way out."

"Maybe not." Mark went into the chamber past the bays and large, safelike boxes and stopped at the back wall. He tapped. "We need to get this open."

"What are you looking for?" Duerr asked.

Mark moved to the far right side of the wall, where he found a red switch. He pushed it up and, with a loud, grating sound, the wall split in half, one side sliding to the left, the other to the right. The space facing them was high and wide enough to fit an average-sized truck. Lights flickered on to reveal a long tunnel. A ramp.

"Well, of course," Duerr said.

Mark knelt and touched mud on the ramp, some of which was molded into the shape of tire tread. "My guess is that this tread isn't from a 1940s vehicle."

Duerr stepped past him and walked up the ramp. Mark followed.

It stretched a hundred yards, or so it seemed to Mark. They reached another switch, which opened a large door. It took both of them to lift it until it latched into place. They stood before a thick curtain of faux foliage. Mark looked to the right and discovered a rope. He pulled on it and the foliage lifted like a set of blinds. When it was high enough for them to slip under, Mark wrapped the rope around a hook that had been installed for that purpose.

From where they stood, they could see a newly formed path that curved through the overgrowth to the main road. A vehicle had driven on it recently.

"I don't think I've felt panic until now," Duerr said.

CHAPTER 35

NOVOSIBIRSK, SIBERIA

SUSAN HAD BEEN taken to the detectives' lounge—an assembly of folding tables and chairs—and was sipping on a dark, bitter, but welcome, cup of instant coffee, when Anton appeared at the door. He had a bandage above his left eye.

"How are you bearing up?" he asked.

"Define 'bearing up,'" she said with a wan smile. She ached all over and her knees were rubbed raw from having been dragged across the blacktop.

Anton pulled back a chair and sat next to her. "Detective Rozvensky has filled me in on what happened."

She replayed it all in her mind. The confusion and chaos had scared her nearly to death and the residual feelings clung to her now. "Who were they?"

"Return to Earth."

"And what were they going to do with me?" She wrapped her arms around herself to keep from shivering, though the room wasn't cold.

"Rozvensky is interrogating the driver of the van to find out. The detective is thrilled to be the first police officer in the world to have captured a Return to Earth agent, by the way."

"I'm glad to have helped." Susan wondered if Duerr knew about this. "Were they planning to execute me?"

"It looks more like attempted kidnapping." Anton touched his bandage. "Otherwise I wouldn't be wearing this and we wouldn't be having this conversation."

Susan thought for a moment. "How did Rozvensky know about their plot?"

"He had his people following us. And they saw that we were also being followed by Return to Earth."

"We were being followed by two different groups?"

"It would seem so. Though it sounds like overkill to me. They should have shared a car and saved on petrol."

Susan smiled.

"The police followed our tails to the water-treatment plant and to the pumping station. They saw everything we were doing."

"Why didn't they take action earlier?"

"Rozvensky wanted to see what Return to Earth was up to. He let it play out so he could catch them in the act."

"He used us as bait?"

Anton nodded.

Indignation rose in her chest. "Bait!" But her anger dissipated almost as quickly as it came, and she slumped in sullen silence. She felt sick. The whole thing could have gone terribly wrong, and she'd have been killed—or in the clutches of Return to Earth. She slowly brought the coffee to her lips and drank as she struggled with feelings of both indignation and relief. After a moment, she asked, "Why kidnap me?"

He shrugged. "Apparently we were getting close to something they didn't want us to find."

The door to the lounge opened and a woman in uniform held it open as two young men in civilian clothes entered. The woman spoke to Anton in Russian, then stepped out again.

Anton stood. "Dr. Hutchinson, may I introduce Corporal Jankowski and PFC Youngman."

"Who are they?" Susan asked, her mind still spinning from all that Anton just told her.

The corporal stepped forward. "We are with the U.S. Army, ma'am."

She was surprised and looked them over, doubting that was possible. "But you aren't dressed like soldiers."

The corporal nodded awkwardly and gestured to his dress trousers, white shirt, and overcoat. "The colonel thought the Russians might resent our showing up in uniform. So we're undercover."

"Colonel who?"

"Colonel Kevin Maklin from The Hague. He sent us here to escort you."

"Kevin sent you?" She felt as if he'd sent flowers.

Jankowski continued: "Our squad is here to protect you and the rest of the WHO team."

"We've been assigned to TSI activities in the past," added Youngman.

"The last mission in Eyam," Jankowski said.

Susan remembered the report about Eyam. "Several soldiers were wounded by a sniper."

"Only flesh wounds," Jankowski said. "Shall we go?"

"We're leaving?"

"Unless you'd rather stay," said Anton.

Susan painfully rose to her feet. "Where are we going?"

"Rozvensky has given us the okay to take you to a safe house. Privates Westcott and Brainerd should have it secured by the time we get there."

Susan turned to Anton. "Safe house? What safe house?"

"I'll explain on the way."

CHAPTER 36

BERCHTESGADEN, GERMANY

MARK STOOD AT the edge of the tunnel and watched as Duerr went about the business of being a police officer. Duerr worked with Inspector Edmund Barth from the BKA, who coordinated forensic efforts with the local police authority. Duerr gave Barth the case background, listing the players and concerns. Mark filled in missing details when asked.

Officers of various ranks and positions crawled over the area—in the tunnel, in the lab, even in the surrounding forest. They worked with silent efficiency, with only an occasional whisper as unobtrusive as a breeze in the pines.

After a while, Duerr began to pace, his head down. Every now and then he would look up at the sky, as if his scowl could keep away the rain or stop the sun from setting. The clouds in the iron-gray sky scowled back.

Barth stood a few yards from them as molds of tire treads were taken from the dirt outside the transportation tunnel. He'd already taken digital photographs—at that moment being matched to national databases—but claimed to be old-fashioned and want physical representations as well. "I'm like the doctor who prefers a traditional thermometer to the new digital types," he explained. He ordered the molds rushed off for analysis.

He turned to Duerr and Mark. "An educated guess. The truck was probably a freight vehicle, large enough to carry a substantial amount of weight." He was a tall, beak-nosed man with a firm mouth and tired eyes. He had a shaggy mop of blond hair, which he kept running his fingers through. He wore a dark suit and black overcoat.

Duerr studied the tracks at his feet. "Could it carry a conventional-size bomb from the Second World War, or two or three?"

"Maybe one. Do you believe there were more?"

"We don't know," Mark said. "We're assuming everything."

Barth looked at Duerr. "Do we have a date when the truck was here?"

"Sometime within the last two or three weeks."

Barth grunted. "That long ago? You're fortunate to have any track marks at all, with the rain we've had lately. But it looks as though the driver attempted to cover his tracks with brush and leaves. That helped us. We still need to narrow down the time frame."

"We're guessing it was the last week of October, based on Weigel's appearance at a conference in Siberia," Duerr said.

"If Weigel was here, where did he stay?" Barth asked.

Mark and Duerr looked at each other. Mark thought Duerr blushed ever so slightly.

"We've been so preoccupied with Knox we didn't ask about Weigel," Mark said.

Duerr shook his head. "I'm slipping up with my detective work."

"Unless Weigel had a private residence here, he must have stayed either at the Hotel Berghaus or the InterContinental," Barth said. "Leave it with me." He drifted off with his cell phone to his ear.

Duerr groaned and slapped his palm against his forehead.

"So, we pick a date when the truck was here—then what?" Mark asked.

"If we can pinpoint a day and time, we may be able to use traffic-camera tapes to identify the truck and its traveling directions," said Duerr.

"Are there that many cameras?"

"More than enough."

Mark felt someone lingering nearby and caught the eye of a local police officer. He was fresh-faced, possibly a new recruit. "If you'll pardon me," he said as he came closer.

"Yes?" Duerr asked.

"It may be unrelated, but something came to mind about a truck."

"What of it?" Duerr asked.

"I was on duty a couple of weeks ago, an afternoon, when we received a complaint from a driver who was nearly run off the road by a truck. It happened on the main road, just around the bend heading back toward Berchtesgaden."

"Oh?"

"The driver was very upset by the incident," the young officer continued. "She came in to our station to lodge a formal complaint."

"Did she give you a description of the truck?"

"Yes. That's why I remember it. It was oversized and gray, without company markings. That's unusual."

"Why is that unusual?" Mark asked.

"Since better roads exist to get across country, trucks don't come to this area unless they're making specific deliveries from Salzburg or Munich to the hotels and smaller businesses. Those trucks are usually identifiable with a company logo or name. Rarely are they unmarked."

"Date and time?" Duerr asked.

"I will find out for you," the young officer said.

"And if she got the truck's license number, I'll see you get a promotion," Duerr said.

The officer blinked twice. "A good word to my superiors will be more than enough. I'll call in and have someone dig up the information."

Duerr turned to Mark and rubbed his hands together. "Good detective work is little more than putting pieces together in a way that makes sense. A seemingly unrelated act, a coincidence, a random event, and suddenly we have hope."

Barth returned. "Your Professor Weigel stayed at the Hotel Berghaus. He was there for one night. Frau Peschak remembers him."

"We'll have to talk to her," Duerr said. "I want details."

"She said she'll bring down refreshments for everyone," Barth said. "A kind gesture."

Rather than stand around and wait, Mark ventured back

down the tunnel to the lab. He found Nora stationed in the hidden filing room, leaning over a cabinet drawer removing files.

"How goes it?" Mark asked.

"I should have learned German in high school when I had the chance. But no, Father Hogan persuaded me to take his Latin class. I agreed only because he was good-looking."

Mark moved closer to her. "Is that an acceptable motivation for attending a class? Isn't that some sort of sin?"

"It could have been if I'd moved beyond thinking he was handsome to something else. But I didn't."

"You're such a good Catholic girl."

"And don't you forget it." She looked back at the file drawer and tossed up her hands. "This is impossible."

"Duerr said he'll find a translator for you."

"Great. When?"

"I'll find out." He had another idea. "What about Georgina? She speaks and reads German."

"She's on her way." Nora straightened fully and rubbed her back. "What's happening out there?"

"We're trying to figure out when the truck was here and where it went."

"Do you really think they took a bomb . . . or bombs?"

"What else do we have?"

Nora nodded to concede his answer. "How is Knox?"

"Still in critical condition. I'm not sure he's regained consciousness. He's probably concussed and I suspect he had internal injuries. Barth arranged to put a guard on his room. It's a miracle he wasn't killed."

"Do you think he finally understands the kind of monsters he was working with?"

"Maybe he will, *if* he survives."

Nora pulled open another file drawer. It screeched and groaned at her, as if bothered about being awakened. "Let's hope these documents help us understand what *we're* dealing with."

· · ·

As the sun set, Frau Peschak and her tattooed waiter brought down trays of tea and coffee for the investigators. Mark took a coffee cup, thanked her, then asked what she remembered of Weigel.

"He was a nice man. Fascinated by the history of the hotel."

"What about it, specifically?" Mark sipped the hot coffee. It was strong stuff.

"The usual things. How the Nazis took it over, what they did with it. I gave him a personal tour of the tunnels below the hotel, at least those we allow the public to see. Though, he was more interested in the layout of the hotel itself."

"The layout?"

She paused then, as if struggling with the right English words. "Not the layout, but the furniture. He was curious about our furniture that predates the Third Reich."

"The hotel has furniture that goes back that far?" Mark asked, then remembered something about the hutch in the dining room.

"A few items."

Duerr appeared and claimed a cup of coffee. He was jubilant. "Now we're getting somewhere."

Frau Peschak took the tray and moved to another group of men. Mark gave Duerr his attention. "Where are we getting?"

"Two o'clock on October twenty-ninth. The woman claimed a truck nearly ran her off the road up here. Using that as our starting point, and after calculating the average speed of a large truck on these roads and the time it takes to travel to any given camera, we'll create a circle radiating from this location in all directions. Then we'll look at the traffic-camera tapes in the cities."

"I hated those kinds of word-logic problems in school. A train leaves Obersalzberg at nine o'clock and travels forty miles an hour—"

"Fortunately, we're not counting on you to do the math," said Duerr. "But a large truck with a large shipment will be easier to spot than most vehicles, particularly if it's unmarked and"—he held up a slip of paper—"we have the vehicle-license number."

Mark brightened. "The woman got it?"

Duerr smiled. "As I said, a seemingly unrelated act, a coincidence, a random event, and suddenly we have hope."

Within an hour, the route of the mysterious truck became clearer. A traffic camera in Berchtesgaden caught the truck at a stoplight. Another camera showed it proceeding north toward Salzburg. There were no sightings in Salzburg, but images came in from outlying towns along the autobahn at just the right times to suggest the truck was journeying toward Munich. A weigh station at the Austrian border also recorded the arrival of the vehicle. Since the driver's papers were in order, no official there felt the need to look in the back of the truck.

"The paperwork states the truck was transporting construction supplies," Duerr said to Mark. They had walked from the mouth of the tunnel to the hotel's lounge.

Barth, who joined them in the lounge, had sent out the German equivalent of an "all-points bulletin" to police stations across Germany and Austria. He sat down heavily, rubbing his face with his hands. "The truck disappeared somewhere near the Munich airport."

"That's bad news," Duerr said.

"But we found it again."

"That's good news." Mark sat up. "Where?"

"Outside the airport perimeter. We know this only because of an incident report from there."

"What kind of incident?" asked Duerr.

"A fire, on the first of November. The truck was completely burned out. Firefighters found nothing inside the truck, nor could they find a cause of the fire, or anyone claiming ownership of the truck."

Mark said, "So they eliminated any evidence."

Barth shrugged. "Wouldn't you?"

"So where did the bombs go?" Duerr asked. "Did they fly them out?"

"We're checking all the airport's records and manifests,"

Barth said. "No plane may take off without its freight accounted for. But so far . . ."

"All right, then. If they didn't fly it out, then where did they take it?" Mark asked.

Duerr lifted a glass and drained the last of his soda water. "It could be here in Germany, right under our noses."

"There must be a laboratory where they work," Mark said. "Surely they can't use a seventy-year-old bomb as is. They'd have to take it somewhere, repurpose it, make sure it's reliable."

"For example . . . ?" Duerr asked.

Mark thought it through. "You'd need a warehouse, an abandoned factory, or an airplane hangar."

Barth suddenly stood. "Then let's go to Munich and find their facility. Since that's where the trail ends, maybe we'll find a way to pick it up again. The area around the airport is full of warehouses, factories, and hangars."

Duerr got to his feet and grabbed his coat. He gestured to Mark, who understood it was a question.

"To Munich," Mark said, and rose on tired legs.

CHAPTER 37

BERCHTESGADEN, GERMANY

NORA WAS STILL sorting through the files when Georgina arrived at the lab, escorted in by a lean, blond, muscular police officer. Though Nora didn't understand German, she sensed Georgina was already midflirt with the man, whose cheeks had turned red by something she said.

Nora practically shouted to break up their little moment and get Georgina's attention.

Georgina said a few parting words to the officer, who bowed slightly and left, then turned to Nora. "Hi. Been busy?"

Nora waved to the files. "Welcome to our new assignment."

"Fun," she said, and walked to the first file cabinet. "All in German?"

"Yes. I've been told that help is on the way," she said, but didn't believe it.

"Where do you want me to start?"

"Let's start with those files." Nora pointed to a handful on the floor. "From the looks of them, they're filled with correspondence and general reports; the rest of those seem to be specific documentation about the victims."

Georgina knelt and looked through the files Nora had assembled. "You're right."

"Have you eaten?"

"Not since breakfast."

"Let's take some of the files up to the hotel and get something. I'm starting to feel dizzy."

• • •

The rain held off and the waiter lit the gas heaters on the large outdoor patio of the Hotel Berghaus. After being stuck inside the file room, Nora felt she could use some fresh air. The gas heaters gave off a pleasant warmth in contrast to the crisp air. Georgina joined her at the table and began to sift through the pile of folders with a grim-faced dedication.

"Stop for a minute," Nora said. "Look at the view. The Alps!"

Georgina glanced at the spectacular view, then returned to the folders. "Great."

Nora thought the view was mesmerizing—everything a soul would need to relax and recover from the stresses of life. A moment later, she heard a chair scuff behind her. She glanced around and noticed a solitary man with close-cropped silver hair chatting with the waiter, though his eyes seemed fixed on them. With so many strangers around, and quite a few to be suspicious of, he worried her.

She looked at Georgina, who was still rifling through the papers.

A voice behind her caused her to jump. "A note for you," he said, handing her a slip of paper on hotel stationery.

She looked up to see the waiter who had served her and Mark the night before. Only now did she realize how strikingly handsome he was, with a strong, narrow face and chin, full lips, and large blue eyes.

"Tea or coffee?" he asked.

"Hot tea, please," she said. "The Milford white tea."

"The Milford white."

"Nothing for me," Georgina said, continuing to go through the files without even a glance at the young man.

Nora held her hand up and the waiter paused before leaving with her drink order. "Who is that man over there?" she asked quietly.

The waiter leaned close. "A businessman."

"What kind of business?"

"Pharmaceuticals or something like that. Why?"

"He keeps looking at us."

The waiter chuckled. "He's here on business and you're two very attractive women. Maybe he thinks he'll get lucky."

"Please make it clear to him that he *won't* get lucky with either of us—and ask him to stop staring."

"Very well," he said, and walked away.

Georgina sneezed. "Musty. I'm going to apply for brown lung disease."

Nora laughed lightly and opened the slip of paper. It was from Mark: "Duerr and I are off to look for bombs in Munich."

Georgina made a soft noise, then held up a piece of paper. "This was jammed between two folders," she said, and unfolded it.

Nora leaned in to see a plain piece of writing paper with a very pleasant cursive filling the page.

Georgina began reading the letter, then gasped.

"What?" Nora asked.

"Listen to this." Georgina began to read aloud.

20 March 1945
Herr General,
Heil Hitler!

We have just received a wire from Central Command in Berlin informing us the Americans' Seventh Army has breached the Siegfried Line, which we thought impenetrable. What we thought to be unthinkable has now happened. The enemy is racing toward the Rhine and, depending upon their course, could be headed directly toward us. Therefore, we have been ordered to seal the laboratory and return to Berlin. In case we are not able to return, here is our report about La Grippe Bombe.

La Grippe Bombe. Nora was breathless. "The influenza bomb."

"Maybe this is the smoking gun we've been looking for," Georgina said.

The waiter returned and placed a tray in front of Nora containing a beautiful porcelain tea set. She noticed again the colorful flowers and vines tattooed on the backs of his hands.

"The water is from melted Alpine snow," the waiter commented. "It'll add to the enjoyment of your tea, I'm sure."

She smiled at him. *"Danke."*

"Nichts zu danken," he replied as he returned the smile, turned, and left.

Nora looked at Georgina, who had finally noticed the waiter and was bug-eyed. "What a beautiful man. I wonder if—"

"Never mind," Nora interrupted as she prepared her tea. She

glanced over her shoulder and noticed that the businessman was gone.

Georgina lifted the letter and continued.

As you will recall, during the first war my forbearers had perfected techniques of placing the influenza infection into foods. The results in America were beyond their wildest expectations— that is, until the Americans brought the dreaded Grippe back to the European front. This unfortunate and unexpected turn of events decimated many of our troops and shut down our offense, ultimately contributing to our Fatherland's untimely and unnecessary defeat.

However, our Führer chose me to restart this endeavor. As I recruited and organized our team, the Führer was pleased to give us preferential laboratories and working conditions in his Führerbunker in Berlin.

Nora held up a hand. *"Führerbunker?"*

Georgina nodded. "It means 'shelter for the leader' or 'Führer's shelter.' Adolf Hitler and Eva Braun committed suicide there at the end of the war."

Nora shook her head. "How romantic."

Georgina went back to the letter.

In our new laboratories, we worked day and night to perfect a system to deliver the virus to our enemies via newly introduced rockets. We tested many of them on several English cities. Our agents in England watched over the medical reports and incidents of illness in the hospitals and reported back to us. Our influenza bombs were not only surprisingly effective at disseminating the germ, but also the English never, to our knowledge, recognized our means of delivery.

Nora topped up her cup with steaming tea as Georgina continued to read.

I must remind you of the work of Dr. Aribert Heim, the chief SS doctor at the Mauthausen work camp, who discovered a powder that, when mixed with desiccated cultures of the influenza virus, seemed to speed the uptake of the flu into the prisoners' systems and resulted in dramatic toxic effects within minutes to hours of ingestion. Additionally—and this is the most remarkable of all—the prisoners passed the virus to other prisoners with amazing ease.

A prisoner or two could be infected, sent to their dormitory, and within 24 to 48 hours they, along with most of their dormitory companions, would be dead or dying. Disposing of the bodies became our only problem.

The doctors discovered that small amounts could be put into the drinking water, and an entire dormitory eliminated almost overnight.

"As if the Nazis needed one more way to murder innocents," Georgina interjected.

Our team was called to mass-produce the powder. The Führer had two hopes for the discovery. First, he wanted the infected powder tested in the various camps to determine if it might not assist him in his "Final Solution to the Jewish Question."

Second, he hoped the infected powder could be introduced, by our brave undercover agents, into the military camps or city water supplies of our enemies, possibly eliminating entire populations of the enemy, thus breaking their spirit to fight.

With the push by the enemy toward Berlin, the Führer insisted that we move our laboratories into the underground facilities below his Berghof. We were housed, along with the SS officers, in the Hotel Berghaus, within walking distance of our new laboratories.

We were able to produce and store large amounts of chemical solvent and virus, mixed together in a powdered form. In addition, we were able to prove that the solvent kept the virus alive and potent for long periods of time. We produced the mixture at a remarkable rate, until this latest turn in the fortunes of the Fatherland. However, when the Americans are defeated and thrust out of the homeland, rest assured that my team and I will immediately return to Berchtesgaden to continue our critical work.

Yours for the
Reich, our Führer, and our Fatherland,
Josef Hermann, PhD

Georgina put the letter down and Nora noticed her hands were trembling. "Such calm. Such pride."

"It's an amazing piece of letter writing. It confirms everything we understood, except for one thing."

"What?"

"Mark and Duerr may be looking for the wrong thing." Nora took out her cell phone. "They're looking for *bombs*. They should be looking for *powder*."

CHAPTER 38

AUTOBAHN TO MUNICH, GERMANY

"A POWDER? WE'RE looking for a *powder*?" Barth exclaimed, then swore at a car that jerked in front of him.

"A powder." Mark looked at the rain as it splashed against the windshield. The autobahn was a black river ahead of them, with red taillights floating like small boats. The occasional passing truck sent a wash over them. They passed a sign for Munich.

"Explain it to me," Duerr said from the backseat.

Mark repeated for Duerr and Barth what Nora had found in the letter. "Nora and Georgina are going through the other files to see if there's more information. But yeah—it looks as if they were storing a powder in the lab, not bombs."

"Are we looking for barrels? Canisters?" Duerr asked.

"What kinds of containers?" asked Barth.

"Probably barrels or drums, if I remember the containers they used at the time. If they had a large supply, Return to Earth would still have needed a big truck to transport everything from the lab."

Barth drove on silently for a moment. "So what's our prevailing theory?"

"Return to Earth has this deadly powder, which they may have used in Siberia," Mark said.

Duerr leaned forward. His face appeared between Mark and Barth. "I'll check with Susan Hutchinson to find out what they may know about it." He leaned back again and Mark heard him dialing.

"Do you think such an old powder would be usable in its

original form or would Return to Earth have to do something to it?" asked Barth.

"Without analyzing the powder, I don't know what its shelf life is." Mark considered the question further. "It must have been viable in its original form or they couldn't have used it so quickly. Unless they were already working on a similar virus, or means of delivery, and Weigel's find merely advanced their work."

"Either way, this is why I followed Return to Earth to Novosibirsk. They may have taken tons of the stuff and used it there," Duerr said. He grunted and his cell phone clicked shut. "My call went directly through to Dr. Hutchinson's voice mail."

"I'll call Kevin Maklin," Mark said.

"Our earlier question is still correct," Barth said. "What kind of laboratory would Return to Earth need to manufacture or improve this powder? Would it be something large and sophisticated, or would they work out of a garage or basement somewhere?"

"My guess is the lab would have to be large and sophisticated," Mark said. "It's not like a cocaine operation or meth lab. This is no cottage industry. The powder has to be contained; otherwise all their lab people would get sick. It would have to be a biosafety lab with at least a BSL-4 rating. There aren't too many of those in the world."

"I need an inventory. We may be able to find them if we can track their supply purchases," said Barth.

Mark's cell phone rang. He saw Digger's name on the screen. "Hey."

"Mac told me to call. I'm still in Cambridge." He sounded bored.

"Did they finish the autopsy on Weigel?"

Digger sighed. "Yes. Technically, he died from injuries sustained in the car crash, but the virus would have had its way with him eventually. No big news there. But the coroner's office found something else." He paused for dramatic effect.

Mark was in no mood for it. "Out with it, Digger. What did they find?"

"A needle puncture on his neck. They believe he was *injected* with the virus."

"To make him the vector?" Mark thought about the letter Nora found, and the rapid transmission of the virus through the concentration-camp prisoners. "But why send Weigel in as a vector when they had powder to put into the water?"

"What powder? What water?" Digger asked.

"I'll explain later."

"Let's make it sooner," Digger said. "I'm heading back to London from here. Unless you need me in Germany. I'd *love* to come to Germany."

"Talk to your boss," Mark said, his mind already racing in other directions. He hung up the phone and pressed it between his palms.

"Did I hear you correctly?" Barth asked.

Mark nodded.

"There's a flaw in the theory," Duerr said. "Return to Earth's activities have been traced to Novosibirsk *before* Weigel arrived. If they had already tampered with the water, why send Weigel?"

Mark groaned, his mind drawing a blank. "They're not making it easy for us, are they?"

Barth's cell phone rang and he tapped his earpiece to answer. Speaking in German, he had an exchange that grew in intensity.

"I wonder what's going on," Mark said.

"*Sshhhh!*" Duerr leaned forward and put a hand on Mark's shoulder. "Apparently, we've had a break."

"What kind of break?" Mark asked, feeling like the odd man out.

Duerr listened, then relayed, "Customs agents have raided a warehouse on the other side of the airport, thinking it was some sort of drug-smuggling operation. No one was there, but three trucks fitting the description of the bulletin that went out earlier were found on-site."

Barth shouted some instructions and hung up. He stepped on the gas and pushed into a line of traffic. Horns blared at him.

"Is it a lab?" Mark asked Barth.

"You'll have to tell me," he replied, then nodded at Duerr. "But here's the intriguing part. On one of the tables they found a package addressed to 'Inspector Martin Duerr.'"

Duerr came forward again. "What? Is it a bomb?"

"Not according to the bomb squad."

"Then what is it?"

"It's a disc player." Barth pressed the car horn and accelerated into the traffic.

CHAPTER 39

BERCHTESGADEN, GERMANY

"GOOD EVENING." A low voice came from the doorway to the file room.

Nora looked up from her place on the floor, where she knelt next to a bottom file drawer.

A man stepped in. He was short, no more than five foot five, and wore khaki trousers, a white shirt, and a sports jacket that hung loosely from his hunched shoulders. He had an elfish face. His thick white hair seemed to shoot upward from the heavy black-framed glasses perched on his nose. He smiled, his lips moving crookedly across his face. "You must be Dr. Nora Richards," he said with a hint of a German accent.

"Yes, I am." Nora stood. The effort made her realize how much her muscles ached. She heard Georgina close a drawer behind her and come to her side. "Who are you?"

"I am Jacob Rosh. I do translation work with the BKA. Inspector Barth told me to come." He looked around. "Though I have to admit this is a most unusual assignment."

Nora was relieved. "We're glad to have you join us, Mr. Rosh—"

"Jacob, please."

"Do you have experience translating documents from the Nazi era, Jacob?" Nora asked.

"Oh, yes. I worked for several years with the Wiesenthal Jewish Documentation Center in Vienna."

"So you're not squeamish or prone to fits of anger or weeping," Nora said.

He chuckled. "Not at all. I believe I have translated the worst the Nazis could chronicle."

"Don't count on it," Georgina said, and turned to another file drawer.

"My work with Nazi documents may be why Inspector Barth asked for me specifically," he said. He rubbed his hands. "So, what are we looking for and where would you like me to begin?"

"We're looking for any references to a project called Liebfraumilch or the Final Solution—"

"I know that well."

"Actually, it's not the Final Solution you may be thinking of," Nora said. "It was also the name for a formula related to germ warfare."

"I see."

"The majority of these files are individual case studies about the effects of the Nazis' work. It's pretty grotesque and depressing reading," said Nora.

"It would be if you could read German," Georgina said. "I'm the one who's depressed now."

Nora ignored her. "What we need is specific information about what the Nazis ultimately created, how much they manufactured, and where it was stored."

"All right." He moved toward the filing cabinet closest to him. "How are we keeping track of what we find?"

Nora pointed to a pile on the floor. "Right now we're putting the most relevant files there, for us to go through more diligently later."

Georgina stepped forward with a clipboard. A yellow pad was tucked under the clip. "We're also writing down the names of Nazis who appear with any frequency—doctors, scientists, soldiers, civilians; anyone who seemed to have intimate knowledge of what went on here in the lab and at the test centers."

Rosh took the clipboard and glanced at it. "By 'test centers' I assume you mean the concentration camps."

"Yes," Nora said.

"And what do you hope to do with these names?" he asked as he flipped a few pages.

"Some of the people connected to this project may still be alive," Nora replied. "We hope we can talk to them."

"Ah, well, in that case I may be more helpful to you than as an interpreter."

"Oh?"

"My work with Wiesenthal's Documentation Center gives me access to their database. They have an exhaustive directory of nearly all living Nazis."

Rosh tapped the clipboard.

"I see the name of Aribert Heim here, one of the most notorious of the Nazi concentration-camp doctors."

"Is he still alive?" Nora asked.

"Some believe he is, some believe he isn't," Rosh answered. "An article in your *New York Times* claimed he had been alive and living in Egypt under a false name—Tarek Farid Hussein—but died of intestinal cancer in Cairo in 1992. But that has never been proven."

"Then strike him from the list," Nora said. "We don't have time to worry about the ones in deep hiding. I need someone who we can talk to now."

Rosh gazed at Nora. "What is the urgency?"

Nora explained about the Nazi weaponry, Return to Earth, and the current Siberian-virus pandemic.

The lines on Rosh's face deepened, and he sighed, as if another crisis related to Nazi efforts were his own burden to bear. "Then I would suggest I run these names through the database as an immediate priority."

Georgina came forward again. "I have a laptop, but I can't get access to any Wi-Fi down here."

Rosh reached behind him and picked up a black briefcase. "I have my own equipment," he said, and moved to the small desk along the opposite wall. "And I'm sure I can."

Within an hour, Nora heard Rosh exclaim, *"Ich habe ihn gefunden!"*

"What?" Nora asked.

Georgina came alongside her. "He found something."

Rosh stood at the desk and turned the computer screen to face them. For the first time, Nora noticed he was wearing a hearing aid.

"Look."

Nora peered at a black-and-white photo of a young man, probably taken in the 1920s.

"This is a local boy from the hills near Lake Traunsee, in the Salzkammergut region," Rosh announced.

Nora shook her head, indicating she didn't know the area.

"It's east of Salzburg," Rosh explained. "His file says he was initially hired by the Nazis as an orderly. He is listed as having worked for Dr. Heinrich Gross in various camps and in various capacities as an assistant of some sort. BKA investigated him once, years ago, and determined there wasn't enough evidence to bring him to justice. According to the database, he may still be alive."

"Where is he?" Nora asked, not wanting to prematurely believe their good fortune.

Rosh scrolled down the screen. "Ebensee, Austria."

"Ebensee? That name keeps turning up in these files."

"Not surprising," Rosh said. "Few people know it, but Ebensee may have been home to the most diabolic of all the concentration camps. The horrors committed there are beyond unimaginable."

"And he still lives there?" Georgina asked. "What's he doing, basking in the glow of warm memories?"

Rosh shrugged. "Perhaps he'll tell us."

Nora looked at the photo. "Does he have a name?"

He gestured at the picture. "Dr. Richards, meet Rudolf Zimmerman."

Nora looked at her watch. "Can we get to him now?"

Rosh shook his head. "It's a couple of hours by car. I suggest we go first thing in the morning."

"We?" Nora asked.

"You'll want an interpreter, I assume."

Nora agreed, but something in his tone made her think he had more to say. She waited.

"And, as it is, I can't allow you to visit him alone," he added.

"Why not?"

"It's against the center's policy to give out private information, for fear people will use it to exact revenge against those presumed innocent."

"I understand," Nora said. "We'll go find Herr Zimmerman first thing in the morning."

CHAPTER 40

MUNICH, GERMANY

THE WAREHOUSE, AS Barth had called it, was a large makeshift building made of corrugated metal. It sat on a plot of patchy grass and dirt behind the razor-wire fence that marked the outer edge of Munich's main airfield. Green and white police cruisers and vans, some with red-and-blue lights flashing, sat in random positions near what appeared to be the building's main entrance. To the side of the building, Mark saw two trucks.

An incoming plane roared overhead, jarring Mark's ears as he, Barth, and Duerr approached the warehouse.

Voices echoed loudly from somewhere inside the metal building. An officer stepped in their path. Duerr reached for his identification, but Barth plowed on. "Let them in," he barked. The officer nodded and moved aside.

The warehouse interior was an open space with no dividing walls. Empty gray metal shelves lined the walls, separated only by random small windows covered with newspaper and encrusted with brown soot and spiderwebs. The center of the room was dominated by tables of the same gray metal as the shelves. The table surfaces were covered in dust. There was no sign of any laboratory equipment, but three black barrels sat next to one of the center tables.

"Well?" Barth asked Mark after getting updated by the officer in charge of the scene.

"The bunker in Obersalzberg looked like a lab. I don't know what this is. What brought the customs agents here?"

"One of the maintenance men at the airport was repairing the fence this morning. He saw the trucks and lots of activity in what he thought was an abandoned building. He thought he ought to check it out."

"A good citizen," Duerr said.

"The man came up to a window and saw through a crack in the covering men and women working at these tables. To him they looked as if they were part of a hospital operating theater, with face masks, latex gloves, scrubs, and plastic shoe covers. He thought he saw them take a white powder out of several barrels and put it into boxes on the tables."

"Is that the dust on the surfaces?" Mark asked, suddenly concerned they were all being exposed to the Nazi virus.

"No. The hazmat people already checked it out. It's just dust. There's no sign of any drugs, or chemicals, or anything unusual," Barth said.

"Not even in the barrels?"

Barth shook his head. "Those are clean as a whistle. Though you'll be interested in this." He strode over to the three barrels and pointed to faded swastikas stenciled on each one—perhaps decades ago.

Mark's heart quickened, and he stepped back. "Those need to be contained, just in case."

"All this will be contained for further forensics," Barth said.

"What happened with your industrious airport employee?" Duerr asked.

"The man reported what he found to airport security. They, along with customs agents, came out to investigate. Technically, it's not their jurisdiction, since this isn't airport property, but they did it anyway."

"Then what?" Duerr asked.

"By the time they got here, it looked like this." They called local police. Barth pointed to a box on the table. Mark noticed that Duerr's name was handwritten on the top flap with black marker. "That box was sitting there. Munich police never heard of an Inspector Martin Duerr, but had the box checked out anyway. It was deemed safe from any exploding device or biochemical exposure. They weren't sure what to do with it. Then the bulletin went out with our names attached and one of the investigators made the connection."

Duerr reached for the box, but his fingers lingered over the unsealed top flaps. "You said they're certain this isn't rigged to blow up?"

"Would I be here otherwise?" Barth asked.

The side and bottom folds of the box were taped with a clear adhesive. "Did they check the tape for fingerprints?" Mark asked.

"No results," Barth said.

Duerr lifted the flaps on top and peered inside. He reached in and pulled out a silver machine. A Post-it was pressed against its flat top. Mark looked over his shoulder and read the note. "This is a personal message to Inspector Duerr. It may be played once and will then erase."

"Needless to say, they didn't play it," Barth said.

Although the machine looked like a small laptop, when Duerr opened the lid, it turned out to be a portable DVD player.

"No fingerprints, no brand name, no serial number, no identifying marks. But we're checking the design and will take it apart once you've viewed the message."

"How can a DVD be automatically erased?"

"It's not using a DVD," Barth replied. He pointed to a circular disc repository. "Normally the DVD would go there, but it's sealed shut. Police scanned the machine and found it's been rigged with a chip. I assume the message is on the chip. The chip will fry itself after it's been played."

"Is there any way to record whatever is on here?" Duerr asked.

"The technical team says there's no way to connect a recorder to the device itself. They were afraid to try, in case they screwed up and the message erased. I've arranged for a videographer to record the playback whenever you're ready."

"I'm ready."

Barth signaled a woman nearby. She carried a large case over, opened it, and took out a digital camera. She set it up, pointed to the screen, then gave them a thumbs-up.

"Quiet!" Barth shouted.

As if on a Hollywood soundstage, various people ran around demanding that investigators stop whatever noise they were making. Mark waited for the "lights, camera, action!"

Duerr pushed the play button.

The screen was black for a moment, then an image appeared of the very warehouse they stood in. Standing around one of the black barrels was a group: maybe a dozen people dressed in surgical garb, just as the airport employee described. But instead of surgical masks, they now wore ski masks. The effect was both incongruous and chilling. *Medical terrorists.*

"Hello, Inspector Duerr." The voice was altered, pitched down and distorted to disguise the speaker's real voice. Mark saw the face mask of the man at center stage move. "We're so glad you finally made it to our little party. Return to Earth has been waiting for you to catch up. But, alas, you are still behind. Even while you stand here, watching this video, we are executing our plan. Did I say 'executing'? Yes, I did, which is the appropriate word for what we are doing. I have chosen to destroy three cities. They have been particularly reckless with regard to our dear Mother Nature, have not been nurturing in their relationships with the earth and its nonhuman inhabitants. They are cruel to our animal friends and abuse the very earth, wind, and sky. And so they will feel firsthand what it is to be experimented upon, to be abused. Millions will come to understand."

The camera slowly zoomed in on the speaker. Mark looked at his eyes and remembered them from a slaughterhouse near Eyam, England, where this same man interrogated Mark and brutally tortured and killed another. Stefan Maier.

Maier held the camera in his gaze for a moment, then said softly, "I am bringing an apocalypse, a day of reckoning, a judgment day. I will grip the necks of these cities and cut off their lifeblood. And, dear inspector, there's nothing you or anyone else can do about it. You will remember only that you were warned and found yourself impotent against a perfect weapon dear Mother Nature has caused to evolve. We will assist her in taking back what is rightfully hers."

The screen went black. The three men stood in silence. The videographer turned off the camera, then whispered something in German. She looked pale.

Mark expected a sizzling sound, followed by smoke, like the recorders in the old *Mission: Impossible* show. But the machine simply died.

"Get that thing analyzed!" Barth ordered. "I want it, and that recording, torn apart for clues. There must be some way of identifying the cities he's talking about and how he's accomplishing his 'apocalypse.'"

"He's already found a means to put the powder in the Siberian water supply," Mark said.

"What are we supposed to do?" Barth asked Mark, his expression now filled with worry. "Wait until people elsewhere start dropping dead?"

"We can attempt to treat the virus, unless WHO determines it is a new strain, but we simply don't have enough medicine, doctors, or hospitals to fight this thing if it gets into the water supplies of major cities. The numbers will overwhelm us before we know it. We're certainly seeing that in Siberia and Japan."

"If he's serious about his threat, then that is likely only a small taste of what's to come," Duerr said.

"What can we do?" Barth asked.

Mark hardly knew what to say. "We've got some of the world's best scientists on the case—but we just don't have enough time."

A chill went down his spine and Mark thought it must be the cold breath of death.

"Return to Earth has won," Duerr said, then walked out of the building.

PART ELEVEN

1991

CHAPTER 41

HAMPSHIRE, ENGLAND

CORNELIUS KNOX SAT in the study of his family's Hampshire home and considered his fortieth birthday, which he'd celebrated only the day before. Somewhere outside the large oak door, he could hear Kenneth and the servants cleaning up the remains of the party. It had been a lavish affair, including the modern gentry of Hampshire County in general, and Winchester in particular.

And not a single friend among them, Cornelius thought.

He looked at the cold hearth and pondered its emptiness. To equate it to his life would be too obvious. But why not? Cold and empty. That's how he felt. His first wife had said as much right before she left him for her tennis instructor. His second wife hadn't said it, but she was a woman who said little—and left him for another woman. His third wife, well, he hadn't met her yet, nor did he expect to. Perhaps he was better off as a grand old bachelor, in the Victorian sense. Women were too much trouble. They expected too much. His grandmother and mother, with their strong wills and scheming manipulations, had shown him that. His poor father . . .

Oh, never mind. Why think about his father now? Or is that what milestone birthdays were for, bringing up the past, reevaluating life?

He ran a finger along the edge of the hardcover book he'd been given for his birthday by Spanky Baldwin, his sometime horse-riding partner. The inscription teased him about his "secret legacy" and hoped he enjoyed the read.

A Professor Hans Weigel titled the book *The Great Conspiracy of Two World Wars*. It regurgitated theories Cornelius had heard, and dismissed, over his lifetime—theories ascribed to his grandfather, who was clearly mad as a loon.

No, Cornelius didn't enjoy his legacy at all and wished he had the means to put the whole scandal to rest once and for all. But how? It had been a nonconversation in the house. His grandmother and father and mother refused to speak of it. Ever.

As a boy, when he fancied himself a rebellious youth, he tried to champion his grandfather's views and spoke of the poor man as a misunderstood outcast. He went so far as to suggest his grandfather had been murdered for his ideas.

The only response had come from his grandmother Margaret: "Oh, stop being so tiresome." And that had been the end of it. For her.

At the time, Cornelius had gone searching in the attic for anything stored there that might shed light on his grandfather. Surely there were papers, essays, documents, or letters that would illuminate the mind of such a controversial man. There was a box. He remembered it now. It contained all kinds of letters and papers from around the Second World War. He had just opened it when his father appeared and chased him away. When he sneaked back later, the box was gone.

Why had his family been so insistent he know nothing at all about his grandfather?

He thought now about the attic. He hadn't been up there for years. And there was no one to stop him from looking. If the box hadn't been destroyed, it might still be there somewhere.

"Kenneth!" he called out.

A moment later, Kenneth appeared at the door in his usual dark trousers, his shirtsleeves rolled up. "Yes, sir?"

"A few years ago, we had new insulation put in the attic. Do you remember?"

"Yes, sir."

"You organized everything, didn't you?"

"Mostly. Why?"

"A box of family things from the war was up there."

"Which war?"

"The second. Why? Did you find something from the first?"

"Your family goes back several generations, sir. I found boxes for each war."

"Is there a box about my grandfather?"

"Philip Edward?" Kenneth asked. "One."

"Show it to me."

"Would you like to go up or shall I have it brought down?"

"Let's be wild and carefree," Cornelius said. "I'll go up with you."

Even at his age, Cornelius thought attics were magical and ghostly places. The slanted eaves, sheet-covered furniture, old lamps, standing mirrors, buckled trunks, dust-filled shafts of light, all evoked the writings of M. R. James, C. S. Lewis, Henry James, and Edgar Allan Poe.

Kenneth led him down the center to an area on the right where wood shelves had been constructed. Boxes and smaller trunks adorned the wood, now warped from the weight. Kenneth folded his arms and glanced through the collection he'd assembled there. "Ah," he finally said, and pulled at a small trunk with leather straps. He lowered it by the handles and tapped the gold lock on the front.

"I'm not sure this is the box I was looking for."

Kenneth gave him a knowing smile. "The box you're looking for no longer exists. Your father destroyed it after you started snooping in it."

Cornelius was astonished. "How do you know that?"

"My predecessor told me when he gave me a tour of the attic. You snooped in the box, so your father had him transfer the contents to this trunk, which could be locked. The box was destroyed."

"Why didn't my father destroy its contents, too, if he didn't want me to see them?"

"He couldn't be bothered to go through everything to make sure he wasn't destroying something important."

Cornelius knelt and fiddled with the solid lock. "Should I assume the key is long gone?"

"Not at all," Kenneth said and, with a rattle of a great many keys, pulled a ring from his pocket. "We keep every key to every lock in the house. Organized and identified."

"You're amazing."

"Thank you, sir."

Cornelius's look served as a rebuke.

Kenneth found the right key and inserted it into the lock. With a metallic click the latch came free. Cornelius lifted the lid.

The trunk had two levels: a removable top shelf molded into compartments and an open bottom. Cornelius looked in the various compartments of the top shelf, through cuff links, his father's medals and citations, his grandfather's military buttons and medallions, and sundry other small items of jewelry and mementos of no particular interest. He removed the shelf. On the left side was a hat sitting carefully atop folded military shirts. Beneath the shirts was a box filled with papers and letters. He remembered the look and feel of the letters from his teenage explorations. He set the box on the floor next to him and looked at what was kept in the right side of the trunk: a stack of diaries from the Collins Publishing Company, each embossed with a year. They started in 1933 and went up to 1945.

Cornelius flicked through the pages and saw his grandmother's meticulous handwriting. Even in the large and small swirls of her cursive he saw the determination and iron will of the woman. But he found nothing in the entries beyond the most mundane of appointments.

"Would you like for me to wait?" Kenneth asked.

"No, that's all right. I know you have a lot of work to do. Thank you."

"Yes, sir."

Cornelius turned his attention to the box of papers and letters, mostly correspondence regarding legal matters for the estates, books that had been ordered, property grievances with various neighbors, county wartime rules and regulations, and invitations to cathedral or council hall events. The envelopes had been sliced open with a sharp opener, the edges clean.

A small stack was bound with a red ribbon, now faded to a brownish pink. Cornelius quickly ascertained that most of the envelopes contained sympathy cards regarding the "untimely death" of Philip Edward Knox. To be killed by a train was a beastly way to die, all had agreed. He flipped through some, ignored others, and was about to put the stack back into the box when he noticed an unopened envelope addressed to his father in sharp, angular cursive. The return address was for a Reverend J. Gillingham, Notting Hill, London.

Cornelius took out his penknife and carefully opened the letter. Inside was a piece of onionskin, popular at the time, with writing on one side, though not much of it.

The letter was dated 17 March 1947.

Dear Sir:

After several attempts to reach you by post and by phone, I can only assume that you are not interested in the leather satchel, which I've begged you to take. It is, as I have said, filled with papers that belonged to your father—though, in keeping his trust, I have not opened the satchel as per his instructions. This is a very unusual situation for me and I am dismayed by your silence. Please contact me immediately or I shall be forced to dispose of the item.

Yours most sincerely,
Rev. John Gillingham

How odd, Cornelius thought. A leather satchel that belonged to his grandfather? Why was it in the possession of a Notting Hill vicar in 1947, three years after his grandfather's death?

He pulled out the stack of letters again and looked for any envelopes or papers from the reverend that might explain this last plea. None were there.

Cornelius's curiosity was inflamed. He imagined a leather satchel filled with his grandfather's papers—papers that could confirm the old man's insanity, or prove true his wild theories.

He wondered.

As he came down the stairs to the main floor, he waved the letter at Kenneth. "I won't be playing cricket today."

• • •

It took several weeks of phone calls and correspondence with the Church of England to learn that the Reverend John Gillingham—vicar at St. Peter's Church until his retirement in 1967—died in 1974. His widow, Wendy, passed away in 1988 after spending two years in a retirement facility in Sunninghill, Berkshire. Church records identified the family's executor as a daughter named Penny Gillingham, with an address in Sunninghill.

Cornelius wrote to Penny, who responded with a mixture of bewilderment and curiosity. But, yes, he was welcome to come and speak with her about this mysterious connection between their two families.

Sunninghill was a small village next to the more famous town of Ascot, home of the Ascot Races. Cornelius had attended the races one year when the Queen and Prince Philip were present, and had even bumped into Prince Charles and a blushing Princess Di shortly after they'd been married. He remembered, without fondness, how he'd had too much champagne and become violently ill in front of the Queen's box. He cringed to think of it.

Penny lived in a block of flats on a cul-de-sac not far from Sunninghill's High Street. She was an attractive blonde, short but shapely, only a few years younger than Cornelius. She spoke in rapid sentences, saying far more than she seemed to intend, giggling and blushing. He discerned that she continued to use her original surname not because she was a feminist but because she had never married. She was quick to make clear she wasn't a lesbian, though—just had never found a man who appreciated her dedication to her parents. She had moved into the Sunninghill flat to be close to her mother's retirement home, only a mile away.

"Now, about this mysterious satchel," she said after pouring their second cup of tea. They sat in the small dining room that adjoined the living room that adjoined a tiny kitchen only a short hallway from a single bedroom. "I don't remember seeing anything like it when I was dealing with my mother's things, but that doesn't mean much. I didn't pay attention to some of what she had, not bothering to unpack all the boxes and all that."

"I would be very surprised if your parents had kept it after all those years," Knox said. He was enjoying the tea and the company. Penny was quirky, but lively and engaging. "Why would they? And the letter I found indicated that your father was going to dispose of the satchel if my father didn't contact him right away. I've no reason to believe that he did."

"Why wouldn't he?" Penny asked.

"My family was ashamed of my grandfather. It's possible he didn't want whatever it was your father had."

"How sad."

"Which part?"

"The part about your father being ashamed of your grandfather. What a terrible thing, to feel ashamed of one's family."

"Do you speak from experience?"

"Not at all. I loved my parents and only felt proud of them."

"Always?" Cornelius asked, thinking of his volatile feelings for his domineering grandmother, his equally domineering mother, and his obsequious father.

She looked out a nearby window, a thoughtful expression on her face. Outside, a gentle breeze shook a tree. "They made plenty of mistakes. What parents don't? But that's why we operate on a principle of forgiveness."

"What principle of forgiveness?"

"That we forgive our parents their mistakes, as they forgive us ours," she said. "It's a variation on the Lord's Prayer. The point is, we're all idiots and step on one another's toes, sometimes accidentally, sometimes willfully. We should forgive as we are forgiven." She giggled and blushed again. "I've made a hash of that statement, I think. Unfortunately, I didn't inherit my father's oratorical gifts. He would have said all that much better than I did."

"Do you think about your parents a lot?"

She hesitated. "I was about to say no. But I suppose I do."

"You miss them."

"Oh, yes. Are your parents still alive?"

"No."

"Do you miss them?"

"Not at all. But that doesn't stop me from thinking about them."

She looked at him and he allowed himself to meet her gaze and to study her chestnut-colored eyes.

"The key," she said.

"What key?" he asked.

"The one to the storage room downstairs. All the flats get one. I put some of my mother's things down there." She was up and away before Cornelius was ready to lose eye contact.

She searched for the key and nearly despaired until she found it hanging from a thumbtack stuck in a corkboard in the kitchen. She led him down the stairs to a basement floor of the building, then to several unmarked doors. She tried the key in one, which proved to be wrong, then moved two doors over and found the correct one. It opened with a rusty groan. She found the switch for the bare lightbulb and it flashed on to reveal a narrow closet filled with cardboard boxes, loose Christmas decorations, a bike, a wicker chair, and what looked like out-of-fashion curtains. Penny pushed in, using her knees to nudge things out of the way. She went as far back as she could and let out a cheer. "Here," she said, and thrust a heavy box into his hands. She picked up another and made her way out again. "We'll start with these two."

"How many boxes are there?"

"A few. But I promise not to bore you with any special memories attached to what we find. We'll search for what you're after and nothing else."

Back upstairs, she insisted on going through the boxes herself while he made them another pot of tea. Another happy exclamation brought him in from the kitchen.

She held in her hands a large parcel wrapped in brown paper retrieved from the second box. "It's the right size to be a satchel," she said. "And it's bulky and heavy."

Cornelius's heart pounded in his throat. He didn't think it was possible. He swallowed and told himself that it wasn't possible. The package could be old laundry.

Penny turned the parcel around and noticed an envelope addressed to her mother attached to the side. "This is my father's handwriting," she said, and tore the envelope away. She opened it, took out a note card with a country landscape on the front, and read.

Darling Wendy

I found our little albatross again and had intended to throw it away. Honestly, it is ridiculous to hold on to it for so many years. But it's a mystery that's become part of the family. It's now a matter of pride that we've resisted temptation and haven't opened it, if only to honor a peculiar acquaintance who entrusted it to us. I saw in the newspaper that there is a new generation of Knoxes in Winchester. Well, one. Perhaps this young man will be interested in the package. Please find the correct address and mail it to him, when you have a chance. I've wrapped it for you.

Your loving husband.

"It's dated 4 June 1974." Penny gasped and her face was bright with realization. "He died of a heart attack the very next day! In the chaos of his death, this must have been put aside."

"Why would he write her such a long note?"

"My mother was like a secretary to him. He was always leaving her notes with specific instructions about what he wanted done. He said it was to avoid confusion. She was gone, visiting her sister, when he died. He always used her time away to tidy up and clear things out. He had his heart attack in the garage, where he probably found this. My aunt Mary likely tossed it into a box when she was helping my mother after he died. She enjoyed throwing things into boxes and putting them away."

"Well, that's truly remarkable."

She presented the package to him like a Christmas gift. "Here. You should open it."

"No, it's yours."

"It is not!" she protested. "You heard his instructions. This was supposed to be sent to you years ago. Now take it. And hurry, because it's heavy."

In reality, he wanted to grab it from her hands, but restrained himself and took the package reluctantly. It was heavy and bulky, reminding him of old newspapers. He tore off the brown wrapping paper and looked in wonder at a burnt-orange leather satchel with zipped compartments and two buckles securing the large flap to the main compartment. A small piece of rectangular leather was stitched to the flap, and on it L.H. was stitched in formal cursive.

"L.H.?" Cornelius asked. The initials meant nothing to him and caused him to hesitate. What if this satchel didn't belong to his family after all?

"No L.H. in your family?"

"None that I know of."

Penny squirmed like a small child. "Go on, then. Open it up."

He did. And knew his life would never be the same.

PART TWELVE

November 8
Present Day

CHAPTER 42

MUNICH, GERMANY

MARK OFTEN WONDERED what he would be doing when the end of the world arrived. He didn't expect he would be sitting in a cramped office in Munich. The place smelled of burned coffee, old cigarettes, and body odor. This was not how he wanted to spend his last days.

Last days. Was this really it? Mark mused on the idea and wondered where God was in the scheme of things. Did he really believe God would somehow save the day? Did he trust in God?

He remembered trying to deal with the grief he'd suffered from the death of his daughter. It all came down to what he *really* believed. Does God exist? If so, is he indifferent to what happens to humankind? Does he get some malicious joy out of torturing creatures on earth? Or . . . he exists and he loves us, even when we don't fully understand what's going on.

These were the times Mark had to wonder. *Do I trust God?*

Mark slept for a couple of hours on a small sofa, then used the shower facilities and a disposable razor in a lacerating attempt to shave. He returned to the office, drank some of the burned coffee, and checked his phone. Donna had tried to call him while he was in the shower. He gazed at the number. Should he call her back and tell her to quarantine herself until he was sure all was well? The outbreak hadn't hit America yet, but it was only a matter of time.

The small flat-screen TV was on and the news caught his eye.

Mark had prayed that Return to Earth's threat was a bluff, mere posturing, but morning news anchors, usually laughing and joking about the latest celebrity gaffes, were now stern-faced and earnest. Seemingly overnight, the so-called Siberian flu had broken out with a vengeance in Athens, Rome, and Budapest.

Hospital spokespersons and doctors spoke to jostling cameras about the masses that had begun to flood into emergency rooms overnight. By morning, staff and facilities were overwhelmed. Disaster plans were being implemented so that schools, city halls, convention centers, hotel ballrooms, and even sports arenas would be opened to accommodate the overflow.

Emergency supplies were already running thin, causing the WHO to rush medications and intravenous fluids to nearby military bases. Government officials were now coordinating with both law enforcement and the military to keep order as each city was placed in mandatory quarantine by the European Union.

Mark hammered out a full report for Mac to distribute to the TSI team and sent it via a secure line. He tried to reach Nora, but his calls went straight to her voice mail. He assumed she'd locked herself in the file room for the night.

No question about it. Return to Earth had made good on their promise. He'd failed and could only wait until they announced the next urban outbreak.

Duerr paced the office and berated himself for being so far behind Return to Earth's scheme. "They played me every step of the way," he grumbled. "I should have moved faster."

Mark nodded. He knew better than most what it was like to blame yourself, even for things completely out of your control.

"We have to come up with a plan of action," Duerr said. He took a deep breath, as if to regain control of his inner turmoil. "I want to talk to Dr. Hutchinson. Siberia is the key to this whole thing." He grabbed his cell phone and made the call. Frustrated, he snapped it closed. "Still going straight to voice mail."

"I'll try Kevin Maklin," Mark said, remembering that he'd planned to do that before reaching Munich. He dialed the number and put the phone on speaker.

"This is Maklin," Kevin said as he picked up.

"Kevin? Mark Carlson here. I'm with Inspector Duerr. We're looking for Susan."

"Don't worry. She's safe."

"Safe?" Mark asked. "Was she *not* safe recently?"

"Hold on." He put a hand over the mouthpiece and spoke to someone in his office. A moment later he said, "Return to Earth tried to kidnap her and—"

"What?"

"Clearly the situation is out of control. I've got men on the ground there. Some of the soldiers who helped you in Eyam."

"Is Susan all right?" Duerr asked.

"For the moment. She's at a safe house. And the Russians are finally taking the whole water-tampering business seriously."

"What water tampering?" Mark asked, wondering if Kevin had already seen his report.

"Susan surreptitiously got water samples from a new treatment plant there and had them tested. The water is tainted with the virus. She's convinced Return to Earth is involved. She wanted you to know you were right in your suspicions, Inspector Duerr."

"Tell her I'm coming. I'm leaving now."

"You're leaving?" Mark asked.

Duerr tossed up his hands. "I should be there. My gut tells me the answer to this thing is there. I can't sit around waiting for their next move. Phone me if you learn anything worthwhile." He was gone.

"What's the plan to stop them?" Kevin asked.

"We're working that out." Mark wondered why he suddenly felt alone in that statement. "If we can't keep them from spreading the virus, then we have to come up with a vaccine, a treatment, or an antidote."

"Let me know what I can do to help," Kevin said. "I'm about to go in to a conference call with the White House and the Joint Chiefs of Staff."

"I will," Mark said. "Keep Susan safe."

"On my life," Kevin said and hung up.

Duerr had rushed past as Barth entered the office. "Where's Duerr going?" Barth asked, hooking a thumb behind him.

"Siberia, I think."

Barth exclaimed in German, then growled, "Now is *not* the time to be rash or impulsive. We must strategize. Interpol agents can be such prima donnas!"

"I need a car," Mark said, realizing his next step. "I want to go to Salzburg to talk to Knox. There may be things he knows that he's now ready to share."

"I'll arrange it." Barth walked out and the office was silent, the first bit of silence Mark experienced in days. The sound was turned down on the television, but the BBC World News ticker-tape report scrolled along the bottom of the screen. *Thousands dead . . . People trying to flee the cities . . . Armed roadblocks surround cities . . .* A reporter stood outside a hospital in Athens. A line of patients—some sitting against walls, some in wheelchairs, and others in stretchers—extended from the emergency-room doors out into a parking lot. Most of them looked like creatures from *Night of the Living Dead.*

Surely it was the end of the world.

CHAPTER 43

NOVOSIBIRSK, SIBERIA

THE SAFE HOUSE was actually a small compound of diplomat apartments near the center of the city. The United States and a number of allies used it for sensitive diplomatic or industrial visits to the region, in lieu of an embassy or consulate. It was high-walled and secure. Most of the guards provided were under the authorization of the Russian military.

Jankowski ran diagnostic tests on the apartment they'd given her to ensure they weren't being bugged or monitored. It was more spacious than she'd expected, like a town house. Better than that, water was supplied from an artesian well. She was pleased to find that all her personal items had been brought over from the hotel.

After a quick shower upstairs, she called Kevin. He sounded relieved to hear her voice.

"Tell me you're all right," he said.

"I'm all right."

"Tell me that you feel nothing but undying gratitude for my help."

"I feel nothing but undying gratitude for your help."

"You're welcome," he said. "I would have come myself, but I'm allergic to parka."

"Is that so? I've never heard of such a condition."

"I'll tell you about it at our next dinner."

They chatted about nothing in particular, mostly as a way to reassure themselves all would be well.

After hanging up, she walked downstairs to the kitchenette, put her laptop on the counter, and turned it on. She turned on a small, counter-top television and sipped a cup of coffee as she made some toast. All the networks were running reports about the epidemic, which was expected to be labeled a pandemic that very day. She punched the mute button and ate while she reviewed reports from the WHO and TSI that had come into her e-mail during the night.

The bad news was relentless. The Japanese epidemic had spread with great speed throughout the islands and to six Southeast Asian countries. In addition, the virus was rumored to have escaped quarantine in China. And that spread didn't include the rising numbers of afflicted in Athens, Rome, and Budapest. It was likely the virus would spread across Europe and Asia within days. From all appearances, the Return to Earth threats were real. A new wave of stress worked through her body.

Stock markets around the world responded to the crisis by falling significantly. Fear that terrorists caused the outbreaks frightened investors. Airline stocks, in particular, had plunged amid worries that more governments would impose travel restrictions. "The Siberian flu is ripping through the markets, creating uncertainty in its wake," declared one London senior trader on the BBC.

Susan couldn't sit still. She moved from one end of the room to the other, wanting to do something—but helpless to know what it was. She put in a call to Grigory.

Grigory picked up and began speaking before she could say a word. "Dr. Hutchinson, I am so sorry about your terrible ordeal. You can be sure that the surviving culprit is being thoroughly interrogated. Within the parameters of the Geneva Conventions, of course."

"I never doubted it," she said. "Now, about the—"

"I want you to stay where you are and rest," he said. "We can survive without you for a few hours."

"But—"

"I'll be in touch." The doctor hung up.

Susan stared at the phone for a moment. She couldn't believe how she'd been summarily dismissed. She hoped to have better luck with Joan Caldwell, her boss at the WHO.

A no-nonsense type, Joan got straight to business. "I'm glad you're safe," she said.

"Thank you."

"I'm sending you a report from our physicians and nurses in the field in Siberia, France, and Japan. Keep it close. We wouldn't want certain details leaked to the public, though you may want to inform your friends at TSI, so they'll know what they're up against."

"Will do."

"I've also seen the test results for the samples you sent from the water-treatment plant. I assume you've seen them."

"No, I haven't."

"Oh. How odd." Joan cupped her hand over the phone and shouted to someone, "They're coming."

"Is there anything I should know now?"

"Although there were no free-floating viral particles in the samples, we found other types of unusual particles."

"What kind?"

"*Nano*particles—packed with the H1N1 Siberian virus."

Susan frowned. "Nanoparticles? Have they identified them? Do they know how they work?"

"Not yet. They're working on it now. Watch for that report."

"Thanks." Susan hung up, then looked at her watch. Mac would soon be arranging a conference call. She went to her laptop again and found the report from her boss. She was distressed to learn of the deaths of WHO personnel she knew well, or had worked with over the years. She sat quietly for a few minutes to think about those who had died.

A pounding on the front door abruptly shattered her solitude and nearly caused her to spill her coffee. She crossed the floor to the small entrance hall and peeked through the peephole. Anton had pushed his face up close and was smiling so that she mostly saw teeth.

She opened the door. "You should consider orthodontics."

He walked straight past her to the kitchen and the coffeepot. "Nice place," he said. "It's bigger than mine. I got a one-bedroom efficiency and nothing in the fridge."

"They like me more." She returned to the counter and her laptop.

"I came for the coffee," he said. Susan noticed that the bandage on his forehead had been changed from a functional white to one with a cartoon character.

"I just spoke to Dr. Tarasov," she said.

"He didn't tell you much, did he?"

"Not really. What do you know?"

"I know that Siberia is the perfect place for a crisis like this."

"Why?"

"Because the temperature is below freezing and they can store the overflow of bodies outside."

"Is that a joke?"

"To a certain kind of person, yes."

"Well?" she asked Anton.

"Two items." Anton sipped his coffee. "The first is a report that came into the academy this morning. Apparently there is an active outbreak of the Spanish flu among the employees of a factory just north of the city. Virtually all have become severely ill over the last couple of days. The plant nurses, who examine everyone entering the plant, have reported that no sick person had been allowed to enter."

"What does that mean? People can carry and spread a virus for hours before they themselves become ill?"

"But there's an interesting and ironic coincidence to this outbreak. The factory produces bottled water. In fact, it's the largest in Russia—the company's name, translated from Russian, means 'Happy Water.'"

"A bottled-water plant with a spontaneous outbreak on the premises?"

Anton nodded. "What's worse is the plant produces about twenty-five hundred two-liter bottles per hour. Just this morning, plant chemists found an unusual residue in the water. They have not identified it yet, but it's likely contaminated water has been shipped out of the plant."

"To where?"

"They're checking their distribution schedule to be certain. But they normally ship all over eastern Russia and to China, Mongolia, Turkistan, and Kazakhstan."

"How much do they ship?"

"Over fifty thousand two-liter bottles a day. About one hundred twenty thousand liters every twenty-four hours."

Susan lowered her head. They were now dealing with numbers that were beyond her ability to imagine. And if the mysterious residue happened to be nanoparticles packed with the virus . . . well, she didn't want to consider *that* proposition.

"There's more," he said.

"I don't know if I want to hear—"

"There was a report of a shoot-out at the Novosibirsk water-treatment plant. A truck was again seen dumping some sort of chemical into the water intake of the plant. Two security officers approached the truck. Both were gunned down and pronounced dead on the scene. Security video showed the entire gruesome event."

"Did they identify the truck?"

"They have. But it was a stolen vehicle."

"Did they shut down the water-treatment plant?" she asked.

Anton nodded. "Yes—and quickly. Fortunately for Novosibirsk, a number of large, deep artesian wells can provide an emergency water supply."

Susan looked out the window. Two buildings sat on the opposite side of a small park, the grass brown and the benches empty. Beyond that was the city skyline. Susan thought about the water pumped into all those buildings and the many people who would drink the mysterious virus-packed nanoparticles. The implications were stunning—this type of technology would allow the virus to be spread with unprecedented ease. A chill traveled down her spine.

"The current water lines will have to be flushed. Repeatedly."

"And citizens are being warned not to use city water, or bottled water from the 'Happy Water' Bottling Plant," he added.

"How are they being warned?"

"Television, radio, automated telephone messages, emergency cell-phone IMs. Even trucks are driving through neighborhoods with loudspeakers."

"We can only hope that'll do the trick." Susan sipped her cold coffee. "Interesting that Grigory didn't mention any of that on the phone."

"And admit that you were right?" Anton said. "I don't think so."

"He better get over that if we're to fight this thing together. I'm going to need his help."

"With what?"

She leaned against the counter and asked, "Anton, what do you know about nanoparticles?"

"Only what's in the literature. It's a new technology that uses microscopic particles to deliver medications into targeted areas of the body."

"Well done. You get a gold star. Imagine being able to deliver radioactive particles or toxic chemotherapy directly into cancer cells, where it would be released. No side effects, no normal tissue affected."

"It'd be wonderful if they can figure it out," he said. "Why are we talking about this?"

"Unidentified nanoparticles were found in the water samples we obtained yesterday." She felt as if yesterday had taken place a year ago. "I'm wondering if they're tied to Happy Water and the Novosibirsk water plant—but I'm sure they're tied to whatever it is Return to Earth is doing, though I don't know how. It's the kind of idea, or technology, that would come from a place like Jotham."

Anton nodded. "Understood. But if you're thinking about breaking into Jotham . . ."

"That's why I need Grigory—alone and away from prying eyes and ears. He has to allow us into that complex."

Anton gazed at her for a moment. "Well. Good luck with that."

"I have to do *something*."

Anton drained the last of his coffee. "Shall I arrange for him to come here?"

"Please."

"And I need another favor."

He watched her and waited.

"Bring me a copy of that video of the shoot-out at the water plant."

CHAPTER 44

EBENSEE, AUSTRIA

EBENSEE WAS A storybook town built in the lap of the Alps. Idyllic, with classic Austrian buildings—square and colorful—set against a backdrop of Traunsee, a beautiful lake resting in a bowl between mountain vistas. A late-morning mist shrouded the tops of the tree-covered peaks.

"Amazing," Nora said, looking at a river that spilled from the lake, splitting the town into a main downtown on one side and a residential area that pushed into the mountains on the other. It was the sort of place where she had always fantasized about spending her honeymoon.

"Yes, amazing," Rosh said as he took a turn from the highway and followed a secondary road toward the center of town. He pointed toward the mountains. "And if I went that way, you would see the original concrete gate that led to the Ebensee concentration camp. It's all that is left to remind the residents of the atrocities committed here. The town now boasts a population of over eight thousand people. Two, perhaps three, times that many died at the hands of the Nazis while trying to build tunnels that proved to be of no use to anyone."

Nora put a hand to her mouth. "Twenty thousand people died?"

Rosh snorted. "This was just a branch office. Tens of thousands more died at Mauthausen, the parent camp. Both sites exercised a policy of extermination. Kill the prisoners by working and starving them to death. The more deaths, the more rewards for the guards."

Nora shook her head, stunned.

He glanced at her. "Sorry to shock you." Rosh slowed the car in order to make his way through winding streets filled with multicolored buildings and shops. Nora marveled at their pristine appearance, devoid of any hint that the Second World War, Nazis, Hitler, or a cruel concentration camp ever existed.

"We'll have to use public parking and walk a few blocks," Rosh said. They had just passed the railway station and he pulled into a lot on the right. He found a spot, put money into the pay-and-display machine, and placed the ticket on the dashboard.

Nora took her briefcase from the backseat while Rosh opened the trunk and took out a large case made of hard plastic.

"What is that?"

"I keep all my work in this." He patted the side. "Laptop, notepads, dictionaries . . . boring interpreter's items." Rosh waved them on. "This way."

They walked from the parking lot down a sliver of a road to a larger strasse. A right and a left, then another right, and they were on a residential street named after someone Nora never heard of.

"Are all the streets named after people?" she asked.

"Mostly. Germans and Austrians are especially proud of their cultural elite—doctors, writers, artists. Citizens cling to their culture wherever they can."

"Not to the Nazi era."

"Certainly not. Though I once heard the Allies wanted to rename the streets after Nazi leaders, just to rub everyone's nose in what the Nazis had done."

"Is that true?"

"I have no idea."

The houses and apartment buildings were large, but not ostentatious. Nora imagined the families living behind those doors and windows, wearing felt hats and lederhosen. She smiled inward at her own silliness.

Rosh stopped. "Here we are."

Nora turned to look at a small fence with the number 9. Beyond it, the walk led to a bungalow that looked like a dainty brown pebble wedged between much larger and more impressive rocks. Her impression was that it had been here first, that everything else was built up around it. Perhaps Zimmerman refused to sell out to the developers.

"Shall we?" Rosh asked.

Nora was suddenly nervous. She wished they had called first or had confirmed he was there. What if he was on a holiday somewhere—or dead?

In her moment of hesitation, the front door opened and a man came out. He was tall, thin, and young—and dressed in black. As he lifted his head, Nora saw that he wore a priest's collar. He came down the walk to them.

"Hello," Nora said.

"English?" the priest asked.

"American," she replied.

"Then, hi," he said and stepped through the gate, closing it behind him. He had long jet-black hair, carefully styled away from a slender face and blue eyes that exuded intelligent warmth.

"Is this the home of Rudolf Zimmerman?" Rosh asked.

The priest looked at them both warily. "Zimmerman? No, I'm sorry. This is the home of Rudolf Brecht."

Nora threw a glance at Rosh. He smiled. "Brecht was his mother's original name. It would make sense for him not to use Zimmerman."

"Who are you?" the priest asked, his eyes darting from one to the other. "What is this about?"

"I am Dr. Nora Richards."

"A tourist? A reporter or writer of some sort?"

"Neither. I work with the government."

"Whose government?" the priest asked, his eyes flickering.

"The United States, but also with whatever governments need my help." She tried to keep it simple. She brought out her NIH identification and held it up for the priest.

"It looks official enough, not that I would know. What is your purpose here?"

"That's a matter I have to take up with Mr. Zimmerman."

"I'm not trying to be nosy," the priest said. "I'm protective. Mr. *Brecht* is not in good health."

"Is he a member of your parish?" Nora asked, thinking of another angle to take.

"Yes."

"A good member? A regular confessor and communicant?"

"You are a Catholic?"

"Yes. And if he's a good Catholic, I have every hope he'll want to help me."

"He's a good man. He has served the Church faithfully since . . . well, the war," the priest said. The way he said "the war" gave Nora the impression the priest was fully aware of Zimmerman's past.

"If that's the case, then your presence may be helpful. Will you join us?" Nora asked.

Rosh cleared his throat. "Dr. Richards, I'm not entirely sure that—"

"If it will help Mr. Brecht, then I will," the priest said.

"We need all the help we can get," said Nora.

"I am Father Luke." The priest smiled and took Nora's hand.

"It may be providential that you're with us, Father."

Father Luke turned to Rosh, and Nora noticed Rosh merely nodded but didn't extend his hand. "Jacob Rosh."

"All right," Father Luke said. "Let's go in."

They followed the priest up the sidewalk to the house.

CHAPTER 45

SALZBURG, AUSTRIA

MARK SAT IN Knox's private room in the Landeskliniken Hospital and watched the television attached to the upper corner of the wall. It was muted, but the visuals and headlines affirmed the devastating spread of the virus.

He looked away from the screen to the empty pale blue walls, then to the institutional bed with silver rails. He listened to the hiss and beep of monitoring equipment. Tubes and wires led to and from Knox.

At a glance, Mark couldn't imagine how Knox had survived the blast. Half his face was lacerated. His right arm was broken in two places. He'd required hundreds of stitches around his torso and legs. The doctors were concerned about liver and kidney damage, but wanted him stabilized before doing any exploratory surgery.

Knox groaned loudly.

Mark looked at the man's face. He'd groaned several times over the past hour and had even opened his eyes once, only to close them and drift off again. This time he moved his left arm and flexed his fingers. He groaned again.

Mark found the remote control and turned off the television.

"Carlson?" Knox asked, his voice a harsh rasp.

Mark turned back to see Knox looking at him. "Be still, Knox. I'll get a nurse."

"No." Knox swallowed hard. "Not yet. We have to talk."

"Are you feeling well enough to—"

"Listen to me!" Knox said as sharply as his feeble breath allowed.

Mark pulled his chair closer, sat on its edge, and leaned toward Knox. "Go on."

"Where am I? Is this the hotel?"

"The Landeskliniken Hospital in Salzburg."

"I was in an explosion at the lab."

"That's right."

"Maier," Knox said. "He betrayed me. He betrayed Weigel."

"It's what he does best."

Knox groaned. "I had a dream. I saw Weigel. He came to me and explained everything."

"What did he tell you?"

"He'd followed leads, found the lab in Obersalzberg, and showed it to Maier. Weigel wanted to tell me immediately, wanted to tell the world, but Maier told him to act normally—to go to Siberia for the conference. Then he was to come to London. To meet me as we'd planned. But something went wrong. Weigel fell ill and came to me. But he was too delirious to communicate anything sensible. In my dream, he said he was annoyed with me. For not understanding what he was trying to say. I was too stupid and afraid." Knox fell silent.

"Was that a dream or what really happened?" Mark asked.

Knox closed his eyes and Mark feared he would lose him again. Suddenly his eyes flew open. "Am I safe?"

"There's a guard outside."

Knox sighed. "Maier won't let me live, you know. I've served my usefulness to him. Just as Weigel did." A tear dropped from his right eye. He winced as it slipped into one of the deep cuts.

"What do you know that would give Maier a reason to kill you? He'd only bother if he thought you had something on him."

"Weigel knew something else. Something he was trying to tell *me*."

"Do you know what it was?"

"I believe it's in the satchel," Knox said.

"What satchel?"

"I put it somewhere safe. On top of the wardrobe." Knox took a slow breath, then exhaled.

"Concentrate, Knox. What satchel? What wardrobe?"

"What a surprise to find it in the possession of that woman.

What was her name? I can't think of it. She was a lovely lady, someone I wanted to get to know better, but once I saw what was inside the satchel, there was no chasing another romance. My course was set. I had a purpose to my life."

"What woman are you talking about?" Mark felt a growing frustration.

"I've squandered it," Knox lamented. "I trusted the wrong people."

"Focus, Knox. *Focus.* Do you have information that can help us?"

"There was that other woman," he said.

Mark put his face in his hands. Was Knox deliriously reminiscing about old girlfriends?

"Agent X," he said.

Mark looked up. "Agent X?"

"It's all in the satchel. You have to get it. The official reports. British Intelligence. The pieces are all there. I simply couldn't put them together then. Things will make sense to me now."

"*Where is it?*" Mark tried to control his sense of urgency.

"Come upstairs. I'll show you." Knox tried to sit up. Pain kept him down.

"You have to stay still." Mark touched him lightly to ease him back. "Tell me where the satchel is."

"On the wardrobe," he said as if he couldn't make it any clearer. "But you must find Agent X."

Knox closed his eyes and was silent again.

"Knox?"

Knox's breathing fell into a steady rhythm.

Mark dashed into the hall, speed-dialing Mac as he went.

CHAPTER 46

NOVOSIBIRSK, SIBERIA

SUSAN TURNED THE details of the conference call over in her mind. The world teetered on the edge of a precipice. For the life of her, she wasn't sure what she could do to pull it back. If Jotham turned out to be a dead end, she would be reduced to nothing more than damage control: trying to limit the death count in Siberia.

She was on her fourth cup of coffee when the doorbell rang. She walked to the door and opened it. Grigory nodded to her, then briskly entered the apartment. "Good morning," he said as he took off his gloves and glanced around the apartment. "This is impressive. Maybe I should go to work for the WHO."

"With your credentials . . ." she began to say, but realized by his expression he wasn't in the mood for more humor.

"You want to talk to me privately."

"About Jotham."

He gave her a disapproving look. "What about it?"

"Grigory, I think we're beyond posturing and saber rattling. I'm not here to invade your turf or to undermine you. You can have all the credit if we successfully defeat this outbreak. But you and I must talk candidly and honestly. Is that possible?"

He eyed her for a moment, as if weighing his options. "It's possible."

She wanted to believe him. "All the evidence suggests that Return to Earth has used Jotham—and may be using it now—to kill your people."

He clasped his hands behind his back and walked to the window. He remained there silent for a while. Susan nearly called his name to get his attention again, but chose to wait.

Without facing her, he began, "In the late 1980s, I worked under a boss who was a recognized genius, but whose moral compass was completely out of whack. He admired how the Roman legions catapulted the bodies of sick animals into the camps of their enemies; discovered how the British and Americans used smallpox against Native Americans; researched how a group of Turkish physicians injected typhus-contaminated serum into Armenian civilians during World War I; studied how the Japanese Army conducted human experimentation with multiple biological agents in Manchuria and spread bubonic plague in China." He turned.

"This was your boss at Jotham?" Susan was horrified.

Grigory nodded. "Under his leadership, Jotham was fully vested in developing bacterial and viral weapons. In my section, we worked on loading the Marburg and Ebola viruses into special long-range strategic and operational missile warheads. We also had warheads that were designed to be loaded with the smallpox virus and with the bubonic plague and anthrax bacteria."

"So Jotham's reputation is well deserved," she said.

Grigory shrugged. "It's odd, but I never really imagined the terror and panic that could be generated by the weapons we were developing there. Maybe I thought we'd never succeed. Mostly we considered statistics, not human beings. Our statisticians predicted that attacking a city of five million people with, say, pneumonic plague would result in at least one hundred fifty thousand serious illnesses and no less than thirty-six thousand deaths. Imagine that occurring in a dozen major cities. Then, it was all academic. But I see the panic now. Any one of these weapons, especially if exploded simultaneously in multiple cities, could destroy entire populations of cities, countries, continents."

"Did Stefan Maier work at Jotham?"

Grigory walked over to a bookshelf and rubbed his finger along the grain. "After the fall of the Soviet Union, research funds were limited. Stefan Maier's funds were not. He came and studied with my boss for most of a year. He kept to himself. He had his own lab and brought in his own technicians. He returns to Jotham every couple of years and pays millions of dollars for his time there."

"Does he still have labs there?"

"Possibly. Probably."

"Did he acquire any of the biological agents, the Spanish flu virus, or anthrax bacteria, or Ebola virus?"

Grigory shook his head. "I don't think so. It's not as if such things are lying around for anyone to take. Jotham's leaders want to keep all biologics to themselves, suspicious they might be used against them."

"What about nanotechnology?"

He faced her, with surprise. "You are a very clever woman."

"Tell me about Jotham's work on nanotechnology," she pressed.

"An entire section has been developing nanotechnology for years. It's an especially exciting field. Imagine the possibilities for humanity."

"I can't imagine Maier is interested in saving human lives."

"No. He wouldn't be."

"Did Maier have access to their nanoparticle research?"

Grigory nodded. "He worked on experiments designed to develop a nanotechnology that would allow toxic biological infectious particles to be loaded into nanoparticles. When inhaled, ingested, or injected, the nanoparticles would dissolve, releasing millions of infectious particles into the victim. The nanoparticles would function like a huge army of microscopic Trojan horses. If the technology worked, it would be the most potent delivery system for biologic warfare ever invented."

"What would cause the particles to release their contents?" Susan tried to contain her growing fear. "What would cause the nanocapsule to dissolve? An enzymatic reaction of some sort?"

"I've heard rumors they have developed a particular particle that can be prepared in cold labs and kept in cold storage. These particles are designed to release their contents when warmed up."

"You mean to room temperature?"

"It would depend upon the nanoparticle. Jotham allegedly designed one to dissolve not at room temperature but at about 37 degrees Celsius, or 98.6 degrees Fahrenheit."

Susan folded her arms and thought about Mark's report. "If

Maier obtained samples of the desiccated H1N1 Spanish flu virus from a Nazi lab in Berchtesgaden and brought it here, he could conceivably inject the virus into nanoparticles. It would be the perfect delivery system. He could place them in water or food systems and, when ingested, they would infect scores of people."

Grigory nodded. "Just a few ingested particles could deliver a fatal dose of the virus."

She moved toward him. "Grigory—"

He looked at her. "It's only a theory. We don't know that it happened, or even that it *could* happen."

"Grigory, we have to assume it *is* happening!" She spun around as her mind worked through a dozen different options and scenarios. "We *must* get into Jotham."

Grigory shook his head. "No one gets into Jotham without the highest security clearance. *I* can't get in anymore."

"Then *find* a way! Get your president on the line. Do something. You owe it to your people, if not to the world."

Grigory stood. "There are limits to what we can do."

"Then I have to assume that you're working with Maier and want to protect him."

"That's ridiculous."

"Is it? Others will assume the same if and when the rubble from this catastrophe clears."

"You're threatening me, Dr. Hutchinson."

"Whatever it takes, Dr. Tarasov."

He put on his gloves and smiled.

Anton reappeared at noon with a smug expression on his face.

"I've got it." He walked to a computer on a corner desk and sat down.

"The security tape?" Susan asked, as she stepped behind him.

"This is a DVD from the Novosibirsk water-treatment plant out by the reservoir." He loaded it into the computer. "Compliments of Detective Rozvensky, though he doesn't know it yet."

"You stole this from him?"

"He shouldn't let things lie around his desk." Anton double-clicked on a file name written in Russian and the DVD began. It revealed a screen displaying various areas of the plant, the images all running simultaneously.

"What am I looking at?"

"Unfortunately," Anton explained, as he adjusted them to each view, "the shots on the screen come from different cameras and rotate. They don't keep a digital record of entire recordings of each camera." He pointed to the box at the upper-right hand of the screen. "This is the camera to watch."

Susan leaned in closer.

"Here it is. See the brown van pulling up just outside the fence?"

Susan could make out a cargo truck. "It looks like a UPS truck."

Anton pointed to the side of the truck. "You can see the company logo just behind the door."

She watched as several men dressed in black, wearing ski masks, exited the side of the van. Two men opened the rear doors and pulled out flexible white tubing. From the blurred image, Susan guessed the tubing was about six inches in diameter. Two other men used a bolt cutter to create an opening in the chain-link fence.

The camera cut to another section of the fence.

"We'll come back to the crime scene in just a moment," Anton said, and clicked the controls until the image he wanted reappeared.

The men cutting the fence were now inside.

"You can see that they're pumping liquid into the plant's water intake." He pointed to the screen. "That's the intake. Here. See the water flowing through the grate. They obviously know exactly where to pump the liquid."

The two men at the water's edge were communicating back and forth to the truck, using hand signals.

"Those are standard military signals," Anton said.

"Were you in the military?"

"I just watch a lot of movies." He tapped a finger on the screen. "Now, here it gets interesting. Watch."

Two security guards could be seen walking toward the front of the truck with their sidearms drawn.

"The guards are shouting something at the men. Look." Anton pointed to the side entrance of the truck. A masked man, with an automatic weapon, leaped from the rear compartment, firing his weapon. Susan gasped as the bright muzzle flame burst from the end of the gun. The security guards were blown backward. One landed in a motionless heap. The other rolled over onto his stomach and tried to crawl away. The masked man stood over him and fired several shots into his back. The guard twitched from the impact of the close-range bullets, then stopped.

Susan's hand covered her mouth as she remembered her own horror with masked men and gunfire.

"Now watch this," Anton said.

The men quickly pulled the tubing back into the truck and slammed the doors as the truck peeled away from the scene.

"There! Do you see it?" Anton waved his hand excitedly at the top of the truck.

"What is it? It looks like an external air-conditioning unit."

"It is." With a few clicks, Anton reversed the video, froze the frame, and expanded the picture to reveal the logo on the truck. The Russian letters became clearer—Счастливое Мороженое.

Susan squinted and looked closely. "Is it Russian for 'UPS' or what?"

"No. And the company name isn't registered with the government," Anton explained. "I already checked them out."

"So what's the name?" Susan asked.

"It says 'Happy Ice Cream.' Now we have to ask why they would use an ice-cream company truck to place chemicals into a water-intake valve."

"Because they had to refrigerate whatever agent they were dumping into the water," Susan replied. She stared at the picture of the truck and thought of her conversation with Grigory. "It's not chemicals, Anton. They were dumping chilled nanoparticles filled with the influenza virus in the cold water."

Anton leaned back in his chair and offered a Russian expletive.

The house telephone rang, startling Susan. She punched the speaker phone on. "Hello?"

"Detective Rozvensky here. The Return to Earth agent we captured this morning talked. We know the location of their base of operations. Come to the front of your compound. You may accompany us on the raid."

"On what basis?"

"As a scientific and medical adviser."

"By whose authority?"

"Dr. Grigory Tarasov. He said you wanted to see Jotham. Now's your chance."

CHAPTER 47

MAC AND DIGGER leaned toward the speakerphone on Mac's desk.

"I don't know what to make of it," Mac said to Mark. "A satchel? Agent X? It could be nonsense."

"Well, so far none of the nonsense has proven to be nonsense," Mark said. "Except for that sentence."

"This is so cool." Digger wiggled in his chair like a little boy. "I've heard about an Agent X in British Intelligence. She was regarded as one of the war's best-kept secrets. The legend surrounding her led many to believe she didn't really exist, but was an amalgam of several female agents. MI5 won't confirm or deny her existence. Nobody knows if she's still alive."

"She's probably in Brazil with Hitler and Elvis," Mac said.

Digger smirked at Mac. "You are not a believer."

"What are we supposed to do?" Mac asked Mark. "I'm managing telephone calls, e-mail messages, faxes, and encrypted Teletypes from people in nearly every position and rank imaginable, from the president's special counsel to Pentagon officials to personal friends seeking assurance from me that all is not lost. The world is on the edge of panic and you want me to go searching for a mythical agent and some sort of satchel?"

"I'll do it!" Digger announced. "I think any lead is a lead worth chasing at this point."

Mac rolled his eyes. "You can take a couple of hours—*max*. I don't want a lot of time spent on this."

"Whatever you say, chief."

"Let me know if you find anything," Mark said and hung up.

Mac brushed his hands over his hair. "Well?"

Digger stood. "I'm on it."

He turned to leave, but Abby Benson was standing in the doorway.

"Yes, Mrs. Benson?"

She seemed to be carefully weighing what she intended to say.

"Speak up," Mac said impatiently. "What is it?"

"You were talking about Agent X?"

"You know about her, don't you?" Digger said. "Sure you would! You worked in those circles, right?"

She gazed at Digger as though she doubted she could trust him with what she knew.

Mac rose from his chair. "Mrs. Benson, if you can save us some time and put the myth to rest, I'd be grateful."

She slowly shook her head. "It's no myth."

Digger nearly leaped up and down. "I knew it!"

She looked at her hands, clasped in front of her. "I know where she is."

CHAPTER 48

EBENSEE, AUSTRIA

ZIMMERMAN'S HOME SEEMED smaller on the inside than it looked from the outside. They squeezed into a narrow front hall.

"Please, put your coats there," the priest said, and pointed to a row of old coats and a worn black hat hung on hooks directly to their left. "Let me talk to him first."

Father Luke went through a door to the right. It was made of leaded windowpanes. Obscured colors shifted in the room beyond.

Rosh hung up his coat, then took Nora's and placed it next to his. She noticed a curtained doorway next to the hooks. Through a slight gap Nora glimpsed a bed and a nightstand. A crucifix hung on the wall above the nightstand. She thought she recognized a prayer book and string of rosary beads resting next to the table lamp.

Directly ahead of them, light shined through a window over a sink. A counter held flour and sugar containers and a stainless-steel coffeepot. She saw just the corner of a chrome-framed table and a chair. The air hinted at the smell of aftershave, cigarettes, and old newspapers.

Father Luke opened the paned door and gestured for them to come in. Rosh tipped his head for Nora to go first, and she entered the small sitting room. The room was crowded with a brown sofa, the arms covered in embroidered cloths, a wingback chair with stained and ragged edges, an old television with a portable radio on top, and a liquor cabinet with a framed family photo. Zimmerman was in the photo, white-haired and smiling, with a round-faced woman, another couple, and three small children. The walls were pale green and adorned with a hodgepodge of store-bought pictures of the Alps and green fields, and one painting of the Madonna and Child.

Zimmerman sat in a wheelchair next to a pair of French doors. Threadbare curtains, a faded concoction of flowers, were pulled open, revealing a modest garden in the back. Nora immediately suspected that Father Luke probably mowed the lawn himself, or got one of the kids at the church to do it.

Zimmerman's head hung forward, as if the weight were too much for his neck to bear. His eyes peered at them over thick glasses. His hair was a thin and white, revealing brown age spots on the scalp below.

"Sit down," Father Luke said, and waved a hand at the couch. It barely fit both Nora and Rosh. From this angle, Nora got a better look at Zimmerman's face. She saw a hint of the young man in the photograph online. The high cheekbones, thin lips, sharp nose. But his pallor and the errant patches of hair that stuck out from his cheeks and chin—probably missed during his last shave—announced that youth had left him a long, long time ago.

A feeding tray was attached to the front of the wheelchair and Zimmerman leaned on it, his bony fingers laced, his veiny hands almost glowing in their whiteness.

"So," Zimmerman began, his voice a harsh whisper. The word *so* came out as "zo," and Nora guessed he didn't speak English often. "You have come for Zimmerman."

"Yes, sir," Nora said. "We need your help."

"Help? Of what help could I be to anyone? Look at me. I could not lift a pinch of salt to help you." He was talking to Nora, but his eyes were drawn to Rosh. His expression became uneasy.

"We need to talk to you about your past. I know it must be painful, but you must understand how urgent it is."

"Why is it urgent?"

"We believe a group of terrorists is using the virus created in Obersalzberg to kill people around the world."

"The virus created in Ober—" He looked distressed and muttered something in German. "This is an absurd idea."

"I'm afraid it isn't," Nora said. "Otherwise, I wouldn't have bothered you."

"Tell me why you believe what you do."

Nora looked at Father Luke, who nodded his encouragement. Rosh sat with his eyes down, his expression grim. "Well . . ." She began, then gave him an abbreviated version of what had happened over the past few days, ending with the outbreaks in Athens, Rome, and Budapest.

"I heard about this," Father Luke said. "We prayed for the families at our early Mass this morning."

"Anything you can tell us, no matter how insignificant you may think it is, might help," Nora said.

Zimmerman looked at her, then at Rosh. "You're a Jew?" he asked Rosh.

Rosh cleared his throat. "Yes, I am."

Zimmerman looked at Nora again. "I have nothing to say with him here."

Nora was startled. *"What?"*

"He must leave."

"Herr Brecht—" Father Luke said.

"No. I'm sincere," Zimmerman said.

Rosh stood. "As you wish."

Nora wanted to say something, to reason with Zimmerman, or apologize to Rosh, but concluded that the lives of untold millions was a factor greater than this affront to Rosh.

"With permission, I'll stroll in the garden."

"Whatever you like," Zimmerman said.

Father Luke opened one of the French doors and Rosh stepped out onto the stone patio. He clasped his hands behind his back and walked toward the nearby fence. Father Luke closed the door again.

"What was that all about?" Father Luke asked Zimmerman. "You do not have a problem with Jews."

"No, I don't," he said sadly. "But I've found they have a problem with me. I can't bear the way they look at me. It's as if, in their eyes, I see the eyes of the ones at the camp. All looking at me. Pointing fingers at me. Their mouths open in silent screams, black like graves. I dream about them every night."

Nora opened her briefcase and took out a notepad. "What can you tell me about the German virus?"

Zimmerman pressed his lips together.

"Tell her what you know, Rudolf. Consider this part of your penance."

"My life is a penance," he growled.

"Then make this part of your ongoing confession," the priest said.

"You're shrewd." Zimmerman moved his body without it actually moving, as if the bones under the loose skin had momentum of their own. "No one else has ever asked me about germ warfare. Do you realize? Of all the questions, that one hasn't come up."

"Until now, no one took those rumors seriously," Nora said.

"What can I tell you? You've found their lab. You know what they did."

"We don't know enough," Nora said. "We found a room full of files, as I told you, but we're just getting started going through them. It'll take weeks to sort out the information and to find vulnerabilities for the virus. We don't have weeks."

His head slowly moved up and down.

"We know they desiccated the virus and stored it in powdered form, that the powder could be spread through food and water. What was the powder stored in?"

"Steel drums, I believe. No, maybe it was wooden barrels. I'm not sure. I never saw them myself." He thought again. "No, I'm not speaking correctly. I did see one. A large wooden barrel, like a wine cask, brought to the camp. I didn't know what it was at the time. Not until later. The powder was given to a group of prisoners—for study, they said. Put in their water. Then doctors from Berlin measured the results: time it took for the virus to take effect, symptoms, death."

"You witnessed that?" Nora asked.

He paused, then said with obvious reluctance, "Yes. I helped tabulate the results. No one told me what I was tabulating. I thought it was simply a flu outbreak. The prisoners were sick with something all the time, so that wouldn't have been unusual."

"You did this work as assistant to Dr. Heinrich Gross?"

Zimmerman's eyes shot to hers, the mere mention of the name having jolted him. "For a time, yes. I was assigned."

Nora sensed the defensiveness behind the answers. Zimmerman probably had years of practice attempting to deflect personal culpability. "Besides Dr. Gross, whom else did you meet? Do you know who was in charge of the work?"

"There were many doctors at many camps. But I believe a Dr. Schmidt was running the project. He had been with the Nazi Party for years. It was rumored that he developed the sickness from the first war."

"Are there code names we should look for in the files? I saw a document calling the virus the Final Solution. Is that what you heard it called?"

"An overused phrase. Someone may have called it that somewhere, but it wasn't commonly known as such. We simply called it La Grippe, like they did in the first war."

"Not Liebfraumilch?"

His eyes told her she had surprised him yet again. "Liebfraumilch," he repeated. "I have not thought about Liebfraumilch since the war's end. In those closing days, it was foremost in my mind—most of us thought about it then, for fear Hitler would execute his plan."

Nora was confused. "His plan? Which plan?"

"We were certain he would put the virus into all the water supplies across Austria and Germany if the Allies broke through the lines into Germany. Even down to the last couple of weeks, we anticipated it. That's why we thought about Liebfraumilch."

"We have to go back a few steps," Nora said. "Isn't Liebfraumilch what we've been talking about? I thought that was another name for the germ-warfare efforts."

He looked at her, perplexed, then shook his head. "Liebfraumilch was a different effort, also headed by Dr. Schmidt."

"If it wasn't the virus, then what was it?"

"It was the *cure*."

Nora froze. "What?" The word was a mere click in her throat.

"Liebfraumilch was the cure for the germ they had isolated. You didn't understand that?" He looked at her. "We'd heard rumors they'd created enough to protect all of Germany, if the virus was used against the Allies and brought back to us. Then we heard other rumors they'd made enough only for the Nazi leadership—the true Aryans—and stored it in Obersalzberg, where the leaders would have easy access to it. A few of us determined that, if the sickness came, we would rush to Obersalzberg to get our own doses of Liebfraumilch."

Father Luke, who had been standing for the conversation, sat next to Nora. He seemed as astonished as Nora felt. "So there may be a cure—a way to fight—this virus?"

"If they're using the same virus, yes. Hitler was adamant the Nazis not repeat the imbecility of the Kaiser's government. He told his scientists that if they created an effective virus, they must also have an equally effective cure."

"Do you know if it worked? Was it ever tested?"

He rubbed a bony finger along his thin nose. "At Ebensee we tested it on prisoners given La Grippe. It cured them all. It didn't matter whether they were just coming down with it or were on death's doorstep. If they were given Liebfraumilch, they lived. If they were given a placebo, they died."

"Do you know where they stored the Liebfraumilch?" she asked.

"Somewhere in Obersalzberg. I don't remember ever being told where. Around Hitler's Berghof, we assumed. Or below the Kehlsteinhaus. Either would make sense."

Nora wanted to stand, but feared her legs would buckle under her. This was monumental news. "Would you mind if I made a call?"

"Are you going to turn me in to the Nazi hunters?"

"I'm going to inform my team there's hope," she said. She dug into her pocket for her phone and realized she must have left it in her coat pocket in the front hall.

Zimmerman said something to Father Luke in German.

"He's tired," Father Luke said to her. "If you don't mind . . ."

Nora understood and thanked Zimmerman for his help. His head hung low and he didn't respond. The weight of his past still rested upon his shoulders.

Nora grabbed her briefcase and walked to the front hallway while Father Luke opened the French doors and beckoned for Rosh to come back in.

Nora put on her coat, but her cell phone wasn't in either pocket. *I must have left it in the car.*

Rosh moved into the front hall silently and put on his coat. She assumed he was still offended for being asked to leave. He stepped through the front door and lingered there. Nora waited until Father Luke joined them outside a moment later.

"I'm sure he'll talk to you again after he's rested," he said.

"We'll only bother him if it's absolutely necessary," Nora assured him. "If he remembers anything more, please call me." She handed the priest her card.

"I'll be praying for you and your work."

"Ach," Rosh suddenly said. "I've left my case inside."

"I'll get it," Father Luke started to say, but Rosh was already past him and through the door.

"Thank you for your help, Father," Nora said. "I doubt he would have cooperated had you not been there."

"I know what you must be thinking, but he is a good man. Following the war, he dedicated his life to trying to make up for his role during the war. But, for some, that's never enough."

"Is there ever enough penance, ever enough forgiveness, for such a time?" Nora asked.

"I want to believe so. God lavishes out his forgiveness to us. How much better would the world be if we gave even a small portion of the same to one another?"

Nora looked toward the door, expecting Rosh to return. "I wonder what's delaying him," Nora said.

A crash came from the sitting room. Nora and Father Luke quickly exchanged looks, then dashed through the doorway. "Herr Zimmerman?" Father Luke called.

They came upon an unexpected scene. Rosh was leaning over Zimmerman, his hands on the old man's throat. Zimmerman was struggling, flailing, his face red.

"Rosh!" Nora shouted.

Rosh ignored her and clung to Zimmerman. The priest dove at Rosh and, together, they crashed onto the sofa. As they slammed against the wall, the pictures and knickknacks rattled, some falling with a crash to the floor. They tumbled to the floor, with Father Luke on top. The priest was spry and strong and quickly drove Rosh face-first into the threadbare carpet.

Rosh's contorted face was turned toward Nora, eyes wild,

white spittle at the corners of his mouth. "He doesn't deserve to live," he snarled. "He killed my family! Do you hear me? *He killed my family!*"

While the priest subdued Rosh, Nora went to Zimmerman. He leaned back in his wheelchair, gasping, his neck rubbed raw and already bruising.

"I'll get help," she said, and raced for the phone in the hall.

CHAPTER 49

NOVOSIBIRSK, SIBERIA

THE BLACK RUSSIAN UAZ—an SUV of sorts—careened through the streets of Novosibirsk, trying to follow the half a dozen police cars and the SWAT van that raced ahead. Susan was sitting next to Anton in back of the vehicle, her muscles tight from trying to keep her position. Every turn slammed her back and forth.

Jankowski was driving, his eyes hawklike and his jaw set as he maneuvered through the streets and the few cars in the way. Susan was grateful the city streets were empty due to the epidemic; traffic would have made the trip even more dangerous.

Youngman was riding shotgun, while Westcott and Brainerd occupied the seat in front of Susan and Anton. Dressed in civilian clothes, they had been given strict instructions by Detective Rozvensky about their role in this raid—they were coming strictly as observers and to investigate the scene once it was deemed safe. But as soon as they were seated, the soldiers brought small black carrying cases out from under their seats and began arming themselves with enough weaponry to launch a civil war.

Susan and Anton exchanged nervous looks.

Brainerd saw their worried expressions and said with an apologetic smile, "They may need our help."

The Jotham complex was some twenty miles southeast of Novosibirsk, in rich woodlands just east of the Ob River. As they drove, a light snow began to fall and looked like static against the gray screen of day.

"Can someone give us a clue about what we're driving into?" Jankowski asked.

Anton brought up a website of information on his iPhone and began throwing out statistics for their general consumption. "More than one hundred lab and administrative buildings. A large campus dedicated to virology research. Time spent in the late 1980s working on biological weapons."

"Security?" Jankowski asked.

"State-of-the-art security systems," Anton replied. "And they need it. They've got labs for investigations of pathogens under P-4 biocontainment-level conditions—the most secure in the world. They're messing around with vaccines and aerosols, viral pathogens and infectious material. The buildings are designed for the highest risk-taking with the most virulent of viruses."

They had come alongside the river and, on the opposite side of the road, drove past thick forest. Signs now appeared and, at various points, Susan could see fences through the trees.

"I assume they're also equipped to keep their personnel from contamination," said Susan.

"The buildings have extensive ventilation systems, hermetic entrances, double-cascade filters for fine purification, waste-piping systems that treat wastewater at a temperature of 135 degrees Celsius, and three independent power-supply sources."

"Where I'd want to live when the end of the world comes," Brainerd said. The other soldiers laughed.

"Only if you like animals," Anton said. "The farm is like Noah's ark. It's one of the biggest animal-testing facilities in western Siberia, and one of the biggest lab-animal sellers in the world."

"Yeah, but they're all mutated with three eyes and six legs," Westcott said, laughing.

"It's possible that the Return to Earth agent was lying," Anton said to Susan. "People will say anything under interrogation."

"Would Grigory Tarasov or Detective Rozvensky do this if they weren't sure?"

"In a heartbeat," Anton said. "Our officials are schoolboys dressed in grown-up clothes. Who wouldn't want the chance for a little fast driving and gun shooting?"

After his conversation with Susan, Grigory apparently tagged

Rozvensky to check into the possibility that Return to Earth was operating out of Jotham. Rozvensky changed his interrogation tactics and learned from the captured driver that the organization did have a facility there. Jotham security, cooperating, confirmed that more than one brown Счастливое Мороженое refrigerator truck had been seen entering the complex. Return to Earth, it seemed, had been very busy.

Susan smiled to herself. Apparently Grigory concluded that an international incident at Jotham was preferable to his looking like the bad guy in this crisis.

"Get ready!" Jankowski said, and tapped the GLONASS unit, the Russian version of a GPS, on the dash.

In their earlier briefing, Rozvensky explained that the mission was being handled as a matter of national security through the office of the president of Russia. Leadership at Jotham reluctantly agreed to cooperate. The team would enter through the front gate and approach on a service road to the rear of the building occupied by Return to Earth—a three-story brick laboratory facility—with police cars strategically placed around the building's perimeter. Each car had three police officers and one SWAT sharpshooter who would take positions. The SWAT van would park outside the main loading dock at the rear of the building. Two SWAT teams would enter through door at each end of the loading dock, while a third team would cover them from the armored van. Susan and her entourage were instructed to stay behind the van, on the far side of a surrounding iron fence, until they were given an "all clear."

Rozvensky had made it clear to Susan that she was being allowed to accompany them on the raid only for medical and technical assistance. Her presence, he had said, might prevent his men from making potentially fatal mistakes if biological materials were present. "But," he added more than once, "you can only enter the facility to investigate when signaled to do so."

Susan had insisted she be allowed to bring her bodyguards—and the hazmat team that followed them.

Rozvensky wasn't pleased with the soldiers coming along, but conceded.

A Russian command screeched over the walkie-talkie next to Youngman.

"We're entering the Jotham complex," Jankowski said, and followed left onto a short driveway leading to a heavily guarded gate. Several guards dressed in black stepped out and saluted them as they passed. Susan remembered the last guard she had dealt with—the one who had betrayed them to Return to Earth at the airport. She hoped she wasn't about to experience a rerun.

The Jotham site looked, for all intents and purposes, like a quaint college campus. The buildings were no more than three stories tall, each with a beautiful facade done in flowing Russian style. Susan noticed that, apart from front windows, the buildings had few windows. Probably to maintain greater environmental control and containment in the labs.

Jankowski ordered, "Put your walkie-talkies on silent and activate your earpieces."

Anton handed her the small communications device and she fumbled to insert it into her ear. In that tiny piece of equipment was a speaker, microphone, and transmitter that allowed each member of the team to hear and be heard by all others on an encrypted signal.

"Lock and load," Jankowski ordered as the vehicles navigated a section that looked like a town square. A brick building that Susan recognized from Rozvensky's pictures sat near a fence by the river.

As the unmarked building loomed closer, Susan's mouth turned as dry as old cotton and her heart beat against her chest like a fist. A couple of the vehicles peeled to the left while the others, including Susan's, sped single file through a gate at the back of the facility and raced to their assigned positions. As the SWAT van skidded to a stop, Jankowski pulled the UAZ to a halt at the gate itself.

The SWAT team members leapt out of the van, one team racing to the left, another to the right, while two snipers quickly climbed ladders attached to the vehicle and got into position on top.

Each soldier in the UAZ hopped out, sidearm drawn. They took position behind each open door. Westcott peered back into the UAZ. "Dr. Hutchinson, Mr. Pushkin, do *not* get out of this vehicle until one of us tells you it's all right. Understood?"

Susan's mouth was so dry she could only nod. They were much closer to the building than she'd expected—only twenty-five yards away, if that. Anton nudged for her to get lower down.

"This is bulletproof glass," he said. "But I wouldn't take any chances."

She ducked, but could still see the Russians moving to the two doors on what looked like a loading dock. They ran in a line behind a lead member hidden behind a body-length protective shield. Directly behind him was a man with a handheld battering ram. The remaining squad members had automatic assault weapons up, in position, and ready to shoot.

Before they could reach the doors, Susan saw something move through an opaque window in one of the metal pull-down garage doors. What looked like the end of a bazooka was thrust out. Youngman shouted, "RPG! Incoming!"

Before anyone could react, the weapon was fired. A projectile shot toward the front of the SWAT van and exploded into the motor, lifting the van in a bright explosion. It crashed back down again and the Russian sharpshooters were thrown to the ground. One lay there for a moment, clearly stunned, then got up as far as his knees. He jerked his head back and forth as if trying to shake his brain back into gear. The other man writhed, clutching his leg. A cacophony of voices shouted Russian in Susan's ear.

Youngman and Brainerd brandished their automatic weapons and held them ready. The remaining Russians began firing, peppering the metal garage door with their large-caliber bullets, shredding it.

No one was attending to the two sharpshooters—still on the ground—now being fired on from a second-story window. The sharpshooter who'd been shaking his head looked dazed as bullets sprayed the ground around him. The other seemed to realize what was happening and began dragging himself slowly across the pavement to the relative safety of the van while the gunman in the window continued firing.

Jankowski swore loudly, then gave a signal for Westcott to follow him. They raced to the SWAT van. Jankowski fired at the window as he ran, causing the sniper inside to pull back. He reached the moving sharpshooter and pulled him behind the van.

Westcott was only a few feet from the downed sharpshooter when shots were fired from a different second-floor window. The sharpshooter rolled and cried out, clutching his side. Jankowski spun around to the side of the van and gave Westcott cover while Westcott pulled the man to safety. Westcott knelt to determine his injuries. Susan pushed at the seat in front of her.

"What are you doing?" Anton asked, grabbing her arm.

"If he's wounded, I have to help."

She had reached the middle seat when Westcott said into his earpiece, "He's all right. The protective vest caught the bullet. He got the wind knocked out of him and a twisted ankle from falling off the van."

Susan watched as the SWAT commander emerged from the rear of the van with the movements of a man caught off guard by the chain of events. Jankowski went to him and put a hand on the man's shoulder. The commander looked at him, then nodded.

"We're good!" Jankowski yelled as he moved to one side of the van and signaled for Westcott to take the one opposite. They both raised their guns to the second-story windows. A sniper came into view for what seemed to Susan a fraction of a second. Jankowski fired once and the man flew backward, his rifle falling out the window. That drew the second sniper to fire at Jankowski, who stepped back as if he'd anticipated the shots. Westcott, from his position, took the second sniper out with a single shot.

As the action around the van played out, Susan heard loud percussions and saw each team using its handheld rams to break open the deadbolts on the loading-dock doors. As the doors flew open, the two men holding the rams stepped back and, in perfect precision, the men behind each threw in a pair of stun grenades. The teams took cover behind the wall. The grenades blew and the SWAT teams rushed into the facility. An explosion of automatic gunfire followed.

Susan watched the building anxiously. The drama, now inside, unfolded in her ear with shouts in Russian punctuated by sporadic bursts of gunfire.

"What are they saying?" Susan asked.

Jankowski nodded. "They are calling for ambulances and doctors."

An eerie silence descended. The soldiers and remaining SWAT members all kept their guns aimed at the building. Everyone waited.

Finally, a SWAT team member came to a side door and waved, calling out in Russian.

"All clear!" said Jankowski.

The SWAT commander raced toward the building as the large metal garage doors began to open.

CHAPTER 50

EBENSEE, AUSTRIA

NORA WATCHED THE ambulance pull away from Zimmerman's bungalow, and offered a small prayer that the old man would recover from Rosh's attack.

Rosh, handcuffed and seated in the back of a police car, looked at her just long enough to scowl, then turned away.

A plainclothes detective approached her. "I think we have all we need from you at this time."

"You have my card if there's anything else I can do."

He nodded and then, almost as an afterthought, pulled her cell phone from his pocket. "This is yours. We got it from *him*." A nod to Rosh.

"Thank you."

He walked away. A moment later, the police car took off with Rosh inside.

A hand touched her gently on the shoulder. She turned to face Father Luke. He looked disheveled from his wrestling match with Rosh. A red scrape marked his cheek, and the area above his right eye looked as if it might swell.

"Are you all right?" he asked her.

"Better than you, I think." She looked back at the bungalow. A uniformed officer stood by the door, writing in a notepad. "The job isn't finished until the paperwork is done," she said.

Father Luke chuckled, but his eyes stayed on her. They were kind eyes.

"What happened in there? I never would have expected Rosh to . . . to snap like that."

"He lost family members in the concentration camp here,"

Father Luke reminded her. "Perhaps being in the same room with a former Nazi was more than he could handle. Or perhaps he came with the intention of doing Herr Zimmerman harm."

Nora looked up at him. "Seriously?"

"Understandably, some people can never forgive. Some dedicate their lives to finding former Nazis and seeking justice. They follow leads, find them, then interview them under the guise of a sympathetic or urgent purpose. If they can get the former Nazis to admit who they are and what they've done in a court of law, then all the better. Sometimes, though, they become judge and jury and don't really want justice, only revenge."

"How do you know so much about this?" Nora asked.

"One can't be a priest in this part of the country and not know about it."

Nora lowered her head. "I feel miserable for having played a part in the whole incident."

"How could you know? You can't bear the responsibility for this."

She hugged herself against a sudden chill. She thought of Mark. "This is what happens when people don't forgive."

"I suppose so," the priest said. "Many who can't forgive become murderers. Not outwardly. But in their hearts they kill."

She looked at the priest. "What do they kill?"

"Love. Grace. Their own humanity. They waste their pain."

"Waste their pain? What do you mean?"

"I tell my parishioners that in every trial we encounter, God wants to teach us something. And sometimes the only time he gets our attention is when he allows us to hurt; enough so that we finally stop to listen."

Nora nodded.

"When I am in pain, when I suffer, God is attempting to do something for my good—to do something in and through me. So, I've learned, it's foolish to waste the pain. I must first forgive he who has harmed me. Then I need to accept the pain, as a gift . . . to seek to understand it. Last, I must learn how to use the healing of forgiveness and the gift of pain to help others I meet along the way."

The police officer at the bungalow called out for Father Luke. "One more question, if you please!"

Father Luke apologized to Nora and walked away.

She took a deep breath and slowly released it. She took out her cell phone and dialed Mark.

"This is Mark," he said. "How are you, Nora?"

"I'm all right. Where are you?"

"At the hospital in Salzburg. Knox woke up, but only to give me some cryptic clues. I was just talking them over with Mac and Digger. Any luck with Zimmerman?"

"Yes," she said. "I have to tell you about Liebfraumilch."

And maybe forgiveness.

CHAPTER 51

SALZBURG, AUSTRIA

CORNELIUS KNOX WAS drawn back to consciousness by a soft whisper. He opened his eyes and got the impression from the light in the room that it was late afternoon.

The painkillers are wrecking my sense of time.

He licked his dry lips and heard the whisper again.

"Cornelius."

It was real, not a dream, and he carefully turned his head to the left. In a chair next to his bed sat a large man in a police uniform. Knox thought he'd seen the man somewhere before. Was he the guard assigned to protect him? He was doing a rotten job of it now. The man's head was slumped to one side and he looked asleep.

Something struck Cornelius as odd. Knox turned his head farther to the left. The guard's shirt was unbuttoned at the top, his shirtsleeves pulled up. Wires led to him from the monitoring equipment, the equipment Knox had been connected to. The soft hums and beeps carried on steadily and rhythmically.

A hand gently touched his right shoulder. Startled, Knox swung his head toward it. He found himself looking up into the face of Stefan Maier. Maier smiled. "Hello, Cornelius."

"What are you doing here?" Knox asked, though he already knew the answer. He looked to the door, which was closed. A man Knox had never seen before stood inside the room in front of the door with his arms clasped behind his back. He wore a police officer's uniform, just like the man in the chair.

"I am astounded you are still alive." Maier made it sound like a compliment.

"No thanks to you. You rigged the lab. You wanted me dead."

"But how fortunate for all of us that it didn't happen," Maier said, smiling. His voice was calm and assuring, approximating a doctor's bedside manner. "We were premature. You are valuable to us yet."

"There's nothing I can or will do for you. You betrayed me. You betrayed Weigel. You've used us and discarded us like . . ." The simile escaped him.

Maier shook his head. "This is where you're mistaken. Weigel betrayed us both. He was holding out on us."

"Oh?" Knox asked, not really interested in whatever lies Maier had worked up.

"Weigel knew about the cure for the virus," Maier said.

"What cure?"

"It's awfully late in the game to act as if you don't know," Maier said.

Knox wondered if maybe the painkillers were still playing tricks on him. "I *don't* know."

"Liebfraumilch?" Maier asked, teasing him. "You don't know what that is?"

"The virus."

Maier chuckled. "Are you stalling for time? Weigel knew where it was hidden. Surely you must know, too. Let me in on your secret."

"I don't know what you're talking about," Knox said firmly. "Where are you getting this information?"

"A solid source."

Knox closed his eyes. "You're talking in riddles."

"Tell me where the Nazis stored Liebfraumilch."

"You know what I know," Knox said. "You know *more* than I know. The lab in Obersalzberg?"

Maier shook his head again. "You refuse to cooperate."

"Willfully I would, yes. But at the moment, my refusal is out of sheer ignorance."

"Then I guess I was wrong," Maier said as he reached up. Knox noticed that Maier was wearing surgical gloves. He placed a syringe into the connecting device on Knox's IV. "I guess you don't have value to me after all."

Knox resisted at first, trying to yank the IV from the back of his hand. Maier was too quick and held his wrist in a firm grip. He nodded to the guard, who came over and restrained Knox's free hand.

A warm feeling worked its way through his body and he thought of his grandfather who had been murdered for the truth. *What am I being murdered for? My ignorance? Yes, my ignorance.* He should have figured this out a long time ago.

He tried to relax. This is what he deserved for shaking hands with the devil.

The warmth intensified, but his willingness to live didn't. He felt as calm as he'd ever felt before. He exhaled in a long, slow breath. Gray spots, then jet black spots burst and spilled into one another, creating a large, dark panorama.

He forced himself to smile at the blackness. Maier thought this was the end, but it wasn't. Knox knew there was time to save his family's reputation and legacy.

It was his last thought.

CHAPTER 52

NOVOSIBIRSK, SIBERIA

AFTER THE SWAT team established there was no further danger from Return to Earth, and the hazmat team had determined that biohazard gear wasn't necessary, Susan, Anton, and her team were allowed in.

They entered through the metal doors to a warehouse of some sort. Three vans were parked inside, one larger than the others. All had Счастливое Мороженое painted on the side. Any one of the three could have been the van Susan had seen in the security video from the water plant.

Her eyes were drawn from the vans to a collection of office doors off to the side. Several bodies were scattered across the floor in front of one of the offices, blood soaking through their coveralls and collecting in puddles around them. SWAT members stood over them.

Susan shivered against the ice-cold air. The metal doors leading to the loading dock were opened, allowing in the naturally frigid air, but this air felt refrigerated. She thought of the security video and the refrigeration unit on the van.

Rozvensky stepped up to her and nodded toward the three vans parked across the warehouse. "Well?"

"I'll look." She started for the first van, but something dripped in front of her. She looked up and saw the body of a man draped across the handrail of a second-story balcony. A second man's hand hung limply over the edge of a rail. She had to wonder what the body count would prove to be.

She shivered and wrapped her arms around her as she walked to the largest van. Behind it sat a row of large, translucent plastic containers that held varying amounts of liquid.

Anton joined her and gazed at the containers. "Whatever they are working with," he said, "they sure have a lot of it."

"Check that none of them are leaking from bullet punctures." He quickly walked up and down the line of containers. All seemed intact.

She stepped back to take in their construction. Stainless-steel pipes interconnected the tops of the containers, with stainless-steel valves at the bottom of each. "No labels indicating hazardous materials," she said, mostly to herself.

Anton was at her side again. "Sadly, terrorists aren't always as compliant with the law as we'd like. They don't label their chemicals. They don't announce their attacks. They don't punctuate properly . . ."

Susan glanced at him, smiled, then turned her attention back to the containers. A coil of six-inch tubing ran along the floor from the bottom of one container to the rear of the van and connected to a large rectangular plastic container sitting in the bed of the van.

"What do you think it is?" Anton asked.

Susan shook her head. "I don't know. But it can't be good."

Rozvensky walked over. "Any ideas?"

"We'll need the hazmat team to collect samples from the containers. They need to be double-bagged and sent via chain-of-evidence transmission to our WHO lab immediately. I want these liquids to be handled with utmost care, Detective—and they must be refrigerated every step of the way."

He nodded. "Anything else?"

"I assume you'll have a forensic IT team run tests on all the communications equipment. I'll want a complete rundown of everything on their computers."

"That goes without saying."

"Does it?"

"Detective Rozvensky!" a voice cried out.

Susan turned to see the SWAT commander and Jankowski kneeling next to one of the bodies. The commander shouted something in Russian and beckoned them over.

"One of them is still alive," Anton said.

Susan and Anton followed the detective to the victim. Susan knelt to administer first aid, but Rozvensky put up his hand for her to stay back. "Don't touch him!" he snapped.

The detective crouched and gruffly slapped the man's face, speaking to him harshly in Russian. The man responded by opening his eyes slightly. Rozvensky asked him a question.

"He's asking him what's in the plastic containers and what they put in the water supply," Jankowski said.

The man tried to chuckle, coughed, and spat up blood.

Rozvensky looked the man over, then ripped at a large blood-stain in his shirt.

"What are you doing?" Susan asked.

Rozvensky exposed a bullet wound in the man's stomach area and shoved a finger into it.

The man screamed.

Rozvensky asked the same question again.

"Stop!" Susan cried.

"If you don't like this, you may leave," Rozvensky said. He dug deeper while the man screamed, then pulled his finger away.

The man sputtered and replied in a harsh whisper.

Anton translated. "It's your worst nightmare."

Rozvensky asked another question, and Susan picked up certain phrases.

Jankowski said, "He asked if it's the Grippe."

"*Nyet,*" the man said, his breaths rattling.

"Then what is it?" Susan asked.

The man's eyes drifted to her. He took a deep raspy breath, sneered at her with trembling lips, and said in English, "Armageddon!"

He reached clumsily for something underneath his coveralls, but Rozvensky grabbed his trembling hand. He nodded to Jankowski, who ripped open the garment. Attached to the man's leg was a small electronic device.

"He's rigged," Jankowski shouted.

Rozvensky leapt to his feet, yelling, "Out! Out!"

Anton took Susan's arm and quickly led her away. "This place may be set to blow up."

They ran.

• • •

As Jankowski pulled the UAZ out of the Jotham complex and back onto the main road, Susan looked back and believed she was losing a great opportunity. She would have liked to tour the entire facility. She suspected she never would.

"Was the one man rigged or do they think he had a detonator for the building?" Brainerd asked Jankowski.

"Would you like to go back to find out?" Jankowski asked him.

Anton was on his cell phone talking to Grigory. The conversation was in Russian, but Susan knew he was giving the doctor an update on what they'd found.

"What did he say?" Susan asked after Anton hung up.

"He said that he's glad our theory proved to be true."

"*Our* theory?" So he was already positioning himself to take credit. *Oh, well, a deal was a deal.*

They reached an intersection that bordered the far edge of the Jotham complex, when the vehicle rocked with what felt like a sudden burst of wind, followed by a deafening explosion.

"What was that?" Jankowski asked.

Anton pointed to the trees, silhouetted by an ominous glow. "It must be that."

Smoke billowed from somewhere on the Jotham property.

After another concussive blast and explosion, Jankowski said, "We're getting out of here." He stepped on the gas and burned rubber as he sped toward Novosibirsk.

They heard a third blast. An orange glow and black smoke poured upward from yet another point on the Jotham site. A distant siren began to wail.

"What should we do?" Susan asked, her heart palpitating. She looked through the back window. She could see three mushroom clouds blossoming from a bright sphere and expanding skyward. It looked as if Jotham were under attack.

"Did Return to Earth rig the entire campus to blow up?"

The fourth blast felt as if a gust of wind were trying to pick up the back of the car. A brown cloud of dirt and sand blew up behind them.

As she watched, a new worry came to her. Viruses and experimental diseases could be airborne, over everyone in Novosibirsk.

This could be the Chernobyl of viral outbreaks.

CHAPTER 53

SALZBURG, AUSTRIA

MARK STEPPED OFF the elevator. He hoped Knox would be awake and ready to talk. Maybe he'd make sense now.

Time was slipping away from them—people were dying at astonishing speeds.

Mark went to the nurses' station. "Is Mr. Knox awake?"

The nurse, who seemed to recognize him from his earlier visit, turned to look at the bank of monitors behind her. "He may be asleep," she said, drawing a conclusion from what she saw on the screens.

Two men came down the hall from the direction of Knox's room. A snapping sound drew Mark's attention to one of the man's hands; a pair of gloves were removed and tossed into a trash can. A doctor, Mark thought instantly as the man passed and went to the elevator. The second man was in a police uniform and Mark wondered if he'd been guarding Knox's door. Why wasn't he there now? Possibly a shift change, he decided.

Mark heard the elevator doors open behind him and assumed the two men had gone. He turned back to the nurse to ask when Knox had last been checked, when panic, like a jolt of electricity, surged through him. He spun to the elevator, but the doors were now closed.

"Come with me," he said to the nurse and dashed down the hall to Knox's room. The nurse shouted after him, but he could hear her following.

He reached the room where Knox lay askew on the bed. A guard sat in the chair next to him, slumped over—attached to all the monitoring equipment that should have been attached to Knox.

"No!" Mark raced to Knox, whose eyes stared vacantly.

The nurse behind him shouted in German, then rushed to the bedside and sounded an alarm to bring doctors and nurses running.

Barth arrived within an hour and immediately took charge of the crime scene. Police officers—both plainclothes and uniformed— were talking to nurses at the duty desk and to various patients. Mark sat in the hall in a visitor's chair, watching the activity in disbelief.

"Two men arrived this afternoon. One identified himself as a replacement guard and the other as Knox's personal physician," Barth said. "Their credentials were in order, so the duty nurse let them through. They drugged the guard and put him in the room with Knox, apparently hooking him up to Knox's monitors so the nurse wouldn't know anything was wrong."

"If any of the wires were pulled loose from Knox, an alarm would have gone off at the duty station," Mark said.

"Apparently it did. But only for a couple of seconds. As the nurse got up to investigate, the alarm stopped. She thought it was a momentary glitch."

"Do they have security tapes of the two men?"

"Yes. From the description they gave me, I would say one was Stefan Maier and the other, his henchman."

Mark clenched his teeth. He'd been only a few feet from the man. Why hadn't he looked at the man's face? Why had he let the snap of the gloves distract him?

"Any guesses as to how he died?"

"The coroner believes they injected his IV with something lethal. An autopsy and toxicology report will tell us exactly what it was."

"That's a surprisingly merciful thing for Maier to do," Mark said.

"I doubt he had time for anything crueler," Barth observed.

Farther down the hall, Mark saw the drugged guard sitting in another chair. He held a cup of coffee, but it shook violently in his hand. The man was red-eyed, as if he'd been crying. He spoke in low tones to the plainclothes detective next to him.

"Is it possible that Maier knows about Liebfraumilch?" Mark wondered aloud.

"It's possible," Barth said.

A feeling of dread rose within Mark. "I've got to go back to Obersalzberg."

"The police are there. They'll be all right."

Mark waved a hand at the dead man's room. "And we've seen how well that works."

Barth looked offended, but quickly let it go. "All right, but you need backup."

"What kind of backup?"

"Do you know how to fire a gun?"

CHAPTER 54

NOVOSIBIRSK, SIBERIA

BACK AT HER office, Susan watched the television news feed and clasped her hand over her mouth. The screen showed images transmitted from a helicopter over Jotham. Multiple buildings were on fire. Huge plumes of smoke continued to mushroom into the night sky. Susan watched carefully, but couldn't tell in which direction the smoke was going. There was no question about it: this attack was effective. The degree of physical devastation alone was truly appalling.

And she came very close to being caught in it.

"What are they reporting?" Grigory asked as he walked into the office. Inspector Martin Duerr followed him. Susan was relieved to see Duerr and stood. They shook hands quickly, then turned to look at the television.

"As if things weren't bad enough," Duerr said.

Anton was crouching close to the screen. "Several buildings in the complex have been bombed or set on fire."

Duerr scowled. "Once again, Return to Earth is covering its tracks."

Susan lifted her cup of coffee, but placed it back on the desk again and sat down. *First the outbreaks, now this.* "Did Detective Rozvensky and his men get out?"

"I heard from Rozvensky," Grigory answered. "He got his remaining men out after they found the detonator on the wounded man. But apparently it wasn't the only one. He believes they had alternate detonators set up that triggered timers once the facility was breached."

"That's a typical terrorist ploy," Duerr said. "Let everyone gather in, thinking it's safe, then blow them all up."

"What about the other buildings?" Susan asked.

Grigory shrugged. "We don't know much more about them than the TV reporters do. The emergency responders, including the police and military, are overwhelmed. A number of victims were caught in the fires and rubble. We don't know when the bombs were planted. They may have been part of a long-term plan of Maier's."

"Still a step behind," Duerr muttered as he poured some coffee from the service.

Susan couldn't avert her eyes from the screen. "What are they doing to protect the citizens from whatever toxins are in that smoke?"

"The military and environmental-protection officials are monitoring the situation," Grigory replied. "They say the winds are blowing the smoke to the southeast, where there is a huge forest and few inhabitants for miles. Those in the predicted path of the fallout are being evacuated."

"Let's hope you people learned something from the Chernobyl disaster," Susan said.

He didn't comment.

Duerr stood next to Susan. "Whatever clues we hoped to find have just gone up in smoke."

"Let's get Rozvensky on the phone and find out if that's true," Grigory said.

"Is everyone cleared for this conversation?" the detective asked through the speaker. "There's no one from the press there, I assume."

"We're all cleared," Susan said. "Grigory, Anton, me, and Inspector Martin Duerr from Interpol."

"Welcome to Siberia, Inspector Duerr. We're sure Return to Earth rigged the bombs, since the first one went off in their main building. What surprised us were the sudden explosions in the other buildings. We have a member of Return to Earth claiming Maier wanted revenge against the site because it specialized in animal experimentation."

"That's handy," Duerr said. "He takes what he can from the facility, then blows it up in the name of his cause."

"What became of your men?" Susan asked.

"Two were killed instantly during the initial ambush."

"I'm sorry," Susan said.

Grigory asked, "Is that it? Has Return to Earth destroyed our best lead to them?"

"More important," Duerr added, "have they effectively destroyed their lab?"

"It wasn't a lab," Rozvensky said.

"What do you mean?" Susan asked.

"I debriefed two of my men who went in through the front of the building. They couldn't find a lab or any other indication that Jotham was the location for their work with viruses."

Susan, Anton, and Duerr looked at one another.

"Then what was it?" Susan asked.

"Possibly a storage facility."

"If that wasn't it, then where is the lab?" Grigory asked.

"We don't know."

Duerr slammed his fist against the wall. "Are we done? Have they closed another door on us?"

"It would seem that . . ." Rozvensky began, then excused himself. It sounded as if he had cupped his hand over the phone's mouthpiece. Muted sounds and jostling could be heard, then he was back. "I have to go. We may have hope."

Susan, Anton, and Duerr sat in a cramped viewing room, facing a large glass partition.

On the other side of the glass was a gray interrogation room. Rozvensky sat at one end of a metal table. A mousy-looking young woman with hunched shoulders and stringy hair sat at the other. She wore a prisoner's uniform and attempted to smoke a cigarette with trembling hands.

According to Rozvensky, the young woman was fleeing the Jotham complex after the explosions started and nearly hit a fire truck while driving the wrong way down a service road. When she crashed into a fire hydrant, a policeman approached to make sure she was all right. She tried to run. He caught her. The sticker on her windshield indicated she was authorized to work in the office inhabited by Return to Earth. The policeman took her into custody.

The police searched her car and found a laptop, now in the hands of Rozvensky's technical people.

Rozvensky began the interview with seemingly cordial questions. The young woman tried to sound belligerent, but Susan saw the fear in her eyes.

Anton gave Susan the play-by-play.

"Rozvensky has her file. She was a communications student in Moscow. He is suggesting that she handles communications for Return to Earth. She denies knowing anything about Return to Earth. She claims she is a secretary for a company called the Maier Foundation."

Duerr folded his arms and grunted. Rozvensky's tone took on a harsh edge.

Anton continued. "He's suggesting she's lying, that her behavior while trying to leave the Jotham complex indicates her guilt."

Rozvensky suddenly hit the table with the palm of his hand. The girl dropped her cigarette.

"He says he doesn't have time for games. Lives are being lost while she wastes his time."

A man entered the interrogation room and handed Rozvensky a slip of paper. He looked it over, then slipped it into her file. He leaned back and smiled, causing her to look worried. He spoke again.

"He is saying they now have incriminating evidence from her laptop. They can prove she used it to electronically detonate the explosives in the buildings."

The young woman began to cry.

"Is that true?" Susan asked.

The man who had entered the interrogation room came into the viewing room. He handed Duerr a folder of information and left. Duerr read it over and sat up.

"The laptop is definitely connected to Return to Earth," Duerr said. "It was used for online calling. Programs with image and sound. And the technicians found a record of numbers and accounts."

"Did they have time to trace the numbers?" Susan asked.

"They did—using not only the numbers, but also the servers used to get to those numbers. It was all there."

A shout from Rozvensky, and Susan looked up. He was on his feet now, leaning over the girl. She was sobbing and talking rapidly.

"She's confessing. Apparently, she did specialize in communications for Return to Earth. They kept everything mobile to make it harder to trace. She was on her way to the office with the laptop when everything started blowing up. She swears she had nothing to do with the explosives. She knew nothing about them. So she panicked and tried to run—the wrong way."

"So not all the members of Return to Earth are as hard as Maier," Susan said.

"She's saying she joined them because of her lover. He recruited her."

Duerr was on his feet, his eyes wide. "The online calls point to one location."

"Where?" Susan asked.

Duerr looked at Susan, his face alight. "A vast tunnel complex where the virus can be stored at a constant cool temperature. Why would they need that?"

"For the same reason they needed refrigerated vans. The transmission of the nanoparticles."

"What is the location, Inspector?" Anton asked.

"Austria."

"Austria!" Susan exclaimed. "Where in Austria?"

As Duerr opened his mouth to speak, they could hear the young woman on the other side of the glass say "Ebensee."

Susan turned to look.

The girl had slumped into her chair, head down, as she said the name over and over. *Ebensee.*

CHAPTER 55

LONDON, ENGLAND

THE BISHOP'S TRUST Retirement Community was located in a renovated manor house only a couple of blocks from the Green in Richmond. The famous Kew Gardens were only a stone's throw in the opposite direction.

Digger followed Abby Benson through the lobby. She gave a friendly nod to the attendant at the reception desk and went straight into an elevator that smelled of disinfectant. She pushed the button for the second floor.

The elevator creaked upward.

"I can't believe I'm going to meet X," Digger said.

"Please try to control yourself."

"So this is where they put agents after they retire?"

"It's a retirement community. Anyone can live here. This happens to be where she wanted to live."

"She must be ancient now."

Abby looked at him. "She's ten years older than I am."

"Still in her prime," Digger said quickly. The elevator stopped and the door opened. Abby stepped into the hall. Digger flinched at the garish wallpaper—bright flowers and swirling vines—set against a deep burgundy carpet, worn at the edges.

"This way." Abby continued down the hall.

"So, what name does she go by?" Digger whispered. "I mean, I assume she was given a new identity, for her own protection."

"Lillian Higgs."

"Didn't you say that's her real name?"

"Yes. But no one outside the intelligence community knows that."

Abby stopped at a door marked with the number 7. She turned to Digger and reminded him, "Best behavior."

"Of course." He tugged at his coat so that it covered more of his Hawaiian shirt.

She pressed a small button, and a chime rang inside. A moment later, a woman whom Digger could only describe as formidable pulled the door open. She was tall and stately, and exuded a rare sense of elegance. The beauty she'd had in her youth had not completely left her. She didn't have the sunless, pale complexion of so many her age, but a natural blush that gave her face an unusual vitality. Her eyes were a steely, but light, blue, keen and inquisitive. Her white hair was styled; she wore a cream blouse and loose, dark pants. The only thing that betrayed her age was the metal walker—a Zimmer frame—that she held in front of her.

"Hello, Abby," she said in a soft voice. "What a pleasant surprise."

Abby gave her a peck on each cheek. "Hello, Lillian. I'm sorry it's taken us so long. The traffic from Chiswick was unbearable. I think people are leaving the city in case the emergency hits London."

"You came quicker than I expected." Her eyes went to Digger and he felt their scrutiny. "You must be Digger. Is that a code name from the service, or did you come up with it all by yourself?"

"It's my own creation."

She gave him a mischievous look, then began to shuffle back inside. "I've made tea."

Her apartment was a three-room unit: a main room with a large window and view looking out toward Kew Gardens; a bedroom through a doorway in the center of one wall; and a kitchenette separated from the main room by a waist-high counter.

Lillian seemed to have made the most of the space and decorated tastefully with strategically placed vases of flowers and assorted leather books on shelves with framed photos and knickknacks. A small television sat on the kitchenette counter, the picture relaying the latest BBC reports of the outbreaks.

Lillian led them to a small table, already set with a teapot and three cups and saucers. "Please, sit." She sat and began to serve.

"I know, I know," Lillian interrupted herself with a wave of her long, slender fingers. "You want to get to the point."

"I wouldn't have put it that way," Abby said.

"But you *could* put it that way," she said with a smile.

"I don't want to take up too much of your time, but, as you know, in our work we have to recognize the importance of random facts and activities that suddenly connect to a larger effort."

"I believe I taught *you* that principle," Lillian teased.

The cups of poured tea sat in front of them. Digger, remembering Abby's concern that he be polite, lifted his and sipped.

"Will you tell us about your connection to Philip Knox?" Abby asked.

Lillian placed her hands in her lap and sat up straight, as if she were a schoolgirl about to recite a poem. "When I worked with the British Intelligence Services, as it was known back in the war, one of my assignments was to explore the wild theories that the Germans had developed germ warfare in the *first* war, and might be doing the same under Hitler's orders. It wasn't a high priority, to be honest. But circumstances led me to believe in the theories' validity. That led me to make contact with Philip Edward Knox."

"You knew him?" Digger asked.

"No. Only his work. I didn't meet him until the day he died— the day I received this little present from a German spy named Ernst." She tapped on the walker. "An ugly fellow with a face like a golf ball. He shot me that day. Shattered my hip. Walking was never the same."

"So it's true. Knox was murdered?"

"Yes. He was thrown in front of that train by Ernst."

"How do you know that?" Abby asked.

"At the end of the war, we got a confession out of a mole in our department. A man named Van Doren. We persuaded him that it was in his best interests to tell us everything. That or face the firing squad. Frankly, I would have allowed him to face the firing squad anyway. He was responsible for the deaths of many good people."

"So you didn't know Knox well?" Abby asked.

She sighed. "No, not at all, but I respected him. He was a voice for the truth that no one wanted to hear. People thought he was crazy but I knew better. He put all the pieces together. And when I took what he knew and combined it with what I'd learned, well, it was a rather frightening thing."

"Did you put those pieces together in one place? Official reports?" Digger asked. "Something our team could look through?"

"I wish that were the case," she said. "I've often wondered . . ." She let her voice fade.

"Wondered what?"

"When Ernst attacked us, when he shot me, I gave Knox a leather satchel of mine. All my and his reports and papers were in it. He dashed off with it and I haven't seen or heard of it since. I long believed Ernst took it from him, but we learned from Van Doren that he didn't. I have no idea where it went."

"Didn't you have copies of your material?"

"I did at the office," she replied. "But a mysterious fire destroyed everything on our floor. Van Doren set it, of course, which is what led us to him. By that time, the war was ending and no one thought it worthwhile to try to re-create what we'd lost."

"What became of Ernst?" Digger asked.

"Oh, he died in some Russian gulag," she said matter-of-factly. "The fool went racing back to Berlin in April 1945 in the vain belief he could fight for victory. I hope the Russians tortured him before he died."

Digger was surprised by the woman's candor.

Abby asked, "Did you ever meet with Knox's grandson—Cornelius?"

"No. I heard him speak once and was tempted to approach him. But the Official Secrets Act prohibited me from ever speaking about what I knew. And by the time Cornelius took up his grandfather's cause, there was nothing more to talk about. The Nazis were part of an ancient past, their work locked up or buried in graves or under Bavaria. Why dig it up?

It would only empower the neo-Nazis—who make a lot of noise now—or create unnecessary unhappiness for the survivors or descendants from that nasty era. Let bygones be bygones, and all that. Though I would have asked him about that satchel. He has made public comments that make me think he's seen inside it."

"He has the satchel," Digger said. "The only problem is he died before he could tell us where it is."

"Ah—really?—that's sad."

"Is there anything in it that might help us?" Abby asked.

"Oh, dear. It's been so many years. I'd have to see it to remember." She gazed at Abby. "What's all this about? You haven't said."

Abby looked to Digger. "Are we permitted to say?"

Digger's eyes went to the television again. "Just watch the news."

"I see," Lillian said. "I wondered about the symptoms they've been reporting. For a moment I thought that perhaps subversives had put their hands on the Nazis' work—the Nazis' virus."

Neither Digger nor Abby spoke.

"The rumors about terrorists . . . are they true?" She looked from Digger to Abby and back again.

"Just between us—yes," Digger said.

"It smelled like terrorists," she said with obvious disdain.

"Is there anything more you can tell us?" Digger asked. "Our team needs to be pointed in the right direction."

"Bavaria. It's where the Germans created the virus—and it's where they developed the treatment."

Digger nodded. "We just learned about that. It took us a while to get there, but we now have a team going through a secret lab found near Hitler's Berghof."

"The Berghof. Good," she said. "And the other one?"

Digger put his cup down. "What other one?"

"There was a second lab. A tunnel under the hotel—"

"*Which* hotel?"

"The Berghaus. It had been converted into SS barracks. There was an entrance into the tunnels somewhere on the ground floor that led to the lab, and to the storage area for their cure."

Digger stood so quickly he nearly knocked the table over. "Will you pardon me?" He reached for his cell phone. "I'm going to step out and make a call."

"Of course you are," Lillian said with a knowing smile. He heard her offer Abby a scone.

CHAPTER 56

BERCHTESGADEN, GERMANY

"I DON'T KNOW," Frau Peschak said. "I wish I knew how to help you."

Nora and Georgina sat with her in the hotel lounge after talking to Digger about the revelation from Lillian Higgs. Daylight had rapidly bled from the sky and drained somewhere behind the Alps. "Think through what you know of the hotel's history. You already know there are tunnels."

She nodded. "There's the obvious one, one floor down. We show it to tourists. But the notion there's an entrance on this main floor is beyond my knowledge."

Nora pointed to Weigel's hand-drawn map, which she'd spread on the table in front of them. "You see this square."

"Yes. It appears to be positioned as the hotel."

Nora tapped her forefinger on the square and the symbol next to it. "I think this L is for *Liebfraumilch*. Professor Weigel knew something about this hotel. You said he was particularly interested in the design of the hotel, the furniture."

"The hutch in the dining room. The only piece of furniture in the hotel that predates the Nazis."

"Let's look at that." Nora stood. "It must have caught Weigel's attention for a reason."

As they walked down the hall, Nora gnawed at her lower lip. The news from Lillian Higgs had energized them, but Knox's death made her anxious. Maier and Return to Earth were still at large in the area. She said to Georgina, "Please make sure the police are still watching out for us."

"I'll call Jens. I believe he's still down at the Berghof lab."

"You have his cell phone number?" asked Nora, noting she called the man by his first name.

Georgina smiled coyly. "Of course."

The hutch covered most of the wall just inside the main doorway. It was made of solid oak and handcrafted with carved barley twists along the side edges and scrollwork along the top. The upper half of the hutch had two glass doors bookending three shelves. Decorative plates, glasses, and cups were stored inside. The lower portion had drawers for linens and two large cabinet doors adorned with carvings of bowls of fruit.

"Has this ever been moved?" Nora asked.

"Years ago, when we painted in here."

"What was behind it?"

"Nothing, really. A small doorway to a crawl space," Frau Peschak said. "Large enough to get through only if you kneel down low."

Nora easily imagined how that doorway might lead to a tunnel. "What's in the crawl space?"

"A small storage room. But it was empty and still is."

Georgina hung up. "Jens is on his way with reinforcements."

"Can we pull the hutch away from the wall?" Nora asked.

"Not alone."

"Where is your help? The waiter with the tattoos?"

"Dietrich?"

"Can he help us?"

Frau Peschak looked about to protest, but turned on her heel and strode from the room.

"Doesn't she understand the urgency of the situation?" Nora asked Georgina.

"She's Bavarian. She doesn't want us making a mess of her hotel."

Frau Peschak returned with Dietrich a moment later. He was in jeans and a flannel shirt and looked as if he'd been doing maintenance work somewhere in the building.

"It will take all four of us," he said, and moved to one end of the hutch.

"Oh, no," Frau Peschak said. "Not with the china still inside."

Another five minutes were lost to the china's removal from

the hutch. Once the hutch was emptied, Nora, Georgina, and Frau Peschak positioned themselves around it, with Dietrich giving instructions from his original place at the far end.

Dietrich counted to three in German and the four of them strained to lift the heavy piece of furniture. At first it wouldn't give, then suddenly moved, and they were able to half carry and half slide it a couple of feet from the wall.

They put it down with a collective groan. Frau Peschak held her back and complained in German. She sat down at one of the tables and rubbed her forehead.

Nora moved around the hutch and looked at the wall behind. Low to the floor, set into the wall, was a square doorway. Frau Peschak was right. One would have to crawl through on hands and knees. "I need a flashlight."

"Easy enough," said Dietrich, who reached into the center drawer of the hutch. He took out a black plastic flashlight and turned it on for her. "I think, though, that I should go in. There might be spiders."

Nora took the flashlight. "Thank you, but I don't mind." She knelt and placed her hand on a small latch in the door, which lifted easily enough. She pushed the door inward and leaned down lower. The flashlight beam exposed a floor made of scarred hardwood. Farther inside were walls of plasterboard. Nora took a deep breath and crawled inside.

"Well?" Georgina called from the other side of the wall.

Nora stood. "It's a room, all right." She shined the beam around the room. A wooden door frame remained on the wall, but the door itself had been covered over. "There was a door here at one time."

Dietrich was kneeling at the small hatch, peering in at her. "Someone must have plastered it over during one of the renovations."

Nora turned slowly in a circle. A yellowed sign with Nazi insignia and bold German exclamations hung loosely from the far wall. *Achtung! Verboten!* and a paragraph underneath. Beneath that was a large black arrow pointing to her right.

"What does this say?" she asked Dietrich as she illuminated the sign.

Dietrich squinted. "They're evacuation instructions for authorized personnel only. It says to go right for the labyrinth."

"It says 'labyrinth'?"

"Network of tunnels," he clarified. He grunted as he crawled in with her.

Nora looked in the direction of the arrow where a wall stood. "I assume that wall wasn't always here."

He went over and ran his hand along three cracks in the plaster. "This could have been a doorway."

"How do we find out?"

Dietrich took two steps back and then gave the wall a violent kick. His heel broke through easily, leaving a hole.

Nora shined the flashlight into the gap and peered into the dark distance. "A tunnel."

Dietrich gently touched her arm and she moved aside. Within minutes, he enlarged the hole in the plaster so she could step through. Nora coughed from the dust and waved her hands at the cobwebs threatening to fly in her face from the ceiling beams above.

"Wish me luck," she said to Dietrich as she made a move to go into the tunnel.

Dietrich put a hand on her shoulder. "I don't think so."

"What's wrong?"

"This network could go for miles in various directions. You could easily get lost and still not find what you're looking for. You can't enter without explicit instructions—or an army of people to search it out."

Nora lifted the beam into the tunnel and saw that, within twenty feet, it split in two directions.

"But that could take days. We don't have days."

"Even so, I won't let you. Not without a map."

CHAPTER 57

ON THE ROAD TO OBERSALZBERG

MARK WAS EN route to Obersalzberg when Digger called from London about the meeting with Lillian Higgs. It had been a success insofar as they now knew about a second lab, under the hotel. But they didn't know how to get to it—and still didn't have the satchel, which might fill in more of the missing pieces.

Mark ran a hand over his face. He was tired and couldn't have felt more defeated. The outbreaks in three cities, Knox's murder . . . There was no escaping reality: they were all being outmaneuvered at every turn. One step forward, two steps back.

He felt puny and childish. *Does God care or not?* The child inside wanted to give an ultimatum: *God, if you care, then fix this situation.* But he, the adult, knew the answer. *God uses people to fix situations. People like me.* At the moment, though, he didn't feel capable of being used by anyone for anything.

His phone rang and he grabbed it. "This is Mark."

"Hi, Mark." It was Donna.

"Hey."

Pause. "You sound tired. Are you all right?"

"Have you seen the news?"

"You mean all the people getting sick and dying? Yes. Health officials are talking about closing the schools here and canceling all large public events. They're screening everyone who crosses the border for sickness."

"Probably a good idea."

"It's too bad, though. I've been helping with a fund-raiser for a local homeless shelter. A lot of planning went into it. We may have to postpone."

"You should. Don't take any chances." He wasn't sure how much he should tell her, and opted for the simplest facts. "We're investigating how it spreads. One thing we know—it spreads easily and it spreads fast."

"You're always so dramatic about these things," she teased.

"Still, you have to take precautions."

"Sure, but you don't expect the public to hide and cancel their lives completely, do you? People have things to do."

"Like what?" Mark asked, irritated. "Shopping? Going out for dinner and drinks? Do you have any idea how these germs get passed from one person to another? All it takes is a server's unwashed hand putting a lemon into your glass of unfiltered water and—"

"Okay, okay. You really are grumpy. I'm sorry I mentioned it."

"I'm sorry, too." He was not feeling at all sorry.

"My counselor suggested that losing our daughter as we did—"

Mark flinched.

"—creates a natural impulse to be overprotective, even paranoid about the world around us. Such a loss causes us to want to insulate ourselves while lashing out at others. We want to keep everyone at a distance."

"Meaning what?" Mark didn't like where the conversation was headed.

"I lashed out at you," she said softly. "And you may be doing the same."

Mark bit his tongue. "Donna, this isn't a good time for navel-gazing."

"Is that what you think this is?"

"It's a bad time," he said, trying to soften his statement.

"When is a good time?"

He groaned to himself. "You have no idea what I'm dealing with."

"That's true. You've never been one to tell," she jabbed. "Look, it's okay. Call me when you get a chance." She hung up.

His groan morphed into a growl. The world was engulfed in

what could become the worst pandemic in history and she wanted to play amateur counseling on the phone? She's probably already gone shopping or to meet a friend for dinner and drinks.

He felt awash in self-pity. When was *he* allowed to hide under the covers?

He hit speed dial for Nora. She picked up after the second ring.

"Where are you?" she asked.

"On my way to you."

"Hurry up. We have work to do."

"Look, I've decided I'm giving up."

"Oh, really."

"All I want to do now is curl up in a fetal position and sleep. You're welcome to join me."

"What?"

"We could have dinner at the hotel, and look out the window at the beautiful mountains, and toast each other as the virus comes to take us away. Then we can die in each other's arms back in one of our rooms."

"Have you been drinking?"

"I wonder if your bed is more comfortable than mine. I mean, if I'm going to die, I want to die comfortably."

"Don't be so morose. Besides, we found the tunnel, but we need a map to navigate through it. I hope you have some ideas about where that satchel is."

"None at all."

"Knox must have given you a clue."

"No clues." Mark's mind went back to living with Nora in a room at the hotel. It was absurd, of course. An indication of how tired he was. Yet he imagined them making the most of what was there: the end table covered with medical journals, the desk stacked with books, the wardrobe stuffed with clothes.

"Mark, are you there?" Nora asked.

The wardrobe. "It's on the wardrobe," Mark said, and tightened his grip on the steering wheel.

"What did you say?"

"No, it's what *Knox* said about the satchel. In his delirium, Knox thought he was in the hotel. He said, 'Come upstairs, I'll show you.' He meant upstairs at the hotel."

"Mark, what are you talking about?"

"Go to Knox's room. The satchel is on top of the wardrobe!" he shouted as he stepped on the gas.

CHAPTER 58

BERCHTESGADEN, GERMANY

FRAU PESCHAK TURNED on the lights in Knox's room, a room that looked like all the others. *No class distinction in this place.*

"The room has been cleaned, of course," Frau Peschak said, and went to the wardrobe. "Nothing else has been touched."

The room smelled of Knox's aftershave, and Nora thought sadly of his death. He'd become lost in his own crusade—and trusted the wrong people.

Nora opened the wardrobe doors. A single suit and white shirt hung there. On a top shelf was a blanket and extra pillow. Nora pulled those out. Nothing was hidden beneath or behind them. She checked the sides and the bottom for a false floor or compartment. Nothing. She stood back and her eyes went to the scrolled woodwork at the top.

Looking around, she saw a chair at the small table and drew it over.

"Be careful," Frau Peschak instructed as Nora stepped unsteadily onto it.

"How often do you polish the tops of the wardrobes?" Nora asked.

"Once a month," Frau Peschak said.

Nora couldn't see beyond the scrollwork and had to reach blindly past to explore the top. She was encouraged—there was enough room for a thick satchel to be hidden from view. At first, she felt only wood and dust. She moved around to the other side and reached again. This time her fingers brushed past something. Standing on her tiptoes, she was able to place her hand firmly on whatever it was. It felt like leather. Her finger hooked around a strap and she pulled the object to the edge, where she could get a better grip. She lifted and a burnt-orange satchel came into view.

Using both hands, she brought it down. Her eyes went immediately to the set of initials embossed on the front.

L.H.

Frau Peschak posted a "Closed" sign for the restaurant, redirecting guests to the Hotel InterContinental so they wouldn't see the mess being made of her hotel. She offered a cursory apology for "investigating" police on the property.

Nora and Georgina took the thick stack of documents from the satchel and spread the papers out on various dining-room tables. Nora was very curious and warily hopeful, but Georgina spoke as if they'd found the Holy Grail. "Wait until Digger sees *this*," she said, circling the satchel and stacks of papers.

Frau Peschak returned with Dietrich and barked instructions at him. He produced a cloth, seemingly out of thin air, and began to polish the hutch.

In the satchel were a variety of reports from Higgs to her superiors, dated as early as 1940.

"According to Digger, Higgs thought the satchel had been taken by the German spy who murdered Philip Knox," said Georgina.

Philip Edward Knox's theories and research, dating back to 1918, were also represented in the collection, as were his articles written under the pseudonym Philip Barrison.

"Philip Barrison?" Georgina said. "Why is that name familiar?"

"I don't know it," Nora said, feeling a hint of melancholy for the man, never to have seen his life and work vindicated.

Nora noticed that the reports from both Higgs and Philip Knox stopped in 1944, which lined up with what Digger had told them.

Cornelius Knox took up the cause in 1991, and articles, Internet printouts, and other pieces were added randomly to the collection. Nora suspected that at some point Knox dispensed with the satchel and began keeping the rest of his exhaustive research in other places, possibly after he partnered with Weigel.

Nora was intrigued by a typed sheet of paper, an intelligence report, about a Dr. Werner Schmidt, who had been relocated from Germany to America after the war. Reading between the lines, Nora surmised that he'd been captured by the Allies and brought to America to spill all he knew about Nazi medicine and science. He didn't last long. He killed himself before they could get anything worthwhile from him. *A true Nazi to the end.*

A translation of a KGB report from the archives of the Soviet Union after the fall of Berlin chronicled a prisoner named Eberhard Ernst; a black-and-white photo showed a brutal-looking man with a pockmarked complexion and harsh scar on his cheek below his right eye. Under interrogation, he confessed to killing a variety of people in Great Britain under orders from a British Intelligence agent named Richard Van Doren.

Nora's focus fell to a group of photos from both American and British reconnaissance flights over Germany. Although out of focus, the photos had been retouched by someone who outlined the various buildings and landmarks.

Nora laid out Weigel's hand-drawn map next to one of the photos and saw that he had captured much of what had been identified years before. Even the shed entrance to the secret lab was marked on the photo, though Nora had no reason to believe anyone understood what it was. Even Knox must not have known.

"Look at this," Georgina said. She pressed her hands against a large, wrinkled yellow sheet that looked like an architect's diagram. A swastika was drawn in the upper left-hand corner but no other labels or identifying marks appeared. Lines went in all directions from no central point. They zigzagged, split off, circled, and abruptly ended. In the upper right-hand corner someone had written, "Where is this?" The handwriting looked feminine, so Nora assumed it was a note from Higgs.

"If we laid this on a grid as you had done with Weigel's map, will it line up with this area?" Nora asked. "If we can find the legend, this may be the map of the network below us."

"I can ask my image-processing friend to try," Georgina said.

"Is it possible Knox had the information to get to Liebfraumilch and didn't know it?"

"Funny if this turns out to be the key to everything," said Georgina. She rolled up the sheet and was about to walk out when she gasped. "The *key*. That's it! I saw the name Philip Barrison while I was helping Mark look for the key."

"What are you talking about?"

Georgina went to her laptop and began clicking away at the keyboard. A moment later, she announced, "Here it is. An unsent e-mail from Weigel to Knox. I got it from Helene's computer. She had a backup of Weigel's Internet account. If the dates are correct, his e-mail was written during his recent trip to this area. Weigel told Knox to ask 'F.P.' for the envelope to Philip Barrison."

"F.P.?" Nora asked.

"Franklin Pierce," Georgina said. "It was the only thing I could think of."

"How about Frau Peschak?"

Nora and Georgina rushed down the hall to the front desk. Frau Peschak was in her office, but came out as soon as she saw the two women arrive.

"Now what?" she asked.

"Do you have an envelope addressed to Philip Barrison?" Nora asked.

"If I do, it would be down here." Frau Peschak looked under the counter. "Ah. I was considering throwing it away. No Philip Barrison has ever come in, nor made arrangements to stay here."

"He already has," Nora said. "May I see it?"

Frau Peschak handed her the envelope. It was letter size and had the name Philip Barrison handwritten in the center. Nora showed it to Georgina. "You spent a while in Weigel's office. Is this his handwriting?"

Georgina nodded. "It sure looks like it."

"Who is this Philip Barrison?" Frau Peschak asked.

"It was a pseudonym of Cornelius Knox's grandfather," Nora explained, then said, "I'm going to open this envelope."

Frau Peschak rolled her eyes. "As if I could stop you."

The door behind them opened. The cold evening air rushed in.

"I hope I'm not interrupting anything," Mark said with a weary smile.

"You're just in time." Nora tore open the envelope and spread the contents on the countertop: a handwritten note, labeled diagrams of the tunnel system, and identifying marks in German. Weigel had translated them into English.

"Thank God," Nora heard herself saying as relief washed over her. "Maybe now the pieces are falling into place."

CHAPTER 59

OBERSALZBERG, GERMANY

CORNELIUS, **THE NOTE** inside the envelope began,

> *Congratulations on getting this far. You have made it further than I since, if you've found this, I am dead. I don't trust Stefan Maier and believe he will ultimately murder me, possibly when I meet him later this evening.*
>
> *So this is my backup plan, my secret which I have kept from him.*
>
> *Enclosed with this note, you will find a map I discovered in the laboratory. It gives specific directions from the hotel to the storage point for Liebfraumilch.*
>
> *The Nazis cleverly had a contingency plan. If I've read the material correctly, there may be hundreds of thousands of treatment doses. There is also a detailed "recipe" for how to quickly manufacture more of the cure.*
>
> *I wish you well, my friend. If I can escape Maier, I will. Perhaps my forthcoming trip to the Akademgorodok will afford me the opportunity. Or perhaps I am wrong about the man and he will behave honorably.*
>
> *With any luck, I will see you in England in a few days and we'll come back and read this note together. Then we'll laugh.*
>
> > *Yours,*
> > *Weigel*

Nora and Mark were standing in the dining room. Nora read the note aloud while Mark looked at the crawl space door behind the hutch.

"So we have Weigel's map of the tunnel system," Mark said. "But there's another one?"

"We're not sure. Georgina is sending something that looked like a map or a diagram to her computer-imaging friend."

Mark clapped his hands together. "Let's not waste any more time. What do we need to go in there?"

"Dietrich is assembling some supplies for us."

"Dietrich?"

"The good-looking waiter."

"Oh."

Georgina returned and said, "That's done. So when do we go in?"

"You're not going in," Mark said.

Georgina frowned.

Mark continued, "You have to stay here to be the point of contact for our team. In case anything happens. Call Mac to let him know what we're doing. We'll try to use our cell phones in there, but I doubt they'll work."

"Texting might," Georgina said. "The signal might not accommodate voice, but texting sometimes gets through. I don't know why."

Dietrich came into the dining room with a small backpack. "I think I have everything we'll need for our little adventure."

"What do you mean 'our'?" Mark asked.

"I'm coming with you."

"Bad idea," Mark said. He zipped up his jacket as a punctuation mark.

Dietrich gazed at Mark with a fixed smile. "You don't know what you'll find in there. If nothing else, you need someone who can read German."

Nora looked at Mark. He didn't have a response.

"I can also help you find your way back."

"Wait. Give me your cell phone," Georgina said to Nora. Nora gave it to her and she leaned over Weigel's map, still spread out on a table. She snapped several pictures of it. "We need a copy of this. I'll send it to Mac and Digger, so they'll have it."

"Have your map pal compare it to the one we found in the satchel," Nora said.

"Right."

While Nora sent the copy of the map to Mac, Dietrich looked at the thin blue lines on the page.

"Do you know anything about maps?" Nora asked him.

"Enough," he said. "Clearly, we're here." He pointed to the structure identified as a barracks. "The storage room is there," he said, and pointed to another position on the map—a structure neither the Nazis nor Weigel had marked.

"Why isn't it labeled?" Mark asked.

"Probably because it's so obvious."

"Obvious?" Nora asked.

"It's not obvious to me," said Mark.

"It's the Kehlsteinhaus," he said. "The storage room is under the Eagle's Nest."

CHAPTER 60

SOMEWHERE OVER RUSSIA

"**HAVE YOU FIGURED** it out?" Susan asked Anton and Duerr. So far they had spent the better part of the flight from Novosibirsk to Austria reading through a pile of documents provided by some long-titled historical information department housed at Novosibirsk State University.

The small Russian military jet bumped against turbulence. Susan dropped into her seat and buckled the seat belt.

"Here." Duerr pointed to a satellite photograph of the Austrian mountains. "Here is Lake Traunsee. It's only about thirty kilometers from Wels, where we'll be landing."

Anton pointed to an area on the south shore of the lake. "This is the location of Ebensee—the town, I mean." His finger drifted over to the edge of a mountain range. "And the Nazis built the Ebensee concentration camp here."

"It looks small. Where is the tunnel?"

Duerr said, "The site had two extensive underground tunnel systems, but we think Return to Earth is using only one. The Nazis called it 'Dachs'—"

"Which means badger," Anton interjected.

"Why do you think they're using that one?"

"A couple of reasons," Duerr replied. "It's a large natural cave. The Nazis liked it because they could simply enlarge it, shape it appropriately, and add an extensive tunnel network connected to the central chambers."

"Shape it appropriately?" Susan asked.

Anton sorted through his documents until he found the one he wanted—a diagram of the cross section of a tunnel and central chamber. "See how the roof is cut up at a sharp angle on each side. This design not only gave extra room at the top of each tunnel or chamber, but also allowed fumes and smoke to be channeled up and out of the complex without poisoning those inside."

"Those inside—meaning the prisoners?" Susan asked.

"Of course not," Anton said. "They didn't want *their soldiers* harmed. It's estimated that twenty to thirty thousand camp inmates were worked to death constructing the various tunnels."

Susan looked at several black-and-white images of skeletal men and women, all dressed in the striped rags of the concentration camps—hollow-eyed and dying—and felt a deep sadness.

"The complex was originally planned as an underground headquarters for the Luftwaffe," Duerr said. "Later, the plans were changed and the site was used for the research and testing of the Wasserfall anti-aircraft rocket, and the intercontinental A9/A10 Amerika-Rakete. It's a huge complex. Perfect for Return to Earth."

"And it's very cold," said Anton. "Even today the tunnels maintain a constant year-round temperature of 8 degrees Celsius."

Duerr smiled at Susan. "That's about 46 degrees Fahrenheit, for those who use the old system."

Susan nodded appreciatively. "That would make it easier to refrigerate."

"This tunnel would also be the better place to hide a secret lab," Anton said. "It's farther away from the town and wouldn't attract as much attention."

"I spoke with Inspector Barth with the BKA. You'll meet him when we land." Duerr opened a manila folder to a small collection of photographs. "According to Barth, about three years ago, a corporation built a small office and lab complex close to the blocked entrance to that tunnel. The surveillance photos show that more cars parked there each day than one would expect for such a small building. Over a period of time, trucks carrying equipment for building renovations came and went. They may have been using those materials to adapt the tunnel. These people could be using the tunnel complex as a lab and no one would know."

He reached down and laid out an additional file. "Last year's sewer, water, and electricity bills. Barth's staff ran comparatives and found the company uses far more utilities than one occupying a normal office building of similar size."

Susan frowned. "And the company?"

"It claims to be a cosmetics manufacturer—a privately held corporation. But it's been controversial locally."

"Why?"

"Apparently some animal-rights activists believe the company uses their labs to test products on animals."

Susan laughed. "That's ironic."

"That's very Stefan Maier," Duerr said. "It's also been a source of contention because, rather than hiring locals, the company flies workers in who live in a company complex in the forest near town. The workers don't interact much with the people in the area."

Susan pointed to the name of the corporation on the documents, all written in German. "What's the name of the corporation?"

Duerr smiled. "Eden von Neuem, which, translated into English, means New Eden or Eden Renewed."

"Like the Garden of Eden," Susan mused. "Or Return to Earth."

Duerr stood and stretched. "I'd better get Barth on the radio."

"Why?"

"We have a lot of planning to do. I'm going to need all the law enforcement Germany and Austria can provide. Return to Earth won't let us just stroll in and bust up their operation. This could get ugly."

CHAPTER 61

OBERSALZBERG, GERMANY

"THESE ARE FOR you," Frau Peschak said from the dining-room doorway. She held out a few sheets of paper retrieved from the fax machine.

"Thank you," Georgina said.

Frau Peschak shot a look at the hutch. "I'm not paying Dietrich for the work he's doing to help you. You can pay him." She walked out.

Georgina laughed to herself, then looked over the fax from her imaging friend: a rough composite of the map she had sent earlier. A cover note told her to look in her e-mail for a more detailed effort. She opened her laptop and logged in to her server. Sitting down, she navigated the screen to make the map details clearer.

"Something to drink?" a man asked. Surprised, she turned to see Jens, her police-officer pal from the underground lab, standing in the door with a tray.

"Shouldn't you be outside guarding my precious life?"

"I have my underlings doing that." He grinned, then looked at the mess of papers on the table and at the diagram on her laptop screen. "Are these the secret tunnels?"

She pointed to the hole in the wall. "*That's* the secret tunnel. I'm still trying to figure out what this is."

Jens put the tray on the table and knelt down to look closer at the screen. Georgina noticed how beautifully fine his blond hair was. "This is curious," he said, standing close to her.

"What?"

"You say the tunnel is there, but it looks to me as if there is another *there*." He rested his finger on top of the symbol for the Kehlsteinhaus.

Georgina isolated that section on the screen and magnified it. "What do you think it means?"

"I may be wrong, but I think it means there's another entrance to the same room from the Eagle's Nest."

Georgina gasped. "*Two* ways in?"

"That would make sense," Jens said, standing up. "If the Nazi leaders were trapped up there, they would want an underground escape route."

Georgina picked up her phone. "I have to let Mark and Nora know."

Jens placed his hand over hers. "No, you don't have to."

She looked up at him, confused. "Why not?" Then she felt the round, metallic barrel of a gun against her neck.

"It's better they don't know."

Georgina was crestfallen. "Oh, please don't tell me you're working with Return to Earth."

He smiled at her.

"You people are like roaches." She felt sick. "When will I ever learn?"

Training the gun on her, he pulled out his cell phone and dialed a number. "I have something for you," he said into the phone.

If ever Nora was inclined to believe in ghosts, this was the time. Shadows rose from dark graves, floated across chipped plaster walls, stretched over arched doorways, and disappeared around corners. And the air was cryptlike. Damp and dead.

Dietrich interpreted the various signs they encountered, most directing personnel to various engineering rooms, electric and plumbing facilities, ventilation shafts, machine-gun positions, and sleeping quarters. Alcoves with ladders led up to hatchways, storage rooms, bathrooms and bedrooms, circular stairways, even prison cells. They occasionally came upon a light switch and would try it, but so far no light was forthcoming.

More than anything else, there were stairs. A lot of stairs. Nora sensed they were slowly ascending the inside of a mountain and regretted she wasn't in better shape. Her calves already ached.

Mark was mostly silent, lost in his own thoughts. He wore a particular expression—a tightness around his eyes—that made her suspect he'd recently talked to Donna.

"How far is it?" she asked, sounding like a small child in the backseat of a car.

"If this map is correct, it's only . . ." Dietrich stopped and converted measurements for her. "A mile or so."

"*Up*," Mark said.

"Up," he agreed.

"I don't know why these missions always take me into tunnels," Mark griped.

Nora said, "At least these tunnels are passable. I'm surprised by their condition. I'd have thought that the Allied bombs would've destroyed them."

"Surprisingly not," Dietrich said. "Even the Eagle's Nest, which is as open and easy a target as you could get, was virtually unharmed."

"I hope there aren't any rats," Mark said. "I hate rats."

"Do you think there are?" Nora asked, shooting her flashlight beam to the ground. Her flesh crawled.

Dietrich laughed. "What would they eat? Besides us, I mean."

"Stop it," she pleaded.

They pressed on. The tunnels seemed endless. Endless walls, endless cement, endless stairs. At the top of one flight, the floor leveled off a few dozen yards, then came to a T-junction. To the left was a short hall with a sign and a locked door to an electrical room. To the right was another short hall with another sign and a locked door to a ventilation shaft. Directly ahead was a wall, mostly bare, except for a metal swastika fastened to its center. Beneath it was the word *Feueraxt* stenciled onto the wall above an iron fire ax and metal bucket of sand hanging from iron clips.

"Did we take a wrong turn?"

Dietrich checked the map. "This is where we should be."

"Are we supposed to go through one of the locked doors?"

"No," he said, and looked at the wall. "We're supposed to go through there."

It was clear to Nora there was no way through. "How are we supposed to continue on?"

Dietrich shined his flashlight on the wall, then pressed both hands against it. "It seems solid enough."

"The wall is fake," Mark said, stepping back and looking at the obstruction. "This is a door. It was the last days of the war. The leadership didn't want everyone racing in a panic for that cure. Only the elite were supposed to get through."

"So the elite would know how to get through this wall?" she asked.

Dietrich unclipped the bucket and upended it onto the floor, kicking at the sand and cigarette butts. "I keep my house key in a pot of flowers on the porch. Maybe the Nazis did the same."

But there was no key or hint about how to get through the wall.

Dietrich then grabbed the fire ax. "It might be as simple as smashing through it."

"Wait," Mark said sharply. He took his flashlight and shined it on the metal swastika. "Does that look right to you?"

Nora and Dietrich looked.

"It's tilted at the wrong angle," Dietrich said. "The Nazis angled it to the right. This one is angled to the left."

"That's what I thought." Mark handed his flashlight to Dietrich and reached up. The symbol was fastened to the wall by a single bolt in its center. He strained to turn the symbol from left to right.

They heard a loud click from somewhere inside the wall and a section of it slid to one side.

Dietrich directed his flashlight beam to the top of the wall. "It's a sliding panel."

"I suppose that was pretty advanced stuff in the 1940s," Mark said, and pushed the panel farther open. "They should have watched more movies."

Nora smelled something like new air. *Not fresh, just new.*

Dietrich picked up the fire ax. Nora looked at him quizzically.

"Just in case," he said.

Just in case of what?

Mark took only a few steps and stopped. He swung his flash-light to the right. "Another light switch. Let's see if this one works."

Nora heard a loud *click*. An electrical hum seemed to vibrate from somewhere behind the walls. A light above them flickered and brightened—as did another farther along the ceiling, then another, and still another until a long row of lights provided a dim yellow glow over the tunnel.

Nora gasped.

The walls of the tunnel were lined with boxes and crates, of odd sizes and shapes, as one might expect to find in a museum receiving room. They moved in and Nora noticed some of the crates were rectangular and thin.

"Paintings?"

"It could be one of Hitler's treasure troves," Dietrich said. "Stuff he stole from the Louvre or Rome."

Nora looked closer at the crates and saw they were still nailed shut. "If only we had more time. I'd love to know what's here."

"If only."

They followed that passage past the crates to a long, open hall. It led them to a large, medieval-looking door, with iron framing, studs, and another swastika in the center. This one was angled correctly.

"I guess we'll use the door handle for this one," Mark said and grabbed the large handle. He pulled the door open on groan-ing hinges.

Nora flinched and put her hand to her nose. Something smelled rotten. Dietrich instantly pulled a handkerchief from his pocket and put it over the lower part of his face. He found a light switch.

The room had been a barracks of some kind and held cots and steamer trunks, a sink, and a mirror. Two skeletons in Nazi SS uniforms were sprawled on the floor.

"Nice Luger." Dietrich reached down to take the gun from the hand of one soldier. The corpse was stiff and brittle, and only reluctantly gave up the gun. Dietrich pocketed the pistol.

"I'd say he shot the other soldier, then killed himself," Mark suggested. "The duty of all good Nazis."

On the opposite end of the small room was another door. A sign warned them about entering without permission. Ignoring it, Dietrich tugged at the handle, then fought to get the door open. They gazed into darkness.

They shined their flashlights into what appeared to be a large room with arches, pillars, and a vaulted ceiling. It reminded Nora of a church crypt. In the center was a single metal desk. Deep into the shadows were barrels. Lots and lots of barrels.

Nora went to the desk and found a dusty binder sitting on top. She wiped the dust off and shined the light of her flashlight on the cover. She chuckled.

"What?" Mark asked.

Nora lifted the notebook and held it toward him. On the front was written "Liebfraumilch."

PART THIRTEEN

November 9
Present Day

CHAPTER 62

EBENSEE, AUSTRIA

IT WAS WELL after midnight when the military jet taxied to a private hangar at the airport in Wels, Austria. No sooner had they departed the jet than Susan, Anton, and Duerr were whisked into Austrian police cars and taken across the airfield to a waiting helicopter.

"What about our soldiers?" Susan asked, looking back at the hangar. In the stark, bright lights of the airfield she saw Jankowski and the others coming off the plane.

"They have their own helicopter," Duerr said. "They're going to the Eagle's Nest. I suspect TSI needs them."

They drove to a blue Bell helicopter. As if on cue, the pilot started the engines and the blades began to spin. Duerr leaned over to Susan. "We'll be working with the GEK, though they're also known as EKO Cobra."

She turned to him, her expression a question mark.

"The Einsatzkommando Cobra," he explained. "Austria's Special Forces."

Anton added, "Some believe they're the best-trained counterterrorist commandos in the world."

"I've never heard of them."

"And that's how they like it."

Their doors were opened. The three jogged to the helicopter and were helped in by a uniformed pilot, who made sure they were buckled safely into their harnesses. He gave them communication headsets.

Within seconds, the helicopter rose from the airfield.

"Welcome aboard," the copilot said thinly into her headset. "I'm Commander Lutz."

Susan found herself looking at a man in profile, whose face reminded her of the side of a cliff. His eyes were tucked beneath a high forehead, as if in a mountain crevice. His nose had been broken in two places, his mouth a razor-thin line set above a sharp jaw.

Lutz continued, "And this is Officer Werner."

Werner nodded without turning around.

"Thanks for your assistance, Commander," Duerr said.

"This flight won't take long. We'll be landing in a patch of field just outside the Ebensee tunnels. My men have already surrounded and taken command of the building complex and living quarters of Eden von Neuem."

"Was anyone hurt?" Duerr asked.

"No shots were fired. The employees were taken completely by surprise. We've also secured the laboratory in the tunnel—and discovered a network of tunnels connecting the lab to the main complex."

"Did you check for explosives?" Duerr asked. "Return to Earth has a reputation for rigging everything."

Lutz gazed at him. "I don't know what you're used to, Inspector. But when we say the site is secured, we mean it is *secured*—not only by our explosives experts, but also by our hazmat specialists."

Smiling, Duerr leaned back in his seat. "Is it possible we're a step ahead of Return to Earth?"

"Or it might be a trap," Anton said.

CHAPTER 63

THE EAGLE'S NEST, GERMANY

"IS THAT WHAT you're looking for?" Dietrich asked Nora in the darkness.

"Yes," she said, her hand on the Liebfraumilch binder.

"Let there be light," Mark announced, and flipped a switch on the wall next to the door.

More humming and buzzing preceded the lights coming on overhead.

Mark reached for Dietrich's fire ax. "If you don't mind."

Dietrich handed him the ax, and Mark stepped to the nearest barrel. He swung the ax in a large arc, smashing it against the top. A white powder puffed out and drifted in the air like smoke. He put down the ax and shined his flashlight into the barrel.

"So this is Liebfraumilch." He sounded unimpressed.

Nora approached the barrel. "I hope you're right—and it's not more desiccated virus."

They looked in the barrel. It could just as easily have been a container of flour or powdered sugar. They clearly had expected something spectacular. Nora couldn't help but feel slightly let down.

"We need to capture a sample of it. A plastic bag or—"

"You won't find a plastic bag in here," Dietrich said, then shoved his hand into his coat pocket. "Wait." He pulled out a couple of store-bought bags of trail mix. "Will this do?"

She nodded.

He opened the sealable pouch and emptied the trail mix into one of his pockets. He blew into the bag, just to get out the remaining bits, then handed it to her.

She scooped a small portion of what she prayed was Liebfrau-milch into it, then did the same again after he handed her the second bag.

"I'll call Georgina to let her know." Nora brought out her cell phone but the signal was too faint for her to make a call. "Then again, maybe I'll try texting her."

She punched out a text message telling Georgina they may have found Liebfraumilch and to use the map to come quickly. As she was about to send the text, she thought to share the news with the rest of the TSI team. After sending the message to the list in her contacts, she looked at Mark. "We need help with this. How do we get others here?"

"I'll go back," Dietrich said as he moved back for the tunnels. "Sit tight."

"Just a minute," she called out to him. She handed him one of the plastic bags of white powder. "Please take this with you. Tell Georgina to have it tested right away. We need to know ex-actly what this is. And we have to make sure it's still viable."

"Thanks for all your help," Mark said.

Dietrich nodded, turned, and was gone.

While Mark wandered through the barrels, Nora sat at the desk and began flipping through the notebook—page after page, paragraph after paragraph, of neatly typed German. There were headings and subheadings, and a section that appeared filled with formulas.

"I know I've said this before but I should have learned German."

"And if we were in France, you'd wish you knew French."

"It's none of my business, but you can talk about it if you want."

"Talk about what?"

"Donna. You talked to her earlier, didn't you?"

"How can you tell?"

"A woman's intuition."

Mark continued drifting among the barrels, like a shopper at a market. He cleared his throat. "If I forgive her, do I have to become part of her life again? Does she have to become part of mine?"

"That's a good question."

"We've changed over the past few years. Neither of us is the same. Putting aside any issues of forgiveness and trust, I don't know that we're compatible anymore. Is that wrong?"

Nora shook her head, wishing she hadn't brought the subject up. She remembered anew why it wasn't her place to speak to their situation. It made her anxious. She had a vested interest in its outcome. She loved Mark. "I don't know. You're divorced—which means you have no formal obligation to do anything. However, you know what it means when a divorced couple reconciles."

"What does it mean?"

"It speaks of God's grace." She had to busy herself with something. She decided to use her cell-phone camera to take photos of the pages and send them on. She suspected the signal wouldn't carry the photos, but at least she'd have them represented somewhere, in case something happened.

In case something happened.

She thought of Return to Earth and wondered what the eco-terrorists were up to while she and Mark were hidden deep in here. Nothing could be worse for them than for their enemies to have a cure.

She noticed a text message from Digger waiting for her. "Well done!" it said. At least some kind of signal was getting out. She wondered why she hadn't received a confirmation from Georgina.

Thud.

Nora looked up. Mark looked around.

Thud. Thud. Thud.

"What is that?" Mark asked.

The sound wasn't coming from the direction of the tunnels, she realized, but from the opposite side of the storeroom.

Mark realized the same thing and moved in the direction of the sound. Together they walked around a large pillar. In the far corner, in the shadows under a stone arch, was a door.

"I guess there *is* another way in," Mark said.

Nora took a couple of steps forward, but Mark touched her

arm and drew her back. He reached behind him and brought a pistol out from under his jacket.

"Where did you get that?" Nora asked, surprised.

"A security measure from Barth." He gently pressed on her arm. "Let's go back to the tunnels."

As they moved to the other side of the pillar again, a blinding white flash and an explosion knocked them to the floor.

CHAPTER 64

EBENSEE, AUSTRIA

AS THE HELICOPTER approached Ebensee, Susan caught a glimpse of Lake Traunsee, a great gash in the mountain that looked dark and unfathomable. The twinkling lights of the city seemed to smile at her. The chopper banked around to face the giant blackness of the mountain range, which seemed like a hole in the fabric of the gray dawn. She thought of the many souls who had been poured into that hole. Tens of thousands.

"We're good to land," Commander Lutz said, and signaled the pilot.

Susan thought the darkness itself seemed to move during their descent, buffeted by the helicopter's rotor blades. A spotlight hit the field as they landed, illuminating the way to the tunnel. Crouching, she and Anton followed Commander Lutz and Duerr away from the helicopter toward a single light that glowed over a large door at the mouth of the tunnel. She stumbled over a rock, and Anton reached out to take her hand.

Two Special Forces soldiers stood erect and alert with assault weapons in their hands. They parted for the four of them, and one opened the tunnel door. It led to a short passageway and another door, also guarded by two soldiers. They walked quickly down the tunnel, through the door, and into a large cavern.

Susan took only a few steps before she stopped, her mouth falling open. It was, without question, one of the largest and most complex laboratory facilities she'd ever seen. Besides the main room, which seemed to extend deep into the mountain, she could see dozens of alcoves carved into the rock, each sealed with a large glass wall. The entrances through the thick Plexiglas were multichambered bioprotective ports. The ceiling, above the endless rows of bright fluorescent lights, contained a large network of ducts. Susan recognized air-conditioning and exhaust ducts.

"It's like something from a *Star Trek* movie," Anton said.

"It's better than that," Susan gasped.

Barth strode across the floor to them and thanked Commander Lutz for all his help. The commander nodded and stepped aside. "It's all yours."

Duerr introduced Barth to Susan and Anton as they moved farther into the vast laboratory.

"Our hazardous-materials technicians have also tested the air and the central facility," Barth said. "At this point, teams have not examined any of the side labs. All have been sealed. We don't see a need for biohazard suits."

Susan was relieved.

He waved a hand for them to follow. "There's some sort of communications center over here."

They walked along a wall, which curved to suit the natural shape of the cave, and came to a large Plexiglas partition. On the other side of it was a control room with a long bank of computer screens. Two stricken men, both in white lab coats, sat handcuffed to metal chairs.

"Apparently these two were trying to shut down the system when our officers came in," Barth said.

Duerr stepped up to the two men. "Explain yourselves."

The two began jabbering in a machine-gun volley of words.

Anton leaned over to Susan. "They say they were only doing their jobs and had no idea they were involved in anything illegal."

She looked at Anton. "You speak German, also?"

Anton smiled.

Barth sneered at the prisoners. "Yes, yes. The SS officers said the same thing after the war."

Duerr turned to the screens. "What's all this?"

The men were suddenly silent.

Duerr laughed. "Nothing to say?"

Barth said, "One member of my team is a tech expert. Tell them what you found, Franz."

An officer standing nearby cleared his throat. "These computers are filled with encrypted files giving data and shipping information about deliveries of something called nanoparticles."

"That would be the microscopic particles packed with the virus," Susan explained.

The officer continued, "In the case of some cities, the data lists specific water-treatment plants Return to Earth intended to infiltrate. In other cases, it lists the reservoirs into which they were going to dump the materials."

"How?" Duerr asked.

"From helicopters." The officer looked at them with a grave expression. "They planned to infect twenty-five cities over the next seven days—the most heavily populated cities in the world having a combined population of more than two hundred and fifty million people."

A screen image flickered and changed. A message appeared indicating someone called Wolfsblood was calling in through the network.

The men in the chairs were agitated. One lowered his head and shook it from side to side, groaning.

"What's that?" Duerr asked, pointing to the screen.

"It's him," the man on the right said. "He's calling. He always calls at this time."

"Who?" Duerr asked. "Who is Wolfsblood?"

The man swallowed hard. "Dr. Maier."

Susan took a step back, as if the name itself delivered a striking blow.

Duerr said, "You have to answer it."

"How?" the man asked, whining. "He'll kill us when he finds out—"

"If you don't cooperate, you're as good as dead anyway. *Answer it*—but don't let him know what's happened here. Do you understand? No code words, no cryptic phrases." Duerr pulled a handgun from an underarm holster and placed it against the technician's forehead. "Anything unusual and I'll shoot you here and now myself."

The rattled man nodded quickly.

Barth unshackled the man. Running his hand through his hair and adjusting his coat, the technician looked as if he were about to make a TV appearance. He glanced nervously at the crowd around him. "Farther back," he said. "You have to get farther out or the camera will pick you up."

Susan and Anton squeezed in close to each other against the wall. He smiled at her.

"Try anything and I'll break your hands."

"Or Kevin will."

Susan looked at him and blushed.

The technician pushed the answer button and a dark, grainy image appeared on the screen.

Susan recognized Maier. He appeared to be using a cell phone for this linkup.

"Konrad?" he said. "What took you so long?"

The man, who was Konrad, stammered. "I'm sorry, sir. I was on the plant floor double-checking the packing equipment. One of the storage units was malfunctioning."

"Is it anything serious?"

"No, sir. I think we have it taken care of."

"You'd better. Where is Gustav?"

Konrad looked at the other man, still handcuffed to the chair. He then looked to Duerr, who waved a hand at him to keep going.

"He's . . ." Konrad looked as if he might freeze up. "He's . . ."

"He's what?"

"In the toilet. He has a stomach bug."

"A stomach bug? Then what is he doing at work? Tell him to go home to bed. I don't want our workers catching or spreading anything."

Susan wondered if Maier recognized the supreme irony of what he'd just said.

"I wanted to check in before the day shift arrives. It's going to be a very busy day. I expect everything to work according to plan, without any hitches. Is there anything to report?"

"Uh . . ." Konrad stammered.

"You're worrying me, Konrad. Is something wrong?"

"No, sir. That storage unit has thrown me off, that's all."

"Do I need to come?"

"No, sir."

Duerr nodded up and down vigorously.

"That is to say—um—yes, sir. Perhaps you should. It would be good for morale to have you here, considering the importance of what we're doing. If you don't mind . . ."

Maier frowned at him. "All right. I will."

Maier's image seemed to freeze. The picture pixilated, then returned to a general desktop window for the network.

Konrad collapsed into the chair.

"When will he get here?" Duerr asked.

"I don't know," Konrad complained, "since I have no idea where he was calling from. We are never allowed to know where he is. Sometimes he's five minutes away, sometimes a day or two."

Barth looked over at Duerr. "Whenever he gets here, we'll be ready."

Duerr looked wistfully at the screen where Maier's image had been. "He won't get away from me this time."

CHAPTER 65

THE EAGLE'S NEST, GERMANY

THE EXPLOSION KNOCKED Nora sideways to the ground.

Stunned, she couldn't imagine what had happened. Her ears rang and pain shot through her knees from her fall. Mark lay prone on the cement floor. He pushed onto all fours and seemed to be looking for something.

She went to him and pulled at his arm. "Get under the desk," she said, wanting protection for them in case of another explosion or if the roof caved in. Her mind raced with possibilities: a still active booby trap set up by the Nazis, perhaps a coincidental gas explosion in the old building.

"I lost the gun," he said, but staggered with her to the desk. They crouched under it, waiting. Mark shook his head as if trying to get his senses back.

Through the ringing in her ears, Nora heard voices and peeked over the desk. A man with a shaved head walked into view and to the barrels, his back to her. Nora's heart lurched. Maier, she thought. A blond-haired uniformed man carrying a black gym bag followed him.

Maier touched the top of the barrel they had opened. He lifted a piece of the splintered wood and jerked his head around. Nora ducked.

Maier spoke sharply and she heard the soles of their shoes scuff loudly against the cement floor as they moved away from the barrels.

Mark whispered, "Run for the tunnels! *Run!*"

Nora instantly obeyed and pushed herself out from under the desk and half ran, half staggered toward the tunnel door. Rough hands suddenly gripped her arms, dragging her back. She saw the blond man in the police uniform approach the desk, his gun on Mark.

"Come out."

"Aren't you one of Barth's men?" Mark asked. "Jens?"

The man crouched and hit Mark with the pistol. "I said to *come out.*"

Nora cried out and was thrown to the ground at Maier's feet. She struggled to get up, but felt the telltale cold of a muzzle pressed against her head.

Maier leaned over her. "Don't fight, Dr. Richards. Let's be friends."

His eyes were penetrating. She saw in them the charisma and potency of a powerful personality and understood how one could look in those eyes and be willing to follow the man. She twisted to look around.

Mark was on his knees. He was rubbing the side of his mouth, blood smeared on his chin.

Nora heard a gentle cough near the door. Georgina sat on the ground, her clothes torn, her face scraped. She smiled sheepishly. "Hi, Nora."

"Klaus. See what's down there," Maier said to the burly, bearded man who'd grabbed Nora. He nodded and disappeared through the doorway to the tunnels.

"Did anyone else come with you?" Maier asked.

"Just us," Nora said.

He gazed at her and she felt like squirming.

He gestured at Jens with his head.

Jens grabbed Nora and pulled her to her feet. Mark was also on his feet and looked as if he might lunge at the man.

Maier held up his hand. "Stay calm."

Jens bound Nora's hands behind her back with duct tape he retrieved from the gym bag. Then he did her ankles. "You should be ashamed," she said to him, knowing she sounded like a clichéd mother. "As a police officer, don't you take an oath?"

"I got a better offer," he said simply.

Klaus returned from the tunnels and shook his head at Maier.

Maier wiggled his fingers and Klaus came forward. "The kit, please."

Klaus reached to his belt and unzipped a pouch. He removed a small black box and handed it to his boss.

Maier took the box and turned to the desk, his back to them. "Everyone is so quiet," he said, amused. "Where's your renowned banter—the witty repartee?"

"I just thought of something," Georgina said proudly. "You'll never get away with this."

Maier turned back to them and held up a syringe, flicking at the top of it with his forefinger. "Not true."

The needle seemed to shine in the dull light. Norah's heart raced.

Maier moved to Mark, who recoiled and took a confrontational stance, like a wrestler.

"Thanks, but I've had my shots," Mark said.

Maier sighed. Klaus came up behind Mark and hit him hard on the back. Mark let out a groan and fell to his knees.

"Stop!" Nora cried out.

Klaus kicked Mark in the side to topple him completely to the floor, then used the flat of his boot to push him onto his stomach. Mark's face was pressed hard against the cement and he puffed angrily. Klaus taped his wrists.

"How did you get in?" Nora asked Maier.

"Through the Eagle's Nest," he said as he walked to Mark. "Georgina showed us the way."

"The other map in the satchel," Georgina said.

"A secret passage in the office of the restaurant there," Maier explained as he knelt next to Mark, the syringe held up. "Those Nazis loved their hidden doors and fake walls. Apparently no one knew it was there. Certainly not the security guard we interrogated."

Mark struggled, but Klaus held him firmly in place. Maier jabbed the needle into his shoulder. Mark winced and growled while the bearded man wrapped duct tape around his ankles.

"So, all kidding aside," Georgina said, "what is this stuff?"

Maier stood and glanced at Georgina. He returned to the black box on the desk. A moment later he turned and nodded to Klaus, who came up behind Georgina and held her.

"Watch where you put your hands, Mr. Beardy," she said.

"You're not my type," he snarled. Klaus pushed her over and bound her wrists and ankles.

Maier came at her. "Thanks for all your help."

"The *same* needle?" Georgina said. "It's not hygienic."

Maier chuckled, then stuck the needle into her shoulder muscle.

"Is this how you did it to Weigel?" Mark asked with a groan.

Maier looked impressed. "Did the mark show up in his autopsy?" He tsked. "And I was so careful, too. But then the jugular does bleed a bit more than the shoulder, eh, Doctor? When they find you, they'll never know."

Back again he went to the desk. Jens tightened his grip on Nora's arm to keep her from squirming.

"What are you pumping into us?" she asked, certain she already knew the answer. "Is it the virus?"

"*The* virus?" he asked, slowly turning and coming toward her. "Not exactly. This is a concentrated form packed into countless microscopic particles. When injected into the body, it works *much* faster than the type the Nazis used."

He smirked at Nora. "I assume you've taken the monoclonal antibody. Don't think for a minute that it's going to protect you. The viral dose I'm about to give you is too high. Better than that"—Maier stooped to hold the needle only inches from her nose—"the wonderful little particles carrying my virus don't release it until the particles have settled inside the cells of the body. The antibody you've taken, which only floats around the bloodstream, will give you *no* protection at all."

She wanted to kick, bite, thrash, anything rather than meekly take the needle. As if feeling her body tense, Jens grabbed a handful of her hair. "I wouldn't," he whispered in her ear.

Maier stuck the needle into her arm. The pinprick felt like fire, the sensation spreading from her arm into the rest of her body. Jens pulled her backward, off balance, half-lowering and half-dropping herself to the floor.

Maier returned to the desk, set the syringe down. He slowly turned, and leaned back, as if they were old friends at a keg party. "I know I'm being melodramatic, but I like the idea of your dying only a few feet from the very thing that might save you."

Nora was having trouble breathing and her throat was constricting. She wondered whether it was the virus or just sheer panic.

"Not that it matters," he added. "We're going to blow it all up anyway. If there's one thing we don't need—it's a cure for our little friend." He nodded toward Jens. "We'll just take one small container." He smiled at Nora. "For personal use."

Nora turned her head and realized that, while Maier was talking, Klaus was taking plastic explosives from a backpack and placing them on several barrels, then connecting them by wires strung from one explosive to the next. He finished with a set of wires attached to a cell phone.

She looked at Mark, who lay still, his eyes closed. Georgina was blinking as if she were having trouble focusing.

"Good-bye," Maier said. He noticed the binder and picked it up, tucking it under his arm. "If you believe in a deity, or a higher power, or an afterlife, I suggest you make your acts of contrition now."

Maier and the two men walked through what was left of the secret doorway, their footsteps echoing down the passageway.

"Well, this is awkward," Georgina said. "Mark, are you faking it or are you really sick?"

Mark opened his eyes. "I don't feel very well at all. I don't think 'faking it' is an option now." He jostled himself so he was sitting upright.

Nora's throat felt tight. She coughed, then said, "Dietrich went back to get help . . ."

"I hope he's fast," Georgina said.

"Is there a timer on the explosives?" Nora asked.

Mark shook his head. "Once they've gotten away, they'll likely trigger the blast with that cell phone." Mark leveraged himself against the desk to get to his feet. "I'll hop over and yank the wires apart."

"Won't that blow us up?" Georgina asked. "I thought breaking the connections sets it off."

"Since when are you an explosive-device expert?" Mark hopped toward the barrels.

"Digger likes movies about bombs," she said.

"Forget about that. There has to be a way to get our hands and feet loose," said Mark. "There are nails sticking out of a few of these barrels."

With great effort, Nora also got to her feet. "I'll see if I can find something sharp in the desk."

"If you two could see yourselves," Georgina said. "It's like watching the Easter parade."

"Stop talking, will you?" Mark snapped. "It's all I can do to think straight. Everything's getting fuzzy."

Georgina rolled around, trying to get to her feet. "My legs aren't working."

"Then *keep* talking, Georgina," Nora suggested. "Stay conscious."

Mark leaned against a barrel, trying to position his wrists over a protruding nail. He stumbled and cried out.

"What's wrong?" Nora asked, alarmed.

"I just gashed my back with that nail."

"Have you had your tetanus booster?" Georgina asked.

Mark glared at her.

Nora busied herself struggling with her bound wrists to get the drawers open on the desk. No scissors, no knives, no letter openers.

Mark hopped across the room to the doorway. "There are shards of metal sticking out from the door." He sounded breathless.

Nora leaned against the desk. Her eyes were burning as if she had a fever. She felt beads of sweat form on her brow.

Georgina coughed violently. A spot of blood hit the floor.

"Mark?" Nora called out. He had disappeared from view. She could hear him grunting from the other side of the doorway.

"I'm doing my best," he said.

Georgina began to writhe and groan.

Nora fell back into the chair next to the desk. She felt drenched and began shivering.

"Got it!" Mark shouted.

He was a blur to Nora as he came around the pillar, flexing his freed hands, his feet now also released. He knelt next to

Georgina. "Did Digger's movies tell you how to disarm the bombs?"

Georgina could only moan in reply.

"All right, then," he said defiantly. "I'm going to rip the wires out."

Nora struggled to stay conscious. She felt a series of chills spread through her body and gritted her teeth to keep them from chattering. She watched Mark move to the barrels. He picked up the cell phone, looked it over, then looked at her . . . He took a deep breath, then unplugged the wires.

Nothing.

Mark smiled and turned toward Nora. He stumbled as he came to her, looking like a man on the deck of a wave-tossed boat. Or maybe that was only how she saw him.

"I'm going to try to inject us with the Liebfraumilch. I'll have to use Maier's syringe." He stumbled around and grabbed Dietrich's backpack. In a side pocket was a plastic bottle of water, some of it spilling as he opened the top. He careened toward the open barrel and scooped some powder into his hand. He dropped the powder into the container, screwed the lid, and shook it violently.

"Looks like it's going into solution." His voice slurred. He sat down on the floor and leaned over Nora.

She looked into his bloodshot eyes. Sweat poured from his face.

Opening her mouth, she tried to speak—wanted to say something of comfort—but could manage only a clicking sound with her dry tongue.

Her eyes stayed fixed on the edge of one of the arches. It reminded her of a church she'd visited in England—Salisbury Cathedral. She remembered its beautiful and holy elegance.

And then she thought of heaven, and nothing else.

CHAPTER 66

THE EAGLE'S NEST, GERMANY

THE NIGHT HAD turned cold. The unprotected parking lot outside the Eagle's Nest didn't help with the chill. Jens shifted from one foot to the other. He ran a hand through his hair and tugged at his police uniform. He didn't like wearing the uniform for this kind of work, but he'd had no time to change. He glanced at Maier, who just closed his cell phone. Jens felt nervous, but wasn't sure why. All had gone well and according to plan.

Maier looked at his watch. "Something isn't right at Ebensee. I'm driving over." He looked thoughtfully at the small container of Liebfraumilch in his hand and then back at the entrance to the Eagle's Nest. "Wait until I'm off the mountain, then detonate the bomb. Make sure it goes off. I don't want any foul-ups."

He went to his car, climbed in, and sped away.

"Not even a thank-you," Klaus said. He shivered. "It's cold. Let's get out of here."

"I hope Michael kept the heat on in the van," Jens said.

The rear lights were a bright red from Michael pressing the brake pedal. The van's exhaust sent ribbons of white into the frosty air.

"We should be driving a hybrid," Klaus said as they walked toward the van. He stopped abruptly. "That wasn't here before." He was pointing to a red car at the far end of the parking lot.

"Yes it was." Jens was bluffing. He wanted to get out of the cold and away from this place. He didn't have time to worry about a couple of lovers making out.

"Are you sure?"

"Yes. Forget about it." They continued on and approached the rear of the van.

"Front or back?"

"Front," Jens said. He held up the wired cell phone. "I want to make sure I have a clear signal when I blow up that storeroom." He looked worried. "The caves aren't going to collapse under us, are they?"

"No. I only set enough to destroy the room and whatever's around it. The manager's office in the Eagle's Nest will get scorched."

Klaus did the coded knock on the back of the van.

"Idiot," Jens said. "He's in the driver's seat."

Klaus tried the handle and the back door opened. He climbed in, closing the door behind him.

Jens was about to go around to the passenger side, when something in the night sky caught his eye. A red star, he thought, but he realized it was moving too quickly to be that. A flashing white dot followed. He heard the beating of helicopter blades echo through the blackness. The aircraft was coming toward them.

Whoever it was, they weren't part of the plan.

Jens swore and ran around the van to the passenger door. "Someone's coming!" he exclaimed to the driver as he climbed in and flipped open the cell phone. He punched in the numbers to detonate the bombs in the storeroom, but nervously fumbled the sequence and had to start over, his eyes focused only on the keypad. "Don't just sit there, get us out of here while I set it off."

He started the sequence again. He heard the approaching helicopter at the same time he realized the van still wasn't moving. "What's keeping you?" he shouted as he looked over at the driver.

It wasn't Michael.

"Dietrich!" Jens cried out. "What are you doing here? You're supposed to be keeping an eye on things at the hotel!"

"A change of plans." He lifted a pistol, the large silencer looking cannonlike to Jens. "What's the code?"

"Code?"

"The 'mission accomplished' code. And don't lie to me. I'll know if you're lying."

"A text message. The numbers 91152. Maier's birth date."

"Thank you." Dietrich looked at him for a moment, then said, "Hitler was a vegetarian, you know."

"What?" There was a sharp puff of air and Jens felt something hammer him in the forehead. But only for a second.

Dietrich wiped his brow with the back of his gloved hand. *This is hard work. I'm going to ask Barth for a raise.*

After sending the confirmation code to Maier, he looked over at Jens, now slumped onto the dashboard. The passenger window was sprayed with gore and dripping red.

Dietrich tried to suppress the pleasure he felt in killing Jens. Nothing he hated more than a cop who worked with the wrong side.

In the back, Klaus and Michael were still. Dead still.

He put the van in drive and moved it to the edge of the parking lot, only a few feet from his car, so the helicopter could make a worry-free landing.

Barth warned him the Americans were coming.

He cut the engine and got out. He looked at the gun in his hand and, taking it by the silencer, threw it like a stick over the precipice.

The helicopter whipped the bitter air into a frenzy as it glided to the ground. Dietrich turned his face away, feeling the cold burn his cheeks. He reached into the inside pocket of his coat and took out his BKA badge.

Bouncing slightly, the helicopter settled and the side door opened. Two German officers and four Americans, decked out in fatigues and assault weapons, leaped out.

Dietrich held up his badge and walked toward them.

CHAPTER 67

WAS IT A dream?

Mark lay on the cold floor, bathed in his own sweat, and watched as the men came running in. One looked a lot like the waiter who'd served him and Nora the other night. What was his name? *Dietrich*? Oh yes, he must have come back.

Then four soldiers dressed in American military fatigues rushed in. He knew them—Jankowski and Brainerd and . . . he couldn't remember all their names. What were they doing here? Weren't they supposed to be in Siberia protecting Susan Hutchinson?

One of the soldiers approached the bombs and held up the wires Mark had pulled out. He seemed agitated by the discovery.

Jankowski came and knelt next to him.

"Dr. Carlson?"

Mark couldn't answer. He was feeling better than he was a little while ago—when that was, he couldn't be sure—but he was weak and unsure he was actually awake and seeing what he thought he was seeing.

"Nora," he managed to say.

"We have her," Jankowski said. "We have all of you. You're safe now."

Mark looked down at his hand and wondered why he was clutching a hypodermic. An odd thing to be holding in his sleep.

Then he smiled and slipped into unconsciousness.

CHAPTER 68

EBENSEE, AUSTRIA

"THE POLICE THINK he's coming," Anton said, interpreting for Susan the German voices on the walkie-talkie.

Though Susan wanted to be in the laboratory when Maier was arrested, Duerr insisted that she and Anton be moved to the safety of the Eden office building in the main complex.

"I think Rozvensky was a fool to have allowed you to participate in the Jotham raid," Duerr said. "I won't make that mistake."

The Eden office building—a modern, three-story structure—looked much the same as any other office building Susan had ever seen. The gray cubicles, meeting rooms, vending machines, and reception desks betrayed nothing of the work being done there.

"It's not him, it's another employee," Anton said.

As the morning arrived, so did many of the workers. They arrived and parked in the garage under the building. As they entered, police officers nabbed them and took them to a large cafeteria-like area. Cell phones, laptops, and any other means of communication were confiscated.

Susan and Anton sat in Maier's office—a large, heavily furnished room with windows that overlooked the mountains and the laboratory. Susan watched a small white golf cart zip across the lot from the office to the lab. *BKA is trying to make it look like business as usual.*

More chatter from the walkie-talkie and Anton, who sat in Maier's leather desk chair, said, "They think he's coming now."

"For real?"

Anton shrugged. "If the employee they interrogated is telling the truth, it's his car."

Susan walked over to a large bookcase and studied the titles on the book spines. They were all foreign-language editions.

The walkie-talkie was alive with different voices. "It's him," Anton said, and sat up. "He's pulled into the parking garage underneath us."

Susan was now worried. "I thought he was going to the lab."

"Maybe he parks here and takes the tunnel to the lab. Don't worry. Plenty of police are on-site to grab him."

The chatter on the walkie-talkie took on a noticeable urgency.

"Maier has disappeared," Anton said, standing.

"How could he disappear in the parking garage?"

"They can't see him on the security cameras. They say he turned into a separate parking structure, exited his car, then disappeared."

"Wouldn't they expect him to have a private entrance? Aren't they covering everything?"

They both heard the sound: an activated mechanism from somewhere behind the bookcase. It sounded to Susan like an elevator. Susan staggered back and waved frantically to Anton. "Do something!"

Anton grabbed the walkie-talkie and shouted, "He's coming up to his office!"

"We have to get out of here." Susan started for the door.

"You go." Anton retrieved a gun from his coat pocket. He waved her on and positioned himself behind the desk, his arms outstretched, the gun clutched in both hands.

It was too late for Susan to escape. The bookcase silently moved aside on a greased transport system, exposing an elevator cab behind it.

Maier stepped off. He wore an overcoat and a suit, and carried a briefcase as any executive might. He froze and gazed at Susan.

"Well," he said calmly. "This *is* a surprise, Dr. Hutchinson."

"Don't move," Anton said from the desk.

Maier smiled, then quickly threw his briefcase at Anton. Anton ducked to avoid being hit by the case. When he raised his head again, Maier had slipped back into the elevator just before the bookcase closed.

"He's on the run!" Anton shouted into the walkie-talkie and dashed into the hall.

Susan felt something was wrong. She moved closer to the bookcase, then realized what it was: the elevator mechanism hadn't engaged. She heard only silence on the other side.

The bookcase suddenly opened again and Maier stepped back in, holding a pistol. His eyes quickly assessed the otherwise vacant room, then settled on Susan. "Come with me," he said and roughly grabbed her arm. She tried pulling away but he overpowered her and dragged her into the elevator.

Maier pushed the call button and stepped behind Susan, holding the gun against her back. "I'm so glad to finally meet you. I've admired your work for years."

Susan didn't speak.

"I assume police are in position all over the building and the lab?"

Susan remained silent.

Maier sighed. "And Liebfraumilch—is that safe?"

Susan wouldn't answer.

The elevator reached the parking-garage level. When the door opened, Susan saw immediately they weren't in an employee lot but a private garage, with its own electric door and, presumably, its own entrance from the main lot. As he nudged her forward, they moved slowly into the concrete area. His car sat to one side.

A stairwell door to the left of the elevator burst open and Anton rushed in. In the instant before Maier could raise his gun, Susan saw the surprise on his face. He fired at Anton, unleashing a deafening roar in Susan's right ear. Instinctively, she doubled over and rammed her elbow into Maier's abdomen. It knocked the wind out of him and he stumbled a few steps back.

Susan bolted to the side and slammed into the wall next to the elevator.

Anton had hit the ground and rolled, his gun up and pointed. He fired a shot at Maier, which blew a hole in the wall over Maier's left shoulder.

Maier dropped to a crouch and shot back, moving like a crab toward his car.

Anton let out a roar of pain, but fired again at Maier. Maier buckled and grabbed his leg. His gun fell to the floor. Susan pushed herself away from the wall and kicked it. The weapon skidded several feet away.

Susan looked at Anton. He had dropped his gun and was lying still, a puddle of blood forming around him. She heard a noise and spun around to see Maier lunging for his gun. Susan got to it first, scooping it up as she stumbled past it. She fell heavily against the stairway door, but held on to the gun. Sliding to the floor, she fumbled, then got the weapon into shooting position so she could fire if she had to.

Maier was now flat on the ground a few feet away. She looked again at Anton, who still wasn't moving. Shouts came from somewhere, but she had no idea where.

Maier tried to get to his feet, cursing as he did.

"Don't!" Susan shouted.

He looked at her with animal-like fury. He extended his hand, palm up, rhythmically flexing his fingers. "Give me the gun," he snarled.

She lifted it with both hands and pointed it at him—her hands and gun shaking.

He moved toward her, "You won't shoot me. You're a doctor."

"I can fix whatever I break."

Anton groaned. At least he was still alive—but for how much longer?

Maier smiled at her, and something about his eyes caught her attention. At first they struck her as beautiful, the kind that might welcome her in and make her feel at home.

He had his weight on his good knee, the other leg extended uselessly, blood pouring from the bullet wound. "Here's an idea. Look away for a few seconds and I'll simply disappear. Otherwise, you'll have to shoot."

She looked into his eyes and now saw something cold and heartless. She considered how all of humanity would benefit if she shot him dead right now.

Susan heard shouts in the stairwell behind her.

"It's over," she said.

Maier smiled. "It's never over. The work will carry on."

Susan was certain he would make a move. He wasn't the sort of man to give up under any conditions. She tightened her hold on the gun, keeping it fixed on him while she moved away from the stairwell door.

More noises drifted in from the other side of the electric garage door. His eyes were drawn to the noises as he lost all composure. He moved from his crouching position and leaned back, stretching his arms as if he might raise his hands. A glint of silver caught Susan's eye as something dropped from Maier's sleeve into his hand.

Maier brought the small blade up, jamming it deep into his neck, twisting his wrist to ensure maximum damage to the carotid artery. Blood pumped, spraying up and out like a garden sprinkler. Maier fell backward onto the pavement.

Susan froze, her arms still outstretched, pistol pointed.

Duerr and several officers crashed through the stairwell door. Duerr first looked at Susan and Anton, then down at Maier.

He sighed and holstered his weapon. "A coward to the end."

Susan dropped the gun, got to her feet, and rushed to help Anton.

PART FOURTEEN

Present Day

CHAPTER 69

NOVEMBER 10, SALZBURG, AUSTRIA

MARK THOUGHT SOMEHOW that a room in a Salzburg hospital should be more quaint and Austrian: heavy, colorful curtains bordered with gold edging, thick cushioned furniture, the smell of strudel wafting through the air. Instead, his room was like any other hospital room in any other city. *How disappointing.*

He considered all this with a postfever weariness that left him wanting to do nothing more than lie perfectly still.

He heard a low voice at the doorway, where a young man in American fatigues stood guard. Jankowski was talking to someone just out of view. *Jankowski.*

He remembered all that happened and sat up quickly—too quickly. The movement made his head spin and sent a sharp pain up his back. Puzzled, he reached behind him and felt under his hospital gown. His fingertips touched stitches. *The nail in the barrel.* He felt an ache in his shoulder as he moved his arm and realized he had likely been given a diphtheria-tetanus-acellular pertussis booster by whoever had sewn him up.

Digger walked in carrying a laptop. Jankowski followed him in, but stayed close to the door.

"It's about time, sleepy boy," Digger said, and dropped his bulk into a bedside chair.

A pale, dark-eyed Georgina followed Digger in. She wore a robe over her hospital gown and walked slowly.

"Hi, Mark," she said, then coughed. She sat in the guest chair next to Digger.

"Are you all right?" Mark asked Georgina.

She nodded. "Not bad, all things considered."

"How's Nora?"

"She's fine. Looks a lot like you."

"How do I look?"

"Like someone who's been injected with a potent virus then had it countered with a sixty-five-year-old remedy—all in the most unhealthy and unsanitary conditions possible."

"Ah," he said.

"You could have killed them, you know," Digger said.

"You came all the way from England to criticize me?"

"Somebody has to. At least until Mac gets here."

Mark settled back into his pillows. "For your information, we were going to die anyway, so I used the syringe and pumped the stuff into us. There's no way I could have known what it was—or if I was giving the right doses. It was Liebfraumilch or death."

"Calm down, Dr. Kildare. I wasn't talking about that," Digger said, waving away the explanation. "I was talking about the bomb. You yanked out those wires."

"So?"

"So, that move triggered a backup timing device. When Janks and the boys showed up, you had five minutes before the place blew sky-high."

"I told him not to do it," Georgina said.

"It's *Jankowski*," the soldier corrected Digger from the doorway. "Nobody calls me *Janks*—twice—and lives."

Digger laughed, then stopped when he saw Jankowski's earnest expression. "Yeah. Sorry."

Jankowski returned to his position in the doorway.

"And besides that—" Digger said.

Mark held up his hand. "If this is going to be a debriefing detailing everything I did wrong, forget about it."

"Whatever," Digger said. "But you have to hear about Liebfraumilch."

"Tell me we saved it. Are the right people in charge of it?"

"Yeah, sure. Who cares? I'm talking about what it's made of."

"What do you mean?"

"It's a bunch of herbs," he said. "I've been looking over the pages from the binder—"

"The one Maier took," Mark said. "Did they catch him?"

"Maier's been dealt with." Digger was getting impatient with Mark's interruptions. "Nora took photos of the pages. They're on Georgina's phone. Anyway, it's made of all these natural things, such as *Andrographis paniculata, Sambucus nigra, Lomatium dissectum, Sanguinaria canadensis, Echinacea angustifolia, Echinacea pallida,* and *Echinacea purpurea, Panax schinseng,* and *Hedera senticosa.*"

"I'm not getting what you're saying," Mark said, thrown by all the Latin.

"The Nazis concocted a cure out of Indian echinacea, European alder, biscuit root, bloodroot, black coneflower, Tibetan ginseng, and even touch-me-not. Just a bunch of roots and herbs!"

"You're kidding."

"All herbs that have shown at least some effectiveness in treating influenza or the common cold. And, apparently, the Germans have a long tradition with them."

"You mean we risked our lives for a bunch of root juice?" Mark moaned.

"Call it what you want," Digger said, "but researchers from Russia, China, and Germany have found that the extract components possess what they call immunostimulant properties. And, believe it or not, studies actually show they increase the ability of white blood cells to fight the virus."

"Great," Mark said. "That makes me feel much better."

"*And*"—Georgina spoke as if she'd been waiting for the chance to interrupt—"I found Nazi documents claiming the recipe was taken from some of the early nineteenth century's best-known German herbalists and tested on concentration-camp prisoners. They refined the recipe based on results and hit the mother lode with Liebfraumilch. They found it virtually one hundred percent effective at rapidly reducing symptoms of the virus, and preventing fatalities."

"That's remarkable," Mark said.

Digger pointed to something on his screen. "And Nazi physicians found they could mix the herbal combination with a preservative that would allow the herbs—in a powdered form and when placed in French oak barrels—to last indefinitely."

"Which is what enabled it to save our lives," Georgina added.

Mark put his hands to his head. "I feel as though I'm listening to a morning talk show. Give it a rest, will you?"

"Are we feeling a little irritable this morning?" Nora asked as she walked in.

"Nora! Please, save me."

"I'd be happy to return the favor," she said. She looked haggard and pale, but Mark would never have said so. He was glad to see her.

She looked at him and frowned.

"Do I look that bad?" he asked.

"It's like looking in the mirror." She sat down on the edge of his bed.

"I could never look so beautiful."

Digger wretched. "I'm going to throw up."

Nora smiled at him. "Take it easy."

"Ironic, isn't it?" Digger asked. "They tested the cure on concentration-camp prisoners. Now the world will benefit because of the prisoners' suffering and pain."

"One of the great moral dilemmas of the universe," Nora said softly, and put her hand on Mark's. "How God can redeem suffering and pain."

Georgina shook her head. "Don't talk to me about suffering and pain."

Mark squeezed Nora's hand and she nodded. "We'll leave it there for now."

Outside, Duerr stepped to Jankowski, shook his hand, then came into the room. "It's getting crowded in here," he said.

"A small reunion," Nora said.

"Inspector Barth will be along shortly. He'll need statements from all of you before you disappear. We've got a huge mess to sort out."

"We're saving the world. What kind of mess is more important than that?" Georgina asked.

"I'm not talking about the world. I'm talking about the paperwork."

"What's happening out there?" Mark asked.

Duerr paced to the window. "Well, the information we obtained from the Ebensee laboratory computers has led us to

Return to Earth cells all over Europe. The members we have captured are giving us even more information. This will set them back years."

"Did you get Jens and Mr. Beardy to talk?" Georgina asked.

"Talk?" Duerr harrumphed. "That'd be difficult. They're dead."

Mark frowned. "How?"

"We're not sure. Barth's agent said he found them that way. We suspect Maier killed them once he had no more use for them."

"Barth's agent? At Obersalzberg?" Nora asked, clearly confused.

"I thought Jens was his agent—and that he double-crossed us."

"Dietrich was also Barth's man."

"Dietrich!" Nora exclaimed.

Georgina leaned forward. "But Frau Peschak said he'd been working for her awhile."

"Three months." Duerr now had command of the room and seemed to enjoy it. "Barth put Dietrich in the hotel as part of a sting operation to identify neo-Nazi groups. They like to frequent the hotel and the surrounding area, to pay homage to Hitler. Barth was about to close down the operation when someone coincidentally made contact with Dietrich, saying they'd pay him lots of money to keep an eye on the hotel—police activity, that sort of thing. Dietrich assumed it was part of a neo-Nazi plot, so he accepted. Only later did he realize it was connected to Return to Earth."

"I hope he took their money," Mark said.

Duerr rubbed his chin. "I wouldn't know about that, though it wouldn't surprise me. Barth says he's a bit of a maverick. Sometimes they're not sure whose side he's on."

"Where is he?" Georgina asked. "I'd like to thank him personally for all his help."

"He's gone. After last night, he disappeared to take a break before his next assignment."

"Did he deliver the sample of Liebfraumilch I sent back with him?" Nora asked.

"No. All our samples came from the storeroom."

"What about Maier?" Mark asked. "Digger said you got him."

Duerr shot a look at Digger, who shrugged. "I didn't get specific."

"Maier is dead."

Nora and Georgina gasped.

"Are you sure?" Mark asked. "He was dead before, remember?"

"No, he's definitely dead." Mark got the impression Duerr didn't want to talk anymore about it. "Well, if you'll pardon me, I have another patient to visit."

"Who?" Mark asked.

"A fellow agent shot by Maier."

"Will he be all right?" Nora asked.

"He is getting good care at the trauma hospital here. Dr. Hutchinson is with him."

"At some point, someone is going to have to tell me everything I've missed," Mark said.

Duerr was at the doorway now. "Another time. When I buy all of you the best meal of your lives. You've done excellent work. *Again.*"

CHAPTER 70

NOVEMBER 10, SALZBURG, AUSTRIA

ANTON HAD BEEN moved from intensive care to a private room. He seemed to be asleep when Susan entered his room. She placed flowers on the bedside table—a small vase of edelweiss.

Opening his eyes, he said, "For me? How lovely."

"I'm glad to be putting them here, rather than at a grave site." She feigned annoyance. "Who taught you to play with guns?"

A faint smile. "I thought the body roll was especially dramatic."

"Dramatic and stupid. Do you have any idea how close Maier's bullet came to causing you permanent damage?" She leaned closer to him. "By permanent, I mean the kind that makes you *dead.*"

"I wouldn't give Maier the satisfaction." He winced as he adjusted himself to look at her. "Duerr told me what Maier did. I would never have thought him the suicide type."

"Me neither." She adjusted the flowers. "If you saw the look in his eyes—like a trapped animal—it might make more sense."

"Pretty gruesome, though."

"You have to get well soon," she said, changing the subject. "I'm flying back to Novosibirsk tomorrow. I'll need your help to get them out of this crisis."

"I'm afraid that won't be possible," a voice said from the door.

Susan turned as Duerr walked in. "Why?"

"Once he's patched up, he's coming back with me."

"You can't take him away from me now," she said, as she

turned back toward Anton, feeling her spirit deflate deep inside her. "You can't leave me."

He shrugged. "I've been summoned."

"He has no choice." Duerr walked over to the foot of the bed. "We have work to do."

"So he was your man all along," she said to Duerr, an accusation.

Duerr nodded.

Susan thought she might tear up. She and Anton had been through so much together. "Thank you for everything."

"Any time I can be of service," Anton said, a boyish grin spreading across his face.

"We'll be speaking again, I'm sure," Duerr said to Susan, then retreated toward the hall.

Susan leaned over Anton and kissed him lightly on the cheek. "Anton, I don't know what to say."

"'Good-bye' suits me just fine. Or '*auf Wiedersehen*,' as they say in this part of the world. Till we meet again."

She squeezed his hand. He gave her a final smile before she turned and walked out.

"I thought we were going to have dinner," Kevin said from the other end of the line.

Susan cradled her cell phone between her shoulder and ear while she signed a form that had been faxed to her at the Villa Excelsior Hotel.

"We will." She dropped the form onto the small table in her room. Faxes, printouts, charts, and data were migrating around the suite in small stacks. "Just as soon as I wrap things up in Siberia. Remember, just because we found a treatment for this pandemic doesn't mean our work is done."

"I've got the report right here," he said. "Liebfraumilch is being effectively distributed and the victims are recovering faster than anyone could have anticipated. Not only are herbalists and pharmaceutical companies rushing to reproduce, test, and market the concoction, but also the Ahaz Pharmaceutical Corporation has developed a specific flu vaccine. If successful, it will be ready for the flu season in the Southern Hemisphere."

"Nice reading, Kevin," she teased.

"And I have it from an inside source that the military and NIH researchers are forging ahead on a new vaccine that has the potential to prevent all forms of the influenza virus and banish the killer once and for all." She heard him shuffling some papers. "So you see? All is right with the world. You should stop long enough to have dinner. And, if you don't, I may have to come there and drag you to dinner myself."

"I know, I know."

She sat at the table and looked out the window. A market square with a large stone fountain sat empty. She felt a sudden surge of sadness that she always felt after the rush of a difficult field assignment. But this one had been by far the most difficult and challenging assignment she had ever experienced.

"Maybe . . ." she whispered. She took a deep breath and slowly let it out. "I'll have to call you back." She hung up, feeling overwhelmed. She put her face in her hands and let the tears come.

Her cell phone rang again. She sniffled, wiped her tears with a tissue, and opened it. "Hello."

"You thought I was joking," said Kevin.

"What?"

"I told you I would come and drag you to dinner if I had to."

The door to her suite opened.

She swung around.

Kevin Maklin stepped inside the room and closed his phone. "So I'm here to do just that."

Susan laughed, then cried, then laughed again.

He slowly walked to the table and, as she stood, took her in his arms and gave her a long kiss.

CHAPTER 71

NOVEMBER 12, MARYLAND, VIRGINIA

MARK AND DONNA held hands across the center of the small café table. She searched his face for a moment, then looked at the ships and museums in Baltimore's Inner Harbor.

He tried to read her expression. "Donna, I think what I'm trying to say is . . . there aren't many people who understand what I do, or why I do it. I'm not sure I understand it myself. But it's my life now—it's what I'm committed to."

"I understand." She looked back at him and slid her hand away from his. "And you're right. We've taken on two very different lives now. Whatever once held us together is gone."

He didn't say anything. He didn't know what to say.

"Daniel warned me about this."

"Daniel?"

"My counselor."

Mark smiled. "Are you seeing him? I mean, *dating*?"

She glanced away and he knew the answer. "It's not what you think. He's become very important to me."

"I'm glad."

She looked into his eyes again. "But . . . can you really forgive me? That was the question I originally put to you."

It seemed like a long time ago. His eyes filled with tears as he reached across the table again, placing his hand over hers. "I can and I do. I forgive you," he said, and meant it.

"Thank you." She dabbed at her mouth with the napkin. She leaned on the table and clasped her hands under her chin. "I suppose she's waiting for you."

He nodded. "We're going to finish that drive we started a couple of weeks ago."

With a touching bravado, she waved her hands at him as if she were dismissing a naughty child. "Then go. Leave me. I'm done with you."

He rose and smiled at her. "See you, Donna."

She also stood. "We'll talk sometime, all right?"

"Sure."

"But *you* call *me*. I never know what country you're in or what disease you're dealing with."

"Got it." He leaned and kissed her lightly on the lips.

"Enjoy your drive." She grabbed her napkin and wiped his mouth. "You don't want her to see that."

"I'm sure she won't mind."

"Then she's a saint."

"You may be right about that."

As he walked to the curb, where Nora waited behind the driver's seat of the car, he felt a pang of loss, like the ending of a long and sad chapter. Or maybe it was the beginning of a new one.

They now stood where their adventure began. A modest grave site behind a quaint church in Charlottesville.

It was colder than it had been, a crisp autumn day with a golden glow of sunlight. Everything seemed exceptionally clear. The Blue Ridge Mountains in the distance appeared closer than ever before.

He gazed at his daughter's grave and prayed silently, without specific words.

"I have something for you," Nora said, reaching into her handbag.

He looked at her. In the glow of the sun, she seemed to shine. *She's radiant in more ways than one.*

Nora brought out a piece of Berghaus stationery and unfolded it. "It's based on something the priest in Ebensee said to me. I thought of you—and wrote it down."

Mark took a deep breath. In the air was a hint of wood smoke from a distant fire. He could see Nora's handwriting on the paper.

Nora read,

> *In every trial we encounter, God wants to teach us something.*
> *Sometimes allowing us to experience pain is the only way He can*
> *get our attention. It's the only way to make us stop and listen.*
> *Through pain, through suffering, God is doing something for my*
> *good—to do something in and through me.*
>
> *So it's foolish to waste the pain on anger and bitterness.*
>
> *But for God to use my pain, I must forgive the one who has*
> *hurt me. Then I need to accept the pain as a gift . . . to seek to*
> *understand it . . . and then to learn how to use the healing of for-*
> *giveness and the gift of pain to help others I meet along the way.*

He nodded, then smiled. There wasn't much to add to such
wisdom.

Nora gave him the paper.

He was touched by the tears that fell from her eyes. He bent
down. He scooped out a small pit in the dark soil of the bed of
flowers on the grave and placed the paper into the hole. Then he
gently covered it and stood. He whispered, "Amen."

He took Nora's hand and they walked silently across the field
to the car.

CHAPTER 72

AT TSI HEADQUARTERS in London, Mac's phone buzzed. Expecting it to be Abby Benson, he answered gruffly, "What?"

"No need to be so rude," said a deep, resonant voice. There was a hint of a Hispanic accent.

Mac frowned, recognizing the voice of Peter Romero, CEO of Ahaz Pharmaceutical Company. "Hello, Peter. It's been a while."

"Too long," Romero said. "I wanted to thank you for your help in our securing the contract to produce the Siberian-flu vaccine. Unfortunately, other companies will have to join us in that effort. But your assistance in helping me obtain an exclusive contract to manufacture Liebfraumilch is much appreciated. Though we won't be calling it that, of course."

Mac was puzzled. "My help? What help?"

"Oh, that's right. You *didn't* help," he said, a jab. "Though you should have."

"I told you I don't work with people I can't trust."

"Yes, I remember words to that effect. Fortunately, we had other people in place."

Mac laughed. "You mean your inside man with the BKA?"

Romero was silent.

"Was it the waiter—what was his name? Dietrich?"

Mac read in Nora's report how Dietrich helped her in the tunnel, and how she'd given him a plastic bag of Liebfraumilch to deliver to Georgina for testing. In the rapid-fire confusion, that bag disappeared, along with Dietrich.

"Well, I just wanted to call because I was thinking about

you," Romero said. "I look forward to the time when we will work together again."

"You'll be waiting a long time."

A pause from Romero, then a deep sigh. "We'll be talking soon."

The line clicked and Mac slowly put the handset back onto the cradle. Romero was definitely up to something, but Mac wasn't going to worry about it now. Whatever it was, he'd find out soon enough.

The phone buzzed again. Mac picked up. It was Duerr.

"Have you heard about the new website?" asked Duerr.

"No, I don't cruise the web the way some people do."

"This time you should. It's a new site claiming to represent Return to Earth."

"We knew they wouldn't go away just because Maier is dead," Mac said, disturbed it was true.

"The site claims that Maier, 'a research biologist,' was cruelly assassinated by Interpol, WHO, and TSI agents."

Mac stiffened. "They mention TSI?"

"Unfortunately, yes. Interpol is looking into it. Meanwhile, they're claiming they will announce a new leader in the near future. So our job is not over."

"I never thought it was."

AFTERWORD

OF COURSE, THE World Health Organization (WHO), Interpol, the U.S. Centers for Disease Control and Prevention (CDC), the U.S. National Institutes of Health (NIH), the U.S. Army Medical Research Institute of Infectious Diseases (USAMRIID), the Laboratory of Molecular Biology in Cambridge, the Siberian branch of the Russian Academy of Medical Sciences, the U.S. Armed Forces Institute of Pathology (AFIP), the U.S. Army Special Forces, the German Bundeskriminalamt (BKA), and the Austrian Einsatzkommando Cobra (EKO) are all very real institutions. However, the use of their names and functions for the purposes of this book is purely fictional.

Most of the geographical locations, landmarks, military installations, hospitals, train stations, hotels, concentration camps, and towns, exist or existed. The events we describe in Fort Riley, Kansas, and Fort Devens, Massachusetts, are, for the most part, historical. We highly recommend the various hotels we mention: the Hotel Adlon in Berlin and Hotel Terminus in London, Hotel Centralnaya in Novosibirsk, Hotel George V in Paris, InterContinental Hotel & Resort in Berchtesgaden, Hotel Vier Jahreszeiten Kempinski in Munich, and Villa Excelsior Hotel in Salzburg. Of course, the experiences you can expect are likely to be much better than those of our characters.

We are indebted to John M. Barry for his definitive work on the H1N1 Spanish influenza of 1918–19, *The Great Influenza: The Epic Story of the Deadliest Plague in History* (Viking, 2004). His meticulous research and vivid writing became an essential foundation for our understanding of the many aspects of this horrible plague and its impact on lives, families, cultures, and continents—and on the course of history itself. The descriptions of the many horrific effects of the Spanish (or Siberia) flu by our fictional doctors were adapted from the reports of doctors who cared for Spanish flu victims in 1917 and 1918 that were unearthed by Mr. Barry.

Our thanks, also, to Kathy Abascal for her book *Herbs & Influenza: How Herbs Used in the 1918 Flu Pandemic Can Be Effective Today* (Tigana Press, 2006), in which she describes how over thirty herbs were used to treat the 1918 Spanish flu pandemic in America, based upon a survey of physicians conducted in 1919. However, the recipe for Liebfraumilch is fictitious. These and other herbs should not be taken, especially in combination, without the guidance of a health-care professional who is trained and experienced in prescribing natural medications. In other words: don't try this at home.

Thanks to John and Suzanne Erskine for their help with details about Fort Riley and Bavaria, and with the documents relating to the execution of the two German spies in Washington, DC, caught giving influenza germs to sailors in a hospital. And to Catherine Duerr for her long-distance assistance on questions pertaining to Berlin. We appreciate Martin Duerr (Catherine's father), Vladislav Rugoliev, and Barbara Anni Peschak Cuff for allowing us to use their names.

Anastasia Flanegin helped us with the Russian language. Alexandr Shinkarenko, MD, and Irina Shinkarenko, MD, assisted us in understanding Russian medical practices. A number of physicians once again assisted us by reviewing the manuscript for medical accuracy: Reginald Finger, MD, MPH; Elaine Eng, MD; Gaylen Kelton, MD; Mary Anne Nelson, MD; Ed Guttery, MD; Roy Stringfellow, MD; and Byron Calhoun, MD. Thanks especially to Gregory Rutecki, MD, not only for reviewing our manuscript, but also for sharing with us his research on biologic agents used in warfare, and Roni Devlin, MD, an infectious disease specialist, for her review and suggestions.

Barb and Katherine Larimore, Elizabeth McCusker, Dave Flower, Alton Gansky, and Valerie Pulver spent many hours combing through, reviewing, and editing our manuscript. We are grateful for their expertise. We'd also like to thank the management and staff of the Colorado Springs and Monument, Colorado, establishments that allowed us to spend many hours occupying their tables to dream up and write this book: Barnes & Nobles booksellers, The Egg and I, Serranos coffee shop, Starbucks, and Panera Bread.

Thanks are in order for Lee Hough and Donna Lewis at Alive Communications, and Ned McLeod, Esq., for technical and legal assistance and advice.

Last, but not least, thanks to David Lambert, Becky Nesbitt, and the teams at Howard and Simon & Schuster for placing their trust in us and applying their considerable skills to making what you have read much, much better than the manuscript we first submitted to them. Nevertheless, any errors remaining are our responsibility and should not be taken as a reflection of the many people and resources we relied on as we wrote this book.

Paul McCusker
Walt Larimore, MD

ABOUT THE AUTHORS

Paul McCusker

Paul is the Peabody Award–winning writer and director of the audio drama *Bonhoeffer: The Cost of Freedom* along with the multiple award-winning audio dramatizations of *The Chronicles of Narnia*, *The Screwtape Letters*, *A Christmas Carol*, and his original series the *Father Gilbert Mysteries*.

Paul is also a writer and director the long-running children's program *Adventures in Odyssey*, writing almost three hundred audio episodes and scripting two of the animated video series and eighteen spin-off novels.

For adults, Paul has written the Gold Medallion–nominated *Epiphany*, *The Mill House*, and *A Season of Shadows*. His plays and musicals have been performed in community theaters across the country. And his lyrics have been put to music by Grammy Award–winning Michael W. Smith. He currently has more than thirty books in print.

Walt Larimore, MD

Dr. Larimore is an award-winning medical journalist, bestselling author, and nationally recognized family physician who has been called one of "America's best known family physicians."

A family physician for thirty years, he has been listed in *Distinguished Physicians of America*, the Best Doctors in America, and *Who's Who in Medicine and Healthcare*. He's been listed in the *Guide to America's Top Family Doctors*, *America's Registry of Outstanding Professionals*, and *2000 Outstanding Intellectuals of the 21st Century*.

In 1996, Dr. Larimore was named America's Outstanding Family Physician Educator (Thomas W. Johnson Award) by the

American Academy of Family Physicians, and in 1999, he and his wife, Barb, were named National Educators of the Year by the Christian Medical Association. In addition, Dr. Larimore was listed as an inaugural member of the Leading Educators of the World (in the field of family medicine) and is listed in the International Biographical Centre of Cambridge, England.

As a Gracie Award–winning medical journalist, he hosted more than eight hundred episodes of the award-winning cable TV show *Ask the Family Physician* on Fox's Health Network (1995–2000) and hundreds of the nationally distributed *Focus on Your Family's Health* radio and TV features (2001–2005).

As an award-winning and bestselling author he has written more than twenty books and was awarded the 2004 Christianity Today Book of the Year Award for cowriting *Workplace Grace: Becoming a Spiritual Influence at Work*. He has been a Gold Medallion Book Award finalist three times—for the *Workplace Grace* book and small-group video series as well as his book *The Highly Healthy Child*.

Dr. Larimore and his childhood sweetheart, Barb, have been married for more than thirty-six years and have two grown children and two grandchildren. They reside in Colorado.

You can learn more about Dr. Larimore at www.DrWalt.com. You can also sign up for his free blog (www.DrWalt.com/blog) and learn more about his other books and resources.

AUTHOR Q&A

Where and how did you guys meet?

WALT: Paul and I met when we both worked at Focus on the Family. We admired each other's work and became friends. When Paul had the idea for the first *TSI* book, he contacted me about writing it with him. It's been a lot of fun working out the plots, characters, and medical science in both books.

Paul, as an author and scriptwriter, you are no stranger to high-adventure stories. Your past works show that you love

speculative fiction that explores the dramatic possibilities of normal people in abnormal situations. So how did you come up with the idea for this novel?

PAUL: The Time Scene Investigators series came to me while I was visiting the small village of Eyam in England. (Readers of *TSI: The Gabon Virus* may remember the importance the village had in the story.) There I began to explore the idea of special team of doctors and scientists who try to solve a current medical crisis by investigating a similar crisis in the past. The medical side of the idea was daunting to me, so I turned to Walt for his help, expertise, and storytelling abilities.

How much of the book is based on fact?

WALT: We're meticulous about our medical and historical research, to make sure the medical facts are correct and our speculative ideas are, at the very least, plausible. We want everyone to remember, though, that this is a work of fiction, not a textbook, so we've used the information in a way that makes for a good story.

PAUL: What's frightening to me is that everything we've written is possible in our world. Any terrorist group that could get their hands on "influenza bombs" would do mankind terrible damage.

What about the historical characters involved in the search for the "influenza bomb," are they historical?

PAUL: Some are based on actual people, and some of the conspiracy material is based on genuine theories, but we've fictionalized everything to create a new mythology.

And is there actually a TSI team at the NIH?

WALT: Not that we know of. But you can never really be sure with the government . . .

Is the Return to Earth Society fictional?

PAUL: The name is, but there are real people and animal-rights groups who genuinely believe that man is no more or less special than any other creature in nature. Some of these groups are very dangerous and readily use violence to accomplish their goals.

One of your main characters, Mark Carlson, endures a lot of emotional conflict in this story. Is there anything from your lives that you tapped into for that part of the story?

WALT: I believe all of us can be deeply wounded and must, at one time or another, come to a place of forgiveness for those who've hurt us. Mark's challenge is one we all face. And then it's a question of how to forgive but still maintain healthy boundaries with those who've hurt us.

PAUL: We also wanted to explore how a lack of forgiveness can destroy a person and lead to terrible circumstances. We don't say that forgiveness is easy—but it is necessary to live a healthy life.

There are a couple of romantic relationships developing in these novels. Which one of you is the romantic?

PAUL: We both like the relational aspects of the stories, but Walt is definitely the romantic. He'd have all kinds of smooching going on if I didn't stop him.

READING GROUP GUIDE

1. Some of the characters in the book deal with forgiving, being forgiven, or refusing to forgive. What was the outcome with each character?

2. Is it reasonable to think that the victims of the Holocaust should forgive those who tortured and murdered their families and friends?

3. What kind of offense do you (or would you) find most difficult to forgive?

4. Do you meditate on an offense over and over? Do you ever feel that you are a prisoner of unforgiveness? When? Why? Do you think this gives you bitterness and anger, or joy and peace?

5. How do you find it in yourself to let go of past offenses, even though you "deserve" to hang on to them?

6. Does forgiving someone mean that the offense is forgotten and has no further consequences?

7. What is the only phrase in the Lord's Prayer with a "condition" attached? (Matthew 6:12)

8. Does forgiveness necessitate reconciliation? If Mark forgave his ex-wife, should he also have considered reuniting with her?

9. What do the authors mean when they say, "Don't waste your pain"? How can you apply this principle to your life?

10. Nora thought it would be wrong to influence Mark in his decision about his ex-wife. Was she right to stay neutral or should she have been more outspoken with her opinions and feelings?

11. Because she felt stifled by Russian bureaucracy, Susan took matters into her own hands. Was she right to do that? How far should one go beyond the boundaries of the law, even if it's for a good cause? Ever? Sometimes? Never? Defend your view.

12. The Return to Earth movement has taken the position that humans have been reckless and irresponsible in their care of nature, and so they've forfeited their right to dominate the world. What do you think of that view?

13. Do you believe groups such as the Return to Earth Society exist? Upon what would they base their beliefs?

14. How do you feel about animal-rights groups that seem to place more emphasis on animal rights than human rights?

15. Was Return to Earth right to take extreme and violent measures to correct where humans have gone wrong?

16. Is it legitimate to believe that humans are no greater than any other creature in nature? Is killing a human to save an animal—or nature—ever justified?

17. Do you believe it is morally or ethically right for governments to develop germ and viral weapons? And if so, under what circumstances should they be used and under what circumstances should they never be used?

18. The Bavarian government destroyed Hitler's Berghof because some people were turning it into a shrine to honor the dictator. Were they right to do that? Is there value in keeping such a place intact as a reminder of the horrors committed under the man's leadership?

19. Philip Knox was tenacious in his belief that German scientists had developed a means to disseminate influenza to their enemies, in spite of being called insane and a paranoid conspiracy theorist. Should Knox have given up? When does it border on obsession or insanity to pursue the truth with such determination?

20. Cornelius Knox joined forces with Stefan Maier to get evidence of a Nazi conspiracy. Maier had his own motives. When Knox learned the truth about Maier's activities, should he have broken off from Maier? Does the end justify the means even if the means are morally questionable?

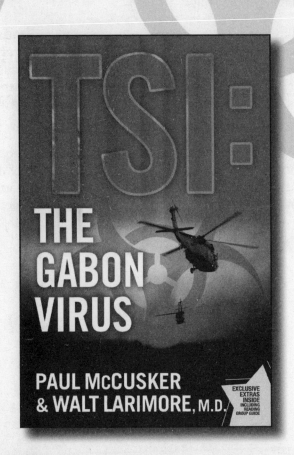